The Visualization Toolkit

An Object-Oriented Approach to 3D Graphics

The Visualization Toolkit

An Object-Oriented Approach To 3D Graphics

Third Edition

Will Schroeder, Ken Martin, Bill Lorensen

with special contributors:
    Lisa Sobierajski Avila, Rick Avila, C. Charles Law

Join the VTK Community at http://www.vtk.org.

Commercial support and consulting is available for this software from Kitware, Inc.
Please visit http://www.kitware.com for more information
or send email to kitware@kitware.com.

Leaders in Visualization Technology

ISBN 1-930934-07-6
90000>

9 781930 934078

QA
76.64
. S36
2002

Kitware

Leaders in Visualization Technology

© 2002 Kitware, Inc.
http://www.kitware.com

The publisher Kitware, Inc. offers discounts on this book when ordered in bulk quantities. The publisher also produces companion works to this text such as *The VTK User's Guide*. For more information contact Kitware, Inc. at kitware@kitware.com. You may also order directly from Kitware's electronic store at http://www.kitware.com/products.

Contributors to this work include the listed authors as well as the following.
Cover Design: Sébastien Barré
Technical Contributors: World-Wide VTK Developer Community at www.vtk.org.

All product names mentioned herein are the trademarks of their respective owners.

This book was previously published by: Pearson Education, Inc. formerly known as Prentice-Hall, Inc.

Printed and produced in the United States of America.
ISBN 1-930934-07-6

Contents

# Preface

*V*isualization is a great field to work in these days. Advances in computer hardware and software have brought this technology into the reach of nearly every computer system. Even the ubiquitous personal computer now offers specialized 3D graphics hardware at discount prices. And with recent releases of the Windows operating systems such as XP, OpenGL has become the defacto standard API for 3D graphics.

We view visualization and visual computing as nothing less than a new form of communication. All of us have long known the power of images to convey information, ideas, and feelings. Recent trends have brought us 2D images and graphics as evidenced by the variety of graphical user interfaces and business plotting software. But 3D images have been used sparingly, and often by specialists using specialized systems. Now this is changing. We believe we are entering a new era where 3D images, visualizations, and animations will begin to extend, and in some cases, replace the current communication paradigm based on words, mathematical symbols, and 2D images. Our hope is that along the way the human imagination will be freed like never before.

This text and companion software offers one view of visualization. The field is broad, including elements of computer graphics, imaging, computer science, computational geometry, numerical analysis, statistical methods, data analysis, and studies in human perception. We certainly do not pretend to cover the field in its entirety. However, we feel that this text does offer you a great opportunity to learn about the fundamentals of visualization. Not only can you learn from the written word and companion images, but the included software will allow you to *practice* visualization. You can start by using the sample data we have provided here, and then move on to your own data and applications. We believe that you will soon appreciate visualization as much as we do.

In this, the third edition of *Visualization Toolkit* textbook, we have added several new features since the first and second editions. Volume rendering is now extensively supported, including the ability to combine opaque surface graphics with volumes. We have added an extensive image processing pipeline that integrates conventional 3D visualization and graphics with imaging. Besides several new filters such as clipping, smoothing, 2D/3D Delaunay triangulation, and new decimation algorithms, we have added several readers and writers, and better support net-based tools such as Java and VRML. VTK now supports cell attributes, and attributes have been generalized into data arrays that are labeled as being scalars, vectors, and so on. Parallel processing, both shared-memory and distributed models, is a major addition. For example, VTK has been used on a large 1024-processor computer at the US National Labs to process nearly a petabyte of data. A suite of 3D widgets is now available in VTK, enabling powerful data interaction techniques. Finally, VTK's cross-platform support has greatly improved with the addition of CMake—a very nice tool for managing the compile process (http://www.cmake.org).

The additions of these features required the support of three special contributors to the text: Lisa Sobierajski Avila, Rick Avila, and C. Charles Law. Rick and Lisa worked hard to create an object-oriented design for volume rendering, and to insure that the design and software is fully compatible with the surface-based rendering system. Charles is the principle architect and implementor for the imaging pipeline. We are proud of the streaming and caching capability of the architecture: It allows us to handle large data sets despite limited memory resources.

Especially satisfying has been the response from users of the text and software. Not only have we received a warm welcome from these wonderful people, but many of them have contributed code, bug fixes, data, and ideas that greatly improved the system. In fact, it would be best to categorize these people as co-developers rather than users of the system. We would like to encourage anyone else who is interested in sharing their ideas, code, or data to contact the VTK user community at http://www.vtk.org, or one of the authors. We would very much welcome any contributions you have to make. Contact us at http://www.kit-ware.com.

Acknowledgments

During the creation of the *Visualization Toolkit* we were fortunate to have the help of many people. Without their aid this book and the associated software might never have existed. Their contributions included performing book reviews, discussing software ideas, creating a supportive environment, and providing key suggestions for some of our algorithms and software implementations.

We would like to first thank our management at the General Electric Corporate R&D Center who allowed us to pursue this project and utilize company facilities: Peter Meenan, Manager of the Computer Graphics and Systems Program, and Kirby Vosburgh, Manager of the Electronic Systems Laboratory. We would also like to thank management at GE Medical Systems who worked with us on the public versus proprietary software issues. This includes John Lalonde, John Heinen, and Steve Roehm.

We thank our co-workers at the R&D Center who have all been supportive: Matt Turek, for proof reading much of the second edition; also Majeid Alyassin, Russell Blue, Jeanette Bruno, Shane Chang, Nelson Corby, Rich Hammond, Margaret Kelliher, Tim Kelliher, Joyce Langan, Paul Miller, Chris Nafis, Bob Tatar, Chris Volpe, Boris Yamrom, Bill Hoffman (now at Kitware), Harvey Cline and Siegwalt Ludke. We thank former co-workers Skip Montanaro (who created a FAQ for us), Dan McLachlan and Michelle Barry. We'd also like to thank our friends and co-workers at GE Medical Systems: Ted Hudacko (who managing the first VTK users mailing list), Darin Okerlund, and John Skinner. Many ideas, helpful hints, and suggestions to improve the system came from this delightful group of people.

The third edition is now published by Kitware, Inc. We very much appreciate the efforts of the many contributors at Kitware who have helped make VTK one of the leading visualization systems in the world today. Sébastien Barré, Andy Cedilnik, Berk Geveci, Amy Henderson, and Brad King have each made significant contributions. Thank also to the folks at GE Global Research such as Jim Miller who continue to push the quality of the system, particularly with the creation of the DART system for regression testing. The US National Labs, led by Jim Ahrens of Los Alamos, has been instrumental in adding parallel processing support to VTK. An additional special thanks to Kitware for accepting the challenge of publishing this book.

Many of the bug fixes and improvements found in the second and third editions came from talented people located around the world. Some of these people are acknowledged in the software and elsewhere in the text, but most of them have contributed their time, knowledge, code, and data without regard for recognition and acknowledgment. It is this exchange of ideas and information with people like this that makes the *Visualization Toolkit* such a fun and exciting project to work on. In particular we would like to thank John Biddiscombe, Charl P. Botha, David Gobbi, Tim Hutton, Dean Inglis, and Prabhu Ramachandran. Thank you very much.

A special thanks to the software and text reviewers who spent their own time to track down some nasty bugs, provide examples, and offer suggestions and improvements. Thank you Tom Citriniti, Mark Miller, George Petras, Hansong Zhang, Penny Rheingans, Paul Hinker, Richard Ellson, and Roger Crawfis. We'd also like to mention that Tom Citriniti at Rensselaer, and Penny Rheingans at the University of Mississippi (now at the University of Maryland Baltimore County) were the first faculty members to teach from early versions of this text. Thank you Penny and Tom for your feedback and extra effort.

Most importantly we would like to thank our friends and loved ones who supported us patiently during this project. We know that you shouldered extra load for us. You certainly saw a lot less of us! But we're happy to say that we're back. Thank you.

Introduction

*V*isualization — "2: the act or process of interpreting in visual terms or of putting into visual form," *Webster's Ninth New Collegiate Dictionary.*

1.1 What Is Visualization?

Visualization is a part of our everyday life. From weather maps to the exciting computer graphics of the entertainment industry, examples of visualization abound. But what is visualization? Informally, visualization is the transformation of data or information into pictures. Visualization engages the primary human sensory apparatus, *vision,* as well as the processing power of the human mind. The result is a simple and effective medium for communicating complex and/or voluminous information.

Terminology

Different terminology is used to describe visualization. *Scientific visualization* is the formal name given to the field in computer science that encompasses user interface, data representation and processing algorithms, visual representations, and other sensory presentation such as sound or touch [McCormick87]. The term *data visualization* is another phrase used to describe visualization. Data visualization is generally interpreted to be more general than scientific visualization, since it implies treatment of data sources beyond the sciences and engineering. Such data sources include financial, marketing, or business data. In addition, the term data visualization is broad enough to include application of statistical methods and other standard data analysis techniques [Rosenblum94]. Another recently emerging term is *information visualization*. This field endeavors to visualize abstract information such as hypertext documents on the World Wide Web, directory/file structures on a computer, or abstract data structures [InfoVis95]. A major challenge facing information visualization researchers is to develop coordinate systems, transformation methods, or structures that meaningfully organize and represent data.

Another way to classify visualization technology is to examine the context in which the data exists. If the data is spatial-temporal in nature (up to three spatial coordinates and the time dimension) then typically methods from scientific visualization are used. If the data exists in higher-dimensional spaces, or abstract spaces, then methods from information visualization are used. This distinction is important, because the human perceptual system is highly tuned to space-time relationships. Data expressed in this coordinate system is inherently understood with little need for explanation. Visualization of abstract data typically requires extensive explanations as to what is being viewed. This is not to say that there is no overlap between scientific and information visualization—often the first step in the information visualization process is to project abstract data into the spatial-temporal domain, and then use the methods of scientific visualization to view the results. The projection process can be quite complex, involving methods of statistical graphics, data mining, and other techniques, or it may be as simple as selecting a lower-dimensional subset of the original data.

In this text we use the term data visualization instead of the more specific terms scientific visualization or information visualization. We feel that scientific visualization is too narrow a description of the field, since visualization techniques have moved beyond the scientific domain and into areas of business, social science, demographics, and information management in general. We also feel that the term data visualization is broad enough to encompass the term information visualization.

Examples of Visualization

Perhaps the best definition of visualization is offered by example. In many cases visualization is influencing peoples' lives and performing feats that a few years ago would have been unimaginable. A prime example of this is its application to modern medicine.

Computer imaging techniques have become an important diagnostic tool in the practice of modern medicine. These include techniques such as X-ray *Computed Tomography* (CT) and *Magnetic Resonance Imaging* (MRI). These techniques use a sampling or data acquisition process to capture information about the internal anatomy of a living patient. This information is in the form of *slice-planes* or cross-sectional images of a patient, similar to conventional photographic X-rays. CT imaging uses many pencil thin X-rays to acquire the data, while MRI combines large magnetic fields with pulsed radio waves. Sophisticated mathematical techniques are used to reconstruct the slice-planes. Typically, many such closely spaced slices are gathered together into a *volume* of data to complete the study.

As acquired from the imaging system, a slice is a series of numbers representing the attenuation of X-rays (CT) or the relaxation of nuclear spin magnetization (MRI) [Krestel90]. On any given slice these numbers are arranged in a matrix, or regular array. The amount of data is large, so large that it is not possible to understand the data in its raw form. However, by assigning to these numbers a gray scale value, and then displaying the data on a computer screen, structure emerges. This structure results from the interaction of the human visual system with the spatial organization of the data and the gray-scale values we have chosen. What the computer represents as a series of numbers, we see as a cross section through the human body: skin, bone, and muscle. Even more impressive results are possible when we extend these techniques into three dimensions. Image slices can be gathered into volumes and the volumes can be processed to reveal complete anatomical structures. Using modern techniques, we can view the entire brain, skeletal system, and vascular system on a living patient without interventional surgery. Such capability has revolutionized modern medical diagnostics, and will increase in importance as imaging and visualization technology matures.

Another everyday application of visualization is in the entertainment industry. Movie and television producers routinely use computer graphics and visualization to create entire worlds that we could never visit in our physical bodies. In these cases we are visualizing other worlds as we imagine them, or past worlds we suppose existed. It's hard to watch the movies such as *Jurassic Park* and *Toy Story* and not gain a deeper appreciation for the awesome Tyrannosaurus Rex, or to be charmed by *Toy Story*'s heroic Buzz Lightyear.

Morphing is another popular visualization technique widely used in the entertainment industry. Morphing is a smooth blending of one object into another. One common application is to morph between two faces. Morphing has also been used effectively to illustrate car design changes from one year to the next. While this may seem like an esoteric application, visualization techniques are used routinely to present the daily weather report. The use of isovalue, or contour, lines to display areas of constant temperature, rainfall, and barometric pressure has become a standard tool in the daily weather report.

Many early uses of visualization were in the engineering and scientific community. From its inception the computer has been used as a tool to simulate physical processes such as ballistic trajectories, fluid flow, and structural mechanics. As the size of the computer simulations grew, it became necessary to transform the resulting calculations into pictures. The amount of data overwhelmed the ability of the human to assimilate and understand it. In fact, pictures were so important that early visualizations were created by manually plotting data. Today, we can take advantage of advances in computer graphics and computer hardware. But, whatever the technology, the application of visualization is the same: to display the results of simulations, experiments, measured data, and fantasy; and to use these pictures to communicate, understand, and entertain.

1.2 Why Visualize?

Visualization is a necessary tool to make sense of the flood of information in today's world of computers. Satellites, supercomputers, laser digitizing systems, and digital data acquisition systems acquire, generate, and transmit data at prodigious rates. The Earth-Orbiting Satellite (EOS) transmits terabytes of data every day. Laser scanning systems generate over 500,000 points in a 15 second scan [Waters91]. Supercomputers model weather patterns over the entire earth [Chen93]. In the first four months of 1995, the New York Stock Exchange processed, on average, 333 million transactions per day [NYTimes]. Without visualization, most of this data would sit unseen on computer disks and tapes. Visualization offers some hope that we can extract the important information hidden within the data.

There is another important element to visualization: It takes advantage of the natural abilities of the human vision system. Our vision system is a complex and powerful part of our bodies. We use it and rely on it in almost everything we do. Given the environment in which our ancestors lived, it is not surprising that certain senses developed to help them survive. As we described earlier in the example of a 2D MRI scan, visual representations are easier to work with. Not only do we have strong 2D visual abilities, but also we are adept at integrating different viewpoints and other visual clues into a mental image of a 3D object or plot. This leads to interactive visualization, where we can manipulate our viewpoint. Rotating about the object helps to achieve a better understanding. Likewise, we have a talent for recognizing temporal changes in an image. Given an animation consisting of hundreds of frames, we have an uncanny ability to recognize trends and spot areas of rapid change.

With the introduction of computers and the ability to generate enormous amounts of data, visualization offers the technology to make the best use of our highly developed visual senses. Certainly other technologies such as statistical analysis, artificial intelligence, mathematical filtering, and sampling theory will play a role in large-scale data processing. However, because visualization directly engages the vision system and human brain, it remains an unequaled technology for understanding and communicating data.

Visualization offers significant financial advantages as well. In today's competitive markets, computer simulation teamed with visualization can reduce product cost and improve time to market. A large cost of product design has been the expense and time required to create and test design prototypes. Current design methods strive to eliminate these physical prototypes, and replace them with digital equivalents. This digital prototyping requires the ability to create and manipulate product geometry, simulate the design under a variety of operating conditions, develop manufacturing techniques, demonstrate product maintenance and service procedures, and even train operators on the proper use of the product before it is built. Visualization plays a role in each case. Already CAD systems are used routinely to model product geometry and design manufacturing procedures. Visualization enables us to view the geometry, and see special characteristics such as surface curvature. For instance, analysis techniques such as finite element, finite difference, and boundary element techniques are used to simulate product performance; and visualization is used to view the results. Recently, human ergonomics and anthropometry are being analyzed using computer techniques in combination with visualization [MDHMS]. Three-dimensional graphics and visualization are being used to create training sequences. Often these are incorporated into a hypertext document or World Wide Web (WWW) pages. Another practical use of graphics and visualization has been in-flight simulators. This has been shown to be a significant cost-savings as compared to flying real airplanes and is an effective training method.

1.3 Imaging, Computer Graphics, and Visualization

There is confusion surrounding the difference between imaging, computer graphics, and visualization. We offer these definitions.

- *Imaging*, or image processing, is the study of 2D pictures, or images. This includes techniques to transform (e.g., rotate, scale, shear), extract information from, analyze, and enhance images.

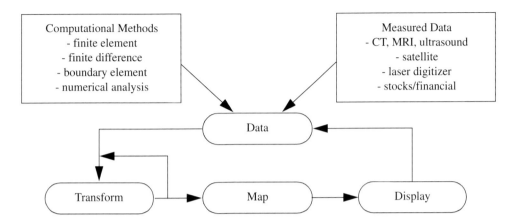

Figure 1–1 The visualization process. Data from various sources is repeatedly transformed to extract, derive, and enhance information. The resulting data is mapped to a graphics system for display.

- *Computer graphics* is the process of creating images using a computer. This includes both 2D paint-and-draw techniques as well as more sophisticated 3D drawing (or rendering) techniques.

- *Visualization* is the process of exploring, transforming, and viewing data as images (or other sensory forms) to gain understanding and insight into the data.

Based on these definitions we see that there is overlap between these fields. The output of computer graphics is an image, while the output of visualization is often produced using computer graphics. Sometimes visualization data is in the form of an image, or we wish to visualize object geometry using realistic rendering techniques from computer graphics.

Generally speaking we distinguish visualization from computer graphics and image processing in three ways.

1. The dimensionality of data is three dimensions or greater. Many well-known methods are available for data of two dimensions or less; visualization serves best when applied to data of higher dimension.

2. Visualization concerns itself with data transformation. That is, information is repeatedly created and modified to enhance the meaning of the data.

3. Visualization is naturally interactive, including the human directly in the process of creating, transforming, and viewing data.

Another perspective is that visualization is an activity that encompasses the process of exploring and understanding data. This includes both imaging and computer graphics as well as data processing and filtering, user interface methodology, computational techniques, and software design. **Figure 1–1** depicts this process.

As this figure illustrates we see that the visualization process focuses on data. In the first step data is acquired from some source. Next, the data is transformed by various methods, and then mapped to a form appropriate for presentation to the user. Finally, the data is rendered or displayed, completing the process. Often, the process repeats as the data is better understood or new models are developed. Sometimes the results of the visualization can directly control the generation of the data. This is often referred to as *analysis steering*. Analysis steering is an important goal of visualization because it enhances the interactivity of the overall process.

1.4 Origins of Data Visualization

The origin of visualization as a formal discipline dates to the 1987 NSF report *Visualization in Scientific Computing* [McCormick87]. That report coined the term *scientific visualization*. Since then the field has grown rapidly with major conferences, such as IEEE Visualization, becoming well established. Many large computer graphics conferences, for example ACM SIGGRAPH, devote large portions of their program to visualization technology.

Of course, data visualization technology had existed for many years before the 1987 report referenced [Tufte83]. The first practitioners recognized the value of presenting data as images. Early pictorial data representations were created during the eighteenth century with the arrival of statistical graphics. It was only with the arrival of the digital computer and the development of the field of computer graphics, that visualization became a practicable discipline.

The future of data visualization and graphics appears to be explosive. Just a few decades ago, the field of data visualization did not exist and computer graphics was viewed as an offshoot of the more formal discipline of computer science. As techniques were created and computer power increased, engineers, scientists, and other researchers began to use graphics to understand and communicate data. At the same time, user interface tools were being developed. These forces have now converged to the point where we expect computers to adapt to humans rather than the other way around. As such, computer graphics and data visualization serve as the window into the computer, and more importantly, into the data that computers manipulate. Now, with the visualization window, we can extract information from data and analyze, understand, and manage more complex systems than ever before.

Dr. Fred Brooks, Kenan Professor of Computer Science at the University of North Carolina at Chapel Hill and recipient of the John von Neumann Medal of the IEEE, puts it another way. At the award presentation at the ACM SIGGRAPH '94, Dr. Brooks stated that computer graphics and visualization offer "intelligence amplification" (IA) as compared to artificial intelligence (AI). Besides the deeper philosophical issues surrounding this issue (e.g., human before computer), it is a pragmatic observation. While the long-term goal of AI has been to develop computer systems that could replace humans in certain applications, the lack of real progress in this area has lead some researchers to view the role of computers as amplifiers and assistants to humans. In this view, computer graphics and visualization play a significant role, since arguably the most effective human/computer interface is visual. Recent gains in computer power and memory are only accelerating this trend, since it is the interface between the human and the computer that often is the obstacle to the effective application of the computer.

1.5 Purpose of This Book

There currently exist texts that define and describe data visualization, many of them using case studies to illustrate techniques and typical applications. Some provide high-level descriptions of algorithms or visualization system architectures. Detailed descriptions are left to academic journals or conference proceedings. What these texts lack is a way to *practice* visualization. Our aim in this text is to go beyond descriptions and provide tools to learn about and apply visualization to your own application area. In short, the purpose of the book is fourfold.

1. Describe visualization algorithms and architectures in detail.

2. Demonstrate the application of data visualization to a broad selection of case studies.

3. Provide a working architecture and software design for application of data visualization to real-world problems.

4. Provide effective software tools packaged in a C++ class library. We also provide language bindings for the interpreted languages Tcl, Python, and Java.

   Taken together, we refer to the text and software as the *Visualization Toolkit*, or VTK for short. Our hope is that you can use the text to learn about the fundamental concepts of visualization, and then adapt the computer code to your own applications and data.

1.6 What This Book Is Not

The purpose of this book is not to provide a rigorous academic treatise on data visualization. Nor do we intend to include an exhaustive survey of visualization technology. Our goal is to bridge the formal discipline of data visualization with practical application, and to provide a solid technical overview of this emerging technology. In many cases we refer you to the included software to understand implementation details. You may also wish to refer to the appropriate references for further information.

1.7 Intended Audience

Our primary audience is computer users who create, analyze, quantify, and/or process data. We assume a minimal level of programming skill. If you can write simple computer code to import data and know how to run a computer program, you can practice data visualization with the software accompanying this book.

   As we wrote this book we also had in mind educators and students of introductory computer graphics and visualization courses. In more advanced courses this text may not be rigorous enough to serve as asole reference. In these instances, this book will serve well as a companion text, and the software is well suited as a foundation for programming projects and class exercises.

   Educators and students in other disciplines may also find the text and software to be valuable tools for presenting results. Courses in numerical analysis, computer science, business simulation, chemistry, dynamic systems, and engineering simulations, to name a few, often require large-scale programming projects that create large amounts of data. The software tools provided here are easy to learn and readily adapted to different data sources. Students can incorporate this software into their work to display and analyze their results.

1.8 How to Use This Book

There are a number of approaches you can take to make effective use of this book. The particular approach depends on your skill level and goals. Three likely paths are as follows:

> *Novice.* You're a novice if you lack basic knowledge of graphics, visualization, or object-oriented principles. Start by reading Chapter 2 if you are unfamiliar with object-oriented principles, Chapter 3 if you are unfamiliar with computer graphics, and Chapter 4 if you are unfamiliar with visualization. Continue by reading the application studies in Chapter 12. You can then move on to the CD-ROM and try out some programming examples. Leave the more detailed treatment of algorithms and data representation until you are familiar with the basics and plan to develop your own applications.

> *Hacker.* You're a hacker if you are comfortable writing your own code and editing other's. Review the examples in Chapters 3, 4, and 12. At this point you will want to acquire the companion software guide to this text (*The VTK User's Guide*) or become familiar with the programming resources at `http://www.vtk.org`. Then retrieve the examples from the CD-ROM and start practicing.

> *Researcher/Educator.* You're a researcher if you develop computer graphics and/or visualization algorithms or if you are actively involved in using and evaluating such systems. You're an educator if you cover aspects of computer graphics and/or visualization within your courses. Start by reading Chapters 2, 3, and 4. Select appropriate algorithms from the text and examine the associated source code. If you wish to extend the system, we recommend that you acquire the companion software guide to this text (*The VTK User's Guide*) or become familiar with the programming resources at `http://www.vtk.org`.

1.9 Software Considerations and Example Code

In writing this book we have attempted to strike a balance between practice and theory. We did not want the book to become a user manual, yet we did want a strong correspondence between algorithmic presentation and software implementation. (Note: *The VTK User's Guide* published by Kitware, Inc. `http://www.kitware.com` is recommended as a companion text to this book.) As a result of this philosophy, we have adopted the following approach:

> *Application versus Design.* The book's focus is the application of visualization techniques to real-world problems. We devote less attention to software design issues. Some of these important design issues include: memory management, deriving new

classes, shallow versus deep object copy, single versus multiple inheritance, and interfaces to other graphics libraries. Software issues are covered in the companion text *The VTK User's Guide* published by Kitware, Inc.

Theory versus Implementation. Whenever possible, we separate the theory of data visualization from our implementation of it. We felt that the book would serve best as a reference tool if the theory sections were independent of software issues and terminology. Toward the end of each chapter there are separate implementation or example sections that are implementation specific. Earlier sections are implementation free.

Documentation. This text contains documentation considered essential to understanding the software architecture, including object diagrams and condensed object descriptions. More extensive documentation of object methods and data members is embedded in the software (in the `.h` header files) and on CD-ROM or on-line at `http://www.vtk.org`. In particular, the Doxygen generated manual pages contain detailed descriptions of class relationships, methods, and other attributes.

We use a number of conventions in this text. Imported computer code is denoted with a typewriter font, as are external programs and computer files. To avoid conflict with other C++ class libraries, all class names in VTK begin with the "vtk" prefix. Methods are differentiated from variables with the addition of the "()" postfix. (Other conventions are listed in *VTK User's Guide*.)

All images in this text have been created using the *Visualization Toolkit* software and data found on the included CD-ROM or from the Web site `http://www.vtk.org`. In addition, every image has source code (sometimes in C++ and sometimes a Tcl script). We decided against using images from other researchers because we wanted you to be able to practice visualization with every example we present. Each computer generated image indicates the originating file. Files ending in `.cxx` are C++ code, files ending in `.tcl` are Tcl scripts. Hopefully these examples can serve as a starting point for you to create your own applications.

To find the example code you will want to search in one of three areas. The standard VTK distribution includes an `VTK/Examples` directory where many well-documented examples are found. The VTK testing directories `VTK/*/Testing`, for example, `VTK/Graphics/Testing/Tcl`, contain some of the example code used in this text. These examples use the data found in the VTKData distribution. Finally, a separate software distribution, the VTKTextbook distribution, contains examples and data that do not exist in the standard VTK distribution. The VTK, VTKData, and VTKTextbook distributions are found on the included CD-ROM and/or on the web site at `http://www.vtk.org`.

1.10 Chapter-by-Chapter Overview

Chapter 2: Object-Oriented Design

This chapter discusses some of the problems with developing large and/or complex software systems and describes how object-oriented design addresses many of these problems. This chapter defines the key terms used in object-oriented modelling and design and works through a real-world example. The chapter concludes with a brief look at some object-oriented languages and some of the issues associated with object-oriented visualization.

Chapter 3: Computer Graphics Primer

Computer graphics is the means by which our visualizations are created. This chapter covers the fundamental concepts of computer graphics from an application viewpoint. Common graphical entities such as cameras, lights, and geometric primitives are described along with some of the underlying physical equations that govern lighting and image generation. Issues related to currently available graphics hardware are presented, as they affect how and what we choose to render. Methods for interacting with data are introduced.

Chapter 4: The Visualization Pipeline

This chapter explains our methodology for transforming raw data into a meaningful representation that can than be rendered by the graphics system. We introduce the notion of a visualization pipeline, which is similar to a data flow diagram from software engineering. The differences between process objects and data objects are covered, as well as how we resolved issues between performance and memory usage. We explain the advantages to a pipeline network topology regarding execution ordering, result caching, and reference counting.

Chapter 5: Basic Data Representation

There are many types of data produced by the variety of fields that apply visualization. This chapter describes the data objects that we use to represent and access such data. A flexible design is introduced where the programmer can interact with most any type of data using one consistent interface. The three high level components of data (structure, cells, and data attributes) are introduced, and their specific subclasses and components are discussed.

Chapter 6: Fundamental Algorithms

Where the preceding chapter deals with data objects, this one introduces process objects. These objects encompass the algorithms that transform and manipulate data. This chapter looks at commonly used techniques for isocontour extraction, scalar generation, color mapping, and vector field display, among others. The emphasis of this chapter is to provide the reader with a basic understanding of the more common and important visualization algorithms.

Chapter 7: Advanced Computer Graphics

This chapter covers advanced topics in computer graphics. The chapter begins by introducing transparency and texture mapping, two topics important to the main thrust of the chapter: volume rendering. Volume rendering is a powerful technique to see inside of 3D objects, and is used to visualize volumetric data. We conclude the chapter with other advanced topics such as stereoscopic rendering, special camera effects, and 3D widgets.

Chapter 8: Advanced Data Representation

Part of the function of a data object is to store the data. The first chapter on data representation discusses this aspect of data objects. This chapter focuses on basic geometric and topological access methods, and computational operations implemented by the various data objects. The chapter covers such methods as coordinate transformations for data sets, interpolation functions, derivative calculations, topological adjacency operations, and geometric operations such as line intersection and searching.

Chapter 9: Advanced Algorithms

This chapter is a continuation of *Fundamental Algorithms* and covers algorithms that are either more complex or less widely used. Scalar algorithms such as dividing cubes are covered along with vector algorithms such as stream ribbons. A large collection of modelling algorithms is discussed, including triangle strip generation, polygon decimation, feature extraction, and implicit modelling. We conclude with a look at some visualization algorithms that utilize texture mapping.

Chapter 10: Image Processing

While 3D graphics and visualization is the focus of the book, image processing is an important tool for pre-processing and manipulating data. In this chapter we focus on several important image processing algorithms, as well as describe how we use a streaming data representation to process large datasets.

Chapter 11: Visualization on the Web

The Web is one of the best places to share your visualizations. In this chapter we show you how to write Java-based visualization applications, and how to create VRML (Virtual Reality Modelling Language) data files for inclusion in your own Web content.

Chapter 12: Applications

In this chapter we tie the previous chapters together by working through a series of case studies from a variety of application areas. For each case, we briefly describe the application and what information we expect to obtain through the use of visualization. Then, we walk through the design and resulting source code to demonstrate the use of the tools described earlier in the text.

1.11 Legal Considerations

We make no warranties, expressly or implied, that the computer code contained in this text is free of error or will meet your requirements for any particular application. Do not use this code in any application where coding errors could result in injury to a person or loss of property. If you do use the code in this way, it is at your own risk. The authors and publisher disclaim all liability for direct or consequential damages resulting from your use of this code.

The computer code contained in this text is copyrighted. We grant permission for you to use, copy, and distribute this software for any purpose. However, you may not modify and then redistribute the software. Some of the algorithms presented here are implementations of patented software. If you plan to use this software for commercial purposes, please insure that applicable patent laws are observed. See the README file in the VTK/Patented directory for more information.

Some of the data on the CD-ROM may be freely distributed or used (with appropriate acknowledgment). Refer to the local README files or other documentation for details.

Several registered trademarks are used in this text. UNIX is a trademark of UNIX System Laboratories. Sun Workstation and XGL are trademarks of Sun Microsystems, Inc. Microsoft, MS, MS-DOS, and Windows are trademarks of Microsoft Corporation. The X Window System is a trademark of the Massachusetts Institute of Technology. Starbase and HP are trademarks of Hewlett-Packard Inc. Silicon Graphics and OpenGL, are trademarks of Silicon Graphics, Inc. Macintosh is a trademark of Apple Computer. RenderMan is a trademark of Pixar.

1.12 Bibliographic Notes

A number of visualization texts are available. The first six texts listed in the reference section are good general references ([Nielson90], [Patrikalakis91], [Brodlie92], [Wolff93], [Rosenblum94], and [Gallagher95]). Gallagher [Gallagher95] is particularly valuable if you are from a computational background. Wolff and Yaeger [Wolff93] contains many beautiful images and is oriented towards Apple Macintosh users. The text includes a CD-ROM with images and software.

You may also wish to learn more about computer graphics and imaging. Foley and van Dam [FoleyVanDam90] is the basic reference for computer graphics. Another recommended text is [BurgerGillies89]. Suggested reference books on computer imaging are [Pavlidis82] and [Wolberg90].

Two texts by Tufte [Tufte83] [Tufte90] are particularly impressive. Not only are the graphics superbly done, but the fundamental philosophy of data visualization is articulated. He also describes the essence of good and bad visualization techniques.

Another interesting text is available from Siemens, a large company offering medical imaging systems [Krestel90]. This text describes the basic concepts of imaging technology, including MRI and CT. This text is only for those users with a strong mathematical background. A less mathematical overview of MRI is available from [SmithRanallo89].

To learn more about programming with *Visualization Toolkit*, we recommend the text *The VTK User's Guide* [UsersGuide]. This text has an extensive example suite as well as descriptions of the internals of the software. Programming resources including a detailed description of API's, VTK file formats, and class descriptions are provided.

1.13 References

[Brodlie92]
K. W. Brodlie et al. *Scientific Visualization Techniques and Applications*. Springer-Verlag, Berlin, 1992.

[BurgerGillies89]
P. Burger and D. Gillies. *Interactive Computer Graphics Functional, Procedural and Device-Level Methods*. Addison-Wesley Publishing Company, Reading, MA, 1989.

[Chen93]
P. C. Chen. "A Climate Simulation Case Study." In *Proceedings of Visualization '93*. pp. 397–401, IEEE Computer Society Press, Los Alamitos, CA, 1993.

[FoleyVanDam90]
J. D. Foley, A. van Dam, S. K. Feiner, and J. F. Hughes. *Computer Graphics Principles and Practice (2d Ed)*. Addison-Wesley, Reading, MA, 1990.

[Gallagher95]
R. S. Gallagher (ed). *Computer Visualization Graphics Techniques for Scientific and Engineering Analysis*. CRC Press, Boca Raton, FL, 1995.

[Krestel90]
E. Krestel (ed). *Imaging Systems for Medical Diagnostics*. Siemens-Aktienges, Munich, 1990.

[InfoVis95]
The First Information Visualization Symposium. IEEE Computer Society Press, Los Alamitos, CA, 1995.

[McCormick87]
B. H. McCormick, T. A. DeFanti, and M. D. Brown. "Visualization in Scientific Computing." Report of the NSF Advisory Panel on Graphics, Image Processing and Workstations, 1987.

[MDHMS]
McDonnell Douglas Human Modeling System Reference Manual. Report MDC 93K0281. McDonnell Douglas Corporation, Human Factors Technology, Version 2.1, July 1993.

[Nielson90]
G. M. Nielson and B. Shriver (eds). *Visualization in Scientific Computing*. IEEE Computer Society Press, Los Alamitos, CA, 1990.

[NYTimes]
The New York Times Business Day, Tuesday, May 2, 1995.

[Patrikalakis91]
N. M. Patrikalakis (ed). *Scientific Visualization of Physical Phenomena*. Springer-Verlag, Berlin, 1991.

[Pavlidis82]
T. Pavlidis. *Graphics and Image Processing*. Computer Science Press, Rockville, MD, 1982.

[Rosenblum94]
L. Rosenblum et al. *Scientific Visualization Advances and Challenges*. Harcourt Brace & Company, London, 1994.

[SmithRanallo89]
   H. J. Smith and F. N. Ranallo. *A Non-Mathematical Approach to Basic MRI.* Medical Physics Publishing Corporation, Madison, WI, 1989.

[Tufte83]
   E. R. Tufte. *The Visual Display of Quantitative Information.* Graphics Press, Cheshire, CT,
   1990.

[Tufte90]
   E. R. Tufte. *Envisioning Information.* Graphics Press, Cheshire, CT, 1990.

[UsersGuide]
   W. Schroeder, ed. *The VTK User's Guide.* Kitware, Inc. `http://www.kitware.com`.

[Waters91]
   K. Waters and D. Terzopoulos. "Modeling and Animating Faces Using Scanned Data." *Visualization and Computer Animation.* 2:123–128, 1991.

[Wolberg90]
   G. Wolberg. *Digital Image Warping.* IEEE Computer Society Press, Los Alamitos, CA,
   1990.

[Wolff93]
   R. S. Wolff and L. Yaeger. *Visualization of Natural Phenomena.* TELOS, Springer-Verlag,
   Santa Clara, CA, 1993.

Object-Oriented Design

Object-oriented systems are becoming widespread in the computer industry for good reason. Object-oriented systems are more modular, easier to maintain, and easier to describe than traditional procedural systems. Since the *Visualization Toolkit* has been designed and implemented using object-oriented design, we devote this chapter to summarizing the concepts and practice of object-oriented design and implementation.

2.1 Introduction

Today's software systems try to solve complex, real-world problems. A rigorous software design and implementation methodology can ease the burden of this complexity. Without such a methodology, software developers can find it difficult to meet a system's specifications. Furthermore, as specifications change and grow, a software system that does not have a solid, underlying architecture and design will have difficulty adapting to these expanding requirements.

Our visualization system is a good example of complex software that needs to be designed with extensibility in mind. Data visualization is a rapidly expanding field, with visualization techniques being introduced each year. Any system that hopes to incorporate future innovations must have an underlying design that supports the addition of new material without a significant impact on the existing system.

Object-oriented design is a software engineering methodology that deals comfortably with complexity and provides a framework for later changes and additions. The object-oriented design process attempts to divide a complex task into small and simple pieces called objects. The objects are computer abstractions that model physical or abstract pieces of the system being simulated. Object-oriented design methodologies provide mechanisms to identify the abstractions that exist within a system and to model the behavior of the objects.

2.2 Goals of Good Software Design

The quality of a software design is difficult to measure, but some qualitative aspects can guide us. A good software design should be robust, understandable, extendible, modular, maintainable, and reusable.

A robust system handles exceptional conditions gracefully and behaves consistently. Robustness gives software developers confidence that the underlying components of the system will behave as expected, even when the system is used under different circumstances than the original implementor intended.

An understandable system can be used by someone other than the original implementor. The use of the system should seem logical and sensible. The names of the components of the system should be derived from the problem domain.

Extendable systems accept new tasks while still doing the tasks they were originally intended to perform. A system should accept new forms of data and new algorithms without disrupting existing software. Adding a new primitive to the system should not cause large portions of the system to be modified. Experience shows that the more existing code that is modified in a system, the more likely errors will be introduced.

Modular software systems minimize the number of relationships that exist between components of a system. System components that are tightly coupled should be grouped together logically and obey common naming conventions and protocols.

Software maintenance is often ignored during system design. Nevertheless, the total cost of a system includes maintenance as well as the original development. A software system is maintainable if problems are easily isolated and the repair of one problem does not introduce problems in unrelated parts of the system.

Finally, the economics of software development require that we leverage as much of our past work as possible. In an ideal world, the implementation of a new technique in an existing system should be a simple task. This is seldom the case in software systems. Creation of reusable software components can reduce duplication of effort and promote consistent interfaces within a system. However, as we see throughout this book, creating software that can be reused often takes extra effort. A short-term view of productivity by one individual conflicts with the long-term view of the productivity of a software development organization.

2.3 Object-Oriented Concepts

Objects are the dominating concepts in object-oriented systems. Objects are abstractions that encapsulate the properties and behavior of the entities within a system. Each object has an identity that distinguishes it from other objects in the system. Often, the distinguishable aspects of an object are obvious. For example, a difference in color, location on a screen, size, or contents distinguishes one window from another on a computer desktop. But, appearances can be deceiving, and even two objects that share all the same characteristics may still have different identities. Two automobiles may have the same manufacturer, model, options and colors, but remain two different cars. The real world distinguishes the two cars by a vehicle identification number. Likewise, programming systems that deal with multiple entities need an identity mechanism. A pointer to allocated memory or a variable name in a system-managed symbol table are often used to distinguish objects in a system. In a database system, a set of identifier keys (called an *n*-tuple) identifies an entity in a system.

But, how do object-oriented systems differ from conventional, procedural programming systems? The major difference is in the way the two approaches treat data abstraction. Conventional systems limit abstraction to data typing, while object-oriented systems create abstractions for both the data and the operations that can be applied to the data. In fact, an object-oriented system keeps the data and operations together in one programming construct called an object. Together, the data and operations comprise an object's *properties*. When an operation is applied to an object, the programming language's dynamic-binding mechanism executes the procedure that is appropriate for that object. This is not the case in procedure-oriented systems. The programmer must supply logic to decide which procedure to call. Systems that handle multiple types are often littered with case statements to select the appropriate procedure for an operation. As new types are added to these systems, the code that dispatches operations based on data type must be extended to handle the new type. For example, in a program to display different types of primitives, the following pseudo code shows how a procedure-oriented system differs from an object-oriented system.

Procedure oriented (in C):

```
Primitive *aPrim;

. . .

DrawPrimitive (aPrim)

. . .

procedure DrawPrimitive (aPrim)

{

    if (aPrim->type == TRIANGLE) then DrawTriangle (aPrim)

    else if (aPrim->type == SQUARE) then DrawSquare (aPrim)

    else if (aPrim->type == CIRCLE) then DrawCircle (aPrim)

. . .

}
```

Object-oriented (in C++):

```
...

aPrim->Draw ();

...
```

Later in this project's existence, someone may want to add a new primitive, let's say a quadratic. The person assigned with such a formidable task must search the existing system for all occurrences of the if statements in the first example and add a test for the new quadratic type. Of course, a good programmer will have isolated the code in one location, as we have done here, so the task is easier. Nevertheless, that programmer must first realize that the original programmer was skilled enough to modularize the drawing code, then find the code (without necessarily knowing the procedure name) and modify the code. To complicate matters, a system built by more than one programmer will undoubtedly be under a configuration management system, requiring a check-out, edit, and check-in cycle.

The object-oriented programmer has an easier task. Consulting the design document that defines the object properties for a primitive, this programmer adds a draw operation to the quadratic object. The new primitive is available to the system without changing any existing code! Of course, this is an oversimplified example. But think about past programs you have written and remember how hard it was to add a new data type. Were your changes isolated to the new code you added? Did you have to edit code that you did not write and maybe did not understand? Keep this example in mind as you read our object-oriented implementation of a data visualization library.

Before describing object-oriented design and programming in more detail, we provide an observation and prediction. Over the several years that we have designed and implemented software using an object-oriented methodology, we have observed that newcomers to the technique will say, "But this is how I already write programs. My systems are modular; they're robust; I can easily add to them." If you still feel that way after reading this book, do not fault the object-oriented approach. Rather, we have failed as authors. However, such a negative response is unlikely. In our experience, users become comfortable with this approach in a short time. Especially when they are introduced to objects through an existing, well-designed object-oriented system. You will reach the "aha" stage, after which it will be difficult to begin a software project without looking for the objects in the problem.

2.4 Object-Oriented Terminology

As with any software engineering design methodology, object-oriented design has its own terminology. Unfortunately, not everyone agrees on what that is. We adopt much of our terminology from Rumbaugh [Rumbaugh91] and, since the *Visualization Toolkit* is written in C++, from Stroustrup [Stroustrup84]. For the most part, Rumbaugh's terminology is independent of programming language, while Stroustrup is specific to implementation in C++. The transition from design to programming will be painless though, and the mappings between the two terminologies are mostly obvious. Where we think there might be confusion, we will point out the correspondences.

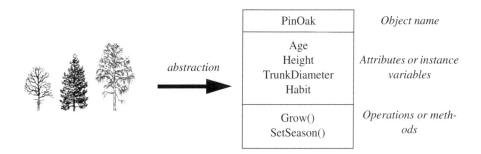

Figure 2–1 Mapping a real-world object into an object abstraction. The real-world objects are various types of trees. One of these objects (a pin oak tree) is mapped into the computer object we call PinOak.

What Is an Object?

An *object* is an abstraction that models the state and behavior of entities in a system. Abstraction is a mental process that extracts the essential aspects of a situation for a particular purpose. Entities are things in the system that have identity. Chairs, airplanes, and cameras are objects that correspond to physical entities in the real world. Binary trees, symbol tables, and ordered collections are objects that exist only within the world of computer science.

Figure 2–1 is an example of the abstraction that occurs when we map the state and behavior of a system component to an object. Here, the object is a particular type of tree: a pin oak. In this application we desire to simulate the growth of various types of trees over the course of a season. For our purpose we have decided that the important state variables are the tree's age, trunk diameter, height, and habit (i.e., growing form). To capture the behavior of the pin oak we have methods to simulate growth and seasonal effects corresponding to spring, summer, fall, and winter. There are also methods (not shown) for setting and getting current state variables.

We call the state of an object its *attributes* (also called *instance variables*) and define its behavior by the *operations* that can be applied to it. Attributes have a name, a data type, and a data value. The data type of an attribute may be a primitive type in the programming language (such as a char or float in C++), or another object. For example, the vtkTransform object in our visualization system has an attribute of type vtkMatrix4x4, another object. vtkMatrix4x4 in turn has attributes that are an array of primitive values declared as float values in C++.

Operations are functions or transformations that can be applied to an object. Operations define the behavior of the object. The operations for a particular object are implemented in procedures we call *methods*.

Together, the attributes and operations of an object comprise its *properties*. A two-dimensional line graph could have attributes that include an *x* and *y* axis, a legend, and a connected set of points. This graph has methods that draw the graph in a window. It also has methods that let a user specify the axes, data to draw, and legend to use.

Objects that share the same properties can be grouped using the process of *classification*. An object class, usually just called a class, specifies the properties that all objects in the class have. The class only specifies the names of the properties, not their specific values. Different classes can (and usually do) have properties with names that exist in other classes. Many classes in our visualization system have an attribute named Position. Although both a camera and actor in our visualization system have this attribute, the effect on each is different because they are different classes. Attribute names are shared by all objects in a given class, but separate storage is allocated for each object's attribute values.

When an operation with the same name is applied to objects of different classes we call the operation *polymorphic*. For example, our visualization system has an operation named Render() that can be applied to many different objects. The implementation of an operation for a particular class is called a method. The print operation for a vtkMatrix4x4 object is implemented in its print method. That is, there exists code that knows how to print objects of class vtkMatrix4x4 and not objects of other classes. Objects know which method to use because they are kept within each object's data structure. In most systems the code for the methods is shared by all objects in the same class. Some programming languages, including C++, define a method by combining an operation name with its argument types. This process is called overloading an operation and is a powerful technique that permits the same name to be used for logically similar operations. For example, the class definition below defines three methods for calculating the square of a number. Even though these methods have the same operation name, they are unique because C++ uses both the operation name and the operations argument types.

```
class math
{
float square(float x);
int square(int x);
double square(double x);
}
```

To use a member of a class for some purpose, we create an instance of the class (the process of *instantiation*). Instance creation establishes the identity of the instance including specifying its initial state. The instance's class serves as a template for the instance during creation, defining the names of each of its attributes and operations. Creation establishes the similarities and differences between this instance and other instances of the same class. The similarities are the names and type of its attributes and the methods that implement its operations. The differences are the specific values of the attributes. The details of how one creates an instance of a class vary from programming language to programming language. In C++, a program creates an instance using a declarative form such as

```
vtkActor aBall;
```

which creates an object from the program stack, or by applying the new operation

```
vtkActor *aBall = new vtkActor;
```

which creates the object from the program heap.

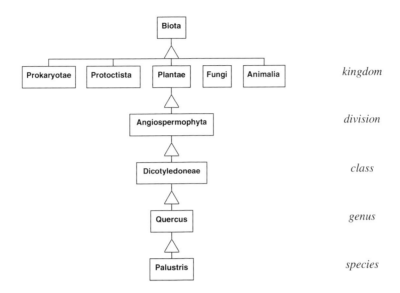

Figure 2–2 Inheritance hierarchy for pin oak tree.

Inheritance

Inheritance is a programming mechanism that simplifies adding new classes to a system when they differ in small ways from currently existing classes. The notion of inheritance is adopted from the observation that most systems can be specified using a hierarchical classification system. A fine example of a classification system is the phyla of life on earth.

Earlier we created an object corresponding to a pin oak tree. The properties of the tree can be more thoroughly described using inheritance (**Figure 2–2**). The classification shown here is based on the five kingdom system of Margulis and Schwartz [Margulis88]. In this system, biota is classified as belonging to one of the five kingdoms Prokaryotae (bacteria), Protoctista (algae, protozoans and slime molds), Fungi (mushrooms, molds, lichens), Plantae (mosses, ferns, cone-bearing, and flowering plants), and Animalia (animals with and without backbones). Below this level we have the classifications division, class, order, family, genus, and species. The figure shows the kingdom, division, class, genus, and species of the pin oak.

Organizing objects into an inheritance hierarchy provides many benefits. Properties of a general classification are also properties of its subclassification. For example, we know that all species of genus *Quercus* form acorns. From the software point of view this means any instance variables and methods of a *superclass* are automatically inherited by its *subclass*. This allows us to make changes to a number of objects simultaneously by modifying their superclass. Furthermore, if we desire to add a new class (say a red oak tree) to the hierarchy we can do so without duplicating existing functionality. We need only differentiate the new class from the others by adding new instance variables or overloading existing methods.

The ability to quickly add new classes that are slightly different from currently existing classes promotes the extensibility of a system. Inheritance can be derived top-down using a process called *specialization*, or it can be created bottom-up, combining similar classes during a process called *generalization*. The use of inheritance implies a class hierarchy with one or more classes being the superclasses of one or more subclasses. A subclass inherits the operations and attributes of its superclasses. In C++, subclasses are called *derived* classes and superclasses are called *base* classes. A subclass can add additional operations and attributes that modify the properties it inherited from its superclasses. Through this inheritance, an object can exhibit its superclass's behavior plus any additional behavior it wishes. It can also restrict, or override, operations implemented by its superclass.

Classes that exist only to act as superclasses for their subclasses are called *abstract* classes. Instance creation of an abstract class is generally prohibited. Abstract classes are useful for gathering attributes and methods that all subclasses will use. They can also define protocols for behavior for their subclasses. This is a powerful use of inheritance that will show up in the design of our visualization system. Abstract classes can enforce complex sequence, control protocols, and ensure uniform behavior. They remove the responsibility of complex protocols from the individual subclasses and isolate the protocol in the superclass.

An example of a simple plotting package illustrates the power of abstract classes. Consider a data presentation application that allows for a variety of two-dimensional plotting. This application must support line charts and horizontal and vertical bar charts. The design process identifies properties common to all plots including title, axes, and legend. We then create an abstract class called TwoDPlot to contain these common attributes. Common behavior can also be captured in TwoDPlot within its plot method:

```
Method Plot
{
Draw the border
Scale the data
Draw the axes
Draw the data
Draw the title
Draw the legend
}
```

An abstract class may or may not provide default behavior for each operation. In this example, default behavior for border and title drawing might be provided. Then subclasses of TwoDPlot would define their own functions for the other methods. The protocol specification explicitly spells out what methods a subclass of TwoDPlot should respond to. In the above example, subclasses will need to define their own methods for drawing the axis, data, and legend. Some subclasses might use TwoDPlot's methods for drawing the border, others might require their own version of this method. The abstract interface defined in TwoDPlot makes it easier to add new classes of 2D plots and the resulting subclasses tend to be more uniform and consistent.

Another mechanism, *delegation*, is useful for isolating and reusing behavior. Using delegation, an object applies operations to one of its attributes that is an object. As an example, in the *Visualization Toolkit* the vtkTransform object delegates its Identity() operation to its vtkMatrix4x4 attribute. This instance of vtkMatrix4x4 then performs the operation. There are

many more useful object-oriented concepts, but for the time being we have enough information to describe how we can use objects to design a system.

2.5 Object-Oriented Modelling and Design

The design of any large software system is a formidable task and the first steps in system
design are often the most challenging. No matter what design technique we choose, we must
have a thorough understanding of the system's application domain. It would be difficult to
see how one could design a fly-by-wire airplane control system without a detailed knowledge
of the underlying hardware control systems. Of course, all flight system software is not
designed by aeronautical engineers, so some form of system specification must exist. The
depth of information in the specifications varies from application to application.

Object-oriented system design begins with a modelling step that extracts objects and
their relationships with other objects from a problem statement or software requirement specification. First, the designer must completely understand the problem being solved. This
often requires an in-depth knowledge of the problem domain or access to detailed specifications of the problem being solved. Then, major abstractions must be identified within the system. The abstractions will become, at this high level of design, the first set of objects. For
example, a system that keeps track of an investment portfolio will need objects such as
stocks, bonds, and mutual funds. In a computer animation system we might need actors, cameras, and lights. A medical computed tomography system will have a table, X-ray source,
detectors, and gantry. Our visualization system will have models, isosurfaces, streamlines,
and cut planes. During this modelling step, we search the problem domain for objects, properties, and relationships. Later, during multiple passes through the design, the model will be
expanded.

Modelling is a step in most design processes regardless of whether we are designing a
ship, house, electronics system, or software. Each discipline follows a methodology that uses
techniques specifically created to make the design process efficient and worthwhile. These
techniques are so-called "tools of the trade." An electrical engineer uses schematics and logic
diagrams, an architect uses drawings and mock-ups, and a ship builder uses scale models.
Likewise, software designers need tools that can help create a model of the system. The software tools should have enough expressive power to help the software designer evaluate a
design against a specification and help communicate that design to others on the software
team.

We use the Object Modeling Technique (OMT) developed at GE by Jim Rumbaugh
and his colleagues [Rumbaugh91]. OMT uses three models to specify an object-oriented
design: an object model, a dynamic model, and a functional model. Each model describes a
different aspect of the system and each has a corresponding diagramming technique that
helps us analyze, design, and implement software systems.

The Object Model

The object model identifies each object in the system, its properties, and its relationships to
other objects in the system. For most software systems, the object model dominates the
design. The OMT graphical technique uses rectangles to depict object classes, and a variety

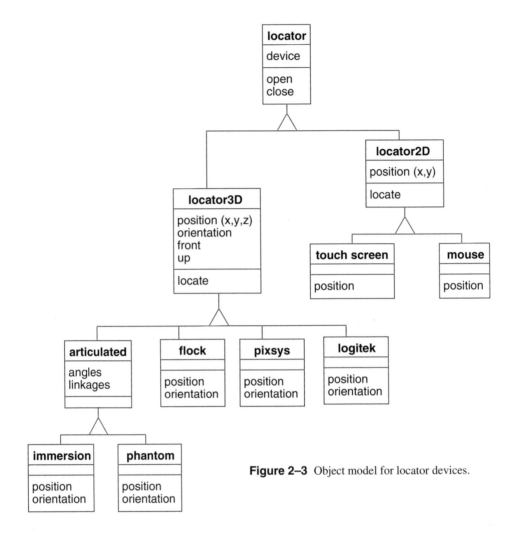

Figure 2–3 Object model for locator devices.

of connectors to depict inheritance and other object-object relations. Object classes are represented as solid rectangles. Instances are represented as dotted rectangles. The name of the
class or instance occupies the top of the rectangle. A line separates the class name from the
next section that contains the attributes; a third section describes the methods. Relationships
between objects are shown with line segments connecting the two related objects. In OMT,
relationships are called associations and they can have various cardinalities: one-to-one, one-
to-many, and many-to-many. Special associations that represent containers of other objects
are called aggregations. Associations can be labeled with roles. (Roles are names given to
associations and are used to further describe the nature of the association.) OMT represents
inheritance with a triangle, with the superclass attached to the apex, and subclasses attached
to the base of the triangle. **Figure 2–3** shows an object model for locator devices in a virtual
reality system.

The first object in the class hierarchy is locator. This abstract class specifies common attributes and methods for all locators. The subclasses of locator are locator2D and locator3D. In the current rendition of this object model, the locator only has one attribute, a device and two methods, open() and close(). The two subclasses of locator, locator2D and locator3D are also abstract classes, containing attributes and methods that distinguish them from each other based on their spatial dimensionality. For example, locator3D has an x, y, z position while locator2D has an x, y position. Both locators have a locate() method that updates the current position. In the 3D locator class, locate() also updates the orientation. The subclasses of locator3D include hardware from three different manufacturers: flock, pixsys, and logitek, as well as an articulated positioner abstract class. The three object classes for the hardware contain methods specific to each device. Each method knows how to convert the hardware specific codes returned by the device. They know that to be considered a locator3D subclass, they must implement a position and orientation operation that will provide x, y, z coordinates and three angular rotations that can be composed into a transformation matrix. The object model also shows us that the articulated locator has angles and linkages. Two specific articulated locators are immersion and phantom. An object model diagrammed in this fashion serves as a starting point for design and discussion. It reveals common methods and attributes as well as the distinguishing characteristics of each class.

Later, during implementation, we will convert these object models into software objects. The particular computer language we choose for implementation will dictate the details of the conversion.

The Dynamic Model

The object model describes the static portion of a system while the dynamic model details the sequences of events and time dependencies of the system. OMT uses state diagrams to model system dynamics. Dynamic models are frequently used to design control systems and user interfaces. Our visualization system has limited sequence and control aspects, so we will not dwell on state diagrams. But, if we were designing a user-friendly interface for a digital wristwatch, the state diagram in **Figure 2–4** would be useful.

The ovals in the diagram show a state; the arrows show a transition from one state to another; and the labels on the arrows show an event that causes the state transition. This example shows three display states and multiple setting states. The event b1 means button one is pressed. This watch has three buttons. The diagram shows what happens in each state when any of the three buttons is pressed. The diagram clearly shows that b1 is used to move between display modes for time, date, and alarm. B2 changes from display mode into setting mode or selects the field to change in a given mode. B3 increments the selected field by one unit. The state diagram also shows what happens when illegal buttons are pressed. If the watch is displaying time and button 3 is pressed, nothing happens. If button 3 is pressed when the watch is displaying the alarm, the alarm on/off is toggled.

The Functional Model

The functional model shows how data flows through the system and how processes and algorithms transform the data. It also shows functional dependencies between processes. Exposing these relationships will affect the associations in the object model. The major components

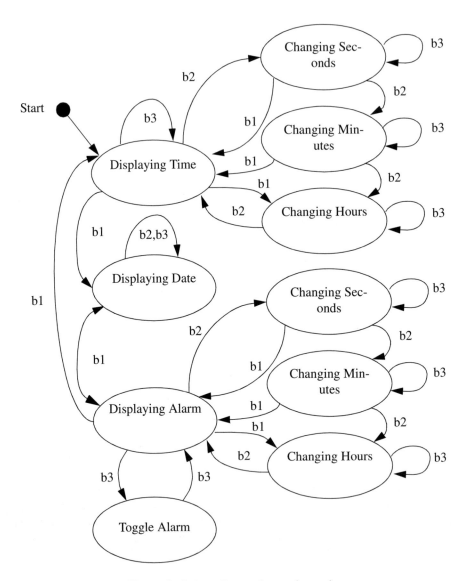

Figure 2–4 State diagram for a wristwatch.

of a data flow diagram (DFD) are data sources, data sinks, and processes. Data sources and sinks are represented as rectangles. Ellipses show processes. Data stores are shown within two horizontal lines. DFDs are useful to describe the overall flow in the system. They can also be used to describe any process that transforms one data representation into another. Processes identified in the DFD during function modelling may turn up as operations or objects in the object model.

Figure 2–5 shows a data flow diagram for a 3D medical imaging system. The diagram shows the data acquisition on the computed tomography (CT) or magnetic resonance imaging

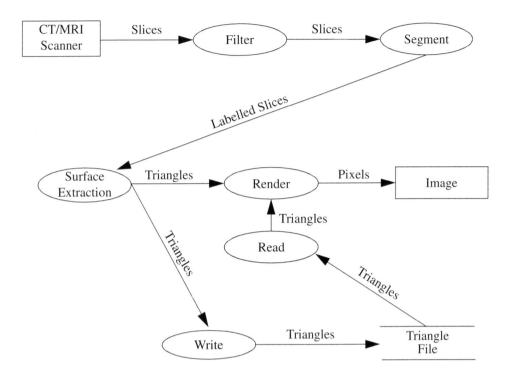

Figure 2–5 Data flow diagram.

(MRI) scanner. The series of cross-sectional slices provided by the scanner is first processed by image processing filters to enhance features in the gray scale slices. A segment process identifies tissues and produces labels for the various tissues present in the slices. These labeled slices are then passed through a surface extraction process to create triangles that lie on the surface of each tissue. The render process transforms the geometry into an image. Alternatively, the write process stores the triangles in a file. Later, the triangles can be read and rendered into an image. We defer the decision whether to make the processes objects or operations until later. Chapter 4 uses DFDs to model the visualization pipeline.

2.6 Object-Oriented Programming Languages

The choice of computer programming language is a religious issue. Every computer language has its evangelists and followers. Most of our experience in object-oriented languages is with C and C++. C itself does not have object-oriented facilities, but an object-oriented methodology and strict coding guidelines permit the development of object-oriented code. We chose C++ for the *Visualization Toolkit* because it has built-in support for the notion of classes, dynamic binding of methods to objects, and inheritance. C++ is also widely available on many UNIX platforms and personal computers.

Simula [Birtwistle79] is usually acknowledged as the first object-oriented language, but Smalltalk [Goldberg83] is probably the best-known language. Smalltalk was developed at the Xerox Palo Alto Research Center (PARC) in the seventies and eighties. Well before its time, Smalltalk provided not just a language, but also an operating system and programming environment built with objects. When you use Smalltalk, you live and breathe objects. For the object-oriented purist, there is no substitute. Smalltalk spin-offs include window systems, workstations, and the desktop paradigm. Both Apple Computer and Microsoft acknowledge the influence that Smalltalk and Xerox PARC had on the Macintosh and Windows. Smalltalk was probably conceived 10 years too early for widespread commercial acceptance. During Smalltalk's infancy and adolescence, the complexity of software was much lower than today's systems. FORTRAN served the scientific and engineering community, COBOL was the choice for business applications and the computer science community embraced C. The use of abstractions was limited to mathematicians and other abstract thinkers. Programming was considered an art form and programmers concentrated on clever implementations of algorithms. Each new task often required a new program. Technical programmers did use numerical libraries for common mathematical operations, but any notions of common abstractions at a higher level were relatively few.

2.7 Object-Oriented Visualization

Don't underestimate the investment required to design a system. Although object-oriented technologies have tremendous potential to produce good software designs, these techniques do not guarantee a good design. The visualization system we present in this text has its roots in an animation [Lorensen89] and visualization system [Schroeder92] that we developed over a 10-year period. The initial design, which identified 25 classes for computer animation of industrial applications, took four software professionals 10 months (almost 3.5 person years) to complete. During this design stage the developers produced zero (!) lines of code. The subsequent implementation took one month, or ten percent of the effort. This system still serves our visualization group even after 20 other software developers have added over 500 classes to the system. The original 25 classes still exist in the system today.

As a reader, we hope that you can benefit from our experience in visualization system design. We have tried to assist you by describing the properties (attributes and methods) of many of the *Visualization Toolkit* classes in each chapter's "Putting It All Together" section. There are also included a series of object diagrams generated by the Doxygen documentation system that will give you a quick overview of object relationships such as superclass and subclass. This documentation can be found on the CD-ROM or on-line at `http://www.vtk.org`. In the next chapter we will also explain the decisions we made to design the VTK object-oriented toolkit.

2.8 Chapter Summary

This chapter introduced object-oriented concepts and terminology. The emphasis was on dealing with complexity and how object-oriented technology provides mechanisms to reduce the complexity of software.

Model building is an important part of any design methodology. We introduced three models and notations. The object model describes the objects in a system and their static relationships, attributes, and methods. Object diagrams succinctly present this static information. The dynamic model focuses on the time dependent aspects of the system. State transition diagrams are used to model the sequence and control portions of the system. The functional model shows how objects in the system transform data or other objects. The data flow diagram is a convenient notation for showing functional dependencies.

There are several choices available today for object-oriented implementations. Although it is possible to implement an object-oriented system in a non-object-oriented language such as C, the methodology is best served by an object-oriented language. We have chosen C++ to implement the *Visualization Toolkit*.

The emphasis in this book is on architecture, data structure design, and algorithms. The object-oriented aspects of the system are important, but what the system does is far more important.

2.9 Bibliographic Notes

There are several excellent textbooks on object-oriented design. Both [Rumbaugh91] and [Birtwistle79] present language-independent design methodologies. Both books emphasize modelling and diagramming as key aspects of design. [Meyer88] also describes the OO design process in the context of Eiffel, an OO language. Another popular book has been authored by Booch [Booch91].

Anyone who wants to be a serious user of object-oriented design and implementation should read the books on Smalltalk [Goldberg83][Goldberg84] by the developers of Smalltalk at Xerox Parc. In another early object-oriented programming book, [Cox86] describes OO techniques and the programming language Objective-C. Objective-C is a mix of C and Smalltalk and was used by Next Computer in the implementation of their operating system and user interface.

There are many texts on object-oriented languages. CLOS [Keene89] describes the Common List Object System. Eiffel, a strongly typed OO language is described by [Meyer88]. Objective-C [Cox86] is a weakly typed language.

Since C++ has become a popular programming language, there now many class libraries available for use in applications. [Gorlen90] describes an extensive class library for collections and arrays modeled after the Smalltalk classes described in [Goldberg83]. [Stepanov94] and [Musser94] describe the Standard Template Library, a framework of data structures and algorithms that is now a part of the ANSI C++ standard. Open Inventor [Inventor] is a C++ library supporting interactive 3D computer graphics. The Insight Segmentation and Registration Toolkit (ITK) is a relatively new class library often used in combination with VTK [ITK] for medical data processing. VXL is a C++ library for computer vision research and implementation [VXL]. Several mathematical libraries such as VNL (a part of VXL) and Blitz++ [Blitz] are also available. A wide variety of other C++ toolkits are available, Google searches [Google] are the best way to find them.

C++ texts abound. The original description by the author of C++ [Stroustrup84] is a must for any serious C++ programmer. Another book [Ellis90] describes standard extensions to the language. These days the UML book series—of which [Booch98] and [Rumbaugh98] are quite popular—are highly recommended resources. Several books on generic programming [Austern99] and STL [Musser96] are also useful. Check with your colleagues for their favorite C++ book.

To keep in touch with new developments there are conferences, journals, and Web sites. The strongest technical conference on object-oriented topics is the annual Object-Oriented Programming Systems, Languages, and Applications (*OOPSLA*) conference. This is where researchers in the field describe, teach and debate the latest techniques in object-oriented technology. The bimonthly *Journal of Object-Oriented Programming* (JOOP) published by SIGS Publications, NY, presents technical papers, columns, and tutorials on the field. Resources on the World Wide Web include the Usenet newsgroups *comp.object* and *comp.lang.c++*.

2.10 References

[Austern99]
> M. H. Austern. *Generic Programming and the STL*. Addison-Wesley 1999. ISBN 0-2-1-30956-4.

[Birtwistle79]
> G. M. Birtwistle, O. Dahl, B. Myhrhaug, and K. Nygaard. *Simula Begin*. Chartwell-Bratt Ltd, England, 1979.

[Blitz]
> `http://www.oonumerics.org/blitz/`.

[Booch91]
> G. Booch. *Object-Oriented Design with Applications*. Benjamin/Cummings Publishing Co., Redwood City, CA, 1991.

[Booch98]
> G. Booch, I. Jacobson, J. Rumbaugh. *The Unified Modeling Language User Guide*. Addison-Wesley 1998, ISBN 0201571684.

[Cox86]
> B. J. Cox. *Object-Oriented Programming: An Evolutionary Approach*. Addison-Wesley, Reading, MA, 1986.

[Ellis90]
> M. Ellis and B. Stroustrup. *The Annotated C++ Reference Manual*. Addison-Wesley, Reading, MA, 1990.

[Goldberg83]
> A. Goldberg, D. Robson. *Smalltalk-80: The Language and Its Implementation*. Addison-Wesley, Reading, MA, 1983.

[Goldberg84]
> A. Goldberg. *Smalltalk-80: The Interactive Programming Environment*. Addison-Wesley, Reading, MA, 1984.

[Google]
> `http://www.google.com`.

[Gorlen90]
> K. Gorlen, S. Orlow, and P. Plexico. *Data Abstraction and Object-Oriented Programming*. John Wiley & Sons, Ltd., Chichester, England, 1990.

[Inventor]
    http://oss.sgi.com/projects/inventor/.

[ITK]
    The Insight Software Consortium. http://www.itk.org.

[Keene89]
    S. Keene. *Object-Oriented Programming in Common Lisp: A Programmer's Guide to CLOS*. Addison-Wesley, Reading, MA, 1989.

[Lorensen89]
    W. E. Lorensen, B. Yamrom. "Object-Oriented Computer Animation." *Proceedings of IEEE NAECON*, 2:588-595, Dayton, Ohio, May 1989.

[Margulis88]
    L. Margulis and K. V. Schwartz. *Five Kingdoms an Illustrated Guide to the Phyla of Life on Earth*. W. H. Freeman & Co., New York, 1988.

[Meyer88]
    B. Meyer. *Object-Oriented Software Construction*. Prentice Hall International, Hertford-shire, England, 1988.

[Musser94]
    D. Musser and A. Stepanov. "Algorithm-Oriented Generic Libraries." *Software Practice and Experience*. 24(7):623–642, July 1994.

[Musser96]
    D. R. Musser and A. Saini. *STL Tutorial and Reference Guide*. Addison-Wesley 1996. ISBN 0-201-63398-1.

[Rumbaugh91]
    J. Rumbaugh, M. Blaha, W. Premerlani, F. Eddy, and W. Lorensen. *Object-Oriented Modeling and Design*. Prentice Hall, Englewood Cliffs, NJ, 1991.

[Rumbaugh98]
    J. Rumbaugh, G. Booch, and I. Jacobson. *The Unified Modeling Language Reference Manual*. Addison-Wesley 1998, ISBN: 020130998X.

[Schroeder92]
    W. J. Schroeder, W. E. Lorensen, G. Montanaro, and C. Volpe. "Visage: An Object-Oriented Scientific Visualization System." In *Proceedings of Visualization '92*. pp. 219–226, IEEE Computer Society Press, Los Alamitos, CA, October 1992.

[Stepanov94]
    A. Stepanov and M. Lee. *The Standard Template Library*. ISO Programming Language C++ Project. Doc. No. X3J16/94-0095, WG21/N0482, May 1994.

[Stroustrup84]
    B. Stroustrup. *The C++ Programming Language*. Addison-Wesley, Reading, MA, 1986.

[VXL]
    http://vxl.sourceforge.net/.

2.11 Exercises

2.1   Answer the following questions about a program you have written.

    a) How much time did you spend on design and implementation?

    b) What methodology, if any, did you use?

     c) Could you easily extend the system?

     d) Could anyone extend the system?

2.2   Identify the major objects and operations for the following applications.

     a) An airline reservation system.

     b) An adventure game.

     c) A 2D plotting package.

     d) An automatic teller machine.

2.3   Draw an object diagram for each example in Exercise 2.2.

2.4   Computer animation uses concepts from graphics and movie making. Identify the major objects and operations in a computer animation system.

2.5   For the animation system in Exercise 2.4, design control and looping objects that will allow flexible control of the properties of the actors in the system. If we call these control and looping objects scenes and cues, how would you expect them to look?

2.6   Draw a state diagram for your wristwatch using Figure 2–4 as an example.

2.7   Draw a data flow diagram for calculating the surface area and volume of a sphere and cylinder.

Computer Graphics Primer

Computer graphics is the foundation of data visualization. Practically speaking, we can say that visualization is the process that transforms data into a set of graphics primitives. The methods of computer graphics are then used to convert these primitives into pictures or animations. This chapter discusses basic computer graphics principles. We begin by describing how lights and physical objects interact to form what we see. Then we examine how to simulate these interactions using computer graphics techniques. Hardware issues play an important role here since modern computers have built-in hardware support for graphics. The chapter concludes with a series of examples that illustrate our object-oriented model for 3D computer graphics.

3.1 Introduction

Computer graphics is the process of generating images using computers. We call this process *rendering*. There are many types of rendering processes, ranging from 2D paint programs to sophisticated 3D techniques. In this chapter we focus on basic 3D techniques for visualization.

We can view rendering as the process of converting graphical data into an image. In data visualization our goal is to transform data into graphical data, or *graphics primitives*, that are then rendered. The goal of our rendering is not so much image realism as it is information content. We also strive for interactive graphical displays so we can interact with the data. This chapter explains the process of rendering an image from graphical data. We begin

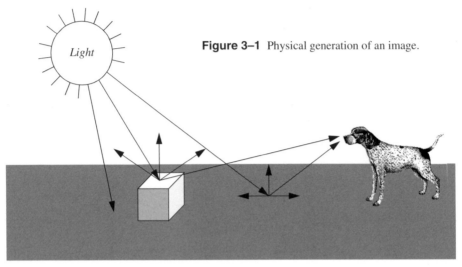

Figure 3–1 Physical generation of an image.

by looking at the way lights, cameras, and objects (or actors) interact in the world around us. From this foundation we explain how to simulate this process on a computer.

A Physical Description of Rendering

Figure 3–1 presents a simplified view of what happens when we look at an object, in this case a cube. Rays of light are emitted from a light source in all directions. (In this example we assume that the light source is the sun.) Some of these rays happen to strike the cube whose surface absorbs some of the incident light and reflects the rest of it. Some of this reflected light may head towards us and enter our eyes. If this happens, then we "see" the object. Likewise, some of the light from the sun will strike the ground and some small percentage of it will be reflected into our eyes.

As you can imagine, the chances of a ray of light traveling from the sun through space to hit a small object on a relatively small planet are low. This is compounded by the slim odds that the ray of light will reflect off the object and into our eyes. The only reason we can see is that the sun produces such an enormous amount of light that it overwhelms the odds. While this may work in real life, trying to simulate it with a computer can be difficult. Fortunately, there are other ways to look at this problem.

A common and effective technique for 3D computer graphics is called *ray-tracing* or *ray-casting*. Ray-tracing simulates the interaction of light with objects by following the path of each light ray. Typically, we follow the ray backwards from the viewer's eyes and into the world to determine what the ray strikes. The direction of the ray is in the direction we are looking (i.e., the view direction) including effects of perspective (if desired). When a ray intersects an object, we can determine if that point is being lit by our light source. This is done by tracing a ray from the point of intersection towards the light. If the ray intersects the light, then the point is being lit. If the ray intersects something else before it gets to the light, then that light will not contribute to illuminating the point. For multiple light sources we just repeat this process for each light source. The total contributions from all the light sources, plus any ambient scattered light, will determine the total lighting or shadow for that point. By following the light's path backwards, ray tracing only looks at rays that end up entering the viewer's eyes. This dramatically reduces the number of rays that must be computed by a simulation program.

Having described ray tracing as a rendering process, it may be surprising that many members of the graphics community do not use it. This is because ray tracing is a relatively slow image generation method since it is typically implemented in software. Other graphics techniques have been developed that generate images using dedicated computer hardware. To understand why this situation has emerged, it is instructive to briefly examine the taxonomy and history of computer graphics.

Image-Order and Object-Order Methods

Rendering processes can be broken into two categories: *image-order* and *object-order*. Ray tracing is an image-order process. It works by determining what happens to each ray of light, one at a time. An object-order process works by rendering each object, one at a time. In the above example, an object-order technique would proceed by first rendering the ground and then the cube.

To look at it another way consider painting a picture of a barn. Using an image-order algorithm you would start at the upper left corner of the canvas and put down a drop of the correct color paint. (Each paint drop is called a picture element or *pixel*.) Then you would move a little to the right and put down another drop of paint. You would continue until you reached the right edge of the canvas, then you would move down a little and start on the next row. Each time you put down a drop of paint you make certain it is the correct color for each pixel on the canvas. When you are done you will have a painting of a barn.

An alternative approach is based on the more natural (at least for many people) object-order process. We work by painting the different objects in our scene, independent of where the objects actually are located on the scene. We may paint from back to front, front-to-back, or in arbitrary order. For example, we could start by painting the sky and then add in the ground. After these two objects were painted we would then add in the barn. In the image-order process we worked on the canvas in a very orderly fashion; left to right, top to bottom. With an object-order process we tend to jump from one part of the canvas to another, depending on what object we are drawing.

The field of computer graphics started out using object-order processes. Much of the early work was closely tied to the hardware display device, initially a vector display. This was little more than an oscilloscope, but it encouraged graphical data to be drawn as a series of line segments. As the original vector displays gave way to the currently ubiquitous raster displays, the notion of representing graphical data as a series of objects to be drawn was preserved. Much of the early work pioneered by Bresenham [Bresenham65] at IBM focused on how to properly convert line segments into a form that would be suitable for line plotters. The same work was applied to the task of rendering lines onto the raster displays that replaced the oscilloscope. Since then the hardware has become more powerful and capable of displaying much more complex primitives than lines.

It wasn't until the early 1980s that a paper by Turner Whitted [Whitted80] prompted many people to look at rendering from a more physical perspective. Eventually ray tracing became a serious competitor to the traditional object-order rendering techniques, due in part to the highly realistic images it can produce. Object-order rendering has maintained its popularity because there is a wealth of graphics hardware designed to quickly render objects. Ray tracing tends to be done without any specialized hardware and therefore is a time-consuming process.

Surface versus Volume Rendering

The discussion to this point in the text has tacitly assumed that when we render an object, we are viewing the surfaces of objects and their interactions with light. However, common objects such as clouds, water, and fog, are translucent, or scatter light that passes through them. Such objects cannot be rendered using a model based exclusively on surface interactions. Instead, we need to consider the changing properties inside the object to properly render them. We refer to these two rendering models as *surface rendering* (i.e., render the surfaces of an object) and *volume rendering* (i.e., render the surface and interior of an object).

Generally speaking, when we render an object using surface rendering techniques, we mathematically model the object with a surface description such as points, lines, triangles, polygons, or 2D and 3D splines. The interior of the object is not described, or only implicitly represented from the surface representation (i.e., surface is the boundary of the volume). Although techniques do exist that allow us to make the surface transparent or translucent, there are still many phenomena that cannot be simulated using surface rendering techniques alone (e.g., scattering or light emission). This is particularly true if we are trying to render data interior to an object, such as X-ray intensity from a CT scan.

Volume rendering techniques allow us to see the inhomogeneity inside objects. In the prior CT example, we can realistically reproduce X-ray images by considering the intensity values from both the surface and interior of the data. Although it is premature to describe this process at this point in the text, you can imagine extending our ray tracing example from the previous section. Thus rays not only interact with the surface of an object, they also interact with the interior.

In this chapter we focus on surface rendering techniques. While not as powerful as volume rendering, surface rendering is widely used because it is relatively fast compared to volume rendering, and allows us to create images for a wide variety of data and objects. Chapter 7 describes volume rendering in more detail.

Visualization Not Graphics

Although the authors would enjoy providing a thorough treatise on computer graphics, such a discourse is beyond the scope of this text. Instead we make the distinction between visualization (exploring, transforming, and mapping data) and computer graphics (mapping and rendering). The focus will be on the principles and practice of visualization, and not on 3D computer graphics. In this chapter and Chapter 7 we introduce basic concepts and provide a working knowledge of 3D computer graphics. For those more interested in this field, we refer you to the texts recommended in the "Bibliographic Notes" on page 78 at the end of this chapter.

One of the regrets we have regarding this posture is that certain rendering techniques are essentially visualization techniques. We see this hinted at in the previous paragraph, where we use the term "mapping" to describe both visualization and computer graphics. There is not currently and will likely never be a firm distinction between visualization and

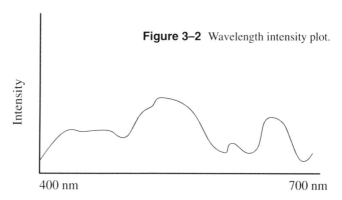

Figure 3–2 Wavelength intensity plot.

graphics. For example, many researchers consider volume rendering to be squarely in the field of visualization because it addresses one of the most important forms of visualization data. Our distinction is mostly for our own convenience, and offers us the opportunity to finish this text. We recommend that a serious student of visualization supplement the material presented here with deeper books on computer graphics and volume rendering.

In the next few pages we describe the rendering process in more detail. We start by describing several color models. Then we examine the primary components of the rendering process. There are sources of light such as the sun, objects we wish to render such as a cube or sphere (we refer to these objects as *actors*), and there is a camera that looks out into the world. These terms are taken from the movie industry and tend to be familiar to most people. Actors represent graphical data or objects, lights illuminate the actors, and the camera constructs a picture by projecting the actors onto a view plane. We call the combination of lights, camera, and actors the *scene*, and refer to the rendering process as rendering the scene.

3.2 Color

The electromagnetic spectrum visible to humans contains wavelengths ranging from about 400 to 700 nanometers. This light that enters our eyes consists of different *intensities* of these wavelengths, an example of which is shown in **Figure 3–2**. This intensity plot defines the color of the light, a different plot results in a different color. Unfortunately, we may not notice the difference since the human eye throws out most of this information. There are three types of color receptors in the human eye. Each type responds to a subset of the 400 to 700 nanometer wavelength range as in **Figure 3–3**. Any color we see gets coded by our eyes into these three overlapping responses. This is a great reduction from the amount of information that actually comes into our eyes. As a result, the human eye is incapable of recognizing differences in any colors whose intensity curves, when applied to the human eye's response curves, result in the same triplet of responses. This also implies that we can store and represent colors in a computer using a simplified form without the human eye being able to recognize the difference.

The two simplified component systems that we use to describe colors are RGB and HSV color systems. The RGB system represents colors based on their red, green, and blue

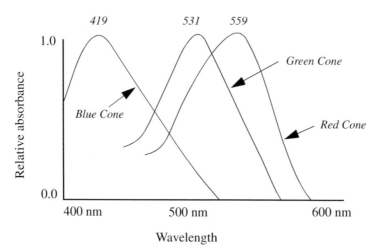

Figure 3–3 Relative absorbance of light by the three types of cones in the human retina [Dartnall83].

intensities. This can be thought of as a three dimensional space with the axes being red, green, and blue. Some common colors and their RGB components are shown in **Figure 3–4**.

The HSV system represents colors based on their hue, saturation, and value. The value component is also known as the brightness or intensity component, and represents how much light is in the color. A value of 0.0 will always give you black and a value of 1.0 will give you something bright. The hue represents the dominant wavelength of the color. Hue is often illustrated using a circle as in **Figure 3–5**. Each location on the circumference of this circle represents a different hue and can be specified using an angle. When we specify a hue we use the range from zero to one, where zero corresponds to zero degrees on the hue circle and one corresponds to 360 degrees. The saturation indicates how much of the hue is mixed into the color. For example, we can set the value to one, which gives us a bright color, and the hue to 0.66, to give us a dominant wavelength of blue. Now if we set the saturation to one, the color will be a bright primary blue. If we set the saturation to 0.5, the color will be sky blue, a blue with more white mixed in. If we set the saturation to zero, this indicates that there is no more of the dominant wavelength (hue) in the color than any other wavelength. As a result, the final color will be white (regardless of hue value). **Figure 3–4** lists HSV values for some common colors.

3.3 Lights

One of the major factors controlling the rendering process is the interaction of light with the actors in the scene. If there are no lights, the resulting image will be black and rather uninformative. To a great extent it is the interaction between the emitted light and the surface (and in some cases the interior) of the actors in the scene that defines what we see. Once rays of light interact with the actors in a scene, we have something for our camera to view.

Color	RGB	HSV
Black	0,0,0	*,*,0
White	1,1,1	*,0,1
Red	1,0,0	0,1,1
Green	0,1,0	1/3,1,1
Blue	0,0,1	2/3,1,1
Yellow	1,1,0	1/6,1,1
Cyan	0,1,1	1/2,1,1
Magenta	1,0,1	5/6,1,1
Sky Blue	1/2,1/2,1	2/3,1/2,1

Figure 3–4 Common colors in RGB and HSV space.

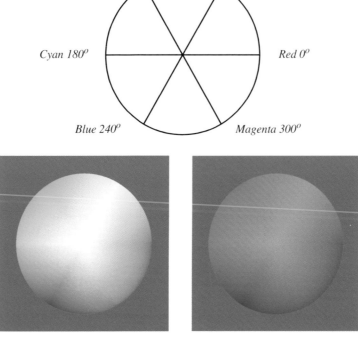

Figure 3–5 On the top, circular representation of hue. The other two images on the bottom are slices through the HSV color space. The first slice has a value of 1.0, the other has a value of 0.5.

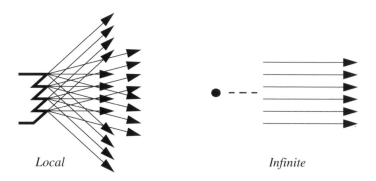

Figure 3–6 Local light source with a finite volume versus an infinite point light source.

Of the many different types of lights used in computer graphics, we will discuss the simplest, the infinitely distant, point light source. This is a simplified model compared to the lights we use at home and work. The light sources that we are accustomed to typically radiate from a region in space (a filament in an incandescent bulb, or a light-emitting gas in a fluorescent light). The point source lighting model assumes that the light is emitted in all directions from a single point in space. For an infinite light source, we assume that it is positioned infinitely far away from what it is illuminating. This is significant because it implies that the incoming rays from such a source will be parallel to each other. The emissions of a local light source, such as a lamp in a room, are not parallel. **Figure 3–6** illustrates the differences between a local light source with a finite volume, versus an infinite point light source. The intensity of the light emitted by our infinite light sources also remains constant as it travels, in contrast to the actual $1/\text{distance}^2$ relationship physical lights obey. As you can see this is a great simplification, which later will allow us to use less complex lighting equations.

3.4 Surface Properties

As rays of light travel through space, some of them intersect our actors. When this happens, the rays of light interact with the surface of the actor to produce a color. Part of this resulting color is actually not due to direct light, but rather from *ambient* light that is being reflected or scattered from other objects. An ambient lighting model accounts for this and is a simple approximation of the complex scattering of light that occurs in the real world. It applies the intensity curve of the light source to the color of the object, also expressed as an intensity curve. The result is the color of the light we see when we look at that object. With such a model, it is important to realize that a white light shining on a blue ball is indistinguishable from a blue light shining on a white ball. The ambient lighting equation is

$$R_c = L_c \cdot O_c \qquad\qquad \textbf{(3-1)}$$

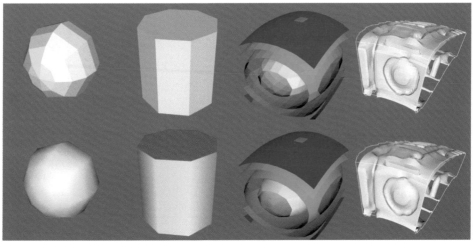

Figure 3–7 Flat and Gouraud shading. Different shading methods can dramatically improve the look of an object represented with polygons. On the top, flat shading uses a constant surface normal across each polygon. On the bottom, Gouraud shading interpolates normals from polygon vertices to give a smoother look.

where R_c is the resulting intensity curve, L_c is the intensity curve of the light, and O_c is the color curve of the object. To help keep the equations simple we assume that all of the direction vectors are normalized (i.e., have a magnitude of one).

Two components of the resulting color depend on direct lighting. *Diffuse lighting*, which is also known as Lambertian reflection, takes into account the angle of incidence of the light onto an object. **Figure 3–7** shows the image of a cylinder that becomes darker as you move laterally from its center. The cylinder's color is constant; the amount of light hitting the surface of the cylinder changes. At the center, where the incoming light is nearly perpendicular to the surface of the cylinder, it receives more rays of light per surface area. As we move towards the side, this drops until finally the incoming light is parallel to the side of the cylinder and the resulting intensity is zero. The contribution from diffuse lighting is expressed in **Equation 3-2** and illustrated in **Figure 3–9**.

$$R_c = L_c O_c [\vec{O}_n \cdot (-\vec{L}_n)]$$
(3-2)

where R_c is the resulting intensity curve, L_c is the intensity curve for the light, and O_c is the color curve for the object. Notice that the diffuse light is a function of the relative angle between incident light vector $\vec{L}_n$ and the surface normal of the object $\vec{O}_n$. As a result diffuse lighting is independent of viewer position.

Specular lighting represents direct reflections of a light source off a shiny object. **Figure 3–10** shows a diffusely lit ball with varying specular reflection. The specular intensity (which varies between the top and bottom rows) controls the intensity of the specular lighting. The specular power, O_{sp}, indicates how shiny an object is, more specifically it indicates how quickly specular reflections diminish as the reflection angles deviate from a perfect

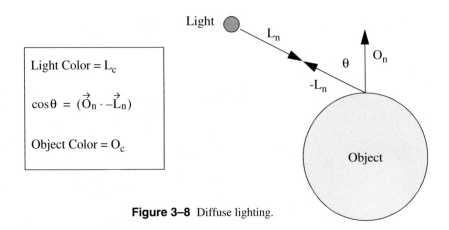

Figure 3–8 Diffuse lighting.

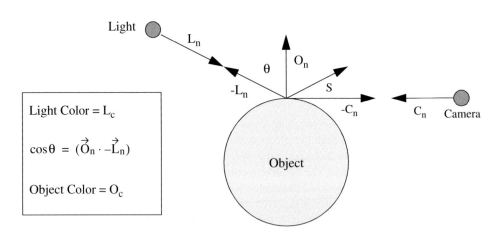

Figure 3–9 Specular lighting.

reflection. Higher values indicate a faster dropoff, and therefore a shinier surface. Referring to **Figure 3–9**, the equation for specular lighting is

$$R_c = L_c O_c [\vec{S} \cdot (-\vec{C}_n)]^{O_{sp}}$$

$$\vec{S} = 2[\vec{O}_n \cdot (-\vec{L}_n)]\vec{O}_n + \vec{L}_n$$

(3-3)

where $\vec{C}_n$ is the direction of projection for the camera and $\vec{S}$ is the direction of specular reflection.

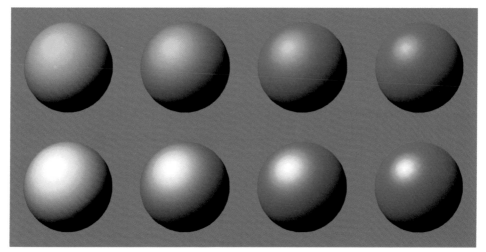

Figure 3–10 Effects of specular coefficients. Specular coefficients control the apparent "shininess" of objects. The top row has a specular intensity value of 0.5; the bottom row 1.0. Along the horizontal direction the specular power changes. The values (from left to right) are 5, 10, 20, and 40 (`SpecularSpheres.cxx`)

We have presented the equations for the different lighting models independently. We can apply all lighting models simultaneously or in combination. **Equation 3-4** combines ambient, diffuse and specular lighting into one equation.

$$R_c = O_{ai}O_{ac}L_c - O_{di}O_{dc}L_c(\vec{O}_n \cdot \vec{L}_n) + O_{si}O_{sc}L_c[\vec{S} \cdot (-\vec{C}_n)]^{O_{sp}} \tag{3-4}$$

The result is a color at a point on the surface of the object. The constants O_{ai}, O_{di}, and O_{si} control the relative amounts of ambient, diffuse and specular lighting for an object. The constants O_{ac}, O_{dc}, and O_{sc} specify the colors to be used for each type of lighting. These six constants along with the specular power are part of the surface material properties. (Other properties such as transparency will be covered in later sections of the text.) Different combinations of these property values can simulate dull plastic and polished metal. The equation assumes an infinite point light source as described in "Lights" on page 38. However the equation can be easily modified to incorporate other types of directional lighting.

3.5 Cameras

We have light sources that are emitting rays of light and actors with surface properties. At every point on the surface of our actors this interaction results in some composite color (i.e., combined color from light, object surface, specular, and ambient effects). All we need now to render the scene is a camera. There are a number of important factors that determine how a 3D scene gets projected onto a plane to form a 2D image (see **Figure 3–11**). These are the

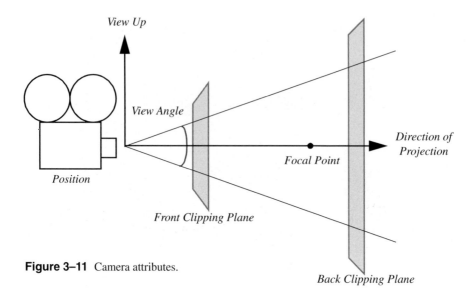

Figure 3–11 Camera attributes.

position, orientation, and focal point of the camera, the method of camera *projection*, and the location of the camera *clipping planes*.

The position and focal point of the camera define the location of the camera and where it points. The vector defined from the camera position to the focal point is called the *direction of projection*. The camera image plane is located at the focal point and is typically perpendicular to the projection vector. The camera orientation is controlled by the position and focal point plus the camera *view-up* vector. Together these completely define the camera view.

The method of projection controls how the actors are mapped to the image plane. *Orthographic projection* is a parallel mapping process. In orthographic projection (or parallel projection) all rays of light entering the camera are parallel to the projection vector. *Perspective projection* occurs when all light rays go through a common point (i.e., the viewpoint or center of projection). To apply perspective projection we must specify a perspective angle or camera view angle.

The front and back *clipping planes* intersect the projection vector, and are usually perpendicular to it. The clipping planes are used to eliminate data either too close to the camera or too far away. As a result only actors or portions of actors within the clipping planes are (potentially) visible. Clipping planes are typically perpendicular to the direction of projection. Their locations can be set using the camera's clipping range. The location of the planes are measured from the camera's position along the direction of projection. The front clipping plane is at the minimum range value, and the back clipping plane is at the maximum range value. Later on in Chapter 7, when we discuss stereo rendering, we will see examples of clipping planes that are not perpendicular to the direction of projection.

Taken together these camera parameters define a rectangular pyramid, with its apex at the camera's position and extending along the direction of projection. The pyramid is truncated at the top with the front clipping plane and at the bottom by the back clipping plane. The resulting *view frustum* defines the region of 3D space visible to the camera.

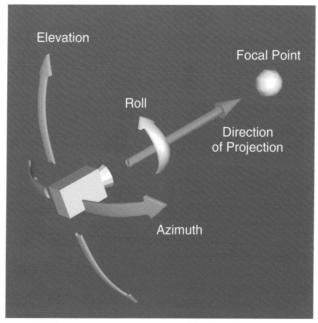

Figure 3–12 Camera movements around focal point (`camera.tcl`).

While a camera can be manipulated by directly setting the attributes mentioned above, there are some common operations that make the job easier. **Figure 3–12** and **Figure 3–13** will help illustrate these operations. Changing the *azimuth* of a camera rotates its position around its view up vector, centered at the focal point. Think of this as moving the camera to the left or right while always keeping the distance to the focal point constant. Changing a camera's *elevation* rotates its position around the cross product of its direction of projection and view up centered at the focal point. This corresponds to moving the camera up and down. To *roll* the camera, we rotate the view up vector about the view plane normal. Roll is sometimes called twist.

The next two motions keep the camera's position constant and instead modify the focal point. Changing the *yaw* rotates the focal point about the view up centered at the camera's position. This is like an azimuth, except that the focal point moves instead of the position. Changes in *pitch* rotate the focal point about the cross product of the direction of projection and view up centered at the camera's position. *Dollying* in and out moves the camera's position along the direction of projection, either closer or farther from the focal point. This operation is specified as the ratio of its current distance to its new distance. A value greater than one will dolly in, while a value less than one will dolly out. Finally, *zooming* changes the camera's view angle, so that more or less of the scene falls within the view frustum.

Once we have the camera situated, we can generate our 2D image. Some of the rays of light traveling through our 3D space will pass through the lens on the camera. These rays then strike a flat surface to produce an image. This effectively projects our 3D scene into a 2D image. The camera's position and other properties determine which rays of light get cap-

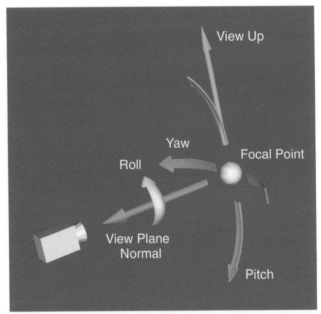

Figure 3–13 Camera movements centered at camera position (`camera2.tcl`).

tured and projected. More specifically, only rays of light that intersect the camera's position, and are within its viewing frustum, will affect the resulting 2D image.

This concludes our brief rendering overview. The light has traveled from its sources to the actors, where it is reflected and scattered. Some of this light gets captured by the camera and produces a 2D image. Now we will look at some of the details of this process.

3.6 Coordinate Systems

There are four coordinate systems commonly used in computer graphics and two different ways of representing points within them (**Figure 3–14**). While this may seem excessive, each one serves a purpose. The four coordinate systems we use are: *model*, *world*, *view*, and *display*.

The model coordinate system is the coordinate system in which the model is defined, typically a local Cartesian coordinate system. If one of our actors represents a football, it will be based on a coordinate system natural to the football geometry (e.g., a cylindrical system). This model has an inherent coordinate system determined by the decisions of whoever generated it. They may have used inches or meters as their units, and the football may have been modeled with any arbitrary axis as its major axis.

The world coordinate system is the 3D space in which the actors are positioned. One of the actor's responsibilities is to convert from the model's coordinates into world coordinates. Each model may have its own coordinate system but there is only one world coordinate system. Each actor must scale, rotate, and translate its model into the world coordinate system. (It may also be necessary for the modeller to transform from its natural coordinate system

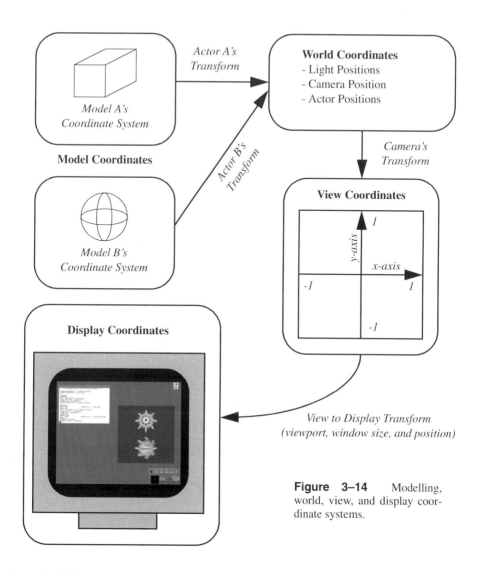

Figure 3–14 Modelling, world, view, and display coordinate systems.

into a local Cartesian system. This is because actors typically assume that the model coordinate system is a local Cartesian system.) The world coordinate system is also the system in which the position and orientation of cameras and lights are specified.

The view coordinate system represents what is visible to the camera. This consists of a pair of x and y values, ranging between $(-1,1)$, and a z depth coordinate. The x, y values specify location in the image plane, while the z coordinate represents the distance, or range, from the camera. The camera's properties are represented by a four by four transformation matrix (to be described shortly), which is used to convert from world coordinates into view coordinates. This is where the perspective effects of a camera are introduced.

The display coordinate system uses the same basis as the view coordinate system, but instead of using negative one to one as the range, the coordinates are actual x, y pixel locations on the image plane. Factors such as the window's size on the display determine how the view coordinate range of (-1,1) is mapped into pixel locations. This is also where the *view-port* comes into effect. You may want to render two different scenes, but display them in the same window. This can be done by dividing the window into rectangular viewports. Then, each renderer can be told what portion of the window it should use for rendering. The view-port ranges from (0,1) in both the *x* and *y* axis. Similar to the view coordinate system, the *z*-value in the display coordinate system also represents depth into the window. The meaning of this *z*-value will be further described in the section titled "Z-Buffer" on page 57.

3.7 Coordinate Transformation

When we create images with computer graphics, we project objects defined in three dimensions onto a two-dimensional image plane. As we saw earlier, this projection naturally includes perspective. To include projection effects such as vanishing points we use a special coordinate system called *homogeneous coordinates*.

The usual way of representing a point in 3D is the three element Cartesian vector (x, y, z). Homogeneous coordinates are represented by a four element vector (x_h, y_h, z_h, w_h). The conversion between Cartesian coordinates and homogeneous coordinates is given by:

$$x = \frac{x_h}{w_h} \qquad y = \frac{y_h}{w_h} \qquad z = \frac{z_h}{w_h} \tag{3-5}$$

Using homogeneous coordinates we can represent an infinite point by setting w_h to zero. This capability is used by the camera for perspective transformations. The transformations are applied by using a 4×4 *transformation matrix*. Transformation matrices are widely used in computer graphics because they allow us to perform translation, scaling, and rotation of objects by repeated matrix multiplication. Not all of these operations can be performed using a 3×3 matrix.

For example, suppose we wanted to create a transformation matrix that translates a point (x, y, z) in Cartesian space by the vector (t_x, t_y, t_z). We need only construct the translation matrix given by

$$T_T = \begin{bmatrix} 1 & 0 & 0 & t_x \\ 0 & 1 & 0 & t_y \\ 0 & 0 & 1 & t_z \\ 0 & 0 & 0 & 1 \end{bmatrix} \tag{3-6}$$

and then postmultiply it with the homogeneous coordinate (x_h, y_h, z_h, w_h). To carry this example through, we construct the homogeneous coordinate from the Cartesian coordinate (x, y, z) by setting $w_h = 1$ to yield $(x, y, z, 1)$. Then, to determine the translated point

(x', y', z') we premultiply the current position by the transformation matrix T_T to yield the translated coordinate. Substituting into **Equation 3-6** we have the result

$$\begin{bmatrix} x' \\ y' \\ z' \\ w' \end{bmatrix} = \begin{bmatrix} 1 & 0 & 0 & t_x \\ 0 & 1 & 0 & t_y \\ 0 & 0 & 1 & t_z \\ 0 & 0 & 0 & 1 \end{bmatrix} \cdot \begin{bmatrix} x \\ y \\ z \\ 1 \end{bmatrix} \tag{3-7}$$

Converting back to Cartesian coordinates via **Equation 3-5** we have the expected solution

$$x' = x + t_x$$
$$y' = y + t_y \tag{3-8}$$
$$z' = z + t_z$$

The same procedure is used to scale or rotate an object. To scale an object we use the transformation matrix

$$T_S = \begin{bmatrix} s_x & 0 & 0 & 0 \\ 0 & s_y & 0 & 0 \\ 0 & 0 & s_z & 0 \\ 0 & 0 & 0 & 1 \end{bmatrix} \tag{3-9}$$

where the parameters s_x, s_y, and s_z are scale factors along the x, y, and z axes. Similarly, we can rotate an object around the x axes by angle θ using the matrix

$$T_{R_x} = \begin{bmatrix} 1 & 0 & 0 & 0 \\ 0 & \cos\theta & -\sin\theta & 0 \\ 0 & \sin\theta & \cos\theta & 0 \\ 0 & 0 & 0 & 1 \end{bmatrix} \tag{3-10}$$

Around the y axis we use

$$T_{R_y} = \begin{bmatrix} \cos\theta & 0 & \sin\theta & 0 \\ 0 & 1 & 0 & 0 \\ -\sin\theta & 0 & \cos\theta & 0 \\ 0 & 0 & 0 & 1 \end{bmatrix} \tag{3-11}$$

and around the z axis we use

$$T_{R_z} = \begin{bmatrix} \cos\theta & -\sin\theta & 0 & 0 \\ \sin\theta & \cos\theta & 0 & 0 \\ 0 & 0 & 1 & 0 \\ 0 & 0 & 0 & 1 \end{bmatrix}$$

(3-12)

Another useful rotation matrix is used to transform one coordinate axes $x - y - z$ to another coordinate axes $x' - y' - z'$. To derive the transformation matrix we assume that the unit x' axis makes the angles $(\theta_{x'x}, \theta_{x'y}, \theta_{x'z})$ around the $x - y - z$ axes (these are called direction cosines). Similarly, the unit y' axis makes the angles $(\theta_{y'x}, \theta_{y'y}, \theta_{y'z})$ and the unit z' axis makes the angles $(\theta_{z'x}, \theta_{z'y}, \theta_{z'z})$. The resulting rotation matrix is formed by placing the direction cosines along the rows of the transformation matrix as follows

$$T_R = \begin{bmatrix} \cos\theta_{x'x} & \cos\theta_{x'y} & \cos\theta_{x'z} & 0 \\ \cos\theta_{y'x} & \cos\theta_{y'y} & \cos\theta_{y'z} & 0 \\ \cos\theta_{z'x} & \cos\theta_{z'y} & \cos\theta_{z'z} & 0 \\ 0 & 0 & 0 & 1 \end{bmatrix}$$

(3-13)

Rotations occur about the coordinate origin. It is often more convenient to rotate around the center of the object (or a user-specified point). Assume that we call this point the object's center O_c. To rotate around O_c we must first translate the object from O_c to the origin, apply rotations, and then translate the object back to O_c.

Transformation matrices can be combined by matrix multiplication to achieve combinations of translation, rotation, and scaling. It is possible for a single transformation matrix to represent all types of transformation simultaneously. This matrix is the result of repeated matrix multiplications. A word of warning: The order of the multiplication is important. For example, multiplying a translation matrix by a rotation matrix will not yield the same result as multiplying the rotation matrix by the translation matrix.

3.8 Actor Geometry

We have seen how lighting properties control the appearance of an actor, and how the camera in combination with transformation matrices is used to project an actor to the image plane. What is left to define is the geometry of the actor, and how we position it in the world coordinate system.

Modelling

A major topic in the study of computer graphics is modelling or representing the geometry of physical objects. Various mathematical techniques have been applied including combinations of points, lines, polygons, curves, and splines of various forms, and even implicit mathematical functions. This topic is beyond the scope of the text. The important point here is that there is an underlying geometric model that specifies where an object is located in the model coordinate system.

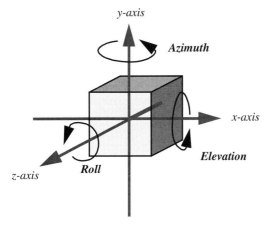

Figure 3–15 Actor coordinate system.

In data visualization, modelling takes a different role. Instead of directly creating geometry to represent an object, visualization algorithms *compute* these forms. Often the geometry is abstract (like a contour line) and has little relationship to real world geometry. We will see how these models are computed when we describe visualization algorithms in Chapters 6 and 9.

The representation of geometry for data visualization tends to be simple, even though computing the representations is not. These forms are most often primitives like points, lines, and polygons, or visualization data such as volume data. We use simple forms because we desire high performance and interactive systems. Thus we take advantage of computer hardware (to be covered in "Graphics Hardware" on page 52) or special rendering techniques like volume rendering (see "Volume Rendering" on page 206).

Actor Location and Orientation

Every actor has a transformation matrix that controls its location and scaling in world space. The actor's geometry is defined by a model in model coordinates. We specify the actor's location using orientation, position, and scale factors along the coordinate axes. In addition, we can define an origin around which the actor rotates. This feature is useful because we can rotate the actor around its center or some other meaningful point.

The orientation of an actor is determined by rotations stored in an orientation vector (O_x, O_y, O_z). This vector defines a series of rotational transformation matrices. As we saw in the previous section on transformation matrices, the order of application of the transformations is not arbitrary. We have chosen a fixed order based on what we think is natural to users. The order of transformation is a rotation by O_y around the y axis, then by O_x around the x axis, and finally by O_z around the z axis. This ordering is arbitrary and is based on the standard camera operations. These operations (in order) are a camera azimuth, followed by an elevation, and then a roll (**Figure 3–15**).

All of these rotations take place around the origin of the actor. Typically this is set to the center of its bounding box, but it can be set to any convenient point. There are many different methods for changing an actor's orientation. RotateX(), RotateY(), and RotateZ() are common methods that rotate about their respective axes. Many systems also include a

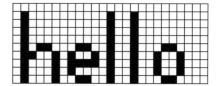

Figure 3–16 A pixel array for the word "hello."

method to rotate about a user-defined axis. In the *Visualization Toolkit* the RotateXYZ() method is used to rotate around an arbitrary vector passing through the origin.

3.9 Graphics Hardware

Earlier we mentioned that advances in graphics hardware have had a large impact on how rendering is performed. Now that we have covered the fundamentals of rendering a scene, we look at some of the hardware issues. First, we discuss raster devices that have replaced vector displays as the primary output device. Then, we look at how our programs communicate to the graphics hardware. We also examine the different coordinate systems used in computer graphics, hidden line/surface removal, and z-buffering.

Raster Devices

Usually, we see computer graphics in a printed picture or displayed on a computer monitor. Occasionally, we see something on TV or in a movie. All of these mediums are raster devices. A raster device represents an image using a two dimensional array of picture elements called pixels. For example, the word "hello" can be represented as an array of pixels.

In **Figure 3–16**, the word "hello" is written within a pixel array that is twenty-five pixels wide and ten pixels high. Each pixel stores one bit of information, whether it is black or white. This is how a black and white laser printer works, for each point on the paper it either prints a black dot or leaves it the color of the paper. Due to hardware limitations, raster devices such as laser printers and computer monitors do not actually draw accurate square pixels like those in **Figure 3–16**. Instead, they tend to be slightly blurred and overlapping. Another hardware limitation of raster devices is their resolution. This is what causes a 300 dpi (dots per inch) laser printer to produce more detailed output than a nine pin dot matrix printer. A 300 dpi laser printer has a resolution of 300 pixels per inch compared to roughly 50 dpi for the dot matrix printer.

Color computer monitors typically have a resolution of about 80 pixels per inch, making the screen a pixel array roughly one thousand pixels in width and height. This results in over one million pixels, each with a value that indicates what color it should be. Since the hardware in color monitors uses the RGB system, it makes sense to use that to describe the colors in the pixels. Unfortunately, having over one million pixels, each with a red, green, and blue component, can take up a lot of memory. This is part of what differentiates the variety of graphics hardware on the market. Some companies use 24 bits of storage per pixel, others use eight, some advanced systems use more than 100 bits of storage per pixel. Typically, the more bits per pixel the more accurate the colors will be.

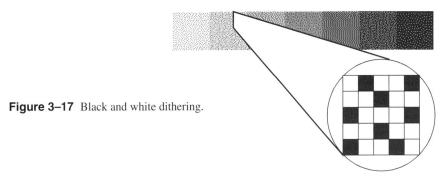

Figure 3–17 Black and white dithering.

One way to work around color limitations in the graphics hardware is by using a technique called *dithering*. Say, for example, that you want to use some different shades of gray, but your graphics hardware only supports black and white. Dithering lets you approximate shades of gray by using a mixture of both black and white pixels. In **Figure 3–17**, seven gray squares are drawn using a mixture of black and white pixels. From a distance the seven squares look like different shades of gray even though up close, it's clear that they are just different mixtures of black and white pixels. This same technique works just as well for other colors. For example, if your graphics hardware supports primary blue, primary green, and white but not a pastel sea green, you can approximate this color by dithering the green, blue, and white that the hardware does support.

Interfacing to the Hardware

Now that we have covered the basics of display hardware, the good news is that you rarely need to worry about them. Most graphics programming is done using higher-level primitives than individual pixels. **Figure 3–18** shows a typical arrangement for a visualization program. At the bottom of the hierarchy is the display hardware that we already discussed; chances are your programs will not interact directly with it. The top three layers above the hardware are the layers you may need to be concerned with.

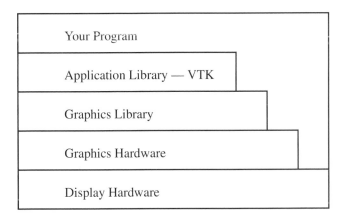

Figure 3–18 Typical graphics interface hierarchy.

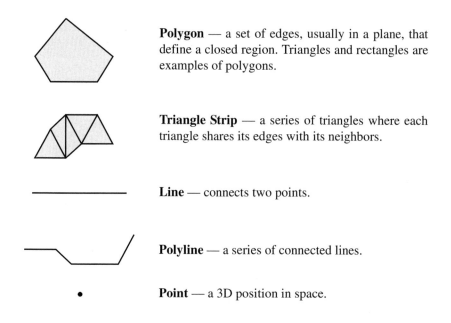

Polygon — a set of edges, usually in a plane, that define a closed region. Triangles and rectangles are examples of polygons.

Triangle Strip — a series of triangles where each triangle shares its edges with its neighbors.

Line — connects two points.

Polyline — a series of connected lines.

Point — a 3D position in space.

Figure 3–19 Graphics primitives.

Many programs take advantage of application libraries as a high-level interface to the graphics capabilities of a system. The *Visualization Toolkit* accompanying this book is a prime example of this. It allows you to display a complex object or graph using just a few commands. It is also possible to interface to a number of different graphics libraries, since different libraries may be supported on different hardware platforms.

The graphics library and graphics hardware layers both perform similar functions. They are responsible for taking high-level commands from an application library or program, and executing them. This makes programming much easier by providing more complex primitives to work with. Instead of drawing pixels one at a time, we can draw primitives like polygons, triangles, and lines, without worrying about the details of which pixels are being set to which colors. **Figure 3–19** illustrates some high-level primitives that all mainstream graphics libraries support.

This functionality is broken into two different layers because different machines may have vastly different graphics hardware. If you write a program that draws a red polygon, either the graphics library or the graphics hardware must be able to execute that command. On high-end systems, this may be done in the graphics hardware, on others it will be done by the graphics library in software. So the same commands can be used with a wide variety of machines, without worrying about the underlying graphics hardware.

The fundamental building block of the primitives in **Figure 3–19** is a point (or vertex). A vertex has a position, normal, and color, each of which is a three element vector. The position specifies where the vertex is located, its normal specifies which direction the vertex is facing, and its color specifies the vertex's red, green, and blue components. A polygon is built by connecting a series of points or vertices as shown in **Figure 3–20**. You may be won-

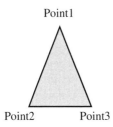

Point1

Point2   Point3

Figure 3–20 An example polygon.

```
Point1
   position=(1,3,0)
   normal=  (0,0,1)
   color=   (.8,.8,.8)
Point2
   position=(0,0,0)
   normal=  (0,0,1)
   color=   (.8,.8,.8)
Point3
   position=(2,0,0)
   normal=  (0,0,1)
   color=   (.8,.8,.8)

Polygon1
   points= (1,2,3)
```

Vertex Normal   Vertex Normal

Polygon Normal

Figure 3–21 Vertex and polygon normals.

dering why each vertex has a normal, instead of having just one normal for the entire polygon. A planar polygon can only be facing one direction regardless of what the normals of its vertices indicate. The reason is that sometimes a polygon is used as an approximation of something else, like a curve. **Figure 3–21** shows a top-down view of a cylinder. As you can see, it's not really a cylinder but rather a polygonal approximation of the cylinder drawn in gray. Each vertex is shared by two polygons and the correct normal for the vertex is not the same as the normal for the polygon. Similar logic explains why each vertex has a color instead of just having one color for an entire polygon.

When you limit yourself to the types of primitives described above, there are some additional properties that many graphics systems support. Edge color and edge visibility can be used to highlight the polygon primitives that make up an actor. Another way to do this is by adjusting the representation from *surface* to *wireframe* or *points*. This replaces surfaces such as polygons with either their boundary edges or points respectively. While this may not make much sense from a physical perspective, it can help in some illustrations. Using edge visibility when rendering a CAD model can help to show the different pieces that comprise the model.

Rasterization

At this point in the text we have described how to represent graphics data using rendering primitives, and we have described how to represent images using raster display devices. The question remains, how do we convert graphics primitives into a raster image? This is the topic we address in this section. Although a thorough treatise on this topic is beyond the scope of this text, we will do our best to provide a high-level overview.

The process of converting a geometric representation into a raster image is called *rasterization*. This process is also called *scan conversion*. In the description that follows we assume that the graphics primitives are triangle polygons. This is not as limiting as you might think, because any general polygon can be tessellated into a set of triangles. Moreover, other surface representations such as splines are usually tessellated by the graphics system into triangles or polygons. (The method described here is actually applicable to convex polygons.)

Most of today's hardware is based on object-order rasterization techniques. As we saw earlier in this chapter, this means processing our actors in order. And since our actors are represented by polygon primitives, we process polygons one at a time. So although we describe the processing of one polygon, bear in mind that many polygons and possibly many actors are processed.

The first step is to transform the polygon using the appropriate transformation matrix. We also project the polygon to the image plane using either parallel or orthographic projection. Part of this process involves clipping the polygons. Not only do we use the front and back clipping planes to clip polygons too close or too far, but we must also clip polygons crossing the boundaries of the image plane. Clipping polygons that cross the boundary of the view frustum means we have to generate new polygon boundaries.

With the polygon clipped and projected to the image plane, we can begin scan-line processing (**Figure 3–22**). The first step identifies the initial scan-line intersected by the projected polygon. This is found by sorting the vertices' y values. We then find the two edges joining the vertex on the left and right sides. Using the slopes of the edges along with the data values we compute delta data values. These data are typically the R, G, and B color components. Other data values include transparency values and z depth values. (The z values are necessary if we are using a z-buffer, described in the next section.) The row of pixels within the polygon (i.e., starting at the left and right edges) is called a *span*. Data values are interpolated from the edges on either side of the span to compute the internal pixel values. This process continues span-by-span, until the entire polygon is filled. Note that as new vertices are encountered, it is necessary to recompute the delta data values.

The shading of the polygon (i.e., color interpolation across the polygon) varies depending on the actor's interpolation attribute. There are three possibilities: *flat*, *Gouraud*, or *Phong shading*. **Figure 3–7** illustrates the difference between flat and Gouraud interpolation. Flat shading calculates the color of a polygon by applying the lighting equations to just one normal (typically the surface normal) of the polygon. Gouraud shading calculates the color of a polygon at all of its vertices using the vertices' normals and the standard lighting equations. The interior and edges of the polygon are then filled in by applying the scan-line interpolation process. Phong shading is the most realistic of the three. It calculates a normal at every location on the polygon by interpolating the vertex normals. These are then used in the lighting equations to determine the resulting pixel colors. Both flat and Gouraud shading are com-

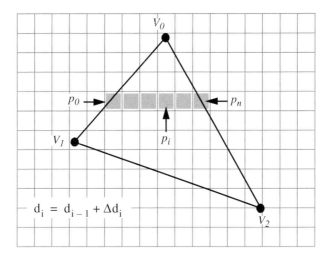

Figure 3–22 Rasterizing a convex polygon. Pixels are processed in horizontal spans (or scan-lines) in the image plane. Data values d_i at point p_i are interpolated along the edges and then along the scan-line using delta data values. Typical data values are RGB components of color.

monly used methods. The complexity of Phong shading has prevented it from being widely supported in hardware.

Z-Buffer

In our earlier description of the rendering process, we followed rays of light from our eye through a pixel in the image plane to the actors and back to the light source. A nice side effect of ray tracing is that viewing rays strike the first actor they encounter and ignore any actors that are hidden behind it. When rendering actors using the polygonal methods described above, we have no such method of computing which polygons are hidden and which are not. We cannot generally count on the polygons being ordered correctly. Instead, we can use a number of hidden-surface methods for polygon rendering.

One method is to sort all of our polygons from back to front and then render them in that order. This is called the painter's algorithm or painter's sort, and has one major weakness illustrated in **Figure 3–23**. Regardless of the order in which we draw these three triangles, we cannot obtain the desired result, since each triangle is both in front of, and behind, another triangle. There are algorithms that sort and split polygons as necessary to treat such a situation [Carlson85]. This requires more initial processing to perform the sorting and splitting. If the geometric primitives change between images or the camera view changes, then this processing must be performed before each render.

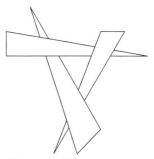

Figure 3–23 Problem with Painter's algorithm.

Another hidden surface algorithm, z-buffering, takes care of this problem and does not require sorting. Z-buffering takes advantage of the z-value (i.e., depth value along direction of projection) in the view coordinate system. Before a new pixel is drawn, its z-value is compared against the current z-value for that pixel location. If the new pixel would be in front of the current pixel, then it is drawn and the z-value for that pixel location is updated. Otherwise the current pixel remains and the new pixel is ignored.

Z-buffering has been widely implemented in hardware because of its simplicity and robustness. The downside to z-buffering is that it requires a large amount of memory, called a z-buffer, to store a z-value of every pixel. Most systems use a z-buffer with a depth of 24 or 32 bits. For a 1000 by 1000 display that translates into three to four megabytes just for the z-buffer. Another problem with z-buffering is that its accuracy is limited depending on its depth. A 24-bit z-buffer yields a precision of one part in 16,777,216 over the height of the viewing frustum. This resolution is often insufficient if objects are close together. If you do run into situations with z-buffering accuracy, make sure that the front and back clipping planes are as close to the visible geometry as possible.

3.10 Putting It All Together

This section provides an overview of the graphics objects and how to use them in VTK.

The Graphics Model

We have discussed many of the objects that play a part in the rendering of a scene. Now it's time to put them together into a comprehensive object model for graphics and visualization.

In the *Visualization Toolkit* there are seven basic objects that we use to render a scene. There are many more objects behind the scenes, but these seven are the ones we use most frequently. The objects are listed in the following and illustrated in **Figure 3–24**.

1. vtkRenderWindow — manages a window on the display device; one or more renderers draw into an instance of vtkRenderWindow.

2. vtkRenderer — coordinates the rendering process involving lights, cameras, and actors.

3. vtkLight — a source of light to illuminate the scene.

4. vtkCamera — defines the view position, focal point, and other viewing properties of the scene.

5. vtkActor — represents an object rendered in the scene, both its properties and position in the world coordinate system. (*Note:* vtkActor is a subclass of vtkProp. vtkProp is a more general form of actor that includes annotation and 2D drawing classes. See "Assemblies and Other Types of vtkProp" on page 75 for more information.)

6. vtkProperty — defines the appearance properties of an actor including color, transparency, and lighting properties such as specular and diffuse. Also representational properties like wireframe and solid surface.

7. vtkMapper — the geometric representation for an actor. More than one actor may refer to the same mapper.

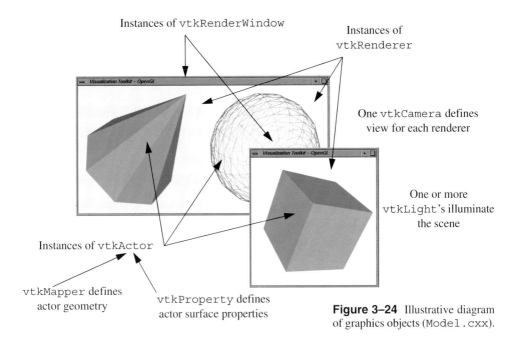

Instances of vtkRenderWindow

Instances of vtkRenderer

One vtkCamera defines view for each renderer

One or more vtkLight's illuminate the scene

Instances of vtkActor

vtkMapper defines actor geometry

vtkProperty defines actor surface properties

Figure 3–24 Illustrative diagram of graphics objects (Model.cxx).

The class vtkRenderWindow ties the rendering process together. It is responsible for managing a window on the display device. For PCs running Windows, this will be a Microsoft display window, for Linux and UNIX systems this will be an X window, and on the Mac (OSX) a Quartz window. In VTK, instances of vtkRenderWindow are device independent. This means that you do not need to be concerned about what underlying graphics hardware or software is being used, the software automatically adapts to your computer as instances of vtkRenderWindow are created. (See "Achieving Device Independence" on page 61 for more information.)

In addition to window management, vtkRenderWindow objects are used to manage renderers and store graphics specific characteristics such as size, position, window title, *window depth*, and the *double buffering* flag. The depth of a window indicates how many bits are allocated per pixel. Double buffering is a technique where a window is logically divided into two buffers. At any given time one buffer is currently visible to the user. Meanwhile, the second buffer can be used to draw the next image in an animation. Once the rendering is complete, the two buffers can be swapped so that the new image is visible. This common technique allows animations to be displayed without the user seeing the actual rendering of the primitives. High-end graphics systems perform double buffering in hardware. A typical system would have a rendering window with a depth of 72 bits. The first 24 bits are used to store the red, green, and blue (RGB) pixel components for the front buffer. The next 24 bits store the RGB values for the back buffer. The last 24 bits are used as a z-buffer.

The class vtkRenderer is responsible for coordinating its lights, camera, and actors to produce an image. Each instance maintains a list of the actors, lights, and an active camera in a particular scene. At least one actor must be defined, but if lights and a camera are not defined, they will be created automatically by the renderer. In such a case the actors are centered in the image and the default camera view is down the z-axis. Instances of the class vtkRenderer also provide methods to specify the background and ambient lighting colors. Methods are also available to convert to and from world, view, and display coordinate systems.

One important aspect of a renderer is that it must be associated with an instance of the vtkRenderWindow class into which it is to draw, and the area in the render window into which it draws must be defined by a rectangular *viewport*. The viewport is defined by normalized coordinates (0,1) in both the *x* and *y* image coordinate axes. By default, the renderer draws into the full extent of the rendering window (viewpoint coordinates (0,0,1,1)). It is possible to specify a smaller viewport. and to have more than one renderer draw into the same rendering window.

Instances of the class vtkLight illuminate the scene. Various instance variables for orienting and positioning the light are available. It is also possible to turn on/off lights and set the color of the light. Normally at least one light is "on" to illuminate the scene. If no lights are defined and turned on, the renderer constructs a light automatically. Lights in VTK can be either positional or infinite. Positional lights have an associated cone angle and attenuation factors. Infinite lights project light rays parallel to one another.

Cameras are constructed by the class vtkCamera. Important parameters include camera position, focal point, location of front and back clipping planes, view up vector, and field of view. Cameras also have special methods to simplify manipulation. These include elevation, azimuth, zoom, and roll. Similar to vtkLight, an instance of vtkCamera will be created automatically by the renderer if none is defined.

Instances of the class vtkActor represent objects in the scene. In particular, vtkActor combines object properties (color, shading type, etc.), geometric definition, and orientation in the world coordinate system. This is implemented behind the scenes by maintaining instance variables that refer to instances of vtkProperty, vtkMapper, and vtkTransform. Normally you need not create properties or transformations explicitly, since these are automatically created and manipulated using vtkActor's methods. You do need to create an instance of vtkMapper (or one of its subclasses). The mapper ties the data visualization pipeline to the graphics device. (We will say more about the pipeline in the next chapter.)

There are other classes of actors with specialized behavior, implemented as subclasses of vtkActor (see "Assemblies and Other Types of vtkProp" on page 75 for more information). One example is vtkFollower. Instances of this class always face the active camera. This is useful when designing signs or text that must be readable from any camera position in the scene.

Instances of the class vtkProperty affect the rendered appearance of an actor. When actors are created, a property instance is automatically created with them. It is also possible to create property objects directly and then associate the property object with one or more actors. In this way actors can share common properties.

Finally, vtkMapper (and its subclasses) defines object geometry and, optionally, vertex colors. We will examine the mapping process in more detail in "Mapper Design" on page 184. For now assume that vtkMapper is an object that represents geometry and other types of visualization data. In addition, vtkMapper refers to a table of colors (i.e., vtkLookupTable) that are used to color vertices. (We discuss mapping of data to colors in "Color Mapping" on page 151.)

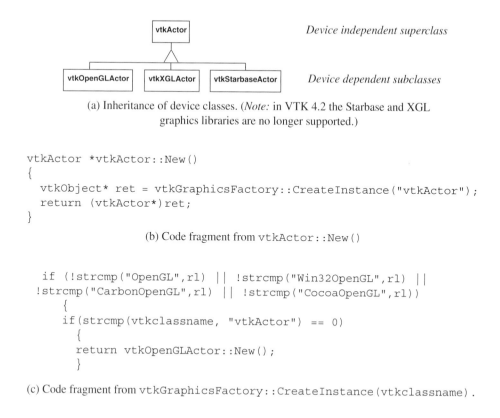

(a) Inheritance of device classes. (*Note:* in VTK 4.2 the Starbase and XGL graphics libraries are no longer supported.)

```
vtkActor *vtkActor::New()
{
  vtkObject* ret = vtkGraphicsFactory::CreateInstance("vtkActor");
  return (vtkActor*)ret;
}
```

(b) Code fragment from `vtkActor::New()`

```
  if (!strcmp("OpenGL",rl) || !strcmp("Win32OpenGL",rl) ||
 !strcmp("CarbonOpenGL",rl) || !strcmp("CocoaOpenGL",rl))
    {
    if(strcmp(vtkclassname, "vtkActor") == 0)
      {
      return vtkOpenGLActor::New();
      }
```

(c) Code fragment from `vtkGraphicsFactory::CreateInstance(vtkclassname)`.

Figure 3–25 Achieving device independence using (a) inheritance and object factories (b) and (c).

There is another important object, vtkRenderWindowInteractor, that captures events for a renderer in the rendering window. vtkRenderWindowInteractor captures these events and then triggers certain operations like camera dolly, pan, and rotate, actor picking, into/out of stereo mode, and so on. Instances of this class are associated with a rendering window using the SetRenderWindow() method.

Achieving Device Independence

A desirable property of applications built with VTK is that they are device independent. This means that computer code that runs on one operating system with a particular software/hardware configuration runs unchanged on a different operating system and software/hardware configuration. The advantage of this is that the programmer does not need to expend effort porting an application between different computer systems. Also, existing applications do not need to be rewritten to take advantage of new developments in hardware or software technology. Instead, VTK handles this transparently by a combination of inheritance and a technique known as *object factories*.

Figure 3–25(a) illustrates the use of inheritance to achieve device independence. Certain classes like vtkActor are broken into two parts: a device independent superclass and a device dependent subclass. The trick here is that the user creates a device dependent subclass by invoking the special constructor New() in the device independent superclass. For example we would use (in C++)

```
vtkActor *anActor = vtkActor::New()
```

to create a device dependent instance of vtkActor. The user sees no device dependent code, but in actuality anActor is a pointer to a device dependent subclass of vtkActor. **Figure 3–25**(b) is a code fragment of the constructor method New() which uses VTK's object factory mechanism. In turn, the vtkGraphicsFactory (used to instantiate graphical classes) produces the appropriate concrete subclass when requested to instantiate an actor as shown in **Figure 3–25**(c).

The use of object factories as implemented using the New() method allows us to create device independent code that can move from computer to computer and adapt to changing technology. For example, if a new graphics library became available, we would only have to create a new device dependent subclass, and then modify the graphics factory to instantiate the appropriate subclass based on environment variables or other system information. This extension would be localized and only done once, and all applications based on these object factories would be automatically ported without change.

Examples

This section works through some simple applications implemented with VTK graphics objects. The focus is on the basics: how to create renderers, lights, cameras, and actors. Later chapters tie together these basic principles to create applications for data visualization.

Render a Cone. The following C++ code uses most of the objects introduced in this section to create an image of a cone. The vtkConeSource generates a polygonal representation of a cone and vtkPolyDataMapper maps the geometry (in conjunction with the actor) to the graphics library. (The source code to this example can be found in Cone.cxx. The source code contains additional documentation as well.)

```
#include "vtkConeSource.h"
#include "vtkPolyDataMapper.h"
#include "vtkRenderWindow.h"
#include "vtkCamera.h"
#include "vtkActor.h"
#include "vtkRenderer.h"

int main( int argc, char *argv[] )
{
  vtkConeSource *cone = vtkConeSource::New();
  cone->SetHeight( 3.0 );
  cone->SetRadius( 1.0 );
  cone->SetResolution( 10 );
```

```
vtkPolyDataMapper *coneMapper = vtkPolyDataMapper::New();
coneMapper->SetInput( cone->GetOutput() );

vtkActor *coneActor = vtkActor::New();
coneActor->SetMapper( coneMapper );

vtkRenderer *ren1= vtkRenderer::New();
ren1->AddActor( coneActor );
ren1->SetBackground( 0.1, 0.2, 0.4 );

vtkRenderWindow *renWin = vtkRenderWindow::New();
renWin->AddRenderer( ren1 );
renWin->SetSize( 300, 300 );

int i;
for (i = 0; i < 360; ++i)
  {
  // render the image
  renWin->Render();
  // rotate the active camera by one degree
  ren1->GetActiveCamera()->Azimuth( 1 );
  }

cone->Delete();
coneMapper->Delete();
coneActor->Delete();
ren1->Delete();
renWin->Delete();

return 0;
}
```

Some comments about this example. The include files vtk___.h include class definitions for the objects in VTK necessary to compile this example. We use the constructor New() to create the objects in this example, and the method Delete() to destroy the objects. In VTK the use of New() and Delete() is mandatory to insure device independence and properly manage reference counting. (See *VTK User's Guide* for details.) In this example the use of Delete() is really not necessary because the objects are automatically deleted upon program termination. But generally speaking, you should always use a Delete() for every invocation of New(). (Future examples will not show the Delete() methods in the scope of the main() program to conserve space, nor show the required #include statements.)

The data representing the cone (a set of polygons) in this example is created by linking together a series of objects into a *pipeline* (which is the topic of the next chapter). First a polygonal representation of the cone is created with a vtkConeSource and serves as input to the data mapper as specified with the SetInput() method. The SetMapper() method associates the mapper's data with the coneActor. The next line adds coneActor to the renderer's list of actors. The cone is rendered in a loop running over 360°. Since there are no cameras or lights

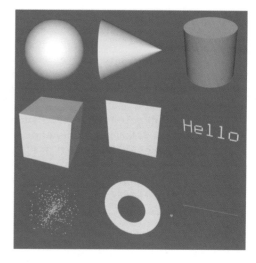

Figure 3–26 Examples of source objects that procedurally generate polygonal models. These nine images represent just some of the capability of VTK. From upper left in reading order: sphere, cone, cylinder, cube, plane, text, random point cloud, disk (with or without hole), and line source. Other polygonal source objects are available; check subclasses of vtkPolyDataSource.

defined in the above example, VTK automatically generates a default light and camera as a convenience to the user. The camera is accessed through the GetActiveCamera() method, and a one degree azimuth is applied as shown. Each time a change is made to any objects a Render() method is invoked to produce the corresponding image. Once the loop is complete all allocated objects are destroyed and the program exits.

There are many different types of source objects in VTK similar to vtkConeSource. **Figure 3–26** shows several additional source objects. In the next chapter we will learn more about source and other types of filters.

Events and Observers. A visualization toolkit like VTK is frequently used in interactive applications or may be required to provide status during operation. In addition, integration with other packages such as GUI toolkits is a common task. Supporting such features requires a mechanism for inserting user functionality into the software. In VTK, the *command/observer* design pattern [Gamma95] is used for this purpose.

Fundamental to this design pattern as implemented in VTK is the concept of *events*. An event is a signal that an important operation has occurred in the software. For example, if the user presses the left mouse button in the render window, VTK will invoke the LeftButton-PressEvent. Observers are objects that register their interest in a particular event or events. When one of these events is invoked, the observer receives notification and may perform any valid operation at that point; that is, execute the command associated with the observer. The benefit of the command/observer design pattern is that is simple in concept and implementation, yet provides significant power to the user. However it does require the software implementation to invoke events as it operates.

In the next example, an observer watches for the StartEvent invoked by the renderer just as it begins the rendering process. The observer in turn executes its associated command which simply prints out the camera's current position.

```
#include "vtkCommand.h"

// Callback for the interaction
```

```cpp
class vtkMyCallback : public vtkCommand
{
public:
  static vtkMyCallback *New()
    { return new vtkMyCallback; }
  virtual void Execute(vtkObject *caller, unsigned long, void*)
    {
      vtkRenderer *ren =
              reinterpret_cast<vtkRenderer*>(caller);
      cout << ren->GetActiveCamera()->GetPosition()[0] << " "
           << ren->GetActiveCamera()->GetPosition()[1] << " "
           << ren->GetActiveCamera()->GetPosition()[2] << "\n";
    }
};


int main( int argc, char *argv[] )
{
  vtkConeSource *cone = vtkConeSource::New();
  cone->SetHeight( 3.0 );
  cone->SetRadius( 1.0 );
  cone->SetResolution( 10 );

  vtkPolyDataMapper *coneMapper = vtkPolyDataMapper::New();
  coneMapper->SetInput( cone->GetOutput() );
  vtkActor *coneActor = vtkActor::New();
  coneActor->SetMapper( coneMapper );

  vtkRenderer *ren1= vtkRenderer::New();
  ren1->AddActor( coneActor );
  ren1->SetBackground( 0.1, 0.2, 0.4 );

  vtkRenderWindow *renWin = vtkRenderWindow::New();
  renWin->AddRenderer( ren1 );
  renWin->SetSize( 300, 300 );

  vtkMyCallback *mo1 = vtkMyCallback::New();
  ren1->AddObserver(vtkCommand::StartEvent,mo1);
  mo1->Delete();

  int i;
  for (i = 0; i < 360; ++i)
    {
    // render the image
    renWin->Render();
    // rotate the active camera by one degree
    ren1->GetActiveCamera()->Azimuth( 1 );
    }

  cone->Delete();
```

```
      coneMapper->Delete();
      coneActor->Delete();
      ren1->Delete();
      renWin->Delete();

      return 0;
   }
```

The observer is created by subclassing from the class vtkCommand. The Execute() method is required to be implemented by any subclass of vtkCommand (i.e., the method id pure virtual). The resulting subclass, vtkMyCommand, is instantiated and then registered with the renderer instance ren1 using the AddObserver() method. In this case the StartEvent is observed.

This simple example does not demonstrate the true power of the command/observer design pattern. Later in this chapter ("Interpreted Code" on page 69) we will see how this functionality is used to integrate a simple GUI into VTK. In Chapter 7 three-dimensional interaction widgets will be introduced ("3D Widgets and User Interaction" on page 241).

Creating Multiple Renderers. The next example is a bit more complex and uses multiple renderers that share a single rendering window. We use viewports to define where the renderers should draw. (This C++ code can be found in Cone3.cxx.)

```
      vtkRenderer *ren1= vtkRenderer::New();
      ren1->AddActor( coneActor );
      ren1->SetBackground( 0.1, 0.2, 0.4 );
      ren1->SetViewport(0.0, 0.0, 0.5, 1.0);

      vtkRenderer *ren2= vtkRenderer::New();
      ren2->AddActor( coneActor );
      ren2->SetBackground( 0.2, 0.3, 0.5 );
      ren2->SetViewport(0.5, 0.0, 1.0, 1.0);
//
      vtkRenderWindow *renWin = vtkRenderWindow::New();
      renWin->AddRenderer( ren1 );
      renWin->AddRenderer( ren2 );
      renWin->SetSize( 600, 300 );

      ren1->GetActiveCamera()->Azimuth(90);

      int i;
      for (i = 0; i < 360; ++i)
        {
        // render the image
        renWin->Render();
        // rotate the active camera by one degree
        ren1->GetActiveCamera()->Azimuth( 1 );
        ren2->GetActiveCamera()->Azimuth( 1 );
        }
```

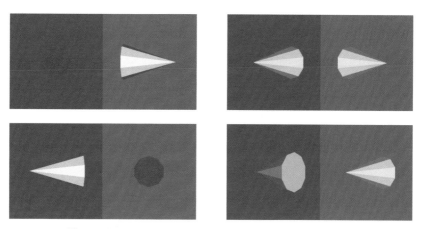

Figure 3–27 Four frames of output from `Cone3.cxx`.

As you can see, much of the code is the same as the previous example. The first difference is that we create two renderers instead of one. We assign the same actor to both renderers, but set each renderer's background to a different color. We set the viewport of the two renderers so that one is on the left half of the rendering window and the other is on the right. The rendering window's size is specified as 600 by 300 pixels, which results in each renderer drawing into a viewport of 300 by 300 pixels.

A good application of multiple renderers is to display different views of the same world as demonstrated in this example. Here we adjust the first renderer's camera with a 90 degree azimuth. We then start a loop that rotates the two cameras around the cone. **Figure 3–27** shows four frames from this animation.

Properties and Transformations. The previous examples did not explicitly create property or transformation objects or apply actor methods that affect these objects. Instead, we accepted default instance variable values. This procedure is typical of VTK applications. Most instance variables have been preset to generate acceptable results, but methods are always available for you to override the default values.

This example creates an image of two cones of different colors and specular properties. In addition, we transform one of the objects to lay next to the other. The C++ source code for this example can be found in `Cone4.cxx`.

```
vtkActor *coneActor = vtkActor::New();
coneActor->SetMapper( coneMapper );
coneActor->GetProperty()->SetColor(0.2, 0.63, 0.79);
coneActor->GetProperty()->SetDiffuse(0.7);
coneActor->GetProperty()->SetSpecular(0.4);
coneActor->GetProperty()->SetSpecularPower(20);

vtkProperty *property = vtkProperty::New();
property->SetColor(1.0, 0.3882, 0.2784);
property->SetDiffuse(0.7);
property->SetSpecular(0.4);
```

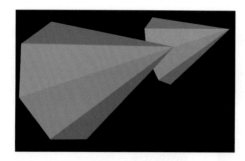

Figure 3–28 Modifying properties and transformation matrix (`Cone4.cxx`).

```
property->SetSpecularPower(20);

vtkActor *coneActor2 = vtkActor::New();
coneActor2->SetMapper(coneMapper);
coneActor2->GetProperty()->SetColor(0.2, 0.63, 0.79);
coneActor2->SetProperty(property);
coneActor2->SetPosition(0, 2, 0);

vtkRenderer *ren1= vtkRenderer::New();
  ren1->AddActor( coneActor );
  ren1->AddActor( coneActor2 );
  ren1->SetBackground( 0.1, 0.2, 0.4 );
```

We set the actor coneActor properties by modifying the property object automatically created by the actor. This differs from actor coneActor2, where we create a property directly and then assign it to the actor. ConeActor2 is moved from its default position by applying the SetPosition() method. This method affects the transformation matrix that is an instance variable of the actor. The resulting image is shown in **Figure 3–28**.

Introducing vtkRenderWindowInteractor. The previous examples are not interactive. That is, it is not possible to directly interact with the data without modifying and recompiling the C++ code. One common type of interaction is to change camera position so that we can view our scene from different vantage points. In the *Visualization Toolkit* we have provided a suite of convenient objects to do this: vtkRenderWindowInteractor and vtkInteractorStyle.

Instances of the class vtkRenderWindowInteractor capture windowing system specific mouse and keyboard events in the rendering window, and then translate these events into VTK events. For example, mouse motion in an X11 or Windows application (occurring in a render window) would be translated by vtkRenderWindowInteractor into VTK's Mouse-MoveEvent. Any observers registered for this event would be notified (see "Events and Observers" on page 64). Typically an instance of vtkInteractorStyle is used in combination with vtkRenderWindowInteractor to define a behavior associated with particular events. For example, we can perform camera dolly, pan, and rotation by using different mouse button and motion combinations. The following example shows how to instantiate and use these objects. This example is the same as our first example with the addition of the interactor and interactor style. The example C++ code is in `Cone5.cxx`.

```
vtkRenderWindowInteractor *iren =
vtkRenderWindowInteractor::New();
  iren->SetRenderWindow(renWin);

vtkInteractorStyleTrackballCamera *style =
  vtkInteractorStyleTrackballCamera::New();
iren->SetInteractorStyle(style);

iren->Initialize();
iren->Start();
```

After the interactor is created using its New() method, we must tell it what render window to capture events in using the SetRenderWindow() method. In order to use the interactor we have to initialize and start the event loop using the Initialize() and Start() methods, which works with the event loop of the windowing system to begin to catch events. Some of the more useful events include the "w" key, which draws all actors in wireframe; the "s" key, which draws the actors in surface form; the "3" key, which toggles in and out of 3D stereo for those systems that support this; the "r" key, which resets camera view; and the "e" key, which exits the application. In addition, the mouse buttons rotate, pan, and dolly about the camera's focal point. Two advanced features are the "u" key, which executes a user-defined function; and the "p" key, which picks the actor under the mouse pointer.

Interpreted Code. In the previous example we saw how to create an interactor style object in conjunction with vtkRenderWindowInteractor to enable us to manipulate the camera by mousing in the render window. Although this provides flexibility and interactivity for a large number of applications, there are examples throughout this text where we want to modify other parameters. These parameters range from actor properties, such as color, to the name of an input file. Of course we can always write or modify C++ code to do this, but in many cases the turn-around time between making the change and seeing the result is too long. One way to improve the overall interactivity of the system is to use an interpreted interface. Interpreted systems allow us to modify objects and immediately see the result, without the need to recompile and relink source code. Interpreted languages also provide many tools, such as GUI (Graphical User Interface) tools, that simplify the creation of applications.

Figure 3–29 In VTK the C++ library is automatically wrapped with the interpreted languages Tcl, Python, and Java.

The *Visualization Toolkit* has built into its compilation process the ability to automatically generate language bindings to the interpreted languages Tcl, Python, and Java [Ousterhout94]. This so-called wrapping process automatically creates a layer between the C++ VTK library and the interpreter as illustrated in **Figure 3–29**. There is a one-to-one mapping between C++ methods and Tcl functions for most objects and methods in the system. To demonstrate this, the following example repeats the previous C++ example except that it is implemented with a Tcl script. (The script can be found in Cone5.tcl.)

```
package require vtk
package require vtkinteraction

vtkConeSource cone
cone SetHeight 3.0
cone SetRadius 1.0
cone SetResolution 10

vtkPolyDataMapper coneMapper
coneMapper SetInput [cone GetOutput]

vtkActor coneActor
coneActor SetMapper coneMapper

vtkRenderer ren1
ren1 AddActor coneActor
ren1 SetBackground 0.1 0.2 0.4

vtkRenderWindow renWin
renWin AddRenderer ren1
renWin SetSize 300 300

vtkRenderWindowInteractor iren
iren SetRenderWindow renWin

vtkInteractorStyleTrackballCamera style
iren SetInteractorStyle style

iren AddObserver UserEvent {wm deiconify .vtkInteract}

iren Initialize

wm withdraw .
```

The example begins by loading some shared libraries defining various VTK classes. Next the standard visualization pipeline is created from the vtkConeSource and vtkPolyDataMapper. The rendering classes are created exactly the same as with the C++ example. One major addition is an observer to watch for a UserEvent in the rendering window (by default a "keypress-u"). The observer triggers the invocation of a Tcl script to raise a Tk interactor GUI widget called .vtkInteract. This GUI, which allows the direct typing of Tcl statements, is shown in **Figure 3–30** and is defined by the Tcl command package require vtkinteraction which was executed earlier in the script. (Note: Tk is a popular GUI toolkit for interpreted languages and is distributed as part of Tcl.)

As we can see from this example, the number of lines of code is less for the Tcl example than for equivalent C++ code. Also, many of the complexities of C++ are hidden using the interpreted language. Using this user-interface GUI we can create, modify, and delete objects, and modify their instance variables. The resulting changes appear as soon as a Render() method is applied or mouse events in the rendering window cause a render to occur.

Figure 3–30 Using Tcl and Tk to build an interpreted application (`Cone5.tcl`).

We encourage you to use Tcl (or one of the other interpreters) for rapid creation of graphics and visualization examples. C++ is best used when you desire higher performing applications.

Transformation Matrices

Transformation matrices are used throughout *Visualization Toolkit*. Actors (subclasses of vtkProp3D—see "Assemblies and Other Types of vtkProp" on page 75) use them to position and orient themselves. Various filters, including vtkGlyph3D and vtkTransformFilter, use transformation matrices to implement their own functionality. As a user you may never use transformation matrices directly, but understanding them is important to successful use of many VTK classes.

The most important aspect to applying transformation matrices is to understand the order in which the transformations are applied. If you break down a complex series of transformations into simple combinations of translation, scaling, and rotation, and keep careful track of the order of application, you will have gone a long way to mastering their use.

A good demonstration example of transformation matrices is to examine how vtkActor uses its internal matrix. vtkActor has an internal instance variable Transform to which it delegates many of its methods or uses the matrix to implement its methods. For example, the RotateX(), RotateY(), and RotateZ() methods are all delegated to Transform. The method SetOrientation() uses Transform to orient the actor.

The vtkActor class applies transformations in an order that we feel is natural to most users. As a convenience, we have created instance variables that abstract the transformation matrices. The Origin (o_x, o_y, o_z) specifies the point that is the center of rotation and scaling. The Position (p_x, p_y, p_z) specifies a final translation of the object. Orientation (r_x, r_y, r_z) defines the rotations about the *x*, *y* and *z* axes. Scale (s_x, s_y, s_z) defines scale factors for the *x*, *y*, and *z* axes. Internally, the actor uses these instance variables to create the following sequence of transformations (see **Equation 3-6**, **Equation 3-9**, **Equation 3-13**).

$$T = T_T(p_x + o_x, p_y + o_y, p_z + o_z)T_{R_z}T_{R_x}T_{R_y}T_S T_T(-o_x, -o_y, -o_z) \qquad \textbf{(3-14)}$$

The term $T_T(x, y, z)$ denotes the translations in the x, y, and z directions. Recall that we premultiply the transformation matrix times the position vector. This means the transformations are read from right to left. In other words, **Equation 3-14** proceeds as follows:

1. Translate the actor to its origin. Scaling and rotation will occur about this point. The initial translation will be countered by a translation in the opposite direction after scaling and rotations are applied.

2. Scale the geometry.

3. Rotate the actor about the y, then x, and then z axes.

4. Undo the translation of step 1 and move the actor to its final location.

The order of the transformations is important. In VTK the rotations are ordered to what is natural in most cases. We recommend that you spend some time with the software to learn how these transformations work with your own data.

Probably the most confusing aspect of transformations are rotations and their effect on the Orientation instance variable. Generally orientations are not set directly by the user, and most users will prefer to specify rotations with the RotateX(), RotateY(), and RotateZ() methods. These methods perform rotations about the x, y, and z axes in an order specified by the user. New rotations are applied to the right of the rotation transformation. If you need to rotate your actor about a single axis, the actor will rotate exactly as you expect it will, and the resulting orientation vector will be as expected. For example, the operation RotateY(20) will produce an orientation of (0,20,0) and a RotateZ(20) will produce (0,0,20). However, a RotateY(20) followed by a RotateZ(20) will not produce (0,20,20) but produce an orientation of (6.71771, 18.8817, 18.8817)! This is because the rotation portion of **Equation 3-14** is built from the rotation order z, then x, and then y. To verify this, a RotateZ(20) followed by a RotateY(20) does produce an orientation of (0,20,20). Adding a third rotation can be even more confusing.

A good rule of thumb is to only use the SetOrientation() method to either reset the orientation to (0,0,0) or to set just one of the rotations. The RotateX(), RotateY(), and RotateZ() methods are preferred to SetOrientation() when multiple angles are needed. Remember that these rotations are applied in reverse order. **Figure 3–31** illustrates the use of the rotation methods. We turn off the erase between frames using the render window's EraseOff() method so we can see the effects of the rotations. Note that in the fourth image the cow still rotates about her own y axis even though an x axis rotation preceded the y rotation.

We have seen that VTK hides some of the complexities of matrix transformations by using instance variables that are more natural than a transformation matrix. But there will be times when the predefined order of transformations performed by the actor will not be sufficient. vtkActor has an instance variable UserMatrix that contains a 4 x 4 transformation matrix. This matrix is applied before the transformation composed by the actor. As you become more comfortable with 4 x 4 transformation matrices you may want to build your own matrix. The object vtkTransform creates and manipulates these matrices. Unlike an actor, an instance of vtkTransform does not have an instance variable for position, scale, origin, etc. You control the composition of the matrix directly. The following statements create an identical 4 x 4 matrix that the actor creates:

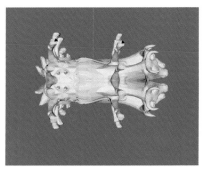

(a) Six rotations about the *x* axis.

(b) Six rotations about the *y* axis.

(c) Six rotations about the *z* axis.

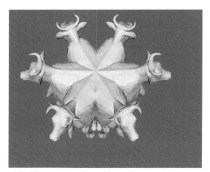

(d) First a rotation about the *x* axis, then
six rotations about the *y* axis.

Figure 3–31 Rotations of a cow about her axes. In this model, the *x* axis is from the left to right; the *y* axis is from bottom to top; and the *z* axis emerges from the image. The camera location is the same in all four images (rotations.tcl).

```
vtkTransform *myTrans = vtkTransform::New ();
myTrans->Translate (position[0],position[1],position[2]);
myTrans->Translate (origin[0],origin[1],origin[2]);
myTrans->RotateZ (orientation[2]);
myTrans->RotateX (orientation[0]);
myTrans->RotateZ (orientation[1]);
myTrans->Scale (scale[0],scale[1],scale[2]);
myTrans->Translate (-origin[0],-origin[1],-origin[2]);
```

Compare this sequence of transform operations with the transformation in **Equation 3-14**.

Our final example shows how the transform built with vtkTransform compares with a transform built by vtkActor. In this example, we will transform our cow so that she rotates about the world coordinate origin (0,0,0). She will appear to be walking around the origin. We accomplish this in two ways: one using vtkTransform and the actor's UserMatrix, then using the actor's instance variables.

First, we will move the cow five feet along the *z* axis then rotate her about the origin. We always specify transformations in the reverse order of their application:

Figure 3–32 The cow "walking" around the global origin (`walkCow.tcl`).

```
vtkTransform *walk = vtkTransform::New();
  walk->RotateY(0,20,0);
  walk->Translate(0,0,5);
vtkActor *cow=vtkActor::New();
  cow->SetUserMatrix(walk->GetMatrix());
```

These operations produce the transformation sequence:

$$T = T_{R_y} T_S T_T(0, 0, 5) \tag{3-15}$$

Now we do the same using the cow's instance variables:

```
vtkActor *cow=vtkActor::New();
  cow->SetOrigin(0,0,-5);
  cow->RotateY(20);
  cow->SetPosition(0,0,5);
```

When the actor builds its transform it will be:

$$T = T_T(0, 0, 5 - (-5)) T_{R_y} T_S T_T(0, 0, -(-5)) \tag{3-16}$$

Canceling the minus signs in the right-most translation matrix and combining the position and origin translation produce the equivalent transform that we built with vtkTranform. **Figure 3–32** shows the cow rotating with the specified transformation order. Your preference

Figure 3–33 The cow rotating about a vector passing through her nose. (a) With origin (0,0,0). (b) With origin at (6.1,1.3,.02). (`walkCow.tcl`).

is a matter of taste and how comfortable you are with matrix transformations. As you become more skilled (and your demands are greater) you may prefer to always build your transformations. VTK gives you the choice.

There is one final and powerful operation that affects an actor's orientation. You can rotate an actor about an arbitrary vector positioned at the actor's origin. This is done with the actor's (and transform's) RotateWXYZ() method. The first argument of the operation specifies the number of degrees to rotate about the vector specified by the next three arguments. **Figure 3–33** shows how to rotate the cow about a vector passing through her nose. At first, we leave the origin at (0,0,0). This is obviously not what we wanted. The second figure shows the rotation when we change the cow's rotation origin to the tip of her nose.

Assemblies and Other Types of vtkProp

Often it is desirable to collect actors into a hierarchy of transform-dependent groups. For example, a robot arm may be represented by rigid links connected at joints such as the shoulder joint, upper arm, elbow, lower arm, wrist joint, and hand. In such a configuration, when the shoulder joint rotates, the expected behavior is that the entire arm rotates since the links are connected together. This is an example of what is referred to as an *assembly* in VTK. vtkAssembly is just one of many actor-like classes in VTK. As **Figure 3–34** shows, these classes are arranged into a hierarchy of vtkProps. (In stage and film terminology, a prop is something that appears or is used on stage.)

Assemblies are formed in VTK by instantiating a vtkAssembly and then adding *parts* to it. A part is any instance of vtkProp3D—including other assemblies. This means that assemblies can be formed into hierarchies (as long as they do not contain self-referencing loops). Assemblies obey the rules of transformation concatenation illustrated in the previous section (see "Transformation Matrices" on page 71). Here is an example of how to create a simple assembly hierarchy (from `assembly.tcl`).

```
vtkSphereSource sphere
vtkPolyDataMapper sphereMapper
    sphereMapper SetInput [sphere GetOutput]
vtkActor sphereActor
```

```
        sphereActor SetMapper sphereMapper
        sphereActor SetOrigin 2 1 3
        sphereActor RotateY 6
        sphereActor SetPosition 2.25 0 0
        [sphereActor GetProperty] SetColor 1 0 1

    vtkCubeSource cube
    vtkPolyDataMapper cubeMapper
        cubeMapper SetInput [cube GetOutput]
    vtkActor cubeActor
        cubeActor SetMapper cubeMapper
        cubeActor SetPosition 0.0 .25 0
        [cubeActor GetProperty] SetColor 0 0 1

    vtkConeSource cone
    vtkPolyDataMapper coneMapper
        coneMapper SetInput [cone GetOutput]
    vtkActor coneActor
        coneActor SetMapper coneMapper
        coneActor SetPosition 0 0 .25
        [coneActor GetProperty] SetColor 0 1 0

    vtkCylinderSource cylinder
    vtkPolyDataMapper cylinderMapper
        cylinderMapper SetInput [cylinder GetOutput]
        cylinderMapper SetResolveCoincidentTopologyToPolygonOffset
    vtkActor cylinderActor
        cylinderActor SetMapper cylinderMapper
        [cylinderActor GetProperty] SetColor 1 0 0

    vtkAssembly assembly
        assembly AddPart cylinderActor
        assembly AddPart sphereActor
        assembly AddPart cubeActor
        assembly AddPart coneActor
        assembly SetOrigin 5 10 15
        assembly AddPosition 5 0 0
        assembly RotateX 15

    ren1 AddActor assembly
    ren1 AddActor coneActor
```

Note that in this example various actors are added to the assembly with the AddPart()
method. The top-level element of the assembly is the only prop in the hierarchy added to the
renderer (with AddActor()). Note also that the coneActor appears twice: once as a part of the
assembly, and once as a separate actor added to the renderer with AddActor(). As you might
imagine, this means that the rendering of assemblies requires concatenation of transformation
matrices to insure the correct positioning of each vtkProp3D. Furthermore, hierarchical
assemblies require special treatment during picking (i.e., graphically selecting props) since a

Figure 3–34 The vtkProp hierarchy. Props that can be transformed in 3D space are a subclass of vtkProp3D. Images can be drawn effectively with vtkImageActor. Overlay text and graphics use vtkActor2D. Hierarchical groups of vtkProps are gathered into a vtkPropAssembly. Volume rendering uses vtkVolume. Collections of transformable props create a vtkAssembly. Level-of-detail rendering uses vtkLODProp3D and vtkLODActor. A vtkFollower allows faces a specified camera and is used for billboards.

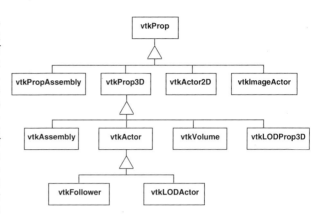

vtkProp can appear more than once in different assembly hierarchies. Picking issues are discussed in more detail in "Picking" on page 290.

As **Figure 3–34** indicates, there are other types of vtkProp as well. Most of these will be informally described in the many examples found in this book. In particular, extensive coverage is given to vtkVolume when we describe volume rendering (see "Volume Rendering" on page 206).

3.11 Chapter Summary

The process of generating an image using a computer is called rendering. Computer graphics is the field of study that encompasses rendering techniques. Computer graphics forms the foundation of data visualization.

Three-dimensional rendering techniques simulate the interaction of lights and cameras with objects, or actors, to generate images. A scene consists of a combination of lights, cameras, and actors. Object-order rendering techniques generate images by rendering actors in a scene in order. Image-order techniques render the image one pixel at a time. Polygon-based graphics hardware is based on object-order techniques. Ray tracing or ray-casting is an image-order technique.

Lighting models require a specification of color. We saw both the RGB (red-green-blue) and HSV (hue-saturation-value) color models. The HSV model is a more natural model than the RGB model for most users. Lighting models also include effects due to ambient, diffuse, and specular lighting.

There are four important coordinate systems in computer graphics. The model system is the 3D coordinate system where our geometry is defined. The world system is the global Cartesian system. All modeled data is eventually transformed into the world system. The view coordinate system represents what is visible to the camera. It is a 2D system scaled from (-1,1). The display coordinate system uses actual pixel locations on the computer display.

Homogeneous coordinates are a 4D coordinate system in which we can include the effects of perspective transformation. Transformation matrices are 4×4 matrices that operate on homogeneous coordinates. Transformation matrices can represent the effects of translation, scaling, and rotation of an actor. These matrices can be multiplied together to give combined transformations.

Graphics programming is usually implemented using higher-level graphics libraries or hardware systems. These dedicated systems offer better performance and easier implementation of graphics applications. Common techniques implemented in these systems include dithering and *z*-buffering. Dithering is a technique to simulate colors by mixing combinations of available colors. Z-buffering is a technique to perform hidden-line and hidden-surface removal.

The *Visualization Toolkit* uses a graphics model based on lights, cameras, actors, and renderers. The renderers draw into rendering windows. Actor properties are represented by a property object and their geometry by a mapper object. Taken together, the instantiations of these various classes form a scene. Interaction with the objects in a scene is facilitated by the vtkRenderWindowInteractor and vtkInteractorStyle classes. These use the command/observer design pattern that triggers and responds to events. Users can observe particular events and write callbacks that can perform arbitrary tasks, easily extending the toolkit for a particular application.

3.12 Bibliographic Notes

This chapter provides the reader with enough information to understand the basic issues and terms used in computer graphics. There are a number of good text books that cover computer graphics in more detail and are recommended to readers who would like a more thorough understanding. The bible of computer graphics is [FoleyVanDam90]. For those wishing for less intimidating books [BurgerGillies89] and [Watt93] are useful references. You also may wish to peruse proceedings of the ACM SIGGRAPH conferences. These include papers and references to other papers for some of the most important work in computer graphics. [Carlson85] provides a good introduction for those who wish to learn more about the human vision system.

3.13 References

[Bresenham65]
    J. E. Bresenham."Algorithm for Computer Control of a Digital Plotter." *IBM Systems Journal*, 4(1): 25–30, January 1965.

[BurgerGillies89]
    P. Burger and D. Gillies. *Interactive Compute Graphics Functional, Procedural and Device-Level Methods*. Addison-Wesley, Reading, MA, 1989.

[Carlson85]
    N. R. Carlson. *Physiology of Behaviour (3d Edition)*. Allyn and Bacon Inc., Newton, MA, 1985.

[Dartnall83]
    H. J. A. Dartnall, J. K. Bowmaker, and J. D. Mollon. "Human Visual Pigments: Microspectrophotometric Results from the Eyes of Seven Persons." *Proceedings of the Royal Society*, London, 1983.

[FoleyVanDam90]

J. D. Foley, A. van Dam, S. K. Feiner, and J. F. Hughes. *Computer Graphics Principles and Practice (2d Edition)*. Addison-Wesley, Reading, MA, 1990.

[Fuchs80]

H. Fuchs, Z. M. Kedem, and B. F. Naylor. "On Visible Surface Generation By A Priori Tree Structure." *Computer Graphics (SIGGRAPH '80)*, 14(3):124–133, 1980.

[Gamma95]

E. Gamma, R. Helm, R. Johnson, J. Vlissides. *Design Patterns Elements of Reusable Object-Oriented Software*. Addison-Wesley 1995. ISBN0-201-63361-2.

[Ousterhout94]

J. K.Ousterhout. *Tcl and the Tk Toolkit*. Addison-Wesley Publishing Company, Reading, MA, 1994.

[Watt93]

A. Watt. *3D Computer Graphics (2d Edition)*. Addison-Wesley, Reading, MA, 1993.

[Whitted80]

T. Whitted. "An Improved Illumination Model for Shaded Display." *Communications of the ACM*, 23(6):343–349, 1980.

3.14 Exercises

3.1 Estimate the odds of a ray of light being emitted from the sun, traveling to earth and hitting a one meter square picnic blanket. You can assume that the sun is a point light source that emits light uniformly in all directions. The approximate distance from the sun to the earth is 150,000,000 km.

a) What are the odds when the sun is directly overhead?

b) What are the odds when the sun is inclined 45 degrees relative to the surface normal of the picnic blanket?

c) What assumptions or approximations did you make?

3.2 Proceeding from your result of Exercise 3.1, what are the difficulties in determining the odds of a ray of light traveling from the sun to hit the picnic blanket and then entering a viewer's eye?

3.3 The color cyan can be represented in both the HSV and RGB color spaces as shown in **Figure 3–4**. These two representations for cyan do not yield the same wavelength intensity plots. How do they differ?

3.4 The vtkSphereSource class generates a polygonal model of a sphere. Using the examples at the end of this chapter as starting points, create a program to display a white sphere. Set the ambient and diffuse intensities to 0.5. Then add a for-loop to this program that adjusts the ambient and diffuse color of this sphere so that as the loop progresses, the diffuse color goes from red to blue, and the ambient color goes from blue to green. You might also try adjusting other lighting parameters such as specular color, ambient, diffuse, and specular intensity.

3.5 Using the vtkSphereSource as described in Exercise 3.4, create a program to display the sphere with a light source positioned at (1,1,1). Then extend this program by adding a for-loop that will adjust the active camera's clipping range so that increasing portions of the interior of the sphere can be seen. By increasing the first value of the clipping range, you will be adjusting the position of the front clipping plane. Once the front clipping plane starts intersecting the sphere, you should be able to see inside of it. The default radius of the vtkSphereSource is 0.5, so make sure that you adjust the clipping range in increments less than 1.0.

3.6   Modify the program presented in "Render a Cone" on page 62 so that the user can enter in a world coordinate in homogenous coordinates and the program will print out the resulting display coordinate. Refer to the reference page for vtkRenderer for some useful methods.
a) Are there any world coordinates that you would expect to be undefined in display coordinates?
b) What happens when the world coordinates are behind the camera?

3.7   Consider rasterizing a ten by ten pixel square. Contrast the approximate difference in the number of arithmetic operations that would need to be done for the cases where it is flat, Gouraud, or Phong shaded.

3.8   When using a z-buffer, we must also interpolate the z-values (or depth) when rasterizing a primitive. Working from Exercise 3.7, what is the additional burden of computing z-buffer values while rasterizing our square?

3.9   vtkTransform has a method GetOrientation() that looks at the resulting transformation matrix built from a series of rotations and provides the single x, y, and z rotations that will reproduce the matrix. Specify a series of rotations in a variety of orders and request the orientation with GetOrientation(). Then apply the rotations in the same order that vtkActor does and verify that the resulting 4 x 4 transformation matrix is the same.

3.10 vtkTransform, by default, applies new transformations at the right of the current transformation. The method PostMultiply() changes the behavior so that the transformations are applied to the left.
a) Use vtkTransform to create a transform using a variety of transformation operators including Scale(), RotateXYZ(), and Translate(). Then create the same matrix with PostMultiplyOn().
b) Applying rotations at the right of a series of transformations in effect rotates the object about its own coordinate system. Use the rotations.tcl script to verify this. Can you explain this?
c) Applying rotations at the left of a series of transformations in effect rotates the object about the world coordinate system. Modify the rotations.tcl script to illustrate this. (Hint: you will have to create an explicit transform with vtkTransform and set the actor's transform with SetUserMatrix().)

The Visualization Pipeline

In the previous chapter we created graphical images using simple mathematical models for lighting, viewing, and geometry. The lighting model included ambient, diffuse, and specular effects. Viewing included the effects of perspective and projection. Geometry was defined as a static collection of graphics primitives such as points and polygons. In order to describe the process of visualization we need to extend our understanding of geometry to include more complex forms. We will see that the visualization process transforms data into graphics primitives. This chapter examines the process of data transformation and develops a model of data flow for visualization systems.

4.1 Overview

Visualization transforms data into images that efficiently and accurately convey information about the data. Thus, visualization addresses the issues of *transformation* and *representation*.

Transformation is the process of converting data from its original form into graphics primitives, and eventually into computer images. This is our working definition of the visualization process. An example of such a transformation is the process of extracting stock prices and creating an *x-y* plot depicting stock price as a function of time.

Representation includes both the internal data structures used to depict the data and the graphics primitives used to display the data. For example, an array of stock prices and an array of times are the computational representation of the data, while the *x-y* plot is the graphical representation. Visualization transforms a computational form into a graphical form.

From an object-oriented viewpoint, transformations are processes in the functional model, while representations are the objects in the object model. Therefore, we characterize the visualization model with both functional models and object models.

A Data Visualization Example

A simple mathematical function for a quadric will clarify these concepts. The function

$$F(x, y, z) = a_0 x^2 + a_1 y^2 + a_2 z^2 + a_3 xy + a_4 yz + a_5 xz + a_6 x + a_7 y + a_8 z + a_9 \qquad \textbf{(4-1)}$$

is the mathematical representation of a quadric. **Figure 4–1**(a) shows a visualization of **Equation 4-1** in the region $-1 \leq x, y, z \leq 1$. The visualization process is as follows. We sample the data on a regular grid at a resolution of $50 \times 50 \times 50$. Three different visualization techniques are then used. On the left, we generate 3D surfaces corresponding to the function $F(x, y, z) = c$ where c is an arbitrary constant (i.e., the isosurface value). In the center, we show three different planes that cut through the data and are colored by function value. On the right we show the same three planes that have been contoured with constant valued lines. Around each we place a wireframe outline.

The Functional Model

The functional model in **Figure 4–1**(b) illustrates the steps to create the visualization. The oval blocks indicate operations (processes) we performed on the data, and the rectangular blocks represent data stores (objects) that represent and provide access to data. Arrows indicate the direction of data movement. Arrows that point into a block are inputs; data flowing out of a block indicate outputs. The blocks also may have local parameters that serve as additional input. Processes that create data with no input are called data *source* objects, or simply sources. Processes that consume data with no output are called *sinks*. Processes with both an input and an output are called *filters*.

The functional model shows how data flows through the system. It also describes the dependency of the various parts upon one another. For any given process to execute correctly, all the inputs must be up to date. This suggests that functional models require a synchronization mechanism to insure that the correct output will be generated.

The Visualization Model

In the examples that follow we will frequently use a simplified representation of the functional model to describe visualization processes (**Figure 4–1**(c)). We will not explicitly distinguish between sources, sinks, data stores, and process objects. Sources and sinks are implied based on the number of inputs or outputs. Sources will be process objects with no input. Sinks will be process objects with no output. Filters will be process objects with at least one input and one output. Intermediate data stores will not be represented. Instead we will assume that they exist as necessary to support the data flow. Thus, as **Figure 4–1**(c) shows, the *Lines* data store that the *Outline* object generates (**Figure 4–1**(b)) are combined into the single object *Outline*. We use oval shapes to represent objects in the visualization model.

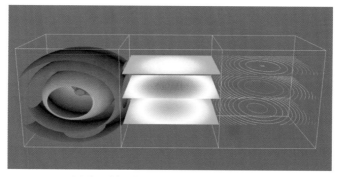

(a) Quadric visualization (`Sample.cxx`)

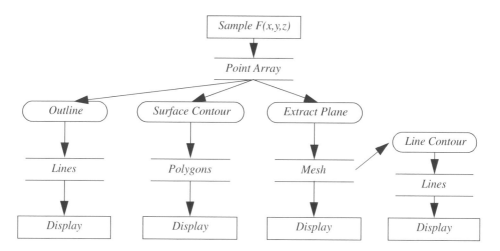

(b) Functional model

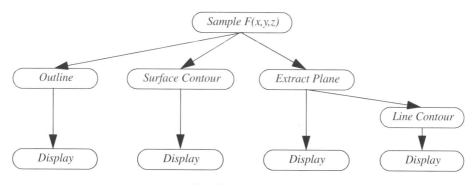

(c) Visualization network

Figure 4–1 Visualizing a quadric function $F(x,y,z) = c$.

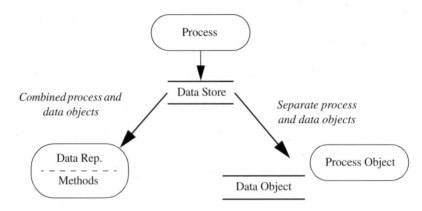

Figure 4–2 Object model design choices. One basic choice is to combine processes and data stores into a single object. This is the usual object-oriented choice. Another choice creates separate data objects and process objects.

The Object Model

The functional model describes the flow of data in our visualization, the object model describes which modules operate on it. But what *are* the objects in the system? At first glance, we have two choices (**Figure 4–2**).

The first choice combines data stores (object attributes) with processes (object methods) into a single object. In the second choice we use separate objects for data stores and processes. There is actually a third alternative: a hybrid combination of these two choices.

The conventional object-oriented approach (our first choice above) combines data stores and processes into a single object. This view follows the standard definition that objects contain a data representation combined with procedures to operate on the data. One advantage of this approach is that the processes, which are the data visualization algorithms, have complete access to the data structures, resulting in good computational performance. But this choice suffers from several drawbacks.

- From a user's perspective, processes are often viewed as independent of data representation. In other words, processes are naturally viewed as objects in the system. For example, we often say we want to "contour" data, meaning creating lines or surfaces corresponding to a constant data value. To the user it is convenient to have a single contour object to operate on different data representations.

- We must duplicate algorithm implementation. As in the previous contouring example, if we bind data stores and processes into a single object, the contour operation must be recreated for each data type. This results in duplicating code even though the implementations of an algorithm may be functionally and structurally similar. Modifying such algorithms also means modifying a large amount of code, since they are implemented across many objects.

- Binding data stores and algorithms together results in complex, data dependent code. Some algorithms may be much more complex than the data they operate on, with large numbers of instance variables and elaborate data structures. By combining many such algorithms with a data store, the complexity of the object greatly increases, and the simple meaning of the object becomes lost.

The second choice separates the data stores and processes. That is, one set of objects represents and provides access to the data, while another set of objects implements all operations on the data. Our experience shows that this is natural to users, although it may be considered unconventional to the object-oriented purist. We also have found that the resulting code is simple, modular, and easy for developers to understand, maintain, and extend.

One disadvantage to the second choice is that the interface between data representation and process is more formal. Thus the interface must be carefully designed to insure good performance and flexibility. Another disadvantage is that strong separation of data and process results in duplicate code. That is, we may implement operations that duplicate algorithms and that cannot be considered strictly data access methods. One example of such a situation is computing data derivatives. This operation is more than simple data access, so strictly speaking it doesn't belong in the data object methods. So to compute derivatives we would have to duplicate the code each time we needed derivatives computed. (Or create a procedural library of functions or macros!)

As a result of these concerns we use the hybrid approach in the *Visualization Toolkit*. Our approach is closest to the second choice described above, but we have selected a small set of critical operations that we implement within the data objects. These operations have been identified based on our experience implementing visualization algorithms. This effectively combines the first two choices to receive the maximum benefit and fewest disadvantages of each.

4.2 The Visualization Pipeline

In the context of data visualization, the functional model of **Figure 4–1**(c) is referred to as the *visualization pipeline* or *visualization network*. The pipeline consists of objects to represent data (data objects), objects to operate on data (process objects), and an indicated direction of data flow (arrow connections between objects). In the text that follows, we will frequently use visualization networks to describe the implementation of a particular visualization technique.

Data Objects

Data objects represent information. Data objects also provide methods to create, access, and delete this information. Direct modification of the data represented by the data objects is not allowed except through formal object methods. This capability is reserved for process objects. Additional methods are also available to obtain characteristic features of the data. This includes determining the minimum and maximum data values, or determining the size or the number of data values in the object.

Data objects differ depending upon their internal representation. The internal representation has significant impact on the access methods to the data, as well as on the storage efficiency or computational performance of process objects that interact with the data object.

Hence, different data objects may be used to represent the same data depending on demands for efficiency and process generality.

Process Objects

Process objects operate on input data to generate output data. A process object either derives new data from its inputs, or transforms the input data into a new form. For example, a process object might derive pressure gradient data from a pressure field or transform the pressure field into constant value pressure contours. The input to a process object includes both one or more data objects as well as local parameters to control its operation. Local parameters include both instance variables or associations and references to other objects. For example, the center and radius are local parameters to control the generation of sphere primitives.

Process objects are further characterized as *source objects*, *filter objects*, or *mapper objects*. This categorization is based on whether the objects initiate, maintain, or terminate visualization data flow.

Source objects interface to external data sources or generate data from local parameters. Source objects that generate data from local parameters are called *procedural* objects. The previous example of **Figure 4–1** uses a procedural object to generate function values for the quadric function of **Equation 4-1**. Source objects that interface to external data are called *reader* objects since the external file must be read and converted to an internal form. Source objects may also interface to external data communication ports and devices. Possible examples include simulation or modelling programs, or data acquisition systems to measure temperature, pressure, or other similar physical attributes.

Filter objects require one or more input data objects and generate one or more output data objects. Local parameters control the operation of the process object. Computing weekly stock market averages, representing a data value as a scaled icon, or performing union set operations on two input data sources are typical example processes of filter objects.

Mapper objects correspond to the sinks in the functional model. Mapper objects require one or more input data objects and terminate the visualization pipeline data flow. Usually mapper objects are used to convert data into graphical primitives, but they may write out data to a file or interface with another software system or devices. Mapper objects that write data to a computer file are termed *writer* objects.

4.3 Pipeline Topology

In this section we describe how to connect data and process objects to form visualization networks.

Pipeline Connections

The elements of the pipeline (sources, filters, and mappers) can be connected in a variety of ways to create visualization networks. However, there are two important issues that arise when we try to assemble these networks: *type* and *multiplicity*.

Type means the form or type of data that process objects take as input or generate as output. For example, a sphere source object may generate as output a polygonal or faceted

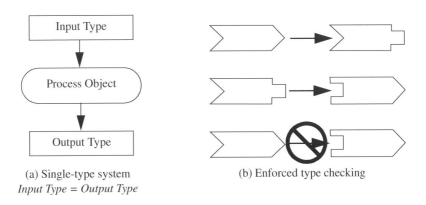

Figure 4–3 Maintaining compatible data type. (a) Single-type systems require no type checking. (b) In multiple-type systems only compatible types can be connected together.

representation, an implicit representation (e.g., parameters of a conic equation), or a set of occupancy values in a discretized representation of 3D space. Mapper objects might take as input polygonal, triangle strip, line, or point geometric representations. The input to a process object must be specified correctly for successful operation.

There are two general approaches to maintain proper input type. One approach is to design with type-less or single-type systems. That is, create a single type of data object and create filters that operate only on this one type (**Figure 4–3**(a)). For example, we could design a general *DataSet* that represents any form of data that we're interested in, and the process objects would only input *DataSets* and generate *DataSets*. This approach is simple and elegant, but inflexible. Often, particularly useful algorithms (i.e., process objects) will operate only on specific types of data and to generalize them results in large inefficiencies in representation or data access. A typical example is a data object that represents structured data such as pixmaps or 3D volumes. Because the data is structured it can easily be accessed as planes or lines. However, a general representation will not include this capability because typically data is not structured.

Another approach to maintain proper input type is to design typed systems (**Figure 4–3**(b)). In typed systems only objects of compatible type are allowed to be connected together. That is, more than one type is designed, but type checking is performed on the input to insure proper connection. Depending on the particular computer language, type checking can be performed at compile, link, or run time. Although type checking does insure correct input type, this approach often suffers from an explosion of types. If not careful, the designers of a visualization system may create too many types, resulting in a fragmented, hard to use and understand system. In addition, the system may require a large number of *type-converter* filters. (Type-converter filters serve only to transform data from one form to another.) Carried to extremes, excessive type conversion results in computationally and memory wasteful systems.

The issue of multiplicity deals with the number of input data objects allowed, and the number of output data objects created during the operation of a process object (**Figure 4–4**). We know that all filter and mapper objects require at minimum one input data object, but in

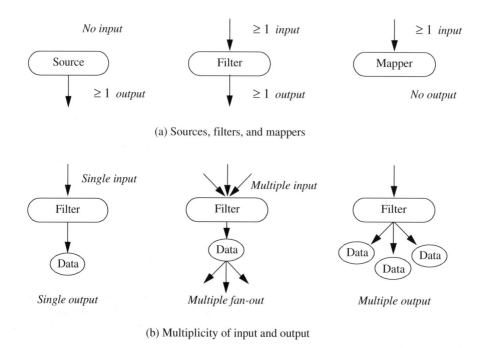

(a) Sources, filters, and mappers

(b) Multiplicity of input and output

Figure 4–4 Multiplicity of input and output. (a) Definition of source, filter, and mapper objects. (b) Various types of input and output.

general these filters can operate sequentially across a list of input. Some filters may naturally require a specific number of inputs. A filter implementing boolean operations is one example. Boolean operations such as union or intersection are implemented on data values two at a time. However, even here more than two inputs may be defined as a recursive application of the operation to each input.

We need to distinguish what is meant by multiplicity of output. Most sources and filters generate a single output. *Multiple fan-out* occurs when an object generates an output that is used for input by more than one object. This would occur, for example, when a source object is used to read a data file, and the resulting data is used to generate a wireframe outline of the data, plus contours of the data (e.g., **Figure 4–1**(a)). *Multiple output* occurs when an object generates two or more output data objects. An example of multiple output is generating x, y, and z components of a gradient function as distinct data objects. Combinations of multiple fan-out and multiple output are possible.

Loops

In the examples described so far, the visualization networks have been free of cycles. In graph theory these are termed directed, acyclic graphs. However, in some cases it is desirable to introduce feedback loops into our visualization networks. Feedback loops in a visualization network allow us to direct the output of a process object upstream to affect its input.

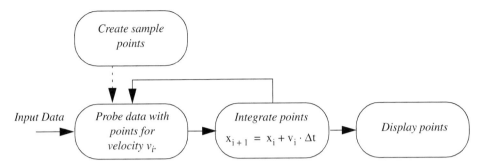

Figure 4–5 Looping in a visualization network. This example implements linear integration. The sample points are created to initialize the looping process. The output of the integration filter is used in place of the sample points once the process begins.

Figure 4–5 shows an example of a feedback loop in a visualization network. We seed a velocity field with an initial set of random points. A probe filter is used to determine the velocity (and possibly other data) at each point. Each point is then repositioned in the direction of its associated vector value, possibly using a scale factor to control the magnitude of motion. The process continues until the points exit the data set or until a maximum iteration count is exceeded.

We will discuss the control and execution of visualization networks in the next section. However, loops pose no special problem in visualization networks. We need only make sure that the combined operation of the filters in the loop does not enter an infinite loop or nonterminating recursive state. Typically, we limit the number of executions of the loop in order to view intermediate results. However, it is possible to execute the loop repeatedly to process data as required.

4.4 Executing the Pipeline

So far we have seen the basic elements of the visualization network and ways to connect these elements together. In this section we discuss how to control the execution of the network.

To be useful, a visualization network must process data to generate a desired result. The complete process of causing each process object to operate is called the *execution* of the network.

Most often the visualization network is executed more than once. For example, we may change the parameters of, or the input to, a process object. This is typically due to user interaction: The user may be exploring or methodically varying input to observe results. After one or more changes to the process object or its input, we must execute the network to generate up-to-date results.

For highest performance, the process objects in the visualization network must execute *only* if a change occurs to their input. In some networks, as shown in **Figure 4–6**, we may have parallel branches that need not execute if objects are modified local to a particular branch. In this figure, we see that object D and the downstream objects E and F must execute

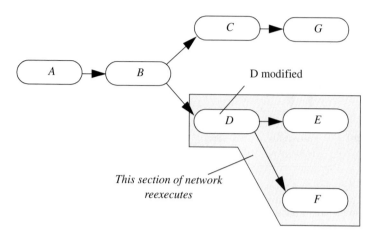

Figure 4–6 Network execution. Parallel branches need not execute if changes are local to a particular branch.

because D's input parameter is changed, and objects E and F depend on D for their input. The other objects need not execute because there is no change to their input.

We can control the execution of the network using either a *demand-driven* or *event-driven* approach. In the demand-driven approach, we execute the network only when output is requested, and only that portion of the network affecting the result. In the event-driven approach, every change to a process object or its input causes the network to reexecute. The advantage of the event-driven approach is that the output is always up to date (except during short periods of computation). The advantage of the demand driven approach is that large numbers of changes can be accumulated without intermediate computation. The demand-driven approach minimizes computation and results in more interactive visualization networks.

The execution of the network requires synchronization between process objects. We want to execute a process object only when all of its input objects are up to date. There are generally two ways to synchronize network execution: explicit or implicit control (**Figure 4–7**).

Explicit Execution

Explicit control means directly tracking the changes to the network, and then directly controlling the execution of the process objects based on an explicit dependency analysis. The major characteristic of this approach is that a centralized *executive* is used to coordinate network execution. This executive must track changes to the parameters and inputs of each object, including subsequent changes to the network topology (**Figure 4–7**(a)).

The advantage of this approach is that synchronization analysis and update methods are local to the single executive object. In addition, we can create dependency graphs and perform analysis of data flow each time output is requested. This capability is particularly important if we wish to decompose the network for parallel computing or to distribute execution across a network of computers.

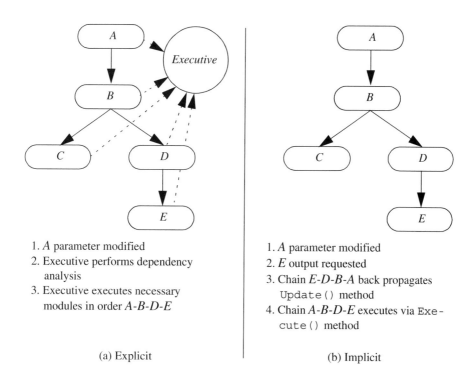

1. *A* parameter modified
2. Executive performs dependency
   analysis
3. Executive executes necessary
   modules in order *A-B-D-E*

1. *A* parameter modified
2. *E* output requested
3. Chain *E-D-B-A* back propagates
   `Update()` method
4. Chain *A-B-D-E* executes via `Exe-`
   `cute()` method

(a) Explicit

(b) Implicit

Figure 4–7 Explicit and implicit network execution.

The disadvantage of the explicit approach is that each process object becomes dependent upon the executive, since the executive must be notified of any change. Also, the executive cannot easily control execution if the network execution is conditional, since whether to execute or not depends on the local results of one or more process objects.

The explicit approach may be either demand-driven or event-driven. In the event-driven approach, the executive is notified whenever a change to an object occurs (typically in response to a user-interface event), and the network is immediately executed. In the demand-driven approach, the executive accumulates changes to object inputs and executes the network based on explicit user demand.

The explicit approach with a central executive is typical of many commercial visualization systems such as AVS, Irix Explorer, and IBM Data Explorer. Typically these systems use a visual-programming interface to construct the visualization network. Often these systems are implemented on parallel computers, and the ability to distribute computation is essential.

Implicit Execution

Implicit control means that a process object executes only if its local input or parameters change (**Figure 4–7**(b)). Implicit control is implemented using a two-pass process. First, when output is requested from a particular object, that object requests input from its input

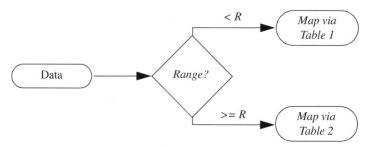

Figure 4–8 Examples of conditional execution. Depending upon range, data is mapped through different color lookup tables.

objects. This process is recursively repeated until source objects are encountered. The source objects then execute if they have changed or their external inputs have changed. Then the recursion unwinds as each process object examines its inputs and determines whether to execute. This procedure repeats until the initial requesting object executes and terminates the process. These two steps are called the *update* and *execution* passes.

Implicit network execution is naturally implemented using *demand-driven* control. Here network execution occurs only when output data is requested. Implicit network execution may also be event-driven if we simply request output each time an appropriate event is encountered (such as change to object parameter).

The primary advantage of the implicit control scheme is its simplicity. Each object only need keep track of its internal modification time. When output is requested, the object compares its modification time with that of its inputs, and executes if out of date. Furthermore, process objects need only know about their direct input, so no global knowledge of other objects (such as a network executive) is required.

The disadvantage of implicit control is that it is harder to distribute network execution across computers or to implement sophisticated execution strategies. One simple approach is to create a queue that executes process objects in order of network execution (possibly in a distributed fashion). Of course, once a central object is introduced back into the system, the lines between implicit and explicit control are blurred.

Conditional Execution

Another important capability of visualization networks is conditional execution. For example, we may wish to map data through different color lookup tables depending upon the variation of range in the data. Small variations can be amplified by assigning more colors within the data range, while we may compress our color display by assigning a small number of colors to the data range (**Figure 4–8**).

The conditional execution of visualization models (such as that shown **Figure 4–1**(c)) can be realized in principle. However, in practice we must supplement the visualization network with a conditional language to express the rules for network execution. Hence, conditional execution of visualization networks is a function of implementation language. Many visualization systems are programmed using the visual programming style. This approach is basically a visual editor to construct data flow diagrams directly. It is difficult to express conditional execution of networks using this approach. Alternatively, in a procedural programming language, conditional execution of networks is straightforward. We defer discussion of this topic until "Putting It All Together" on page 97.

4.5 Memory and Computation Trade-off

Visualization is a demanding application, both in terms of computer memory and computational requirement. Data streams on the order of 1 to 100 megabytes are not uncommon. Many visualization algorithms are computationally expensive, in part due to input size, but also due to the inherent algorithm complexity. In order to create applications that have reasonable performance, most visualization systems have various mechanisms to trade off memory and computation costs.

Static and Dynamic Memory Models

Memory and computation trade-offs are important performance issues when executing visualization networks. In the networks presented thus far, the output of a process object is assumed to be available to downstream process objects at all times. Thus, network computation is minimized. However, the computer memory requirement to preserve object output can be huge. Networks of only a few objects can tie up extensive computer memory resources.

An alternative approach is to save intermediate results only as long as they are needed by other objects. Once these objects finish processing, the intermediate result can be discarded. This approach results in extra computation each time output is requested. The memory resources required are greatly reduced at the expense of increased computation. Like all trade-offs, the proper solution depends upon the particular application and the nature of the computer system executing the visualization network.

We term these two approaches as *static* and *dynamic* memory models. In the static model intermediate data is saved to reduce overall computation. In the dynamic model intermediate data is discarded when it is no longer needed. The static model serves best when small, variable portions of the network reexecute, and when the data sizes are manageable by the computer system. The dynamic model serves best when the data flows are large, or the same part of the network executes each time. Often, it is desirable to combine both the static and dynamic models into the same network. If an entire leg of the network must execute each time, it makes no sense to store intermediate results, since they are never used. On the other hand, we may wish to save an intermediate result at a branch point in the network, since the data will more likely be reused. A comparison of the static and dynamic memory model for a specific network is shown in **Figure 4–9**.

As this figure shows, the static model executes each process object only once, storing intermediate results. In the dynamic model, each process object releases memory after downstream objects complete execution. Depending upon the implementation of the dynamic model, process object B may execute once or twice. If a thorough dependency analysis is performed, process B will release memory only after both objects C and D execute. In a simpler implementation, object B will release memory after C and subsequently, D executes.

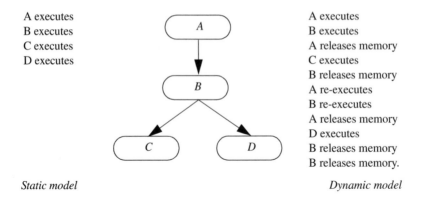

A executes
B executes
C executes
D executes

A executes
B executes
A releases memory
C executes
B releases memory
A re-executes
B re-executes
A releases memory
D executes
B releases memory
B releases memory.

Static model   *Dynamic model*

Figure 4–9 Comparison of static versus dynamic memory models for typical network. Execution begins when output is requested from objects *C* and *D*. In more complex dynamic models, we can prevent *B* from executing twice by performing a more thorough dependency analysis.

Figure 4–10 Reference counting to conserve memory resource. Each filter *A*, *B*, and *C* shares a common point representation. Other data is local to each object.

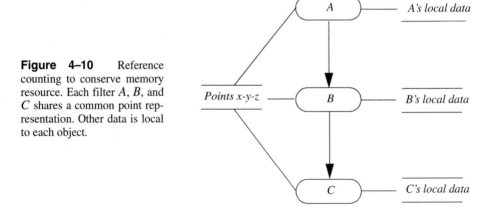

Reference Counting

Another valuable tool to minimize memory cost is to share storage using reference counting. To use reference counting, we allow more than one process object to refer to the same data object. For example, assume that we have three objects *A*, *B*, and *C* that form a portion of a visualization network as shown in **Figure 4–10**. Also assume that these objects modify only part of their input data, leaving the data object that specifies *x-y-z* coordinate position unchanged. Then to conserve memory resources we can allow the output of each process object to refer to the single data object representing these points. Data that is changed remains local to each filter and is not shared.

4.6 Programming Models

Visualization systems are by their very nature designed for human interaction. As a result they must be easy to use. On the other hand, visualization systems must readily adapt to new data, and must be flexible enough to allow rapid data exploration. To meet these demands, a variety of programming models have been developed.

Visualization Models

At the highest level are applications. Visualization applications have finely tailored user-interfaces that are specific to an application area, e.g., fluid flow visualization. Applications are the easiest to use, but are the least flexible. It is very difficult or impossible for the user to extend applications into a new domain because of inherent logistical issues. Commercial turn-key visualization software is generally considered to be application software.

At the opposite end of the spectrum are programming libraries. A conventional programming library is a collection of procedures that operate on a library-specific data structure. Often these libraries are written in conventional programming languages such as C or FORTRAN. These offer great flexibility and can be easily combined with other programming tools and techniques. Programming libraries can be extended or modified by the addition of user-written code. Unfortunately, the effective use of programming libraries requires skilled programmers. Furthermore, non graphics/visualization experts cannot easily use programming libraries because there is no notion of how to fit (or order) the procedures together correctly. These libraries also require extensive synchronization schemes to control execution as input parameters are varied.

Most commercial systems lie between these two extremes. These typically use a *visual programming* approach to construct visualization networks. The basic idea is to provide graphical tools and libraries of modules or process objects. Modules may be connected subject to input/output type constraints, using simple graphical layout tools. In addition, user interface tools allow association of interface widgets with object input parameters. System execution is generally transparent to the user by way of an internal execution executive.

Alternative Visual Programming Models

There are two other graphics and visualization programming models that bear mentioning. These are *scene graphs* and the *spreadsheet* model.

Scene graphs are typically found in 3D graphics systems such as OpenInventor [Wernecke94]. Scene graphs are acyclic tree-structures that represent objects, or nodes, in an order defined by the tree layout. The nodes may be geometry (called shape nodes), graphics properties, transformations, manipulators, lights, cameras, and so forth, that define a complete scene. The parent/child relationship controls how properties and transformations are applied to the nodes as they are rendered, or how the objects relate to other objects in the scene (e.g., which objects the lights shine on). Scene graphs are not used to control the execution of a visualization pipeline, rather they are used to control the rendering process. Scene graphs and visualization pipelines may be used together in the same application. In such a case the visualization pipeline is the generator of the shape nodes, and the scene graph controls the rendering of the scene including the shapes.

Scene graphs have found wide use in the graphics community because of their ability to compactly and graphically represent a scene. In addition, scene graphs have been popularized by their recent use in Web tools such as VRML and Java3D. See Chapter 11 for more information.

Another recently introduced technique for visual programming is the spreadsheet technique of Levoy [Levoy94]. In the spreadsheet model, we arrange operations on a regular grid similar to the common electronic accounting spreadsheets. The grid consists of rows and columns of cells, where each cell is expressed as a computational combination of other cells. The combination is expressed for each cell by using a simple programming language to add, subtract, or perform other more complex operations. The result of the computation (i.e., a visual output) is displayed in the cell.

Although visual programming systems are widely successful, they suffer two drawbacks. First, they are not as tailored as an application and require extensive programming, albeit visual, to be so. Second, visual programming is too limited for detailed control, so constructing complex low-level algorithms and user-interfaces is not feasible. What is required is a visualization system that provides the "modularity" and automatic execution control of a visual system, and the low-level programming capability of a programming library. Object-oriented systems have the potential to provide these capabilities. Carefully crafted object libraries provide the ease of use of visual systems with the control of programming libraries. That is a major goal of the *Visualization Toolkit* described in this text.

4.7 Data Interface Issues

At this point in the text you may be wondering how to apply a visualization pipeline towards your own data. The answer depends on the type of data you have, preferences in programming style, and required complexity. Although we have not described particular types of data (we will in the next chapter), there are three general approaches you may wish to consider when interfacing your data to a visualization system.

Programming Interface

The most powerful and flexible approach is to directly program your application to read, write, and process data. There is almost no limit to what you can achieve using this approach. Unfortunately, in a complex system like VTK this requires a level of expertise that may be beyond your time budget to obtain. (If you are interested in this approach using VTK, you'll have to become familiar with the objects in the system. You will also want to refer to the Doxygen-generated manual pages (on-line at http://www.vtk.org or CD-ROM). The companion text *The VTK User's Guide* is also helpful.

Typical applications requiring a programming interface are interfacing to data files that are not currently supported by the system or generating synthetic data (e.g., from a mathematical relationship) where no data file is available. Also, sometimes it is useful to directly code your data in the form of a program, and then execute the program to visualize the results. (This is exactly what many of the VTK examples do.)

File Interface (Readers / Writers)

In this chapter we saw that readers are source objects, and writers are mappers. What this means from a practical point of view is that readers will ingest data from a file, create a data object, and then pass the object down the pipeline for processing. Similarly, writers ingest a data object and then write the data object to a file. Thus, readers and writers will interface to your data well if VTK supports your format, *and* you only need to read or write a *single* data object. If your data file format is not supported by the system, you will need to interface to your data via the programming interface. Or, if you wish to interface to a collection of objects, you will probably want to see whether an exporter or importer object (described in the next section) exists to support your application.

Examples of readers include vtkSTLReader (read stereo-lithography files) and vtk-BYUReader (read MOVIE.BYU format data files). Similarly the objects vtkSTLWriter and vtkBYUWriter can be used to write data files. To see which readers and writers are supported by VTK, see the *VTK User's Guide* or refer to the Web pages at http://www.vtk.org for the current Doxygen manual pages.

System Interface (Importers / Exporters)

Importers and *exporters* are objects in the system that read or write data files consisting of more than one object. Typically importers and exporters are used to save or restore an entire scene (i.e., lights, cameras, actors, data, transformations, etc.). When an importer is executed, it reads one or more files and may create several objects. For example, in VTK the vtk3DSImporter imports a *3D Studio* file and creates a rendering window, renderer, lights, cameras, and actors. Similarly, the vtkVRMLExporter creates a VRML file given a VTK render window. The VRML file contains cameras, lights, actors, geometry, transformations, and the like, indirectly referred to by the rendering window provided.

In the *Visualization Toolkit*, there are several importers and exporters. To see which importers and exporters are supported by VTK, see the *VTK User's Guide*. You may also want to check the Web pages at http://www.vtk.org for the current Doxygen manual pages. If the exporter you are looking for does not exist, you will have to develop your own using the programming interface. **Figure 4–11** shows an image created from a *3D Studio* model and saved as a *Renderman* RIB file.

4.8 Putting It All Together

In the previous sections we have treated a variety of topics relating to the visualization model. In this section we describe the particular implementation details that we have adopted in the *Visualization Toolkit*.

Procedural Language Implementation

The *Visualization Toolkit* is implemented in the procedural language C++. A class library containing data and process objects facilitates visualization application building. Supporting

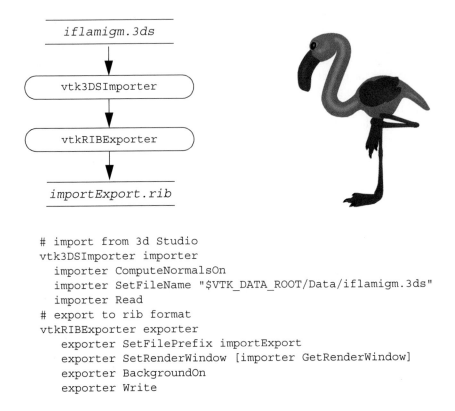

```
# import from 3d Studio
vtk3DSImporter importer
   importer ComputeNormalsOn
   importer SetFileName "$VTK_DATA_ROOT/Data/iflamigm.3ds"
   importer Read
# export to rib format
vtkRIBExporter exporter
   exporter SetFilePrefix importExport
   exporter SetRenderWindow [importer GetRenderWindow]
   exporter BackgroundOn
   exporter Write
```

Figure 4–11 Importing and exporting files in VTK. An importer creates a vtkRenderWindow that describes the scene. Exporters use an instance of vtkRenderWindow to obtain a description of the scene (3dsToRIB.tcl and flamingo.tcl).

abstract objects are available to derive new objects. The visualization pipeline is designed to connect directly to the graphics subsystem described in the previous chapter.

A visual programming interface could be implemented using the class library provided. However, for real-world applications the procedural language implementation provides several advantages. This includes straightforward implementation of conditional network execution and looping, and simple interfacing to other systems such as graphical user-interfaces.

Strongly Typed

With the choice of C++ as the implementation language, strong type checking is mandatory. Most type checking is performed at compile time by the C++ compiler. There is one case where the type checking occurs at run time. This occurs when there is one or more special requirements on input data type.

In this case we find that there are certain filters that operate on a special part of their input data. An example of such a case is the tube filter vtkTubeFilter. This filter creates a tube around any lines found in its input data. Lines are represented using the type vtkPolyData, which represents the graphics primitives we saw in the previous chapter (i.e., points, lines, polygons, and triangle strips). Sometimes the input data will not contain lines. At run time vtkTubeFilter will detect this and issue an error. So even though the compiler is satisfied, there are additional run-time checks that are not.

We would like to mention that one solution to this case is to create more data types. Instead of creating a single type that consists of points, lines, polygons, and triangle strips, we could create four different types of points, lines, polygons, and triangle strips. This certainly is a viable solution, but in our opinion the result is that too many data types are introduced into the system. The result is that the system is harder to understand and use and is less efficient.

Implicit Control of Execution

We have implemented implicit control of visualization network execution. Execution of the network occurs when output is requested from an object (i.e., demand-driven). This approach is simple to implement, is nearly transparent to the user of the system, and accommodates conditional execution and looping. On parallel computers or other special hardware, implicit control can be used in conjunction with an explicit load-balancing scheme by breaking the network into smaller subnetworks.

Our implementation is based on two key methods: Update() and Execute(). If you understand these methods, then you understand the basis for the implicit execution techniques found in VTK.

The Update() method is generally initiated when the user requests the system to render a scene. As part of the process the actors send a Render() method to their mappers. At this point network execution begins. The mapper invokes the Update() method on its input(s). These in turn recursively invoke the Update() method on their input(s). This process continues until a source object is encountered. At this point the source object compares its modified time to the last time it executed. If it has been modified more recently than executed, it re-executes via the Execute() method. The recursion then unwinds with each filter comparing its input time to its execution time. Execute() is called where appropriate. The process terminates when control is returned to the mapper.

This process is extremely simple, but depends upon keeping track of modified time and execution time properly. If you create a filter or source and fail to keep track of modification time correctly, you will encounter cases where your pipeline does not execute properly.

Multiple Input / Output

The *Visualization Toolkit* pipeline architecture has been designed to support multiple inputs and outputs. In practice, you will find that most filters and sources actually generate a single output and filters accept a single input. This is because most algorithms (which sources and filters represent) tend to be single input/output in nature. There are exceptions and we will describe some of these shortly.

The visualization pipeline architecture is depicted in **Figure 4–12**. This figure shows how filters and data objects are connected together to form a visualization network. For the case shown here (i.e., objects with single input/output) the input data is represented by the

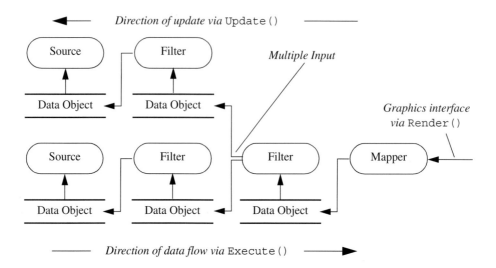

Figure 4–12 Description of implicit execution process implemented in VTK. The Update() method is initiated via the Render() method from the actor. Data flows back to mapper via Execute() method. Arrows connecting objects indicate direction of Update() process.

Input instance variable and is set using the SetInput() method. The output data is represented by the Output instance variable and is accessed using the GetOutput() method. To connect filters together we generally use the C++ statement

```
filter2->SetInput(filter1->GetOutput());
```

where filter1 and filter2 are filter objects of compatible type. (The C++ compiler will enforce proper type.)

The trick to this architecture is that data objects know which filters "own" them. That is, if a filter creates an output data object, the data object knows which filter created it. This allows us to delegate certain messages from a filter through the data object to the connected filter. For example, if filter2 receives an Update() method, it forwards it to its input data object, which in turn forwards it to its owning filter (if any). In this case filter1 is the owning filter of the data object. This process continues until a source object is reached, where the propagation of the Update() method terminates.

You probably already have seen how this approach can be extended to multiple inputs and multiple outputs. The difference is that when a filter receives a message to be forwarded (e.g., Update()), it sends it to all its inputs. Also, when a filter executes, it must update all its outputs. Let's look at some concrete examples.

vtkGlyph3D is an example of a filter that accepts multiple inputs and generates a single output. The inputs to vtkGlyph3D are represented by the Input and Source instance variables. The purpose of vtkGlyph3D is to copy the geometry defined by the data in Source to each point defined by Input. The geometry is modified according to the Source data values (e.g., scalars and vectors). (For more information about glyphs see "Glyphs" on page 178.) If you study the source code for this object carefully, you will see that the object implements its own Update() method (overloading its superclass method). To use the vtkGlyph3D object in C++ code you would do something like

```
glyph = vtkGlyph3D::New();
  glyph->SetInput(foo->GetOutput());
  glyph->SetSource(bar->GetOutput());
  ...
```

where foo and bar are filters returning the appropriate type of output.

The class vtkExtractVectorComponents is an example of a filter with a single input and multiple outputs. This filter extracts the three components of a 3D vector into separate scalar components. Its three outputs are named VxComponent, VyComponent, and VzComponent. An example use of the filter follows:

```
vz = vtkExtractVectorComponents::New();
foo = vtkDataSetMapper::New();
  foo->SetInput(vz->GetVzComponent());
  ...
```

Several other special objects having multiple inputs or outputs are also available. Some of the more notable classes are vtkMergeFilter, vtkAppendFilter, and vtkAppendPolyData. These filters combine multiple pipeline streams and generate a single output. The class vtk-ProbeFilter takes two inputs. The first input is the data we wish to probe. The second input supplies a set of points that are used as probe points. Some process objects take a list of input data. The vtkBooleanStructuredPoints object performs set operations on volume datasets. The first data item in the list is used to initialize the set operation. Each subsequent item in the list is combined with the result of previous operations using a boolean operation specified by the user.

For more details regarding the object design of filters and data objects, please see Chapters 5 and 6.

Support of Looping and Conditional Execution

Our implementation supports network looping and conditional execution. Each loop executes only once each time the network is updated. Multiple loop executions can be effected by updating the network multiple times.

Conditional execution is implemented by using the conditional constructs of the C++ language in conjunction with a local update method available to each process object.

Flexible Computation / Memory Trade-off

By default, networks constructed using the *Visualization Toolkit* store intermediate computational results (i.e., favor computation). However, a single class variable can be set to discard intermediate data when they are no longer needed (i.e., favor memory). In addition, a local parameter can be set within each process object to control this trade-off at object level.

This global variable is set as follows. Given the data object O, (or the output of a filter obtained using O=filter->GetOutput()), invoke O->SetGlobalReleaseDataFlagOn() to enable data release. To enable data release for a particular object use O->SetReleaseDataFlagOn(). Appropriate methods exist to disable memory release as well.

High-Level Object Design

At this point in the text it is premature to describe design details. However, there are two important classes that affect many of the objects in the text. These are the classes vtkObject and vtkObjectBase.

vtkObjectBase is the base object for almost all inheritance hierarchies found in VTK. vtkObjectBase implements data object reference counting (See "Reference Counting" on page 94.) Subclasses of vtkObjectBase may be shared by other objects, without duplicating memory. It also defines an API for objects to print information about themselves.

vtkObject is a subclass of vtkObjectBase. It provides methods and instance variables to control run-time debugging and maintains internal object modification time. In particular, the method Modified() is used to update the modification time, and the method GetMTime() is used to retrieve it. vtkObject also provides a framework for the event callbacks that we saw in the previous chapter (see "Events and Observers" on page 64).

Note that we do not always include vtkObject and vtkObjectBase in object diagrams to conserve space. Refer to the source code for a definitive statement.

Examples

We will now demonstrate some of the features of the visualization pipeline with four examples. Some of the objects used here will be unfamiliar to you. Please overlook missing details until we cover the information later in the book. The goal here is to provide a flavor and familiarity with the software architecture and its use.

Simple Sphere. The first example demonstrates a simple visualization pipeline. A polygonal representation of a sphere is created with the source object (vtkSphereSource). The sphere is passed through a filter (vtkElevationFilter) that computes the height of each point of the sphere above a plane. The plane is perpendicular to the z-axis, and passes through the point (0,0,-1). The data is finally mapped (vtkDataSetMapper) through a lookup table. The mapping process converts height value into colors, and interfaces the sphere geometry to the rendering library. The mapper is assigned to an actor, and then the actor is displayed. The visualization network, a portion of code, and output image are shown in **Figure 4–13**.

The execution of the pipeline occurs implicitly when we render the actor. Each actor asks its mapper to update itself. The mapper in turn asks its input to update itself. This process continues until a source object is encountered. Then the source will execute if modified since the last render. Then the system walks through the network and executes each object if its input or instance variables are out of date. When completed, the actor's mapper is up to date and an image is generated.

Now let's reexamine the same process of pipeline execution by following method invocation. The process begins when the actor receives a Render() message from a renderer. The actor in turn sends a Render() message to its mapper. The mapper begins network execution

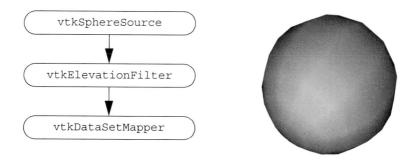

```
vtkSphereSource *sphere = vtkSphereSource::New();
  sphere->SetPhiResolution(12); sphere->SetThetaResolution(12);

vtkElevationFilter *colorIt = vtkElevationFilter::New();
  colorIt->SetInput(sphere->GetOutput());
  colorIt->SetLowPoint(0,0,-1);
  colorIt->SetHighPoint(0,0,1);

vtkDataSetMapper *mapper = vtkDataSetMapper::New();
  mapper->SetInput(colorIt->GetOutput());

vtkActor *actor = vtkActor::New();
  actor->SetMapper(mapper);
```

Figure 4–13 A simple sphere example (`ColorSph.cxx`).

by asking its input to update itself via the Update() operation. This causes a cascade of Update() methods as each filter in turn asks its input to update itself. If branching in the pipeline is present, the update method will branch as well. Finally, the cascade terminates when a source object is encountered. If the source object is out of date, it will send itself an Execute() command. Each filter will send itself an Execute() as necessary to bring itself up to date. Finally, the mapper will perform operations to transform its input into rendering primitives.

In the *Visualization Toolkit*, the Update() method is public while the Execute() method is protected. Thus, you can manually cause network execution to occur by invoking the Update() operation. This can be useful when you want to set instance variables in the network based on the results of upstream execution, but do not want the whole network to update. The Execute() method is protected because it requires a certain object state to exist. The Update() method insures that this state exists.

One final note. The indentation of the code serves to indicate where objects are instantiated and modified. The first line (i.e., the New() operator) is where the object is created. The indented lines that follow indicate that various operations are being performed on the object. We encourage you to use a similar indenting scheme in your own work.

Warped Sphere. This example extends the pipeline of the previous example and shows the effects of type checking on the connectivity of process objects. We add a transform filter (vtkTransformFilter) to nonuniformly scale the sphere in the *x-y-z* directions.

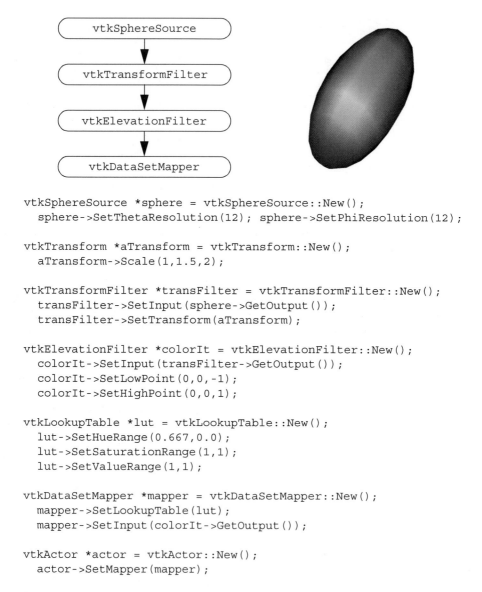

```
vtkSphereSource *sphere = vtkSphereSource::New();
    sphere->SetThetaResolution(12); sphere->SetPhiResolution(12);

vtkTransform *aTransform = vtkTransform::New();
    aTransform->Scale(1,1.5,2);

vtkTransformFilter *transFilter = vtkTransformFilter::New();
    transFilter->SetInput(sphere->GetOutput());
    transFilter->SetTransform(aTransform);

vtkElevationFilter *colorIt = vtkElevationFilter::New();
    colorIt->SetInput(transFilter->GetOutput());
    colorIt->SetLowPoint(0,0,-1);
    colorIt->SetHighPoint(0,0,1);

vtkLookupTable *lut = vtkLookupTable::New();
    lut->SetHueRange(0.667,0.0);
    lut->SetSaturationRange(1,1);
    lut->SetValueRange(1,1);

vtkDataSetMapper *mapper = vtkDataSetMapper::New();
    mapper->SetLookupTable(lut);
    mapper->SetInput(colorIt->GetOutput());

vtkActor *actor = vtkActor::New();
    actor->SetMapper(mapper);
```

Figure 4–14 The addition of a transform filter to the previous example (StrSph.cxx).

The transform filter only operates on objects with explicit point coordinate representation (i.e., a subclass of vtkPointSet). However, the elevation filter generates the more general form vtkDataSet as output. Hence we cannot connect the transform filter to the elevation filter. But we can connect the transform filter to the sphere source, and then the elevation filter to the transform filter. The result is shown in **Figure 4–14**. (Note: an alternative method is to use vtkCastToConcrete to perform run-time casting.)

The C++ compiler enforces the proper connections of sources, filters, and mappers. To decide which objects are compatible, we check the type specification of the SetInput() method. If the input object returns an output object or a subclass of that type, the two objects are compatible and may be connected.

Generating Oriented Glyphs. This example demonstrates the use of an object with multiple inputs. vtkGlyph3D places 3D icons or glyphs (i.e., any polygonal geometry) at every input point. The icon geometry is specified with the instance variable Source, and the input points are obtained from the Input instance variable. Each glyph may be oriented and scaled in a variety of ways, depending upon the input and instance variables. In our example we place cones oriented in the direction of the point normals (**Figure 4–14**).

The visualization network branches at vtkGlyph3D. If either branch is modified, then this filter will reexecute. Network updates must branch in both directions, and both branches must be up to date when vtkGlyph3D executes. These requirements are enforced by the Update() method, and pose no problem to the implicit execution method.

Disappearing Sphere. In our last example we construct a visualization network with a feedback loop, and show how we can use procedural programming to change the topology of the network. The network consists of four objects: vtkSphereSource to create an initial polygonal geometry, vtkShrinkFilter to shrink the polygons and create a gap or space between neighbors, vtkElevationFilter to color the geometry according to height above the x-y plane, and vtkDataSetMapper to map the data through a lookup table and interface to the rendering library. The network topology, a portion of the C++ code, and output are shown in **Figure 4–14**.

After vtkSphereSource generates an initial geometry (in response to a render request), the input of vtkShrinkFilter is changed to the output of the vtkElevationFilter. Because of the feedback loop, vtkShrinkFilter will always reexecute. Thus, the behavior of the network is to reexecute each time a render is performed. Because the shrink filter is reapplied to the same data, the polygons become smaller and smaller and eventually disappear.

4.9 Chapter Summary

The visualization process is naturally modelled using a combination of functional and object models. The functional model can be simplified and used to describe visualization networks. The object model specifies the components of the visualization network.

Visualization networks consist of process objects and data objects. Data objects represent information; process objects transform the data from one form to another. There are three types of process objects — sources have no input and at least one output; filters have at least one input and output; sinks, or mappers, terminate the visualization network.

The execution of the network can be controlled implicitly or explicitly. Implicit control means that each object must insure its input is up to date, thereby distributing the control mechanism. Explicit control means that there is a centralized executive to coordinate the execution of each object.

Many techniques are available to program visualization networks. Direct visual programming is most common in commercial systems. At a higher level, applications provide

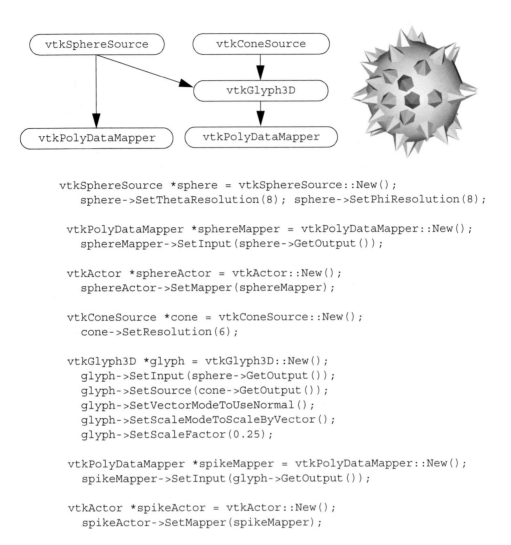

```
vtkSphereSource *sphere = vtkSphereSource::New();
   sphere->SetThetaResolution(8); sphere->SetPhiResolution(8);

vtkPolyDataMapper *sphereMapper = vtkPolyDataMapper::New();
   sphereMapper->SetInput(sphere->GetOutput());

vtkActor *sphereActor = vtkActor::New();
   sphereActor->SetMapper(sphereMapper);

vtkConeSource *cone = vtkConeSource::New();
   cone->SetResolution(6);

vtkGlyph3D *glyph = vtkGlyph3D::New();
   glyph->SetInput(sphere->GetOutput());
   glyph->SetSource(cone->GetOutput());
   glyph->SetVectorModeToUseNormal();
   glyph->SetScaleModeToScaleByVector();
   glyph->SetScaleFactor(0.25);

vtkPolyDataMapper *spikeMapper = vtkPolyDataMapper::New();
   spikeMapper->SetInput(glyph->GetOutput());

vtkActor *spikeActor = vtkActor::New();
   spikeActor->SetMapper(spikeMapper);
```

Figure 4–15 An example of multiple inputs and outputs (Mace.cxx).

tailored but more rigid interfaces to visualize information. At the lowest level, subroutine or object libraries provide the greatest flexibility. The *Visualization Toolkit* contains an object library implemented in C++ for constructing visualization networks.

4.10 Bibliographic Notes

The practical way to learn about the visualization process is to study commercially available systems. These systems can be categorized as either direct visual programming environments or as applications. Common visual programming systems include AVS [AVS89], Iris

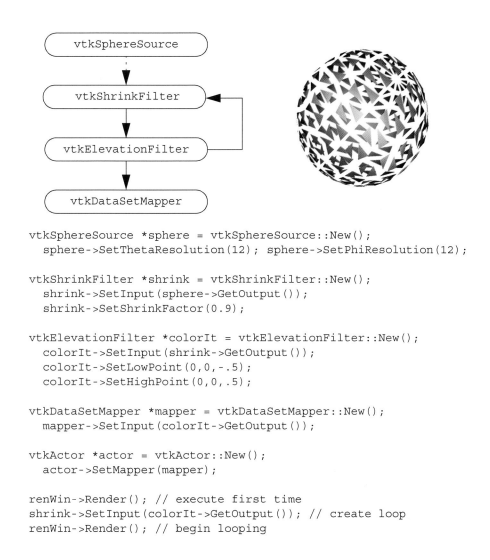

```
vtkSphereSource *sphere = vtkSphereSource::New();
  sphere->SetThetaResolution(12); sphere->SetPhiResolution(12);

vtkShrinkFilter *shrink = vtkShrinkFilter::New();
  shrink->SetInput(sphere->GetOutput());
  shrink->SetShrinkFactor(0.9);

vtkElevationFilter *colorIt = vtkElevationFilter::New();
  colorIt->SetInput(shrink->GetOutput());
  colorIt->SetLowPoint(0,0,-.5);
  colorIt->SetHighPoint(0,0,.5);

vtkDataSetMapper *mapper = vtkDataSetMapper::New();
  mapper->SetInput(colorIt->GetOutput());

vtkActor *actor = vtkActor::New();
  actor->SetMapper(mapper);

renWin->Render(); // execute first time
shrink->SetInput(colorIt->GetOutput()); // create loop
renWin->Render(); // begin looping
```

Figure 4–16 A network with a loop (LoopShrk.cxx).

Explorer [IrisExplorer], IBM Data Explorer [DataExplorer], aPE [aPE90], and Khoros [Rasure91]. Application systems generally provide less flexibility than visual programming systems, but are better tailored to a particular problem domain. PLOT3D [PLOT3D] is an early example of a tool for CFD visualization. This has since been superseded by FAST [FAST90]. FieldView is another popular CFD visualizer [FieldView91]. VISUAL3 [VISUAL3] is a general tool for unstructured or structured grid visualization. PV-WAVE [Charal90] can be considered a hybrid system, since it has both simple visual programming techniques to interface to data files as well as a more structured user-interface than the visual programming environments. Wavefront's DataVisualizer [DataVisualizer] is a general-purpose visualization tool. It is unique in that it is part of a powerful rendering and animation package. A nice system for visualizing 3D gridded data (such as that produced by numerical weather models) is VIS5D. Find out more at the VIS5D Web site `http://www.ssec.wisc.edu/~billh/vis5d.html`.

Although many visualization systems claim to be object-oriented, this is often more in appearance than implementation. Little has been written on object-oriented design issues for visualization. VISAGE [VISAGE92] presents an architecture similar to that described in this chapter. Favre [Favre94] describes a more conventional object-oriented approach. His dataset classes are based on topological dimension and both data and methods are combined into classes.

4.11 References

[aPE90]
  D. S. Dyer. "A Dataflow Toolkit For Visualization." *IEEE Computer Graphics and Applications.* 10(4):60–69, July 1990.

[AVS89]
  C. Upson, T. Faulhaber Jr., D. Kamins and others. "The Application Visualization System: A Computational Environment for Scientific Visualization." *IEEE Computer Graphics and Applications.* 9(4):30–42, July 1989.

[Charal90]
  S. Charalamides. "New Wave Technical Graphics Is Welcome." *DEC USER*, August 1990.

[DataExplorer]
  Data Explorer Reference Manual. IBM Corp, Armonk, NY, 1991.

[DataVisualizer]
  Data Visualizer User Manual. Wavefront Technologies, Santa Barbara, CA, 1990.

[FAST90]
  G. V. Bancroft, F. J. Merritt, T. C. Plessell, P. G. Kelaita, R. K. McCabe, and A. Globus. "FAST: A Multi-Processed Environment for Visualization." In *Proceedings of Visualization '90.* pp. 14–27, IEEE Computer Society Press, Los Alamitos, CA, 1990.

[Favre94]
  J. M. Favre and J. Hahn. "An Object-Oriented Design for the Visualization of Multi-Variate Data Objects." In *Proceedings of Visualization '94.* pp. 319–325, IEEE Computer Society Press, Los Alamitos, CA, 1994.

[FieldView91]
  S. M. Legensky. "Advanced Visualization on Desktop Workstations." In *Proceedings of Visualization '91.* pp. 372–378, IEEE Computer Society Press, Los Alamitos, CA, 1991.

[Haeberli88]
  P. E. Haeberli. "ConMan: A Visual Programming Language for Interactive Graphics." *Computer Graphics (SIGGRAPH '88).* 22(4):103–11, 1988.

[IrisExplorer]
  Iris Explorer User's Guide. Silicon Graphics Inc., Mountain View, CA, 1991.

[Levoy94]
  M. Levoy. "Spreadsheets for Images." In *Proceedings of SIGGRAPH '94.* pp. 139–146, 1994.

[PLOT3D]
   P. P. Walatka and P. G. Buning. *PLOT3D User's Manual*. NASA Fluid Dynamics Division, 1988.

[Rasure91]
   J. Rasure, D. Argiro, T. Sauer, and C. Williams. "A Visual Language and Software Development Environment for Image Processing." *International Journal of Imaging Systems and Technology*. 1991.

[VISAGE92]
   W. J. Schroeder, W. E. Lorensen, G. D. Montanaro, and C. R. Volpe. "VISAGE: An Object-Oriented Visualization System." In *Proceedings of Visualization '92*. pp. 219–226, IEEE Computer Society Press, Los Alamitos, CA, 1992.

[VISUAL3]
   R. Haimes and M. Giles. "VISUAL3: Interactive Unsteady Unstructured 3D Visualization." AIAA Report No. AIAA-91-0794. January 1991.

[Wernecke94]
   J. Wernecke. *The Inventor Mentor*. Addison-Wesley Publishing Company, ISBN 0-201-62495-8, 1994.

4.12 Exercises

4.1   Consider the following 2D visualization techniques: *x-y* plotting, bar charts, and pie charts. For each technique:
      a) Construct functional models.
      b) Construct object models.

4.2   A *height field* is a regular array of 2D points $h = f(x, y)$ where h is an altitude above the point *(x,y)*. Height fields are often used to represent terrain data. Design an object-oriented system to visualize height fields.
      a) How would you represent the height field?
      b) What methods would you use to access this data?
      c) Develop one process object (i.e., visualization technique) to visualize a height field. Describe the methods used by the object to access and manipulate the height field.

4.3   Describe how you would implement an explicit control mechanism for network execution.
      a) How do process objects register their input data with the executive?
      b) How is the executive notified of object modification?
      c) By what method is the executive notified that network execution is necessary?
      d) Describe an approach for network dependency analysis. How does the executive invoke execution of the process objects?

4.4   Visual programming environments enable the user to construct visualization applications by graphically connecting process objects.
      a) Design a graphical notation to represent process objects, their input and output, and data flow direction.
      b) How would you modify instance variables of process objects (using a graphical technique)?

c) By what mechanism would network execution be initiated?

d) How would you control conditional execution and looping in your network?

e) How would you take advantage of parallel computing?

f) How would you distribute network execution across two or more computers sharing a network connection?

4.5   Place oriented cylinders (instead of cones) on the mace in **Figure 4–14**. (*Hint:* use vtk-CylinderSource.)

4.6   The implicit update method for the visualization network used by VTK is simple to implement and understand. However, it is prone to a common programming error. What is this error?

4.7   Experiment with the transformation object in **Figure 4–14**.

a) Translate the actor with vtkTransform's Translate() method.

b) Rotate the actor with the RotateX(), RotateY(), and RotateZ() methods.

c) Scale the actor with the Scale() method.

d) Try combinations of these methods. Does the actor transform in ways that you expect?

4.8   Visualize the following functions. (*Hint:* use vtkSampleFunction and refer to **Figure 4–1**.)

a) $F(x, y, z) = x^2$

b) $F(x, y, z) = x + 2y + 3z + 1$

c) $F(x, y, z) = x^2 + y^2 - (\cos z + 1)$

Basic Data Representation

*I*n Chapter 4 we developed a working definition of the visualization process: mapping information into graphics primitives. We saw how this mapping proceeds through one or more steps, each step transforming data from one form, or data representation, into another. In this chapter we examine common data forms for visualization. The goal is to familiarize you with these forms, so that you can visualize your own data using the tools and techniques provided in this text.

5.1 Introduction

To design representational schemes for data we need to know something about the data we might encounter. We also need to keep in mind design goals, so that we can design efficient data structures and access methods. The next two sections address these issues.

Characterizing Visualization Data

Since our aim is to visualize data, clearly we need to know something about the character of the data. This knowledge will help us create useful data models and powerful visualization systems. Without a clear understanding of the data, we risk designing inflexible and limited visualization systems. In the following we describe important characteristics of data. These characteristics are the discrete nature of data, whether it is regular or irregular, and its topological dimension.

First, visualization data is *discrete*. This is because we use digital computers to acquire, analyze, and represent our data, and typically measure or sample information at a finite number of points. Hence, all information is necessarily represented in discrete form.

Consider visualizing the simple continuous function $y = x^2$. If we are using a conventional digital computer, we must discretize this equation to operate on the data it represents (we are ignoring symbolic/analog computers and methods). For example, to plot this equation we would sample the function in some interval, say $(-1,1)$, and then compute the value y of the function at a series of discrete points $x = x_i$ in this interval. The resulting points $((x_0,y_0), (x_1,y_1), (x_2,y_2), ... (x_n,y_n))$ connect the points with straight line segments. Thus, our (continuous) data is represented by a discrete sampling.

Because of the discrete character of the data we do not know anything about regions in between data values. In our previous example, we know that data is generated from the function $y = x^2$, but, generally speaking, when we measure and even compute data, we cannot infer data values between points. This poses a serious problem, because an important visualization activity is to determine data values at arbitrary positions. For example, we might probe our data and desire data values even though the probe position does not fall on a known point.

There is an obvious solution to this problem: interpolation. We presume a relationship between neighboring data values. Often this is a linear function, but we can use quadratic, cubic, spline, or other interpolation functions. Chapter 8 discusses interpolation functions in greater detail, but for now suffice it to say that interpolation functions generate data values in between known points.

A second important characteristic of visualization data is that its structure may be *regular* or *irregular* (alternatively, *structured* or *unstructured*). Regular data has an inherent relationship between data points. For example, if we sample on an evenly spaced set of points, we do not need to store all the point coordinates, only the beginning position of the interval, the spacing between points, and the total number of points. The point positions are then known implicitly, which can be taken of advantage of to save computer memory.

Data that is not regular is irregular data. The advantage of irregular data is that we can represent information more densely where it changes quickly and less densely where the change is not so great. Thus, irregular data allows us to create adaptive representational forms, which can be beneficial given limited computing resources.

Characterizing data as regular or irregular allows us to make useful assumptions about the data. As we saw a moment ago, we can store regular data more compactly. Typically, we can also compute with regular data more efficiently relative to irregular data. On the other hand, irregular data gives us more freedom in representing data and can represent data that has no regular patterns.

Finally, data has a topological *dimension*. In our example $y = x^2$, the dimension of the data is one, since we have the single independent variable x. Data is potentially of any dimension from 0D points, to 1D curves, 2D surfaces, 3D volumes, and even higher dimensional regions.

The dimension of the data is important because it implies appropriate methods for visualization and data representation. For example, in 1D we naturally use *x-y* plots, bar charts, or pie charts, and store the data as a 1D list of values. For 2D data we might store the data in a matrix, and visualize it with a deformed surface plot (i.e., a *height field* — see Exercise 4.2).

In this chapter and Chapter 8, we show how these characteristics: discrete, regular/ irregular, and data dimension, shape our model of visualization data. Keep these features in mind as you read these chapters.

Design Criterion

Visualizing data involves interfacing to external data, mapping into internal form, processing the data, and generating images on a computer display device. We pose the question: What form or forms should we use to represent data? Certainly many choices are available to us. The choice of representation is important because it affects the ability to interface to external data and the performance of the overall visualization system. To decide this issue we use the following design criteria:

Compact. Visualization data tends to be large, so we need compact storage schemes to minimize computer memory requirements.

Efficient. Data must be computationally accessible. We want to retrieve and store data in constant time (i.e., independent of data size). This requirement offers us the opportunity to develop algorithms that are linear, or $O(n)$, in time complexity.

Mappable. There are two types of mappings. First, data representations need to efficiently map into graphics primitives. This ensures fast, interactive display of our data. Second, we must be able to easily convert external data into internal visualization data structures. Otherwise, we suffer the burden of complex conversion processes or inflexible software.

Minimal Coverage. A single data representation cannot efficiently describe all possible data types. Nor do we want different data representations for every data type we encounter. Therefore, we need a minimal set of data representations that balances efficiency against the number of data types.

Simple. A major lesson of applied computation is that simple designs are preferable to complex designs. Simple designs are easier to understand, and therefore, optimize. The value of simplicity cannot be overemphasized. Many of the algorithms and data representations in this text assign high priority to this design criterion.

The remainder of this chapter describes common visualization data forms based on these design criteria. Our basic abstraction is the *data object*, a general term for the various concrete visualization data types which are the subclasses of data object.

5.2 The Data Object

The most general form of data found in VTK is the data object. A data object can be thought of as a collection of data without any form. Data objects represent the data that is processed by the visualization pipeline (see the previous chapter and **Figure 4–2**). Taken by themselves, data objects carry little useful information. It is only when they are organized into some structure that they provide a form that we can operate on with visualization algorithms.

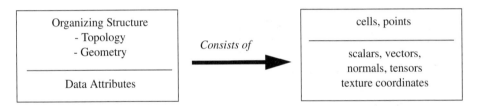

Figure 5–1 The architecture of a dataset. A dataset consists of an organizing structure, with both topological and geometric properties, and attribute data associated with the structure.

5.3 The Dataset

Data objects with an organizing *structure* and associated *data attributes* (**Figure 5–1**).form *datasets*. The dataset is an abstract form; we leave the representation and implementation of the structure to its concrete subclasses. Most algorithms (or process objects) in VTK operate on datasets.

The structure has two parts: *topology* and *geometry*. Topology is the set of properties invariant under certain geometric transformations [Weiler86]. Here we consider the transformations: rotation, translation, and nonuniform scaling. Geometry is the instantiation of the topology, the specification of position in 3D space. For example, saying that a polygon is a "triangle," specifies topology. By providing point coordinates, we specify geometry.

Dataset attributes are supplemental information associated with geometry and/or topology. This information might be a temperature value at a point or the inertial mass of a cell.

Our model of a dataset assumes that the structure consists of *cells* and *points*. The cells specify the topology, while the points specify the geometry. Typical attributes include scalars, vectors, normals, texture coordinates, and tensors.

The definition of the structure of a dataset as a collection of cells and points is a direct consequence of the discrete nature of our data. Points are located where data is known and the cells allow us to interpolate between points. We give detailed descriptions of dataset structure and attributes in the following sections.

5.4 Cell Types

A dataset consists of one or more cells (**Figure 5–2** and **Figure 5–3**). Cells are the fundamental building blocks of visualization systems. Cells are defined by specifying a *type* in combination with an ordered list of points. The ordered list, often referred to as the *connectivity list*, combined with the type specification, implicitly defines the topology of the cell. The x-y-z point coordinates define the cell geometry.

Figure 5–4 shows one cell type, a hexahedron. The ordered list is a sequence of point ids that index into a point coordinate list. The topology of this cell is implicitly known: we know that (8,10) is one of the 12 edges of the hexahedron, and that (8,10,22,21) is one of its six faces.

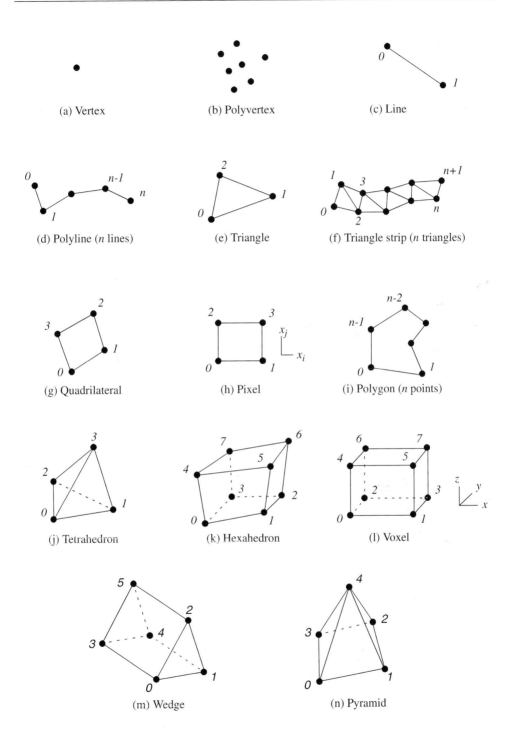

Figure 5–2 Linear cell types found in VTK. Numbers define ordering of the defining points.

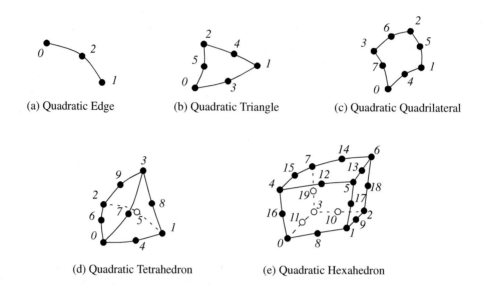

(a) Quadratic Edge (b) Quadratic Triangle (c) Quadratic Quadrilateral

(d) Quadratic Tetrahedron (e) Quadratic Hexahedron

Figure 5–3 Non-linear cell types found in VTK.

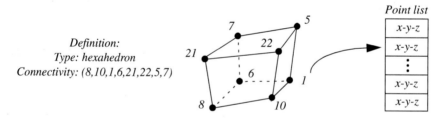

Figure 5–4 Example of a hexahedron cell. The topology is implicitly defined by the ordering of the point list.

Mathematically, we represent a cell by the symbol C_i. Then the cell is an ordered sequence of points $C_i = \{p_1, p_2, ..., p_n\}$ with $p_i \in P$, where P is a set of n-dimensional points (here $n=3$). The type of cell determines the sequence of points, or cell topology. The number of points n defining the cell is the *size* of the cell. A cell C_i "uses" a point p_i when $p_i \in C_i$. Hence the "use set" $U(p_i)$ is the collection of all cells using p_i:

$$U(p_i) = \{C_i : p_i \in C_i\} \qquad (5\text{-}1)$$

The importance of "uses" and "use sets" will become evident in Chapter 8 when we explore the topology of datasets.

Although we define points in three dimensions, cells may vary in topological dimension. Vertices, lines, triangles, and tetrahedron are examples of topologically 0, 1, 2, and 3-D cells, respectively, embedded in three-dimensional geometric space. Cells can also be primary or composite. Composite cells consist of one or more primary cells, while primary cells cannot be decomposed into combinations of other primary cell types. A triangle strip, for example, consists of one or more triangles arranged in compact form. The triangle strip is a composite cell because it can be broken down into triangles, which are primary cells.

Certainly there are an infinite variety of possible cell types. In the *Visualization Toolkit* each cell type has been chosen based on application need. We have seen how some cell types: vertex, line, polygon, and triangle strip (**Figure 3–19**) are used to represent geometry to the graphics subsystem or library. Other cell types such as the tetrahedron and hexahedron are common in numerical simulation. The utility of each cell type will become evident through the practice of visualization throughout this book. A description of the cell types found in the *Visualization Toolkit*—including their classification as linear, nonlinear, or other—is given in the following sections.

Linear Cells

Linear cells are characterized by linear or constant interpolation functions (see "Interpolation Functions" on page 257 for more information). As a result, cells of dimension one or greater are characterized by straight edges. Thus any edge may be characterized by two vertex id's (v_1, v_2). The following are the linear cells currently found in VTK.

Vertex. The vertex is a primary zero-dimensional cell. It is defined by a single point.

Polyvertex. The polyvertex is a composite zero-dimensional cell. The polyvertex is defined by an arbitrarily ordered list of points.

Line. The line is a primary one-dimensional cell. It is defined by two points. The direction along the line is from the first point to the second point.

Polyline. The polyline is a composite one-dimensional cell consisting of one or more connected lines. The polyline is defined by an ordered list of $n+1$ points, where n is the number of lines in the polyline. Each pair of points $(i, i+1)$ defines a line.

Triangle. The triangle is a primary two-dimensional cell. The triangle is defined by a counter-clockwise ordered list of three points. The order of the points specifies the direction of the surface normal using the right-hand rule.

Triangle Strip. The triangle strip is a composite two-dimensional cell consisting of one or more triangles. The points defining the triangle strip need not lie in a plane. The triangle strip is defined by an ordered list of $n+2$ points, where n is the number of triangles. The ordering of the points is such that each set of three points $(i, i+1, i+2)$ with $0 \leq i \leq n$ defines a triangle.

Quadrilateral. The quadrilateral is a primary two-dimensional cell. It is defined by an ordered list of four points lying in a plane. The quadrilateral is convex and its edges must not intersect. The points are ordered counterclockwise around the quadrilateral, defining a surface normal using the right-hand rule.

Pixel. The pixel is a primary two-dimensional cell defined by an ordered list of four points. The cell is topologically equivalent to the quadrilateral with the addition of geometric constraints. Each edge of the pixel is perpendicular to its adjacent edges, and lies parallel to one of the coordinate axes x-y-z. Hence, the normal to the pixel is also parallel to one of the coordinate axes.

The ordering of the points defining the pixel is different from the quadrilateral cell. The points are ordered in the direction of increasing axis coordinate, starting with x, then y, then z. The pixel is a special case of the quadrilateral and is used to improve computational performance.

One important note is that the definition of the pixel cell given here is different from the usual definition for a pixel. Normally pixels are thought of as constant-valued "picture-elements" in an image (see "Graphics Hardware" on page 52). The definition given here implies that four picture-elements form the four corner points of the pixel cell. We normally use the term pixel to describe a pixel cell, but the meaning of the term will vary depending on context.

Polygon. The polygon is a primary two-dimensional cell. The polygon is defined by an ordered list of three or more points lying in a plane. The polygon normal is implicitly defined by a counterclockwise ordering of its points using the right-hand rule.

The polygon may be nonconvex, but may not have internal loops, and it cannot self-intersect. The polygon has n edges, where n is the number of points in the polygon.

Tetrahedron. The tetrahedron is a primary three-dimensional cell. The tetrahedron is defined by a list of four nonplanar points. The tetrahedron has six edges and four triangular faces as shown in **Figure 5–2**.

Hexahedron. The hexahedron is a primary three-dimensional cell consisting of six quadrilateral faces, twelve edges, and eight vertices. The hexahedron is defined by an ordered list of eight points as shown in **Figure 5–2**. The faces and edges must not intersect any other faces and edges, and the hexahedron must be convex.

Voxel. The voxel is a primary three-dimensional cell. The voxel is topologically equivalent to the hexahedron with additional geometric constraints. Each face of the voxel is perpendicular to one of the coordinate x-y-z axes. The defining point list is ordered in the direction of increasing coordinate value as shown in **Figure 5–2**. The voxel is a special case of the hexahedron and is used to improve computational performance.

Similar to pixels, our definition of a voxel cell differs from the conventional definition of the term voxel. Typically, a voxel is referred to as a constant-valued "volume element". Using our definition, eight volume elements form the eight corner points of the voxel cell. We normally use the term voxel to describe a voxel cell, but the meaning of the term will vary depending on the context.

Wedge. The wedge is a primary three-dimensional cell consisting of three quadrilateral faces, two triangular faces, nine edges, and six vertices. The wedge is defined by an ordered list of six points as shown in **Figure 5–2**. The faces and edges must not intersect any other faces and edges, and the wedge must be convex.

Pyramid. The pyramid is a primary three-dimensional cell consisting of one quadrilateral face, four triangular faces, eight edges, and five vertices. The pyramid is defined by an ordered list of five points as shown in **Figure 5–2**. The four points defining the quadrilateral base plane must be convex; the fifth apex point must not be co-planar with the base points.

Nonlinear Types

It is common in numerical analysis to use nonlinear cells. Nonlinear cells provide more accurate interpolation functions (see "Interpolation Functions" on page 257) and better model curved geometry. In VTK, only nonlinear cell types with quadratic interpolation functions are supported. Such cells are constructed by adding mid-edge nodes and extending the connectivity list to reflect the addition of the mid-edge nodes.

One significant difference between linear and nonlinear cells is the way they are rendered and operated on by various visualization algorithms. Linear cells are readily converted to linear graphics primitives, which are then processed by the graphics library. Nonlinear cells, on the other hand, do not often have direct support in graphics libraries. (One exception are the family of non-uniform rational B-splines or NURBS. And even these are generally tessellated by the graphics library into linear primitives.) Therefore, nonlinear cells must be treated specially by the visualization system. Some possibilities include:

1. Tessellating nonlinear cells into linear cells and then operating on the linear cells.

2. Develop custom rendering and visualization algorithms to operate directly on nonlinear cells.

3. Program custom rendering operations in the graphics library.

These issues are active topics in visualization research. In VTK, tessellation methods are currently employed since once tessellated, a cell can be processed by existing linear algorithms. The difficulty with solutions 2) and 3) above is that the effort to create new rendering and visualization algorithms is significant, possibly requiring different solutions for each type of nonlinear cell. Furthermore, it is likely that the performance found in dedicated rendering hardware would far outstrip any software rendering solution for higher order cells. The difficulty with 1) above is that the tessellation must be performed carefully or unacceptable error can be introduced into visualization. Or, if the cell is over-tessellated, an excessive number of linear primitives will result. Future research points to developing adaptive methods that tessellate on a selected error metric.

VTK tessellates quadratic cells using a fixed subdivision as shown in **Figure 5–5**. This generally works well for quadratic cells due to the lower order of interpolation, and the few number of points defining the cell.

Quadratic Edge. The quadratic edge is a primary one-dimensional cell. It is defined by three points. The first two points define the endpoints of the edge; the third point is located in the center of the edge as shown in **Figure 5–3**. The direction along the line is from the first point to the second point.

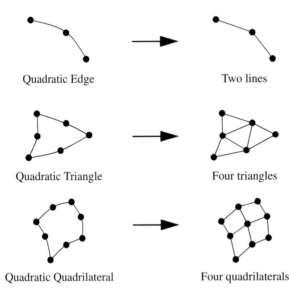

Quadratic Edge   Two lines

Quadratic Triangle   Four triangles

Quadratic Quadrilateral   Four quadrilaterals

Figure 5–5 Decomposing nonlinear cells into linear cells. The quadratic tetrahedron is tessellated into six linear tetrahedron; the quadratic hexahedron is tessellated into eight linear hexahedra. Note that some tessellations require the addition of new points.

Quadratic Triangle. The quadratic triangle is a primary two-dimensional cell. It is defined by six points. The first three points are located at the vertices of the triangle; the next three are located in the middle of each of the three edges as shown in **Figure 5–3**.

Quadratic Quadrilateral. The quadratic quadrilateral is a primary two-dimensional cell. It is defined by eight points. The first four points are located at the vertices of the quadrilateral; the next four are located in the middle of each of the four edges as shown in **Figure 5–3**

Quadratic Tetrahedron. The quadratic tetrahedron is a primary three-dimensional cell. It is defined by ten points. The first four points are located at the vertices of the tetrahedron; the next six are located in the middle of each of the six edges as shown in **Figure 5–3**.

Quadratic Hexahedron. The quadratic hexahedron is a primary three-dimensional cell. It is defined by twenty points. The first eight points are located at the vertices of the hexahedron; the next twelve are located in the middle of each of the twelve edges as shown in **Figure 5–3**.

5.5 Attribute Data

Attribute data is information associated with the structure of the dataset. This structure includes both the dataset geometry and topology. Most often, attribute data is associated with dataset points or cells, but sometimes attribute data may be assigned to cell components such as edges or faces. Attribute data may also be assigned across the entire dataset, or across a group of cells or points. We refer to this information as attribute data because it is an attribute to the structure of the dataset. Typical examples include temperature or velocity at a point, mass of a cell, or heat flux into and out of a cell face.

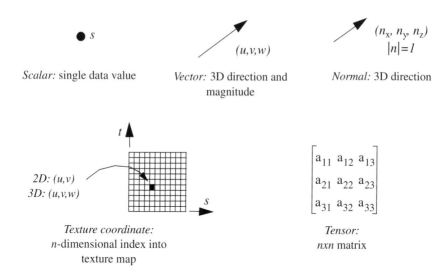

Figure 5–6 Attribute data.

Attribute data is often categorized into specific types of data. These categories have been created in response to common data forms. Visualization algorithms are also categorized according to the type of data they operate on.

Single-valued functions, such as temperature or pressure, are examples of scalar data, which is one attribute type. More generally, attribute data can be treated as n-dimensional data arrays. For example, the single-valued function temperature can be treated as a 1×1 array, while velocity can be treated as a 3×1 array of components in the x, y, and z directions. This abstract model for data attribute can be extended throughout the visualization system. Some systems extend this model to include the structure of the data. For example, a 3D image dataset (i.e., a volume) can be represented as a 3D array of $1 \times m \times n$ data values. Unstructured data can be represented as a 3D vector of position, plus an array of connectivity. We refer to this general approach as the hyperdata model for visualization data (see "Other Data Abstractions" on page 126).

In the following sections we describe data attributes using the simpler type-specific model (**Figure 5–6**). We also limit ourselves to three-dimensional structure, since the dataset structure and graphics are assumed to be three-dimensional.

Scalars

Scalar data is data that is single valued at each location in a dataset. Examples of scalar data are temperature, pressure, density, elevation, and stock price. Scalar data is the simplest and most common form of visualization data.

Vectors

Vector data is data with a magnitude and direction. In three dimensions this is represented as a triplet of values (u, v, w). Examples of vector data include flow velocity, particle trajectory, wind motion, and gradient function.

Normals

Normals are direction vectors: that is, they are vectors of magnitude $|n|=1$. Normals are often used by the graphics system to control the shading of objects. Normals also may be used by some algorithms to control the orientation or generation of cell primitives, such as creating ribbons from oriented lines.

Texture Coordinates

Texture coordinates are used to map a point from Cartesian space into a 1-, 2-, or 3-dimensional texture space. The texture space is usually referred to as a *texture map*. Texture maps are regular arrays of color, intensity, and/or transparency values that provide extra detail to rendered objects. One application of texturing in two dimensions is to "paste" a photograph onto one or more polygons, yielding a detailed image without a large number of graphics primitives. (Texture mapping is covered in more detail in Chapter 7.)

Tensors

Tensors are complex mathematical generalizations of vectors and matrices. A tensor of rank k can be considered a k-dimensional table. A tensor of rank 0 is a scalar, rank 1 is a vector, rank 2 is a matrix, and a tensor of rank 3 is a three-dimensional rectangular array. Tensors of higher rank are k-dimensional rectangular arrays.

General tensor visualization is an area of current research. Efforts thus far have been focused on two-dimensional, rank 2 tensors, which are 3×3 matrices. The most common form of such tensors are the stress and strain tensors, which represent the stress and strain at a point in an object under load. VTK only treats real-valued, symmetric 3×3 tensors.

5.6 Types of Datasets

A dataset consists of an organizing structure plus associated attribute data. The structure has both topological and geometric properties and is composed of one or more points and cells. The type of a dataset is derived from the organizing structure, and specifies the relationship that the cells and points have with one another. Common dataset types are shown in **Figure 5–7**.

A dataset is characterized according to whether its structure is regular or irregular. A dataset is regular if there is a single mathematical relationship within the composing points and cells. If the points are regular, then the geometry of the dataset is regular. If the topological relationship of cells is regular, then the topology of the dataset is regular. Regular (or structured) data can be implicitly represented, at great savings in memory and computation.

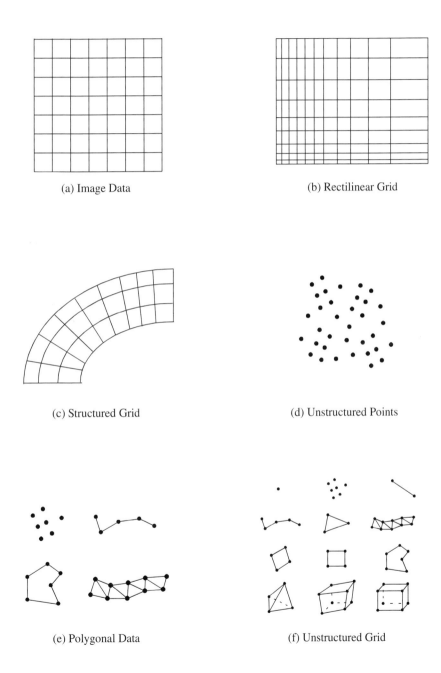

(a) Image Data   (b) Rectilinear Grid

(c) Structured Grid   (d) Unstructured Points

(e) Polygonal Data   (f) Unstructured Grid

Figure 5–7 Dataset types. The unstructured grid consists of all cell types.

Irregular (or unstructured) data must be explicitly represented, since there is no inherent pattern that can be compactly described. Unstructured data tends to be more general, but requires greater memory and computational resources.

Polygonal Data

We have already seen how graphics libraries are designed to render such geometric primitives as lines and polygons. These primitives also are frequently generated or consumed by computational geometry and visualization algorithms. In the *Visualization Toolkit*, we call this collection of graphics primitives *polygonal data*. The polygonal dataset consists of vertices, polyvertices, lines, polylines, polygons, and triangle strips. The topology and geometry of polygonal data is unstructured, and the cells that compose that dataset vary in topological dimension. The polygonal dataset forms a bridge between data, algorithms, and high-speed computer graphics.

Vertices, lines, and polygons form a minimal set of primitives to represent 0-, 1-, and 2-dimensional geometry. We have included polyvertex, polyline, and triangle strip cells for convenience, compactness, and performance. Triangle strips in particular are high-performing primitives. To represent n triangles with a triangle strip requires just $n+2$ points, compared to the $3n$ points for conventional representations. In addition, many graphics libraries can render triangle strips at higher speeds than triangle polygons.

Our minimal selection of cells is based on common application and performance, representing a subset of the cells available in some graphics libraries. Other types include quadrilateral meshes, Bezier curves and surfaces, and other spline types such as NURBS (Non-Uniform Rational B-Splines) [Mortenson85]. Spline surfaces are generally used to accurately model and visualize geometry. Few visualization algorithms (other than geometry visualization) have been developed that require spline surfaces.

Image Data

An image dataset is a collection of points and cells arranged on a regular, rectangular lattice. The rows, columns, and planes of the lattice are parallel to the global *x-y-z* coordinate system. If the points and cells are arranged on a plane (i.e., two-dimensional) the dataset is referred to as a pixmap, bitmap, or image. If the points and cells are arranged as stacked planes (i.e., three-dimensional) the dataset is referred to as a volume. Keep in mind that the term image data refers to images, volumes, or one-dimensional point arrays collectively. Note that some authors have referred to image data as uniform grids and structured points. (Structured points was the terminology used in earlier versions of VTK.)

Image data consist of line elements (1D), pixels (2D), or voxels (3D). Image data is regular in both geometry and topology and can be implicitly represented. The representational scheme requires only data dimensions, an origin point, and the data spacing. The dimension of the data is a 3-vector (n_x, n_y, n_z), specifying the number of points in the *x*, *y*, and *z* directions. The origin point is the position in three-dimensional space of the minimum *x-y-z* point. Each pixel (2D) or voxel (3D) in a image dataset is identical in shape, the spacing specifying the length in the *x-y-z* directions.

The regular nature of the topology and geometry of the image dataset suggests a natural *i-j-k* coordinate system. The number of points in the dataset is $n_x \times n_y \times n_z$ while the number of cells is $(n_x - 1) \times (n_y - 1) \times (n_z - 1)$. A particular point or cell can be selected by specifying the three indices i-j-k. Similarly, a line is defined by specifying two out of three indices, and a plane by specifying a single index.

The simplicity and compactness of representation are desirable features of image data. It is an efficient structure to traverse and compute with. For this reason image data is rivaled only by polygonal data as the most common form of visualization dataset. The major disadvantage with image data is the so-called "curse of dimensionality." To obtain greater data resolution we must increase the dimensions of the dataset. Increasing the dimensions of an image results in an $O(n^2)$ increase in memory requirement, while volumes require an $O(n^3)$ increase. Therefore, to resolve a small feature using image data may require more disk space or computer memory than is available.

Image datasets are often used in imaging and computer graphics. Volumes are frequently generated from medical imaging technologies such as Computed Tomography (CT) and Magnetic Resonance Imaging (MRI). Sometimes volumes are used to sample mathematical functions or numerical solutions.

Rectilinear Grid

The rectilinear grid dataset is a collection of points and cells arranged on a regular lattice. The rows, columns, and planes of the lattice are parallel to the global x-y-z coordinate system. While the topology of the dataset is regular, the geometry is only partially regular. That is, the points are aligned along the coordinate axis, but the spacing between points may vary.

Like the image dataset, rectilinear grids consist of pixels (2D) or voxels (3D). The topology is represented implicitly by specifying grid dimensions. The geometry is represented by maintaining a list of separate x, y, and z coordinates. To obtain the coordinates of a particular point, values from each of the three lists must be appropriately combined.

Structured Grid

A structured grid is a dataset with regular topology and irregular geometry. The grid may be warped into any configuration in which the cells do not overlap or self-intersect.

The topology of the structured grid is represented implicitly by specifying a 3-vector of dimensions (n_x, n_y, n_z). The geometry is explicitly represented by maintaining an array of point coordinates. The composing cells of a structured grid are quadrilaterals (2D) or hexahedron (3D). Like image data, the structured grid has a natural coordinate system that allows us to refer to a particular point or cell using topological i-j-k coordinates.

Structured grids are commonly found in finite difference analysis. Finite difference is a numerical analysis technique to approximate the solution to partial differential equations. Typical applications include fluid flow, heat transfer, and combustion.

Unstructured Points

Unstructured points are points irregularly located in space. There is no topology in an unstructured point dataset, and the geometry is completely unstructured. The vertex and poly-vertex cells are used to represent unstructured points.

Unstructured points are a simple but important type of dataset. Often data has no inherent structure, and part of the visualization task is to discover or create it. For example, consider a piston in a car instrumented with temperature gauges. The number of gauges and their location is chosen at a finite set of points, resulting in temperature values at "unrelated" (at least in terms of visualization topology) positions on the surface of the piston. To visualize the surface temperature, we have to create an interpolation surface and scheme to fill in intermediate values.

Unstructured points serve to represent such unstructured data. Typically, this data form is transformed into another more structured form for the purposes of visualization. Algorithms for transforming unstructured points into other forms are described in "Visualizing Unstructured Points" on page 337.

Unstructured Grid

The most general form of dataset is the unstructured grid. Both the topology and geometry are completely unstructured. Any cell type can be combined in arbitrary combinations in an unstructured grid. Hence the topology of the cells ranges from 0D (vertex, polyvertex) to 3D (tetrahedron, hexahedron, voxel). In the *Visualization Toolkit* any dataset type can be expressed as an unstructured grid. We typically use unstructured grids to represent data only when absolutely necessary, because this dataset type requires the most memory and computational resources to represent and operate on.

Unstructured grids are found in fields such as finite element analysis, computational geometry, and geometric modelling. Finite element analysis is a numerical solution technique for partial differential equations (PDEs). Applications of finite element analysis include structural design, vibration, dynamics, and heat transfer. (This compares to finite difference analysis for PDEs. One advantage of finite element analysis is that the constraint on regular topology is removed. Hence complex domains can be more easily meshed.)

5.7 Other Data Abstractions

Other data models have been proposed besides the dataset model presented here. We briefly examine two other models that have been applied successfully. These are the AVS field model and the model of Haber, Lucas, and Collins, adapted in modified form by the commercial IBM Data Explorer system. The section concludes with a brief comparison between these two models and VTK's data model.

The Application Visualization System

AVS (the Application Visualization System) was the first large-scale, commercial visualization system [AVS89]. Much of the early growth, visibility, and successful application of visualization technology was achieved because of the direct application of AVS or the influence of AVS on other researchers. AVS is a data-flow visualization system with a crisp user interface to create, edit, and manipulate visualization networks. Using an explicit executive to control execution of networks, AVS can run distributed and parallel visualization applications. Since the AVS architecture is open, researchers and developers can and have donated filters for use by others.

The AVS data model consists of primitive data and aggregate data. Primitive data are fundamental representations of data such as byte, integer, real, and string. Aggregate types are complex organizations of primitive types and include fields, colormaps, geometries, and pixel maps. Fields can be considered AVS' fundamental data type, and will be described in detail shortly. Colormaps are used to map functional values (i.e., scalar values) into color and transparency values. Geometries consist of graphics primitives such as points, lines, and polygons, and are used by the geometric renderer to display objects. A pixel map is the rendered image, or output, of a visualization.

The field is the most interesting part of the AVS data model. In general, it is an *n*-dimensional array with scalar or vector data at each point. A scalar is a single value, while a vector is two or more values (not necessarily three). The field array can have any number of dimensions, and the dimensions can be of any size. There is no implicit structure to the field, instead, a *mapping* function is defined. That is, either an implicit or explicit relationship from data elements to coordinate points is specified. Thus a field is a mapping between two kinds of space: the *computational space* of the field data and the *coordinate* space, which is typically the global coordinate system. AVS supports three types of mappings: uniform (i.e., structured), rectilinear, and irregular (i.e., unstructured).

The Data Explorer

The data model of Haber, Lucas, and Collins [Haber91] is based on the mathematics of fiber bundles. The goal of their work is to create a general model for piecewise representations of fields on regular and irregular grids. They refer to their model as the *field data model*, but their definition of the word *field* is different from the AVS model. A field is an object composed of a *base* and *dependent data*. Informally, the base is a manifold whose coordinates are the independent variables for the field, and the dependent data relate the values of dependent variables to the independent variables of the base. Visualization data consists of *field elements* that describe the base and dependent variables over a local region.

The Visualization Toolkit

There are similarities and differences between these data models and VTK's dataset model. The greatest difference is that these other models are more abstract. They are capable of representing a wider range of data and are more flexible. In particular, the AVS field model is capable of representing arbitrary streams of numbers in a simple and elegant manner. The field data model of Haber et al. is also powerful: The authors show how this data representation can be used to exploit regularity in data to obtain compact representations. On the other hand, all these models (including VTK's) share the notion of structure versus data. The AVS field model introduces structure by using a mapping function. The field data of the Haber et al. model resembles VTK's dataset model, in that the base is equivalent to VTK's cells, and the field data model's dependent data is analogous to VTK's attribute data.

The difference in level of abstraction raises important issues in the design of visualization systems. In the following discussion we will refer to data models as abstract or concrete, where the relative level of abstraction is lower in concrete models. In general, abstract and concrete classes compare as follows:

- Abstract models are more flexible and capable of representing a wider range of data forms than concrete models.

- Abstract models lend themselves to compact computer code.

- Concrete models are easier to describe, interface, and implement than abstract models.

- The level of abstraction influences the computer code and/or database interface to the data model. Abstract models result in abstract code and data representations; concrete models result in concrete code and data representations.

- The complexity of abstract models can be hidden by creating simpler, application-specific interfaces. However, this requires extra effort. Concrete models, on the other hand, cannot be made more abstract by modifying interfaces.

The design of computer systems demands careful attention to the balance between abstract and concrete systems. Visualization systems, in particular, must be carefully designed because they interface to other systems and data models. Models that are too abstract can result in confusing computer code and interfaces, and can be misused because of user misunderstanding. On the other hand, concrete models are limited in flexibility and capability, but tend to be easier to learn and apply.

In the design of the *Visualization Toolkit*, we chose to use a more concrete data model relative to the AVS and field data models. Our decision was based on the premise that the system was to be informative as well as functional, and we wanted to clearly demonstrate basic concepts. On the other hand, VTK's data model is general enough to support our practice of visualization. Our experience with users also has shown us that VTK's data model is easier for the casual visualization user to understand than the more abstract models. If you decide to design your own system, we recommend that you examine other data models. However, we feel that the clarity of code manifested in the *Visualization Toolkit* is an example of a well-balanced trade-off between design abstraction and simplicity.

5.8 Putting It All Together

In this section we will describe the implementation details of the dataset types covered previously. We will also show you how to create these datasets through a variety of C++ examples.

Memory Allocation and Data Arrays

Because of the size and scope of data, memory must be carefully managed to create efficient visualization systems. In the *Visualization Toolkit*, we use contiguous data arrays as the basis for most data structures. Contiguous arrays can be created, deleted, and traversed faster than alternative data structures, such as linked lists or arrays of pointers to structures. In VTK, we refer to these as *data arrays*, and represent them with the class vtkDataArray.

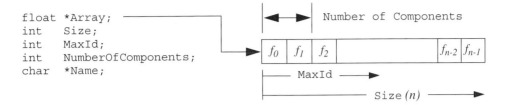

```
float  *Array;
int    Size;
int    MaxId;
int    NumberOfComponents;
char   *Name;
```

Figure 5–8 Implementation of contiguous array. This example is a fragment of the class definition `vtkFloatArray`.

Contiguous arrays also can be easily transmitted across a network, particularly if the information in the array is independent of computer memory address. Memory independence avoids the overhead of mapping information from one memory location to another. Therefore, in VTK we access information based on an "id", an integer index into an array-like object. Data arrays are 0-offset just like C++ arrays. That is, given n data values, we successively access these values using the ids $(0, 1, 2, …, n - 1)$.

An important design decision was to not represent data using arrays of objects (e.g., a separate class for cells and/or points). Our experience has shown that such designs severely impact performance due to the cost of construction and deletion. Instead, we focus on designing classes at a higher level of abstraction. From the perspective of performance, the object-oriented approach serves best at the application level, not at the level of implementation.

The class vtkFloatArray is an example of a contiguous array. We will use this class to describe how contiguous arrays are implemented in VTK. As shown in **Figure 5–8**, the instance variable Array is a pointer to memory of type float. The allocated length of the array is given by Size. The array is dynamic, so an attempt to insert data beyond the allocated size automatically generates a Resize() operation. When resized, the array approximately doubles in size each time. The MaxId field is an integer offset defining the end of inserted data. If no data has been inserted, then MaxId is equal to -1. Otherwise, MaxId is an integer value where $0 \leq \text{MaxId} < \text{Size}$.

The Tuple Abstraction

Many visualization data are defined by multiple component values. An x-y-z coordinate triplet or RGBA color pixel value are two such examples. To represent such data in a contiguous data array, the *tuple* data abstraction is introduced. As **Figure 5–8** illustrates, the contiguous array is grouped into smaller subarrays with NumberOfComponents components. These subarrays are

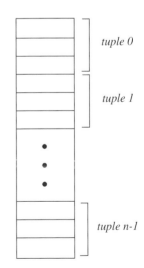

Figure 5–9 Data array structure. In this example, each tuple has three components.

called tuples, and for a given array the tuple size, or NumberOfComponents, is constant for all tuples as shown in **Figure 5–9**.

Representing Data With Data Arrays

Attribute data and points, as well as several other data objects, are represented with data arrays in VTK. Certain attribute data, such as points, vectors, normals, and tensors, are required to have a tuple size consistent with their definition. For example, points, vectors and normals require a data array with a tuple size of three; tensors a tuple size of nine (i.e., a 3×3 matrix). Scalars do not place any requirement on the tuple size. Algorithms that process such scalar data generally operate on the first component of each tuple. (Filters exist in VTK to split multi-component data arrays into separate arrays, and to combine separate data arrays into a single array. See vtkSplitFields and vtkMergeFields.)

Abstract/Concrete Data Array Objects

Visualization data comes in many forms—floating point, integer, byte, and double precision—to name just a few simple types. More complex types such as character strings or multidimensional identifiers also are possible. Given this variety of types, how do we represent and manipulate such data using data arrays? The answer is to provide run-time solutions via abstract data objects, and compile-time solutions using templated C++ code.

Abstract data objects are objects that provide uniform methods to create, manipulate, and delete data using dynamic binding. In C++ we use the virtual keyword to declare methods as dynamically bound. Dynamic binding allows us to execute a method belonging to a concrete object by manipulating that object's abstract superclass (see **Figure 5–10**).

Consider the abstract class vtkDataArray. We can access the data value at associated point id 129 by executing the method float s = GetTuple1(129). Since the virtual GetTuple1() method returns a floating-point data value, each subclass of vtkDataArray must also return a floating-point value. Although the subclass is free to represent data in any possible form, it must transform its data representation into a floating-point value. This process may be as simple as a cast from a built-in type to floating-point value, or it may be a complex mapping of data. For example, if our data consists of character strings, we could conceivably create an alphabetical list and map the string into a location in the list, and then cast the location into a float value.

While this run-time oriented interface is convenient for writing general algorithms that do not depend on a particular data type, the conversion of native representation to float type is problematic. First, the conversion operation can affect performance adversely, since the data access methods are called frequently, virtual functions are slower than in-line or non-virtual invocations, and the cast operator is slow in many cases. Second, a complex type such as double loses precision during conversion to float. To remedy these problems, it is possible to access data in its native form and process it accordingly. In this approach C++ templates are used.

To use templates it is necessary to obtain raw, typed pointers to data, and to know the type of data. vtkDataArray and its associated subclasses provides this functionality. With this information it is possible to switch on the type of data into a function templated over that

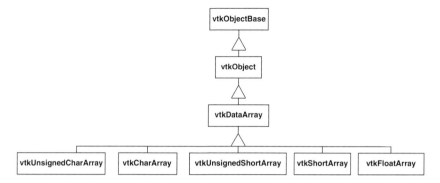

Figure 5–10 Data array object diagram. vtkDataArray is an abstract base class. Subclasses of vtkDataArray implement type specific representation and operations. Note: not all concrete data array subclasses are shown in this diagram.

type. A typical code fragment using this functionality is found in most imaging filters, almost all of which are templated as follows:

```
switch (outData->GetScalarType())
  {
  case VTK_CHAR:
    { typedef char VTK_TT;
    func(arg1, arg2, arg3, VTK_TT* arg4, VTK_TT* arg5); }
    break;
  case VTK_UNSIGNED_CHAR:
    { typedef unsigned char VTK_TT;
    func(arg1, arg2, arg3, VTK_TT* arg4, VTK_TT* arg5); }
    break;

...for all types.....

  }
```

In practice this code is simplified using macros, and the static_cast<> C++ operator is used to perform the cast. Note that the function func is a templated function. The compiler will instantiate the function for the appropriate type. In most cases all native types are represented in the switch statement, so func is expanded accordingly.

Using compile-time oriented methods such as templates avoids the need to cast each data access into a particular type (e.g., float). While it does complicate the code somewhat and result in larger object code, it is generally faster than run-time virtual methods. This approach becomes problematic as the number of types increases. For example, some filters such as vtkImageShiftScale use doubly nested templates to resolve the potential difference in input and output types. The code is more complex and much larger than the generic run-time approach.

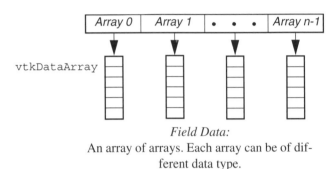

Figure 5–11 Data object representation as field data. A field can be represented as an array of arrays. Each array has a specified type, length, tuple size, and name. The association of a data array with points or cells, and its labeling as a particular attribute type, forms point and cell attribute data.

Field Data:
An array of arrays. Each array can be of different data type.

Data Object Representation

Data objects are implemented in VTK as an array of vtkDataArrays as shown in **Figure 5–11**. vtkDataObject is an general representation of visualization data. It serves to encapsulate instance variables and methods for visualization network execution (see previous chapter), as well as representing data. Internally, data is represented with an instance of the class vtkFieldData. Very few algorithms directly operate on data objects; rather most algorithms require the specification of an organizing structure in order to process the data. The dataset specifies that organizing structure as described in the following section.

Dataset Representation

Five datasets are implemented in VTK: vtkPolyData, vtkImageData, vtkStructuredGrid, vtkRectilinearGrid, and vtkUnstructuredGrid. The unstructured points dataset is not implemented, but can be represented using either vtkPolyData or vtkUnstructuredGrid.

We use a different internal data representation for each dataset type. By using different representations we minimize data structure memory requirements and implement efficient access methods. It would have been possible to use vtkUnstructuredGrid to represent all dataset types, but the memory and computational overhead are unacceptable for large data. The following sections describe how we represent the dataset.

vtkImageData. The simplest and most compact representation is vtkImageData. Both the dataset points and cells are represented implicitly by specifying the dimensions, data spacing, and origin. The dimensions define the topology of the dataset, while the origin and spacing specify the geometry. The vtkImageData dataset type can represent 1D line samples, 2D images, and 3D volumes. (Note: in earlier versions of VTK, vtkImageData was known as vtkStructuredPoints. There are still remnants of this terminology in the code base.)

There is an implicit ordering of both the points and cells composing vtkImageData. Both the cells and points are numbered in the direction of increasing x, then y, then z. The total number of points is $n_x \times n_y \times n_z$ where n_x, n_y, and n_z are the dimensions of vtkImageData. The total number of cells is $(n_x - 1) \times (n_y - 1) \times (n_z - 1)$.

vtkRectilinearGrid. While the topology of vtkRectilinearGrid is regular, the geometry can be described as "semi-regular." The topology is implicitly represented by specifying data dimensions along the x, y, and z coordinate axes. The geometry is defined using three arrays of coordinate values along these axes. These three coordinate arrays can be combined to determine the coordinates of any point in the dataset. In VTK, we represent the arrays using three instances of vtkDataArray. The numbering of points and cells is implicit in exactly the same way as described for vtkImageData.

vtkStructuredGrid. Like vtkImageData, the topology of vtkStructuredGrid is regular and is defined by specifying dimensions in the topological i-j-k coordinate system. However, the geometry of vtkStructuredGrid is realized by specifying point coordinates in the global x-y-z coordinate system.

The abstract data class vtkPoints is used to represent the point coordinates. vtkPoints refers to an underlying instance of vtkDataArray which actually holds the representation of the points as a contiguous array of three-component tuples. A particular point coordinate may be retrieved or inserted by specifying a particular point id. The numbering of the points and cells is implicit in the same fashion as vtkImageData. Care must be taken to insure that the number of points in the data array is the same as that implied by the dimensions of the grid.

vtkPolyData. Unlike vtkImageData and vtkStructuredGrid, the topology of vtkPolyData is not regular, so both the topology and geometry of the dataset must be explicitly represented. The point data in vtkPolyData is represented using the vtkPoints class similar to vtkStructuredGrid.

The *Visualization Toolkit* uses the class vtkCellArray to explicitly represent cell topology. This class is a list of connectivity for each cell. The structure of the list is a sequence of integer numbers (**Figure 5–12**). The first number in the list is a count (the number of points in the cell connectivity), and the next series of numbers is the cell connectivity. (Each number in the connectivity list is an index into an instance of a point coordinate list.) Sequences of count followed by the connectivity list are repeated until each cell is enumerated. Additional information such as the number of cells in the list and current position in the list (for traversal purposes) is also maintained by vtkCellArray.

Notice that type information is not directly represented in this structure. Instead, vtkPolyData maintains four separate lists to vertices, lines, polygons, and triangle strips. The vertex list represents cells of type vtkVertex and vtkPolyVertex. The lines list represents cells of type vtkLine and vtkPolyLine. The polygon list represents cells of type vtkTriangle, vtkQuad, and vtkPolygon. The triangle strip list represents cells of the single type vtkTriangleStrip. As a result, the cell type is known from the particular list the cell is defined in, plus the number of points that define the cell.

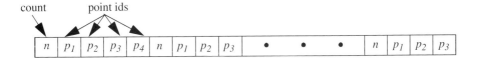

Figure 5–12 vtkCellArray structure to represent cell topology.

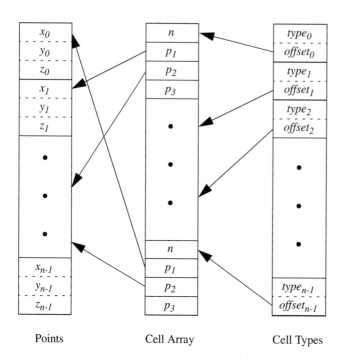

Figure 5–13 The data structure of the class `vtkUnstructuredGrid`. (This is a subset of the complete structure. See Chapter 8 for complete details.)

Points   Cell Array   Cell Types

Our design of the vtkPolyData class is based on two important requirements. First, we want an efficient interface to external graphics libraries. Second, we wish to aggregate cells according to topology. The four separate lists provide efficient interface because graphics libraries have separate vertex, line, polygon, and triangle strip primitives. As a result, in VTK no run-time checking is required to match the different cell types with the appropriate "load primitive" function, since the type is known from the list in which the primitive resides. The four lists also separate cells into 0-, 1-, and 2-dimensional types. This is useful because visualization algorithms often treat data of varying topological order differently.

vtkUnstructuredGrid. The dataset type vtkUnstructuredGrid is the most general in terms of its ability to represent topological and geometric structure. Both points and cells are explicitly represented using derived classes of vtkPoints and vtkCellArray. The class vtkUnstructuredGrid is similar to vtkPolyData except that vtkUnstructuredGrid must be capable of representing all cell types, not just the limited graphics types (i.e., vertices, lines, polygons, and triangle strips) of vtkPolyData.

Another distinguishing characteristic of vtkUnstructuredGrid is that we represent type information differently. In vtkPolyData we categorized cells into four separate lists, thereby representing cell type indirectly. In vtkUnstructuredGrid we add the additional class vtkCellTypes to represent cell type explicitly.

The vtkCellTypes is an array of supplemental information. For each cell, an integer flag defines the cell type. Another variable is used to record the location of the cell definition in the corresponding vtkCellArray (**Figure 5–13**).

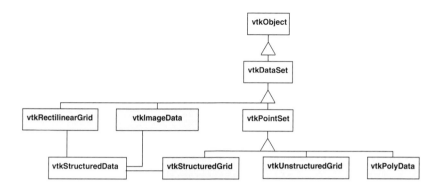

Figure 5–14 Dataset object diagram. The five datasets (shaded) are implemented in VTK.

Besides representing cell type, this design also enables random access to cells. Because the length of a cell connectivity list varies, the vtkCellArray class cannot locate a particular cell without traversing its data structure from the origin. With the added class vtkCellTypes, however, it is possible to directly access a cell with a single dereference (i.e., using the offset value).

The vtkCellTypes may also be added to the vtkPolyData data representation — and indeed it has. However, our reasons for this addition are not to represent type explicitly, but rather to provide random access to the cells and enable many topological operations. We will expand on this idea in Chapter 8.

Object Model. The five datasets are implemented as shown in **Figure 5–14**. As this object diagram illustrates, these concrete datasets are subclasses of the abstract class vtkDataSet. Two additional classes are introduced as well. The class vtkStructuredData contributes instance variables and methods for structured data. vtkStructuredData is not in an inheritance relationship with the datasets; rather the structured datasets shown delegate to it in order to implement some of their methods. (This was done to avoid multiple inheritance.) Subclasses of the class vtkPointSet represent their points explicitly, that is, through an instance of vtkPoints or its subclasses. vtkPointSet provides methods and instance variables to manipulate the point data, as well as a general searching capability to find points and cells. (See "Searching" on page 279.)

Cell Representation

In the *Visualization Toolkit* each cell type has been implemented by creating specific classes. Each cell is a subclass of the abstract type vtkCell. Cell topology is represented by a list of ordered point ids, and cell geometry is represented by a list of point coordinates. The object diagram for vtkCell and its subclasses is shown in **Figure 5–15**.

The abstract class vtkCell specifies methods that each cell must implement. These methods provide a defined interface to the cell's geometry and topology. Additional methods perform computation on the cell. These methods will be discussed in detail in Chapter 8.

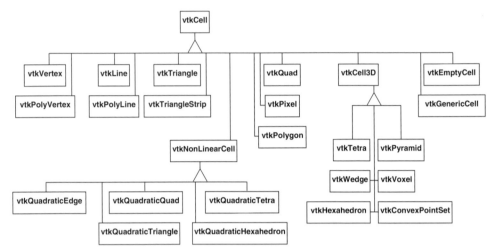

Figure 5–15 Object diagram for twenty concrete cell types in VTK. vtkEmptyCell represents NULL cells. vtkGenericCell can represent any type of cell. Three-dimensional cells are subclasses of vtkCell3D. Higher order cells are subclasses of vtkNonLinearCell.

Data Attributes

Data attributes are associated with the structure of a dataset. The dataset model is built on points and cells, so it is natural to associate data attributes with points and cells as well. Intermediate structure features, such as cell edges or faces, are not explicitly represented so we cannot easily associate data attributes with them.

In VTK data attributes are associated with the points and cells of the dataset. There is no association of data attributes to intermediate topological features such as triangle edges or hexahedron faces. (Here we refer to data attributes associated with points as *point attributes*, and data attributes associated with cells as *cell attributes*.) Our design choice is based on the following rationale.

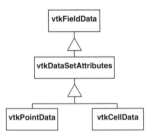

Figure 5–16 Inheritance hierarchy for representing data set attributes.

- Data acquisition and numerical simulation systems typically measure and/or compute the results at point locations, or at the center of cells.

- Boundary attribute information (e.g., on faces and edges) can be maintained as cell data ordered according to the topology of the cell.

- The VTK data model is based on points and cells for reasons of compactness and efficiency. Representing attribute data on cell boundaries would require expanding this representation to support a small number of situations requiring direct support of attribute data on cell boundaries. If in the future a more complex data structure is required to represent boundary attribute data, this is best encapsulated into a single class rather than forcing the abstraction throughout the system.

One difficulty with maintaining both cell data and point data representations is that possible inconsistencies in the data may arise. For example, if a cell's scalar value is 0.5, and its points have scalar values other than 0.5, which is the correct value? Priority schemes can be devised to resolve such situations although the user must recognize that such inconsistencies may exist.

To represent dataset attributes we use the organizing classes vtkPointData and vtkCellData, both of which are subclasses of the class vtkFieldData as shown in **Figure 5–16**. The class vtkDataSetAttributes serves to coordinate the movement of data from one process object to the next. It provides methods for copying, interpolating, and moving data between input and output. Another important feature of vtkDataSetAttributes is that it provides the ability to assign a data array to represent a particular data attribute. For example, the method SetScalars() is used to specify which data array is to be treated as the scalars in the field.

There is a one-to-one correspondence between each dataset point and its attribute data. Point attributes are accessed by way of the point id. For example, to access the scalar value of point id 129 in the dataset instance aDataSet, we use

```
aDataSet->GetPointData()->GetScalars()->GetScalar(129);
```

This statement assumes that the scalar data has been defined for this dataset and is non-NULL.

Examples

In the examples that follow we show manual creation and manipulation of datasets. Typically, these operations are not performed directly by users of VTK. Instead, source objects are used to read data files or generate data. This is more convenient than the manual techniques shown here and should be used whenever possible.

Creation of datasets is a two step process. First the geometry and topology of the dataset must be defined. Depending on the type of dataset, the geometry and topology definition will proceed differently. Then the point and/or cell attribute data is created and associated with the dataset. Remember that there is a one-to-one relationship between the attribute data and the points and cells in the dataset.

Create a Polygonal Dataset. In our first example we create a polygonal representation of a cube. The cube is defined by eight points and six quadrilateral faces. We also create eight scalar values associated with the eight vertices of the cube. **Figure 5–17** shows the key C++ code fragments used to create the data, and the resulting image.

The geometry of the cube is defined using an instance of the class vtkPoints. By default, the underlying type of vtkPoints is a vtkFloatArray. The topology of the cube (i.e., polygons) is defined with an instance of the class vtkCellArray. These define the points and polygons of the cube, respectively. Scalar data is represented by an instance of the class vtkIntArray.

As this example shows, polygonal data is created by constructing pieces (e.g., points, cells, and point attribute data), and then assembling the pieces to form the complete dataset. If the name of the instance of vtkPolyData is cube, we can summarize these three steps as follows:

```
vtkPolyData *cube = vtkPolyData::New();
vtkPoints *points = vtkPoints::New();
vtkCellArray *polys = vtkCellArray::New();
vtkFloatArray *scalars = vtkFloatArray::New();

for (i=0; i<8; i++) points->InsertPoint(i,x[i]);
for (i=0; i<6; i++) polys->InsertNextCell(4,pts[i]);
for (i=0; i<8; i++) scalars->InsertTuple1(i,i);

cube->SetPoints(points);
points->Delete();
cube->SetPolys(polys);
polys->Delete();
cube->GetPointData()->SetScalars(scalars);
scalars->Delete();
```

Figure 5–17 Creation of polygonal cube (Cube.cxx).

1. Create instance of subclass of vtkPoints to define geometry (i.e., point coordinates). Use the operator cube->SetPoints() to associate the points with the dataset.

2. Create instances of vtkCellArray to define topology for vertices, lines, polygons, and triangle strips. Use the operators cube->SetVerts(), cube->SetLines(), cube->SetPolys(), and cube->SetStrips() to associate the cells with the dataset.

3. Create point and/or attribute data. Every dataset has two fields representing vtkPointData and vtkCellData. Use the operator pd=cube->GetPointData() to retrieve the pointer to the point attribute data. Use the operator pd=cube->GetCellData() to retrieve the pointer to the cell attribute data. Associate the attribute data with the dataset using the operators pd->SetScalars(), pd->SetVectors(), pd->SetNormals(), pd->SetTensors(), and pd->SetTCoords() (and similar for cell data).

Polygonal data supports the following cell types: vertices, polyvertices, lines, polylines, triangles, quadrilaterals, polygons, and triangle strips. Point and cell attribute data does not need to be defined — you can create none, some, or all of the point and cell attributes in any combination.

The most confusing aspect of this example is the Delete() method. To prevent memory leaks we must use a Delete() method (VTK's destructor) after every New() method. It is apparent from the example that the instance's points, polys, and scalars are referred to by another object (e.g., cube). So doesn't invocation of the Delete() method pose a problem?

The answer is no. Certain data objects in VTK are reference counted to conserve memory resources (i.e., subclasses of vtkObjectBase). That means they can be shared between objects. For most objects the Delete() will invoke the destructor. Reference counted objects act a little differently. The Delete() method simply decrements the reference count. This may or may not destroy the object depending on whether it is being used by another object. In this example the points, polys, and scalars are used by the polygonal dataset cube, so they are not deleted when Delete() is invoked. They will be freed once we free the dataset cube, that is, when their reference count drops to zero. (See the *VTK User's Guide* for more information about memory management.)

Create an Image Data Dataset. In this example, we create an image dataset (i.e., an instance of vtkImageData). The topology of the dataset is defined by specifying the data dimensions. The geometry is defined by the data spacing and origin. The spacing specifies the length, width, and height of each voxel. The origin specifies the position in 3D space of the "lower-left" corner of the data. In our example we set the origin and spacing of the dataset so that its center lies at the origin, and the bounds of the dataset are (-0.5,0.5, -0.5,0.5, -0.5,0.5).

In this example we create scalar data along with the image data dataset. The scalar values are computed from the implicit function for a sphere

$$F(x, y, z) = (x^2 + y^2 + z^2) - R^2 \qquad (5\text{-}2)$$

with the radius $R = 0.4$. The scalar data is stored in an instance of vtkFloatArray and assigned to the point attribute data of the dataset.

To complete this example, a contour filter is used to generate a surface of scalar value $F(x, y, z) = 0$. Note that this functionality (in a more general form) is available from the source object vtkSampleFunction in combination with vtkSphere. **Figure 5–18** shows the key C++ code fragment used to create the data and contour the scalar field, and the resulting image.

Image data datasets are easy to construct because both the geometry and topology are implicitly defined. If the name of the instance of vtkImageData is vol, we can summarize the steps to create the dataset as follows:

1. Define the topology of the dataset using the operator vol->SetDimensions().

2. Define the geometry of the dataset using the operators vol->SetOrigin() and vol->SetSpacing().

3. Create point and/or attribute data and associate it with the dataset.

You do not need to specify origin and data spacing. By default the data spacing is (1,1,1) in the *x-y-z* directions, and the origin is (0,0,0). Thus if the dimensions of the dataset are $n_x \times n_y \times n_z$, the default length, width, and height of the dataset will be $(n_x - 1, n_y - 1, n_z - 1)$.

The topological dimension of the dataset is implicitly known from its instance variables. For example, if any of the dimensions (n_x, n_y, n_z) is equal to one (and the other two are greater than one), the topological dimension of the dataset is two.

Create a Structured Grid Dataset. In the next example we create a vtkStructuredGrid dataset. Topology is implicitly defined from the dimensions of the dataset. The geometry is explicitly defined by providing an object to represent the point coordinates. In this example we use an instance of vtkPoints and assume that the structured grid is warped according to the equation for a cylinder

$$x = r_i \cos\theta$$
$$y = r_i \sin\theta \qquad\qquad (5\text{-}3)$$
$$z = z_i$$

We arbitrarily choose the number of points in the tangential direction to be thirteen, the number of points in the radial direction to be eleven, and the number of points in the axis direction to be eleven (i.e., dimensions are $13 \times 11 \times 11$).

Vectors are generated tangential to the cylinder and of magnitude proportional to the radius. To display the data we draw small, oriented lines at each point as shown in **Figure 5– 19**. (This technique is called a *hedgehog*. See "Hedgehogs and Oriented Glyphs" on page 161.)

The creation of a structured grid dataset is partially explicit and partially implicit. Geometry is created explicitly be creating an instance of vtkPoints, while the topology is created implicitly by specifying dataset dimensions. If the name of the instance of vtkStructuredGrid is sgrid, the following three steps are used to create it.

1. Specify the dataset geometry by creating an instance of vtkPoints. Use the operator sgrid->SetPoints() to associate the points with the dataset.

2. The dataset topology is specified using the operator sgrid->SetDimensions(). Make sure the number of points created in item number 1 above is equal to the implied number of points $n_x \cdot n_y \cdot n_z$.

3. Create point and/or cell attribute data and associate it with the dataset.

The topological dimension of the dataset is implied by the specified dimensions. For example, if any of the dimensions (n_x, n_y, n_z) is equal to one, the topological dimension of the dataset is two. If two of the three dimensions (n_x, n_y, n_z) are equal to one, the topological dimension of the dataset is one.

Create a Rectilinear Grid Dataset. A rectilinear grid is regular in topology and semi-regular in geometry. Similar to a structured grid or image data dataset, topology is implicitly represented by specifying grid dimensions. Because the grid is axis-aligned but the point coordinates along each axis may vary, we need three data arrays to represent the geometry of

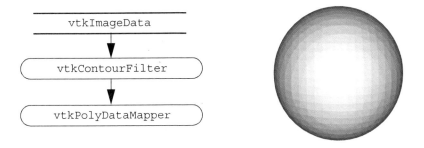

```
vtkImageData *vol = vtkImageData::New();
  vol->SetDimensions(26,26,26);
  vol->SetOrigin(-0.5,-0.5,-0.5);
  sp = 1.0/25.0;
  vol->SetSpacing(sp, sp, sp);

vtkFloatArray *scalars = vtkFloatArray::New()
for (k=0; k<26; k++)
   {
   z = -0.5 + k*sp;
   kOffset = k * 26 * 26;
   for (j=0; j<26; j++)
      {
      y = -0.5 + j*sp;
      jOffset = j * 26;
      for (i=0; i<26; i++)
         {
         x = -0.5 + i*sp;
         s = x*x + y*y + z*z - (0.4*0.4);
         offset = i + jOffset + kOffset;
         scalars->InsertTuple1(offset,s);
         }
      }
   }
vol->GetPointData()->SetScalars(scalars);
scalars->Delete();
```

Figure 5–18 Creating a image data dataset. Scalar data is generated from the equation for a sphere. Volume dimensions are 26^3 (Vol.cxx).

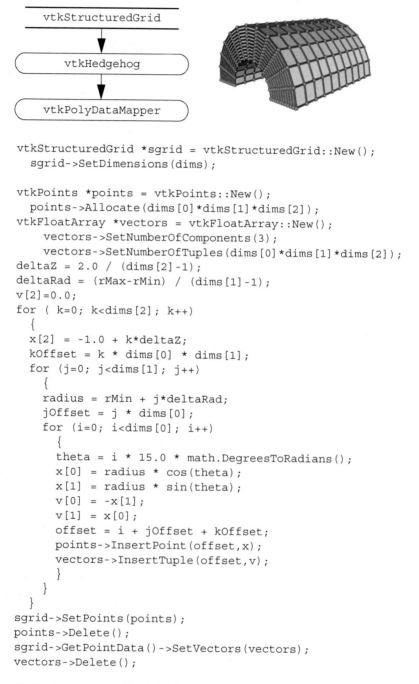

```
vtkStructuredGrid *sgrid = vtkStructuredGrid::New();
  sgrid->SetDimensions(dims);

vtkPoints *points = vtkPoints::New();
  points->Allocate(dims[0]*dims[1]*dims[2]);
vtkFloatArray *vectors = vtkFloatArray::New();
    vectors->SetNumberOfComponents(3);
    vectors->SetNumberOfTuples(dims[0]*dims[1]*dims[2]);
deltaZ = 2.0 / (dims[2]-1);
deltaRad = (rMax-rMin) / (dims[1]-1);
v[2]=0.0;
for ( k=0; k<dims[2]; k++)
  {
  x[2] = -1.0 + k*deltaZ;
  kOffset = k * dims[0] * dims[1];
  for (j=0; j<dims[1]; j++)
    {
    radius = rMin + j*deltaRad;
    jOffset = j * dims[0];
    for (i=0; i<dims[0]; i++)
      {
      theta = i * 15.0 * math.DegreesToRadians();
      x[0] = radius * cos(theta);
      x[1] = radius * sin(theta);
      v[0] = -x[1];
      v[1] = x[0];
      offset = i + jOffset + kOffset;
      points->InsertPoint(offset,x);
      vectors->InsertTuple(offset,v);
      }
    }
  }
sgrid->SetPoints(points);
points->Delete();
sgrid->GetPointData()->SetVectors(vectors);
vectors->Delete();
```

Figure 5–19 Creating a structured grid dataset of a semicylinder. Vectors are created whose magnitude is proportional to radius and oriented in tangential direction (SGrid.cxx).

the dataset, one array for each of the *x-y-z* axes. Note that the cell types of the rectilinear dataset are pixels and voxels.

For maximum flexibility when creating rectilinear grids, in VTK we use three vtkDataArray objects to define the axes arrays. This means that different native data type (e.g., unsigned char, int, float, and so on) can be used for each axes.

To summarize the process of creating an instance of vtkRectilinearGrid, we follow four steps. In this example (shown in **Figure 5–20**), we assume that the name of the vtkRectilinearGrid instance is rgrid.

1. Create the dataset geometry by creating three instance of vtkDataArray, one for each of the *x-y-z* coordinate axes. We will assume that the number of values in each scalar is n_x, n_y, and n_z.

2. Each of the three instances is assigned to the *x*, *y*, and *z* axes using the rgrid->SetXCoordinates(), rgrid->SetYCoordinates(), and rgrid->SetZCoordinates() methods, respectively.

3. The dataset topology is specified using the operator rgrid->SetDimensions(). Make sure the number of points created in item number 1 above is equal to the implied number of points $n_x \cdot n_y \cdot n_z$.

4. Create point and/or cell attribute data and associate it with the dataset.

The topological dimension of the dataset is implied by the specified dimensions. For example, if any of the dimensions (n_x, n_y, n_z) is equal to one, the topological dimension of the dataset is two. If two of the three dimensions (n_x, n_y, n_z) are equal to one, the topological dimension of the dataset is one.

Create an Unstructured Grid Dataset. Unstructured grid datasets are the most general dataset type in both topology and geometry. In this example we "artificially" create an unstructured grid using an instance of vtkUnstructuredGrid (**Figure 5–21**). The grid contains examples of each cell type except for pixels and voxels. (Pixels and voxels are generally used internally to process image data datasets. They can be explicitly created and manipulated as long as the required relationship of point geometry is observed.) Creating the dataset structure requires creating points to define the geometry and various cells to define the topology. (Note that in the finite element world we would refer to these as *nodes* and *elements*.)

To summarize the process of creating an instance of vtkUnstructuredGrid, we follow five steps. We assume the name of vtkUnstructuredGrid instance is ugrid.

1. Allocate memory for the dataset. Use the operator ugrid->Allocate(). This operator takes two optional parameters related to the size of the data. The first is the size of the connectivity list, and the second is the amount to extend storage (if necessary). As a rule of thumb, use the number of cells times the average number of points defining each cell for both parameters. Exact values for these parameters are not important, although the choice may affect performance. If you fail to execute this operation before inserting data, the software will break.

2. Create an instance of a subclass of vtkPoints to define the dataset geometry. Use the operator ugrid->SetPoints() to associate the points with the dataset.

3. Create the dataset topology on a cell by cell basis by using the cell insertion operator

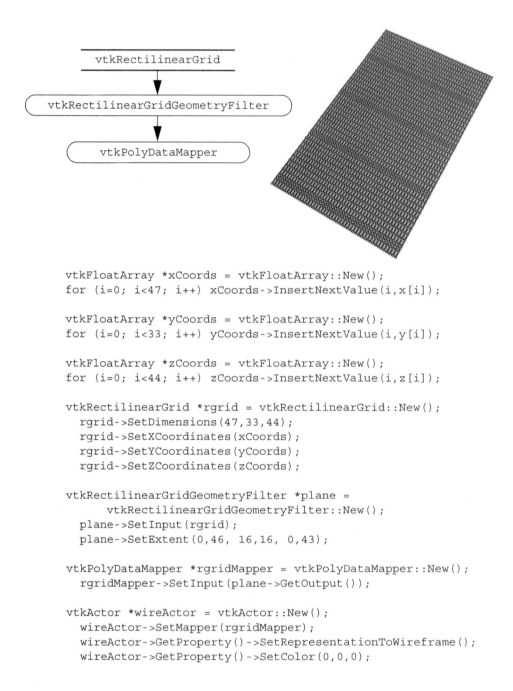

```
vtkFloatArray *xCoords = vtkFloatArray::New();
for (i=0; i<47; i++) xCoords->InsertNextValue(i,x[i]);

vtkFloatArray *yCoords = vtkFloatArray::New();
for (i=0; i<33; i++) yCoords->InsertNextValue(i,y[i]);

vtkFloatArray *zCoords = vtkFloatArray::New();
for (i=0; i<44; i++) zCoords->InsertNextValue(i,z[i]);

vtkRectilinearGrid *rgrid = vtkRectilinearGrid::New();
  rgrid->SetDimensions(47,33,44);
  rgrid->SetXCoordinates(xCoords);
  rgrid->SetYCoordinates(yCoords);
  rgrid->SetZCoordinates(zCoords);

vtkRectilinearGridGeometryFilter *plane =
      vtkRectilinearGridGeometryFilter::New();
  plane->SetInput(rgrid);
  plane->SetExtent(0,46, 16,16, 0,43);

vtkPolyDataMapper *rgridMapper = vtkPolyDataMapper::New();
  rgridMapper->SetInput(plane->GetOutput());

vtkActor *wireActor = vtkActor::New();
  wireActor->SetMapper(rgridMapper);
  wireActor->GetProperty()->SetRepresentationToWireframe();
  wireActor->GetProperty()->SetColor(0,0,0);
```

Figure 5–20 Creating a rectilinear grid dataset. The coordinates along each axis are defined using an instance of vtkDataArray (RGrid.cxx).

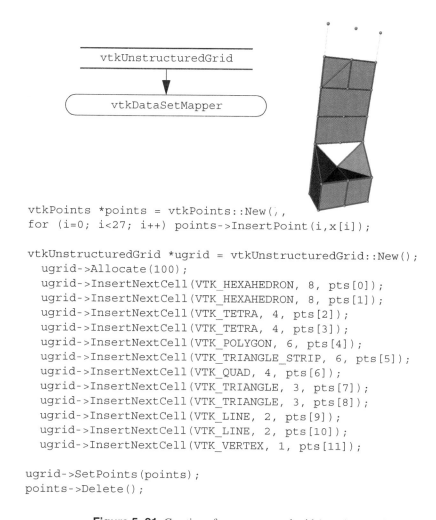

```
vtkPoints *points = vtkPoints::New(),
for (i=0; i<27; i++) points->InsertPoint(i,x[i]);

vtkUnstructuredGrid *ugrid = vtkUnstructuredGrid::New();
    ugrid->Allocate(100);
    ugrid->InsertNextCell(VTK_HEXAHEDRON, 8, pts[0]);
    ugrid->InsertNextCell(VTK_HEXAHEDRON, 8, pts[1]);
    ugrid->InsertNextCell(VTK_TETRA, 4, pts[2]);
    ugrid->InsertNextCell(VTK_TETRA, 4, pts[3]);
    ugrid->InsertNextCell(VTK_POLYGON, 6, pts[4]);
    ugrid->InsertNextCell(VTK_TRIANGLE_STRIP, 6, pts[5]);
    ugrid->InsertNextCell(VTK_QUAD, 4, pts[6]);
    ugrid->InsertNextCell(VTK_TRIANGLE, 3, pts[7]);
    ugrid->InsertNextCell(VTK_TRIANGLE, 3, pts[8]);
    ugrid->InsertNextCell(VTK_LINE, 2, pts[9]);
    ugrid->InsertNextCell(VTK_LINE, 2, pts[10]);
    ugrid->InsertNextCell(VTK_VERTEX, 1, pts[11]);

ugrid->SetPoints(points);
points->Delete();
```

Figure 5–21 Creation of an unstructured grid (UGrid.cxx).

ugrid->InsertNextCell(). There are various flavors of this operator, use the appropriate one.

4. Create point and/or cell attribute data and associate it with the dataset.

5. Complete the creation process by executing the ugrid->Squeeze() operator. This operator reclaims any extra memory consumed by the data structures. Although this step is not required, it will return memory resource back to the computer system.

The creation of unstructured grid datasets is somewhat different from the creation of the other dataset types. This is because of the unstructured nature of the data, and the complex nature of the internal data structures.

5.9 Chapter Summary

A dataset represents visualization data. The dataset has an organizing structure, with topological and geometric components, and associated attribute data. The structure of a dataset consists of cells (topology) and points (geometry). An important characteristic of the structure is whether its geometry and topology are regular or irregular (or equivalently, structured or unstructured). Regular data is more compact and usually more computationally efficient than irregular data. However, irregular data is more flexible in representation capability than regular data.

Important dataset types include polygonal data, rectilinear grid, image data, structured grids, and unstructured grids. The polygonal dataset type is used to represent graphics data, as well as many kinds of visualization data. The unstructured grid is the most general type, consisting of arbitrary combinations of all possible cell types.

Attribute data consists of scalars, vectors, tensors, texture coordinates, and normals. Other arrays may also be includes as part of attribute data since it is a type of field data. In the *Visualization Toolkit*, attribute data is associated with both the dataset point and cells.

5.10 Bibliographic Notes

A variety of representation schemes have been proposed for each dataset type described here. These schemes vary depending on design goals. For example, even the simple volume representation has been implemented with other more complex schemes such as run-length encoding and octrees [Bloomenthal88]. A description of more general representation schemes is available in [Haber91], the AVS field model [AVS89], and the compact cell structure [Schroeder94]. An overview of dataset types can be found in [Gelberg90]. Some structures for those mathematically oriented can be found in [Brisson90] and [Poluzzi93]. Haimes [VISUAL3] describes an efficient data structure for unstructured grid visualization.

If you are interested in more details on finite element methods see the classic Zienkiewicz [Zienkiewicz87] or [Gallagher75]. Information about both finite difference and finite element methods is available in [Lapidus82].

5.11 References

[AVS89]
   C. Upson, T. Faulhaber, Jr., D. Kamins, and others. "The Application Visualization System: A Computational Environment for Scientific Visualization." *IEEE Computer Graphics and Applications*. 9(4):30–42, July 1989.

[Bloomenthal88]
   J. Bloomenthal. "Polygonization of Implicit Surfaces." *Computer Aided Geometric Design*. 5(4):341–355, November 1988.

[Brisson90]
   E. Brisson. "Representing Geometric Structures in *d*-Dimensions: Topology and Order." *ACM Symposium on Computational Geometry*. ACM Press, NY, 1989.

[Gallagher75]
   R. H. Gallagher. *Finite Element Analysis: Fundamentals.* Prentice Hall, Upper Saddle River, NJ, 1975.

[Gelberg90]
   L. Gelberg, D. Kamins, D. Parker, and J. Stacks. "Visualization Techniques for Structured and Unstructured Scientific Data." *SIGGRAPH '90 Course Notes for State of the Art Data Visualization.* August 1990.

[Haber91]
   R. B. Haber, B. Lucas, N. Collins. "A Data Model for Scientific Visualization with Provisions for Regular and Irregular Grids." In *Proceedings of Visualization '91.* pp. 298–395, IEEE Computer Society Press, Los Alamitos, CA, 1991.

[Lapidus82]
   L. Lapidus and G. F. Pinder. *Numerical Solution of Partial Differential Equations in Science and Engineering.* John Wiley and Sons, New York, 1987.

[Mortenson85]
   M. E. Mortenson. *Geometric Modeling.* John Wiley and Sons, New York, 1985.

[Poluzzi93]
   A. Paoluzzi, F. Bernardini, C. Cattani, and V. Ferrucci. "Dimension-Independent Modeling with Simplicial Complexes." *ACM Transactions on Graphics.* 12(1):56–102, 1993.

[Schroeder94]
   W. J. Schroeder and B. Yamrom. "A Compact Cell Structure for Scientific Visualization." *SIGGRAPH '93 and '94 Course Notes for Advanced Techniques for Scientific Visualization.*

[VISUAL3]
   R. Haimes and M. Giles. "VISUAL3: Interactive Unsteady Unstructured 3D Visualization." AIAA Report No. AIAA-91-0794. January 1991.

[Weiler86]
   K. J. Weiler. *Topological Structures for Geometric Modeling.* PhD thesis, Rensselaer Polytechnic Institute, Troy, NY, May 1986.

[Zienkiewicz87]
   O. C. Zienkiewicz and R. L. Taylor. *The Finite Element Method, vol. 1.* McGraw-Hill Book Co., New York, 4th ed. 1987.

5.12 Exercises

5.1   Consider a pixmap of dimensions 100^2. Compare the memory requirements to represent this data using:

a) an image dataset,

b) a structured grid dataset,

c) a polygonal mesh of quadrilaterals,

d) an unstructured grid of quadrilateral cells,

e) and a triangle strip mesh of 100 strips of 200 triangles each.

5.2   Consider a volume of dimensions 100^3. Compare the memory requirements to represent this data using:

a) an image dataset,

b) a structured grid dataset,

c) and an unstructured grid of hexahedral cells.

5.3   Develop a representational scheme for a rectilinear grid. How does this compare (in memory requirement) to a structured grid?

5.4   Consider a volume of dimensions 100^3. Compute the memory requirements for the following point attribute types:

a) unsigned character scalars (1 byte per scalar),

b) float scalars (4 bytes per scalar),

c) float vectors,

d) and double-precision tensors (3x3 tensors).

5.5   List three examples of scalar data.

5.6   List three examples of vector data.

5.7   List three examples of tensor data.

5.8   Is it possible to have more than one scalar field in a dataset? If so, how would this information be represented?

5.9   A common method to represent cell connectivity is to list point ids with the last id negated. For example, triangle (8,7,3) would be represented (8,7,-3). The negative index represents end of cell definition. What are the advantages and disadvantages of this scheme as compared to the VTK cell array structure?

5.10   How many different ways can a hexahedral cell be decomposed into tetrahedron? Are there compatibility issues between neighboring hexahedra?

5.11   Write a program to create and display a structured grid in the form of a hollow cylinder (i.e., cylinder with a hole through it).

5.12   Write a program to create and display an unstructured grid in the form of a hollow cylinder.

5.13   Write a program to create and display a polygonal octahedron.

Fundamental Algorithms

We have seen how to represent basic types of visualization data such as image data, structured grids, unstructured grids, and polygonal data. This chapter explores methods to transform this data to and from these various representations, eventually generating graphics primitives that we can render. These methods are called *algorithms*, and are of special interest to those working in the field of visualization. Algorithms are the verbs that allow us to express our data in visual form. By combining these verbs appropriately, we can reduce complex data into simple, readily comprehensible sentences that are the power of data visualization.

6.1 Introduction

The algorithms that transform data are the heart of data visualization. To describe the various transformations available, we need to categorize algorithms according to the *structure* and *type* of transformation. By structure we mean the effects that transformation has on the topology and geometry of the dataset. By type we mean the type of dataset that the algorithm operates on.

Structural transformations can be classified in four ways, depending on how they affect the geometry, topology, and attributes of a dataset.

- *Geometric transformations* alter input geometry but do not change the topology of the dataset. For example, if we translate, rotate, and/or scale the points of a polygonal dataset, the topology does not change, but the point coordinates, and therefore the geometry, does.

- *Topological transformations* alter input topology but do not change geometry and attribute data. Converting a dataset type from polygonal data to unstructured grid data, or from image data to unstructured grid, changes the topology but not the geometry. More often, however, the geometry changes whenever the topology does, so topological transformation is uncommon.

- *Attribute transformations* convert data attributes from one form to another, or create new attributes from the input data. The structure of the dataset remains unaffected. Computing vector magnitude or creating scalars based on elevation are data attribute transformations.

- *Combined transformations* change both dataset structure and attribute data. For example, computing contour lines or surfaces is a combined transformation.

We also may classify algorithms according to the type of data they operate on, or the type of data they generate. By type, we most often mean the type of attribute data, such as scalars or vectors. Typical categories include:

- *Scalar algorithms* operate on scalar data. For example, the generation of contour lines of temperature on a weather map.

- *Vector algorithms* operate on vector data. Showing oriented arrows of airflow (direction and magnitude) is an example of vector visualization.

- *Tensor algorithms* operate on tensor matrices. An example of a tensor algorithm is to show the components of stress or strain in a material using oriented icons.

- *Modelling algorithms* generate dataset topology or geometry, or surface normals or texture data. Modelling algorithms tend to be the catch-all category for many algorithms, since some do not fit neatly into any single category mentioned above. For example, generating glyphs oriented according to the vector direction and then scaled according to the scalar value, is a combined scalar/vector algorithm. For convenience we classify such an algorithm as a modelling algorithm, because it does not fit squarely into any other category.

Algorithms also can be classified according to the type of data they process. This is the most common scheme found in the visualization literature. However, this scheme is not without its problems. Often the categories overlap, resulting in confusion. For example, a category (not mentioned above) is *volume visualization*, which refers to the visualization of volume data (or in our terminology, image data). This category was initially created to describe the visualization of scalar data arranged on a volume, but more recently, vector (and even tensor) data has been visualized on a volume. Hence, we have to qualify our techniques to *volume vector visualization*, or other potentially confusing combinations.

In the text that follows, we will use the attribute type classification scheme: scalar, vector, tensor, and modelling. In cases where the algorithms operate on a particular dataset type, we place them in the appropriate category according to our best judgment. Be forewarned, though, that alternative classification schemes do exist, and may be better suited to describing the true nature of the algorithm.

Generality Versus Efficiency

Most algorithms can be written specifically for a particular dataset type, or more generally, treating any dataset type. The advantage of a specific algorithm is that it is usually faster than a comparable general algorithm. (See "Other Data Abstractions" on page 126 where we discussed the trade-off between abstract and concrete forms.) An implementation of a specific algorithm also may be more memory efficient and its implementation may better reflect the relationship between the algorithm and the dataset type it operates on.

One example of this is contour surface creation. Algorithms for extracting contour surfaces were originally developed for volume data, mainly for medical applications. The regularity of volumes lends itself to efficient algorithms. However, the specialization of volume-based algorithms precludes their use for more general datasets such as structured or unstructured grids. Although the contour algorithms can be adapted to these other dataset types, they are less efficient than those for volume datasets.

Our presentation of algorithms favors the more general implementations. In some special cases we will describe performance improving techniques for particular dataset types. Refer to the bibliography at the end of each chapter for detailed descriptions of specialized algorithms.

6.2 Scalar Algorithms

Scalars are single data values associated with each point and/or cell of a dataset. (Recall that in the *Visualization Toolkit* we associate data with points.) Because scalar data is commonly found in real-world applications, and because scalar data is so easy to work with, there are many different algorithms to visualize it.

Color Mapping

Color mapping is a common scalar visualization technique that maps scalar data to colors, and displays the colors on the computer system. The scalar mapping is implemented by indexing into a *color lookup table*. Scalar values serve as indices into the lookup table.

The mapping proceeds as follows. The lookup table holds an array of colors (e.g., red, green, blue components or other comparable representations). Associated with the table is a minimum and maximum *scalar range (min, max)* into which the scalar values are mapped. Scalar values greater than the maximum range are clamped to the maximum color, scalar values less than the minimum range are clamped to the minimum color value. Then, for each scalar value s_i, the index i into the color table with n entries (and 0-offset) is given by **Figure 6–1**.

A more general form of the lookup table is called a *transfer function*. A transfer function is any expression that maps scalar value into a color specification. For example, **Figure 6–2** maps scalar values into separate intensity values for the red, green, and blue color components. We can also use transfer functions to map scalar data into other information such as local transparency. (Transfer functions are discussed in more detail in "Transparency and Alpha Values" on page 201 and "Volume Rendering" on page 206.) A lookup table is a

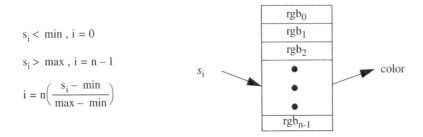

$$s_i < min \, , \, i = 0$$

$$s_i > max \, , \, i = n - 1$$

$$i = n\left(\frac{s_i - min}{max - min}\right)$$

Figure 6–1 Mapping scalars to colors via a lookup table.

discrete sampling of a transfer function. We can create a lookup table from any transfer function by sampling the transfer function at a set of discrete points.

Color mapping is a one-dimensional visualization technique. It maps one piece of information (i.e., a scalar value) into a color specification. However, the display of color information is not limited to one-dimensional displays. Often we use color information mapped onto 1D, 2D, or 3D objects. This is a simple way to increase the information content of our visualizations.

The key to color mapping for scalar visualization is to choose the lookup table entries carefully. **Figure 6–3** shows four different lookup tables used to visualize gas density as fluid flows through a combustion chamber. The first lookup table is grayscale. Grayscale tables often provide better structural detail to the eye. The other three images in **Figure 6–3** use different color lookup tables. The second uses rainbow hues from blue to red. The third uses rainbow hues arranged from red to blue. The last table uses a table designed to enhance contrast. Careful use of colors can often enhance important features of a dataset. However, any type of lookup table can exaggerate unimportant details or create visual artifacts because of unforeseen interactions between data, color choice, and human physiology.

Designing lookup tables is as much art as it is science. From a practical point of view, tables should accentuate important features, while minimizing less important or extraneous details. It is also desirable to use palettes that inherently contain scaling information. For example, a color rainbow scale from blue to red is often used to represent temperature scale, since many people associate "blue" with cold temperatures, and "red" with hot temperatures.

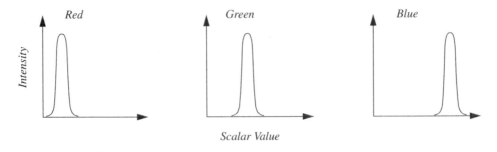

Figure 6–2 Transfer function for color components red, green, and blue as a function of scalar value.

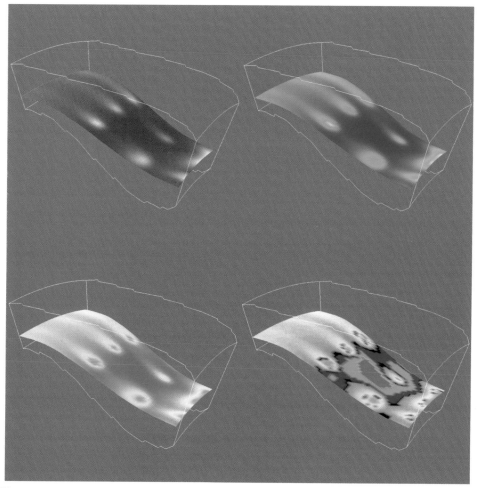

Figure 6–3 Flow density colored with different lookup tables. Top-left: grayscale; Top-right rainbow (blue to red); lower-left rainbow (red to blue); lower-right large contrast (`rainbow.tcl`).

However, even this scale is problematic: a physicist would say that blue is hotter than red, since hotter objects emit more blue light (i.e., shorter wavelength) than red. Also, there is no need to limit ourselves to "linear" lookup tables. Even though the mapping of scalars into colors has been presented as a linear operation (**Figure 6–1**), the table itself need not be linear. That is, tables can be designed to enhance small variations in scalar value using logarithmic or other schemes.

There is another element to visualization that is the artistic, or aesthetic, quality. Good visualizations represent a balance between effective communication of information and aesthetically pleasing presentation. While it is true in this day of mass media that information is often sacrificed for the sake of image, improving the comfort level and engaging the human observer more deeply in the presentation of data improves the effectiveness of communication.

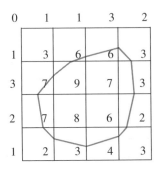

Figure 6–4   Contouring a 2D structured grid with contour line value = 5.

Contouring

A natural extension to color mapping is *contouring*. When we see a surface colored with data values, the eye often separates similarly colored areas into distinct regions. When we contour data, we are effectively constructing the boundary between these regions. These boundaries correspond to contour lines (2D) or surfaces (3D) of constant scalar value.

Examples of 2D contour displays include weather maps annotated with lines of constant temperature (isotherms), or topological maps drawn with lines of constant elevation. Three-dimensional contours are called *isosurfaces*, and can be approximated by many polygonal primitives. Examples of isosurfaces include constant medical image intensity corresponding to body tissues such as skin, bone, or other organs. Other abstract isosurfaces such as surfaces of constant pressure or temperature in fluid flow also may be created.

Consider the 2D structured grid shown in **Figure 6–4**. Scalar values are shown next to the points that define the grid. Contouring always begins by selecting a scalar value, or contour value, that corresponds to the contour lines or surfaces generated. To generate the contours, some form of interpolation must be used. This is because we have scalar values at a finite set of points in the dataset, and our contour value may lie between the point values. Since the most common interpolation technique is linear, we generate points on the contour surface by linear interpolation along the edges. If an edge has scalar values 10 and 0 at its two end points, and if we are trying to generate a contour line of value 5, then edge interpolation computes that the contour passes through the midpoint of the edge.

Once the points on cell edges are generated, we can connect these points into contours using a few different approaches. One approach detects an edge intersection (i.e., the contour passes through an edge) and then "tracks" this contour as it moves across cell boundaries. We know that if a contour edge enters a cell, it must exit a cell as well. The contour is tracked until it closes back on itself, or exits a dataset boundary. If it is known that only a single contour exists, then the process stops. Otherwise, every edge in the dataset must be checked to see whether other contour lines exist.

Another approach uses a divide and conquer technique, treating cells independently. This is the *marching squares* algorithm in 2D, and *marching cubes* [Lorensen87] in 3D. The basic assumption of these techniques is that a contour can only pass through a cell in a finite number of ways. A case table is constructed that enumerates all possible topological *states* of a cell, given combinations of scalar values at the cell points. The number of topological states depends on the number of cell vertices, and the number of inside / outside relationships a vertex can have with respect to the contour value. A vertex is considered inside a contour if its scalar value is larger than the scalar value of the contour line. Vertices with scalar values less than the contour value are said to be outside the contour. For example, if a cell has four vertices and each vertex can be either inside or outside the contour, there are $2^4 = 16$ possible ways that the contour passes through the cell. In the case table we are not interested in where the contour passes through the cell (e.g., geometric intersection), just how it passes through the cell (i.e., topology of the contour in the cell).

Figure 6–5 shows the sixteen combinations for a square cell. An index into the case table can be computed by encoding the state of each vertex as a binary digit. For 2D data represented on a rectangular grid, we can represent the 16 cases with 4 bit index. Once the proper case is selected, the location of the contour line / cell edge intersection can be calculated using interpolation. The algorithm processes a cell and then moves, or *marches* to the next cell. After all cells are visited, the contour will be completed. In summary, the marching algorithms proceed as follows:

1. Select a cell.

2. Calculate the inside / outside state of each vertex of the cell.

3. Create an index by storing the binary state of each vertex in a separate bit.

4. Use the index to look up the topological state of the cell in a case table.

5. Calculate the contour location (via interpolation) for each edge in the case table.

This procedure will construct independent geometric primitives in each cell. At the cell boundaries duplicate vertices and edges may be created. These duplicates can be eliminated by using a special coincident point-merging operation. Note that interpolation along each edge should be done in the same direction. If not, numerical round-off will likely cause points to be generated that are not precisely coincident, and will not merge properly.

There are advantages and disadvantages to both the edge-tracking and marching cubes approaches. The marching squares algorithm is easy to implement. This is particularly important when we extend the technique into three dimensions, where isosurface tracking becomes much more difficult. On the other hand, the algorithm creates disconnected line segments and points, and the required merging operation requires extra computation resources. The track-

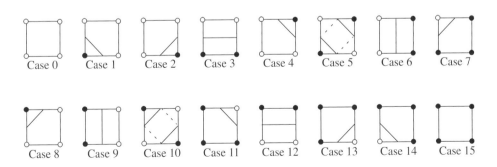

Figure 6–5 Sixteen different marching squares cases. Dark vertices indicate scalar value is above contour value. Cases 5 and 10 are ambiguous.

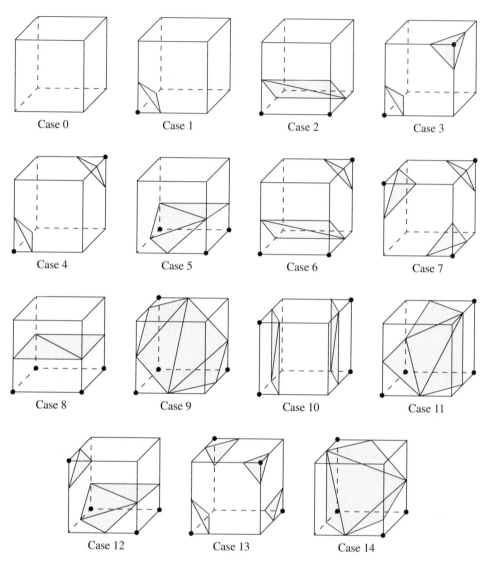

Figure 6–6 Marching cubes cases for 3D isosurface generation. The 256 possible cases have been reduced to 15 cases using symmetry. Dark vertices are greater than the selected isosurface value.

ing algorithm can be implemented to generate a single polyline per contour line, avoiding the need to merge coincident points.

As mentioned previously, the 3D analogy of marching squares is marching cubes. Here, there are 256 different combinations of scalar value, given that there are eight points in a cubical cell (i.e., 2^8 combinations). **Figure 6–6** shows these combinations reduced to 15 cases by using arguments of symmetry. We use combinations of rotation and mirroring to produce topologically equivalent cases.

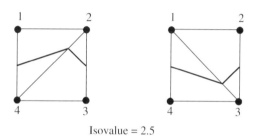

Isovalue = 2.5

Figure 6–7 Using marching triangles or marching tetrahedra to resolve ambiguous cases on rectangular lattice (only face of cube is shown). Choice of diagonal orientation may result in "bumps" in contour surface. In 2D, diagonal orientation can be chosen arbitrarily, but in 3D diagonal is constrained by neighbor.

An important issue is *contouring ambiguity*. Careful observation of marching squares cases numbered 5 and 10 and marching cubes cases numbered 3, 6, 7, 10, 12, and 13 show that there are configurations where a cell can be contoured in more than one way. (This ambiguity also exists when using an edge tracking approach to contouring.) Contouring ambiguity arises on a 2D square or the face of a 3D cube when adjacent edge points are in different states, but diagonal vertices are in the same state.

In two dimensions, contour ambiguity is simple to treat: for each ambiguous case we implement one of the two possible cases. The choice for a particular case is independent of all other choices. Depending on the choice, the contour may either extend or break the current contour as illustrated in **Figure 6–8**. Either choice is acceptable since the resulting contour lines will be continuous and closed (or will end at the dataset boundary).

In three dimensions the problem is more complex. We cannot simply choose an ambiguous case independent of all other ambiguous cases. For example **Figure 6–9** shows what happens if we carelessly implement two cases independent of one another. In this figure we have used the usual case 3 but replaced case 6 with its *complementary* case. Complementary cases are formed by exchanging the "dark" vertices with "light" vertices. (This is equivalent to swapping vertex scalar value from above the isosurface value to below the isosurface value, and vice versa.) The result of pairing these two cases is that a hole is left in the isosurface.

Several different approaches have been taken to remedy this problem. One approach tessellates the cubes with tetrahedron, and uses a *marching tetrahedra* technique. This works because the marching tetrahedra exhibit no ambiguous cases. Unfortunately, the marching tetrahedra algorithm generates isosurfaces consisting of more triangles, and the tessellation of a cube with tetrahedra requires making a choice regarding the orientation of the tetrahedra. This choice may result in artificial "bumps" in the isosurface because of interpolation along the face diagonals as shown in **Figure 6–7**. Another approach evaluates the asymptotic behavior of the surface, and then chooses the cases to either join or break the contour. Nielson and Hamann [Nielson91] have developed a technique based on this approach they call the *asymptotic decider*. It is based on an analysis of the variation of the scalar variable across an ambiguous face. The analysis determines how the edges of isosurface polygons should be connected.

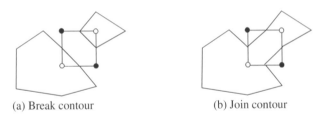

(a) Break contour   (b) Join contour

Figure 6–8 Choosing a particular contour case will break (a) or join (b) the current contour. Case shown is marching squares case 10.

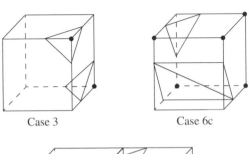

Case 3   Case 6c

Figure 6–9 Arbitrarily choosing marching cubes cases leads to holes in the isosurface.

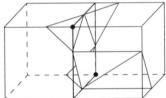

A simple and effective solution extends the original 15 marching cubes cases by adding additional complementary cases. These cases are designed to be compatible with neighboring cases and prevent the creation of holes in the isosurface. There are six complementary cases required, corresponding to the marching cubes cases 3, 6, 7, 10, 12, and 13. The complementary marching cubes cases are shown in **Figure 6–10**.

We can extend the general approach of marching squares and marching cubes to other topological types. In VTK we use marching lines, triangles, and tetrahedra to contour cells of these types (or composite cells that are composed of these types). In addition, although we speak of regular types such as squares and cubes, marching cubes can be applied to any cell type topologically equivalent to a cube (e.g., hexahedron or noncubical voxel).

Figure 6–11 shows four applications of contouring. In **Figure 6–11**(a) we see 2D contour lines of CT density value corresponding to different tissue types. These lines were generated using marching squares. **Figure 6–11**(b) through **Figure 6–11**(d) are isosurfaces created by marching cubes. **Figure 6–11**(b) is a surface of constant image intensity from a computed tomography (CT) X-ray imaging system. (**Figure 6–11**(a) is a 2D subset of this data.) The intensity level corresponds to human bone. **Figure 6–11**(c) is an isosurface of constant flow density. **Figure 6–11**(d) is an isosurface of electron potential of an iron protein molecule. The image shown in **Figure 6–11**(b) is immediately recognizable because of our familiarity with human anatomy. However, for those practitioners in the fields of computational fluid dynam-

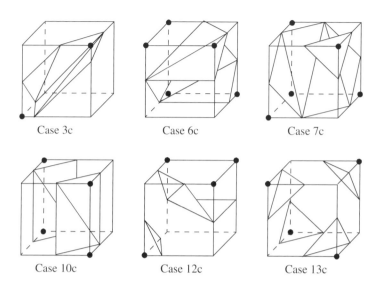

Case 3c   Case 6c   Case 7c

Case 10c   Case 12c   Case 13c

Figure 6–10 Marching cubes complementary cases.

ics and molecular biology, **Figure 6–11**(c) and **Figure 6–11**(d) are equally familiar. As these examples show, methods for contouring are powerful yet general techniques for visualizing data from a variety of fields.

Scalar Generation

The two visualization techniques presented thus far, color mapping and contouring, are simple, effective methods to display scalar information. It is natural to turn to these techniques first when visualizing data. However, often our data is not in a form convenient to these techniques. The data may not be single-valued (i.e., a scalar), or it may be a mathematical or other complex relationship. That is part of the fun and creative challenge of visualization: We must tap our creative resources to convert data into a form we can visualize.

For example, consider terrain data. We assume that the data is x-y-z coordinates, where x and y represent the coordinates in the plane, and z represents the elevation above sea level. Our desired visualization is to color the terrain according to elevation. This requires creating a colormap — possibly using white for high altitudes, blue for sea level and below, and various shades of green and brown corresponding to elevation between sea level and high altitude. We also need scalars to index into the colormap. The obvious choice here is to extract the z coordinate. That is, scalars are simply the z-coordinate value.

This example can be made more interesting by generalizing the problem. Although we could easily create a filter to extract the z-coordinate, we can create a filter that produces elevation scalar values where the elevation is measured along any axis. Given an oriented line starting at the (low) point p_l (e.g., sea level) and ending at the (high) point p_h (e.g., mountain top), we compute the elevation scalar s_i at point $p_i = (x_i, y_i, z_i)$ using the dot product as shown in **Figure 6–12**. The scalar is normalized using the magnitude of the oriented line, and

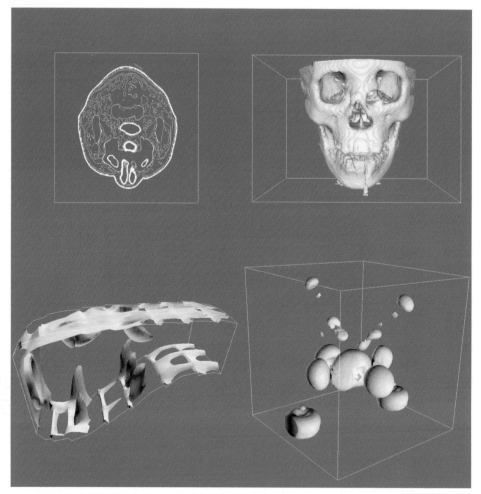

Figure 6–11 Contouring examples. (a) Marching squares used to generate contour lines (`headSlic.tcl`); (b) Marching cubes surface of human bone (`head-Bone.tcl`); (c) Marching cubes surface of flow density (`combIso.tcl`); (d) Marching cubes surface of iron-protein (`ironPIso.tcl`).

may be clamped between minimum and maximum scalar values (if necessary). The bottom half of this figure shows the results of applying this technique to a terrain model of Honolulu, Hawaii. A lookup table of 256 ranging from deep blue (water) to yellow-white (mountain top) is used to color map this figure.

Part of the creative practice of visualization is selecting the best technique for given data from the palette of available techniques. Often this requires creative mapping by the user of the visualization system. In particular, to use scalar visualization techniques we need only to create a relationship to generate a unique scalar value. Other examples of scalar mapping include an index value into a list of data, computing vector magnitude or matrix determinate, evaluating surface curvature, or determining distance between points. Scalar generation,

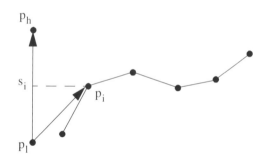

$$s_i = \frac{(p_i - p_l) \cdot (p_h - p_l)}{|p_h - p_l|^2}$$

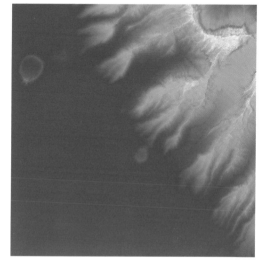

Figure 6–12 Computing scalars using normalized dot product. Bottom half of figure illustrates technique applied to terrain data from Honolulu, Hawaii (`hawaii.tcl`).

when coupled with color mapping or contouring, is a simple, yet effective, technique for visualizing many types of data.

6.3 Vector Algorithms

Vector data is a three-dimensional representation of direction and magnitude. Vector data often results from the study of fluid flow, or when examining derivatives (i.e., rate of change) of some quantity.

Hedgehogs and Oriented Glyphs

A natural vector visualization technique is to draw an oriented, scaled line for each vector (**Figure 6–13**(a)). The line begins at the point with which the vector is associated and is oriented in the direction of the vector components (v_x, v_y, v_z). Typically, the resulting line must be scaled up or down to control the size of its visual representation. This technique is often referred to as a *hedgehog* because of the bristly result.

There are many variations of this technique (**Figure 6–13**(b)). Arrows may be added to indicate the direction of the line. The lines may be colored according to vector magnitude, or

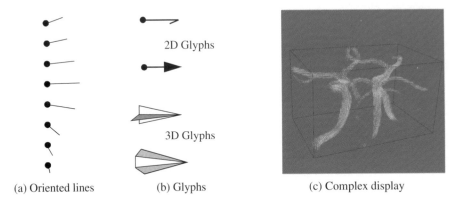

(a) Oriented lines   (b) Glyphs   (c) Complex display

Figure 6–13 Vector visualization techniques: (a) oriented lines; (b) using oriented glyphs; (c) complex vector visualization (`complexV.tcl`).

some other scalar quantity (e.g., pressure or temperature). Also, instead of using a line, oriented "glyphs" can be used. By glyph we mean any 2D or 3D geometric representation such as an oriented triangle or cone.

Care should be used in applying these techniques. In 3D it is often difficult to understand the position and orientation of a vector because of its projection into a 2D image. Also, using large numbers of vectors can clutter the display to the point where the visualization becomes meaningless. **Figure 6–13**(c) shows 167,000 3D vectors (using oriented and scaled lines) in the region of the human carotid artery. The larger vectors lie inside the arteries, the smaller vectors lie outside the arteries and are randomly oriented (measurement error) but small in magnitude. Clearly the details of the vector field are not discernible from this image.

Scaling glyphs also poses interesting problems. In what Tufte has termed a "visualization lie," [Tufte83] scaling a 2D or 3D glyph results in nonlinear differences in appearance. The surface area of an object increases with the square of its scale factor, so two vectors differing by a factor of two in magnitude may appear up to four times different based on surface area. Such scaling issues are common in data visualization, and great care must be taken to avoiding misleading viewers.

Warping

Vector data is often associated with "motion." The motion is in the form of velocity or displacement. An effective technique for displaying such vector data is to "warp" or deform geometry according to the vector field. For example, imagine representing the displacement of a structure under load by deforming the structure. Or if we are visualizing the flow of fluid, we can create a flow profile by distorting a straight line inserted perpendicular to the flow.

Figure 6–14 shows two examples of vector warping. In the first example the motion of a vibrating beam is shown. The original undeformed outline is shown in wireframe. The second example shows warped planes in a structured grid dataset. The planes are warped accord-

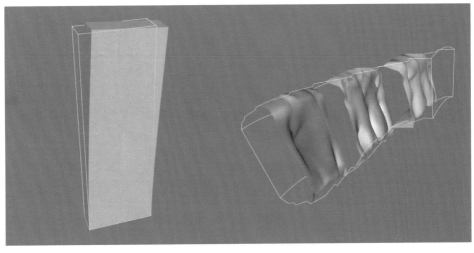

(a) Vibration of beam   (b) Momentum profiles

Figure 6–14 Warping geometry to show vector field; (a) Beam displacement (`vib.tcl`); (b) Flow momentum (`velProf.tcl`).

ing to flow momentum. The relative back and forward flow are clearly visible in the deformation of the planes.

Typically, we must scale the vector field to control geometric distortion. Too small a distortion may not be visible, while too large a distortion can cause the structure to turn inside out or self-intersect. In such a case the viewer of the visualization is likely to lose context, and the visualization will become ineffective.

Displacement Plots

Vector displacement on the surface of an object can be visualized with displacement plots. A displacement plot shows the motion of an object in the direction perpendicular to its surface. The object motion is caused by an applied vector field. In a typical application the vector field is a displacement or strain field.

Vector displacement plots draw on the ideas in "Scalar Generation" on page 159. Vectors are converted to scalars by computing the dot product between the surface normal and vector at each point (**Figure 6–15**(a)). If positive values result, the motion at the point is in the direction of the surface normal (i.e., positive displacement). Negative values indicate that the motion is opposite the surface normal (i.e., negative displacement).

A useful application of this technique is the study of vibration. In vibration analysis, we are interested in the eigenvalues (i.e., natural resonant frequencies) and eigenvectors (i.e., mode shapes) of a structure. To understand mode shapes we can use displacement plots to indicate regions of motion. There are special regions in the structure where positive displacement changes to negative displacement. These are regions of zero displacement. When plotted on the surface of the structure, these regions appear as the so-called *modal* lines of

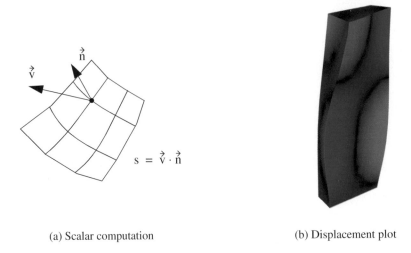

(a) Scalar computation   (b) Displacement plot

Figure 6–15 Vector displacement plots. (a) Vector converted to scalar via dot product computation; (b) Surface plot of vibrating plate. Dark areas show nodal lines. Bright areas show maximum motion (dispPlot.tcl).

vibration. The study of modal lines has long been an important visualization tool for under-standing mode shapes.

Figure 6–15(b) shows modal lines for a vibrating rectangular beam. The vibration mode in this figure is the second torsional mode, clearly indicated by the crossing modal lines. (The aliasing in the figure is because of the coarseness of the analysis mesh.) To create the figure we combined the procedure of **Figure 6–15**(a) with a special lookup table. The lookup table was arranged with dark areas in the center (i.e., corresponds to zero dot product) and bright areas at the beginning and end of the table (corresponds to 1 or -1 dot product). As a result, regions of large normal displacement are bright and regions near the modal lines are dark.

Time Animation

Some of the techniques described so far can be thought of as moving a point or object over a small time step. The hedgehog line is an approximation of a point's motion over a time period whose duration is given by the scale factor. In other words, if velocity $\vec{V} = dx/dt$, then the displacement of a point is

$$dx = \vec{V} \, dt \qquad\qquad \textbf{(6-1)}$$

This suggests an extension to our previous techniques: repeatedly displace points over many time steps. **Figure 6–16** shows such an approach. Beginning with a sphere S centered about some point C, we move S repeatedly to generate the bubbles shown. The eye tends to

Figure 6–16 Time animation of a point C. Although the spacing between points varies, the time increment between each point is constant.

trace out a path by connecting the bubbles, giving the observer a qualitative understanding of the fluid flow in that area. The bubbles may be displayed as an animation over time (giving the illusion of motion) or as a multiple exposure sequence (giving the appearance of a path).

Such an approach can be misused. For one thing, the velocity at a point is instantaneous. Once we move away from the point the velocity is likely to change. Using **Equation 6-1** above assumes that the velocity is constant over the entire step. By taking large steps we are likely to jump over changes in the velocity. Using smaller steps we will end in a different position. Thus the choice of step size is a critical parameter in constructing accurate visualization of particle paths in a vector field.

To evaluate **Equation 6-1** we can express it as an integral:

$$\vec{x}(t) = \int_t \vec{V} dt \tag{6-2}$$

Although this form cannot be solved analytically for most real world data, its solution can be approximated using numerical integration techniques. Accurate numerical integration is a topic beyond the scope of this book, but it is known that the accuracy of the integration is a function of the step size dt. Since the path is an integration throughout the dataset, the accuracy of the cell interpolation functions, as well as the accuracy of the original vector data, plays an important role in realizing accurate solutions. No definitive study is yet available that relates cell size or interpolation function characteristics to visualization error. But the lesson is clear: the result of numerical integration must be examined carefully, especially in regions of large vector field gradient. However, as with many other visualization algorithms, the insight gained by using vector integration techniques is qualitatively beneficial, despite the unavoidable numerical errors.

The simplest form of numerical integration is Euler's method,

$$\vec{x}_{i+1} = \vec{x}_i + \vec{V}_i \Delta t \tag{6-3}$$

where the position at time $\vec{x}_{i+1}$ is the vector sum of the previous position plus the instantaneous velocity times the incremental time step Δt.

Euler's method has error on the order of $O(\Delta t^2)$, which is not accurate enough for some applications. One such example is shown in **Figure 6–17**. The velocity field describes perfect rotation about a central point. Using Euler's method we find that we will always diverge and, instead of generating circles, will generate spirals instead.

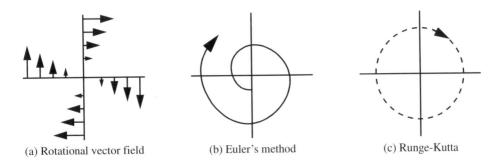

(a) Rotational vector field   (b) Euler's method   (c) Runge-Kutta

Figure 6–17 Euler's integration (b) and Runge-Kutta integration of order 2 (c) applied to uniform rotational vector field (a). Euler's method will always diverge.

In this text we will use the Runge-Kutta technique of order 2 [Conte72]. This is given by the expression

$$\vec{x}_{i+1} = \vec{x}_i + \frac{\Delta t}{2}(\vec{V}_i + \vec{V}_{i+1})$$ (6-4)

where the velocity $\vec{V}_{i+1}$ is computed using Euler's method. The error of this method is $O(\Delta t^3)$. Compared to Euler's method, the Runge-Kutta technique allows us to take a larger integration step at the expense of one additional function evaluation. Generally this trade-off is beneficial, but like any numerical technique, the best method to use depends on the particular nature of the data. Higher-order techniques are also available, but generally not necessary, because the higher accuracy is countered by error in interpolation function or inherent in the data values. If you are interested in other integration formulas, please check the references at the end of the chapter.

One final note about accuracy concerns. The errors involved in either perception or computation of visualizations is an open research area. The discussion in the preceding paragraph is a good example of this. There we characterized the error in streamline integration using conventional numerical integration arguments. But there is a problem with this argument. In visualization applications, we are integrating across cells whose function values are continuous, but whose derivatives are not. As the streamline crosses the cell boundary, subtle effects may occur that are not treated by the standard numerical analysis. Thus the standard arguments need to be extended for visualization applications.

Integration formulas require repeated transformation from global to local coordinates. Consider moving a point through a dataset under the influence of a vector field. The first step is to identify the cell that contains the point. This operation is a search (see "Searching" on page 273), plus a conversion to local coordinates. Once the cell is found, then the next step is to compute the velocity at that point by interpolating the velocity from the cell points. The point is then incrementally repositioned (using the integration formula **Equation 6-4**). The process is then repeated until the point exits the dataset or the distance or time traversed exceeds some specified value.

This process can be computationally demanding. There are two important steps we can take to improve performance.

1. *Improving search procedures.* There are two distinct types of searches. Initially, the starting location of the particle must be determined by a global search procedure. Once the initial location of the point is determined in the dataset, an incremental search procedure can then be used. Incremental searching is efficient because the motion of the point is limited within a single cell, or at most across a cell boundary. Thus, the search space is greatly limited, and the incremental search is faster relative to the global search.

2. *Coordinate transformation.* The cost of a coordinate transformation from global to local coordinates can be reduced if either of the following conditions are true: the local and global coordinate systems are identical with one another (or vary by x-y-z translation), or if the vector field is transformed from global space to local coordinate space. The image data coordinate system is an example of a local coordinates which are parallel to global coordinates, hence global to local coordinate transformation can be greatly accelerated. If the vector field is transformed into local coordinates (either as a preprocessing step or on a cell-by-cell basis), then the integration can proceed completely in local space. Once the integration path is computed, selected points along the path can be transformed into global space for the sake of visualization.

Streamlines

A natural extension of the previous time animation techniques is to connect the point position $\vec{x}(t)$ over many time steps. The result is a numerical approximation to a particle trace represented as a line.

Borrowing terminology from the study of fluid flow, we can define three related line representation schemes for vector fields.

- *Particle traces* are trajectories traced by fluid particles over time.

- *Streaklines* are the set of particle traces at a particular time t_i that have previously passed through a specified point x_i.

- *Streamlines* are integral curves along a curve s satisfying the equation

$$s = \int_t \vec{V}\, ds, \quad \text{with } s = s(x, t) \qquad \text{(6-5)}$$

for a particular time $\dot{t}$.

Streamlines, streaklines, and particle traces are equivalent to one another if the flow is steady. In time-varying flow, a given streamline exists only at one moment in time. Visualization systems generally provide facilities to compute particle traces. However, if time is fixed, the same facility can be used to compute streamlines. In general, we will use the term streamline to refer to the method of tracing trajectories in a vector field. Please bear in mind the differences in these representations if the flow is time-varying.

Figure 6–18 shows forty streamlines in a small kitchen. The room has two windows, a door (with air leakage), and a cooking area with a hot stove. The air leakage and temperature

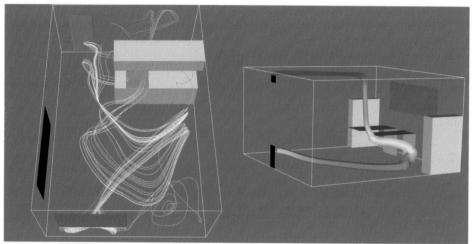

Figure 6–18 Flow velocity computed for a small kitchen (top and side view). Forty streamlines start along the rake positioned under the window. Some eventually travel over the hot stove and are convected upwards (`Kitchen.cxx`).

variation combine to produce air convection currents throughout the kitchen. The starting positions of the streamlines were defined by creating a *rake*, or curve (and its associated points). Here the rake was a straight line. These streamlines clearly show features of the flow field. By releasing many streamlines simultaneously we obtain even more information, as the eye tends to assemble nearby streamlines into a "global" understanding of flow field features.

Many enhancements of streamline visualization exist. Lines can be colored according to velocity magnitude to indicate speed of flow. Other scalar quantities such as temperature or pressure also may be used to color the lines. We also may create constant time dashed lines. Each dash represents a constant time increment. Thus, in areas of high velocity, the length of the dash will be greater relative to regions of lower velocity. These techniques are illustrated in **Figure 6–19** for airflow around a blunt fin. This example consists of a wall with half a rounded fin projecting into the fluid flow. (Using arguments of symmetry, only half of the domain was modeled.) Twenty-five streamlines are released upstream of the fin. The boundary layer effects near the junction of the fin and wall are clearly evident from the streamlines. In this area, flow recirculation is apparent, as well as the reduced flow speed.

6.4 Tensor Algorithms

As we mentioned earlier, tensor visualization is an active area of research. However there are a few simple techniques that we can use to visualize 3×3 real symmetric tensors. Such tensors are used to describe the state of displacement or stress in a 3D material. The stress and strain tensors for an elastic material are shown in **Figure 6–20**.

In these tensors the diagonal coefficients are the so-called normal stresses and strains, and the off-diagonal terms are the shear stresses and strains. Normal stresses and strains act perpendicular to a specified surface, while shear stresses and strains act tangentially to the

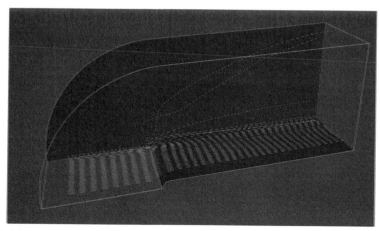

Figure 6–19 Dashed streamlines around a blunt fin. Each dash is a constant time increment. Fast moving particles create longer dashes than slower moving particles. The streamlines also are colored by flow density scalar (`bluntStr.cxx`).

surface. Normal stress is either compression or tension, depending on the sign of the coefficient.

A 3×3 real symmetric matrix can be characterized by three vectors in 3D called the eigenvectors, and three numbers called the eigenvalues of the matrix. The eigenvectors form a 3D coordinate system whose axes are mutually perpendicular. In some applications, particularly the study of materials, these axes also are referred to as the principle axes of the tensor and are physically significant. For example, if the tensor is a stress tensor, then the principle axes are the directions of normal stress and no shear stress. Associated with each eigenvector is an eigenvalue. The eigenvalues are often physically significant as well. In the study of vibration, eigenvalues correspond to the resonant frequencies of a structure, and the eigenvectors are the associated mode shapes.

Mathematically we can represent eigenvalues and eigenvectors as follows. Given a matrix **A**, the eigenvector $\vec{x}$ and eigenvalue λ must satisfy the relation

$$A \cdot \vec{x} = \lambda \vec{x} \qquad\qquad\qquad \textbf{(6-6)}$$

For **Equation 6-6** to hold, the matrix determinate must satisfy

$$\det|A - \lambda I| = 0 \qquad\qquad\qquad \textbf{(6-7)}$$

Expanding this equation yields a nth degree polynomial in λ whose roots are the eigenvalues. Thus, there are always n eigenvalues, although they may not be distinct. In general, **Equation 6-7** is not solved using polynomial root searching because of poor computational performance. (For matrices of order 3 root searching is acceptable because we can solve for the eigenvalues analytically.) Once we determine the eigenvalues, we can substitute each into **Equation 6-7** to solve for the associated eigenvectors.

We can express the eigenvectors of the 3×3 system as

$$\vec{v}_i = \lambda_i \vec{e}_i, \text{ with } i = 1, 2, 3 \qquad\qquad\qquad \textbf{(6-8)}$$

$$\begin{bmatrix} \sigma_x & \tau_{xy} & \tau_{xz} \\ \tau_{yx} & \sigma_y & \tau_{yz} \\ \tau_{zx} & \tau_{zy} & \sigma_z \end{bmatrix}$$

$$\begin{bmatrix} \dfrac{\partial u}{\partial x} & \left(\dfrac{\partial u}{\partial y}+\dfrac{\partial v}{\partial z}\right) & \left(\dfrac{\partial u}{\partial z}+\dfrac{\partial w}{\partial x}\right) \\ \left(\dfrac{\partial u}{\partial y}+\dfrac{\partial v}{\partial z}\right) & \dfrac{\partial v}{\partial y} & \left(\dfrac{\partial v}{\partial z}+\dfrac{\partial w}{\partial y}\right) \\ \left(\dfrac{\partial u}{\partial z}+\dfrac{\partial w}{\partial x}\right) & \left(\dfrac{\partial v}{\partial z}+\dfrac{\partial w}{\partial y}\right) & \dfrac{\partial w}{\partial z} \end{bmatrix}$$

(a) Stress tensor   (b) Strain tensor

Figure 6–20 Stress and strain tensors. Normal stresses in the x-y-z coordinate directions indicated as $\sigma_x, \sigma_y, \sigma_z$, shear stresses indicated as τ_{ij}. Material displacement represented by u, v, w components.

with $\vec{e}_i$ a unit vector in the direction of the eigenvalue, and λ_i the eigenvalues of the system. If we order eigenvalues such that

$$\lambda_1 \geq \lambda_2 \geq \lambda_3 \qquad\qquad\qquad\qquad \textbf{(6-9)}$$

then we refer to the corresponding eigenvectors $\vec{v}_1$, $\vec{v}_2$, and $\vec{v}_3$ as the *major, medium,* and *minor* eigenvectors.

Tensor Ellipsoids

This leads us to the tensor ellipsoid technique for the visualization of real, symmetric 3×3 matrices. The first step is to extract eigenvalues and eigenvectors as described in the previous section. Since eigenvectors are known to be orthogonal, the eigenvectors form a local coordinate system. These axes can be taken as the *minor, medium,* and *major* axes of an ellipsoid. Thus, the shape and orientation of the ellipsoid represent the relative size of the eigenvalues and the orientation of the eigenvectors.

To form the ellipsoid we begin by positioning a sphere at the tensor location. The sphere is then rotated around its origin using the eigenvectors, which in the form of **Equation 6-8** are direction cosines. The eigenvalues are used to scale the sphere. Using 4×4 transformation matrices and referring to **Equation 3-6, Equation 3-9,** and **Equation 3-13,** we form the ellipsoid by transforming the sphere centered at the origin using the matrix T

$$T = T_T \cdot T_R \cdot T_S \qquad\qquad\qquad\qquad \textbf{(6-10)}$$

(remember to read right-to-left). The eigenvectors can be directly plugged in to create the rotation matrix, while the point coordinates x-y-z and eigenvalues $\lambda_1 \geq \lambda_2 \geq \lambda_3$ are inserted into the translation and scaling matrices. A concatenation of these matrices forms the final transformation matrix T.

Figure 6–21(a) depicts the tensor ellipsoid technique. In **Figure 6–21**(b) we show this technique to visualize material stress near a point load on the surface of a semi-infinite

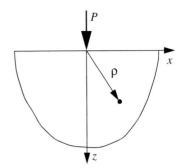

(a) Tensor ellipsoid   (b) Point load on semiinfinite domain

$$\sigma_x = -\frac{P}{2\pi\rho^2}\left(\frac{3zx^2}{\rho^3} - (1-2v)\left(\frac{z}{\rho} - \frac{\rho}{\rho+z} + \frac{x^2(2\rho+z)}{\rho(\rho+z)^2}\right)\right)$$

$$\sigma_y = -\frac{P}{2\pi\rho^2}\left(\frac{3zy^2}{\rho^3} - (1-2v)\left(\frac{z}{\rho} - \frac{\rho}{\rho+z} + \frac{y^2(2\rho+z)}{\rho(\rho+z)^2}\right)\right)$$

$$\sigma_z = -\frac{3Pz^3}{2\pi\rho^5}$$

$$\tau_{xy} = \tau_{yx} = -\frac{P}{2\pi\rho^2}\left(\frac{3xyz}{\rho^3} - (1-2v)\left(\frac{xy(2\rho+z)}{\rho(\rho+z)^2}\right)\right)$$

$$\tau_{xz} = \tau_{zx} = -\frac{3Pxz^2}{2\pi\rho^5}$$

c) Analytic solution

$$\tau_{yz} = \tau_{zy} = -\frac{3Pyz^2}{2\pi\rho^5}$$

Figure 6–21 Tensor ellipsoids. (a) Ellipsoid oriented along eigenvalues (i.e., principle axes) of tensor; (b) Pictorial description of Boussinesq's problem; (c) Analytic results according to Saada.

domain. (This is the so-called Boussinesq's problem.) From Saada [Saada74] we have the analytic expression for the stress components in Cartesian coordinates shown in **Figure 6–21**(c). Note that the z-direction is defined as the axis originating at the point of application of the force P. The variable ρ is the distance from the point of load application to a point x-y-z. The orientation of the x and y axes are in the plane perpendicular to the z axis. (The rotation in the plane of these axes is unimportant since the solution is symmetric around the z axis.) (The parameter v is Poisson's ratio which is a property of the material. Poisson's ratio relates the lateral contraction of a material to axial elongation under a uniaxial stress condition. See [Saada74] or [Timoshenko70] for more information.)

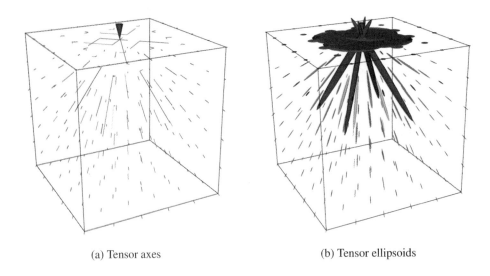

(a) Tensor axes   (b) Tensor ellipsoids

Figure 6–22 Tensor visualization techniques; (a) Tensor axes (`TenAxes.tcl`); (b) Tensor ellipsoids (`TenEllip.tcl`).

In **Figure 6–22** we visualize the analytical results of Boussinesq's problem from Saada. The left-hand portion of the figure shows the results by displaying the scaled and oriented principal axes of the stress tensor. (These are called *tensor axes*.) In the right-hand portion we use tensor ellipsoids to show the same result. Tensor ellipsoids and tensor axes are a form of *glyph* (see "Glyphs" on page 178) specialized to tensor visualization.

A certain amount of care must be taken to visualize this result since there is a stress singularity at the point of contact of the load. In a real application loads are applied over a small area and not at a single point. Also, plastic behavior prevents stress levels from exceeding a certain point. The results of the visualization, as with any computer process, are only as good as the underlying model.

6.5 Modelling Algorithms

Modelling algorithms are the catch-all category for our taxonomy of visualization techniques. Modelling algorithms have one thing in common: They create or change dataset geometry or topology.

Source Objects

As we have seen in previous examples, source objects begin the visualization pipeline. Source objects are used to create geometry such as spheres, cones, or cubes to support visualization context or are used to read in data files. Source objects also may be used to create dataset attributes. Some examples of source objects and their use are as follows.

Modelling Simple Geometry. Spheres, cones, cubes, and other simple geometric objects can be used alone or in combination to model geometry. Often we visualize real-world applications such as air flow in a room and need to show real-world objects such as furniture, windows, or doors. Real-world objects often can be represented using these simple geometric representations. These source objects generate their data procedurally. Alternatively, we may use reader objects to access geometric data defined in data files. These data files may contain more complex geometry such as that produced by a 3D CAD (Computer-Aided Design) system.

Supporting Geometry. During the visualization process we may use source objects to create supporting geometry. This may be as simple as three lines to represent a coordinate axis or as complex as tubes wrapped around line segments to thicken and enhance their appearance. Another common use is as supplemental input to objects such as streamlines or probe filters. These filters take a second input that defines a set of points. For streamlines, the points determine the initial positions for generating the streamlines. The probe filter uses the points as the position to compute attribute values such as scalars, vectors, or tensors.

Data Attribute Creation. Source objects can be used as procedures to create data attributes. For example, we can procedurally create textures and texture coordinates. Another use is to create scalar values over a uniform grid. If the scalar values are generated from a mathematical function, then we can use the visualization techniques described here to visualize the function. In fact, this leads us to a very important class of source objects: implicit functions.

Implicit Functions

Implicit functions are functions of the form

$$F(x, y, z) = c \qquad \text{(6-11)}$$

where c is an arbitrary constant. Implicit functions have three important properties.

- *Simple geometric description.* Implicit functions are convenient tools to describe common geometric shapes. This includes planes, spheres, cylinders, cones, ellipsoids, and quadrics.

- *Region separation.* Implicit functions separate 3D Euclidean space into three distinct regions. These regions are inside, on, and outside the implicit function. These regions are defined as $F(x, y, z) < 0$, $F(x, y, z) = 0$, and $F(x, y, z) > 0$, respectively.

- *Scalar generation.* Implicit functions convert a position in space into a scalar value. That is, given an implicit function we can sample it at a point (x_i, y_i, z_i) to generate a scalar value c_i.

An example of an implicit function is the equation for a sphere of radius R

$$F(x, y, z) = x^2 + y^2 + z^2 - R^2 \qquad \text{(6-12)}$$

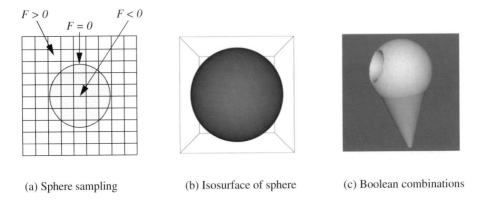

(a) Sphere sampling   (b) Isosurface of sphere   (c) Boolean combinations

Figure 6–23 Sampling functions: (a) 2D depiction of sphere sampling; (b) Isosurface of sampled sphere; (c) Boolean combination of two spheres, a cone, and two planes. (One sphere intersects the other, the planes clip the cone.) (Refer to `sphere.tcl` and `iceCream.tcl`.)

This simple relationship defines the three regions $F(x, y, z) = 0$ (on the surface of the sphere), $F(x, y, z) < 0$ (inside the sphere), and $F(x, y, z) > 0$ (outside the sphere). Any point may be classified inside, on, or outside the sphere simply by evaluating **Equation 6-12**.

Implicit functions have a variety of uses. This includes geometric modelling, selecting data, and visualizing complex mathematical descriptions.

Modelling Objects. Implicit functions can be used alone or in combination to model geometric objects. For example, to model a surface described by an implicit function, we sample F on a dataset and generate an isosurface at a contour value c_i. The result is a polygonal representation of the function. **Figure 6–23**(b) shows an isosurface for a sphere of radius=1 sampled on a volume. Note that we can choose nonzero contour values to generate a family of offset surfaces. This is useful for creating blending functions and other special effects.

Implicit functions can be combined to create complex objects using the boolean operators union, intersection, and difference. The union operation $F \cup G$ between two functions $F(x, y, z)$ and $G(x, y, z)$ at a point (x_0, y_0, z_0) is the minimum value

$$F \cup G = \min(F(x_0, y_0, z_0), G(x_0, y_0, z_0)) \qquad \text{(6-13)}$$

The intersection between two implicit functions is given by

$$F \cap G = \max(F(x_0, y_0, z_0), G(x_0, y_0, z_0)) \qquad \text{(6-14)}$$

The difference of two implicit functions is given by

$$F - G = \max(F(x_0, y_0, z_0), -G(x_0, y_0, z_0)) \qquad \text{(6-15)}$$

Figure 6–23(c) shows a combination of simple implicit functions to create an ice-cream cone. The cone is created by clipping the (infinite) cone function with two planes. The ice

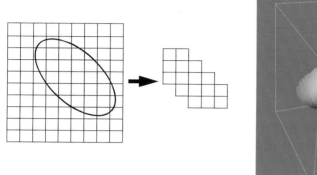

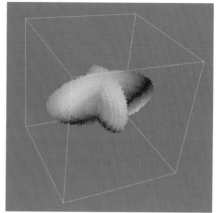

(a) Selecting data with implicit function   (b) Selecting data with boolean combination

Figure 6–24 Implicit functions used to select data: (a) 2D cells lying in ellipse are selected; (b) Two ellipsoids combined using the union operation used to select voxels from a volume. Voxels shrunk 50 percent (`extractD.tcl`).

cream is constructed by performing a difference operation on a larger sphere with a smaller offset sphere to create the "bite." The resulting surface was extracted using surface contouring with isosurface value 0.0.

Selecting Data. We can take advantage of the properties of implicit functions to select and cut data. In particular we will use the region separation property to select data. (We defer the discussion on cutting to "Cutting" on page 180.)

Selecting or extracting data with an implicit function means choosing cells and points (and associated attribute data) that lie within a particular region of the function. To determine whether a point x-y-z lies within a region, we simply evaluate the point and examine the sign of the result. A cell lies in a region if all its points lie in the region.

Figure 6–24(a) shows a 2D implicit function, here an ellipse, used to select the data (i.e., points, cells, and data attributes) contained within it. Boolean combinations also can be used to create complex selection regions as illustrated in **Figure 6–24**(b). Here, two ellipses are used in combination to select voxels within a volume dataset. Note that extracting data often changes the structure of the dataset. In **Figure 6–24** the input type is a image data dataset, while the output type is an unstructured grid dataset.

Visualizing Mathematical Descriptions. Some functions, often discrete or probabilistic in nature, cannot be cast into the form of **Equation 6-11**. However, by applying some creative thinking we can often generate scalar values that can be visualized. An interesting example of this is the so-called *strange attractor*.

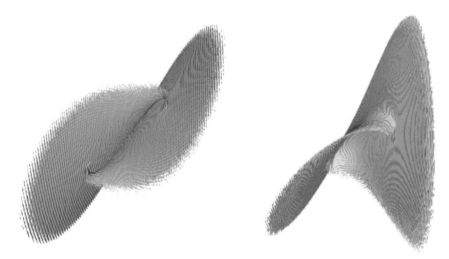

Figure 6–25 Visualizing a Lorenz strange attractor by integrating the Lorenz equations in a volume. The number of visits in each voxel is recorded as a scalar function. The surface is extracted via marching cubes using a visit value of 50. The number of integration steps is 10 million, in a volume of dimensions 200^3. The surface roughness is caused by the discrete nature of the evaluation function (`Lorenz.cxx`).

Strange attractors arise in the study of nonlinear dynamics and chaotic systems. In these systems, the usual types of dynamic motion — equilibrium, periodic motion, or quasi-periodic motion — are not present. Instead, the system exhibits chaotic motion. The resulting behavior of the system can change radically as a result of small perturbations in its initial conditions.

A classical strange attractor was developed by Lorenz in 1963 [Lorenz63]. Lorenz developed a simple model for thermally induced fluid convection in the atmosphere. Convection causes rings of rotating fluid and can be developed from the general Navier-Stokes partial differential equations for fluid flow. The Lorenz equations can be expressed in nondimensional form as

$$\frac{dx}{dt} = \sigma(y - x)$$

$$\frac{dy}{dt} = \rho x - y - xz \qquad\qquad \textbf{(6-16)}$$

$$\frac{dz}{dt} = xy - \beta z$$

where x is proportional to the fluid velocity in the fluid ring, y and z measure the fluid temperature in the plane of the ring, the parameters σ and ρ are related to the Prandtl number and Raleigh number, respectively, and β is a geometric factor.

Figure 6–26 Distance functions to a point, line, and triangle.

Certainly these equations are not in the implicit form of **Equation 6-11**, so how do we visualize them? Our solution is to treat the variables x, y, and z as the coordinates of a three-dimensional space, and integrate **Equation 6-16** to generate the system "trajectory", that is, the state of the system through time. The integration is carried out within a volume and scalars are created by counting the number of times each voxel is visited. By integrating long enough, we can create a volume representing the "surface" of the strange attractor, **Figure 6–25**. The surface of the strange attractor is extracted by using marching cubes and a scalar value specifying the number of visits in a voxel.

Implicit Modelling

In the previous section we saw how implicit functions, or boolean combinations of implicit functions, could be used to model geometric objects. The basic approach is to evaluate these functions on a regular array of points, or volume, and then to generate scalar values at each point in the volume. Then either volume rendering (see "Volume Rendering" on page 206), or isosurface generation in combination with surface rendering, is used to display the model.

An extension of this approach, called implicit modeling, is similar to modeling with implicit functions. The difference lies in the fact that scalars are generated using a distance function instead of the usual implicit function. The distance function is computed as a Euclidean distance to a set of generating primitives such as points, lines, or polygons. For example, **Figure 6–26** shows the distance functions to a point, line, and triangle. Because distance functions are well-behaved monotonic functions, we can define a series of offset surfaces by specifying different isosurface values, where the value is the distance to the generating primitive. The isosurfaces form approximations to the true offset surfaces, but using high volume resolution we can achieve satisfactory results.

Used alone the generating primitives are limited in their ability to model complex geometry. By using boolean combinations of the primitives, however, complex geometry can be easily modeled. The boolean operations union, intersection, and difference (**Equation 6-13**, **Equation 6-14**, and **Equation 6-15**, respectively) are illustrated in **Figure 6–27**. **Figure 6–28** shows the application of implicit modeling to "thicken" the line segments in the text symbol "HELLO". The isosurface is generated on a $110 \times 40 \times 20$ volume at a distance offset of 0.25 units. The generating primitives were combined using the boolean union operator. Although Euclidean distance is always a nonnegative value, it is possible to use a signed distance function for objects that have an outside and an inside. A negative distance is the

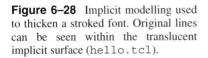

Original   Union   Intersection   Difference

Figure 6–27 Boolean operations using points and lines as generating primitives.

Figure 6–28 Implicit modelling used to thicken a stroked font. Original lines can be seen within the translucent implicit surface (`hello.tcl`).

negated distance of a point inside the object to the surface of the object. Using a signed distance function allows us to create offset surfaces that are contained within the actual surface.

Another interesting feature of implicit modeling is that when isosurfaces are generated, more than one connected surface can result. These situations occur when the generating primitives form concave features. **Figure 6–29** illustrates this situation. If desired, multiple surfaces can be separated by using the connectivity algorithm described in "Connectivity" on page 356.

Glyphs

Glyphs, sometimes referred to as icons, are a versatile technique to visualize data of every type. A glyph is an "object" that is affected by its input data. This object may be geometry, a dataset, or a graphical image. The glyph may orient, scale, translate, deform, or somehow alter the appearance of the object in response to data. We have already seen a simple form of glyph: hedgehogs are lines that are oriented, translated and scaled according to the position and vector value of a point. A variation of this is to use oriented cones or arrows. (See "Hedgehogs and Oriented Glyphs" on page 161.)

More elaborate glyphs are possible. In one creative visualization technique Chernoff [Chernoff73] tied data values to an iconic representation of the human face. Eyebrows, nose, mouth, and other features were modified according to financial data values. This interesting technique built on the human capability to recognize facial expression. By tying appropriate data values to facial characteristics, rapid identification of important data points is possible.

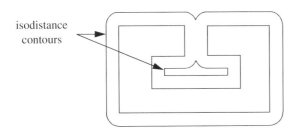

isodistance
contours

Figure 6–29 Concave features can result in multiple contour lines/surfaces.

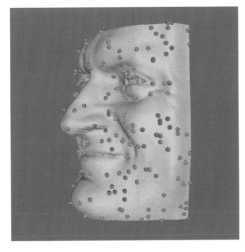

Figure 6–30 Glyphs indicate surface normals on model of human face. Glyph positions are randomly selected (`spikeF.tcl`).

In a sense, glyphs represent the fundamental result of the visualization process. Moreover, all the visualization techniques we present can be treated as concrete representations of an abstract glyph class. For example, while hedgehogs are an obvious manifestation of a vector glyph, isosurfaces can be considered a topologically two-dimensional glyph for scalar data. Delmarcelle and Hesselink [Delmarcelle95] have developed a unified framework for flow visualization based on types of glyphs. They classify glyphs according to one of three categories.

- *Elementary icons* represent their data across the extent of their spatial domain. For example, an oriented arrow can be used to represent surface normal.

- *Local icons* represent elementary information plus a local distribution of the values around the spatial domain. A surface normal vector colored by local curvature is one example of a local icon, since local data beyond the elementary information is encoded.

- *Global icons* show the structure of the complete dataset. An isosurface is an example of a global icon.

This classification scheme can be extended to other visualization techniques such as vector and tensor data, or even to nonvisual forms such as sound or tactile feedback. We have found this classification scheme to be helpful when designing visualizations or creating visualization techniques. Often it gives insight into ways of representing data that can be overlooked.

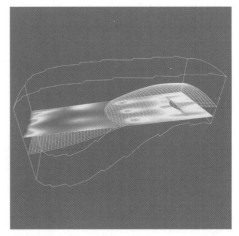

Figure 6–31 Cut through structured grid with plane. The cut plane is shown solid shaded. A computational plane of constant k value is shown in wireframe for comparison (cut.tcl). The colors correspond to flow density. Cutting surfaces are not necessarily planes: implicit functions such as spheres, cylinders, and quadrics can also be used.

Figure 6–30 is an example of glyphing. Small 3D cones are oriented on a surface to indicate the direction of the surface normal. A similar approach could be used to show other surface properties such as curvature or anatomical key-points.

Cutting

Often we want to cut through a dataset with a surface and then display the interpolated data values on the surface. We refer to this technique as *data cutting* or simply *cutting*. The data cutting operation requires two pieces of information: a definition for the surface and a dataset to cut. We will assume that the cutting surface is defined by an implicit function. A typical application of cutting is to slice through a dataset with a plane, and color map the scalar data and/or warp the plane according to vector value.

A property of implicit functions is to convert a position into a scalar value (see "Implicit Functions" on page 173). We can use this property in combination with a contouring algorithm (e.g., marching cubes) to generate cut surfaces. The basic idea is to generate scalars for each point of each cell of a dataset (using the implicit cut function), and then contour the surface value $F(x, y, z) = 0$.

The cutting algorithm proceeds as follows. For each cell, function values are generated by evaluating $F(x, y, z)$ for each cell point. If all the points evaluate positive or negative, then the surface does not cut the cell. However, if the points evaluate positive and negative, then the surface passes through the cell. We can use the cell contouring operation to generate the isosurface $F(x, y, z) = 0$. Data attribute values can then be computed by interpolating along cut edges.

Figure 6–31 illustrates a plane cut through a structured grid dataset. The plane passes through the center of the dataset with normal (–0.287, 0, 0.9579). For comparison purposes a portion of the grid geometry is also shown. The grid geometry is the grid surface $k=9$ (shown in wireframe). A benefit of cut surfaces is that we can view data on (nearly) arbitrary surfaces. Thus, the structure of the dataset does not constrain how we view the data.

We can easily make multiple planar cuts through a structured grid dataset by specifying multiple isovalues for the cutting algorithm. **Figure 6–32** shows 100 cut planes generated perpendicular to the camera's view plane normal. Rendering the planes from back to front

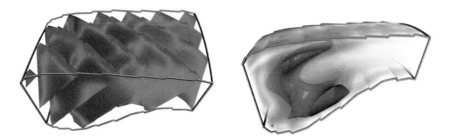

Figure 6–32 100 cut planes with opacity of 0.05. Rendered back-to-front to simulate volume rendering (PseudoVolumeRendering.tcl).

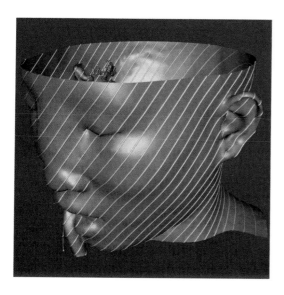

Figure 6–33 Cutting a surface model of the skin with a series of planes produces contour lines (cutModel.tcl). Lines are wrapped with tubes for visual clarity.

with an opacity of 0.05 produces a simulation of volume rendering. (See "Volume Rendering" on page 206.)

This example illustrates that cutting the volumetric data in a structured grid dataset produced polygonal cells. Similarly, cutting polygonal data produces lines. Using a single plane equation, we can extract "contour lines" from a surface model defined with polygons. **Figure 6–33** shows contours extracted from a surface model of the skin. At each vertex in the surface model we evaluate the equation of the plane $F(x, y, z) = c$ and store the value of the function as a scalar value. Cutting the data with 46 isovalues from 1.5 to 136.5 produces contour lines that are 3 units apart.

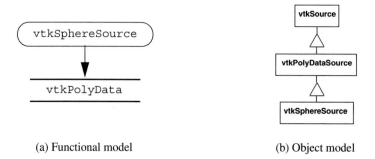

(a) Functional model   (b) Object model

Figure 6–34 Source object design. Example shown is a source object that creates a polygonal representation of a sphere.

6.6 Putting It All Together

Process Object Design

Algorithms are implemented in the *Visualization Toolkit* as process objects. These objects may be either sources, filters, or mappers (See "The Visualization Pipeline" on page 85.) In this section we will describe how these objects are implemented.

Source Design. Source objects have no visualization data for input and one or more outputs, **Figure 6–34**. To create a source object, inheritance is used to specify the type of dataset that the process object creates for output. **Figure 6–34** illustrates this for the concrete source object vtkSphereSource. This class inherits from vtkSource, indicating that it is a source object, and vtkPolyData, indicating that it creates polygonal data on output.

The convenience object vtkPolyDataSource has been created to simplify subclass derivation. For example, vtkBYUReader is also of type vtkPolyDataSource. The major difference between vtkSphereSource and vtkBYUReader is the implementation of the virtual method Execute(). This method actually creates its output data. If you derive a source object you do not need to make it a subclass of any convenience object (e.g., vtkPolyDataSource) but you should derive it from vtkSource. This is especially true when multiple-output objects are created, since no convenience classes exist expressly for derivation in this case.

Filter Design. Filter objects have one or more inputs and one or more outputs as shown in **Figure 6–35**. (You may also refer to "Multiple Input / Output" on page 99.) To create a filter object, inheritance is used to specify the type of input and output data objects. **Figure 6–35** illustrates this for the concrete source object vtkContourFilter (which implements marching cubes and other contouring techniques). It is worth examining this object diagram in detail since it is the basis for the architecture of the visualization pipeline.

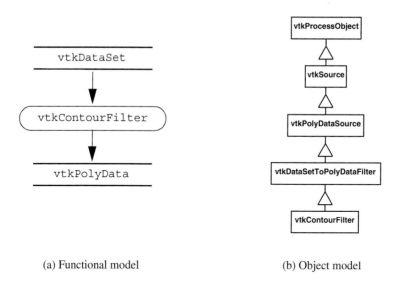

(a) Functional model   (b) Object model

Figure 6–35 Filter object design. The example shown is for an object that receives a general dataset as input and creates polygonal data on output.

The superclasses of vtkContourFilter are vtkProcessObject, vtkSource, vtkPolyDataSource, and vtkDataSetToPolyDataFilter. Although the inheritance of vtkContourFilter from vtkSource may be confusing at first glance, the meaning is this: the filter is a source of visualization data. The class vtkPolyDataSource specifies the type of data vtkContourFilter produces on output (i.e., a vtkPolyData), while vtkDataSetToPolyDataFilter specifies the type of input (i.e., dataset). Note that inheritance from vtkPolyDataSource and vtkDataSetToPolyDataFilter is optional—this functionality could be implemented directly in vtkContourFilter. These optional superclasses are simply convenience objects to make class derivation a little easier.

What is left for vtkContourFilter to implement is its Execute() method (as well as constructor, print method, and any other methods special to this class). Thus the primary difference between classes with equivalent inheritance hierarchies is the implementation of the Execute() method.

As we mentioned a moment ago, the class vtkDataSetToPolyDataFilter enforces filter input and output type with the type checking features of the C++ compiler. It accepts input type vtkDataSet (or subclasses) and produces vtkPolyData on output. Since vtkDataSet is a base class for all data types, this filter will accept any type as input. Specialized filters are derived from other classes. For example, filters that accept polygonal data might be derived from vtkPolyDataToPolyDataFilter, and filters that accept unstructured grid datasets might be derived from vtkUnstructuredGridToPolyDataFilter.

We encourage you to examine the source code carefully for a few filter and source objects. The architecture is simple enough that you can grasp it quickly.

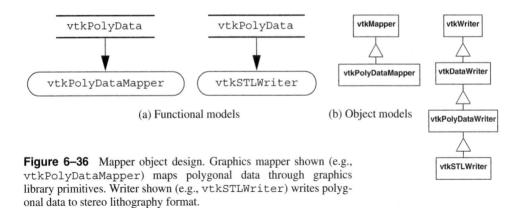

(a) Functional models   (b) Object models

Figure 6–36 Mapper object design. Graphics mapper shown (e.g., vtkPolyDataMapper) maps polygonal data through graphics library primitives. Writer shown (e.g., vtkSTLWriter) writes polygonal data to stereo lithography format.

Mapper Design. Mapper objects have one or more inputs and no visualization data output, **Figure 6–36**. Two different types of mappers are available in the *Visualization Toolkit*: graphics mappers and writers. Graphics mappers interface geometric structure and data attributes to the graphics library; writers write datasets to disk or other I/O devices.

Since mappers take datasets as input, type enforcement is required. Each mapper implements this functionality directly. For example, both classes vtkPolyDataMapper and vtkSTLWriter implement a SetInput() method to enforce the input to be of type vtkPolyData. Other mappers and writers enforce input type as appropriate.

Although writers and mappers do not create visualization data, they both have methods similar to the Execute() method of the sources and filters. Each subclass of vtkMapper must implement the Render() method. This method is exchanged by the graphics system actors and its associated mappers during the rendering process. The effect of the method is to map its input dataset to the appropriate rendering library/system. Subclasses of the class vtkWriter must implement the WriteData() method. This method causes the writer to write its input dataset to disk (or other I/O device).

Color Maps

Color maps are created in the *Visualization Toolkit* using instances of the class vtkLookupTable. This class allows you to create a lookup table using HSVA (e.g., hue, saturation, value, and alpha opacity value) specification. Although we discussed the HSV color system in Chapter 3, we haven't yet defined alpha opacity. We shall do so in Chapter 7, but until then consider the alpha value to be the opacity of an object. Alpha values of one indicate that the object is opaque, while alpha values of zero indicate that the object is transparent.

The procedure for generating lookup table entries is to define pairs of values for HSVA. These pairs define a linear ramp for hue, saturation, value, and opacity. When the Build() method is invoked, these linear ramps are used to generate a table with the number of table entries requested. Alternatively, vtkLookupTable also enables you to load colors directly into the table. Thus, you build custom tables that cannot be simply expressed as linear ramps of HSVA values.

To demonstrate this procedure, we specify a starting and ending value for each of the components of HSVA, then we will create a rainbow lookup table from blue to red by using the following C++ code.

```
vtkLookupTable *lut=vtkLookupTable::New();
    lut->SetHueRange(0.6667, 0.0);
    lut->SetSaturationRange(1.0, 1.0);
    lut->SetValueRange(1.0, 1.0);
    lut->SetAlphaRange(1.0, 1.0);
    lut->SetNumberOfColors(256);
    lut->Build();
```

Since the default values for SaturationRange, ValueRange, AlphaRange, and the number of lookup table colors are (1,1), (1,1), (1,1), and 256, respectively, we can simplify this process to the following

```
vtkLookupTable *lut=vtkLookupTable::New();
    lut->SetHueRange(0.6667, 0.0);
    lut->Build();
```

(The default values for HueRange are (0.0, 0.6667) — a red to blue color table.)
       To build a black and white lookup table of 256 entries we use

```
vtkLookupTable *lut=vtkLookupTable::New();
    lut->SetHueRange(0.0, 0.0);
    lut->SetSaturationRange(0.0, 0.0);
    lut->SetValueRange(0.0, 1.0)
```

In some cases you may want to specify colors directly. You can do this by specifying the number of colors, building the table, and then inserting new colors. When you insert colors, the RGBA color description system is used. For example, to create a lookup table of the three colors red, green, and blue, use the following C++ code.

```
vtkLookupTable *lut=vtkLookupTable::New();
    lut->SetNumberOfColors(3);
    lut->Build();
    lut->SetTableValue(0, 1.0, 0.0, 0.0, 1.0);
    lut->SetTableValue(0, 0.0, 1.0, 0.0, 1.0);
    lut->SetTableValue(0, 0.0, 0.0, 1.0, 1.0);
```

Lookup tables in the *Visualization Toolkit* are associated with the graphics mappers. Mappers will automatically create a red to blue lookup table if no table is specified, but if you want to create your own, use the mapper->SetLookupTable(lut) operation where mapper is an instance of vtkMapper or its subclasses.
       A few final notes on using lookup tables.

- Mappers use their lookup table to map scalar values to colors. If no scalars are present, the mappers and their lookup tables do not control the color of the object. Instead the

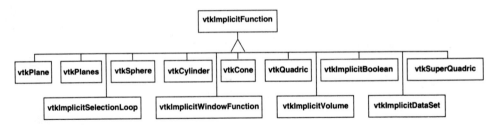

Figure 6–37 Inheritance hierarchy of `vtkImplicitFunction` and subclasses.

vtkProperty object associated with the vtkActor class does. Use vtkProperty's method actor->GetProperty()->SetColor(r,g,b) where r, g, and b are floating-point values specifying color.

- If you want to prevent scalars from coloring your object, use vtkMapper's method mapper->ScalarVisibilityOff() to turn off color mapping. Then the actor's color will control the color of the object.

- The scalar range (i.e., the range into which the colors are mapped) is specified with the mapper. Use the method mapper->SetScalarRange(min, max).

You can also derive your own lookup table types. Look at vtkLogLookupTable for an example. This particular lookup table inherits from vtkLookupTable. It performs logarithmic mapping of scalar value to table entry, a useful capability when scalar values span many orders of magnitude.

Implicit Functions

As we have seen, implicit functions can be used for visualizing functions, creating geometry, and cutting or selecting datasets. VTK includes several implicit functions including a single plane (vtkPlane), multiple convex planes (vtkPlanes), spheres (vtkSphere), cones (vtkCone), cylinders (vtkCylinder), and the general quadric (vtkQuadric). The class vtkImplicitBoolean allows you to create boolean combinations of these implicit function primitives. Other implicit functions can be added to VTK by deriving from the abstract base class vtkImplicitFunction.

The existing inheritance hierarchy for implicit functions is shown in **Figure 6–37**. Subclasses of vtkImplicitFunction must implement the two methods Evaluate() and Gradient(). The method Evaluate() returns the value of the function at point (x,y,z), while the method Gradient() returns the gradient vector to the function at point (x,y,z).

Contouring

Scalar contouring is implemented in the *Visualization Toolkit* with vtkContourFilter. This filter object accepts as input any dataset type. Thus, vtkContourFilter treats every cell type and each cell type must provide a method for contouring itself.

Contouring in VTK is implemented using variations of the marching cubes algorithm presented earlier. That is, a contour case table is associated with each cell type, so each cell

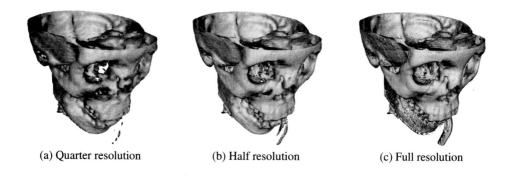

| (a) Quarter resolution | (b) Half resolution | (c) Full resolution |

Resolution	Specific (w/ normals)	General (no normals)	Factor	General (w/ normals)	Factor
64 x 64 x 93	1.000	2.889	2.889	7.131	7.131
128 x 128 x 93	5.058	11.810	2.330	23.260	4.600
256 x 256 x 93	37.169	51.620	1.390	87.230	2.350

Figure 6–38 The cost of generality. Isosurface generation of three volumes of different sizes are compared. The results show normalized execution times for two different implementations of the marching-cubes isosurface algorithm. The specialized filter is vtkMarchingCubes. The general algorithms are first vtkContourFilter and then in combination with vtkPolyDataNormals.

will generate contouring primitives as appropriate. For example, the tetrahedron cell type implements "marching tetrahedron" and creates triangle primitives, while the triangle cell type implements "marching triangles" and generates lines segments.

The implication of this arrangement is that vtkContourFilter will generate point, line, and surface contouring primitives depending on the combination of input cell types. Thus vtkContourFilter is completely general. We have created another contour filter, vtkMarchingCubes, that is specific to the dataset type image data (in particular, 3D volumes). These two filters allow us to compare (at least for this one algorithm) the cost of generality.

Recall from "Generality Versus Efficiency" on page 151 the issues regarding the trade-offs between general and specific algorithms. **Figure 6–38** shows a comparison of CPU times for a volume dataset at $64 \times 64 \times 93$, $128 \times 128 \times 93$, and $256 \times 256 \times 93$ resolution. The volume is a CT dataset of a human head. Three cases were run. In the first case the vtkMarchingCubes object was used. The output of this filter is triangles plus point normals. In the second case vtkContourFilter was run. The output of this filter is just triangles. In the last case vtkContourFilter was combined with vtkPolyDataNormals (to generate point normals). The output of the combined filters is also triangles plus point normals.

The execution times are normalized to the smallest dataset using the vtkMarchingCubes object. The results are clear: The specific object outperforms the general object by a factor of 1.4 to 7, depending on data size and whether normals are computed. The larger differences occur on the smaller datasets. This is because the ratio of voxel cells containing the isosurface to the total number of voxels is larger for smaller datasets. (Generally the total number of voxels increases as the resolution cubed, while the voxels containing the isosurface increase as the resolution squared.) As a result, more voxels are processed in the smaller datasets relative to the total number of voxels than in the larger datasets. When the datasets become larger, more voxels are "empty" and are not processed.

Although these results do not represent all implementations or the behavior of other algorithms, they do point to the cost of generality. Of course, there is a cost to specialization as well. This cost is typically in programmer time, since the programmer must rewrite code to adapt to new circumstances and data. Like all trade-offs, resolution of this issue requires knowledge of the application.

An example use of vtkContourFilter is shown in **Figure 6–39**. This example is taken from **Figure 4–1**, which is a visualization of a quadric function. The class vtkSampleFunction samples the implicit quadric function using the vtkQuadric class. Although vtkQuadric does not participate in the pipeline in terms of data flow, it is used to define and evaluate the quadric function. It is possible to generate one or more isolines/isosurfaces simultaneously using vtkContourFilter. As **Figure 6–39** shows, we use the GenerateValues() method to specify a scalar range, and the number of contours within this range (including the initial and final scalar values). vtkContourFilter generates duplicate vertices, so we can use vtkCleanPolyData to remove them. To improve the rendered appearance of the isosurface, we use vtkPolyDataNormals to create surface normals. (We describe normal generation in Chapter 9.)

Cutting

vtkCutter performs cutting of all VTK cell types. The SetValue() and GenerateValues() methods permit the user to specify which multiple scalar values to use for the cutting. vtkCutter requires an implicit function that will be evaluated at each point in the dataset. Then each cell is cut using the cell's Contour method. Any point attributes are interpolated to the resulting cut vertices. The sorting order for the generated polygonal data can be controlled with the SortBy method. The default sorting order, SortByValue(), processes cells in the inner loop for each contour value. SortByCell() processes the cutting value in the inner loop and produces polygonal data that is suitable for back-to-front rendering (see **Figure 6–32**). (The sorting order is useful when rendering with opacity as discussed in Chapter 7.) Notice the similarity of this filter to the vtkContourFilter. Both of these objects contour datasets with multiple isovalues. vtkCutter uses an implicit function to calculate scalar values while vtkContourFilter uses the scalar data associated with the dataset's point data.

Glyphs

The vtkGlyph3D class provides a simple, yet powerful glyph capability in the *Visualization Toolkit*. vtkGlyph3D is an example of an object that takes multiple inputs (**Figure 6–40**). One input, specified with the SetInput() method, defines a set of points and possible attribute data

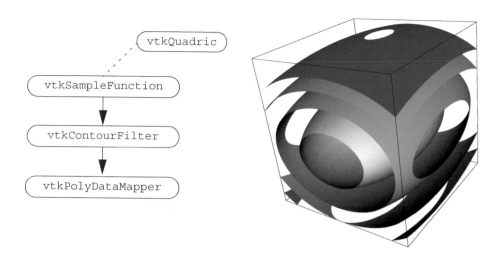

```
// Define implicit function
vtkQuadric *quadric = vtkQuadric::New();
  quadric->SetCoefficients(.5,1,.2,0,.1,0,0,.2,0,0);
vtkSampleFunction *sample = vtkSampleFunction::New();
  sample->SetSampleDimensions(50,50,50);
  sample->SetImplicitFunction(quadric);
vtkContourFilter *contour = vtkContourFilter::New();
  contour->SetInput(sample->GetOutput());
  contour->GenerateValues(5,0,1.2);
vtkPolyDataMapper *contourMapper = vtkPolyDataMapper::New();
  contourMapper->SetInput(contour->GetOutput());
  contourMapper->SetScalarRange(0,1.2);
vtkActor *contourActor = vtkActor::New();
  contourActor->SetMapper(contourMapper);

// Create outline
vtkOutlineFilter *outline = vtkOutlineFilter::New();
  outline->SetInput(sample->GetOutput());
vtkPolyDataMapper *outlineMapper = vtkPolyDataMapper::New();
  outlineMapper->SetInput(outline->GetOutput());
vtkActor *outlineActor = vtkActor::New();
  outlineActor->SetMapper(outlineMapper);
  outlineActor->GetProperty()->SetColor(0,0,0);
```

Figure 6–39 Contouring quadric function. Pipeline topology, C++ code, and resulting image are shown (contQuad.cxx).

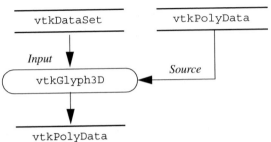

Figure 6–40 Data flow into and out of the `vtkGlyph3D` class.

at those points. The second input, specified with the SetSource() method, defines a geometry to be copied to every point in the input dataset. The source is of type vtkPolyData. Hence, any filter, sequence of filters creating polygonal data, or a polygonal dataset may be used to describe the glyph's geometry.

The behavior of an instance of vtkGlyph3D depends on the nature of the input data and the value of its instance variables. Generally, the input Source geometry will be copied to each point of the Input dataset. The geometry will be aligned along the input vector data and scaled according to the magnitude of the vector or the scalar value. In some cases, the point normal is used rather than the vector. Also, scaling can be turned on or off.

We saw how to use vtkGlyph3D in the example given in **Figure 4–14**. Cones were used as the glyph and were located at each point on the sphere, oriented along the sphere's surface normal.

Streamlines

Streamlines and particle motion require numerical integration to guide a point through the vector field. Vector visualization algorithms that we will see in later chapters also require numerical integration. As a result, we designed an object hierarchy that isolates the numerical integration process into a single base class. The base class is vtkStreamer and it is responsible for generating a particle path through a vector field of specified length (expressed as elapsed time). Each derived class of vtkStreamer takes advantage of this capability to move through the vector field but implements its own particular representational technique to depict particle motion. Streamlines (vtkStreamLine) draw connected lines while particle motion is shown by combining the output of vtkStreamPoints with the vtkGlyph3D object. Using vtkGlyph3D we can place spheres or oriented objects such as cones or arrows at points on the particle path created by vtkStreamPoints. The inheritance hierarchy for vtkStreamer and subclasses is shown in **Figure 6–41**.

The integration method in vtkStreamer is implemented as a virtual function. Thus it can be overloaded as necessary. Possible reasons for overloading include implementing an integration technique of higher or lower accuracy, or creating a technique specialized to a particular dataset type. For example, the search process in a volume is much faster than it is for other dataset types, therefore, highly efficient vector integration techniques can be constructed.

The vector integration technique in VTK will accommodate any cell type. Thus, integration through cells of any topological dimension is possible. If the cells are of topological

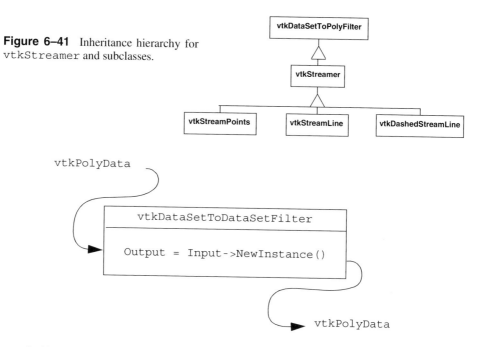

Figure 6–41 Inheritance hierarchy for
vtkStreamer and subclasses.

Figure 6–42 Depiction of data flow for abstract filter output. The output object type is the same as the input type.

dimension 2 or less, the integration process constrains particle motion to the surface (2D) or line (1D). The particle may only leave a cell by passing through the cell boundary, and traveling to a neighboring cell, or exiting the dataset.

Abstract Filters

Attribute transformations create or modify data attributes without changing the topology or geometry of a dataset. Hence filters that implement attribute transformation (e.g., vtkElevationFilter) can accept any dataset type as input, and may generate any dataset type on output. Unfortunately, because filters must specialize the particular type of data they output, at first glance it appears that filters that create general dataset types on output are not feasible. This is because the type vtkDataSet is an abstract type and must be specialized to allow instantiation.

Fortunately, there is a a solution to this dilemma. The solution is to use the "virtual constructor" NewInstance(). Although C++ does not allow virtual constructors, we can simulate it by creating a special virtual function that constructs a copy of the object that it is invoked on. For example, if this function is applied to a dataset instance of type vtkPolyData, the result will be a copy of that instance (**Figure 6–42**). (Note that we use reference counting to make copies and avoid duplicating memory.) The virtual constructor function NewInstance() is implemented in a number of VTK classes including datasets and cells.

Using the virtual constructor we can construct filters that output abstract data types like vtkDataSet. We simply apply NewInstance() to the input of the filter. This will then return a pointer to a concrete object that is the output of the filter. The result is a general filter object that can accept any dataset type for input and creates the general vtkDataSet type as output. In VTK, this functionality has been implemented in the abstract class vtkDataSetToDataSetFilter.

There are other filters that implement variations of this delegation technique. The class vtkPointSetToPointSetFilter is similar to vtkDataSetToDataSetFilter. This class takes as input any dataset whose geometry is explicitly defined via an instance of vtkPoints (or subclass), and generates on output an object of the same type (i.e., vtkPointSet). The class vtkMergeFilter combines dataset structure and point attributes from one or more input datasets. For example, you can read multiple files and combine the geometry/topology from one file with different scalars, vectors, and normals from other files.

One difficulty using abstract filter types is that the output type may not match with the input type of a downstream filter. For example, the output of vtkElevationFilter is specified as vtkDataSet even though the input may be of type vtkPolyData, and we know from the previous discussion that the actual output type will be vtkPolyData. This difficulty is removed by using the filter vtkCastToConcrete, which allows you to run-time cast to the appropriate output type. In this case we would use the GetPolyDataOutput() from vtkCastToConcrete. After checking the validity of the cast, this method returns a dataset cast to vtkPolyData. Of course, this process requires that the input to vtkCastToConcrete be set before the output is requested.

Visualizing Blood Flow

In this example we'll combine a few different techniques to visualize blood flow in the human carotid arteries. Our data contains both vectors that represent the velocity of blood and scalars that are proportional to the magnitude of the velocity (i.e., speed).

We can provide context for the visualization by creating an isosurface of speed. This isosurface shows regions of fastest blood flow, and is similar to, but not the same as, the actual surface of the arteries. However, it provides us with a visual cue to the structure of the arteries.

The first vector visualization technique we'll use is to generate vector glyphs (**Figure 6–43**). Unfortunately, we cannot just create glyphs at each point because of the number of points (over 167,000 points). To do so would result in a confusing mess, and the interactive speed would be poor. Instead, we'll use two filters to select a subset of the available points. These filters are vtkThresholdPoints and vtkMaskPoints.

vtkThresholdPoints allows us to extract points that satisfy a certain threshold criterion. In our example, we choose points whose speed is greater than a specified value. This eliminates a large number of points, since most points lie outside the arteries and have a small speed value.

The filter vtkMaskPoints allows us to select a subset of the available points. We specify the subset with the OnRatio instance variable. This instance variable indicates that every OnRatio point is to be selected. Thus, if the OnRatio is equal to one, all points will be selected, and if the OnRatio is equal to ten, every tenth point will be selected. This selection

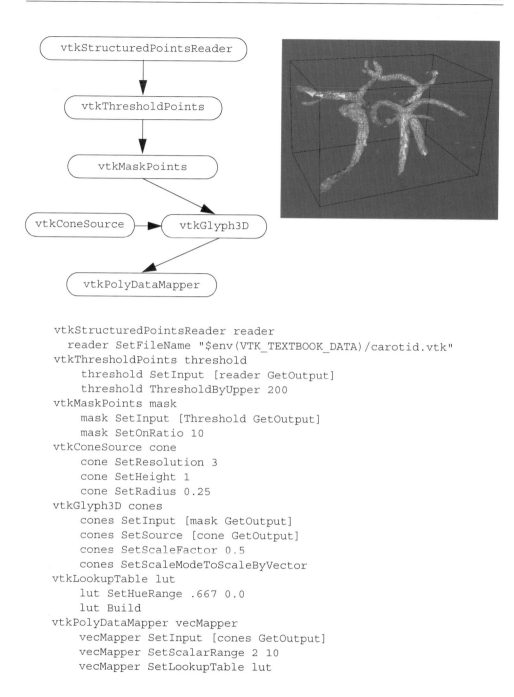

```
vtkStructuredPointsReader reader
    reader SetFileName "$env(VTK_TEXTBOOK_DATA)/carotid.vtk"
vtkThresholdPoints threshold
    threshold SetInput [reader GetOutput]
    threshold ThresholdByUpper 200
vtkMaskPoints mask
    mask SetInput [Threshold GetOutput]
    mask SetOnRatio 10
vtkConeSource cone
    cone SetResolution 3
    cone SetHeight 1
    cone SetRadius 0.25
vtkGlyph3D cones
    cones SetInput [mask GetOutput]
    cones SetSource [cone GetOutput]
    cones SetScaleFactor 0.5
    cones SetScaleModeToScaleByVector
vtkLookupTable lut
    lut SetHueRange .667 0.0
    lut Build
vtkPolyDataMapper vecMapper
    vecMapper SetInput [cones GetOutput]
    vecMapper SetScalarRange 2 10
    vecMapper SetLookupTable lut
```

Figure 6–43 Visualizing blood flow in human carotid arteries. Cone glyphs indicate flow direction and magnitude. The code fragment shown is from the Tcl script `thrshldV.tcl` and shows creation of vector glyphs.

can be either uniform or random. Random point selection is set using the RandomModeOn()
and RandomModeOff() methods.

After selecting a subset of the original points, we can use the vtkGlyph3D filter in the
usual way. A cone's orientation indicates blood flow direction, and its size and color correspond to the velocity magnitude. **Figure 6–43** shows the pipeline, sample code, and a resulting image from this visualization. Note that we've implemented the example using the
interpreted language Tcl. See Chapter 11 if you want more information about Tcl.

In the next part of this example we'll generate streamtubes of blood velocity. Again we
use an isosurface of speed to provide us with context. The starting positions for the streamtubes were determined by experimenting with the data. Because of the way the data was measured and the resolution of the velocity field, many streamers travel outside the artery. This is
because the boundary layer of the blood flow is not captured due to limitations in data resolution. Consequently, as the blood flows around curves, there is a component of the velocity
field that directs the streamtube outside the artery. As a result it is hard to find starting positions for the streamtubes that yield interesting results. We use the source object
vtkPointSource in combination with vtkThresholdPoints to work around this problem.
vtkPointSource generates random points centered around a sphere of a specified radius. We
need only find an approximate position for the starting points of the streamtubes and then
generate a cloud of random seed points. vtkThresholdPoints is used to cull points that may be
generated outside the regions of high flow velocity.

Figure 6–44 shows the pipeline, sample Tcl code, and a resulting image from the visualization. Notice that the isosurface is shown in wireframe. This provides context, yet allows
us to see the streamtubes within the isosurface.

6.7 Chapter Summary

Visualization algorithms transform data from one form to another. These transformations can
change or create new structure and/or attributes of a dataset. Structural transformations
change either the topology or geometry of a dataset. Attribute transformations change dataset
attributes such as scalars, vectors, normals, or texture coordinates.

Algorithms are classified according to the type of data they operate on. Scalar, vector,
and tensor algorithms operate on scalar, vector, and tensor data, respectively. Modelling
algorithms operate on dataset geometry or topology, texture coordinates, or normals. Modelling algorithms also may include complex techniques that may represent combinations of different data types.

Algorithms can be designed and implemented for general types of data or specialized
for a specific type. General algorithms are typically less efficient than their specialized counterparts. Conversely, general algorithms are more flexible and do not require rewriting as
new dataset types are introduced.

Important scalar algorithms include color mapping and contouring. Color maps are
used to map scalar values to color values. Contouring algorithms create isosurfaces or isolines to indicate areas of constant scalar value.

Glyphs such as hedgehogs are useful for visualizing vector data. These techniques are
limited by the number of glyphs that can be displayed at one time. Particle traces or stream-

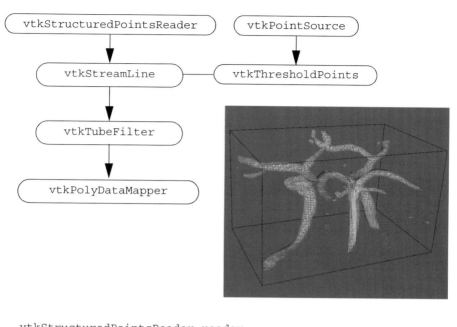

```
vtkStructuredPointsReader reader
    reader SetFileName "$env(VTK_TEXTBOOK_DATA)/carotid.vtk"
vtkPointSource source
    source SetNumberOfPoints 25
    source SetCenter 133.1 116.3 5.0
    source SetRadius 2.0
vtkThresholdPoints threshold
    threshold SetInput [reader GetOutput]
    threshold ThresholdByUpper 275
vtkStreamLine streamers
    streamers SetInput [reader GetOutput]
    streamers SetSource [source GetOutput]
    streamers SetMaximumPropagationTime 100.0
    streamers SetIntegrationStepLength 0.2
    streamers SpeedScalarsOn
    streamers SetTerminalSpeed .1
vtkTubeFilter tubes
    tubes SetInput [streamers GetOutput]
    tubes SetRadius 0.3
    tubes SetNumberOfSides 6
    tubes SetVaryRadiusToVaryRadiusOff
vtkPolyDataMapper streamerMapper
    streamerMapper SetInput [tubes GetOutput]
    streamerMapper SetScalarRange 2 10
```

Figure 6–44 Visualizing blood flow in the human carotid arteries. Streamtubes of flow vectors (streamV.tcl).

lines are another important algorithm for vector field visualization. Collections of particle traces can convey something of the structure of a vector field.

Real, symmetric 3×3 tensors can be characterized by their eigenvalues and eigenvectors. Tensors can be visualized using tensor ellipsoids or oriented axes.

Implicit functions and sampling techniques can be used to make geometry, cut data, and visualize complex mathematical descriptions. Glyphs are objects whose appearance is associated with a particular data value. Glyphs are flexible and can be created to visualize a variety of data.

6.8 Bibliographic Notes

Color mapping is a widely studied topic in imaging, computer graphics, visualization, and human factors. References [Durrett87] [Ware88] [Rheingans92] provide samples of the available literature. You also may want to learn about the physiological and psychological effects of color on perception. The text by Wyszecki and Stiles [Wyszecki82] serves as an introductory reference.

Contouring is a widely studied technique in visualization because of its importance and popularity. Early techniques were developed for 2D data [Watson92]. Three dimensional techniques were developed initially as contour connecting methods [Fuchs77] — that is, given a series of 2D contours on evenly spaced planes, connect the contours to create a closed surface. Since the introduction of marching cubes, many other techniques have been implemented. (A few of these include [Nielson91] [Montani94] and [Durst88]). A particularly interesting reference is given by Livnat et al. [Livnat96]. They show a contouring method with the addition of a preprocessing step that generates isocontours in near optimal time.

Although we barely touched the topic, the study of chaos and chaotic vibrations is a delightfully interesting topic. Besides the original paper by Lorenz [Lorenz63], the book by Moon [Moon87] is a good place to start.

Two- and three-dimensional vector plots have been used by computer analysts for many years [Fuller80]. Streamlines and streamribbons also have been applied to the visualization of complex flows [Volpe89]. Good general references on vector visualization techniques are given in [Helman90] and [Richter90].

Tensor visualization techniques are relatively few in number. Most techniques are glyph oriented [Haber90] [deLeeuw93]. We will see a few more techniques in Chapter 9.

Blinn [Blinn82], Bloomental [Bloomenthal88] [Bloomenthal97] and Wyvill [Wyvill86] have been important contributors to implicit modeling. Implicit modeling is currently popular in computer graphics for modeling "soft" or "blobby" objects. These techniques are simple, powerful, and are becoming widely used for advanced computer graphics modeling.

6.9 References

[Abraham85]
R. H. Abraham and Christopher D. Shaw. *Dynamics The Geometry of Behavior.* Aerial Press, Santa Cruz, CA, 1985.

[Blinn82]
   J. F. Blinn. "A Generalization of Algebraic Surface Drawing." *ACM Transactions on Graphics*. 1(3):235–256, July 1982.

[Bloomenthal88]
   J. Bloomenthal. "Polygonization of Implicit Surfaces." *Computer Aided Geometric Design*. 5(4):341–355, November 1982.

[Bloomenthal97]
   J. Bloomenthal, editor. *Introduction to Implicit Surfaces*. Morgan Kaufmann Publishers, Inc., San Francisco, CA., 1997.

[Chernoff73]
   H. Chernoff. "Using Faces to Represent Pints in *K*-Dimensional Space Graphically." *J. American Statistical Association*. 68:361–368, 1973.

[Cline93]
   H. Cline, W. Lorensen, and W. Schroeder. "3D Phase Contrast MRI of Cerebral Blood FLow and Surface Anatomy." *Journal of Computer Assisted Tomography*. 17(2):173–177, March/April 1993.

[Conte72]
   S. D. Conte and C. de Boor. *Elementary Numerical Analysis*. McGraw-Hill Book Company, 1972.

[deLeeuw93]
   W. C. de Leeuw and J. J. van Wijk. "A Probe for Local Flow Field Visualization." In *Proceedings of Visualization '93*. pp. 39–45, IEEE Computer Society Press, Los Alamitos, CA, 1993.

[Delmarcelle95]
   T. Delmarcelle and L. Hesselink. "A Unified Framework for Flow Visualization." In *Computer Visualization Graphics Techniques for Scientific and Engineering Analysis*. R. S. Gallagher, ed. CRC Press, Boca Raton, FL, 1995.

[Durrett87]
   H. J. Durrett, ed. *Color and the Computer*. Academic Press, Boston, MA, 1987.

[Durst88]
   M. J. Durst. "Additional Reference to Marching Cubes." *Computer Graphics*. 22(2):72–73, 1988.

[Fuchs77]
   H. Fuchs, Z. M. Kedem, and S. P. Uselton. "Optimal Surface Reconstruction from Planar Contours." *Communications of the ACM*. 20(10):693–702, 1977.

[Fuller80]
   A. J. Fuller and M.L.X. dosSantos. "Computer Generated Display of 3D Vector Fields." *Computer Aided Design*. 12(2):61–66, 1980.

[Haber90]
   R. B. Haber and D. A. McNabb. "Visualization Idioms: A Conceptual Model to Scientific Visualization Systems." *Visualization in Scientific Computing*, G. M. Nielson, B. Shriver, L. J. Rosenblum, ed. IEEE Computer Society Press, pp. 61–73, 1990.

[Helman90]
   J. Helman and L. Hesselink. "Representation and Display of Vector Field Topology in Fluid Flow Data Sets." *Visualization in Scientific Computing*. G. M. Nielson, B. Shriver, L. J. Rosenblum, eds. IEEE Computer Society Press, pp. 61–73, 1990.

[Livnat96]
Y. Livnat, H. W. Shen, C. R. Johnson. "A Near Optimal Isosurface Extraction Algorithm for Structured and Unstructured Grids." *IEEE Transactions on Visualization and Computer Graphics*. Vol. 2, No. 1, March 1996.

[Lorensen87]
W. E. Lorensen and H. E. Cline. "Marching Cubes: A High Resolution 3D Surface Construction Algorithm." *Computer Graphics*. 21(3):163–169, July 1987.

[Lorenz63]
E. N. Lorenz. "Deterministic Non-Periodic Flow." *Journal of Atmospheric Science*. 20:130–141, 1963.

[Montani94]
C. Montani, R. Scateni, and R. Scopigno. "A Modified Look-Up Table for Implicit Disambiguation of Marching Cubes." *Visual Computer*. (10):353–355, 1994.

[Moon87]
F. C. Moon. *Chaotic Vibrations*. Wiley-Interscience, New York, NY, 1987.

[Nielson91]
G. M. Nielson and B. Hamann. "The Asymptotic Decider: Resolving the Ambiguity in Marching Cubes." In *Proceedings of Visualization '91*. pp. 83–91, IEEE Computer Society Press, Los Alamitos, CA, 1991.

[Rheingans92]
P. Rheingans. "Color, Change, and Control for Quantitative Data Display." In *Proceedings of Visualization '92*. pp. 252–259, IEEE Computer Society Press, Los Alamitos, CA, 1992.

[Richter90]
R. Richter, J. B. Vos, A. Bottaro, and S. Gavrilakis. "Visualization of Flow Simulations." *Scientific Visualization and Graphics Simulation*. D. Thalmann editor, pp. 161–171, John Wiley and Sons, 1990.

[Saada74]
A. S. Saada. *Elasticity Theory and Applications*. Pergamon Press, Inc., New York, NY, 1974.

[Timoshenko70]
S. P. Timoshenko and J. N. Goodier. *Theory of Elasticity, 3d Edition*. McGraw-Hill Book Company, New York, NY, 1970.

[Tufte83]
E. R. Tufte. *The Visual Display of Quantitative Information*. Graphics Press, Cheshire, CT, 1990.

[Volpe89]
G. Volpe. "Streamlines and Streamribbons in Aerodynamics." Technical Report AIAA-89-0140, 27th Aerospace Sciences Meeting, 1989.

[Ware88]
C. Ware. "Color Sequences for Univariate Maps: Theory, Experiments and Principles." *IEEE Computer Graphics and Applications*. 8(5):41–49, 1988.

[Watson92]
D. F. Watson. *Contouring: A Guide to the Analysis and Display of Spatial Data*. Pergamon Press, 1992.

[Wyszecki82]

   G. Wyszecki and W. Stiles. *Color Science: Concepts and Methods, Quantitative Data and Formulae.* John Wiley and Sons, 1982.

[Wyvill86]

   G. Wyvill, C. McPheeters, B. Wyvill. "Data Structure for Soft Objects." *Visual Computer.* 2(4):227–234, 1986.

6.10 Exercises

6.1   Sketch contour cases for marching triangles. How many cases are there?

6.2   Sketch contour cases for marching tetrahedron. How many cases are there?

6.3   A common visualization technique is to animate isosurface value. The procedure is to smoothly vary isosurface value over a specified range.
       a) Create an animation sequence for the quadric example (**Figure 4–1**).
       b) Create an animation sequence for the head sequence (**Figure 6–11**(b)).

6.4   Marching cubes visits each cell during algorithm execution. Many of these cells do not contain the isosurface. Describe a technique to improve the performance of isosurface extraction by eliminating visits to cells not containing isosurface. (*Hint:* use a preprocessing step to analyze data. Assume that many isosurfaces will be extracted and that the preprocessing step will not count against execution time.)

6.5   Scan-line rasterization proceeds along horizontal spans in graphics hardware (see "Rasterization" on page 56). Interpolation of color occurs along horizontal spans as well.
       a) Show how the orientation of a polygon affects interpolated color.
       b) Discuss potential problems caused by orientation dependent viewing of visualizations.

6.6   Write a program to simulate beam vibration. Use the code associated with **Figure 6–14**(a) as your starting point.

6.7   Using the filters vtkStreamLine, vtkMaskPoints, and vtkGlyph3D, create a visualization consisting of oriented glyphs along a streamline.

6.8   Visualize the following functions.
       a) Scalar $S(x, y, z) = \sin(xy)$, for x,y between 0 and π.
       b) The effective stress field (a scalar field) from **Figure 6–21**.
       c) The vector field described in the combustor data (i.e., combq.bin and combxyz.bin).

6.9   Tensor ellipsoids are based on an ellipsoidal glyph. Describe two other glyphs that you might use.

6.10   Write a source object to generate a polygonal representation of a torus.

6.11   Design a glyph to convey airplane heading, speed, and altitude, and proximity (i.e., distance) to other planes.

6.12 Morphing is a process to smoothly blend images (2D) or geometry (3D) between two known images or geometry. Using an implicit modeling approach, how would you morph a torus into a cube?

6.13 Describe a technique to visualize vector information by animating a color map. (*Hint:* By choosing a map carefully, you can give the illusion of motion across a surface.)

6.14 Isoline contours of different values are typically shown together in one image.
a) Describe the advantages and disadvantages of displaying isosurfaces simultaneously.
b) What two graphics properties might you adjust to improve the display of multiple isosurfaces?

6.15 Describe a parallel algorithm for marching cubes. Use a parallel architecture of your choice.

6.16 Decomposition can greatly increase the speed of an operation.
a) Prove that 3D Gaussian smoothing can be decomposed into three 1D operations.
b) Give the complexity of the decomposed filter and the same filter implemented as a 3D convolution.
c) Under what conditions can constant smoothing be decomposed into 1D operations.

Advanced Computer Graphics

Chapter 3 introduced fundamental concepts of computer graphics. A major topic in that chapter was how to represent and render geometry using surface primitives such as points, lines, and polygons. In this chapter our primary focus is on volume graphics. Compared to surface graphics, volume graphics has a greater expressive range in its ability to render inhomogeneous materials, and is a dominant technique for visualizing 3D image (volume) datasets.

We begin the chapter by describing two techniques that are important to both surface and volume graphics. These are simulating object transparency using simple blending functions, and using texture maps to add realism without excessive computational cost. We also describe various problems and challenges inherent to these techniques. We then follow with a focused discussion on volume graphics, including both object-order and image-order techniques, illumination models, approaches to mixing surface and volume graphics, and methods to improve performance. Finally, the chapter concludes with an assortment of important techniques for creating more realistic visualizations. These techniques include stereo viewing, antialiasing, and advanced camera techniques such as motion blur, focal blur, and camera motion.

7.1 Transparency and Alpha Values

Up to this point in the text we have focused on rendering opaque objects — that is, we have assumed that objects reflect, scatter, or absorb light at their surface, and no light is transmitted through to their interior. Although rendering opaque objects is certainly useful, there are many applications that can benefit from the ability to render objects that transmit light. One important application of transparency is volume rendering, which we will explore in greater detail later in the chapter. Another simple example makes objects translucent so that we can see inside of the region bounded by the surface, as shown in **Figure 12–4**. As demonstrated in this example, by making the skin semitransparent, it becomes possible to see the internal organs.

Transparency and its complement, opacity, are often referred to as *alpha* in computer graphics. For example, a polygon that is 50 percent opaque will have an alpha value of 0.5 on a scale from zero to one. An alpha value of one represents an opaque object and zero represents a completely transparent object. Frequently, alpha is specified as a property for the entire actor, but it also can be done on a vertex basis just like colors. In such cases, the RGB specification of a color is extended to RGBA where A represents the alpha component. On many graphics cards the frame buffer can store the alpha value along with the RGB values. More typically, an application will request storage for only red, green, and blue on the graphics card and use back-to-front blending to avoid the need for storing alpha.

Unfortunately, having transparent actors introduces some complications into the rendering process. If you think back to the process of ray tracing, viewing rays are projected from the camera out into the world, where they intersect the first actor they come to. With an opaque actor, the lighting equations are applied and the resulting color is drawn to the screen. With a semitransparent actor we must solve the lighting equations for this actor, and then continue projecting the ray farther to see if it intersects any other actors. The resulting color is a composite of all the actors it has intersected. For each surface intersection this can be expressed as **Equation 7-1**.

$$R = A_s R_s + (1 - A_s)R_b$$
$$G = A_s G_s + (1 - A_s)G_b$$
$$B = A_s B_s + (1 - A_s)B_b \qquad \textbf{(7-1)}$$
$$A = A_s + (1 - A_s)A_b$$

In this equation subscript s refers to the surface of the actor, while subscript b refers to what is behind the actor. The term $1 - A_s$ is called the transmissivity, and represents the amount of light that is transmitted through the actor. As an example, consider starting with three polygons colored red, green, and blue each with a transparency of 0.5. If the red polygon is in the front and the background is black, the resulting RGBA color will be (0.4, 0.2, 0.1, 0.875) on a scale from zero to one (**Figure 7–1**).

It is important to note that if we switch the ordering of the polygons, the resulting color will change. This underlies a major technical problem in using transparency. If we ray-trace a scene, we will intersect the surfaces in a well-defined manner — from front to back. Using this knowledge we can trace a ray back to the last surface it intersects, and then composite the color by applying **Equation 7-1** to all the surfaces in reverse order (i.e., from back to front). In object-order rendering methods, this compositing is commonly supported in hardware, but unfortunately we are not guaranteed to render the polygons in any specific order. Even though our polygons are situated as in **Figure 7–1**, the order in which the polygons are ren-

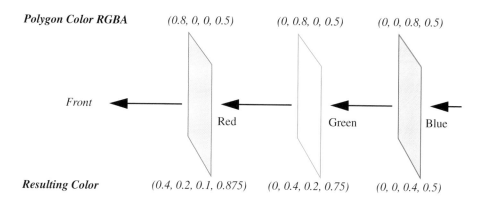

Figure 7–1 Alpha compositing.

dered might be the blue polygon, followed by the red, and finally the green polygon. Consequently, the resulting color is incorrect.

If we look at the RGBA value for one pixel we can see the problem. When the blue polygon is rendered, the frame buffer and z-buffer are empty, so the RGBA quad (0,0,0.8,0.5) is stored along with the its z-buffer value. When the red polygon is rendered, a comparison of its z-value and the current z-buffer indicates that it is in front of the previous pixel entry. So **Equation 7-1** is applied using the frame buffer's RGBA value. This results in the RGBA value (0.4,0,0.2,0.75) being written to the buffer. Now, the green polygon is rendered and the z comparison indicates that it is behind the current pixel's value. Again this equation is applied, this time using the frame buffer's RGBA value for the surface and the polygon's values from behind. This results in a final pixel color of (0.3,0.2, 0.175,0.875), which is different from what we previously calculated. Once the red and blue polygons have been composited and written to the frame buffer, there is no way to insert the final green polygon into the middle where it belongs.

One solution to this problem is to sort the polygons from back to front and then render them in this order. Typically, this must be done in software requiring additional computational overhead. Sorting also interferes with actor properties (such as specular power), which are typically sent to the graphics engine just before rendering the actor's polygons. Once we start mixing up the polygons of different actors, we must make sure that the correct actor properties are set for each polygon rendered.

Another solution is to store more than one set of RGBAZ values in the frame buffer. This is costly because of the additional memory requirements, and is still limited by the number of RGBAZ values you can store. Some new techniques use a combination of multiple RGBAZ value storage and multipass rendering to yield correct results with a minimum performance hit [Hodges92].

The second technical problem with rendering transparent objects occurs less frequently, but can still have disastrous effects. In certain applications, such as volume rendering, it is desirable to have thousands of polygons with small alpha values. If the RGBA quad is stored in the frame buffer as four eight-bit values, then the round-off can accumulate over many polygons, resulting in gross errors in the output image. This may be less of a problem in the future if graphics hardware begins to store 16 or more bits per component for texture and the frame buffer.

7.2 Texture Mapping

Texture mapping is a technique to add detail to an image without requiring modelling detail. Texture mapping can be thought of as pasting a picture to the surface of an object. The use of texture mapping requires two pieces of information: a *texture map* and *texture coordinates*. The texture map is the picture we paste, and the texture coordinates specify the location where the picture is pasted. More generally, texture mapping is a table lookup for color, intensity, and/or transparency that is applied to an object as it is rendered. Textures maps and coordinates are most often two-dimensional, but three-dimensional texture maps and coordinates are supported by most new graphics hardware.

The value of texture mapping can be shown through the simple example of rendering a wooden table. The basic geometry of a table can be easily created, but achieving the wood grain details is difficult. Coloring the table brown is a good start, but the image is still unrealistic. To simulate the wood grain we need to have many small color changes across the surface of the table. Using vertex colors would require us to have millions of extra vertices just to get the small color changes. The solution to this is to apply a wood grain texture map to the original polygons. This is like applying an oak veneer onto inexpensive particleboard, and this is the strategy used by video games to provide realistic scenes with low numbers of polygons for interactivity.

There are several ways in which we can apply texture data. For each pixel in the texture map (commonly called a *texel* for texture element), there may be one to four components that affect how the texture map is pasted onto the surface of the underlying geometry. A texture map with one component is called an *intensity map*. Applying an intensity map results in changes to the intensity (or value in HSV) of the resulting pixels. If we took a gray scale image of wood grain, and then texture-mapped it onto a brown polygon, we would have a reasonable looking table. The hue and saturation of the polygon would still be determined by the brown color, but the intensity would be determined from the texture map. A better looking table could be obtained by using a color image of the wood. This is a three-component texture map, where each texel is represented as a RGB triplet. Using an RGB map allows us to obtain more realistic images, since we would have more than just the intensity changes of the wood.

By adding alpha values to an intensity map we get two components. We can do the same to an RGB texture map to get a four component RGBA texture map. In these cases, the alpha value can be used to make parts of the underlying geometry transparent. A common trick in computer graphics is to use RGBA textures to render trees. Instead of trying to model the complex geometry of a tree, we just render a rectangle with an RGBA texture map applied to it. Where there are leaves or branches, the alpha is one, where there are gaps and open space, the alpha is zero. As a result, we can see through portions of the rectangle, giving the illusion of viewing through the branches and leaves of a tree.

Besides the different ways in which a texture map can be defined, there are options in how it interacts with the original color of the object. A common option for RGB and RGBA maps is to ignore the original color; that is, just apply the texture color as specified. Another

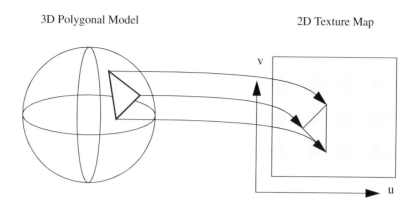

Figure 7–2 Vertex texture coordinates.

option is to modulate the original color by the texture map color (or intensity) to produce the final color.

While we have been focusing on 2D texture maps, they can be of any dimension, though the most common are 2D and 3D. Three-dimensional texture maps are used for textures that are a function of 3D space, such as wood grain, stone, or X-ray intensity (i.e., CT scan). In fact, a volumetric dataset is essentially a 3D texture. We can perform high-speed volume rendering by passing planes through a 3D texture and compositing them using translucent alpha values in the correct order. Techniques for performing volume rendering using texture mapping hardware will be discussed later in this chapter.

A fundamental step in the texture mapping process is determining how to map the texture onto the geometry. To accomplish this, each vertex has an associated texture coordinate in addition to its position, surface normal, color, and other point attributes. The texture coordinate maps the vertex into the texture map as shown in **Figure 7–2**. The texture coordinate system uses the parameters (u,v) and (u,v,t) or equivalently (r,s) or (r,s,t) for specifying 2D and 3D texture values. Points between the vertices are linearly interpolated to determine texture map values.

Another approach to texture mapping uses procedural texture definitions instead of a texture map. In this approach, as geometry is rendered, a procedure is called for each pixel to calculate a texel value. Instead of using the (u,v,t) texture coordinates to index into an image, they are passed as arguments to the procedural texture that uses them to calculate its result. This method provides almost limitless flexibility in the design of a texture; therefore, it is almost impossible to implement in dedicated hardware. Most commonly, procedural textures are used with software rendering systems that do not make heavy use of existing graphics hardware.

While texture maps are generally used to add detail to rendered images, there are important visualization applications.

- Texture maps can be generated procedurally as a function of data. One example is to change the appearance of a surface based on local data value.

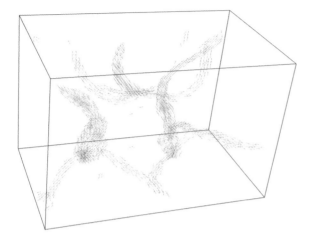

Figure 7–3   One frame from a vector field animation using texture maps (`animVectors.tcl`).

- Texture coordinates can be generated procedurally as a function of data. For example, we can *threshold* geometry by creating a special texture map and then setting texture coordinates based on local data value. The texture map consists of two entries: fully transparent ($\alpha = 0$) and fully opaque ($\alpha = 1$). The texture coordinate is then set to index into the transparent portion of the map if the scalar value is less than some threshold, or into the opaque portion otherwise.

- Texture maps can be animated as a function of time. By choosing a texture map whose intensity varies monotonically from dark to light, and then "moving" the texture along an object, the object appears to crawl in the direction of the texture map motion. We can use this technique to add apparent motion to things like hedgehogs to show vector magnitude. **Figure 7–3** is an example of a texture map animation used to simulate vector field motion.

These techniques will be covered in greater detail in Chapter 9. (See "Texture Algorithms" on page 344.)

7.3 Volume Rendering

Until now we have concentrated on the visualization of data through the use of geometric primitives such as points, lines, and polygons. For many applications such as architectural walk-throughs or terrain visualization, this is obviously the most efficient and effective representation for the data. In contrast, some applications require us to visualize data that is inherently volumetric (which we refer to as 3D image or volume datasets). For example, in biomedical imaging we may need to visualize data obtained from an MR or CT scanner, a confocal microscope, or an ultrasound study. Weather analysis and other simulations also produce large quantities of volumetric data in three or more dimensions that require effective visualization techniques. As a result of the popularity and usefulness of volume data over the last several decades, a broad class of rendering techniques known as volume rendering has emerged. The purpose of volume rendering is to effectively convey information within volumetric data.

In the past, researchers have attempted to define volume rendering as a process that operates directly on the dataset to produce an image without generating an intermediate geometric representation. With recent advances in graphics hardware and clever implementations, developers have been able to use geometric primitives to produce images that are identical to those generated by direct volume rendering techniques. Due to these new techniques, it is nearly impossible to define volume rendering in a manner that is clearly distinct from geometric rendering. Therefore, we choose a broad definition of volume rendering as any method that operates on volumetric data to produce an image.

The next several sections cover a variety of volume rendering methods that use direct rendering techniques, geometric primitive rendering techniques, or a combination of these two methods, to produce an image. Some of the direct volume rendering techniques discussed in this chapter generate images that are nearly identical to those produced by geometric rendering techniques discussed in earlier chapters. For example, using a ray casting method to produce an isosurface image is similar, though not truly equivalent, to rendering geometric primitives that were extracted with the marching cubes contouring technique described in Chapter 6.

The two basic surface rendering approaches described in Chapter 3, image-order and object-order, apply to volume rendering techniques as well. In an image-order method, rays are cast for each pixel in the image plane through the volume to compute pixel values, while in an object-order method the volume is traversed, typically in a front-to-back or back-to-front order, with each voxel processed to determine its contribution to the image. In addition, there are other volume rendering techniques that cannot easily be classified as image-order or object-order. For example, a volume rendering technique may traverse both the image and the volume simultaneously, or the image may be computed in the frequency domain rather than the spatial domain.

Since volume rendering is typically used to generate images that represent an entire 3D dataset in a 2D image, several new challenges are introduced. Classification must be performed to assign color and opacity to regions within the volume, and volumetric illumination models must be defined to support shading. Furthermore, efficiency and compactness are of great importance due to the complexity of volume rendering methods and the size of typical volumetric datasets. A geometric model that consists of one million primitives is generally considered large, while a volumetric dataset with one million voxels is quite small. Typical volumes contain between ten and several hundred million voxels, with datasets of a billion or more voxels becoming more common. Clearly care must be taken when deciding to store auxiliary information at each voxel or to increase the time required to process each voxel.

7.4 Image-Order Volume Rendering

Image-order volume rendering is often referred to as ray casting or ray tracing. The basic idea is that we determine the value of each pixel in the image by sending a ray through the pixel into the scene according to the current camera parameters. We then evaluate the data encountered along the ray using some specified function in order to compute the pixel value. As we will demonstrate throughout this chapter, ray casting is a flexible technique that can be used to render any 3D image dataset, and can produce a variety images. Also, it is relatively easy to extend a basic ray casting technique designed for volumetric data sets that have uniform

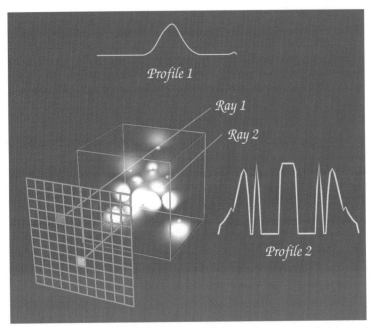

Figure 7–4 Image-order volume rendering. High potential iron protein data courtesy of Scripps Clinic, La Jolla, CA.

voxels to work on rectilinear or structured grids. Unfortunately, basic ray casting is also fairly slow; therefore, later in this chapter we will discuss a number of acceleration methods that can be used to improve performance, though often with some additional memory requirements or loss in flexibility.

The ray casting process is illustrated in **Figure 7–4**. This example uses a standard orthographic camera projection; consequently, all rays are parallel to each other and perpendicular to the view plane. The data values along each ray are processed according to the ray function, which in this case determines the maximum value along the ray and converts it to a gray scale pixel value where the minimum scalar value in the volume maps to transparent black, and the maximum scalar value maps to opaque white.

The two main steps of ray casting are determining the values encountered along the ray, and then processing these values according to a ray function. Although in implementation these two steps are typically combined, we will treat them independently for the moment. Since the specific ray function often determines the method used to extract values along the ray, we will begin by considering some of the basic ray function types.

Figure 7–5 shows the data value profile of a ray as it passes through 8 bit volumetric data where the data values can range between 0 and 255. The x-axis of the profile indicates distance from the view plane while the y-axis represents data value. The results obtained from four different simple ray functions are shown below the profile. For display purposes we convert the raw result values to gray scale values using a method similar to the one in the previous example.

The first two ray functions, maximum value and average value, are basic operations on the scalar values themselves. The third ray function computes the distance along the ray at

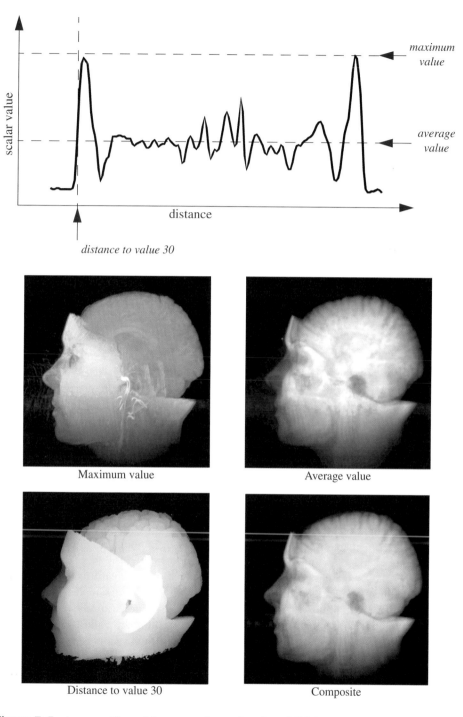

Figure 7–5 A ray profile and four example ray functions. MRI head data courtesy of Siemens Medical Systems, Inc., Iselin, NJ.

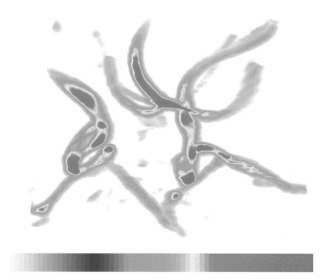

Figure 7–6 A maximum intensity projection created with a ray casting technique. Intensity values are mapped through the color lookup table shown at the bottom of the image before display.

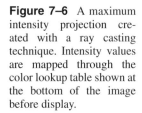

which a scalar value at or above 30 is first encountered, while the fourth uses an alpha compositing technique, treating the values along the ray as samples of opacity accumulated per unit distance. Unlike the first three ray functions, the result of the compositing technique is not a scalar value or distance that can be represented on the ray profile.

The maximum intensity projection, or MIP, is probably the simplest way to visualize volumetric data. This technique is fairly forgiving when it comes to noisy data, and produces images that provide an intuitive understanding of the underlying data. One problem with this method is that it is not possible to tell from a still image where the maximum value occurred along the ray. For example, consider the image of a carotid artery shown in **Figure 7–6**. We are unable to fully understand the structure of the blood vessels from this still image since we cannot determine whether some vessel is in front of or behind some other vessel. This problem can be solved by generating a small sequence of images showing the data rotating, although for parallel camera projections even this animation will be ambiguous. This is due to the fact that two images generated from cameras that view the data from opposite directions will be identical except for a reflection about the Y axis of the image.

Later in this chapter, during the classification and illumination discussions, we will consider more complex ray functions. Although the colorful, shaded images produced by the new methods may contain more information, they may also be more difficult to interpret, and often easier to misinterpret, than the simple images of the previous examples. For that reason, it is beneficial to use multiple techniques to visualize your volumetric data.

A volume is represented as a 3D image dataset where scalar values are defined at the points of the regular grid, yet in ray casting we often need to sample the volume at arbitrary locations. To do this we must define an interpolation function that can return a scalar value for any location between grid points. The simplest interpolation function, which is called zero-order, constant, or nearest neighbor interpolation, returns the value of the closest grid point. This function defines a grid of identical rectangular boxes of uniform value centered on grid points, as illustrated in 2D on the left side of **Figure 7–7**. In the image on the right we see an example of trilinear interpolation where the value at some location is defined by using

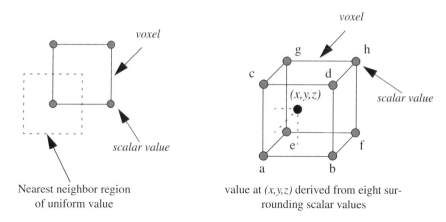

Figure 7–7 A 2D example of nearest neighbor interpolation (left) and a 3D example of trilinear interpolation (right).

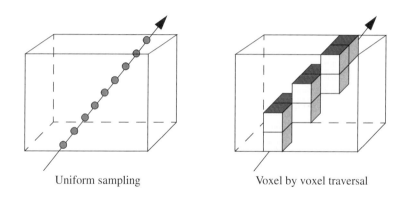

Figure 7–8 Two basic ray traversal methods for volume rendering.

linear interpolation based on distance along each of the three axes. In general, we refer to the region defined by eight neighboring grid points as a voxel. In the special case where a discrete algorithm is used in conjunction with nearest neighbor interpolation, we may instead refer to the constant-valued regions as voxels.

To traverse the data along a ray, we could sample the volume at uniform intervals or we could traverse a discrete representation of the ray through the volume, examining each voxel encountered, as illustrated in **Figure 7–8**. The selection of a method depends upon factors such as the interpolation technique, the ray function, and the desired trade-off between image accuracy and speed.

The ray is typically represented in parametric form as

$$(x, y, z) = (x_0, y_0, z_0) + (a, b, c)t \qquad \text{(7-2)}$$

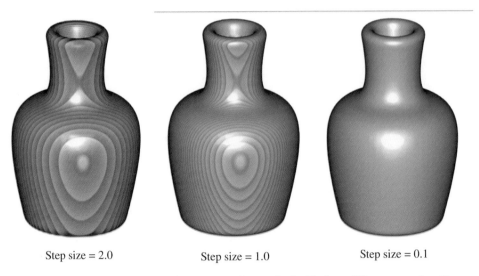

Step size = 2.0   Step size = 1.0   Step size = 0.1

Figure 7–9 Images generated using a ray casting method with three different step sizes. Vase data courtesy of SUNY Stony Brook.

where (x_0, y_0, z_0) is the origin of the ray (either the camera position for perspective viewing transformations or a pixel on the view plane for parallel viewing transformations), and (a, b, c) is the normalized ray direction vector. If t1 and t2 represent the distances where the ray enters and exits the volume respectively, and delta_t indicates the step size, then we can use the following code fragment to perform uniform distance sampling:

```
t = t1;
v = undefined;
while ( t < t2 )
   {
   x = x0 + a * t;
   y = y0 + b * t;
   z = z0 + c * t;
   v = EvaluateRayFunction( v, t );
   t = t + delta_t;
   }
```

One difficulty with the uniform distance sampling method is selecting the step size. If the step size is too large, then our sampling might miss features in the data, yet if we select a small step size, we will significantly increase the amount of time required to render the image. This problem is illustrated in **Figure 7–9** using a volumetric dataset with grid points that are one unit apart along the X, Y, and Z axes. The images were generated using step sizes of 2.0, 1.0, and 0.1 units, where the 0.1 step-size image took nearly 10 times as long to generate as the 1.0 step-size image, which in turn took twice as long to render as the 2.0 step-size image. A compositing method was used to generate the images, where the scalar values within the dataset transition sharply from transparent black to opaque white. If the step size is

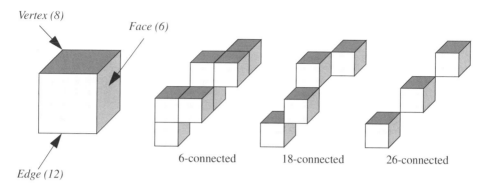

Vertex (8)

Face (6)

Edge (12)

6-connected   18-connected   26-connected

Figure 7–10 Discrete ray classification.

too large, a banding effect appears in the image highlighting regions of the volume equidistant from the ray origin along the viewing rays. To reduce this effect when a larger step size is desired for performance reasons, the origin of each ray can be bumped forward along the viewing direction by some small random offset, which will produce a more pleasing image by eliminating the regular pattern of the aliasing.

In some cases it may make more sense to examine each voxel along the ray rather than taking samples. For example, if we are visualizing our data using a nearest neighbor interpolation method, then we may be able to implement a more efficient algorithm using discrete ray traversal and integer arithmetic. Another reason for examining voxels may be to obtain better accuracy on certain ray functions. We can easily compute the exact maximum value encountered along a ray within each voxel when using trilinear interpolation by taking the first derivative of the interpolation function along the ray and solving the resulting equation to compute the extrema. Similarly, we can find the exact location along the ray where a selected value is first encountered to produce better images of isovalue surfaces within the volume.

A 3D scan conversion technique, such as a modified Bresenham method, can be used to transform the continuous ray into a discrete representation. The discrete ray is an ordered sequence of voxels $v_1, v_2, ... v_n$, and can be classified as 6-connected, 18-connected, or 26-connected as shown in **Figure 7–10**. Each voxel contains 6 faces, 12 edges, and 8 vertices. If each pair of voxels v_i, v_{i+1} along the ray share a face then the ray is 6-connected, if they share a face or an edge the ray is 18-connected, and if they share a face, an edge, or a vertex the ray is 26-connected. Scan converting and traversing a 26-connected ray requires less time than a 6-connected ray but is more likely to miss small features in the volume dataset.

If we are using a parallel viewing transformation and our ray function can be efficiently computed using a voxel by voxel traversal method, then we can employ a templated ray casting technique [Yagel92b] with 26-connected rays to generate the image. All rays are identical in direction; therefore, we only need to scan convert once, using this "template" for every ray. When these rays are cast from pixels on the image plane, as shown in the left image of **Figure 7–11**, then some voxels in the dataset will not contribute to the image. If instead we cast the rays from the voxels in the base plane of the volume that is most parallel to the image plane, as shown in the right image, then the rays fit together snugly such that every voxel in

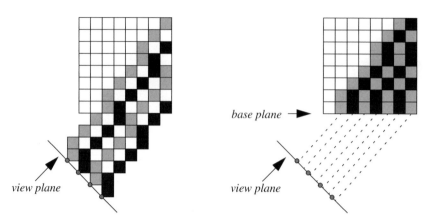

Figure 7–11 Ray casting with templated discrete rays. If the rays originate from the image plane (left) then voxels are missed in the volume. If instead the rays originate from a base plane of the volume (right), each voxel is visited exactly once.

the dataset is visited exactly once. The image will appear warped because it is generated from the base plane, so a final resampling step is required to project this image back onto the image plane.

7.5 Object-Order Volume Rendering

Object-order volume rendering methods process samples in the volume based on the organization of the voxels in the dataset and the current camera parameters. When an alpha compositing method is used, the voxels must be traversed in either a front-to-back or back-to-front order to obtain correct results. This process is analogous to sorting translucent polygons before each projection in order to ensure correct blending. When graphics hardware is employed for compositing, a back-to-front ordering is typically preferred since it is then possible to perform alpha blending without the need for alpha bitplanes in the frame buffer. If a software compositing method is used, a front-to-back ordering is more common since partial image results are more visually meaningful, and can be used to avoid additional processing when a pixel reaches full opacity. Voxel ordering based on distance to the view plane is not always necessary since some volume rendering operations, such as MIP or average, can be processed in any order and still yield correct results.

Figure 7–12 illustrates a simple object-order, back-to-front approach to projecting the voxels in a volume for an orthographic projection. Voxel traversal starts at the voxel that is furthest from the view plane and then continues progressively to closer voxels until all voxels have been visited. This is done within a triple nested loop where, from the outer to the inner loop, the planes in the volume are traversed, the rows in a plane are processed, and finally the voxels along a row are visited. Figure 7–12 shows an ordered labeling of the first seven voxels as the volume is projected. Processing voxels in this manner does not yield a strict ordering from the furthest to the closest voxel. However, it is sufficient for orthographic

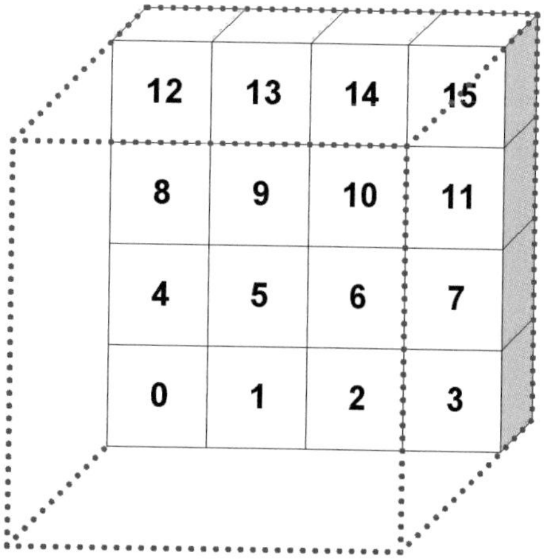

Figure 7–12 Object-order, back-to-front volume rendering.

projections since it does ensure that the voxels that project to a single pixel are processed in the correct order.

When a voxel is processed, its projected position on the view plane is determined and an operation is performed at that pixel location using the voxel and image information. This operator is similar to the ray function used in image-order ray casting techniques. Although this approach to projecting voxels is both fast and efficient, it often yields image artifacts due to the discrete selection of the projected image pixel. For instance, as we move the camera closer to the volume in a perspective projection, neighboring voxels will project to increasingly distant pixels on the view plane, resulting in distracting "holes" in the image.

A volume rendering technique, called splatting, addresses this problem by distributing the energy of a voxel across many pixels. Splatting is an object-order volume rendering technique proposed by Westover [Westover90] and, as its name implies, it projects the energy of a voxel onto the image plane one splat, or footprint, at a time. A kernel with finite extent is placed around each data sample. The footprint is the projected contribution of this sample onto the image plane, and is computed by integrating the kernel along the viewing direction and storing the results in a 2D footprint table. **Figure 7–13** illustrates the projection of a Gaussian kernel onto the image plane that may then be used as a splatting footprint. For a parallel viewing transform and a spherically symmetric kernel, the footprint of every voxel is identical except for an image space offset. Therefore, the evaluation of the footprint table and the image space extent of a sample can be performed once as a preprocessing step to volume rendering. Splatting is more difficult for perspective volume rendering since the image space extent is not identical for all samples. Accurately correcting for perspective effects in a splatting approach would make the algorithm far less efficient. However, with a small loss of accuracy we can still use the generic footprint table if we approximate the image plane extent of an ellipsoid with an ellipse.

There are several important considerations when utilizing a splatting approach for volume rendering. The type of kernel, the radius of the kernel, and the resolution of the footprint table will all impact the appearance of the final image. For example, a kernel radius that is smaller than the distance between neighboring samples may lead to gaps in the image, while

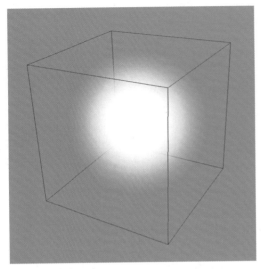

Figure 7–13 A Gaussian kernel is projected onto the view plane to produce a splat footprint.

a larger radius will lead to a blurry image. Also, a low resolution footprint table is faster to precompute, but a high resolution table allows us to use nearest neighbor sampling for faster rendering times without a significant loss in image accuracy.

Texture mapping as described earlier in this chapter was originally developed to provide the appearance of high surface complexity when rendering geometric surfaces. As texture mapping methods matured and found their way into standard graphics hardware, researchers began utilizing these new capabilities to perform volume rendering [Cabral94]. There are two main texture-mapped volume rendering techniques based on the two main types of texture hardware currently available. Two-dimensional texture-mapped volume rendering makes use of 2D texture mapping hardware whereas 3D texture-mapped volume rendering makes use less commonly available 3D texture mapping graphics hardware.

We can decompose texture-mapped volume rendering into two basic steps. The first is a sampling step where the data samples are extracted from the volume using some form of interpolation. Depending on the type of texture hardware available, this may be nearest neighbor, bilinear, or trilinear interpolation and may be performed exclusively in hardware or through a combination of both software and hardware techniques. The second step is a blending step where the sampled values are combined with the current image in the frame buffer. This may be a simple maximum operator or it may be a more complex alpha compositing operator.

Texture-mapped volume renderers sample and blend a volume to produce an image by projecting a set of texture-mapped polygons that span the entire volume. In 2D texture-mapped volume rendering the dataset is decomposed into a set of orthographic slices along the axis of the volume most parallel to the viewing direction. The basic rendering algorithm consists of a loop over the orthogonal slices in a back-to-front order, where for each slice, a 2D texture is downloaded into texture memory. Each slice, which is a rectangular polygon, is projected to show the entire 2D texture. If neighboring slices are far apart relative to the image size, then it may be necessary to use a software bilinear interpolation method to extract additional slices from the volume in order to achieve a desired image accuracy. The image on

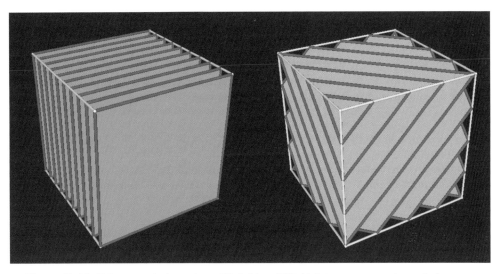

Figure 7–14 Volume rendering using a 2D (left) and 3D (right) texture mapping technique.

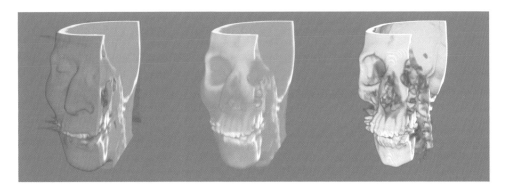

Figure 7–15 2D texture-mapped volume rendering. The images were generated using three different mappings of scalar value to opacity. CT data (256x256x225) courtesy of North Carolina Memorial Hospital.

the left side of **Figure 7–14** illustrates the orthogonal slices that are rendered using a 2D texture mapping approach. Several example images generated using 2D texture-mapped volume rendering are shown in **Figure 7–15**.

The performance of this algorithm can be decomposed into the software sampling rate, the texture download rate, and the texture-mapped polygon scan conversion rate. The software sampling step is required to create the texture image, and is typically dependent on view direction due to cache locality when accessing volumetric data stored in a linear array. Some implementations minimize the software sampling cost at the expense of memory by precomputing and saving images for the three major volume orientations. The texture download rate is the rate at which this image can be transferred from main memory to texture mapping memory. The scan conversion of the polygon is usually limited by the rate at which the graphics hardware can process pixels in the image, or the pixel fill rate. For a given hardware implementation, the download time for a volume is fixed and will not change based on viewing parameters. However, reducing the relative size of the projected volume will reduce the number of samples processed by the graphics hardware that, in turn, will increase volume rendering rates at the expense of image quality.

Unlike 2D hardware, 3D texture hardware is capable of loading and interpolating between multiple slices in a volume by utilizing 3D interpolation techniques such as trilinear interpolation. If the texture memory is large enough to hold the entire volume, then the rendering algorithm is simple. The entire volume is downloaded into texture memory once as a preprocessing step. To render an image, a set of equally spaced planes along the viewing direction and parallel to the image plane is clipped against the volume. The resulting polygons, illustrated in the image on the right side of **Figure 7–14**, are then projected in back-to-front order with the appropriate 3D texture coordinates.

For large volumes it may not be possible to load the entire volume into 3D texture memory. The solution to this problem is to break the dataset into small enough subvolumes, or bricks, so that each brick will fit in texture memory. The bricks must then be processed in back-to-front order while computing the appropriately clipped polygon vertices inside the bricks. Special care must be taken to ensure that boundaries between bricks do not result in image artifacts.

Similar to a 2D texture mapping method, the 3D algorithm is limited by both the texture download and pixel fill rates of the machine. However, 3D texture mapping is superior to the 2D version in its ability to sample the volume, generally yielding higher quality images with fewer artifacts. Since it is capable of performing trilinear interpolation, we are able to sample at any location within the volume. For instance, a 3D texture mapping algorithm can sample along polygons representing concentric spheres rather than the more common view-aligned planes.

In theory, a 3D texture-mapped volume renderer and a ray casting volume renderer perform the same computations, have the same complexity, $O(n^3)$, and produce identical images. Both sample the entire volume using either nearest neighbor or trilinear interpolation, and combine the samples to form a pixel value using, for example, a maximum value or compositing function. Therefore, we can view 3D texture mapping and standard ray casting methods as functionally equivalent. The main advantage to using a texture mapping approach is the ability to utilize relatively fast graphics hardware to perform the sampling and blending operations. However, there are currently several drawbacks to using graphics hardware for volume rendering. Hardware texture-mapped volume renderings tend to have more artifacts than software ray casting techniques due to limited precision within the frame buffer for storing partial results at each pixel during blending. In addition, only a few ray functions are supported by the hardware, and advanced techniques such as shading are more difficult to achieve. However, these limitations are beginning to disappear as texture mapping hardware evolves. Through the use of extensions to the OpenGL standard, per pixel vectors can be defined allowing for hardware shaded volume texture mapping. Other extensions have allowed for maximum intensity projections, and deeper framebuffers eliminate artifacts.

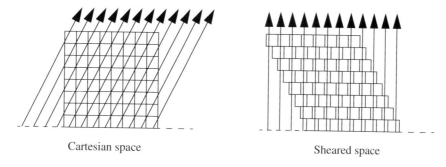

Cartesian space   Sheared space

Figure 7–16 On the left, orthographic rays are cast from the base plane of the volume. In the right image the volume is sheared such that these rays become perpendicular to the base plane.

7.6 Other Volume Rendering Methods

Not all volume rendering methods fall cleanly into the image-order or object-order categories. For example, the shear-warp method [Lacroute94] of volume rendering traverses both image and object space at the same time. The basic idea behind this method is similar to that of templated ray casting. If we cast rays from the base plane of the volume for an orthographic projection, then it is possible to shear the volume such that the rays become perpendicular to the base plane, as shown in **Figure 7–16**. Looking at the problem this way, it is clear to see that if all rays originate from the same place within the voxels on the base plane, then these rays intersect the voxels on each subsequent plane of the volume at consistent locations. Using bilinear interpolation on the 2D planes of the dataset, we can precompute one set of interpolation weights for each plane. Instead of traversing the volume by evaluating samples along each ray, an object-order traversal method can be used to visit voxels along each row in each plane in a front-to-back order through the volume. There is a one-to-one correspondence between samples in a plane of the volume and pixels on the image plane, making it possible to traverse both the samples and the pixels simultaneously. As in templated ray casting, a final resampling (warping) operation must be performed to transform the image from sheared space on the base plane to cartesian space on the image plane.

Shear-warp volume rendering is essentially an efficient variant of ray casting. The correspondence between samples and pixels allows us to take advantage of a standard ray casting technique known as early ray termination. When we have determined that a pixel has reached full opacity during compositing, we no longer need to consider the remaining samples that project onto this pixel since they do not contribute to the final pixel value. The biggest efficiency improvement in shear-warp volume rendering comes from run-length encoding the volume. This compression method removes all empty voxels from the dataset, leaving only voxels that can potentially contribute to the image. Depending on the classification of the data, it is possible to achieve a greater than 10:1 reduction in voxels. As we step through the compressed volume, the number of voxels skipped due to run-length encoding also indicates the number of pixels to skip in the image. One drawback to this method is that it requires three copies of the compressed volume to allow for front-to-back traversal from all

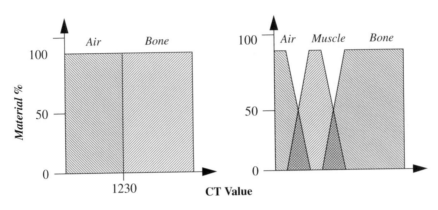

Figure 7–17 Transfer functions that classify CT densities into material percentages. A simple binary classification used to define a bone isosurface (left) and a gradual transition from air to muscle to bone (right) is shown.

view directions. In addition, if we wish to use a perspective viewing transformation then we may need to traverse all three compressed copies of the volume in order to achieve the correct traversal order.

Volume rendering can also be performed using the Fourier slice projection theorem [Totsuka92] that states that if we extract a slice of the volume in the frequency domain that contains the center and is parallel to the image plane, then the 2D spectrum of that slice is equivalent to the 2D image obtained by taking line integrals through the volume from the pixels on the image plane. Therefore we can volume render the dataset by extracting the appropriate slice from the 3D Fourier volume, then computing the 2D inverse Fourier transform of this slice. This allows us to render the image in $O(n^2 \log n)$ time as opposed to the $O(n^3)$ complexity required by most other volume rendering algorithms.

Two problems that must be addressed when implementing a frequency domain volume renderer are the high cost of interpolation when extracting a slice from the Fourier volume, and the high memory requirements (usually two double precision floating-point values per sample) required to store the Fourier volume. Although some shading and depth cues can be provided with this method, occlusion is not possible.

7.7 Volume Classification

Classifying the relevant objects of interest within a dataset is a critical step in producing a volume rendered image. This information is used to determine the contribution of an object to the image as well as the object's material properties and appearance. For example, a simple binary classification of whether a data sample corresponds to bone within a CT dataset is often performed by specifying a density threshold. When the scalar value at a voxel is greater than this threshold, it is classified as bone, otherwise it is considered air. This essentially specifies an isosurface in the volume at the transition between air and bone. If we plot this operation over all possible scalar values we will get the binary step function shown on the left in **Figure 7–17**. In volume rendering we refer to this function as a transfer function. A trans-

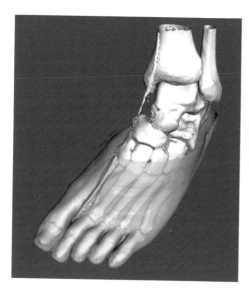

Figure 7–18 Volume rendering using a gradient magnitude opacity transfer function. Rendering performed with Kitware's VolView volume rendering system. The Visible Man CT data is courtesy of The National Library of Medicine.

fer function is responsible for mapping the information at a voxel location into different values such as material, color, or opacity. The strength of volume rendering is that it can handle transfer functions of much greater complexity than a binary step function. This is often necessary since datasets contain multiple materials and classification methods cannot always assign a single material to a sample with 100 percent probability. Using advanced image segmentation and classification techniques, the single component volume can be processed into multiple material percentage volumes [Drebin88]. Referring back to our CT example, we can now specify a material percentage transfer function that defines a gradual transition from air to muscle, then from muscle to bone, as shown on the right in **Figure 7–17**.

In addition to material percentage transfer functions, we can define four independent transfer functions that map scalar values into red, green, blue, and opacity values for each material in the dataset. For simplicity, these sets of transfer functions are typically preprocessed into one function each for red, green, blue and opacity at the end of the classification phase. During rendering we must decide how to perform interpolation to compute the opacity and color at an arbitrary location in the volume. We could interpolate scalar value then evaluate the transfer functions, or we could evaluate the transfer functions at the grid points then interpolate the resulting opacities and colors. These two methods will produce different image results. It is generally considered more accurate to classify at the grid points then interpolate to obtain color and opacity; although if we interpolate then classify, the image often appears more pleasing since high frequencies may be removed by the interpolation.

Classifying a volume based on scalar value alone is often not capable of isolating an object of interest. A technique introduced by Levoy [Levoy88] adds a gradient magnitude dimension to the specification of a transfer function. With this technique we can specify an object in the volume based on a combination of scalar value and the gradient magnitude. This allows us to define an opacity transfer function that can target voxels with scalar values in a range of densities and gradients within a range of gradient magnitudes. This is useful for avoiding the selection of homogeneous regions in a volume and highlighting fast-changing regions. **Figure 7–18** shows a CT scan of a human foot. The sharp changes in the volume,

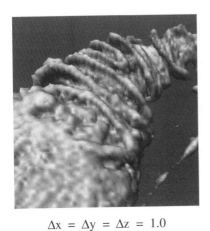
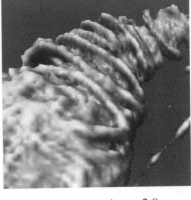

$$\Delta x = \Delta y = \Delta z = 1.0$$

$$\Delta x = \Delta y = \Delta z = 2.0$$

Figure 7–19 A comparison of shaded images with two different step sizes used during normal estimation. Confocal microscopy data courtesy of Howard Hughes Medical Institute, SUNY Stony Brook.

such as the transition from air to skin and flesh to bone, are shown. However, the homogeneous regions, such as the internal muscle, are mostly transparent.

If we are using a higher-order interpolation function such as tri-cubic interpolation then we can analytically compute the gradient vector at any location in the dataset by evaluating the first derivative of the interpolation function. Although we can use this approach for trilinear interpolation, it may produce undesirable artifacts since trilinear interpolation is not continuous in its first derivative across voxel boundaries. An alternative approach is to employ a finite differences technique to approximate the gradient vector:

$$g_x = \frac{f(x + \Delta x, y, z) - f(x - \Delta x, y, z)}{2\Delta x}$$

$$g_y = \frac{f(x, y + \Delta y, z) - f(x, y - \Delta y, z)}{2\Delta y} \tag{7-3}$$

$$g_z = \frac{f(x, y, z + \Delta z) - f(x, y, z - \Delta z)}{2\Delta z}$$

where $f(x, y, z)$ represents the scalar value at location (x, y, z) in the dataset according to the interpolation function, and g_x, g_y, and g_z are the partial derivatives of this function along the x, y, and z axes respectively. The magnitude of the gradient at (x, y, z) is the length of the resulting vector (g_x, g_y, g_z). This vector can also be normalized to produce a unit normal vector. The choice of Δx, Δy, and Δz are critical as shown in **Figure 7–19**. If these values are too small, then the gradient vector field derived from **Equation 7-3** may contain high frequencies, yet if these values are too large we will lose small features in the dataset.

It is often the case that transfer functions based on scalar value and even gradient magnitude are not capable of fully classifying a volume. Ultrasound data is an example of particularly difficult data that does not perform well with simple segmentation techniques. While no one technique exists that is universally applicable, there exists a wide variety of techniques that produce classification information at each sample. For instance, [Kikinis96] provides techniques for classifying the human brain. In order to properly handle this information a volume renderer must access the original volume and a classification volume. The classification volume usually contains material percentages for each sample, with a set of color and opacity transfer functions for each material used to define appearance.

7.8 Volumetric Illumination

The volume rendered images that we have shown so far in this chapter do not include any lighting effects. Scientist sometimes prefer to visualize their volumes using these simpler methods because they fear that adding lighting effects to the image will interfere with their interpretation. For example, in a maximum intensity projection, a dark region in the image clearly indicates the lack of high opacity values in the corresponding region of the volume, while a dark feature in a shaded image may indicate either low opacity values or values with gradient directions that point away from the light source.

There are several advantages to lighting that can often justify the additional complexity in the image. First, consider the fact that volume rendering is a process of creating a 2D image from 3D data. The person viewing that data would like to be able to understand the 3D structure of the volume from that image. Of course, if you were to look at a photograph of a skeleton it would be easy to understand its structure from the 2D representation. The two main clues that you received from the picture are occlusion and lighting effects. If you were to view a video of the skeleton, you would receive the additional clue of motion parallax. A static image showing a maximum intensity projection does not include occlusion or lighting effects, making it difficult to understand structure. An image generated with a compositing technique does include occlusion, and the compositing ray function can be modified to include shading as well. A comparison of these three methods is shown in **Figure 7–20** for a CT scan of a human foot.

To accurately capture lighting effects, we could use a transport theory illumination model [Krueger91] that describes the intensity of light I arriving at a pixel by the path integral along the ray:

$$I(t_0, \vec{\omega}) = \int_{t_0}^{\infty} Q(t) e^{-\int_{t_0}^{t} \sigma_a(t') + \sigma_{sc}(t') dt'} dt \qquad (7\text{-}4)$$

If we are using camera clipping planes, then t_0 and ∞ would be replaced by the distance to the near clip plane t_{near} and the distance to the far clip plane t_{far} respectively. The contribution $Q(t)$ from each sample at a distance t along the ray $\vec{\omega}$ is attenuated according to how much intensity is lost on the way from t to t_0 due to absorption $\sigma_a(t')$ and scattering

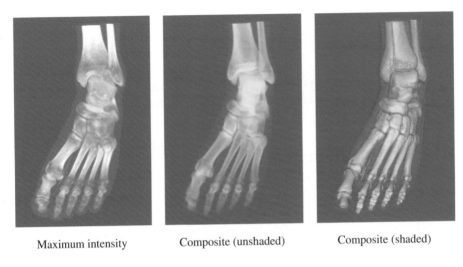

Maximum intensity   Composite (unshaded)   Composite (shaded)

Figure 7–20 A comparison of three volume rendering techniques. A maximum intensity projection does not include occlusion or shading. A composite image includes occlusion and can include shading.

$\sigma_{sc}(t')$. The contribution at t can be defined as:

$$Q(t) = E(t) + \sigma_{sc}(t) \int_{4\pi} \rho_{sc}(\vec{\omega}' \to \vec{\omega}) I(t, \vec{\omega}') d\vec{\omega}' \tag{7-5}$$

The contribution consists of the amount of light directly emitted by the sample $E(t)$, plus the amount of light coming from all directions that is scattered by this sample back along the ray. The fraction of light arriving from the $\vec{\omega}'$ direction that is scattered into the $\vec{\omega}$ direction is defined by the scattering function $\rho_{sc}(\vec{\omega}' \to \vec{\omega})$. To compute the light arriving from all directions due to multiple bounce scattering, we must recursively compute the illumination function.

　　If scattering is accurately modelled, then basing the ray function on the transport theory illumination model will produce images with realistic lighting effects. Unfortunately, this illumination model is too complex to evaluate, therefore approximations are necessary for a practical implementation. One of the simplest approximations is to ignore scattering completely, yielding the following intensity equation:

$$I(t_0, \vec{\omega}) = \int_{t_0}^{\infty} E(t) e^{-\int_{t_0}^{t} \sigma_a(t') dt'} dt \tag{7-6}$$

We can further simplify this equation by allowing $\alpha(t)$ to represent both the amount of light emitted per unit length and the amount of light absorbed per unit length along the ray. The outer integral can be replaced by a summation over samples along the ray within some clipping range, while the inner integral can be approximated using an over operator:

$$I(t_{near}, \vec{\omega}) = \sum_{t=t}^{t \geq t_{far}} \alpha(t) \prod_{t'=t}^{t' < t} (1 - a(t'))$$

(7-7)

This equation is typically expressed in its recursive form:

$$I(t_n, \vec{\omega}) = \alpha(t_n) + (1 - \alpha(t_n))I(t_{n+1}, \vec{\omega})$$

(7-8)

which is equivalent to the simple compositing method using the over operator that was described previously. Clearly in this case we have simplified the illumination model to the point that this ray function does not produce images that appear to be realistic.

If we are visualizing an isosurface within the volumetric data, then we can employ the surface illumination model described in Chapter 3 to capture ambient and diffuse lighting as well as specular highlights. There are a variety of techniques for estimating the surface normal needed to evaluate the shading equation. If the image that is produced as a result of volume rendering contains the distance from the view plane to the surface for every pixel, then we can post-process the image with a 2D gradient estimator to obtain surface normals. The gradient at some pixel (x_p, y_p) can be estimated with a central difference technique by:

$$\frac{\partial Z}{\partial x} = \frac{Z(x_p + \Delta x, y_p) - Z(x_p - \Delta x, y_p)}{2\Delta x}$$

$$\frac{\partial Z}{\partial y} = \frac{Z(x_p, y_p + \Delta y) - Z(x_p, y_p - \Delta y)}{2\Delta y}$$

(7-9)

$$\frac{\partial Z}{\partial z} = 1$$

The results are normalized to produce a unit normal vector. As with the 3D finite differences gradient estimator given in **Equation 7-3**, care must be taken when selecting Δx and Δy. Typically, these values are simply the pixel spacing in x and y so that neighboring pixel values are used to estimate the gradient, although larger values can be used to smooth the image.

One problem with the 2D gradient estimation technique described above is that normals are computed from depth values that may represent disjoint regions in the volume, as shown in **Figure 7–21**. This may lead to a blurring of sharp features on the edges of objects. To reduce this effect, we can locate regions of continuous curvature in the depth image, then estimate the normal for a pixel using only other pixel values that fall within the same curvature region [Yagel92a]. This may require reducing our Δx and Δy values, or using an off-centered differences technique to estimate the components of the gradient. For example, the x component of the gradient could be computed with a forward difference:

$$\frac{\partial Z}{\partial x} = \frac{Z(x_p + \Delta x, y_p) - Z(x_p, y_p)}{\Delta x}$$

(7-10)

or a backward difference:

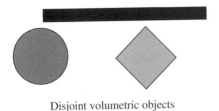

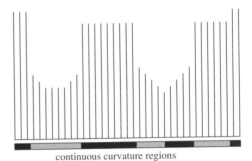

Disjoint volumetric objects

continuous curvature regions

Figure 7–21   A scene (left) and the corresponding depth image (right) used in 2D gradient estimation.

Corresponding depth image

$$\frac{\partial Z}{\partial x} = \frac{Z(x_p, y_p) - Z(x_p - \Delta x, y_p)}{\Delta x} \qquad (7\text{-}11)$$

Although 2D gradient estimation is not as accurate as the 3D version, it is generally faster and allows for quick lighting and surface property changes without requiring us to recompute the depth image. However, if we wish to include shading effects in an image computed with a compositing technique, we need to estimate gradients at many locations within the volume for each pixel. A 3D gradient estimation technique is more suitable for this purpose. An illumination equation for compositing could be written as:

$$I(t_{near}, \vec{\omega}) = \sum_{t=t}^{t \ge t_{far}} \alpha(t)(I_a + I_d + I_s) \prod_{t'=t}^{t' < t} (1 - a(t')) \qquad (7\text{-}12)$$

where the ambient illumination I_a, the diffuse illumination I_d, and the specular illumination I_s are computed as in surface shading using the estimated volume gradient in place of the surface normal. In this equation, $\alpha(t)$ represents the amount of light reflected per unit length along the ray, with $1 - \alpha(t)$ indicating the fraction of light transmitted per unit length.

As in classification, we have to make a decision about whether to directly compute illumination at an arbitrary location in the volume, or to compute illumination at the grid points and then interpolate. This is not a difficult decision to make on the basis of accuracy since it is clearly better to estimate the gradient at the desired location rather than interpolate from neighboring estimations. On the other hand, if we do interpolate from the grid points then we can precompute the gradients for the entire dataset once, and use this to increase rendering performance for both classification and illumination. The main problem is the amount of memory required to store the precomputed gradients. A naive implementation would store a floating-point value (typically four bytes) per component of the gradient per scalar value. For a dataset with 256^3 one-byte scalars, this would increase the storage requirement from 16 Mbytes to 218 Mbytes.

In order to reduce the storage requirements, we could quantize the precomputed gradients by using some number of bits to represent the magnitude of the vector, and some other number of bits to encode the direction of the vector. Quantization works well for storing the

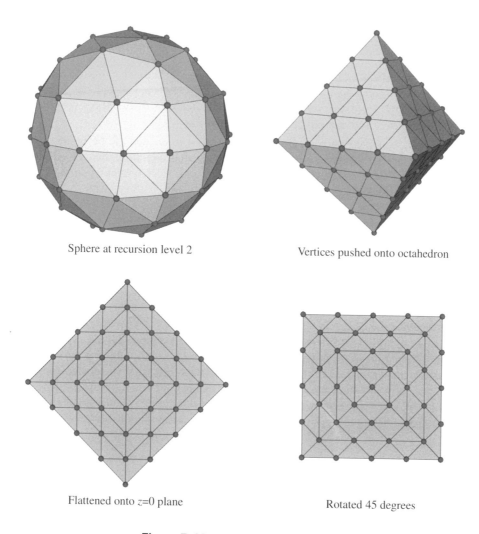

Sphere at recursion level 2

Vertices pushed onto octahedron

Flattened onto *z*=0 plane

Rotated 45 degrees

Figure 7–22 Gradient direction encoding.

magnitude of the gradient, but does not provide a good distribution of directions if we simply divide the bits among the three components of the vector. A better solution is to use the uniform fractal subdivision of an octahedron into a sphere as the basis of the direction encoding, as shown in **Figure 7–22**. The top left image shows the results obtained after the recursive replacement of each triangle with four new triangles, with a recursion depth of two. The vector directions encoded in this representation are all directions formed by creating a ray originating at the sphere's center and passing through a vertex of the sphere. The remaining images in this figure illustrate how these directions are mapped into an index. First we push all vertices back onto the original faces of the octahedron, then we flatten this sphere onto the $z = 0$ plane. Finally, we rotate the resulting grid by $45°$. We label the vertices in the grid with indices starting at 0 at the top left vertex and continue across the rows then down the columns to index 40 at the lower right vertex. These indices represent only half of the encoded normals because when we flattened the octahedron, we placed two vertices on top of each other on all but the edge locations. Thus, we can use indices 41 through 81 to represent vectors with a negative z component. Vertices on the edges represent vectors with out a z component, and although we could represent them with a single index, using two keeps the indexing scheme more consistent and, therefore, easier to implement.

The simple example above requires only 82 values to encode the 66 unique vector directions. If we use an unsigned short to store the encoded direction, then we can use a recursion depth of 6 when generating the vertices. This leads to 16,642 indices representing 16,386 unique directions.

Once the gradients have been encoded for our volume, we need only compute the illumination once for each possible index and store the results in a table. Since data samples with the same encoded gradient direction may have different colors, this illumination value represents the portion of the shading equation that is independent of color. Each scalar value may have separate colors defined for ambient, diffuse, and specular illumination; therefore, the precomputed illumination is typically an array of values.

Although using a shading table leads to faster rendering times, there are some limitations to this method. Only infinite light sources can be supported accurately since positional light sources would result in different light vectors for data samples with the same gradient due to their different positions in the volume. In addition, specular highlights are only captured accurately for orthographic viewing directions where the view vector does not vary based on sample position. In practice, positional light sources are often approximated by infinite light sources, and a single view direction is used for computing specular highlights since the need for fast rendering often outweighs the need for accurate illumination.

7.9 Regions of Interest

One difficulty in visualizing volumetric data with the methods presented thus far is that in order to study some feature in the center of the volume we must look through other features in the dataset. For example, if we are visualizing a tomato dataset, then we will be unable to see the seeds within the tomato using a maximum intensity projection because the seeds have lower intensity than the surrounding pulp. Even using a compositing technique, it is difficult to visualize the seeds since full opacity may be obtained before reaching this area of the dataset.

We can solve the problem of visualizing internal features by defining a region of interest within our volume, and rendering only this portion of the dataset as shown in **Figure 7–23**. There are many techniques for defining a region of interest. We could use the near and far clipping planes of the camera to exclude portions of the volume. Alternatively, we could use six orthographic clipping planes that would define a rectangular subvolume; we could use a set of arbitrarily oriented half-space clipping planes; or we could define the region of interest as the portion of the volume contained within some set of closed geometric objects. Another approach would be to create an auxiliary volume with binary scalar values that define a mask indicating which values in the volume should be considered during rendering.

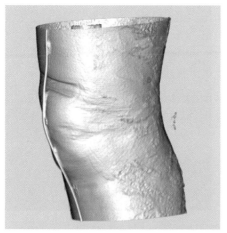
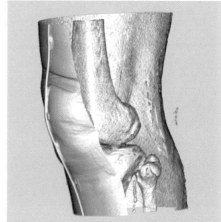
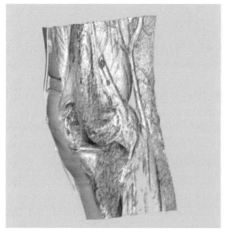

Figure 7–23 Volume rendering with regions of interest. On the upper left, full-resolution volume rendering. On the upper right, the use of axis-aligned cropping planes. Lower left, the use of arbitrary clipping planes. Renderings performed using Kitware's VolView product; Visible Human Data is courtesy of The National Library of Medicine.

All of these region of interest methods are fairly simple to implement using an image-order ray casting approach. As a preprocessing step to ray casting, the ray is clipped against all geometric region definitions. The ray function is then evaluated only along segments of the ray that are within the region of interest. The mask values are consulted at each sample to determine if its contribution should be included or excluded.

For object-order methods we must determine for each sample whether or not it is within the region of interest before incorporating its contribution into the image. If the underlying graphics hardware is being utilized for the object-order volume rendering as is the case with a texture mapping approach, hardware clipping planes may be available to help support regions of interest.

7.10 Intermixing Volumes and Geometry

Although the volume is typically the focus of the image in volume visualization, it is often helpful to add geometric objects to the scene. For example, showing the bounding box of the

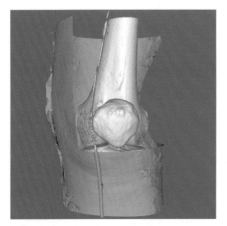 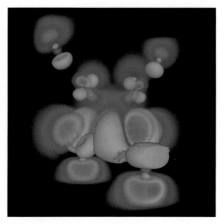

Figure 7–24 Two volumes rendered with both geometric and volumetric techniques. The Visible Woman CT data is courtesy of The National Library of Medicine.

dataset or the position and orientation of cut planes can improve the viewer's understanding of the volumetric data. Also, it can be useful to visualize volumetric data using both geometric and volumetric methods within the same image. The left image in **Figure 7–24** shows a CT scan of a human knee where a contouring method is used to extract the skin isosurface. This isosurface is rendered as triangles using standard graphics hardware. The upper-right portion of the skin is cut to reveal the bone beneath, which is rendered using a software ray casting technique with a compositing ray function. In the right image, the wave function values of an iron protein are visualized using both geometric isosurface and volume rendering techniques.

When using graphics hardware to perform volume rendering, as is the case with a texture mapping approach, intermixing opaque geometry in the scene is trivial. All opaque geometry is rendered first, then the semitransparent texture-mapped polygons are blended in a back-to-front order into the image. If we wish to include semitransparent geometry in the scene, then this geometry and the texture-mapped polygons must be sorted before rendering. Similar to a purely geometric scene, this may involve splitting polygons to obtain a sorted order.

If a software volume rendering approach is used, such as an object-order splatting method or an image-order ray casting method, opaque geometry can be incorporated into the image by rendering the geometry, capturing the results stored in the hardware depth buffer, and then using these results during the volume rendering phase. For ray casting, we would simply convert the depth value for a pixel into a distance along the view ray and use this to bound the segment of the ray that we consider during volume rendering. The final color computed for a pixel during volume rendering is then blended with the color produced by geometric rendering using the over operator. In an object-order method, we must consider the depth of every sample and compare this to the value stored in the depth buffer at each pixel within the image extent of this sample. We accumulate this sample's contribution to the volume rendered image at each pixel only if the sample is in front of the geometry for that pixel. Finally, the volume rendered image is blended over the geometric image.

7.11 Efficient Volume Rendering

Rendering a volumetric dataset is a computationally intensive task. If n is the size of the volume on all three dimensions and we visit every voxel once during a projection, the complexity of volume rendering is $O(n^3)$. Even a highly optimized software algorithm will have great difficulty projecting a moderately sized volume of $512 \times 512 \times 512$ or approximately 134 million voxels at interactive rates. If every voxel in the volume contributes in some way to the final image and we are unwilling to compromise image quality, our options for efficiency improvements are limited. However, it has been observed that many volumetric datasets contain large regions of empty or uninteresting data that are assigned opacity values of 0 during classification. In addition, those areas that contain interesting data may be occupied by coherent or nearly homogeneous regions. There have been many techniques developed that take advantage of these observations.

Space leaping refers to a general class of efficiency improvement techniques that attempt to avoid processing regions of a volume that will not contribute to the final image. One technique often used is to build an octree data structure which hierarchically contains all of the important regions in the volume. The root node of the octree contains the entire volume and has eight child nodes, each of which represents 1/8 of the volume. These eight subregions are created by dividing the volume in half along the x, y, and z axes. This subdivision continues recursively until a node in the octree represents a homogeneous region of the volume. With an object-order rendering technique, only the nonempty leaf nodes of the octree would be traversed during rendering thereby avoiding all empty regions while efficiently processing all contributing homogeneous regions. Similarly, an image-order ray casting technique would cast rays through the leaf nodes, with the regular structure of the octree allowing us to quickly step over empty nodes.

A hybrid space leaping technique [Sobierajski95] makes use of graphics hardware to skip some of the empty regions of the volume during software ray casting. First, a polygonal representation is created that completely contains or encloses all important regions in the volume. This polygonal representation is then projected twice — first using the usual less than operator on the depth buffer and the second time using a greater than operator on the depth buffer. This produces two depth images that contain the closest and farthest distance to relevant data for every pixel in the image. These distances are then used to clip the rays during ray casting.

An alternate space-leaping technique for ray casting involves the use of an auxiliary distance volume [Zuiderveld92], with each value indicating the closest distance to a nontransparent sample in the dataset. These distance values are used to take larger steps in empty regions of the volume while ensuring that we do not step over any nontransparent features in the volume. Unfortunately, the distance volume is computationally expensive to compute accurately, requires additional storage, and must be recomputed every time the classification of the volume is modified.

One difficulty with these space-leaping techniques is that they are highly data dependent. On a largely empty volume with a small amount of coherent data we can speed up volume rendering by a substantial amount. However, when a dataset is encountered that is entirely made up of high-frequency information such as a typical ultrasound dataset, these techniques break down and will usually cause rendering times to increase rather than decrease.

7.12 Interactive Volume Rendering

Generating a volume rendered image may take anywhere from a fraction of a second to tens of minutes depending on a variety of factors including the hardware platform, image size, data size, and rendering technique. If we are generating the image for the purpose of medical diagnostics we clearly would like to produce a high quality image. On the other hand, if the image is produced during an interactive session then it may be more important to achieve a desired rendering update rate. Therefore, it is clear that we need to be able to trade off quality for speed as necessary based on application. As opposed to our discussion on efficiency improvements, the techniques described here do not preserve image quality. Instead, they allow a controlled degradation in quality in order to achieve speed.

Since the time required for image-order ray casting depends mostly on the size of the image in pixels and the number of samples taken along the ray, we can adjust these two values to achieve a desired update rate. The full-size image can be generated from the reduced resolution image using either a nearest neighbor or bilinear interpolation method. If bilinear interpolation is used, the number of rays cast can often be reduced by a factor of two along each image dimension during interaction, resulting in a four-times speed-up, without a noticeable decrease in image quality. Further speed-ups can be achieved with larger reductions, but at the cost of blurry, less detailed images.

We can implement a progressive refinement method for ray casting if we do not reduce the number of samples taken along each ray. During interaction we can compute only every n^{th} ray along each image dimension and use interpolation to fill in the remaining pixels. When the user stops interacting with the scene the interpolated pixels are progressively filled in with their actual values.

There are several object-order techniques available for achieving interactive rendering rates at the expense of image quality. If a splatting algorithm is used, then the rendering speed is dependent on the number of voxels in the dataset. Reduced resolution versions of the data can be precomputed, and a level of resolution can be selected during interaction based on the desired frame rate. If we use a splatting method based on an octree representation, then we can include an approximate scalar value and an error value in each parent node where the error value indicates how much the scalar values in the child nodes deviate from the approximate value in the parent node. Hierarchical splatting [Laur91] can be performed by descending the octree only until a node with less than a given error tolerance is encountered. The contribution of this region of the volume on the image can be approximated by rendering geometric primitives for the splat [Shirley90], [Wilhelms91]. Increasing the allowed error will decrease the time required to render the data by allowing larger regions to be approximated at a higher level in the octree.

When using a texture mapping approach for volume rendering, faster rendering speeds can be achieved by reducing the number of texture-mapped polygons used to represent the volume. This is essentially equivalent to reducing the number of samples taken along the ray in an image-order ray casting method. Also, if texture download rates are a bottleneck, then a reduced resolution version of the volume can be loaded into texture memory for interaction. This is similar to reducing both the number of rays cast and the number of samples taken along a ray in an image-order method.

7.13 Volume Rendering Future

In the past two decades, volume rendering has evolved from a research topic with algorithms that required many minutes to generate an image on a high-end workstation to an area of active development with commercial software available for home computers. Yet as the demand for volume rendering increases, so do the challenges. The number of voxels in a typical dataset is growing, both due to advances in acquisition hardware and increased popularity of volume rendering in areas such as simulation and volume graphics [Kaufman93]. New methods are needed in order to satisfy the conflicting needs of high quality images and interactivity on these large datasets. In addition, time dependent datasets that contain volumetric data sampled at discrete time intervals present new challenges for interpolation, image accuracy, and interactivity while providing new opportunities in classification and interpolation methods.

Most of the volume rendering discussion in this chapter focused on regular volumetric datasets. Although it is clearly possible to extend most ray casting and object-order methods to visualize rectilinear grid, structured grid, and even irregular data, in practice it is difficult to provide both high quality images and interactivity with these methods. Rendering techniques for these data types continues to be an area of active research in volume visualization [Cignoni96], [Silva96], [Wilhelms96].

7.14 Stereo Rendering

In our practice of computer graphics so far, we have used a number of techniques to simulate 3D graphics on a 2D display device. These techniques include the use of perspective and scale, shading to confer depth, and motion/animation to see all sides of an object. However, one of the most effective techniques to simulate 3D viewing is *binocular parallax*.

Binocular parallax is a result of viewing 3D objects with our two eyes. Since each eye sees a slightly different picture, our mind interprets these differences to determine the depth of objects in our view. There have been a number of "3D" movies produced that take advantage of our binocular parallax. Typically, these involve wearing a set of special glasses while watching the movie.

This effect can be valuable in our efforts to visualize complex datasets and CAD models. The additional depth cues provided by stereo viewing aid us in determining the relative positions of scene geometry as well as forming a mental image of the scene. There are several different methods for introducing binocular parallax into renderings. We will refer to the overall process as *stereo rendering*, since at some point in the process a stereo pair of images is involved.

To generate correct left and right eye images, we need information beyond the camera parameters that we introduced in Chapter 3. The first piece of information we need is the separation distance between the eyes. The amount of parallax generated can be controlled by adjusting this distance. We also need to know if the resulting images will be viewed on one or two displays. For systems that use two displays (and hence two view planes), the parallax can be correctly produced by performing camera azimuths to reach the left and right eye positions. Head mounted displays and booms are examples of two display systems. Unfortunately, this doesn't work as well for systems that have only one view plane. If you try to

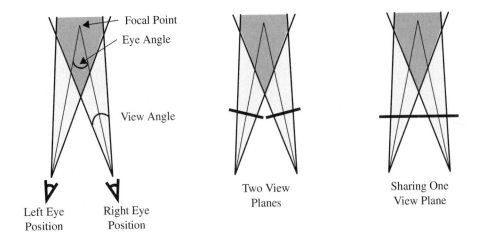

Figure 7–25 Stereo rendering and binocular parallax.

display both the left and right views on a single display, they are forced to share the same view plane as in **Figure 7–25**. Our earlier camera model assumed that the view plane was perpendicular to the direction of projection. To handle this nonperpendicular case, we must translate and shear the camera's viewing frustum. Hodges provides some of the details of this operation as well as a good overview on stereo rendering [Hodges92].

Now let's look at some of the different methods for presenting stereoscopic images to the user. Most methods are based on one of two main categories: *time multiplexed* and *time parallel* techniques. Time multiplexed methods work by alternating between the left and right eye images. Time parallel methods display both images at once in combination with a process to extract left and right eye views. Some methods can be implemented as either a time multiplexed or a time parallel technique.

Time multiplexed techniques are most commonly found in single display systems, since they rely on alternating images. Typically this is combined with a method for also alternating which eye views the image. One cost-effective time multiplexed technique takes advantage of existing television standards such as NTSC and PAL. Both of these standards use interlacing, which means that first the even lines are drawn on the screen and then the odd. By rendering the left eye image to the even lines of the screen and the right eye image to the odd, we can generate a stereo video stream that is suitable for display on a standard television. When this is viewed with both eyes, it appears as one image that keeps jumping from left to right. A special set of glasses must be worn so that when the left eye image is being displayed, the user's left eye can see and similarly for the right eye. The glasses are designed so that each lens consists of a liquid crystal shutter that can either be transparent or opaque, depending on what voltage is applied to it. By shuttering the glasses at the same rate as the television is interlacing, we can assure that the correct eye is viewing the correct image.

There are a couple of disadvantages to this system. The resolutions of NTSC and PAL are both low compared to a computer monitor. The refresh rate of NTSC (60 Hz) and PAL (50 Hz) produces a fair amount of flicker, especially when you consider that each eye is updated at half this rate. Also, this method requires viewing your images on a television, not the monitor connected to your computer.

To overcome these difficulties, some computer manufacturers offer stereo ready graphics cards. These systems use liquid crystal shuttered glasses to directly view the computer monitor. To obtain the alternating stereo images, the left eye image is rendered to the top half of the screen and the right eye image to the bottom. Then the graphics card enters a special stereo mode where it doubles the refresh rate of the monitor. So a monitor that initially displays both images at 60Hz begins to alternate between the left and right eye at a rate of 120Hz. This results in each eye getting updated at 60Hz, with its original horizontal resolution and half of its original vertical resolution. For this process to work, your application must take up the entire screen while rendering.

Some more recent graphics cards have a left image buffer and a right image buffer for stereo rendering. While this requires either more memory or a lower resolution, it does provide for stereo rendering without having to take over the entire screen. For such a card, double buffering combined with stereo rendering results in quad buffering, which can result in a large number of bits per pixel. For example: 24 bits for an RGB color, another 24 bits for the back buffer's color, plus 24 bits for the z-buffer results in 72 bits per pixel. Now double that for the two different views and you have 144 bits per pixel or 18 megabytes for a 1K by 1K display.

Time parallel techniques display both images at the same time. Headmounted displays and booms have two separate screens, one for each eye. To generate the two video streams requires either two graphics cards or one that can generate two separate outputs. The rendering process then involves just rendering each eye to the correct graphics card or output. Currently, the biggest disadvantage to this approach is the cost of the hardware required.

In contrast, SIRDS (Single Image Random Dot Stereograms) require no special hardware. Both views are displayed in a single image, as in **Figure 7–26**. To view such an image the user must focus either in front of, or behind, the image. When the user's focal point is correct, the two triangular cutouts in the top of the image will appear as one and the image should appear focused. This works because dot patterns repeat at certain intervals. Here, only the depth information is present in the resulting image. This is incorporated by changing the interval between patterns just as our ocular disparity changes with depth.

The next two techniques for stereo rendering can be implemented using either the time parallel or time multiplexed methods. The distinction is slightly blurred because most of the time parallel methods can be multiplexed, though typically there is no advantage to it. Both of these methods have been used by the movie industry to produce "3D" movies. The first is commonly called red-blue (or red-green or red-cyan) stereo and requires the user to wear a pair of glasses that filter entering light. The left eye can only see the image through a red filter, the right through a blue filter. The rendering process typically involves generating images for the two views, converting their RGB values into intensity, and then creating a resulting image. This image's red values are taken from the left eye image intensities. Likewise the blue values (a mixture of blue and green) are taken from the right eye image intensities. The resulting image has none of the original hue or saturation, but it does contain both original images' intensities. (An additional note: red-green methods are also used because the human eye is more sensitive to green than blue.) The benefits of this technique are that the resulting images can be displayed on a monitor, paper, or film, and all one needs to view them is an inexpensive pair of glasses.

Figure 7–26 Single image random dot stereogram of a tetrahedron.

The second technique is similar to the first but it preserves all the color information from the original images. It separates the different views by using polarized light. Normally, the light we see has a mixture of polarization angles, but there are lenses that can filter out a subset of these angles. If we project a color image through a vertical polarizing filter, and then view it through another vertical filter, we will see the original image, just slightly dimmer because we've filtered out all the horizontally polarized light. If we place a horizontal filter and a vertical filter together, all the light is blocked. Polarized stereo rendering typically projects one eye's image through a vertical filter and the other through a horizontal filter. The user wears a pair of glasses containing a vertical filter over one eye and a horizontal filter over the other. This way each eye views the correct image.

All the methods we have discussed for stereo rendering have their advantages and disadvantages, typically revolving around cost and image quality. At the end of this chapter we will look at an example program that renders stereo images using the red-blue technique.

Figure 7–27 Wireframe image and antialiased equivalent.

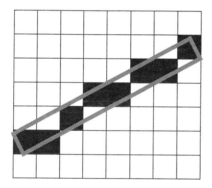 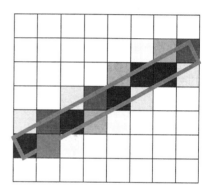

Figure 7–28 A one pixel wide line (outlined in gray) draw using a winner take all approach (left) and a coverage approach (right).

7.15 Aliasing

At one point or another most computer users have run into aliasing problems. This "stair-stepping" occurs because we represent continuous surface geometry with discrete pixels. In computer graphics the most common aliasing problem is jagged edges when rendering lines or surface boundaries, as in **Figure 7–27**.

The aliasing problem stems from the rasterization process as the graphics system converts primitives, such as line segments, into pixels on the screen. For example, the quickest way to rasterize a line is to use an all or nothing strategy. If the line passes through the pixel, then the pixel is set to the line's color; otherwise, it is not altered. As can be seen in **Figure 7–28**, this results in the stair-stepped appearance.

There are several techniques for handling aliasing problems, and they are collectively known as *antialiasing* techniques. One approach to antialiasing is to change how the graphics system rasterizes primitives. Instead of rasterizing a line using an all or nothing approach, we look at how much of the pixel the line occupies. The resulting color for that pixel is a mixture of its original color and the line's color. The ratio of these two colors is determined by the line's occupancy. This works especially well when working primarily with wireframe models. A similar approach breaks each pixel down into smaller subpixels. Primitives are rendered using an all or nothing strategy, but at subpixel resolutions. Then the subpixels are averaged to determine the resulting pixel's color. This tends to require much more memory.

A good result can be obtained by breaking each pixel into 10 subpixels, which requires about 10 times the memory and rendering time. If you don't have access to hardware subpixel rendering, you can approximate it by rendering a large image and then scaling it down. Using a program such as pnmscale, which does bilinear interpolation, you can take a 1000 by 1000 pixel image and scale it down to a 500 by 500 antialiased image. If you have a graphics library that can render into memory instead of the screen, large images such as 6000 by 6000 pixels can be scaled down into high quality results, still at high resolutions such as 2000 by 2000. This may seem like overkill, but on a standard 600dpi color printer this would result in a picture just over three inches on a side.

The last method of antialiasing we will look at uses an accumulation buffer to average a few possibly aliased images together to produce one antialiased result. An accumulation buffer is just a segment of memory that is set aside for performing image operations and storage. The following fragment of C++ code illustrates this process.

```
for (imageNum = 0; imageNum < imageTotal; imageNum++)
  {
  // Jitter the camera and focal point by less than one pixel
  // Render an image
  // add the image to the accumulation buffer
  }
// Divide the accumulation buffer by imageTotal
// Display the resulting antialiased image
```

Instead of using one image with eight subpixels per pixel, we can use eight images without subpixels. The antialiasing is achieved by slightly translating the camera's position and focal point between each image. The amount of translation should be within one pixel of magnitude and perpendicular to the direction of projection. Of course, the camera's position is specified in world coordinates not pixels, but **Equation 7-13** will do the trick. We calculate the new camera position and focal point (i.e., p_{new} and f_{new}) from the offset to avoid difficulties surrounding the transformation matrix at the camera's position.

$$f_{new} = (f M_{WD} + O_p) M_{DW}$$
$$O_w = f_{new} - f \qquad\qquad (7\text{-}13)$$
$$p_{new} = p + O_w$$

In this equation O_p is the offset in pixel coordinates, O_w is the offset in world coordinates, f is the camera focal point, p is the camera position, and the transformation matrices M_{WD} and M_{DW} transform from world coordinates to display coordinates and from display coordinates to world coordinates, respectively.

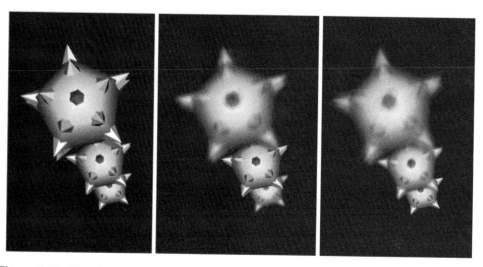

Figure 7–29 Three images showing focal depth. The first has no focal depth, the second is focused on the center object, the third image is focused on the farthest object.

7.16 Camera Tricks

In the previous section we saw how to combine an accumulation buffer and small camera translations to produce an antialiased image. In this section we will cover a few other camera techniques of interest. You may have noticed that with computer generated images all actors are in focus. With a real camera you have to set the focal depth to match the distance of the object you are photographing. Anything that is closer or farther than your focal depth will appear out of focus. This is because a real camera has a lens that lets light pass through a finite area. The camera model we have introduced has a point lens, where all the light travels through at exactly the same point. (See **Figure 7–29** for a comparison.)

We can simulate a finite camera lens by rendering many images, each with a slightly different camera position but the same focal point. Then we accumulate these images and take the average. The resulting image simulates a camera lens with focal depth. The different camera positions are determined by selecting random points from the lens you are trying to simulate. Larger diameter lenses will produce more distortion and vice versa. Increasing the number of random points will improve the precision of your result. Typically 10 to 30 samples is desirable. The images in **Figure 7–29** were created using 30 sample points.

Another difference between a real camera and a computer camera is in the shutter speed. Our model generates an image for a single moment in time; in contrast, a photograph captures what the camera views while its shutter is open. Fast moving objects appear blurred because of changes in their position during the small time that the shutter is open. This effect, known as *motion blur*, can also be simulated with our camera model (**Figure 7–30**). Instead of rendering one image and displaying it, we render a few subframes that are accumulated, averaged, and finally displayed. This is similar to the antialiasing and focal depth techniques

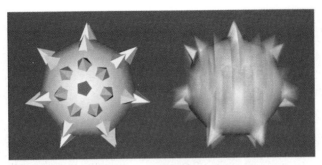

Figure 7–30 Motion blur. Rapidly moving objects appear blurry when recorded on film or videotape. To simulate motion blur with a computer camera, multiple images (or subframes) can be accumulated and averaged. This figure was generated by accumulating 21 subframes.

that we just discussed. In both of those techniques, the camera is jittered while the actors remain fixed in time. To implement motion blur we don't jitter the camera; we increment the scene's time between each subframe. Moving objects or camera movements will result in differences between each subframe. The resulting image approximates the effects of photographing moving objects over a finite time.

7.17 Mouse-Based Interaction

There's no doubt that being able to interactively view an object aids in understanding and recognizing its important features. Using a pointing device (e.g., a mouse or trackball) is certainly the most common method for controlling such movements. The software that accompanies this book contains the vtkRenderWindowInteractor object that translates mouse and keyboard events into modifications to the camera and actors. For example, while the user holds the left mouse button down, the vtkRenderWindowInteractor rotates the camera towards the current pointer position. The farther the pointer is from the center of the window, the faster the camera rotates.

Most of these interactions are straightforward, but there are a few issues associated with rotations. When rotating around an object, one must decide what to do with the view-up vector. We can keep it perpendicular to the direction of projection as we rotate, or we can leave it unchanged. This results in two different types of rotations. If we keep our view-up vector orthogonal to the direction of projection, we will rotate all around the object much like a plane flying around the globe. This is shown in the left half of **Figure 7–31**. If we leave the view-up vector unchanged, our plane will start flying backwards at the north and south poles, as shown in the right half of **Figure 7–31**.

The advantage of a constant view-up vector is that some objects have a natural sense of up and down (e.g., terrain). Elevation and azimuth operations remain consistent as we move around the object. On the other hand, there are singular points where the view-up vector and direction of projection become parallel. In these cases the camera viewing transformation matrix is undefined. Then we have to modify the view-up vector or use the perpendicular view-up / direction of projection method to handle this situation. If the data you are working

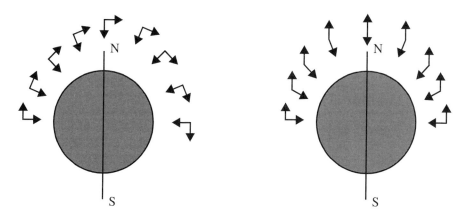

Figure 7–31 Rotations using an orthogonalized view-up vector (left) and a constant view-up vector (right).

with has a well-defined up and down, then it probably makes sense to leave the view-up constant during rotations; otherwise, it makes sense to keep it orthogonal to the direction of projection.

7.18 3D Widgets and User Interaction

Chapter 3 provided an introduction to interaction techniques for graphics (see "Introducing vtkRenderWindowInteractor" on page 68). In the context of visualization, interaction is an essential feature of systems that provide methods for data exploration and query. The classes vtkRenderWindowInteractor and vtkInteractorStyle are core constructs used in VTK to capture windowing-system specific events in the render window, translate them into VTK events, and then take action as appropriate to the event invocation. In Chapter 3 we saw how these classes could be used to manipulate the camera and actors to interactively produce a desired view. This functionality, however, is relatively limited in its ability to interact with data. For example, users often whish to interactively control the positioning of streamline starting points, control the orientation of a clipping plane, or transform an actor. While using interpreted languages (see "Interpreted Code" on page 69) can go a long way to provide this interaction, in some situations the ability to see what you are doing when placing objects is essential. Therefore, it is apparent that a variety of user interaction techniques is required by the visualization system if it is to successfully support real-world applications.

3D widgets are a logical extension of the pervasive 2D widgets found on most computer systems, providing interactive capabilities similar to their 2D counterparts except that they function in the richer 3D space. 3D widgets are capable of providing the variety of user interaction techniques required by a visualization system. Unlike 2D widgets, however, 3D widgets are relatively new technology, and because their application is in the context of a richer space, there is no consensus as to what widgets might constitute a complete set of functionality. Several popular 3D widget sets, for example Open Inventor [Wernecke94], the Brown University 3D Widgets Library [Zeleznik93], and the University of Utah's SCIRUN

3D widgets [Purciful95], have distinctly different components in their widget toolbox. The widget sets vary according to the perceived purpose of the graphical environment in which they exist

3D widgets are a recent addition (see **Figure 7–32**) to VTK. In principal, the core functionality is simple: events captured by the vtkRenderWindow are in turn translated into VTK events. Observers which have registered themselves with the vtkRenderWindow receive these VTK events, take the appropriate action, and then may either pass the event along to the next observer in the list, or abort further processing of the event. (Note: observers can be prioritized according to the order in which they receive events.)

It is the implementation of 3D widgets, that is, what they can do with the events, that makes them so powerful. As **Figure 7–32** shows, widgets typically provide a representation in the scene that can be selected and manipulated. For example, a vtkLineWidget can be used to position a rake of streamline seed points and represents itself with a thick line (tube) and two spherical end points. Widgets also may directly manipulate an underlying class—the vtk-ScalarBarWidget enables the user to interactively size, orient (horizontal or vertical), and position a vtkScalarBar. Widgets also provide additional functionality such as managing an internal implicit function or transformation matrix (e.g., vtkBoxWidget). The following is a list of widgets currently found in VTK and a brief description of their capabilities.

- vtkScalarBarWidget — manage a vtkScalarBar including positioning, scaling, and orienting it.

- vtkPointWidget — position a point x-y-z location in 3D space. The widget produces a polygonal output.

- vtkLineWidget — place a straight line with a specified subdivision resolution. The widget produces a polygonal output.

- vtkPlaneWidget — orient and position a finite plane. The plane resolution is variable and the widget produces an implicit function and a polygonal output.

- vtkImplicitPlaneWidget — orient and position an unbounded plane. The widget produces an implicit function and a polygonal output. The polygonal output is created by clipping the plane with a bounding box.

- vtkBoxWidget — orient and position a bounding box. The widget produces an implicit function and a transformation matrix.

- vtkImagePlaneWidget — manipulate three orthogonal planes within a 3D volumetric data set. Probing of the planes to obtain data position, pixel value, and window-level is possible.

- vtkSphereWidget — manipulate a sphere of variable resolution. The widget produces an implicit function, a transformation matrix, and enables the control of focal point and position to support such classes as vtkCamera and vtkLight.

- vtkSplineWidget — manipulate an interpolating 3D spline. The widget produces a polygonal data represented by a series of line segments of specified resolution. The widget also directly manages underlying splines for each of the x-y-z coordinate values.

The key to widget design is careful implementation of intuitive, simple user interaction techniques. For example, the end points on the vtkLineWidget (represented as small spheres) can

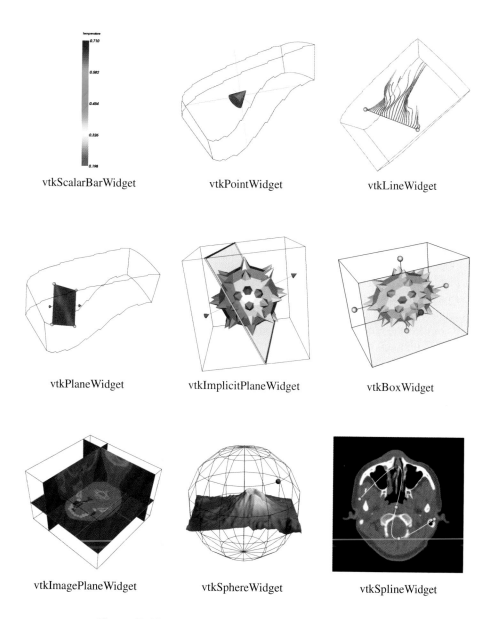

Figure 7–32 Application of some 3D widgets found in VTK.

be selected and dragged to a new position. The vtkLineWidget supports the modifier "Shift" key to lock motion of the end points along the coordinate *x-y-z* axes. The initial direction of motion is used to determine which of the axes the user is moving the end point along. Such attention to detail is essential to successful widget design and will continue to change as the technology evolves in the future.

7.19 Putting It All Together

This chapter has covered a wide variety of topics. In this section we demonstrate applications of each topic to some simple problems.

Texture Mapping

Figure 7–33 shows the complete source code for a simple texture mapping example. You will notice that most of the code is similar to what we used in the preceding examples. The key step here is the creation of a vtkTexture object. This object interfaces between its data input and the texture mapping functions of the graphics library. The vtkTexture instance is associated with an actor. More than one texture instance may be shared between multiple actors. For texture mapping to function properly, texture coordinates must be defined by the actor's modeller.

One interesting note regarding the vtkTexture object. Instances of this class are mappers that have an Input instance variable that is updated during each render. The input type is a vtkImageData dataset type. Thus, a visualization pipeline can be constructed to read, process, and/or generate the texture map. This includes using the object vtkRendererSource, which converts the renderer's image into an image data dataset. The input texture map can be either 2D (a pixmap) or 3D (a volume).

A few words of warning when using textures. Some renderers only support 2D texture, or may not support alpha textures. Also, many rendering systems require that each dimension of the image dataset is an exact power of two. In VTK, non-power of two textures are automatically converted to power of two at the expense of extra computation.

Volume Rendering

This example focuses on volume rendering. The source code shown in example **Figure 7–34** begins by creating the usual objects. Then we use a vtkStructuredPointsReader to read in a volume dataset for a high potential iron protein. We create a vtkPiecewiseFunction object to map the scalar values in the volume dataset to opacity, and a vtkColorTransferFunction object to map the scalar values to color. These two transfer functions are referenced from the vtkVolumeProperty object. In addition, we use the ShadeOn() method of vtkVolumeProperty to enable shading for this volume, and the SetInterpolationTypeToLinear() method to request trilinear interpolation. Since we are using a ray casting approach, we need to create a ray function. In this example we use a vtkVolumeRayCastCompositeFunction object for this purpose. The output of the reader is given to the vtkVolumeRayCastMapper as the scalar input, and the SetVolumeRayCastFunction() method is used to assign the ray function. The vtkVolume object is quite similar to a vtkActor, and the SetVolumeMapper() and SetVolumeProperty() methods are used just like the SetMapper() and SetProperty() methods of vtkActor. Finally, we add this volume to the renderer, adjust the camera, set the desired image update rate and start the interactor.

To produce a maximum intensity projection in **Figure 7–34**, we would simply change the type of the ray function to a vtkVolumeRayCastMIPFunction. We could also produce a

```
vtkBMPReader bmpReader
  bmpReader SetFileName "$VTK_DATA_ROOT/Data/masonry.bmp"
vtkTexture atext
  atext SetInput [bmpReader GetOutput]
  atext InterpolateOn

vtkPlaneSource plane
vtkPolyDataMapper  planeMapper
  planeMapper SetInput [plane GetOutput]
vtkActor planeActor
  planeActor SetMapper planeMapper
  planeActor SetTexture atext

vtkRenderer ren1
vtkRenderWindow renWin
    renWin AddRenderer ren1
vtkRenderWindowInteractor iren
    iren SetRenderWindow renWin

# Add the actors to the renderer
ren1 AddActor planeActor
```

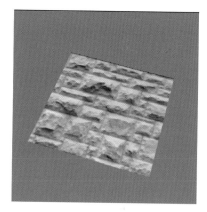

Figure 7–33 Example of texture mapping
(`TPlane.tcl`).

surface image using a vtkVolumeRayCastIsosurfaceFunction where the IsoValue instance
variable would be set to define the surface.

Red-Blue Stereo

In our first example, we will be looking at using red-blue stereo rendering. We start off with
the example shown in **Figure 7–35**, which renders something akin to a mace. Then, in
Figure 7–35 we add in red-blue stereo rendering by adding two lines near the bottom that
invoke the StereoRenderOn() and SetStereoType() methods. Once these two methods have
been invoked, further rendering will be done in stereo. The picture in the upper right corner
displays a grayscale version of the resulting image.

Motion Blur

In our second example, we show how to simulate motion blur using the *Visualization Toolkit*.
As shown in **Figure 7–36**, we begin with our previous example. We then remove the two
lines controlling stereo rendering and add a few lines to create another mace. We position the
first mace in the top of the rendering window and the second mace at the bottom. We then use
the SetSubFrames() method to start performing subframe accumulation. Here, we will perform 21 renders to produce the final image. For motion blur to be noticeable, something must

```
# Create the standard renderer, render window and interactor
vtkRenderer ren1
vtkRenderWindow renWin
    renWin AddRenderer ren1
vtkRenderWindowInteractor iren
    iren SetRenderWindow renWin

# Create the reader for the data
vtkStructuredPointsReader reader
    reader SetFileName "$VTK_DATA_ROOT/Data/ironProt.vtk"

# Create transfer mapping scalar value to opacity
vtkPiecewiseFunction opacityTransferFunction
    opacityTransferFunction AddPoint   20    0.0
    opacityTransferFunction AddPoint   255   0.2

# Create transfer mapping scalar value to color
vtkColorTransferFunction colorTransferFunction
    colorTransferFunction AddRGBPoint       0.0 0.0 0.0 0.0
    colorTransferFunction AddRGBPoint      64.0 1.0 0.0 0.0
    colorTransferFunction AddRGBPoint     128.0 0.0 0.0 1.0
    colorTransferFunction AddRGBPoint     192.0 0.0 1.0 0.0
    colorTransferFunction AddRGBPoint     255.0 0.0 0.2 0.0

# The property describes how the data will look
vtkVolumeProperty volumeProperty
    volumeProperty SetColor colorTransferFunction
    volumeProperty SetScalarOpacity opacityTransferFunction
    volumeProperty ShadeOn
    volumeProperty SetInterpolationTypeToLinear

# The mapper / ray cast function know how to render the data
vtkVolumeRayCastCompositeFunction  compositeFunction
vtkVolumeRayCastMapper volumeMapper
    volumeMapper SetVolumeRayCastFunction compositeFunction
    volumeMapper SetInput [reader GetOutput]

# Set the mapper and the property and
vtkVolume volume
    volume SetMapper volumeMapper
    volume SetProperty volumeProperty

ren1 AddVolume volume
renWin Render
```

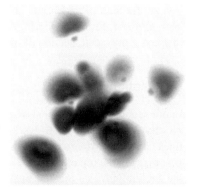

Figure 7–34 Volume rendering of a high potential
iron protein (SimpleRayCast.tcl).

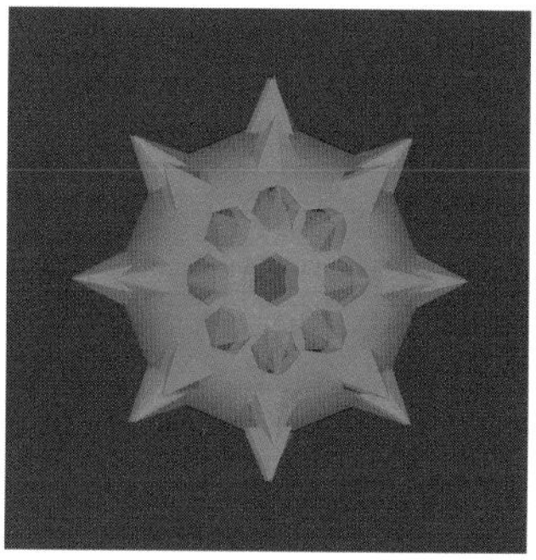

```
vtkRenderer *ren1 = vtkRenderer::New();
vtkRenderWindow *renWin =
      vtkRenderWindow::New();
  renWin->AddRenderer(ren1);
vtkRenderWindowInteractor *iren =
      vtkRenderWindowInteractor::New();
  iren->SetRenderWindow(renWin);

// create the pipline, ball and spikes
vtkSphereSource *sphere =
      vtkSphereSource::New();
  sphere->SetThetaResolution(7);
  sphere->SetPhiResolution(7);
vtkPolyDataMapper *sphereMapper = vtkPolyDataMapper::New();
  sphereMapper->SetInput(sphere->GetOutput());
vtkActor *sphereActor = vtkActor::New();
  sphereActor->SetMapper(sphereMapper);

vtkConeSource *cone = vtkConeSource::New();
  cone->SetResolution(5);
vtkGlyph3D *glyph = vtkGlyph3D::New();
  glyph->SetInput(sphere->GetOutput());
  glyph->SetSource(cone->GetOutput());
  glyph->SetVectorModeToUseNormal();
  glyph->SetScaleModeToScaleByVector();
  glyph->SetScaleFactor(0.25);
vtkPolyDataMapper *spikeMapper = vtkPolyDataMapper::New();
  spikeMapper->SetInput(glyph->GetOutput());
vtkActor *spikeActor = vtkActor::New();
  spikeActor->SetMapper(spikeMapper);

ren1->AddActor(sphereActor);
ren1->AddActor(spikeActor);
ren1->SetBackground(0.2,0.3,0.4);
renWin->SetSize(300,300);

renWin->Render();
ren1->GetActiveCamera()->Zoom(1.4);
renWin->StereoRenderOn();
renWin->SetStereoTypeToRedBlue();
renWin->Render();
```

Figure 7–35 An example of red-blue stereo rendering (Mace3.cxx).

be moving, so we set up a loop to rotate the bottom mace by two degrees between each sub-frame. Over the 21 subframes it will rotate 40 degrees from its initial position. It is important to remember that the resulting image is not displayed until the required number of subframes have been rendered.

```
// changes and additions to the
// preceding example's source
vtkActor *spikeActor2 = vtkActor::New();
  spikeActor2->SetMapper(spikeMapper);

spikeActor2->SetPosition(0,-0.7,0);
sphereActor2->SetPosition(0,-0.7,0);

ren1->AddActor(sphereActor2);
ren1->AddActor(spikeActor2);

// zoom in a little
ren1->GetActiveCamera()->Zoom(1.5);

renWin->SetSubFrames(21);

for (i = 0; i <= 1.0; i = i + 0.05)
  {
  spikeActor2->RotateY(2);
  sphereActor2->RotateY(2);
  renWin->Render();
  }

iren->Start();
```

Figure 7–36   Example of motion blur (MotBlur.cxx).

Focal Depth

Now we will change the previous example to illustrate focal depth. First, we change the position of the bottom mace, moving it farther away from us. Since it is farther away it will appear smaller, so we scale it by a factor of two to maintain reasonable image size. We then remove the code for rendering the subframes and instead set the number of frames for focal depth rendering. We also set the camera's focal point and focal disk to appropriate values. The resulting image and the required changes to the source code are shown in **Figure 7–37**.

vtkLineWidget

There are a variety of 3D widgets in VTK all of which function in a similar fashion. 3D widgets are a subclass of vtkInteractorObserver meaning that they are associated with a vtkRenderWindow and observe events in the render window (). (Note: vtkInteractorStyle— see "Introducing vtkRenderWindowInteractor" on page 68—is also a subclass of vtkInteractorObserver. The interactor style differs from a 3D widget in that it does not have a representation in the scene.) The following example shows the general approach to using a 3D widget using vtkLineWidget as an example (**Figure 7–39**). First the widget is instantiated and then placed. Placing means positioning, scaling, and orienting the widget consistent with the object on which they operate. By default, widgets are enabled with a "keypress-i" event, but the specific event to enable the widget can be modified.

```
// changes to the preceding example

// set the actors position and scale
spikeActor->SetPosition(0,0.7,0);
sphereActor->SetPosition(0,0.7,0);
spikeActor2->SetPosition(0,-1,-10);
sphereActor2->SetPosition(0,-1,-10);
spikeActor2->SetScale(1.5,1.5,1.5);
sphereActor2->SetScale(1.5,1.5,1.5);

// zoom in a little
ren1->GetActiveCamera()->SetFocalPoint(0,0,0);
ren1->GetActiveCamera()->Zoom(1.8);
ren1->GetActiveCamera()->SetFocalDisk(0.05);

renWin->SetFDFrames(11);
renWin->Render();

iren->Start();
```

Figure 7–37 Example of a scene rendered with focal depth (`CamBlur.cxx`).

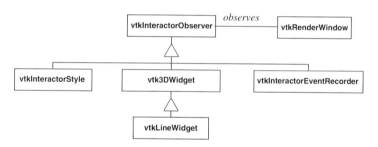

Figure 7–38 Partial class hierarchy for 3D widgets. Each 3D widget observes a particular vtkRender-Window similar to vtkInteractorStyle. Unlike the vtkInteractorStyle which is used to manipulate the camera, 3D widgets have a representation in the scene that can be directly manipulated. More than one vtkInteractorObserver can watch a vtkRenderWindow at a given time, so classes like vtkInteractor-EventRecorder can record an event and pass them on to the next vtkInteractorObserver observing the vtkRenderWindow.

   The widget interfaces with the application through the command/observer event handling mechanism (see "Events and Observers" on page 64). 3D widgets invoke several events, the most important being the StartInteractionEvent, InteractionEvent, and EndInteractionEvents. These events are typically invoked, for example, on mouse down, mouse move, and mouse up, respectively. In the example shown here, Tcl procedures are tied to the StartInteractionEvent and InteractionEvent using the AddObserver() method to produce streamlines as the widget is manipulated. Note that the streamline is seeded with a polygonal dataset each time an InteractionEvent is invoked using the GetPolyData() method. The pipeline update mechanism then automatically executes on the next render since the input to the streamline is modified.

```
vtkRungeKutta4 rk4
vtkPolyData seeds
vtkStreamTracer streamer
     streamer SetInput [reader GetOutput]
     streamer SetSource seeds

vtkRenderWindowInteractor iren
     iren SetRenderWindow renWin

vtkLineWidget lineWidget
     lineWidget SetInteractor iren
     lineWidget SetInput [reader GetOutput]
     lineWidget SetAlignToYAxis
     lineWidget PlaceWidget
     lineWidget GetPolyData seeds
     lineWidget ClampToBoundsOn
     lineWidget SetResolution 25
     [lineWidget GetLineProperty] SetColor 0 0 0
     lineWidget AddObserver StartInteractionEvent
BeginInteraction
     lineWidget AddObserver InteractionEvent
GenerateStreamlines

(skipping material...)

proc BeginInteraction {} { streamline VisibilityOn }
proc GenerateStreamlines {} { lineWidget GetPolyData seeds }
```

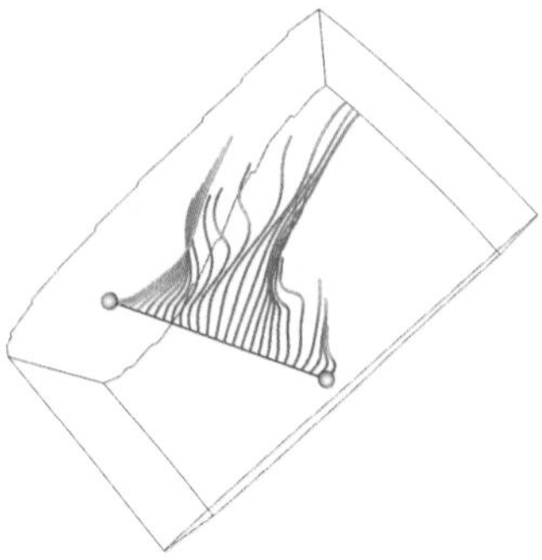

Figure 7–39 Using the vtkLineWidget to produce streamtubes in the combustor dataset. The StartInteractionEvent turns the visibility of the streamlines on; the InteractionEvent causes the streamlines to regenerate themselves (LineWidget.tcl).

7.20 Chapter Summary

Alpha opacity is a graphics method to simulate transparent objects. Compositing is the process of blending translucent samples in order. Alpha compositing requires the data to be ordered properly.

Texture mapping is a powerful technique to introduce additional detail into an image without extensive geometric modelling. Applying 2D texture maps to the surface of an object is analogous to pasting a picture. The location of the texture map is specified via texture coordinates.

Volume rendering is a powerful rendering technique to view the interior of inhomogeneous objects. Most volume rendering techniques can be classified as image-order or object-order, although some are a combination of the two while others do not fall into either category. Object-order techniques generally composite voxels in front-to-back or back-to-front order. Image-order techniques cast rays through pixels in the image plane to sample the volume. Other methods may traverse both the image and the volume at the same time or may operate in the frequency domain. For effective visualization of volumetric data, classification and shading are important considerations. Regions of interest may be used to reduce the amount of data visible in an image. Due to the complexity of volume rendering algorithms, efficiency and methods that allow for interactivity are critical.

Stereo rendering techniques create two separate views for the right and left eyes. This simulates binocular parallax and allows us to see depth in the image. Time multiplexed techniques alternate left and right eye views in rapid succession. Time parallel techniques display both images at the same time.

Raster devices often suffer from aliasing effects. Antialiasing techniques are used to minimize the effects of aliasing. These techniques create blended images that soften the boundary of hard edges.

By using an accumulation buffer we can create interesting effects, including motion blur and focal blur. In motion blurring we accumulate multiple renders as the actors move. To simulate focal blur, we jitter the camera position and hold its focal point constant.

Effective visualizations are inherently interactive. Not only are camera manipulation models required for different types of data, but methods to interact, query, and modify data are essential. 3D widgets are important contributions to this end. They provide intuitive graphical interface to the data through a representation in the scene that can be easily manipulated. 3D widgets also generate supplemental information such as implicit functions, output polygonal data, and transformation matrices that may be applied to objects in the scene.

7.21 Bibliographic Notes

An overview of volume rendering and volume visualization techniques can be found in a tutorial by Kaufman [Kaufman91]. Many of the volume rendering techniques discussed in this chapter are also accessible from research institutions as source code. The shear-warp algorithm is provided within the VolPack rendering library and is available on the Web at `http://www-graphics.stanford.edu/software/volpack/`. SUNY Stony Brook offers a turn-key volume visualization system called VolVis to nonprofit and government organizations. Source code and executable versions are available at `http://www.cs.sunysb.edu/~volvis`. In addition, an application called Vis5D is available that applies volume visualization techniques to time varying atmospheric weather data. Vis5D may be obtained from the Web location `http://vis5d.sourceforge.net`. A commercial volume rendering application, VolView, developed on top of The Visualization Toolkit, is available from Kitware for a 30-day trial at `http://www.kitware.com/products/volview.html`

7.22 References

[Cabral94]

B. Cabral, N. Cam, J. Foran. "Accelerated Volume Rendering and Tomographic Reconstruction Using Texture Mapping Hardware." In *Proceedings of 1994 Symposium on Volume Visualization*. pp. 91–98, October 1994.

[Cignoni96]
   P. Cignoni, C. Montani, E. Puppo, R. Scopigno. "Optimal Isosurface Extraction from Irregular Volume Data." In *Proceedings of 1996 Symposium on Volume Visualization*. pp. 31–38, IEEE Computer Society Press, Los Alamitos, CA, October 1996.

[Drebin88]
   R. A. Drebin, L. Carpenter, P. Hanrahan. "Volume Rendering." *Computer Graphics*. 22(4):64–75 (Siggraph 1988).

[Hodges92]
   L. F. Hodges. "Tutorial: Time-Multiplexed Stereoscopic Computer Graphics." *IEEE Computer Graphics & Applications*. March 1992.

[Kaufman91]
   A. Kaufman (ed.). *Volume Visualization*. IEEE Computer Society Press, Los Alamitos, CA, 1991.

[Kaufman93]
   A. Kaufman, R. Yagel, D. Cohen. "Volume Graphics." *IEEE Computer*. 26(7):51–64, July 1993.

[Kelly94]
   M. Kelly, K. Gould, S. Winner, A. Yen. "Hardware Accelerated Rendering of CSG and Transparency." *Computer Graphics (SIGGRAPH '94)*. pp. 177-184.

[Kikinis96]
   R. Kikinis, M. Shenton, D. Iosifescu, R. McCarley, P. Saiviroonporn, H. Hokama, A. Robatino, D. Metcalf, C. Wible, C. Portas, R. Donnino, F. Jolesz. "A Digital Brain Atlas for Surgical Planning, Model Driven Segmentation and Teaching." *IEEE Transactions on Visualization and Computer Graphics*. 2(3), September 1996.

[Krueger91]
   W. Krueger. "The Application of Transport Theory to Visualization of 3D Scalar Data Fields." *Computers in Physics*. pp. 397–406, July/August 1994.

[Lacroute94]
   P. Lacroute and M. Levoy. "Fast Volume Rendering Using a Shear-Warp Factorization of the Viewing Transformation." In *Proceedings of SIGGRAPH '94*. pp. 451-458, Addison-Wesley, Reading, MA, 1994.

[Laur91]
   D. Laur and P. Hanrahan. "Hierarchical Splatting: A Progressive Refinement Algorithm for Volume Rendering." In *Proceedings of SIGGRAPH '91*. 25:285–288, 1991.

[Levoy88]
   M. Levoy. "Display of Surfaces from Volumetric Data." *IEEE Computer Graphics & Applications*. 8(3), pp. 29–37, May 1988.

[Purciful95]
   J.T. Purciful. "Three-Dimensional Widgets for Scientific Visualization and Animation." Masters Thesis, Dept. of Computer Science, Univ. of Utah, 1995.

[Shirley90]
   P. Shirley and A. Tuchman. "A Polygonal Approximation to Direct Volume Rendering." *Computer Graphics*. 24(5):63–70, 1990.

[Silva96]
   C. Silva, J. S. B. Mitchell, A. E. Kaufman. "Fast Rendering of Irregular Grids." In *Proceedings of 1996 Symposium on Volume Visualization*. pp. 15–22, IEEE Computer Society Press, Los Alamitos, CA, October 1996.

[Sobierajski95]
L. Sobierajski and R. Avila. "A Hardware Acceleration Method for Volumetric Ray Trac-
ing." In *Proceedings of Visualization '95*. pp. 27–34, IEEE Computer Society Press, Los
Alamitos, CA, October 1995.

[Totsuka92]
T. Totsuka and M. Levoy. "Frequency Domain Volume Rendering." *Computer Graphics
(SIGGRAPH '93)*. pp. 271–278, August 1993.

[Wernecke94]
J. Wernecke. *The Inventor Mentor*. Addison-Wesley, Reading MA,1994.

[Westover90]
L. Westover. "Footprint Evaluation for Volume Rendering." *Computer Graphics (SIG-
GRAPH '90)*. 24(4):36, 1990.

[Wilhelms91]
J. Wilhelms and A. Van Gelder. "A Coherent Projection Approach for Direct Volume Rendering." *Computer Graphics (SIGGRAPH '91)*. 25(4):275–284, 1991.

[Wilhelms96]
J. P. Wilhelms, A. Van Gelder, P. Tarantino, J. Gibbs. "Hierarchical and Parallelizable Direct Volume Rendering for Irregular and Multiple Grids." In *Proceedings of Visualization
'96*. pp. 73ê80, IEEE Computer Society Press, Los Alamitos, CA, October 1996.

[Yagel92a]
R. Yagel, D. Cohen, and A. Kaufman. "Normal Estimation in 3D Discrete Space." *The Visual Computer*. pp. 278–291, 1992.

[Yagel92b]
R. Yagel and A. Kaufman. "Template-based Volume Viewing." In *Proceedings of Euro-
graphics '92*. pp. 153–167, September 1992.

[Zeleznik93]
R. C. Zeleznik, K. P. Herndon, D. C. Robbins, N. Huang, T. Meyer, N. Parker, J. F. Hughes.
"An Interactive Toolkit for Constructing 3D Interfaces." *Computer Graphics (Proceedings
of Siggraph '93)*. 27(4):81–84. July 1993.

[Zuiderveld92]
K. J. Zuiderveld, A. h. j. Koning, and M. A. Viergever. "Acceleration of Ray-Casting Using
3D Distance Transforms." In *Proceedings of Visualization and Biomedical Computing*, pp.
324–335, October 1992.

7.23 Exercises

7.1   In astronomy, photographs can be taken that show the movements of the stars over a
period of time by keeping the camera's shutter open. Without accounting for the rotation of the earth, these photographs display a swirl of circular arcs all centered about a
common point. Such time lapse photography is essentially capturing motion blur. If we
tried to simulate these images using the motion blur technique described in this chapter,
they would look different from the photographs. Why is this? How could you change
the simple motion blur algorithm to correct this?

7.2   In **Figure 7–25** we show the difference between stereo rendering with two or one view
planes. If you were viewing a rectangle head-on (its surface normal parallel to your

direction), what artifacts would be introduced by rendering onto one view plane while using the equations for two planes?

7.3   On some graphics systems transparent objects are rendered using a technique called screen door transparency. Basically, every pixel is either completely opaque or completely transparent. Any value in between is approximated using dithering. So a polygon that was 50 percent opaque would be rendered by drawing only half of the pixels. What visual artifacts does this introduce? What blending problems can arise in using such a technique?

7.4   In this chapter we describe a few different techniques for antialiased rendering. One technique involved rendering a large image and then scaling it down to the desired size using bilinear interpolation. Another technique involved rendering multiple images at the desired size using small camera movements and then accumulating them into a final image. When rendering a model with a surface representation, these two techniques will produce roughly the same result. When rendering a model with a wireframe representation there will be significant differences. Why is this?

7.5   You need to create a small image of a volume dataset to include on your web page. The dataset contains 512^3 voxels, and the desired image size is 100^2 pixels. You can use a software object-order method that projects each voxel onto the image, or a software ray casting method that casts one ray for each pixel. Assuming that identical images are created, which method would you select, and why?

7.6   Two software developers implement volume rendering methods. The first developer uses a software ray casting approach, while the second uses a graphics hardware texture mapping approach. The grayscale images are generated and displayed on a workstation with an 8 bit frame buffer (256 levels of gray). They both use the same interpolation method and the same compositing scheme, yet the two methods produce different images even though the same number of samples from identical locations were used to generate the images. Why is this?

7.7   In the classification of some medical dataset, scalar values from 100 to 200 represent skin, 200 to 300 represent muscle and 300 to 400 represent bone. The color transfer functions define skin as tan, muscle as red, and bone as white. If we interpolate scalar value and then perform classification, what classification artifacts may appear in the image?

7.8   The normal encoding example illustrated in **Figure 7–22** produced 82 indices at a recursion depth of two, which would require seven bits of storage. If we instead use a recursion depth of three, how many indices are there? How many unique vector directions does this represent? How many bits of storage does this require?

7.9   Writing an object-order back-to-front projection algorithm is more difficult for a perspective viewing transformation than a parallel viewing transformation. Explain why this is and draw a 2D diagram of the volume and the viewing frustum that illustrates the issues.

Advanced Data Representation

This chapter examines advanced topics in data representation. Topics include topological and geometric relationships and computational methods for cells and datasets.

8.1 Coordinate Systems

We will examine three different coordinate systems: the global, dataset, and structured coordinate systems. **Figure 8–1** shows the relationship between the global and dataset coordinate systems, and depicts the structured coordinate system.

Global Coordinate System

The global coordinate system is a Cartesian, three-dimensional space. Each point is expressed as a triplet of values (x,y,z) along the x, y, and z axes. This is the same system that was described in Chapter 3 (see "Coordinate Systems" on page 46).

The global coordinate system is always used to specify dataset geometry (i.e., the point coordinates), and data attributes such as normals and vectors. We will use the word "position" to indicate that we are using global coordinates.

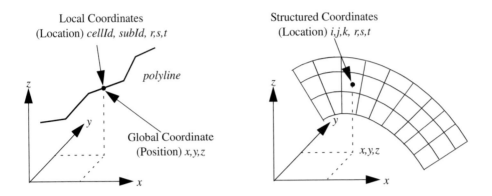

Figure 8–1 Local and global coordinate systems.

Dataset Coordinate System

The dataset, or local, coordinate system is based on combined topological and geometric coordinates. The topological coordinate is used to identify a particular cell (or possibly a sub-cell), and the geometric coordinate is used to identify a particular location within the cell. Together they uniquely specify a location in the dataset. Here we will use the word "location" to refer to local or dataset coordinates.

The topological coordinate is an "id": a unique, nonnegative integer number referring to either a dataset point or cell. For a composite cell, we use an additional "sub-id" to refer to a particular primary cell that composes the composite cell. The sub-id is also unique and non-negative. The id and sub-id together select a particular primary cell.

To specify a location within the primary cell, we use geometric coordinates. These geometric coordinates, or *parametric coordinates*, are coordinates "natural" or canonical to the particular topology and dimension of a cell.

We can best explain local coordinates by referring to an example. If we consider the polyline cell type shown in **Figure 8–1**, we can specify the position of a point by indicating 1) the polyline cell id, 2) the primary cell (i.e., line) sub-id and 3) the parametric coordinate of the line. Because the line is one-dimensional, the natural or parametric coordinate is based on the one-dimensional parameter r. Then any point *along* the line is given by a linear combination of the two end points of the line x_i and x_{i+1}

$$x(r) = (1-r)x_i + rx_{i+1} \tag{8-1}$$

where the parametric coordinate r is constrained between $(0,1)$. In this equation we are assuming that the sub-id is equal to i.

The number of parametric coordinates corresponds to the topological dimension of the cell. Three-dimensional cells will be characterized by the three parametric coordinates (r, s, t). For cells of topological order less than three, we will ignore the last $(3 - n)$ parametric coordinates, where n is the topological order of the cell. For convenience and consistency, we also will constrain each parametric coordinate to range between $(0,1)$.

Every cell type will have its own parametric coordinate system. Later in this chapter we will describe the parametric coordinate systems in detail. But first we will examine another coordinate system, the *structured coordinate system*.

Structured Coordinate System

Many dataset types are structured. This includes image data and structured grids. Because of their inherent structure, they have their own natural coordinate system. This coordinate system is based on the *i-j-k* indexing scheme that we touched on in Chapter 5 (see "Image Data" on page 124).

The structured coordinate system is a natural way to describe components of a structured dataset. By fixing some indices, and allowing the others to vary within a limited range, we can specify points, lines, surfaces, and volumes. For example, by fixing the *i* index $i = i_0$, and allowing the *j* and *k* indices to range between their minimum and maximum values, we specify a surface. If we fix three indices, we specify a point, if we fix two indices, we specify a line, and if we allow three indices to vary, we specify a volume (or sub-volume). The structured coordinate system is generally used to specify a *region of interest* (or ROI). The region of interest is an area that we want to visualize, or to operate on.

There is a simple relationship between the point and cell id of the dataset coordinate system and the structured coordinate system. To obtain a point id p_{id} given the indices (i_p, j_p, k_p) and dimensions (n_x, n_y, n_z) we use

$$p_{id} = i_p + j_p n_x + k_p n_x n_y \tag{8-2}$$

with $0 \le i_p < n_x$, $0 \le j_p < n_y$, $0 \le k_p < n_z$. (We can use this id to index into an array of points or point attribute data.) This equation implicitly assumes an ordering of the points in topological space. Points along the *i* axis vary fastest, followed by the *j* and then the *k* axes. A similar relationship exists for cell id's

$$cell_{id} = i_p + j_p(n_x - 1) + k_p(n_x - 1)(n_y - 1) \tag{8-3}$$

Here we've taken into account that there are one fewer cells along each topological axes than there are points.

8.2 Interpolation Functions

Computer visualization deals with discrete data. The data is either supplied at a finite number of points or created by sampling continuous data at a finite number of points. But we often need information at positions other than these discrete point locations. This may be for rendering or for subsampling the data during algorithm execution. We need to interpolate data from known points to some intermediate point using *interpolation functions*.

Interpolation functions relate the values at cell points to the interior of the cell. Thus, we assume that information is defined at cell points, and that we must interpolate from these points. We can express the result as a weighted average of the data values at each cell point.

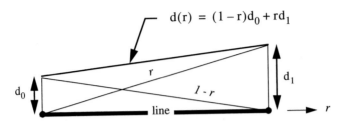

$$d(r) = (1 - r)d_0 + rd_1$$

Figure 8–2 Interpolation is a linear combination of local interpolation functions. Interpolation functions are scaled by data values at cell points.

General Form

To interpolate data from the cell points p_i to a point p that is inside the cell, we need three pieces of information:

1. the data values at each cell point,

2. the parametric coordinates of the point p within the cell, and

3. the cell type including interpolation functions.

Given this information, the interpolation functions are a linear combination of the data values at the cell points

$$d = \sum_{i}^{n-1} W_i \cdot d_i \tag{8-4}$$

where d is the data value at the interior cell location (r,s,t), d_i is the data value at the ith cell point, and W_i is a weight at the ith cell point. The interpolation weights are functions of the parametric coordinates $W_i = W(r,s,t)$. In addition, because we want $d = d_i$ when the interior point coincides with a cell point, we can place additional constraints on the weights

$$W_i = 1, W_j = 0 \text{ when } p = p_i \text{ and } i \neq j \tag{8-5}$$

We also desire the interpolated data value d to be no smaller than the minimum d_i and no larger than the maximum d_i. Thus the weights should also satisfy

$$\sum_i W_i = 1, \quad 0 \leq W_i \leq 1 \tag{8-6}$$

The interpolation functions are of a characteristic shape. They reach their maximum value $W_i = 1$ at cell point p_i, and are zero at all other points. Examining **Equation 8-1**, we draw **Figure 8–2** and see that each interpolation function has the shape of a peaked "hat," and that interpolation is a linear combination of these hat functions, scaled by the data value at each point.

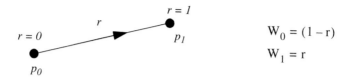

Figure 8–3 Parametric coordinate system and interpolation functions for a line.

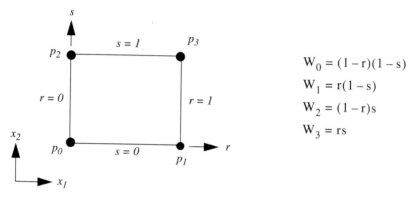

Figure 8–4 Parametric coordinate system and interpolation functions for a pixel.

Equation 8-4 is the general form for cell interpolation. It is used to interpolate any data value defined at the cell points to any other point within the cell. We have only to define the specific interpolation functions W_i for each cell type.

Specific Forms

Each cell type has its own interpolation functions. The weights W_i are functions of the parametric coordinates r, s, and t. In this section we will define the parametric coordinate system and interpolation function for each primary cell type. Composite cells use the interpolation functions and parametric coordinates of their composing primary cells. The only difference in coordinate system specification between primary and composite cells is that composite cells use the additional sub-id to specify a particular primary cell.

Vertex. Vertex cells do not require parametric coordinates or interpolation functions since they are zero-dimensional. The single weighting function is $W_0 = 1$.

Line. Figure 8–3 shows the parametric coordinate system and interpolation functions for a line. The line is described using the single parametric coordinate r.

Pixel. Figure 8–4 shows the parametric coordinate system and interpolation functions for a pixel cell type. The pixel is described using the two parametric coordinates (r,s). Note that the pixel edges are constrained to lie parallel to the global coordinate axes. These are often

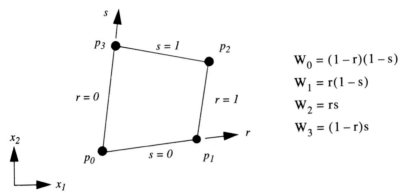

$$W_0 = (1-r)(1-s)$$
$$W_1 = r(1-s)$$
$$W_2 = rs$$
$$W_3 = (1-r)s$$

Figure 8–5 Parametric coordinate system and interpolation functions for a quadrilateral.

referred to as *bilinear interpolation* functions.

Quadrilateral. Figure 8–5 shows the parametric coordinate system and interpolation functions for a quadrilateral cell type. The quadrilateral is described using the two parametric coordinates (r,s).

Triangle. Figure 8–6 shows the parametric coordinate system and interpolation functions for a triangle cell type. The triangle is characterized using the two parametric coordinates (r,s).

Polygon. Figure 8–7 shows the parametric coordinate system and interpolation functions for a polygon cell type. The polygon is characterized using the two parametric coordinates (r,s). The parametric coordinate system is defined by creating a rectangle oriented along the first edge of the polygon. The rectangle also must bound the polygon.

The polygon poses a special problem since we do not know how many vertices define the polygon. As a result, it is not possible to create general interpolation functions in the fash-

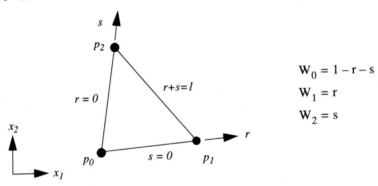

$$W_0 = 1-r-s$$
$$W_1 = r$$
$$W_2 = s$$

Figure 8–6 Parametric coordinate system and interpolation functions for a triangle.

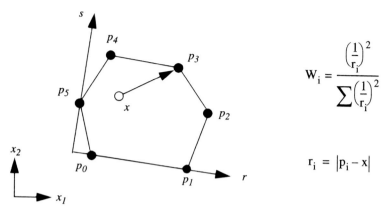

$$W_i = \frac{\left(\frac{1}{r_i}\right)^2}{\sum\left(\frac{1}{r_i}\right)^2}$$

$$r_i = |p_i - x|$$

Figure 8–7 Parametric coordinate system and interpolation functions for a polygon.

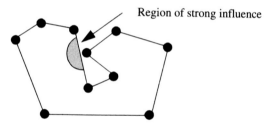

Region of strong influence

Figure 8–8 Potential problem with distance-based interpolation functions.

ion of the previous functions we have seen. Instead, we use a function based on weighted distance squared from each polygon vertex.

The weighted distance squared interpolation functions work well in practice. However, there are certain rare cases where points topologically distant from the interior of a polygon have an undue effect on the polygon interior (**Figure 8–8**). These situations occur only if the polygon is concave and wraps around on itself.

Tetrahedron. Figure 8–9 shows the parametric coordinate system and interpolation functions for a tetrahedron cell type. The tetrahedron is described using the three parametric coordinates (r,s,t).

Voxel. Figure 8–10 shows the parametric coordinate system and interpolation functions for a voxel cell type. The voxel is described using the three parametric coordinates (r,s,t). Note that the voxel edges are constrained to lie parallel to the global coordinate axes. These are often referred to as *trilinear interpolation* functions.

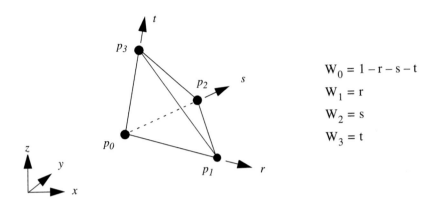

$$W_0 = 1 - r - s - t$$
$$W_1 = r$$
$$W_2 = s$$
$$W_3 = t$$

Figure 8–9 Parametric coordinate system and interpolation functions for a tetrahedron.

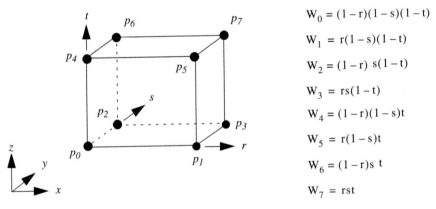

$$W_0 = (1-r)(1-s)(1-t)$$
$$W_1 = r(1-s)(1-t)$$
$$W_2 = (1-r)\,s(1-t)$$
$$W_3 = rs(1-t)$$
$$W_4 = (1-r)(1-s)t$$
$$W_5 = r(1-s)t$$
$$W_6 = (1-r)s\,t$$
$$W_7 = rst$$

Figure 8–10 Parametric coordinate system and interpolation functions for a voxel.

Hexahedron. Figure 8–11 shows the parametric coordinate system and interpolation functions for a hexahedron cell type. The hexahedron is described using the three parametric coordinates (r,s,t).

Wedge. Figure 8–12 shows the parametric coordinate system and interpolation functions for a wedge cell type. The wedge is described using the three parametric coordinates (r,s,t).

Pyramid. Figure 8–13 shows the parametric coordinate system and interpolation functions for a pyramid cell type. The pyramid is described using the three parametric coordinates (r,s,t).

Quadratic Edge. Figure 8–14 shows the parametric coordinate system and interpolation functions for a quadratic edge cell type. The quadratic edge is described using the single parametric coordinate r.

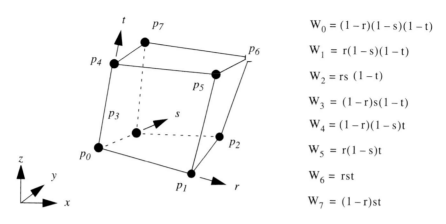

$$W_0 = (1-r)(1-s)(1-t)$$
$$W_1 = r(1-s)(1-t)$$
$$W_2 = rs\ (1-t)$$
$$W_3 = (1-r)s(1-t)$$
$$W_4 = (1-r)(1-s)t$$
$$W_5 = r(1-s)t$$
$$W_6 = rst$$
$$W_7 = (1-r)st$$

Figure 8–11 Parametric coordinate system and interpolation functions for a hexahedron.

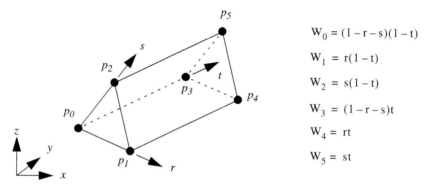

$$W_0 = (1-r-s)(1-t)$$
$$W_1 = r(1-t)$$
$$W_2 = s(1-t)$$
$$W_3 = (1-r-s)t$$
$$W_4 = rt$$
$$W_5 = st$$

Figure 8–12 Parametric coordinate system and interpolation functions for a wedge.

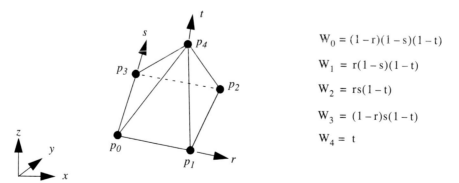

$$W_0 = (1-r)(1-s)(1-t)$$
$$W_1 = r(1-s)(1-t)$$
$$W_2 = rs(1-t)$$
$$W_3 = (1-r)s(1-t)$$
$$W_4 = t$$

Figure 8–13 Parametric coordinate system and interpolation functions for a pyramid.

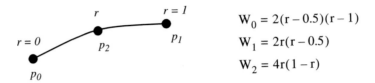

Figure 8–14 Parametric coordinate system and interpolation functions for a quadratic edge.

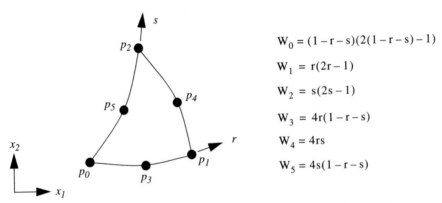

Figure 8–15 Parametric coordinate system and interpolation functions for a quadratic triangle.

Quadratic Triangle. Figure 8–15 shows the parametric coordinate system and interpolation functions for a quadratic triangle cell type. The quadratic triangle is described using the two parametric coordinates (r,s).

Quadratic Quadrilateral. Figure 8–16 shows the parametric coordinate system and interpolation functions for a quadratic quadrilateral cell type. The quadratic quadrilateral is described using the two parametric coordinates (r,s). Note that because the interpolation functions are most easily expressed in the interval (-1,1), a coordinate shift is performed to the (ξ, η) coordinates defined in this range. Also, the notation ξ_i and η_i is introduced. These are the parametric coordinates at the ith point.

Quadratic Tetrahedron. Figure 8–17 shows the parametric coordinate system and interpolation functions for a quadratic tetrahedron cell type. The quadratic tetrahedron is described using the three parametric coordinates (r,s,t).

Quadratic Hexahedron. Figure 8–18 shows the parametric coordinate system and interpolation functions for a quadratic hexahedron cell type. The quadratic hexahedron is described using the three parametric coordinates (r,s,t). Note that because the interpolation functions are most easily expressed in the interval (-1,1), a coordinate shift is performed to the (ξ, η) coordinates defined in this range. Also, the notation ξ_i, η_i and ζ_i is introduced. These are the parametric coordinates at the ith point.

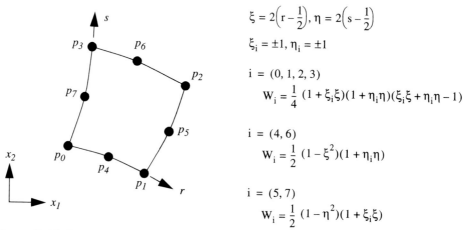

$$\xi = 2\left(r - \frac{1}{2}\right), \eta = 2\left(s - \frac{1}{2}\right)$$

$$\xi_i = \pm 1, \eta_i = \pm 1$$

$$i = (0, 1, 2, 3)$$

$$W_i = \frac{1}{4}(1 + \xi_i\xi)(1 + \eta_i\eta)(\xi_i\xi + \eta_i\eta - 1)$$

$$i = (4, 6)$$

$$W_i = \frac{1}{2}(1 - \xi^2)(1 + \eta_i\eta)$$

$$i = (5, 7)$$

$$W_i = \frac{1}{2}(1 - \eta^2)(1 + \xi_i\xi)$$

Figure 8–16 Parametric coordinate system and interpolation functions for a quadratic quadrilateral. In VTK parametric coordinates (r,s) run between $(0,1)$, hence the coordinate system shift into the (ξ, η) parametric system ranging from $(-1,1)$. Note that ξ_i and η_i refer to the parametric coordinates of the ith point.

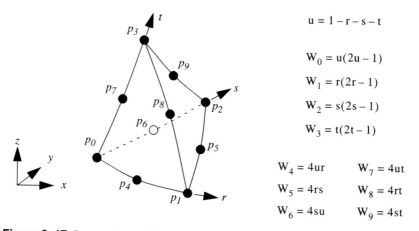

$$u = 1 - r - s - t$$

$$W_0 = u(2u - 1)$$

$$W_1 = r(2r - 1)$$

$$W_2 = s(2s - 1)$$

$$W_3 = t(2t - 1)$$

$$W_4 = 4ur \qquad W_7 = 4ut$$

$$W_5 = 4rs \qquad W_8 = 4rt$$

$$W_6 = 4su \qquad W_9 = 4st$$

Figure 8–17 Parametric coordinate system and interpolation functions for a quadratic tetrahedron. In VTK parametric coordinates (r,s,t) run between $(0,1)$, hence the coordinate system shift into the (ξ, η, ζ) parametric system ranging from $(-1,1)$.

8.3 Coordinate Transformation

Coordinate transformation is a common visualization operation. This may be either transformation from dataset coordinates to global coordinates, or global coordinates to dataset coordinates.

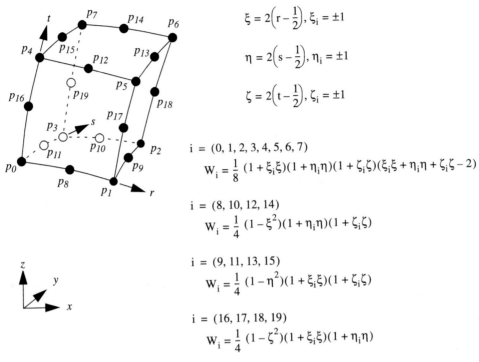

$$\xi = 2\left(r - \frac{1}{2}\right), \ \xi_i = \pm 1$$

$$\eta = 2\left(s - \frac{1}{2}\right), \ \eta_i = \pm 1$$

$$\zeta = 2\left(t - \frac{1}{2}\right), \ \zeta_i = \pm 1$$

$i = (0, 1, 2, 3, 4, 5, 6, 7)$
$$W_i = \frac{1}{8} \, (1 + \xi_i\xi)(1 + \eta_i\eta)(1 + \zeta_i\zeta)(\xi_i\xi + \eta_i\eta + \zeta_i\zeta - 2)$$

$i = (8, 10, 12, 14)$
$$W_i = \frac{1}{4} \, (1 - \xi^2)(1 + \eta_i\eta)(1 + \zeta_i\zeta)$$

$i = (9, 11, 13, 15)$
$$W_i = \frac{1}{4} \, (1 - \eta^2)(1 + \xi_i\xi)(1 + \zeta_i\zeta)$$

$i = (16, 17, 18, 19)$
$$W_i = \frac{1}{4} \, (1 - \zeta^2)(1 + \xi_i\xi)(1 + \eta_i\eta)$$

Figure 8–18 Parametric coordinate system and interpolation functions for a quadratic hexahedron. In VTK parametric coordinates (r,s,t) run between $(0,1)$, hence the coordinate system shift into the (ξ, η, ζ) parametric system ranging from $(-1,1)$. Note that ξ_i, η_i and ζ_i refer to the parametric coordinates of the ith point.

Dataset to Global Coordinates

Transforming between dataset coordinates and global coordinates is straightforward. We start by identifying a primary cell using the cell id and sub-id. Then the global coordinates are generated from the parametric coordinates by using the interpolation functions of **Equation 8-4**. Given cell points $p_i = p_i(x_i, y_i, z_i)$ the global coordinate p is simply

$$p = \sum_{i=0}^{n-1} W_i(r_0, s_0, t_0)p_i \tag{8-7}$$

where the interpolation weights W_i are evaluated at the parametric coordinate (r_0, s_0, t_0).

In the formulation presented here, we have used the same order interpolation functions for both data and cell geometry. (By order we mean the polynomial degree of the interpolating polynomials.) This is termed *iso-parametric* interpolation. It is possible to use different interpolation functions for geometry and data. *Super-parametric* interpolation is used when the order of the interpolation functions for geometry is greater than those used for data. *Sub-parametric* interpolation is used when the order of the interpolation functions for geometry is less than those used for data. Using different interpolation functions is commonly used in numerical analysis techniques such as the finite element method. We will always use the isoparametric interpolation for visualization applications.

Global to Dataset Coordinates

Global to dataset coordinate transformations are expensive compared to dataset to global transformations. There are two reasons for this. First, we must identify the particular cell C_i that contains the global point p. Second, we must solve **Equation 8-4** for the parametric coordinates of p.

To identify the cell C_i means doing some form of searching. A simple but inefficient approach is to visit every cell in a dataset and determine whether p lies inside any cell. If so, then we have found the correct cell and stop the search. Otherwise, we check the next cell in the list.

This simple technique is not fast enough for large data. Instead, we use accelerated search techniques. These are based on spatially organizing structures such as an octree or three-dimensional hash table. The idea is as follows: we create a number of "buckets," or data place holders, that are accessed by their location in global space. Inside each bucket we tag all the points or cells that are partially or completely inside the bucket. Then, to find a particular cell that contains point p, we find the bucket that contains p, and obtain all the cells associated with the bucket. We then evaluate inside/outside for this abbreviated cell list to find the single cell containing p. (See "Searching" on page 273 for a more detailed description.)

The second reason that global to dataset coordinate transformation is expensive is because we must solve the interpolation function for the parametric coordinates of p. Sometimes we can do this analytically, but in other cases we must solve for the parametric coordinates using numerical techniques.

Consider the interpolation functions for a line (**Figure 8–2**). We can solve this equation exactly and find that

$$r = \frac{(x - x_0)}{(x_1 - x_0)} = \frac{(y - y_0)}{(y_1 - y_0)} = \frac{(z - z_0)}{(z_1 - z_0)} \tag{8-8}$$

Similar relations exist for any cell whose interpolation functions are linear combinations of parametric coordinates. This includes vertices, lines, triangles, and tetrahedra. The quadrilateral and hexahedron interpolation functions are nonlinear because they are products of linear expressions for the parametric coordinates. As a result, we must resort to numerical techniques to compute global to dataset coordinate transformations. The interpolation functions for pixels and voxels are nonlinear as well, but because of their special orientation with respect to the x, y, and z coordinate axes, we can solve them exactly. (We will treat pixel and voxel types in greater depth in "Special Techniques for Image Data" on page 277.)

To solve the interpolation functions for parametric coordinates we must use nonlinear techniques for the solution of a system of equations. A simple and effective technique is Newton's method [Conte72].

To use Newton's method we begin by defining three functions for the known global coordinate $p = p(x,y,z)$ in terms of the interpolation functions $W_i = W_i(r,s,t)$

$$f(r, s, t) = 0 = x - \sum W_i x_i$$

$$g(r, s, t) = 0 = y - \sum W_i y_i \tag{8-9}$$

$$h(r, s, t) = 0 = z - \sum W_i z_i$$

and then, expanding the functions using a Taylor's series approximation,

$$f = 0 = f_0 + \frac{\partial f}{\partial r}(r - r_0) + \frac{\partial f}{\partial s}(s - s_0) + \frac{\partial f}{\partial t}(t - t_0) + \cdots$$

$$g = 0 = g_0 + \frac{\partial g}{\partial r}(r - r_0) + \frac{\partial g}{\partial s}(s - s_0) + \frac{\partial g}{\partial t}(t - t_0) + \cdots \tag{8-10}$$

$$h = 0 = h_0 + \frac{\partial h}{\partial r}(r - r_0) + \frac{\partial h}{\partial s}(s - s_0) + \frac{\partial h}{\partial t}(t - t_0) + \cdots$$

we can develop an iterative procedure to solve for the parametric coordinates. This yields the general form

$$\begin{bmatrix} r_{i+1} \\ s_{i+1} \\ t_{i+1} \end{bmatrix} = \begin{bmatrix} r_i \\ s_i \\ t_i \end{bmatrix} - \begin{bmatrix} \frac{\partial f}{\partial r} & \frac{\partial f}{\partial s} & \frac{\partial f}{\partial t} \\ \frac{\partial g}{\partial r} & \frac{\partial g}{\partial s} & \frac{\partial g}{\partial t} \\ \frac{\partial h}{\partial r} & \frac{\partial h}{\partial s} & \frac{\partial h}{\partial t} \end{bmatrix}^{-1} \begin{bmatrix} f_i \\ g_i \\ h_i \end{bmatrix} \tag{8-11}$$

Fortunately, Newton's method converges quadratically (if it converges) and the interpolation functions that we have presented here are well behaved. In practice, **Equation 8-11** converges in just a few iterations.

8.4 Computing Derivatives

Interpolation functions enable us to compute data values at arbitrary locations within a cell. They also allow us to compute the rate of change, or derivatives, of data values. For example, given displacements at cell points we can compute cell strains and stresses — or, given pressure values, we can compute the pressure gradient at a specified location.

To introduce this process, we will begin by examining the simplest case: computing derivatives in a 1D line (**Figure 8–19**). Using geometric arguments, we can compute the derivatives in the r parametric space according to

$$\frac{ds}{dr} = \frac{(s_1 - s_0)}{1} = (s_1 - s_0) \tag{8-12}$$

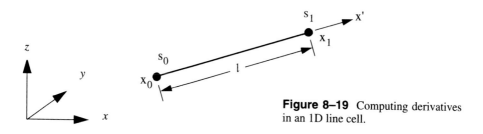

Figure 8–19 Computing derivatives in an 1D line cell.

where s_i is the data value at point i. In the local coordinate system x', which is parallel to the r coordinate system (that is, it lies along the vector $\vec{x}_1 - \vec{x}_0$), the derivative is

$$\frac{ds}{dx'} = \frac{(s_1 - s_0)}{1}$$

(8-13)

where l is the length of the line.

Another way to derive **Equation 8-13** is to use the interpolation functions of **Figure 8–3** and the chain rule for derivatives. The chain rule

$$\frac{d}{dr} = \frac{d}{dx'} \cdot \frac{d}{dr}x'$$

(8-14)

allows us to compute the derivative d/dx' using

$$\frac{d}{dx'} = \left(\frac{d}{dr}\right) / \frac{d}{dr}x'$$

(8-15)

With the interpolation functions we can compute the x' derivatives with respect to r as

$$\frac{d}{dr}x' = \frac{d}{dr}\left(\sum_{i=0}^{1} W_i \cdot x'_i\right) = -x_0' + x_1' = 1$$

(8-16)

which, when combined with **Equation 8-15** and **Equation 8-12** for the s derivatives, yields **Equation 8-13**.

One final step remains. The derivatives in the $\vec{x}$ coordinate system must be converted to the global x-y-z system. We can do this by creating a unit vector $\vec{v}$ as

$$\vec{v} = \frac{(\vec{x}_1 - \vec{x}_0)}{|x_1 - x_0|}$$

(8-17)

where $\vec{x}_0$ and $\vec{x}_1$ are the locations of the two end points of the line. Then the derivatives in the x, y, and z directions can be computed by taking the dot products along the axes.

$$\frac{ds}{dx} = \left(\frac{s_1 - s_0}{1}\right) \vec{v} \cdot (1, 0, 0)$$

$$\frac{ds}{dy} = \left(\frac{s_1 - s_0}{1}\right) \vec{v} \cdot (0, 1, 0)$$ (8-18)

$$\frac{ds}{dz} = \left(\frac{s_1 - s_0}{1}\right) \vec{v} \cdot (0, 0, 1)$$

To summarize this process, derivatives are computed in the local *r-s-t* parametric space using cell interpolation. These are then transformed into a local $x' - y' - z'$ Cartesian system. Then, if the $x' - y' - z'$ system is not aligned with the global $x - y - z$ coordinate system, another transformation is required to generate the result.

We can generalize this process to three dimensions. From the chain rule for partial derivatives

$$\frac{\partial}{\partial x} = \frac{\partial}{\partial r}\frac{\partial r}{\partial x} + \frac{\partial}{\partial s}\frac{\partial s}{\partial x} + \frac{\partial}{\partial t}\frac{\partial t}{\partial x}$$

$$\frac{\partial}{\partial y} = \frac{\partial}{\partial r}\frac{\partial r}{\partial y} + \frac{\partial}{\partial s}\frac{\partial s}{\partial y} + \frac{\partial}{\partial t}\frac{\partial t}{\partial y}$$ (8-19)

$$\frac{\partial}{\partial z} = \frac{\partial}{\partial r}\frac{\partial r}{\partial z} + \frac{\partial}{\partial s}\frac{\partial s}{\partial z} + \frac{\partial}{\partial t}\frac{\partial t}{\partial z}$$

or after rearranging

$$\begin{bmatrix} \frac{\partial}{\partial r} \\ \frac{\partial}{\partial s} \\ \frac{\partial}{\partial t} \end{bmatrix} = \begin{bmatrix} \frac{\partial x}{\partial r} & \frac{\partial y}{\partial r} & \frac{\partial z}{\partial r} \\ \frac{\partial x}{\partial s} & \frac{\partial y}{\partial s} & \frac{\partial z}{\partial s} \\ \frac{\partial x}{\partial t} & \frac{\partial y}{\partial t} & \frac{\partial z}{\partial t} \end{bmatrix} \begin{bmatrix} \frac{\partial}{\partial x} \\ \frac{\partial}{\partial y} \\ \frac{\partial}{\partial z} \end{bmatrix} = J \begin{bmatrix} \frac{\partial}{\partial x} \\ \frac{\partial}{\partial y} \\ \frac{\partial}{\partial z} \end{bmatrix}$$ (8-20)

The 3×3 matrix J is called the Jacobian matrix, and it relates the parametric coordinate derivatives to the global coordinate derivatives. We can rewrite **Equation 8-20** into more compact form

$$\frac{\partial}{\partial r_i} = J \frac{\partial}{\partial x_i}$$ (8-21)

and solve for the global derivatives by taking the inverse of the Jacobian matrix

$$\frac{\partial}{\partial x_i} = J^{-1} \frac{\partial}{\partial r_i}$$ (8-22)

The inverse of the Jacobian always exists as long as there is a one-to-one correspondence

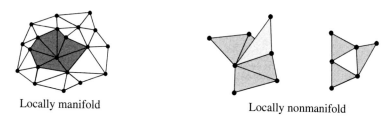

Locally manifold   **Locally nonmanifold**

Figure 8–20 Manifold and nonmanifold surface topology. If the local neighborhood around a vertex is topologically a 2D disk (i.e., a small disk can be placed on the surface without tearing or overlapping), then the surface is manifold at that vertex.

between the parametric and global coordinate systems. This means that for any (r, s, t) coordinate, there corresponds only one (x, y, z) coordinate. This holds true for any of the parametric coordinate systems presented here, as long as pathological conditions such as cell self-intersection or a cell folding in on itself are avoided. (An example of cell folding is when a quadrilateral becomes nonconvex.)

In our one-dimensional example, the derivatives along the line were constant. However, other interpolation functions (e.g., **Figure 8–5**) may yield non-constant derivatives. Here, the Jacobian is a function of position in the cell and must be evaluated at a particular (r, s, t) coordinate value.

8.5 Topological Operations

Many visualization algorithms require information about the topology of a cell or dataset. Operations that provide such information are called *topological operations*. Examples of these operations include obtaining the topological dimension of a cell, or accessing neighboring cells that share common edges or faces. We might use these operations to decide whether to render a cell (e.g., render only one-dimensional lines) or to propagate particles through a flow field (e.g., traversing cells across common boundaries).

Before proceeding we need to define some terms from topology. *Manifold topology* describes a region surrounding a point that is topologically connected. That is, a region around the point is topologically equivalent to a small "disk" (in two-dimensions) or "ball" (in three-dimensions). Topology that is not manifold is termed *nonmanifold*. Examples of manifold and nonmanifold geometry are shown in **Figure 8–20**.

There are some simple rules we can use to decide whether a surface or region approximated with cells is manifold or nonmanifold. In two dimensions, if every edge of a two-dimensional cell is used by exactly one other cell, than the surface is locally manifold. In three dimensions, if every face of a three-dimensional cell is used by exactly one other cell, than the region is locally manifold.

We also will use the term *simplex* on some occasions. A simplex of dimension n is the convex region defined by a set of $n+1$ independent points. A vertex, line, triangle, and tetrahedron are simplices of dimension 0, 1, 2, and 3, respectively as shown in **Figure 8–21**.

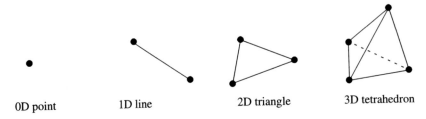

| 0D point | 1D line | 2D triangle | 3D tetrahedron |

Figure 8–21 Simplices of dimension three and lower.

Cell Operations

Cell operations return information about the topology of a cell. Typically, we want to know the topological order of the cell or the topology of the cell boundary.

Given a cell C_i of topological dimension d, the cell is (implicitly) composed of boundary cells of topological order $d-1$ and lower. For example, a tetrahedron is composed of four two-dimensional triangles, six one-dimensional edges, and four zero-dimensional vertices. Cell operations return information about the number of boundary cells of a particular topological dimension, as well as the ordered list of points that define each bounding cell.

Another useful cell operation returns the closest boundary cell of dimension $d-1$ given the parametric coordinates of the cell. This operation ties the geometry to the topology of the cell, as compared to the parametric coordinate system, which ties the topology to the geometry. The closest boundary cell operation is implemented by partitioning each cell into various regions, as illustrated in **Figure 8–22**. To determine the closest boundary cell we need only to identify the parametric region that the point lies in, and then return the appropriate boundary cell.

Another useful cell operation is cell decomposition into simplices. Every cell can be decomposed into a collection of simplices. By doing so, and by operating on the simplex decomposition rather than the cell itself, we can create algorithms that are independent of cell type. For example, if we want to intersect two datasets of varied cell type, without simplex decomposition we would have to create methods to intersect every possible combination of cells. With simplex decomposition, we can create a single intersection operation that operates on only the limited set of simplices. The significant advantage of this approach is that as new cells are added to the visualization system, only the cell object (including its method for simplex decomposition) must be implemented, and no other objects need be modified.

Dataset Operations

Dataset operations return information about the topology of a dataset or topological information about the adjacency of cells. Typical operations include determining the neighbors of a cell or returning a list of all cells that use a particular point.

We can formalize the adjacency operations by continuing the discussion of "Cell Types" on page 114. Adjacency methods are used to obtain information about the neighbors of a cell. A neighbor of a particular cell C_i is simply a cell that shares one or more points in common with C_i. A vertex neighbor is a neighbor that shares one or more vertices. An edge

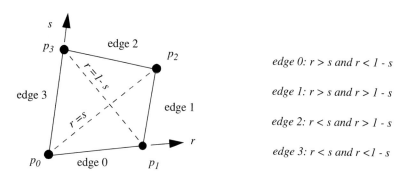

Figure 8–22 Closest boundary cell operation for quadrilateral cell.

neighbor is a neighbor that shares one or more edges. A face neighbor is a cell that shares vertices that define one of the faces of the cell. Note that a face neighbor is also an edge neighbor, and an edge neighbor is also a vertex neighbor.

The adjacency operators are simple set operations. For a particular cell C_i defined by points

$$C_i = \{p_1, p_2, ..., p_n\} = P \tag{8-23}$$

and a point list $\bar{P} = (\bar{p}_1, \bar{p}_2, ..., \bar{p}_n)$ with $\bar{P} \subset P$, where $\bar{P}$ typically corresponds to the points defining a boundary cell of C_i; the neighbors of C_i are the adjacency set $A(\bar{C}, \bar{P})$. The adjacency set is simply the intersection of the use sets for each point, excluding the cell C_i.

$$A(C_i, \bar{P}) = \left(\bigcap^n U(\bar{p}_i) \right) - C_i \tag{8-24}$$

The adjacency set represents a variety of useful information. In a manifold object represented by a polyhedra, for example, each polygon must have exactly one edge neighbor for each of its edges. Edges that have no neighbors are boundary edges; edges that have more than one edge neighbor represent nonmanifold topology. Datasets that consist of three-dimensional cells (e.g., unstructured grids) are topologically consistent only if, for each cell, there is exactly one face neighbor for each face. Faces that have no neighbors are on the boundary of the dataset. More than one face neighbor implies that the neighbors are self-intersecting (in 3D space).

8.6 Searching

Searching is an operation to find the cell containing a specified point p, or to locate cells or points in a region surrounding p. Algorithms requiring this operation include streamline generation, where we need to find the starting location within a cell; probing, where the data values at a point are interpolated from the containing cell; or collision detection, where cells in a certain region must be evaluated for intersection. Sometimes (e.g., image datasets), searching is a simple operation because of the regularity of data. However, in less structured data, the searching operation is more complex.

To find the cell containing p, we can use the following naive search procedure. Traverse all cells in the dataset, finding the one (if any) that contains p. To determine whether a cell contains a point, the cell interpolation functions are evaluated for the parametric coordinates (r,s,t). If these coordinates lie within the cell, then p lies in the cell. The basic assumption here is that cells do not overlap, so that at most a single cell contains the given point p. To determine cells or points lying in the region surrounding p, we can traverse cells or points to see whether they lie within the region around p. For example, we can choose to define the region as a sphere centered at p. Then, if a point or the points composing a cell lie in the sphere, the point or cell is considered to be in the region surrounding p.

These naive procedures are unacceptable for all but the smallest datasets, since they are of order $O(n)$, where n is the number of cells or points. To improve the performance of searching, we need to introduce supplemental data structures to support spatial searching. Such structures are well-known and include MIP maps, octrees, kd-trees, and binary sphere trees (see "Bibliographic Notes" on page 297 at the end of this chapter).

The basic idea behind these spatial search structures is that the search space is subdivided into smaller parts, or buckets. Each bucket contains a list of the points or cells that lie within it. Buckets are organized in structured fashion so that constant or logarithmic time access to any bucket is possible. For example, if we assign a portion of 2D Euclidean space into a grid of n by m buckets, the location of p in a particular bucket can be determined with two subtractions and two divisions: a constant time access. Similarly, the location of p in a nonuniformly subdivided octree is determined in logarithmic time, since recursive insertion into octant children is required. Once the bucket is found, the search is then limited to the points or cells contained within it. In a properly designed spatial search structure, the number of points or cells in a bucket is a small portion of the total number of cells and less than a fixed value. Thus, the time to search within a bucket can be bounded by a fixed constant. The result is that introducing spatial search structures reduces search times to a maximum $O(\log n)$, or better yet $O(n)$.

We have two options when applying spatial search structures. We may insert points into the search structure, or we may insert cells, depending on the application. There are advantages and disadvantages to both approaches. Inserting cells into buckets is not a trivial operation. In general, cells are arbitrarily oriented and shaped, and will not fit completely into a single bucket. As a result, cells often span multiple buckets. To reliably determine whether a cell is in a bucket requires geometric intersection tests, a costly operation. Another approach is to use the *bounding box* of a cell to decide which bucket(s) a cell belongs in. We only need to intersect the bounding box with a bucket to determine whether the cell may belong in the bucket. Unfortunately, even though this operation is generally fast, often cells are associated with buckets even though they may not actually lie inside them, wasting (in large models) memory resources and extra processing time.

Inserting points into a search structure is easier because points can be uniquely placed into a bucket. Inserting points also allows us to search for both points *and* cells. Cells can be found by using p to index into the appropriate bucket. The closest point(s) p_i to p are then located. Using the topological adjacency operator to retrieve the cells using points p_i, we can then search these cells for the cell containing p. This procedure must be used with caution, however, since the closest points may not be used by the cells containing p (**Figure 8–23**).

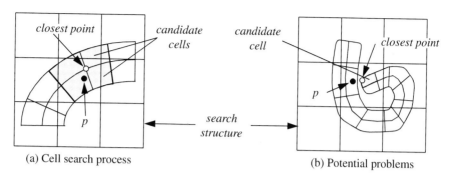

(a) Cell search process   (b) Potential problems

Figure 8–23 Using search structure (containing points) to find cells. (a) Points are associated with appropriate bucket. Point p is used to index into bucket, and closest point(s) p_i
is found. Cells using p_i are evaluated for the cell containing p. (b) Sometimes closest
points p_i are not used by cells containing p.

8.7 Cell / Line Intersection

An important geometric operation is intersection of a line with a cell. This operation can be
used to interactively select a cell from the rendering window, to perform ray-casting for rendering, or to geometrically query data.

In the *Visualization Toolkit* each cell must be capable of intersecting itself against a
line. **Figure 8–24** summarizes these operations for the nine linear primary cell types supported by VTK. (Intersections on composite cells are implemented by intersecting each primitive cell in turn.) Note that the procedure for intersecting higher order cells is the same.

Line/cell intersection for 0D, 1D, and 2D cells follows standard approaches. Intersection against 3D cells is difficult. This is because the surfaces of these cells are described para-
metrically and are not necessarily planar. For example, to intersect a line with a tetrahedron,
we can intersect the line against the four triangular faces of the tetrahedron. Hexahedron,
however, may have nonplanar faces. Thus, we cannot intersect the line against six quadrilateral, planar faces. Instead, we use line/face intersection as an initial guess, and project the
intersection point onto the surface of the cell. This produces an approximate result, but is
accurate enough for most applications.

8.8 Scalars and Colors

There is a close correspondence between scalar data and colors. We touched on this in "Color
Mapping" on page 151, where we saw how to use a color table to map scalar values into a
color specification (i.e., red, green, blue, and alpha, or *RGBA*). There are cases, however,
when we want to circumvent this mapping process. Such cases occur when color data is supplied instead of scalar data.

A common example occurs in imaging. Recall that an image is a regular, two-dimensional array of points. The points define pixels, which in turn form a two-dimensional image
dataset. Images are frequently stored as a pair of dimensions along with data values. The data

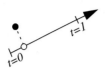

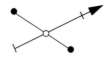

Vertex	Line	Triangle
• project point onto ray	• 3D line intersection	• line/plane intersection
• distance to line must be within tolerance	• distance between lines must be within tolerance	• intersection point must lie in triangle
• t must lie between [0,1]	• s,t must lie between [0,1]	• t must lie between [0,1]

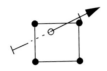

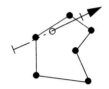

Quadrilateral	Pixel	Polygon
• line/plane intersection	• line/plane intersection	• line/plane intersection
• intersection point must lie in quadrilateral	• intersection point must lie in pixel (uses efficient in/out test)	• intersection point must lie in polygon (uses ray casting for polygon in/out)
• t must lie between [0,1]	• t must lie between [0,1]	• t must lie between [0,1]

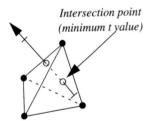

Intersection point (minimum t value)

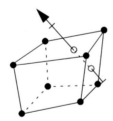

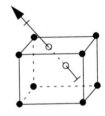

Tetrahedron	Hexahedron	Voxel
• intersect each (triangle) face	• intersect each (quadrilateral) face	• intersect each (pixel) face
• t must lie between [0,1]	• since face may be nonplanar, project previous result onto hexahedron surface	• t must lie between [0,1]
	• t must lie between [0,1]	

Figure 8–24 Summary of line/cell intersection operations for nine primitive cell types. Line is assumed normalized in parametric coordinate t with $0 \leq t \leq 1$.

values may be one of black and white (e.g., a bitmap), grayscale, or color (e.g., a pixmap). Bitmaps and grayscale images can be directly cast into the form of single-values scalar data, and we can use our earlier approach. Pixmaps, however, consist of (at a minimum) three values per pixel of red, green, and blue. (Sometimes, a fourth alpha opacity value may also be included.) Thus, pixmaps cannot be directly cast into scalar form.

To accommodate color data, conversions between multicomponent color data and single-valued scalars must be defined. Each class must act as if it were a scalar: that is, a request for data at a particular point must return a *single* scalar value. This allows us to use standard scalar visualization techniques such as contouring or warping. Thus a mapping from *RGB* or *RGBA* color coordinates to a single scalar value is required.

The simplest conversion is to select one of n components in a color tuple and use that as the scalar value. Another common mapping returns the *luminance Y* of a color. Given three components, *RGB*, the luminance is

$$Y = 0.30R + 0.59G + 0.11B \tag{8-25}$$

If the color includes transparency, *RGBA*, the luminance is

$$Y = A(0.30R + 0.59G + 0.11B) \tag{8-26}$$

Using this abstraction allows us to treat single-valued scalars and scalars consisting of multivalued colors the same. The end result is that we can mix both types of scalar data into our visualization networks.

8.9 Special Techniques for Image Data

A significant attraction of using 2- and 3-dimensional image data is the speed and simplicity of computation. In this section, we will explore specific techniques that exploit the special regular topology and geometry of image data.

Coordinate Transformation

Given a point p we can find the structured coordinates by performing three division operations (**Figure 8–25**). Taking the integer floor function yields the structured coordinates. Taking the fractional part of the result yields the parametric coordinates of the cell. We can then use **Equation 8-3** to convert to dataset coordinates.

Derivative Computation

Because the image dataset is oriented parallel to the coordinate x, y, and z axes, and because the spacing of points in each of these directions is regular, finite difference schemes can be used to compute partial derivatives at the cell points. Referring to **Figure 8–26**, we see that central differences can be used in each of the three directions according to the equation:

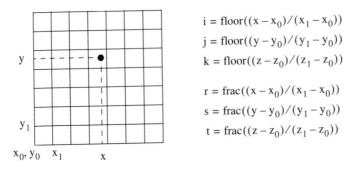

$$i = \text{floor}((x - x_0)/(x_1 - x_0))$$
$$j = \text{floor}((y - y_0)/(y_1 - y_0))$$
$$k = \text{floor}((z - z_0)/(z_1 - z_0))$$

$$r = \text{frac}((x - x_0)/(x_1 - x_0))$$
$$s = \text{frac}((y - y_0)/(y_1 - y_0))$$
$$t = \text{frac}((z - z_0)/(z_1 - z_0))$$

Figure 8–25 Image data coordinate transformation.

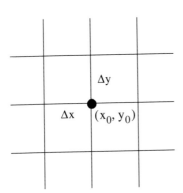

Figure 8–26 Using finite differences to compute derivatives on image data.

$$g_x = \frac{d(x_0 + \Delta x, y_0, z_0) - d(x_0 - \Delta x, y_0, z_0)}{2\Delta x}$$

$$g_y = \frac{d(x_0, y_0 + \Delta y, z_0) - d(x_0, y_0 - \Delta y, z_0)}{2\Delta y} \qquad \text{(8-27)}$$

$$g_z = \frac{d(x_0, y_0, z_0 + \Delta z) - d(x_0, y_0, z_0 - \Delta z)}{2\Delta z}$$

(Note that at the boundary of the dataset, one-sided differences may be used.) We can use these equations to compute derivatives within the cell as well. We simply compute the derivatives at each cell point from **Equation 8-27**, and then use the cell interpolation functions to compute the derivative at the point inside the cell.

Topology

Structured datasets lend themselves to efficient topological operations (i.e., both image data and structured grids). Given a cell id, it is possible to determine vertex, edge, or face neighbors using simple constant time operations. First, given the cell id in a three-dimensional structured dataset, we use a combination of division and modulo arithmetic to compute the structured coordinates

$$
\begin{aligned}
i &= \text{id modulo } (n_x - 1) \\
j &= (\text{id}/(n_x - 1)) \text{ modulo } (n_y - 1) \\
k &= \text{id}/((n_x - 1)(n_y - 1))
\end{aligned}
\tag{8-28}
$$

Face neighbors are determined by incrementing one of the i, j, or k indices. Edge neighbors are determined by incrementing any two indices, while vertex neighbors are found by incrementing all three indices. Care must be taken while incrementing to insure that the indices fall in the range

$$
\begin{aligned}
0 \leq i &< (n_x - 1) \\
0 \leq j &< (n_y - 1) \\
0 \leq k &< (n_z - 1)
\end{aligned}
\tag{8-29}
$$

An attempt to index outside these ranges indicates that the neighbor in question does not exist.

Searching

Given a point $p = (x, y, z)$ we can determine the cell containing p by using the equations given in **Figure 8–25**. These equations generate the structured coordinates (i, j, k), which can then be converted to cell id (i.e., dataset coordinates) using **Equation 8-3**.

To find the closest point to p, we compute the structured coordinates by rounding to the nearest integer value (instead of using the floor function). Thus,

$$
\begin{aligned}
i &= \text{int}((x - x_0)/(x_1 - x_0)) \\
j &= \text{int}((y - y_0)/(y_1 - y_0)) \\
k &= \text{int}((z - z_0)/(z_1 - z_0))
\end{aligned}
\tag{8-30}
$$

8.10 Putting It All Together

In this section we will finish our earlier description of an implementation for unstructured data. We also define a high-level, abstract interface for cells and datasets. This interface allows us to implement the general (i.e., dataset specific) algorithms in the *Visualization Toolkit*. We also describe implementations for color scalars, searching and picking, and conclude with a series of examples to demonstrate some of these concepts.

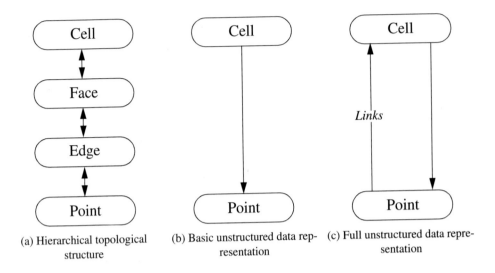

(a) Hierarchical topological structure   (b) Basic unstructured data representation   (c) Full unstructured data representation

Figure 8–27 Enhancing hierarchical unstructured data representation. (a) Conventional topological hierarchy for geometric model. (b) Basic unstructured data hierarchy. (c) Full unstructured data hierarchy. By introducing upward references from points to cells, the unstructured data hierarchy may be efficiently traversed in both directions, and is more compact than conventional topological hierarchies.

Unstructured Topology

In Chapter 5 we described data representations for the unstructured dataset types vtkPolyData and vtkUnstructuredGrid. Close examination of this data structure reveals that operations to retrieve topological adjacency are inefficient. In fact, to implement any operation to retrieve vertex, edge, or face neighbors requires a search of the cell array, resulting in $O(n)$ time complexity. This is unacceptable for all but the smallest applications, since any algorithm traversing the cell array and retrieving adjacency information is at a minimum $O(n^2)$.

The reason for this inefficiency is that the data representation is a "downward" hierarchy (**Figure 8–27**(b)). That is, given a cell we can quickly determine the topological features lower in the topological hierarchy such as faces, edges, and points. However, given a face, edge, or point we must search the cell array to determine the owning cells. To improve the efficiency of this data representation, we must introduce additional information into the hierarchy that allows "upward" hierarchy traversal (similar to that shown in **Figure 8–27**(a)).

The solution to this problem is to extend the unstructured data structure with *cell links*. The cell links array is a list of lists of cells that use each point and corresponds to the upward links of **Figure 8–27**(c). The cell links array transforms the hierarchical structure of **Figure 5–13** into a ring structure. Cells reference their composing points, and points in turn reference the cells that use them. The full unstructured data structure is shown in **Figure 8–28**.

The cell links array is in fact an implementation of the use sets of **Equation 5-1**. We can use this equation to compute adjacency operation in constant time, if the maximum num-

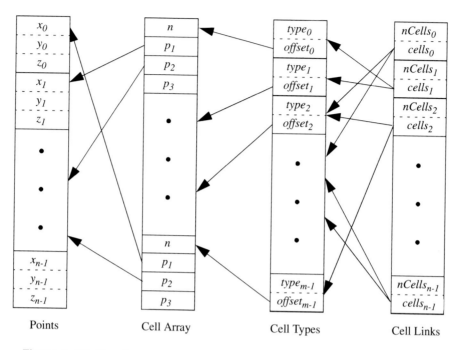

Figure 8–28 Complete unstructured data representation including link lists. There are m cells and n points. The n structures in the link list are lists of cells that use each vertex. Each link list is variable in length.

ber of cells using a point is much smaller than the number of points in a dataset. To see this, we refer to **Equation 8-24** and see that the adjacency operations consist of a finite number of set intersections. Each operation is an intersection of the link lists for each point. If the number of cells in each link list is "small," then the intersection operation can be bounded by a fixed constant in time, and the total operation can be considered a constant time operation.

There are several important characteristics of this data representation.

- The cell links array is an extension of the basic unstructured data representation. As a result, we can defer the construction of the cell links until they are required. Often the cell links are never needed and require no computer resources to compute or store.

- Building the cell links is a linear $O(n)$ operation. Each cell is traversed and for every point that the cell uses, the list of using cells for that point is extended to include the current cell. Building the cell links is only needed once as an initialization step.

- The data representation is compact relative to other topology representation schemes (e.g., the winged-edge structure and the radial-edge structures [Baumgart74] [Weiler88]). These other data structures contain explicit representation of intermediate topology such as edges, loops, faces, or special adjacency information such as adjacent edges (winged-edge structure) or extensive "use" descriptions (radial-edge structure). The compactness of representation is particularly important for visualization, since the data size is typically large.

The unstructured data structure in the *Visualization Toolkit* is implemented using the four classes vtkPoints (and subclasses), vtkCellArray, vtkCellTypes, and vtkCellLinks. The building of this data structure is incremental. At a minimum, the points and cells are represented using vtkPoints and vtkCellArray. If random access or extra type information is required, then the object vtkCellTypes is used. If adjacency information is required, an instance of the class vtkCellLinks is created. These operations are carried out behind the scenes, and generally do not require extra knowledge by the application programmer.

Abstract Interfaces

With the completion of Chapters 5 and 8, we can summarize the abstract interface for cells, datasets, and the point data attributes. These pseudo-code descriptions encapsulate the core functionality of the classes vtkDataSet, vtkCell, and vtkPointData, and their subclasses. All algorithms presented in this text can be implemented using combinations of these methods.

Dataset Abstraction. The dataset is the central data representation in VTK. Datasets are composed of one or more cells and points. Associated with the points are attribute data consisting of scalars, vectors, normals, texture coordinates, and tensors.

type = GetDataObjectType()
> Return the type of dataset (e.g., vtkPolyData, vtkImageData, vtkStructuredGrid, vtkRectilinearGrid, or vtkUnstructuredGrid).

numPoints = GetNumberOfPoints()
> Return the number of points in the dataset.

numCells = GetNumberOfCells()
> Return the number of cells in the dataset.

GetPoint(ptId,x)
> Given a point id, return the *(x,y,z)* coordinates of the point.

cell = GetCell(cellId)
> Given a cell id, return a pointer to a cell object.

type = GetCellType(cellId)
> Return the type of the cell given by cell id.

GetCellTypes(types)
> Return a list of types of cells that compose the dataset.

cells = GetPointCells(ptId)
> Given a point id, return the cells that use this point.

GetCellPoints(cellId, ptIds)
> Given a cell id, return the point ids (e.g., connectivity list) defining the cell.

GetCellNeighbors(cellId, ptIds, neighbors)
> Given a cell id and a list of points composing a boundary face of the cell, return the neighbors of that cell sharing the points.

cellId = FindCell(x, cell, cellId, tol2, subId, pcoords, weights)
> Given a coordinate value x, an initial search cell defined by cell and cellId, and a tolerance measure (squared), return the cell id and sub-id of the cell containing the point and its interpolation function weights. The initial search cell is used to speed up the search process when the position x is known to be near the cell. If no cell is found, cellId < 0 is returned.

pointData = GetPointData()
> Return a pointer to the object maintaining point attribute data. This includes scalars, vectors, normals, tensors, and texture coordinates, as well as any other data arrays that the field carries.

cellData = GetCellData()
> Return a pointer to the object maintaining cell attribute data. This includes scalars, vectors, normals, tensors, and texture coordinates, as well as any other data arrays that the field carries.

bounds = GetBounds()
> Get the bounding box of the dataset.

length = GetLength()
> Return the length of the diagonal of the bounding box of the dataset.

center = GetCenter()
> Get the center of the bounding box of the dataset.

range = GetScalarRange()
> A convenience method to return the (minimum, maximum) range of the scalar attribute data associated with the dataset.

dataSet = NewInstance()
> Make a copy of the current dataset. A "virtual" constructor. (Typically, reference counting methods are used to copy data.)

CopyStructure(dataSet)
> Update the current structure definition (i.e., geometry and topology) with the supplied dataset.

Cell Abstraction. Cells are the atomic structures of VTK. Cells consist of a topology, defined by a sequence of ordered point ids, and a geometry, defined by point coordinates. The cell coordinate consists of a cell id, a subcell id, and a parametric coordinate. The subid specifies a primary cell that lies within a composite cell such as a triangle strip. Cell edges and faces are defined implicitly from the topology of the cell.

type = GetCellType()
> Return the type of the cell. Must be one of the twelve VTK cell types (or the empty cell type).

dim = GetCellDimension()
> Return the topological definition of the cell.

`order = GetInterpolationOrder()`
> Return the degree of the interpolating polynomial of the cell. (The twelve cell types are all degree 1; cells added in the future may be of higher-order.)

`numberPoints = GetNumberOfPoints()`
> Return the number of points that define the cell.

`points = GetPoints()`
> Return a list of point ids defining the cell.

`numberEdges = GetNumberOfEdges()`
> Return the number of edges in the cell.

`edge = GetEdge(i)`
> Given an edge id ($0 \le i <$ numberEdges) return a pointer to a cell that represents an edge of the cell.

`numberFaces = GetNumberOfFaces()`
> Return the number of faces in a cell.

`face = GetFace(i)`
> Given an face id ($0 \le i <$ numberFaces) return a pointer to a cell that represents a face of the cell.

`inOutStatus = CellBoundary(subId, pcoords, poindIds)`
> Given a cell subid and parametric coordinates, return a list of point ids that define the closest boundary face of the cell. Also return whether the point is actually in the cell.

`inOutStatus = EvaluatePosition(x, closestPoint, subId, pcoords, weights, dist2)`
> Given a point coordinate x, return the sub-id, parametric coordinates, and interpolation weights of the cell if x lies inside the cell. The position closestPoint is the closest point on the cell to x (may be the same) and dist2 is the squared distance between them. The method returns an inOutStatus indicating whether x is *topologically* inside or outside the cell. That is, the point may satisfy parametric coordinate conditions but may lie off the surface of the cell (e.g., point lies above polygon). Use both inOutStatus and dist2 to determine whether point is both topologically and geometrically in the cell.

`EvaluateLocation(subId, pcoords, x, weights)`
> Given a point location (i.e., sub-id and parametric coordinates), return the position x of the point and the interpolation weights.

`Contour(value, cellScalars, locator, verts, lines, polys, inputPointData, outputPointData)`
> Given a contour value and scalar values at the cell points, generate contour primitives (vertices, lines, or polygons with associated points and attribute data values). The points are placed in a locator object (see "Searching" on page 279) which merges coincident points, and the attribute data values are interpolated (along the cell edge) from the inputPointData to the outputPointData.

Clip(value, cellScalars, locator, cells, inputPointData,
     outputPointData, insideOut)
> Given a contour value and scalar values at the cell points, clip the cell to generate new cells of the same topological dimension as the original cell. The points are placed in a locator object (see "Searching" on page 279) which merges coincident points, and the attribute data values are interpolated (or copied) from the inputPointData to the outputPointData. The clipped cells are placed in the cells list.

Derivatives(subId, pcoords, values, dim, derivs)
> Given a cell location (i.e., subid and parametric coordinates) and data values at the cell points, return dim*3 derivatives (i.e., corresponds to the x, y, and z directions times dimension of data).

inOutStatus = IntersectWithLine(p1, p2, tol, t, x,
     pcoords, subId)
> Given a finite line defined by the two points p1 and p2 and an intersection tolerance, return the point of intersection x. The parametric coordinate t along the line and cell location at the point of intersection is also returned. Returns a nonzero if intersection occurs.

Triangulate(index, ptIds, points)
> Decompose the cell into simplices of dimension equal to the topological cell dimension. The index is an integer that controls the triangulation if more than one triangulation is possible. The simplices are defined by an ordered list of point ids and their corresponding coordinates.

bounds = GetBounds()
> Return the bounding box of the cell.

Point and Cell Attribute Abstraction. Point and cell attribute data is information associated with the points and cells of a dataset. This information consists of scalars, vectors, normals, tensors, and texture coordinates. There is a one-to-one relationship between the points and cells in a dataset and its corresponding point and cell attribute data. For example, a point scalar value at location 100 is associated with point id 100.

Many of the methods described below deal with moving data from the input to the output of a filter. Since the possibility exists that new types of attribute data could be added in the future, the details of moving data is hidden as much as possible (i.e., minimize the knowledge that the filter has about specific attribute types). Thus, generic functions like CopyData() allow for copying data from the input to the output without knowing what this data is.

CopyScalarsOn() / CopyScalarsOff()
> Turn on/off boolean flag controlling copying of scalar data from input to output of filter.

CopyVectorsOn() / CopyVectorsOff()
> Turn on/off boolean flag controlling copying of vector data from input to output of filter.

`CopyNormalsOn() / CopyNormalsOff()`
Turn on/off boolean flag controlling copying of normal data from input to output of filter.

`CopyTensorsOn() / CopyTensorsOff()`
Turn on/off boolean flag controlling copying of tensor data from input to output of filter.

`CopyTextureCoordsOn() / CopyTextureCoordsOff()`
Turn on/off boolean flag controlling copying of texture coordinates data from input to output of filter.

`CopyAllOn() / CopyAllOff()`
Turn on/off all boolean flags controlling copying of all attribute data from input to output of filter.

`PassData(pointData)`
Transfer all point attribute data (pointData) to the output according to the copy flags listed previously.

`CopyAllocate(pointData)`
Initialize and allocate storage for point-by-point copy process.

`CopyData(pointData, fromId, toId)`
Given point data and a specific point id, copy the point attribute data (pointData) to the output point.

`InterpolateAllocate(pointData)`
Initialize and allocate storage for point-by-point interpolation process.

`InterpolatePoint(pointData, toId, ptIds, weights)`
Given input point data (pointData) and a list of points and their interpolation weights, interpolate data to the specified output point.

`InterpolateEdge(pointData, toId, p1, p2, t)`
From an edge defined by the two points p1 and p2, interpolate the pointData at the edge parametric coordinate t and copy the interpolated attribute data to the output point ptId.

`NullPoint(int ptId)`
Set the data value(s) of the specified output point id to a null value.

`SetScalars() / GetScalars()`
Set / return scalar data. The GetScalars() method may return a NULL value, in which case the scalars are not defined.

`SetVectors() / GetVectors()`
Set / return vector data. The GetVectors() method may return a NULL value, in which case the vectors are not defined.

`SetNormals() / GetNormals()`
Set / return normal data. The GetNormals() method may return a NULL value, in

which case the normals are not defined.

`SetTensors() / GetTensors()`

Set / return tensor data. The GetTensors() method may return a NULL value, in which case the tensors are not defined.

`SetTextureCoords() / GetTextureCoords()`

Set / return texture coordinate data. The GetTextureCoords() method may return a NULL value, in which case the texture coordinates are not defined.

Traversing Intermediate Topology

The dataset abstraction implemented by VTK provides simple techniques to traverse points and cells. Sometimes we want to traverse intermediate topology such as edges or faces. For example, to identify boundary edges in a triangular mesh we must traverse each edge, counting the number of triangles that use each edge. (Recall that boundary edges are used by just one triangle.) Unfortunately, there is no obvious way to traverse edges. The same problem holds true if we want to traverse the faces of a dataset containing 3D cells.

A simple solution is to traverse each cell and then obtain the edges (or faces) that compose the cell. The problem with this approach is that edges and faces are generally used by more than one cell, resulting in multiple visits to the same face or edge. This may be acceptable in some algorithms, but usually we count on visiting each edge or face only once.

A better solution to this problem is to traverse each cell as before, but only process intermediate topology if the current cell has the smallest cell id. (The current cell is the cell being visited in the traversal process.) To determine whether the current cell has the smallest cell id, we obtain all cells using the intermediate topology. This information can be obtained using the topological adjacency operators described earlier (e.g., **Equation 8-24**).

To illustrate this process consider visiting the edges of a triangle mesh. We begin by visiting the first triangle, *t*, and then its edges. For each edge we determine the adjacent triangle(s) (if any) that use the edge. If the id of the adjacent triangle(s) is greater than triangle *t*'s id, or there are no adjacent triangles, then we know to process the current edge. (Of course the first triangle will always have the smallest id — but this will change as the traversal proceeds.) We then continue traversing the triangle list for new *t*'s. In this way all the edges of the mesh will be visited.

Color Scalar Data

Multivalued scalar data, or scalars represented by various color representations, are treated specially by the *Visualization Toolkit*. These data arise, for example, when using a color specification to directly control the color of objects rather than mapping a scalar value through a lookup table. (See "Color Mapping" on page 151 for more information.)

By default, the mapping of scalars into colors proceeds as follows (vtkMapper and subclasses are responsible for implementing this behavior):

- If the scalar type is `unsigned char` with the tuple size ranging between one and four components, the data is considered to be color data.

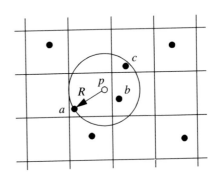

Figure 8–29 Determining closest point to *p* in vtkPointLocator. Initial search in bucket results in point *a*. Search must extend beyond local bucket as a function of search radius *R*, resulting in point *b*.

- Four component data is assumed to be a RGBA (red-green-blue-alpha transparency) color specification. Three component data is assumed to be a RGB color specification. Two component data is assumed to be a IA (intensity-alpha) representation. Single component data is assumed to be a I (intensity) value.

- Any other data type, or data with more than four components, is assumed to represent a scalar value. In that case the scalars are mapped through a lookup table to produce colors during the rendering process.

It is possible to force unsigned char data to be mapped through a lookup table. The vtkMapper method SetColorModeToMapScalars() forces all data—regardless of type—to be mapped through the lookup table.

Searching

The *Visualization Toolkit* provides two classes to perform searches for dataset points and cells. These are vtkPointLocator and vtkCellLocator. (Both of these classes are subclasses of vtkLocator, which is an abstract base class for spatial search objects.) vtkPointLocator is used to search for points and, if used with the topological dataset operator GetPointCells(), to search for cells as well. vtkCellLocator is used to search for cells.

vtkPointLocator is implemented as a regular grid of buckets (i.e., same topology and geometry as an image dataset). The number of buckets can be user-specified, or more conveniently, automatically computed based on the number of dataset points. On average, vtkPointLocator provides constant time access to points. However, in cases where the point distribution is not uniform, the number of points in a bucket may vary widely, giving $O(n)$ worst-case behavior. In practice this is rarely a problem, but adaptive spatial search structures (e.g., an octree) may sometimes be a better choice.

Determining closest point to a point *p* using vtkPointLocator (as well as other spatial search structures) is a three-step process. In the first step, the bucket containing *p* is found using the appropriate insertion scheme. (For vtkPointLocator this is three divisions to determine bucket indices *(i, j, k)*.) Next, the list of points in this bucket is searched to determine the closest point. However, as **Figure 8–29** shows, this may not be the true closest point, since points in neighboring buckets may be closer. Consequently, a final search of neighboring buckets is necessary. The search distance is a function of the distance to the current closest point. Once all neighbors within this distance are searched, the closest point is returned.

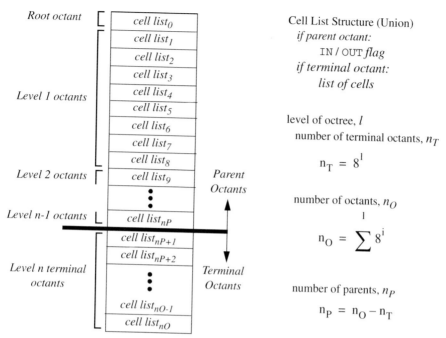

Figure 8–30 Structure of spatial search structure vtkCellLocator. The data structure represents a uniformly subdivided octree.

vtkCellLocator is implemented as a uniformly subdivided octree with some peculiar characteristics (**Figure 8–30**). Conventional octree representations use upward parent and downward children pointers to track parent and children octants. Besides the required list of entities (i.e., points or cells) in each octant, additional information about octant level, center, and size may also be maintained. This results in a flexible structure with significant overhead. The overhead is the memory resources to maintain pointers, plus the cost to allocate and delete memory.

In contrast, vtkCellLocator uses a single array to represent the octree. The array is divided into two parts. The first part contains a list of parent octants, ordered according to level and octant child number. In the second part are the terminal, or leaf octants. The terminal octants are ordered on a regular array of buckets, just the same as vtkLocator. The terminal octants contain a list of the entities inside the octant. The parent octants maintain a value indicating whether the octant is empty, or whether something is inside it. (Both types of information are represented in the same portion of the octant structure.) Because the octree is uniformly subdivided, parent-child relationships, as well as octant locations, can be computed quickly using simple division operations.

The advantage of this structure is that memory can be allocated and deleted quickly. In addition, insertion into the octree is exactly the same as with vtkLocator, and is simpler than conventional octrees. The parent octants provide quick culling capability, since their status (empty or nonempty) allows us to stop certain types of search operations. On the downside, because the octree is uniformly subdivided, this structure is wasteful of memory resources if the data is nonuniformly distributed.

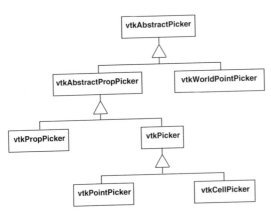

Figure 8–31 The picking hierarchy in VTK. All subclasses of vtkAbstractPropPicker return the picked instance of vtkProp. The information is returned as a vtkAssemblyPath. The assembly path is necessary because some props may exist in an assembly hierarchy. The classes vtkWorldPointPicker and vtkPropPicker are hardware accelerated picking classes. All others use software ray casting.

Our experience with the search structures described here is that they work well for many types of visualization data. However, if your data is non-uniform, you may want to implement your own special search classes.

Picking

The *Visualization Toolkit* provides a variety of classes to perform actor (or vtkProp), point, cell, and world point picking (**Figure 8–31**). Depending on which picker is used, either software-based geometric intersection or hardware picking is used. The following describes each of the picker types in detail.

All pickers are subclasses of vtkAbstractPicker which defines the basic pick interface. The user must specific a selection point in display coordinates for a specified instance of vtkRenderWindow and invoke the Pick() method. At a minimum, the class must return an x-y-z pick position in world coordinates. It is possible to limit the pick candidates to a list of vtkProps (the PickList). The class also invokes the StartPickEvent, PickEvent, and EndPickEvent events that are invoked prior to picking, during picking, and after picking, respectively.

Classes that can return information indicating which vtkProp they have picked are subclasses of vtkAbstractPropPicker. After the pick operation, vtkAbstractPropPicker returns a vtkAssemblyPath. The assembly path is an ordered list of instances of vtkProp and possibly associated 4x4 transformation matrices. The path represents a concatenated hierarchy of assembly nodes if an assembly has been defined (see "Assemblies and Other Types of vtkProp" on page 75 for more information about props and assemblies).

The object vtkPicker intersects a ray defined from camera position to a screen (i.e., pixel) coordinate against the bounding box of all pickable and nontransparent vtkProp3D's. (A vtkProp is pickable if its Pickable instance variable is true.) The result of the vtkPicker pick operation is to return a list of the vtkProp3D's whose bounding box is intersected. The prop closest to the camera position is also returned.

The object vtkPointPicker intersects the ray against the points defining each vtkProp3D, and returns the point coordinate closest to the camera position, as well as the vtkProp3D that the point belongs to. Since screen resolution prevents precise selection of a point, a tolerance around the ray must be specified. The tolerance is expressed as a fraction of the rendering window size. (Rendering window size is measured across the window diagonal.) Points must lie within this tolerance to be picked.

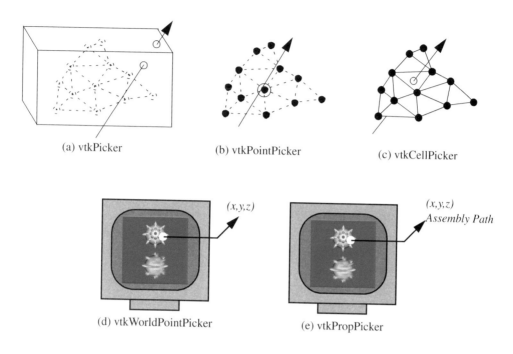

(a) vtkPicker (b) vtkPointPicker (c) vtkCellPicker

(x,y,z)

(x,y,z)
Assembly Path

(d) vtkWorldPointPicker (e) vtkPropPicker

Figure 8–32 Summary of picking operations. The top three pick classes (a)-(c) use software ray casting. The bottom two pick classes (d)-(e) use hardware acceleration.

The object vtkCellPicker intersects the ray with the cells defining each vtkProp3D, and returns the point of intersection, as well as the vtkProp3D that the cell belongs to. If you are trying to select a cell belonging to a particular vtkProp3D, vtkCellPicker is the object to use because it performs surface (or cell) intersection. Unfortunately, vtkCellPicker is the slowest of the pickers because of greater computational requirements.

The class vtkWorldPointPicker returns the (x,y,z) coordinate value of a pick in the rendering window. To determine this information, it combines the display (x,y) values with the z-buffer depth values. Of all the pickers this is the fastest, but it cannot determine the actual cell, point or vtkProp that is selected since it is not a subclass of vtkAbstractPropPicker. (Note: on some systems z-buffer operations are inoperative and this object will not function properly.)

By default picking is performed with the class vtkPropPicker. This class uses hardware-accelerated picking—so it is generally faster than software based picking. Unlike the other hardware accelerated class (vtkWorldPointPicker), it returns the instance of vtkProp that was picked as well as the (x,y,z) world coordinate value

Figure 8–32 summarizes the five concrete picking classes. Picking is built into the vtkRenderWindowInteractor class using the "p" key (see "Introducing vtkRenderWindowInteractor" on page 68). By default a vtkPropPicker is created and used, but you are free to specify your own picker type.

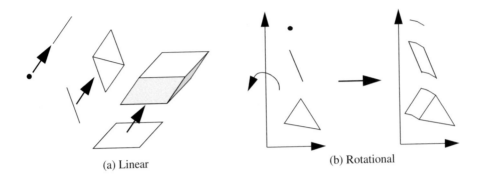

(a) Linear   (b) Rotational

Figure 8–33 Depiction of linear and rotational extrusion.

Examples

To conclude this section, we will examine how some of the dataset, cell, and point attribute operations are used. These operations tend to be used by class developers. You will not need to use them if you build applications by constructing visualization pipelines with existing filters.

Find Free Edges. In our first example we will take a peek inside the filter vtkLinearExtrusionFilter. This filter implements the following modelling operation. Given a polygonal mesh, extrude the mesh in a given direction, constructing a "skirt" or "walls" from the free edges. If the polygonal example is a single square, the result of this operation is a cube. Or, if the polygonal data consists of a single line, the result of the operation is a quadrilateral. A point will generate a line as shown in **Figure 8–33**(a).

Recall that free edges are edges used by only one polygon. We can determine this information using the dataset topology operation GetCellEdgeNeigbors(). We use **Equation 8-24** and the two points defining the edge of the polygon to determine the adjacency set (i.e., the polygons sharing this edge). If no other polygon uses this edge, then the edge is extruded to generate a triangle strip. The C++ pseudo code is as follows.

```
for (cellId=0; cellId < numCells; cellId++)
  {
  cell = mesh->GetCell(cellId);
  if ((dim=cell->GetCellDimension()) == 0)
  //create lines from points
  else if ( dim == 1 )
  // create strips from lines
  else if ( dim == 2 ) // create strips from boundary edges
    {
    numEdges = cell->GetNumberOfEdges();
    for (i=0; i<numEdges; i++)
```

```
    {
    edge = cell->GetEdge(i);
    for (j=0; j<(edge->GetNumberOfPoints()-1); j++)
      {
      p1 = edge->PointIds->GetId(j);
      p2 = edge->PointIds->GetId(j+1);
      mesh.GetCellEdgeNeighbors(cellId, p1, p2, cellIds);
      if ( cellIds->GetNumberOfIds() < 1 )
        {
        //generate triangle strip
        }
      } //for each subedge
    } //for each edge
  } //for each polygon or triangle strip
} //for each cell
```

This same approach is used in the vtkRotationalExtrusionFilter (**Figure 8–33**(b)). The difference between these two functions is that the type of motion is rotational as compared to linear (vtkLinearExtrusionFilter). These two filters can be used to perform some nifty modelling operations. Linear extrusion can be used to create bar charts with arbitrary cross sections, or to sweep out three-dimensional fonts. The rotational extrusion filter can be used to create rotationally symmetric objects such as bottles or wine glasses. Examples of these techniques are shown in **Figure 8–34**.

Find Cells. In this example we combine picking and a topological operation to select cells sharing a common point. Specifically, we use vtkPointPicker and the topological dataset operation GetPointCells(). **Figure 8–35** depicts this operation. We have also included a fragment of C++ code implementing this procedure. Note that this procedure will work for any dataset type, even if the geometry is implicitly defined (e.g., vtkImageData).

The most difficult part of this procedure is the picking process. The selection point must be specified in pixel coordinates. The vtkPointPicker converts these coordinates into world and then dataset coordinates using the renderer in which the pick occurred. (The renderer uses the transformation matrix of its active camera to perform coordinate transformation.)

The picking process is conveniently managed in vtkRenderWindowInteractor. This object allows the specification of functions to execute just before picking and just after picking (i.e., "AddObserver StartPickEvent" and "AddObserver EndPickEvent"). Using this facility we can define a postpicking function to retrieve the point id and then execute the GetPointCells() operation. This process is shown in **Figure 8–35**.

Point Probe. In this example we will show how to build a point probe using the dataset and cell operations described in this chapter. A point probe is defined as follows. Given a (x,y,z) point coordinate, find the cell coordinates (i.e., cell id, subcell id, and parametric coordinates) and the interpolation weights. Once the interpolation weights are found, we can then compute local data values at (x,y,z).

The point probe is implemented using the dataset operation FindCell(). This method requires a point specified in global coordinates (our (x,y,z) value) and a tolerance. The toler-

(a) Linearly extruded fonts to show letter frequency in text (`alphaFreq.cxx`).

(b) Rotationally symmetric objects (`bottle.tcl`).

(c) Rotation in combination with linear displacement and radius variation (`spring.tcl`).

Figure 8–34 Models created using linear and rotational extrusion.

ance is often necessary because of numerical precision or when picking near the surface of 3D cells, or on 0D, 1D, and 2D cells. The FindCell() operation returns the information we require, plus the interpolation weights of the cell containing our point probe. To determine the data value at our probe point, we need to retrieve the data values on the cell points. We can then use the interpolation functions of **Equation 8-4** to determine the probe scalar value.

Figure 8–36 depicts this process and includes C++ code. In the example we use the combustor dataset with the objects vtkCursor3D, vtkProbeFilter, and vtkGlyph3D. The purpose of the cursor is to control the position of the probe point. The class vtkProbeFilter performs the probing operation just described. (This filter has been generalized so that it can handle more than one input point.) vtkGlyph3D is used to place an oriented, scaled cone at the cursor focal point. This gives us visual feedback about the scalar and vector quantities at the probe. Of course, we can extract numeric values and display them to the user if this is important.

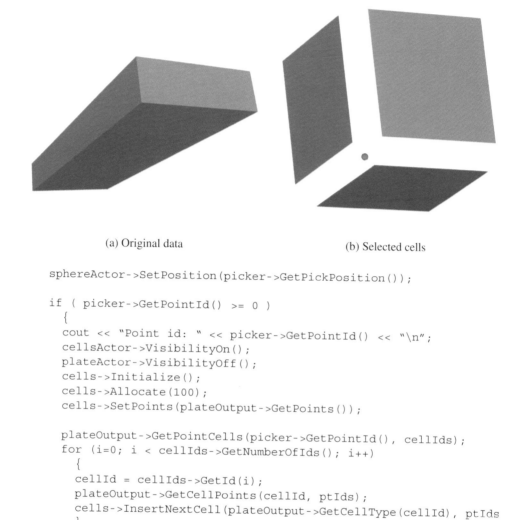

(a) Original data   (b) Selected cells

```
sphereActor->SetPosition(picker->GetPickPosition());

if ( picker->GetPointId() >= 0 )
  {
  cout << "Point id: " << picker->GetPointId() << "\n";
  cellsActor->VisibilityOn();
  plateActor->VisibilityOff();
  cells->Initialize();
  cells->Allocate(100);
  cells->SetPoints(plateOutput->GetPoints());

  plateOutput->GetPointCells(picker->GetPointId(), cellIds);
  for (i=0; i < cellIds->GetNumberOfIds(); i++)
    {
    cellId = cellIds->GetId(i);
    plateOutput->GetCellPoints(cellId, ptIds);
    cells->InsertNextCell(plateOutput->GetCellType(cellId), ptIds
    }
  }
else
  {
  cellsActor->VisibilityOff();
  plateActor->VisibilityOn();
  }
renWin->Render();
```

(c) C++ code (`pickCells.cxx`)

Figure 8–35 Selecting group of cells sharing a common point. (a) Original data. (b) Selected cells sharing point on corner. Cells shrunk for clarity. The small sphere indicates the selected point. (c) C++ code fragment in pick routine.

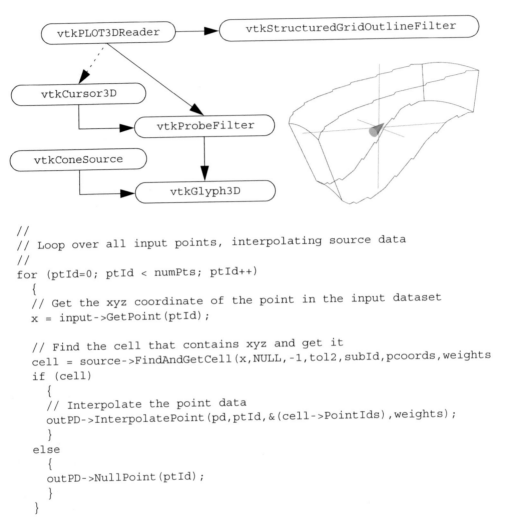

```
//
// Loop over all input points, interpolating source data
//
for (ptId=0; ptId < numPts; ptId++)
    {
    // Get the xyz coordinate of the point in the input dataset
    x = input->GetPoint(ptId);

    // Find the cell that contains xyz and get it
    cell = source->FindAndGetCell(x,NULL,-1,tol2,subId,pcoords,weights
    if (cell)
        {
        // Interpolate the point data
        outPD->InterpolatePoint(pd,ptId,&(cell->PointIds),weights);
        }
    else
        {
        outPD->NullPoint(ptId);
        }
    }
```

Figure 8–36 Creating a point probe. Visualization network shown in diagram above. C++ code shows inner loop of vtkProbeFilter and resulting image for combustor data (probe.cxx).

8.11 Chapter Summary

Three important visualization coordinate systems are the world, dataset, and structured coordinate systems. The world coordinate system is an *x-y-z* Cartesian three-dimensional space. The dataset coordinate system consists of a cell id, subcell id, and parametric coordinates. The structured coordinate system consists of *(i,j,k)* integer indices into a rectangular topological domain.

Visualization data is generally in discrete form. Interpolation functions are used to obtain data at points between the known data values. Interpolation functions vary depending on the particular cell type. The form of the interpolation functions are weighting values located at each of the cells points. The interpolations functions form the basis for conversion from dataset to global coordinates and vice versa. The interpolation functions also are used to compute data derivatives.

Topological operators provide information about the topology of a cell or dataset. Obtaining neighboring cells to a particular cell is an important visualization operation. This operation can be used to determine whether cell boundaries are on the boundary of a dataset or to traverse datasets on a cell-by-cell basis.

Because of the inherent regularity of image datasets, operations can be efficiently implemented compared to other dataset types. These operations include coordinate transformation, derivative computation, topological query, and searching.

8.12 Bibliographic Notes

Interpolation functions are employed in a number of numerical techniques. The finite element method, in particular, depends on interpolation functions. If you want more information about interpolation functions refer to the finite element references suggested below [Cook89] [Gallagher75] [Zienkiewicz87]. These texts also discuss derivative computation in the context of interpolation functions.

Basic topology references are available from a number of sources. Two good descriptions of topological data structures are available from Weiler [Weiler86] [Weiler88] and Baumgart [Baumgart74]. Weiler describes the radial-edge structure. This data structure can represent manifold and nonmanifold geometry. The winged-edge structure described by Baumgart is widely known. It is used to represent manifold geometry. Shephard [Shephard88] describes general finite element data structures — these are similar to visualization structures but with extra information related to analysis and geometric modelling.

There are extensive references regarding spatial search structures. Samet [Samet90] provides a general overview of some. Octrees were originally developed by Meagher [Meagher82] for 3D imaging. See [Williams83], [Bentley75], and [Quinlan94] for information about MIP maps, kd-trees, and binary sphere trees, respectively.

8.13 References

[Baumgart74]
    B. G. Baumgart. "Geometric Modeling for Computer Vision." Ph.D. thesis, Stanford University, Palo Alto, CA, 1974.

[Bentley75]
    J. L. Bentley. "Multidimensional Binary Search Trees Used for Associative Search." *Communications of the ACM*. 18(9):509–516, 1975.

[Conte72]
    S. D. Conte and C. de Boor. *Elementary Numerical Analysis*. McGraw-Hill Book Company, 1972.

[Cook89]
> R. D. Cook, D. S. Malkus, and M. E. Plesha. *Concepts and Applications of Finite Element Analysis*. John Wiley and Sons, New York, 1989.

[Gallagher75]
> R. H. Gallagher. *Finite Element Analysis: Fundamentals*. Prentice Hall, Upper Saddle River, NJ, 1975.

[Meagher82]
> D. J. Meagher. "Efficient Synthetic Image Generation of Arbitrary 3D Objects." In *Proceedings of the IEEE Conference on Pattern Recognition and Image Processing*. pp. 473–478, 1982.

[Quinlan94]
> S. Quinlan. "Efficient Distance Computation Between Non-Convex Objects." In *Proceedings of IEEE International Conference on Robotics and Automation*. 1994.

[Samet90]
> H. Samet. *Design and Analysis of Spatial Data Structures*. Addison-Wesley, Reading, MA, 1990.

[Shephard88]
> M. S. Shephard and P. M. Finnigan. "Toward Automatic Model Generation." *State-of-the-Art Surveys on Computational Mechanics*. A. K. Noor and J. T. Oden, eds., ASME, pp. 335–366, 1989.

[Weiler86]
> K. J. Weiler. *Topological Structures for Geometric Modeling*. Ph.D. thesis, Rensselaer Polytechnic Institute, Troy, NY, May 1986.

[Weiler88]
> K. J. Weiler. "The Radial-Edge Structure: A Topological Representation for Non-Manifold Geometric Boundary Representations." In M. J. Wozny, H. W. McLaughlin, and J. L. Encarnacao, eds., *Geometric Modeling for CAD Applications*. pp. 3–36, North Holland, 1988.

[Williams83]
> L. Williams. "Pyramidal Parametrics." *Computer Graphics (SIGGRAPH '83)*. 17(3):1–11, 1983.

[Zienkiewicz87]
> O. C. Zienkiewicz and R. L. Taylor. *The Finite Element Method — Vol. 1*. McGraw Hill Book Co., NY, 4th ed., 1987.

8.14 Exercises

8.1   Given a volume of dimensions $5 \times 10 \times 15$ with origin $(1.0, 2.0, 3.0)$ and voxel spacing $(0.5, 0.5, 1.0)$.

a) Compute minimum point position.

b) Compute maximum point position.

c) For cell id 342, compute cell minimum point position and maximum point position.

d) What points (list ids) define cell id 342?

e) Given point specified in structured coordinates as $i, j, k = (3, 6, 4)$; $r, s, t = (0.1, 0.2, 0.5)$, compute global coordinates.

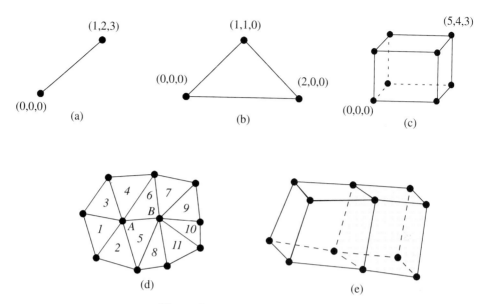

Figure 8–37 Exercise figures.

f) Given point id 342; compute global coordinates.

8.2 Compute global coordinates and interpolation weights for the points specified in dataset coordinates (refer to **Figure 8–37**(a-d)).
a) Line with $r = 0.5$.
b) Triangle with $r, s = (0.25, 0.33)$.
c) Voxel with $r, s, t = (0.25, 0.33, 0.5)$.

8.3 Compute parametric coordinates for cells shown in **Figure 8–37**(a–d).
a) Line with $x, y, z = (0.3, 0.6, 0.9)$.
b) Triangle with $x, y, z = (0.5, 0.25, 0.0)$.
c) Voxel with $x, y, z = (0.5, 0.4, 2.0)$.

8.4 Given the line shown in **Figure 8–37**(a), if scalar data values are $(s_0, s_1) = (0.0, 0.25)$, what are the derivatives in the x, y, z directions?

8.5 Refer to **Figure 8–37**(d) and let the numbers indicate cell ids and the letters indicate point ids.
a) List the cells using point A.
b) List the cells using point B.
c) List cells using edge (A, B) . How does this list correspond to your answers in parts a) and b) above?

8.6 Refer to **Figure 8–37**(e).
a) How many boundary faces are there?
b) How many "internal" faces?

8.7 Describe a procedure to intersect two finite lines. How does tolerance value come into play?

8.8 Describe a procedure to intersect a line and triangle. Are there special characteristics of a triangle that can be used to speed this operation?

8.9 Compare memory requirements for the three unstructured grid data structures shown in **Figure 8–27**. Assume that two cells use each face, four faces use each edge, and six edges use each vertex (i.e., a structured dataset).

8.10 Using the abstract cell and dataset interface, write a program to compute
a) number of points in a dataset,
b) number of cells in a dataset,
c) number of edges in a dataset,
d) number of faces in a dataset.

8.11 Given a volume of dimensions $5 \times 10 \times 15$.
a) How many internal faces are there (i.e. used by two voxels)?
b) How many boundary faces are there (i.e., used by one voxel)?

8.12 Write a general extrusion filter that sweeps an object along a path to construct a new surface. Assume that the path is defined by a sequence of transformation matrices. Can you think of a way to prevent self-intersection?

Advanced Algorithms

We return again to visualization algorithms. This chapter describes algorithms that are either more complex to implement, or less widely used for 3D visualization applications. We retain the classification of algorithms as either scalar, vector, tensor, or modelling algorithms.

9.1 Scalar Algorithms

As we have seen, scalar algorithms often involve mapping scalar values through a lookup table, or creating contour lines or surfaces. In this section, we examine another contouring algorithm, *dividing cubes*, which generates contour surfaces using dense point clouds. We also describe carpet plots. Carpet plots are not true 3D visualization techniques, but are widely used to visualize many types of scalar data. Finally, clipping is another important algorithm related to contouring, where cells are cut into pieces as a function of scalar value.

Dividing Cubes

Dividing cubes is a contouring algorithm similar to marching cubes [Cline88]. Unlike marching cubes, dividing cubes generates point primitives as compared to triangles (3D) or lines (2D). If the number of points on the contour surface is large, the rendered appearance of the contour surface appears "solid." To achieve this solid appearance, the density of the points

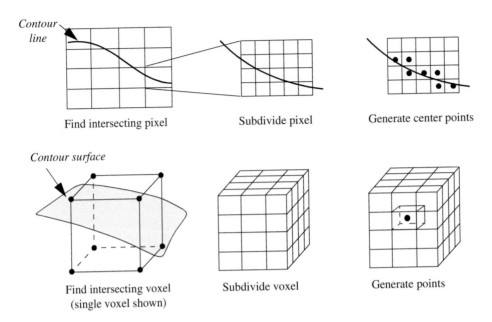

Contour line

Find intersecting pixel   Subdivide pixel   Generate center points

Contour surface

Find intersecting voxel   Subdivide voxel   Generate points
(single voxel shown)

Figure 9–1 Overview of the dividing cubes algorithm. Voxels through which the contour passes are subdivided into subvoxels at less than screen resolution. If the contour passes through a subvoxel, a center point is generated.

must be at or greater than screen resolution. (Also, the points must be rendered using the standard lighting and shading equations used in surface rendering.)

The motivation for dividing cubes is that rendering points is much faster than rendering polygons. This varies depending upon rendering hardware/software. Special purpose hardware has been developed to render shaded points at high speed. In other systems, greater attention has been placed on polygon rendering, and the rendering speed differences are not so great. Also, certain geometric operations such as clipping and merging data are simple operations with points. Comparable operations with polygons are much more difficult to implement.

One disadvantage of creating contours with dense point clouds is that magnification of the surface (via camera zooming, for example) reveals the disconnected nature of the surface. Thus, the point set must be constructed for maximum zoom, or constructed dynamically based on the relative relationship between the camera and contour.

Although dividing cubes was originally developed for volume datasets, it is possible to adapt the algorithm to other dataset types by subdividing in parametric coordinates. Our presentation assumes that we are working with volumes.

Figure 9–1 provides an overview of the dividing cubes algorithm. Like other contouring algorithms, we first choose a contour value. We begin by visiting each voxel and select those through which the isosurface passes. (The isosurface passes through a voxel when there are scalar values both above and below the contour value.) We also compute the gradient at each voxel point for use in computing point normals.

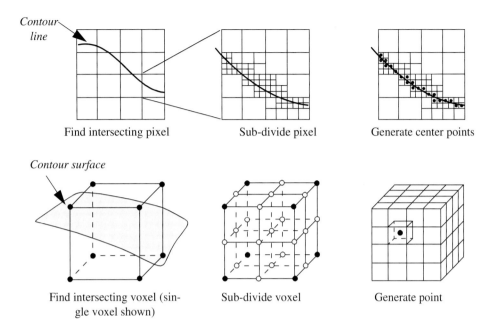

Figure 9–2 Recursive dividing cubes algorithm. Top half of figure shows algorithm depicted in two dimensions. Lower half depicts algorithm in three dimensions.

After selecting a voxel that the isosurface passes through, the voxel is subdivided into a regular grid of $n_1 \times n_2 \times n_3$ subvoxels. The number of divisions is controlled by the width of a voxel w_i in combination with screen resolution R. The screen resolution is defined as the distance between adjacent pixels in world coordinates. We can express the number of divisions n_i along the coordinate axes x_i as

$$n_i = \frac{w_i}{R} \tag{9-1}$$

where the quotient is rounded up to the nearest integer. The scalar values at the subpoints are generated using the interpolation functions for a voxel (see **Figure 8–10**). Then we determine whether the contour passes through each subvoxel. If it does, we simply generate a point at the center of the subvoxel and compute its normal using the standard interpolation functions.

An interesting variation on this algorithm is a recursive implementation as shown in **Figure 9–2**. Instead of subdividing the voxel directly (i.e., procedurally) into a regular grid we recursively divide the voxel (similar to octree decomposition). The voxel is subdivided regularly creating eight subvoxels and 19 new points (12 midedge points, 6 midface points, and 1 midvoxel point). The scalar values at the new points are interpolated from the original voxel using the trilinear interpolation functions. The process repeats for each subvoxel if the isosurface passes through it. This process continues until the size of the subvoxel is less than or equal to screen resolution. In this case, a point is generated at the center of the subvoxel. The collection of all such points composes the dividing cubes' isosurface.

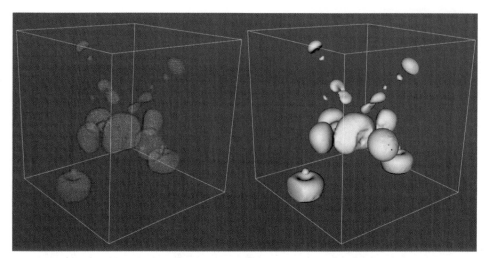

Figure 9–3 Examples of dividing cubes isosurface. The left image consists of 50,078 points, and the right image consists of 2,506,989 points (`dcubes.tcl`).

The advantage of the recursive implementation is that the subdivision process terminates prematurely in those regions of the voxel where the contour cannot pass. On the other hand, the recursive subdivision requires that the voxel subdivision occurs in powers of two. This can generate far more points than the procedural implementation.

Figure 9–3 shows two examples of dividing cubes isosurfaces. The contour surface on the left consists of 50,078 points. Because the points are not generated at display resolution, it is possible to see through the contour surface. The second contour surface on the right is composed of 2,506,989 points. The points are generated at display resolution, and as a result the contour surface appears solid.

As **Figure 9–1** and **Figure 9–2** show, the points generated by dividing cubes do not lie exactly on the contour surface. We can determine the maximum error by examining the size of the terminal subvoxels. Assume that a terminal subvoxel is a cube, and that the length of the side of the cube is given by l. Then the maximum error is half the length of the cube diagonal, or $l\sqrt{3}/2$.

Carpet Plots

A common data form is a 2D image dataset with associated scalar data. *Carpet plots* can visualize data in this form. A carpet plot is created by warping a 2D surface in the direction of the surface normal (or possibly some user-defined direction). The amount of warping is controlled by the scalar value, possibly in combination with a scale factor. Carpet plots are similar to the vector displacement plots (see "Displacement Plots" on page 163).

Although carpet plots are typically applied to image data, they can be used to visualize datasets composed of 2D structured grids or 2D unstructured grids. In their basic form carpet plots can be used to visualize only three variables: two surface position coordinates and a scalar value. However, it is common to introduce another variable by using color mapping on the surface.

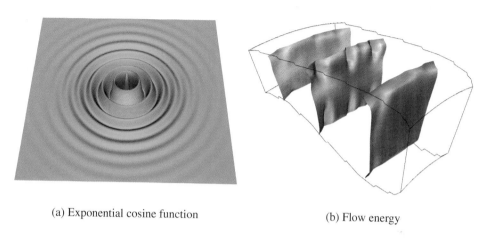

(a) Exponential cosine function   (b) Flow energy

Figure 9–4 Carpet plots. (a) Visualization of an exponential cosine function. Function values are indicated by surface displacement. Colors indicate derivative values (`exp-Cos.cxx`). (b) Carpet plot of combustor flow energy in a structured grid. Colors and plane displacement represent energy values (`warpComb.tcl`).

Figure 9–4 illustrates application of carpet plots. **Figure 9–4**(a) shows the exponential cosine function centered at the origin with points located at radius r

$$F(r) = e^{-r}\cos(10r)$$ **(9-2)**

The function values are used to warp the surface while the function derivatives are used to color it.

Figure 9–4(b) shows a carpet plot that visualizes flow energy in a structured grid. Both displacement and color are used to show the energy values. Although this figure is similar to **Figure 6–14**(b) there are some important differences. **Figure 6–14**(b) displays vector data whereas **Figure 9–4**(b) displays scalar data. **Figure 9–4**(b) deforms the surface in the direction of surface normal (or possibly a user-defined direction). The vector data (i.e., vector orientation) controls the direction of deformation in **Figure 6–14**(b).

Clipping With Scalar Fields

Clipping is a common graphics operation that limits the extent of a polygon so that it does not lie outside the view frustrum (See "Cameras" on page 43.) **Figure 9–5** shows a triangle before and after clipping with an infinite plane. The clip operation transforms a polygon into a polygon. Clipping can also be a powerful modeling tool. Clipping part of a structure can reveal internal details of the surface or other parts contained within the surface. Objects can be split into pieces and the pieces can be individually moved and controlled.

We can do clipping with arbitrary implicit functions using a variation of the "marching" primitives discussed in "Contouring" on page 154. We illustrate the technique for triangles.

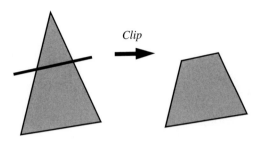

Figure 9–5 Clipping a triangle produces a polygon. The dark line represents an infinite plane.

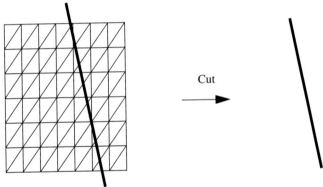

Figure 9–6 Cutting polygons produces lines (`cutPlane.tcl`).

Recall that marching triangles transforms triangles into lines that approximate a scalar value called the isovalue. This is accomplished using the inside/outside relationship that each vertex has with respect to some scalar value. For our purposes here, we use a scalar value that represents the signed distance of the triangle vertex to a plane. This infinite plane, described by an implicit function of the form $F(x, y, z) = n_x x + n_y y + n_z z - d = 0$, partitions space into two infinite half spaces. All points with negative scalar values lie on one side of the plane and all with positive values lie on the other side. **Figure 9–6** shows a finite plane represented by a grid of triangles. The thick line shows the infinite plane defined by $F(x,y,z) = x + y + z - c = 0$. The cut algorithm described in "Cutting" on page 180 creates a set of lines using the contour operations specific to each cell primitive. In this example, the triangle's contour operator extracts lines that lie on the intersection of the infinite plane and the triangles that comprise the finite plane. The contour operation for a triangle uses the eight cases shown in **Figure 9–7** to contour or "cut" each triangle appropriately.

Clipping transforms polygons into polygons. We do clipping with a modified case table for the triangle that outputs polygons shown in **Figure 9–8**. In VTK, each polygonal data cell has a different case table to define the clip operation. Applying the clip algorithm to the polygonal data in **Figure 9–9** using the same scalar field generated with a plane equation produces a new set of triangles.

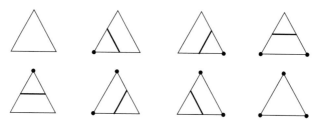

Figure 9–7 The eight cases for cutting (contouring) a triangle. Black dots show triangle vertices that are "inside" the scalar cutting region. Solid lines show the output of the cutting operation.

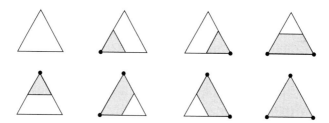

Figure 9–8 The eight cases for clipping a triangle. Black dots show triangle vertices that are "inside" the scalar clipping region. Shaded regions show the output of the clip operation.

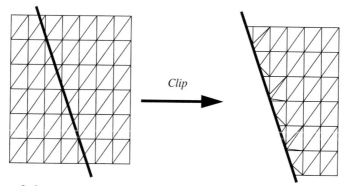

Clip

Figure 9–9 A plane of triangles clipped with a plane function (`clipPlane.tcl`).

Formulating clipping using scalar fields permits more sophisticated operations. Clipping can use scalar data that is computed or scalar data that is part of a polygonal dataset's point attributes. **Figure 9–10** shows a scanned image that is first converted to a quadrilateral mesh with vertex scalar values set to the scanned image intensity. Clipping this quadrilateral mesh with a value equal to 1/2 the maximum intensity of the scanned image produces a polygonal model show in **Figure 9–10**.

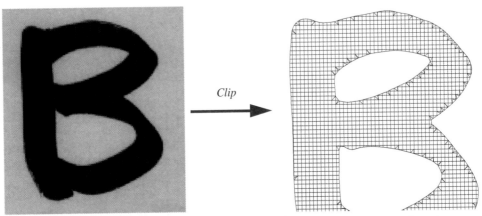

Figure 9–10 A scanned image clipped with a scalar value of 1/2 its maximum intensity produces a mixture of quadrilaterals and triangles (`createBFont.tcl`).

9.2 Vector Algorithms

In Chapter 6 we showed how to create simple vector glyphs and how to integrate particles through a vector field to create streamlines. In this section we extend these concepts to create streamribbons and streampolygons. In addition, we introduce the concept of vector field topology, and show how to characterize a vector field using topological constructs.

Streamribbons and Streamsurfaces

Streamlines depict particle paths in a vector field. By coloring these lines, or creating local glyphs (such as dashed lines or oriented cones), we can represent additional scalar and temporal information. However, these techniques can convey only elementary information about the vector field. Local information (e.g., flow rotation or derivatives) and global information (e.g., structure of a field such as vortex tubes) is not represented. Streamribbons and streamsurfaces are two techniques used to represent local and global information.

A natural extension of the streamline technique widens the line to create a ribbon. The ribbon can be constructed by generating two adjacent streamlines and then bridging the lines with a polygonal mesh. This technique works well as long as the streamlines remain relatively close to one another. If separation occurs, so that the streamlines diverge, the resulting ribbon will not accurately represent the flow, because we expect the surface of the ribbon to be everywhere tangent to the vector field (i.e., definition of streamline). The ruled surface connecting two widely separated streamlines does not generally satisfy this requirement.

The streamribbon provides information about important flow parameters: the vector vorticity and flow divergence. *Vorticity* $\vec{\omega}$ is the measure of rotation of the vector field, expressed as a vector quantity: a direction (axis of rotation) and magnitude (amount of rotation). *Streamwise vorticity* Ω is the projection of $\vec{\omega}$ along the instantaneous velocity vector, $\vec{v}$. Said another way, streamwise vorticity is the rotation of the vector field around the streamline defined as follows.

$$\Omega = \frac{\vec{v} \cdot \vec{\omega}}{|\vec{v}||\vec{\omega}|} \tag{9-3}$$

The amount of twisting of the streamribbon approximates the streamwise vorticity. Flow *divergence* is a measure of the "spread" of the flow. The changing width of the streamribbon is proportional to the cross-flow divergence of the flow.

A streamsurface is a collection of an infinite number of streamlines passing through a *base curve*. The base curve, or *rake*, defines the starting points for the streamlines. If the base curve is closed (e.g., a circle) the surface is closed and a streamtube results. Thus, streamribbons are specialized types of streamsurfaces with a narrow width compared to length.

Compared to vector icons or streamlines, streamsurfaces provide additional information about the structure of the vector field. Any point on the streamsurface is tangent to the velocity vector. Consequently, taking an example from fluid flow, no fluid can pass through the surface. Streamtubes are then representations of constant mass flux. Streamsurfaces show vector field structure better than streamlines or vector glyphs because they do not require visual interpolation across icons.

Streamsurfaces can be computed by generating a set of streamlines from a user-specified rake. A polygonal mesh is then constructed by connecting adjacent streamlines. One difficulty with this approach is that local vector field divergence can cause streamlines to separate. Separation can introduce large errors into the surface, or possibly cause self-intersection, which is not physically possible.

Another approach to computing streamsurfaces has been taken by Hultquist [Hultquist92]. The streamsurface is a collection of streamribbons connected along their edges. In this approach, the computation of the streamlines and tiling of the streamsurface is carried out concurrently. This allows streamlines to be added or removed as the flow separates or converges. The tiling can also be controlled to prevent the generation of long, skinny triangles. The surface may also be "torn", i.e., ribbons separated, if the divergence of the flow becomes too high.

Stream Polygon

The techniques described so far provide approximate measures of vector field quantities such as streamwise vorticity and divergence. However, vector fields contain more information than these techniques can convey. As a result, other techniques have been devised to visualize this information. One such technique is the *stream polygon* [Schroeder91], which serves as the basis for a number of advanced vector and tensor visualization methods. The stream polygon is used to visualize local properties of strain, displacement, and rotation. We begin by describing the effects of a vector field on the local state of strain.

Nonuniform vector fields give rise to local deformation in the region where they occur. If the vector field is displacement in a physical medium such as a fluid or a solid, the deformation consists of local strain (i.e., local distortion) and rigid body motion. To mathematically describe the deformation, we examine a 3D vector $\vec{v} = (u, v, w)$ at a specified point $\vec{x} = (x, y, z)$. Using a first order Taylor's series expansion about $\vec{x}$, we can express the local deformation e_{ij} as

$$e_{ij} = \varepsilon_{ij} + \omega_{ij} \qquad (9\text{-}4)$$

where ε_{ij} is the local strain and ω_{ij} is the local rotation. Note that these variables are expressed as 3×3 tensors. (Compare this equation to that given in **Figure 6–20**. Note that this equation and the following **Equation 9-5** differ in their off-diagonal terms by a factor of 1/2. This is because **Figure 6–20** expresses *engineering shear strain* which is used in the study of elasticity. **Equation 9-5** expresses a tensor quantity and is mathematically consistent.)

The local strain is expressed as a combination of the partial derivatives at $\vec{x}$ as follows.

$$\varepsilon_{ij} = \begin{bmatrix} \dfrac{\partial u}{\partial x} & \dfrac{1}{2}\left(\dfrac{\partial u}{\partial y}+\dfrac{\partial v}{\partial x}\right) & \dfrac{1}{2}\left(\dfrac{\partial u}{\partial z}+\dfrac{\partial w}{\partial x}\right) \\[2ex] \dfrac{1}{2}\left(\dfrac{\partial u}{\partial y}+\dfrac{\partial v}{\partial x}\right) & \dfrac{\partial v}{\partial y} & \dfrac{1}{2}\left(\dfrac{\partial v}{\partial z}+\dfrac{\partial w}{\partial y}\right) \\[2ex] \dfrac{1}{2}\left(\dfrac{\partial u}{\partial z}+\dfrac{\partial w}{\partial x}\right) & \dfrac{1}{2}\left(\dfrac{\partial v}{\partial z}+\dfrac{\partial w}{\partial y}\right) & \dfrac{\partial w}{\partial z} \end{bmatrix} \qquad (9\text{-}5)$$

The terms on the diagonal of ε_{ij} are the normal components of strain. The off-diagonal terms are the shear strain. The local rigid-body rotation is given by

$$\omega_{ij} = \begin{bmatrix} 0 & \dfrac{1}{2}\left(\dfrac{\partial u}{\partial y}-\dfrac{\partial v}{\partial x}\right) & \dfrac{1}{2}\left(\dfrac{\partial u}{\partial z}-\dfrac{\partial w}{\partial x}\right) \\[2ex] \dfrac{1}{2}\left(\dfrac{\partial v}{\partial x}-\dfrac{\partial u}{\partial y}\right) & 0 & \dfrac{1}{2}\left(\dfrac{\partial v}{\partial z}-\dfrac{\partial w}{\partial y}\right) \\[2ex] \dfrac{1}{2}\left(\dfrac{\partial w}{\partial x}-\dfrac{\partial u}{\partial z}\right) & \dfrac{1}{2}\left(\dfrac{\partial w}{\partial y}-\dfrac{\partial v}{\partial z}\right) & 0 \end{bmatrix} \qquad (9\text{-}6)$$

Equation 9-6 can also be represented using tensor notation as

$$\omega_{ij} = -\frac{1}{2}\varepsilon_{ijk}\vec{\omega} \qquad (9\text{-}7)$$

where $\vec{\omega}$ is the vorticity vector referred to in the previous section. The vorticity, or local rigid body rotation is then

$$\vec{\omega} = \begin{bmatrix} \dfrac{\partial w}{\partial y}-\dfrac{\partial v}{\partial z} \\[2ex] \dfrac{\partial u}{\partial z}-\dfrac{\partial w}{\partial x} \\[2ex] \dfrac{\partial v}{\partial x}-\dfrac{\partial u}{\partial y} \end{bmatrix} \qquad (9\text{-}8)$$

For the reader unfamiliar with tensor notation, this presentation is certainly less than

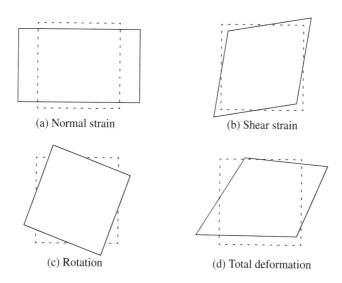

(a) Normal strain   (b) Shear strain

(c) Rotation   (d) Total deformation

Figure 9–11 Components of local deformation due to vector field. Dotted line shows initially undeformed object.

complete. However, the matrices in **Equation 9-5** and **Equation 9-6** directly translate into visual form, which will help clarify the concepts presented here. Referring to **Figure 9–11**, the normal strain, shear strain, and rigid body motion create distinct deformation modes. These modes combine to produce the total deformation. Modes of normal strain cause compression or extension in the direction perpendicular to a surface, while shear strains cause angular distortions. These strains combined with rigid body rotation around an axis yield the total strain at a point.

The essence of the stream polygon technique is to show these modes of deformation. A regular n-sided polygon (**Figure 9–12**) is placed into a vector field at a specified point and then deformed according to the local strain. The components of strain may be shown separately or in combination. The orientation of the normal of the polygon is arbitrary. However, it is convenient to align the normal with the local vector. Then the rigid body rotation about the vector is the streamwise vorticity, and the effects of normal and shear strain are in the plane perpendicular to a streamline passing through the point.

The stream polygon offers other interesting possibilities. The stream polygon may be swept along a trajectory, typically a streamline, to generate tubes. The radius of the tube r can be modified according to some scalar function. One application is to visualize fluid flow. In incompressible flow with no shear, the radius of the tube can vary according to the scalar function vector magnitude. Then the equation

$$r(\vec{v}) = r_{max}\sqrt{\frac{|\vec{v}_{min}|}{|\vec{v}|}} \tag{9-9}$$

represents an area of constant mass flow. As a result, the tube will thicken as the flow slows and narrow as the velocity increases. Each of the n sides of the tube can be colored with a dif-

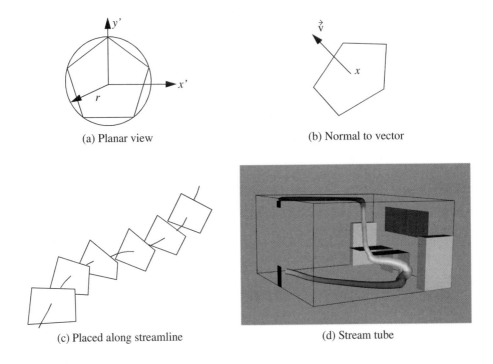

(a) Planar view

(b) Normal to vector

(c) Placed along streamline

(d) Stream tube

Figure 9–12 The stream polygon. (a) Planar view. (b) Aligned with vector. (c) Aligned along streamline. (d) Sweeping polygon to form tube (`officeTube.tcl`).

ferent scalar function, although for visual clarity, at most, one or two functions should be used.

The streamtubes generated by the streampolygon and the streamtubes we described in the previous section are not the same. The streampolygon does not necessarily lie along a streamline. If it does, the streampolygon represents information at a point, while the streamtube is an approximation constructed from multiple streamlines. Also, the radial variation in the tubes constructed from streampolygon sweeps do not necessarily relate to mass flow since the radius in a streampolygon can be tied to an arbitrary scalar variable.

Vector Field Topology

Vector fields have a complex structure characterized by special features called *critical points* [Globus91] [Helman91]. Critical points are locations in the vector field where the local vector magnitude goes to zero and the vector direction becomes undefined. At these points the vector field either converges or diverges, and/or local circulation around the point occurs.

Critical points lie in dataset cells where the u, v, and w components of the vector field each pass through zero. These points are located using an iterative search procedure such as the bi-section technique. Each iteration evaluates the cell interpolation function until the zero vector is found. Once a critical point is found, its local behavior is determined from the matrix of partial derivatives. This is because at the critical point the velocity is zero, and the vector field can be approximated by a first-order expansion of partial derivatives [Helman91]

$$u \approx \frac{\partial u}{\partial x}dx + \frac{\partial u}{\partial y}dy + \frac{\partial u}{\partial z}dz$$

$$v \approx \frac{\partial v}{\partial x}dx + \frac{\partial v}{\partial y}dy + \frac{\partial v}{\partial z}dz \qquad \text{(9-10)}$$

$$w \approx \frac{\partial w}{\partial x}dx + \frac{\partial w}{\partial y}dy + \frac{\partial w}{\partial z}dz$$

The matrix of partial derivatives J can be written in vector notation as

$$\vec{u} = J d\vec{x} \quad \text{with} \quad J = \begin{bmatrix} \dfrac{\partial u}{\partial x} & \dfrac{\partial u}{\partial y} & \dfrac{\partial u}{\partial z} \\[2mm] \dfrac{\partial v}{\partial x} & \dfrac{\partial v}{\partial y} & \dfrac{\partial v}{\partial z} \\[2mm] \dfrac{\partial w}{\partial x} & \dfrac{\partial w}{\partial y} & \dfrac{\partial w}{\partial z} \end{bmatrix} \qquad \text{(9-11)}$$

and is referred to as the Jacobian. The behavior of the vector field in the vicinity of a critical point is characterized by the eigenvalues of J. The eigenvalues consist of an imaginary and real component. The imaginary component describes the rotation of the vector field around the critical point, while the real part describes the relative attraction or repulsion of the vector field to the critical point. In two dimensions the critical points are as shown in **Figure 9–13**.

A number of visualization techniques have been developed to construct vector field topology from an analysis of critical points. These techniques provide a global understanding of the field, including points of *attachment* and *detachment* and field *vortices*. Using a fluid flow analogy, points of attachment and detachment occur on the surface of an object where the tangential component of the vector field goes to zero, and the flow is perpendicular to the surface. Thus, streamlines will begin or end at these points. There is no common definition for a vortex, but generally speaking, vortices are regions of relatively concentrated vorticity (e.g., flow rotation). The study of vortices is important because they represent areas of energy loss, or can have significant impact on downstream flow conditions (e.g., trailing vortices behind large aircraft).

One useful visualization technique creates vector field skeletons that divide the vector field into separate regions. Within each region, the vector field is topologically equivalent to uniform flow. These skeletons are created by locating critical points, and then connecting the critical points with streamlines. In 3D vector field analysis this technique can be applied to the surface of objects to locate lines of flow separation and attachment and other important flow features. Also, in general 3D flow, the regions of uniform flow are separated by surfaces, and creation of 3D flow skeletons is a current research topic.

Vortex visualization is another area of current research. One technique computes the *helicity-density*

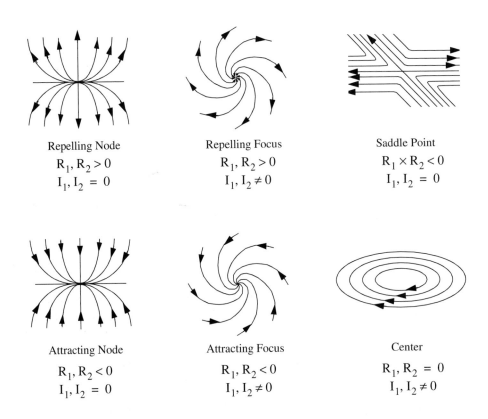

Figure 9–13 Critical points in two dimensions. The real part of the eigenvalues (R_1, R_2) of the matrix of first derivatives control the attraction or repulsion of the vector field. The imaginary part of the eigenvalues (I_1, I_2) controls the rotation.

$$H_d = \vec{v} \cdot \vec{w} = |\vec{v}||\vec{w}| \cos\varphi \qquad \text{(9-12)}$$

This is a scalar function of the vector dot product between the vorticity and the local vector. Large positive values of H_d result in right-handed vortices, while large negative values indicate left-handed vortices. Helicity-density can be conveniently shown using isosurfaces, which gives an indication for the location and structure of a vortex.

9.3 Tensor Algorithms

In Chapter 6 we saw that 3×3 real symmetric tensors can be characterized by the eigenvalues and eigenvectors of the tensor. Recall that we can express the eigenvectors of the system as

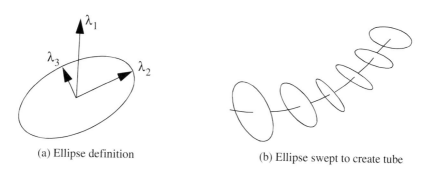

(a) Ellipse definition   (b) Ellipse swept to create tube

Figure 9–14 Creation of hyperstreamlines. An ellipse is swept along a streamline of the eigenfield. Major/minor axes of the ellipse are controlled by the other two eigenvectors.

$$\vec{v}_i = \lambda_i e_i, \text{ with } i = 1, 2, 3 \tag{9-13}$$

where e_i is a unit vector in the direction of the eigenvalue, and λ_i are the eigenvalues. Thus, we can decompose a 3×3 real symmetric tensor field into three vector fields, each field defined by one of the three eigenvectors described in **Equation 9-13**. We call these vector fields *eigenfields*, since they are derived from the eigenvectors of the tensor field.

Decomposition of the tensor field in this fashion provides additional insight into visualizing 3×3 real symmetric tensors. We can directly use the vector field visualization techniques presented previously or use variations of them. One such technique is a novel extension of the streampolygon technique, the method of *hyperstreamlines*.

Hyperstreamlines

Hyperstreamlines are constructed by creating a streamline through one of the three eigenfields, and then sweeping a geometric primitive along the streamline [Delmarcelle93]. Typically, an ellipse is used as the geometric primitive, where the remaining two eigenvectors define the major and minor axes of the ellipse (**Figure 9–14**). Sweeping the ellipse along the eigenfield streamline results in a tubular shape. Another useful generating geometric primitive is a cross. The length and orientation of the arms of the cross are controlled by two of the eigenvectors. Sweeping the cross results in a helical shape since the eigenvectors (and therefore cross arms) will rotate in some tensor fields.

Figure 9–15 shows an example of hyperstreamlines. The data is from a point load applied to a semi-infinite domain. Compare this figure to **Figure 6–22** that used tensor ellipsoids to visualize the same data. Notice that there is less clutter and more information available from the hyperstreamline visualization.

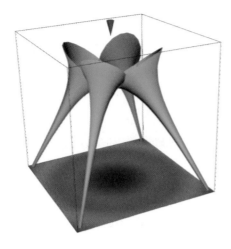

Figure 9–15 Example of hyperstreamlines (Hyper.tcl). The four hyperstreamlines shown are integrated along the minor principle stress axis. A plane (colored with a different lookup table) is also shown.

9.4 Modelling Algorithms

Visualizing Geometry

One of the most common applications of visualization is to view geometry. We may have a geometric representation of a part or complex assembly (perhaps designed on a CAD system) and want to view the part or assembly before it is manufactured. While viewing geometry is better addressed in a text on computer graphics, often there is dataset structure we wish to view in the same way. For example, we may want to see data mapped on a particular portion of the dataset, or view the structure of the dataset itself (e.g., view a finite element mesh).

Three-dimensional datasets have a surface and interior. Typically we want to visualize the surface of the dataset or perhaps a portion of the interior. (Note: volume rendering is a different matter — see "Volume Rendering" on page 206.) To visualize the dataset we must extract a portion of the dataset topology/geometry (and associated data) as some form of surface primitives such as polygons. If the surface of the dataset is opaque, we may also wish to eliminate occluded interior detail.

We have already seen how structured datasets, such as image data or structured grids, have a natural *i-j-k* coordinate system that allow extraction of points, lines, and planes from the interior of the dataset (see "Structured Coordinate System" on page 257). For example, to extract the fifth *i*-plane from a structured grid of dimensions (i_m, j_m, k_m) , we specify the data extents using $(4, 4, 0, (j_m - 1), 0, (k_m - 1))$ (assuming zero-offset addressing).

More generally, we can extract boundary edges and faces from a dataset. A boundary edge is an 1D cell type (e.g., line or polyline), or the edge of a 2D cell used by only that single cell. Similarly, a boundary face is a 2D cell type (e.g., polygon, triangle strip) or the face of a 3D cell used by only that single cell (**Figure 9–16**). We can obtain this information using the topological operators of the previous chapter. Cells of dimensions two or less are extracted as is, while boundary edges and faces are determined by counting the number of cell neighbors

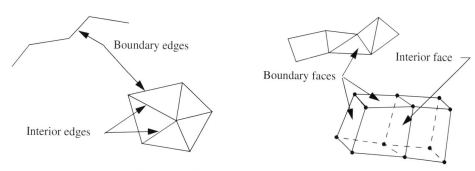

Figure 9–16 Boundary edges and faces.

for a particular topological boundary (i.e., edge or face neighbors). If there are no neighbors, the edge or face is a boundary edge or face, and is extracted.

Using these techniques we can view the structure of our dataset. However, there are also situations where we want more control in the selection of the data. We call this *data extraction*.

Data Extraction

Often we want to extract portions of data from a dataset. This may be because we want to reduce the size of the data, or because we are interested in visualizing only a portion of it.

Reducing dataset size is an important practical capability, because visualization data size can be huge. By reducing data size, reductions in computation and memory requirements can be realized. This results in better interactive response.

We also may need to reduce data size in order to visualize the important features of a large dataset. This can be used to reduce image clutter and improve the effectiveness of the visualization. Smaller data size also enables the visualization user to navigate through and inspect data more quickly relative to larger datasets. Next we describe two techniques to extract data. One is based on *geometry extraction*, and the other is based on *data thresholding*, or *thresholding*.

Geometry Extraction. Geometry extraction selects data based on geometric or topological characteristics. A common extraction technique selects a set of points and cells that lie within a specified range of ids. A typical example is selecting all cells having ids between 0–100, or all cells using point ids 250–500. Finite element analysts use this method frequently to isolate the visualization to just a few key regions.

Another useful technique called *spatial extraction*, selects dataset structure and associated data attributes lying within a specified region in space. For example, a point and radius can be used to select (or deselect) data within an enclosing sphere. Implicit functions are particularly useful tools for describing these regions. Points that evaluate negative are inside the region, while points outside the region evaluate positive; thus, cells whose points are all positive are outside the region, and cells whose points are all negative are inside the region.

Subsampling (**Figure 9–17**) is a method that reduces data size by selecting a subset of

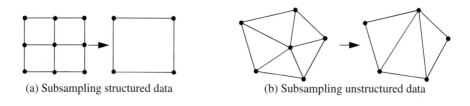

(a) Subsampling structured data   (b) Subsampling unstructured data

Figure 9–17 Subsampling data. (a) Structured data can be subsampled by choosing every nth point. (b) Subsampling unstructured data requires local retriangulation.

the original data. The subset is specified by choosing a parameter n, specifying that every nth data point is to be extracted. For example, in structured datasets such as image data and structured grids, selecting every nth point produces the results shown in **Figure 9–17**(a).

Subsampling modifies the topology of a dataset. When points or cells are not selected, this leaves a topological "hole." Dataset topology must be modified to fill the hole. In structured data, this is simply a uniform selection across the structured i-j-k coordinates. In unstructured data (**Figure 9–17**(b)), the hole must be filled in by using triangulation or other complex tessellation schemes. Subsampling is not typically performed on unstructured data because of its inherent complexity.

A related technique is *data masking*. In data masking we select every nth cell that at a minimum leaves one or more topological "holes" in the dataset. Masking also may change the topology of the dataset, since partial selections of cells from structured datasets can only be represented using unstructured grids. Masking is typically used to improve interactive performance or to quickly process portions of data.

Thresholding. Thresholding extracts portions of a dataset data based on attribute values. For example, we may select all cells having a point with scalar value between $(0,1)$ or all points having a velocity magnitude greater than 1.0.

Scalar thresholding is easily implemented. The threshold is either a single value that scalar values are greater than or less than, or a range of values. Cells or points whose associated scalar values satisfy the threshold criteria can be extracted. Other dataset attribute types such as vectors, normals, or tensors can be extracted in similar fashion by converting the type to a single scalar value. For example, vectors can be extracted using vector magnitude, and tensors using matrix determinate.

A problem with both geometry extraction and thresholding is that the approaches presented thus far extract "atomic" pieces of data, that is, a complete cell. Sometimes the cell may lie across the boundary of the threshold. In this case the cell must be clipped (see "Clipping With Scalar Fields" on page 305) and only a portion of the cell is extracted.

Probing

Probing obtains dataset attributes by sampling one dataset (the input) with a set of points (the probe) as shown in **Figure 9–18**(a). Probing is also called "resampling." Examples include probing an input dataset with a sequence of points along a line, on a plane, or in a volume.

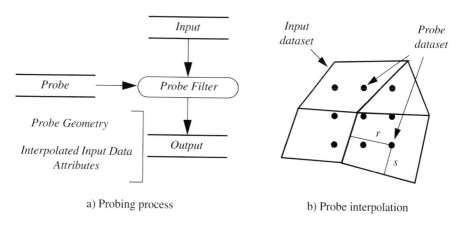

a) Probing process   b) Probe interpolation

Figure 9–18 Probing data. The geometry of one dataset (*Probe*) is used to extractact dataset attributes from another dataset (*Input*).

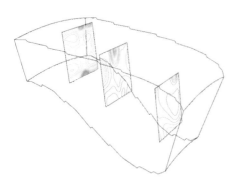

Figure 9–19 Probing data in a combustor. Probes are regular array of 50^2 points that are then passed through a contouring filter (`probeComb.tcl`).

The result of the probing is a new dataset (the output) with the topological and geometric structure of the probe dataset, and point attributes interpolated from the input dataset. Once the probing operation is completed, the output dataset can be visualized with any of the appropriate techniques described in this text.

Figure 9–18(b) illustrates the details of the probing process. For every point in the probe dataset, the location in the input dataset (i.e., cell, subcell, and parametric coordinates) and interpolation weights are determined. Then the data values from the cell are interpolated to the probe point. Probe points that are outside the input dataset are assigned a nil (or appropriate) value. This process repeats for all points in the probe dataset.

Probing can be used to reduce data or to view data in a particular fashion.

• Data is reduced when the probe operation is limited to a subregion of the input dataset, or the number of probe points is less than the number of input points.

• Data can be viewed in a particular fashion by sampling on specially selected datasets. Using a probe dataset consisting of a line enables *x-y* plotting along a line, or using a plane allows surface color mapping or line contouring.

Probing must be used carefully or errors may be introduced. Under-sampling data in a region can miss important high-frequency information or localized data variations. Oversampling data, while not creating error, can give false confidence in the accuracy of the data. Thus the sampling frequency should have a similar density as the input dataset, or if higher density, the visualization should be carefully annotated as to the original data frequency.

One important application of probing converts irregular or unstructured data to structured form using a volume of appropriate resolution as a probe to sample the unstructured data. This is useful if we use volume rendering or other volume visualization techniques to view our data.

Figure 9–19 shows an example of three probes. The probes sample flow density in a structured grid. The output of the probes is passed through a contour filter to generate contour lines. As this figure illustrates, we can be selective with the location and extent of the probe, allowing us to focus on important regions in the data.

Triangle Strip Generation

Triangle strips are compact representations of triangle polygons as described in "Triangle Strip" on page 117. Many rendering libraries include triangle strips as graphics primitives because they are a high-performance alternative to general polygon rendering.

Visualization and graphics data is often represented with triangles. Marching cubes, for example, generates thousands and potentially millions of triangles to represent an isosurface. To achieve greater performance in our visualizations, we can convert triangle polygons into triangle strips. Or, if data is represented using polygons, we can first triangulate the polygons and then create triangle strips.

A simple method to generate triangle strips uses greedy gathering of triangles into a strip (**Figure 9–20**). The method proceeds as follows. An "unmarked" triangle is found to initialize the strip — unmarked triangles are triangles that have not yet been gathered into a triangle strip. Starting with the initial triangle, the strip may grow in one of three directions, corresponding to the three edges of the triangle. We choose to grow the strip in the direction of the first unmarked neighbor triangle we encounter. If there are no unmarked neighbors the triangle strip is complete; otherwise, the strip is extended by adding triangles to the list that satisfy triangle strip topology. The strip is grown until no unmarked neighbor can be found. Additional strips are then created using the same procedure until every triangle is marked.

The length of the triangle strips varies greatly depending on the structure of the triangle mesh. **Figure 9–21**(a) shows triangle strips each of 390 triangles in length from a dataset that was originally structured. Such a case is an exception: unstructured triangle meshes typically average about 5–6 triangles per strip (**Figure 9–21**(b)). Even so, the memory savings are impressive. A triangle strip of length 6 requires 8 points to represent, while 8 triangles require 24 points, for a memory savings of 66.7 percent. Rendering speed may be greatly affected, too, depending upon the capabilities of the rendering system.

Connectivity

Intercell connectivity is a topological property of datasets. Cells are topologically connected when they share boundary features such as points, edges, or faces (**Figure 9–22**). Connectivity is useful in a number of modeling applications, particularly when we want to separate out "parts" of a dataset.

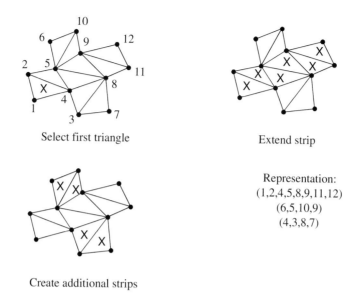

Select first triangle   Extend strip

Create additional strips

Representation:
(1,2,4,5,8,9,11,12)
(6,5,10,9)
(4,3,8,7)

Figure 9–20 Creating triangle strips.

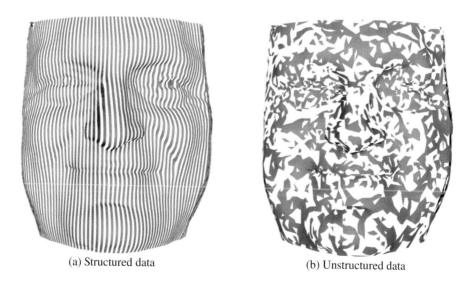

(a) Structured data   (b) Unstructured data

Figure 9–21 Triangle strip examples. (a) Structured triangle mesh consisting of 134 strips each of 390 triangles (`stripF.tcl`). (b) Unstructured triangle mesh consisting of 2227 strips of average length 3.94, longest strip 101 triangles. Images are generated by displaying every other triangle strip (`uStripeF.tcl`).

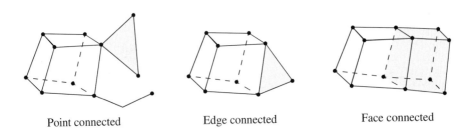

Point connected   Edge connected   Face connected

Figure 9–22 Connected cells.

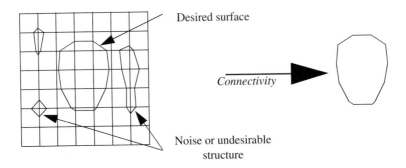

Desired surface

Connectivity

Noise or undesirable
structure

Figure 9–23 Extracting portion of isosurface of interest using connectivity.

One application of connectivity extracts a meaningful portion of an isosurface. If the isosurface is generated from measured data such as an MRI or CT scan, it likely contains "noise" or unimportant anatomical structure. Using connectivity algorithms, we can separate out the part of the isosurface that we desire, either by eliminating noise or undesirable anatomical structure. **Figure 9–23** is an example where a 2D surface of interest (e.g., an isocontour) is extracted from a noisy signal.

Connectivity algorithms can be implemented using a recursive visit method. We begin by choosing an arbitrary cell and mark it "visited". Then, depending upon the type of connectivity desired (i.e., point, edge, face), we gather the appropriate neighbors and mark them visited. This process repeats recursively until all connected cells are visited. We generally refer to such a set of connected cells as a connected "surface" even though the cells may be of a topological dimension other than two.

To identify additional connected surfaces we locate another unvisited cell and repeat the processes described previously. We continue to identify connected surfaces until every cell in the dataset is visited. As each connected surface is identified, it is assigned a surface number. We can use this number to specify the surfaces to extract or we can specify "seed" points or cells and extract the surfaces connected to them.

In some cases the recursion depth of the connectivity algorithm becomes larger than the computer system can manage. In this case, we can specify a maximum recursion depth. When this depth is exceeded, recursion is terminated and the current cells in the recursion are used as seeds to restart the recursion.

Polygon Normal Generation

Gouraud and Phong shading (see Chapter 3) can improve the appearance of rendered polygons. Both techniques require point normals. Unfortunately polygonal meshes do not always contain point normals, or data file formats may not support point normals. Examples include the marching cubes algorithm for general datasets (which typically will not generate surface normals) and the stereo lithography file format (does not support point normals). **Figure 9–24**(a) shows a model defined from stereo-lithography format. The faceting of the model is clearly evident.

To address this situation we can compute surface normals from the polygonal mesh. A simple approach follows. First, polygon normals are computed around a common point. These normals are then averaged at the point, and the normal is renormalized (i.e., $|n| = 1$) and associated with the point. This approach works well under two conditions.

1. The orientation of all polygons surrounding the point are consistent as shown in **Figure 9–24**(b). A polygon is oriented consistently if the order of defining polygon points is consistent with its edge neighbors. That is, if polygon p is defined by points *(1,2,3)*, then the polygon edge neighbor p_{23} must use the edge *(2,3)* in the direction *(3,2)*. If not consistent, then the average point normal may be zero or not accurately represent the orientation of the surface. This is because the polygon normal is computed from a cross product of the edges formed by its defining points.

2. The angular difference in surface normals between adjacent polygons is small. Otherwise, sharp corners or edges will have a washed out appearance when rendered, resulting in an unsatisfactory image (**Figure 9–24**(c)).

To avoid these problems we adopt a more complex polygon normal generation algorithm. This approach includes steps to insure that polygons are oriented consistently, and an edge-splitting scheme that duplicates points across sharp edges.

To orient edges consistently we use a recursive neighbor traversal. An initial polygon is selected and marked "consistent." For each edge neighbor of the initial polygon, the ordering of the neighbor polygon points is checked — if not consistent, the ordering is reversed. The neighbor polygon is then marked "consistent." This process repeats recursively for each edge neighbor until all neighbors are marked "consistent". In some cases there may be more than one connected surface, so that the process may have to be repeated until all polygons are visited.

A similar traversal method splits sharp edges. A sharp edge is an edge shared by two polygons whose normals vary by a user-specified *feature angle*. The feature angle between two polygons is the angle between their normals (**Figure 9–25**(a)). When sharp edges are encountered during the recursive traversal, the points along the edge are duplicated, effectively disconnecting the mesh along that edge (**Figure 9–25**(b)). Then, when shared polygon normals are computed later in the process, contributions to the average normal across sharp edges is prevented.

On some computers limitations on recursion depth may become a problem. Polygonal surfaces can consist of millions of polygons, resulting in large recursion depth. As a result, the depth of recursion can be specified by the user. If recursion depth exceeds the specified

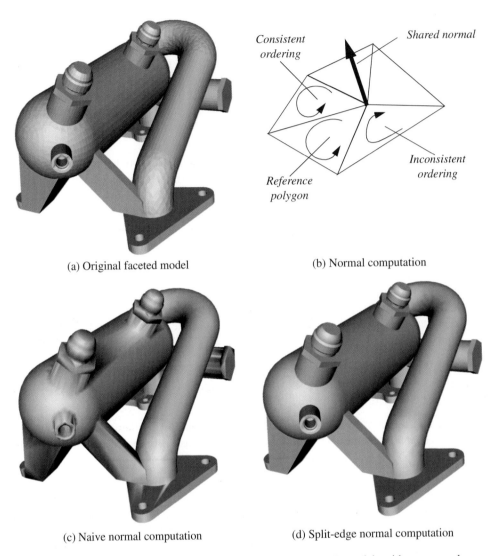

(a) Original faceted model   (b) Normal computation

(c) Naive normal computation   (d) Split-edge normal computation

Figure 9–24   Surface normal generation. (a) Faceted model without normals. (b) Polygons must be consistently oriented to accurately compute normals. (c) Sharp edges are poorly represented using shared normals as shown on the corners of this model. (d) Normal generation with sharp edges split (`Normals.cxx`).

value, the recursion halts and the polygons on the boundary of the recursion become seeds to begin the process again.

Figure 9–24(d) shows the result of the advanced normal generation technique with a feature angle of 60 degrees. Sharp edges are well defined and curved areas lack the faceting evident in the original model. The figure is shown with Gouraud shading.

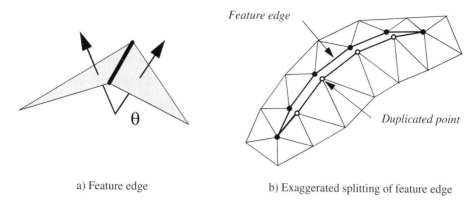

a) Feature edge

b) Exaggerated splitting of feature edge

Figure 9–25 Computing feature angles (a) and splitting edges (b).

Decimation

Various data compression techniques have been developed in response to large data size. The UNIX utilities `compress/uncompress` and the PC utility `zip` compress data files. The MPEG compression algorithm compresses video sequences. These techniques may be loss-less, meaning that no data is lost between the compression/decompression steps, or lossy, meaning that data is lost during compression. The utilities `compress/uncompress` and `zip` are loss-less, while MPEG is lossy.

In graphics, data compression techniques have been developed as well. The subsampling methods we saw earlier in this chapter are an example of simple data compression techniques for visualization data. Another emerging area of graphics data compression is polygon reduction techniques.

Polygon reduction techniques reduce the number of polygons required to model an object. The size of models, in terms of polygon count, has grown tremendously over the last few years. This is because many models are created using digital measuring devices such as laser scanners or satellites. These devices can generate data at tremendous rates. For example, a laser digitizer can generate on the order of 500,000 triangles in a 15-second scan. Visualization algorithms such as marching cubes also generate large numbers of polygons: one to three million triangles from a 512^3 volume is typical.

One polygon reduction technique is the decimation algorithm [Schroeder92a]. The goal of the decimation algorithm is to reduce the total number of triangles in a triangle mesh, preserving the original topology and forming a good approximation to the original geometry. A triangle mesh is a special form of a polygonal mesh, where each polygon is a triangle. If need be, a polygon mesh can be converted to a triangle mesh using standard polygon triangulation methods.

Decimation is related to the subsampling technique for unstructured meshes described in **Figure 9–17**(b). The differences are that

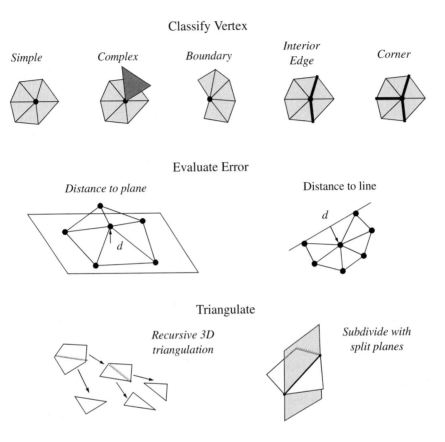

Figure 9–26 Overview of decimation algorithm.

- decimation treats only triangle meshes not arbitrary unstructured grids;

- the choice of which points to delete is a function of a *decimation criterion*, a measure of the local error introduced by deleting a point; and

- the triangulation of the hole created by deleting the point is carried out in a way as to preserve edges or other important features.

Decimation proceeds by iteratively visiting each point in a triangle mesh. For each point, three basic steps are carried out (**Figure 9–26**). The first step classifies the local geometry and topology in the neighborhood of the point. The classification yields one of the five categories shown in the figure: simple, boundary, complex, edge, and corner point. Based on this classification, the second step uses a local error measure (i.e., the decimation criterion) to determine whether the point can be deleted. If the criterion is satisfied, the third step deletes the point (along with associated triangles), and triangulates the resulting hole. A more detailed description of each of these steps and example applications follow.

Point Classification. The first step of the decimation algorithm characterizes the local geometry and topology for a given point. The outcome of classification determines whether the vertex is a potential candidate for deletion, and if it is, which criteria to use.

Each point may be assigned one of five possible classifications: simple, complex, boundary, interior edge, or corner vertex. Examples of each type are shown in **Figure 9–26**.

A *simple point* is surrounded by a complete cycle of triangles, and each edge that uses the point is used by exactly two triangles. If the edge is not used by two triangles, or if the point is used by a triangle not in the cycle of triangles, then the point is *complex*. These are nonmanifold cases.

A point that is on the boundary of a mesh, that is, within a semicycle of triangles, is a *boundary point*.

A simple point can be further classified as an *interior edge* or *corner point*. These classifications are based on the local mesh geometry. If the surface normal angle between two adjacent triangles is greater than a specified *feature angle*, then a *feature edge* exists (see **Figure 9–25**(a)). When a point is used by two feature edges, the point is an interior edge point. If one, three, or more feature edges use the point, the point is a *corner point*.

Complex and corner vertices are not deleted from the triangle mesh; all other vertices become candidates for deletion.

Decimation Criterion. Once we have a candidate point for deletion, we estimate the error that would result by deleting the point and then replacing it (and its associated triangles) with another triangulation. There are a number of possible error measures; but the simplest are based on distance measures of local planarity or local colinearity (**Figure 9–26**).

In the local region surrounding a simple point, the mesh is considered nearly "flat," since there are by definition no feature edges. Hence, simple points use an error measure based on distance to plane. The plane passing through the local region can be computed either using a least-squares plane or by computing an area-averaged plane.

Points classified as boundary or interior edge are considered to lay on an edge, and use a distance to edge error measure. That is, we compute the distance that the candidate point is from the new edge formed during the triangulation process.

A point satisfies the decimation criterion d if its distance measure is less than d. The point can then be deleted. All triangles using the point are deleted as well, leaving a "hole" in the mesh. This hole is patched using a local triangulation process.

Triangulation. After deleting a point, the resulting hole must be retriangulated. Although the hole, defined by a loop of edges, is topologically two dimensional, it is generally non-planar, and therefore general purpose 2D triangulation techniques cannot be used. Instead, we use a special recursive 3D divide-and-conquer technique to triangulate the loop.

Triangulation proceeds as follows. An initial split plane is chosen to divide the loop in half and create two subloops. If all the points in each subloop lie on opposite sides of the plane, then the split is a valid one. In addition, an *aspect ratio* check insures that the loop is not too long and skinny, thereby resulting in needle-like triangles. The aspect ratio is the ratio between the length of the split line to the minimum distance of a point in the subloop to the split plane. If the candidate split plane is not valid or does not satisfy the aspect ratio criterion, then another candidate split plane is evaluated. Once a split plane is found, then the subdivision of each subloop continues recursively until a subloop consists of three edges. In this case, the subloop generates a triangle and halts the recursion.

Occasionally, triangulation fails because no split plane can be found. In this case, the candidate point is not deleted and the mesh is left in its original state. This poses no problem to the algorithm and decimation continues by visiting the next point in the dataset.

Results. Typical compression rates for the decimation algorithm range from 2:1 to 100:1, with 10:1 a nominal figure for "large" (i.e., 10^5 triangles) datasets. The results vary greatly depending upon the type of data. CAD models typically reduce the least because these models have many sharp edges and other detailed features, and the CAD modellers usually produce minimal triangulations. Terrain data, especially if relatively flat regions are present, may reduce at rates of 100:1.

Figure 9–27 shows two applications of decimation to laser digitized data and to a terrain model of Honolulu, Hawaii. In both cases the reduction was on the order of 90 percent for a 10:1 compression ratio. Wireframe images are shown to accentuate the density of the polygonal meshes. The left-hand image in each pair is the original data; the right-hand image is the decimated mesh. Notice the gradations in the decimated mesh around features of high curvature. The advantage of decimation, as compared to subsampling techniques, is that the mesh is adaptively modified to retain more details in areas of high curvature.

Advanced Techniques. Polygon reduction is an active field of research. Many powerful algorithms beyond the decimation algorithm have been presented (see "Bibliographic Notes" on page 362). Although we cannot cover the field in its entirety in this section, there are two notable trends worth addressing. First, progressive schemes [Hoppe96] allow incremental transmission and reconstruction of triangle meshes — this is especially important for Web-based geometry visualization. Second, recent algorithms modify the topology of the mesh [He96] [Popovic97] [Schroeder97]. This feature is essential towards obtaining arbitrary levels of mesh reduction.

A *progressive mesh* is a series of triangle meshes M^i related by the operations

$$(\hat{M} = M^n) \rightarrow M^{n-1} \rightarrow \ldots \rightarrow M^1 \rightarrow M^0 \tag{9-14}$$

where M and M^n represent the mesh at full resolution, and M^0 is a simplified base mesh. The critical characteristic of progressive meshes is that is possible to choose the mesh operations in such a way to make them invertible. Then the operations can be applied in reverse order (starting with the base mesh M^0)

$$M^0 \rightarrow M^1 \rightarrow \ldots \rightarrow M^{n-1} \rightarrow M^n \tag{9-15}$$

to obtain a mesh of desired reduction level (assuming that the reduction level is *less than* the base mesh M^0).

One such invertible operator is an edge collapse and its inverse is the edge split shown in **Figure 9–28**(a). Each collapse of an interior mesh edge results in the elimination of two triangles (or one triangle if the collapsed vertex is on a boundary). The operation is represented by five values

$$\text{Edge Collapse/Split} (v_s, v_t, v_l, v_r, A) \tag{9-16}$$

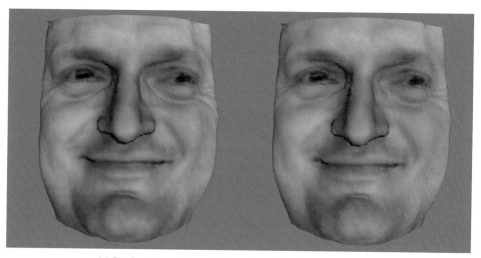

(a) Decimation of laser digitizer data (`deciFran.tcl`).

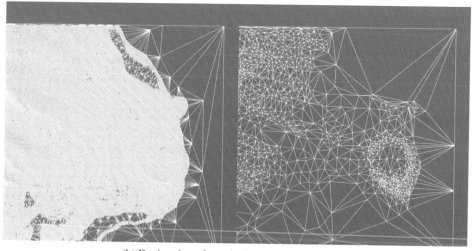

(b) Decimation of terrain data (`deciHawa.tcl`).

Figure 9–27 Examples of decimation algorithm. Triangle meshes are shown in wireframe.

where v_s is the vertex to collapse/split, v_t is the vertex being collapsed to / split from, and v_l and v_r are two additional vertices to the left and right of the split edge. These two vertices in conjunction with v_s and v_t define the two triangles deleted or added. A represents vertex attribute information, which at a minimum contains the coordinates x of the collapsed / split vertex v_s. (Note: in the context of the decimation algorithm, the edge collapse operator replaces the recursive triangulation process.)

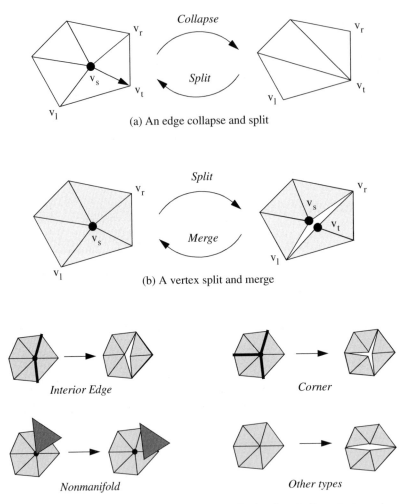

(a) An edge collapse and split

(b) A vertex split and merge

Interior Edge

Corner

Nonmanifold

Other types

(c) Vertex splits applied to various mesh features.Darker lines indicate feature edges.

Figure 9–28 Progressive mesh operators edge collapse/split and vertex split/merge.

While progressive meshes allow us to compactly store and transmit triangle meshes, the problem remains that the size of the base mesh is often larger than desired reduction level. Since in some applications we wish to realize *any* given level, we want the base mesh to contain no triangles

$$(\hat{M} = M^n) \rightarrow M^{n-1} \rightarrow \ldots \rightarrow M^1 \rightarrow (M^0 = M(V, \varnothing)) \qquad \textbf{(9-17)}$$

(some vertices are necessary to initiate the edge split operations). To address this problem, the invertible edge collapse/split operator — which is topology preserving — is extended with a vertex split/merge operator. The vertex split/merge operator modifies the topology of the mesh and allows arbitrary levels of reduction.

A mesh split occurs when we replace vertex v_s with vertex v_t in the connectivity list of one or more triangles that originally used vertex v_s (**Figure 9–28**(b)). The new vertex v_t is given exactly the same coordinate value as v_s. Splits introduce a "crack" or "hole" into the mesh. We prefer not to split the mesh, but at high decimation rates this relieves topological constraint and enables further decimation. Splitting is only invoked when a valid edge collapse is not available, or when a vertex cannot be triangulated (e.g., a nonmanifold vertex). Once the split operation occurs, the vertices v_s and v_t are re-inserted into the priority queue.

Different splitting strategies are used depending on the classification of the vertex (**Figure 9–28**(c)). Interior edge vertices are split along the feature edges, as are corner vertices. Nonmanifold vertices are split into separate manifold pieces. In any other type of vertex splitting occurs by arbitrarily separating the loop into two pieces. For example, if a simple vertex cannot be deleted because a valid edge collapse is not available, the loop of triangles will be arbitrarily divided in half (possibly in a recursive process).

Like the edge collapse/split, the vertex split/merge can also be represented as a compact operation. A vertex split/merge operation can be represented with four values

$$\text{Vertex Split/Merge } (v_s, v_t, v_l, v_r) \tag{9-18}$$

The vertices v_l and v_r define a sweep of triangles (from v_r to v_l) that are to be separated from the original vertex v_s (we adopt a counter-clockwise ordering convention to uniquely define the sweep of triangles).

Figure 9–29 shows the results of applying the topology modifying progressive mesh algorithm to two sets of data. In **Figure 9–29**(a-c), a thin plate with holes is decimated (the darker lines show split edges). The middle image in the sequence shows the limits of topology on the algorithm. It is only when the topology of the mesh is allowed to be modified that the final level of reduction is possible. **Figure 9–29**(d-f) shows the same algorithm applied to CAD data.

Mesh Smoothing

Mesh smoothing is a technique that adjusts the point coordinates of a dataset. The purpose of mesh smoothing is to improve the appearance of a mesh, and/or improve the shape of dataset cells. During smoothing the topology of the dataset is not modified, only the geometry. Applications of mesh smoothing include improving the appearance of isosurfaces, or as a modelling tool to remove surface noise. The appearance of models can be dramatically improved by applying mesh smoothing. **Figure 9–30** is an example of smoothing applied to analytic surface (a semicylinder) with a random surface distortion (smoothCyl.tcl).

A simple, yet effective technique is Laplacian smoothing. The Laplacian smoothing equation for a point p_i at position $\vec{x}_i$ is given by

$$\vec{x}_{i+1} = \vec{x}_i + \lambda \vec{V}_{ij} = \vec{x}_i + \lambda \sum (\vec{x}_j - \vec{x}_i) \quad \forall j:0 \leq j < n \tag{9-19}$$

where $\vec{x}_{i+1}$ is the new coordinate position, and $\vec{x}_j$ are the positions of points p_j "connected" to p_i, and λ is a user-specified weight. Geometrically this relation is depicted in

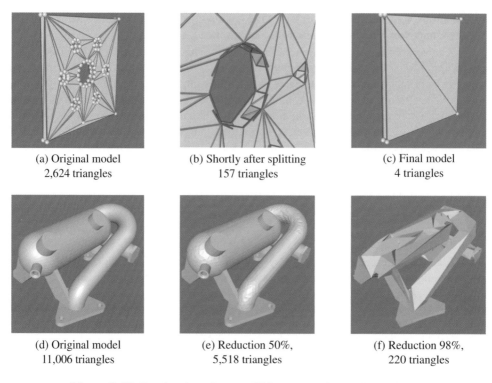

(a) Original model
2,624 triangles

(b) Shortly after splitting
157 triangles

(c) Final model
4 triangles

(d) Original model
11,006 triangles

(e) Reduction 50%,
5,518 triangles

(f) Reduction 98%,
220 triangles

Figure 9–29 Results of topology modifying progressive mesh algorithm.

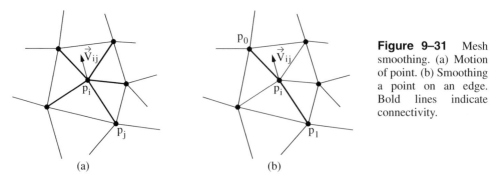

(a)

(b)

Figure 9–31 Mesh smoothing. (a) Motion of point. (b) Smoothing a point on an edge. Bold lines indicate connectivity.

Figure 9–31(a). Here the vertex p_i is connected to the surrounding points p_j via edges. The equation expresses that the new position $\vec{x}_{i+1}$ is offset from the original position $\vec{x}_i$ plus the average vector $\vec{V}_{ij}$ multiplied by λ. Typically, the factor λ is a small number (e.g., 0.01), and the process is executed repeatedly (e.g., 50-100 iterations). Notice that the overall effect of smoothing is to reduce the high frequency surface information. The algorithm will reduce surface curvature and tend to flatten the surface.

Besides adjusting the number of iterations and smoothing factor, smoothing can be controlled by modifying the connections between p_i and its surrounding points p_j. For example, if p_i lies along a fold or sharp edge in the mesh, we may want to only use the two

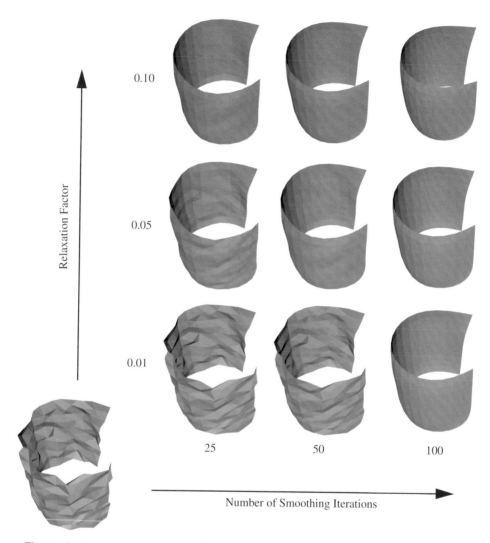

Figure 9–30 Mesh smoothing applied to a semicylinder. Lower left image is the original model. On the *x*-axis the number of smoothing iterations is modified. On the *y*-axis the relaxation factor is modified.

edge end points to compute the smoothing vector $\vec{V}_{ij}$, limiting the motion of p_i along the edge (**Figure 9–31**(b)). We can also anchor p_i to prevent any motion. Anchoring is useful for points that are located on "corners" or other special features such as nonmanifold attachments. One benefit of anchoring and controlling point connectivity is that we can limit the amount of shrinkage in the mesh. It also tends to produce better overall results. (In **Figure 9–30** the boundary points of the surface are constrained to move along the boundary, while the points at sharp corners are anchored.)

Although Laplacian smoothing works well in most cases, there are applications of Laplacian smoothing that can badly damage the mesh. Large numbers of smoothing iterations, or large smoothing factors, can cause excessive shrinkage and surface distortion. Some objects, like spheres or the cylinder shown in **Figure 9–30**, will lose volume with each iteration, and can even shrink to a point. In rare cases it is possible for the mesh to pull itself "inside-out." Situations like this occur when the average vector moves p_i across a mesh boundary, causing some of the attached triangles to overlap or intersect.

Mesh smoothing is particularly useful when creating models that do not require high accuracy. As we have seen, smoothing modifies point coordinates and, therefore, surface geometry. Use smoothing to improve the appearance of models, but characterize error carefully if you are going to measure from a smoothed surface. Alternatively, you may want to design your own smoothing algorithms that better fit the underlying data.

Swept Volumes and Surfaces

Consider moving an object (e.g., your hand) over some path (e.g., raise your hand). How can we visualize this motion? The obvious answer is to form a time-animation sequence as the hand is moved. But what if we wish to statically represent the motion as well as the space that is traversed by the hand? Then we can use *swept surfaces* and *swept volumes*.

A swept volume is the volume of space occupied by an object as it moves through space along an arbitrary trajectory. A swept surface is the surface of the swept volume. Together, swept volumes and swept surfaces can statically represent the motion of objects.

Past efforts at creating swept surfaces and volumes have focused on analytical techniques. The mathematical representation of various 3D geometric primitives (e.g., lines, polygons, splines) was extended to include a fourth dimension of time (the path). Unfortunately, these approaches have never been practically successful, partly due to mathematical complexity and partly due to problem degeneracies.

Degeneracies occur when an *n*-dimensional object moves in such a way that its representation becomes *(n-1)*-dimensional. For example, moving a plane in the direction of its normal, sweeps out a 3D "cubical" volume. Sweeping the plane in a direction perpendicular to its normal, however, results in a degenerate condition, since the plane sweeps out a 2D "rectangle."

Instead of creating swept surfaces analytically, numerical approximation techniques can be used [Schroeder94]. Implicit modeling provides the basis for an effective technique to visualize object motion via swept surfaces and volumes. The technique is immune to degeneracies and can treat any geometric representation for which a distance function can be computed, such as the VTK cell types.

The technique to generate swept surfaces and volumes using an implicit modeling approach proceeds as follows. The geometric model, or part, and a path describing the parts motion, or sweep trajectory ST, must be defined. Then we use the following steps as depicted in **Figure 9–32**.

1. Generate an implicit model from the part. This results in an implicit representation in the form of a volume. We call this the implicit model V_I.

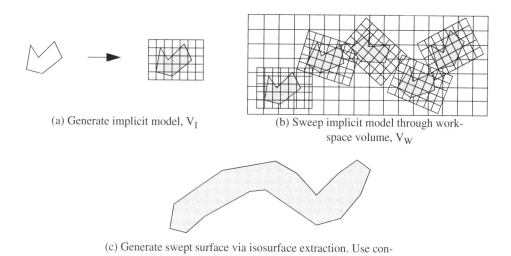

(a) Generate implicit model, V_I (b) Sweep implicit model through work-
                                                  space volume, V_W

(c) Generate swept surface via isosurface extraction. Use connectivity to extract single surface.

Figure 9–32 Overview of swept surface technique.

2. Construct another volume, the workspace volume V_W, that strictly bounds V_I as it
   moves along the path ST . Then sweep V_I through V_W by moving in small steps, Δx,
   along ST . At each step, s, sample V_I with the workspace volume V_W. We use a boolean union operation to perform the sampling.

3. Extract isosurface, or offset surface(s) from V_W using a contouring algorithm such as
   marching cubes.

4. Step 3 may create multiple connected surfaces. If a single surface is desired, use connectivity to extract the single "largest" surface (in terms of number of triangles). This
   surface is an approximation to the swept surface, and the volume it encloses is an
   approximation to the swept volume.

There are a few points that require additional explanation. This algorithm uses two volumes,
the implicit model and the workspace volume. Both are implicit models, but the workspace
volume is used to accumulate the part as it moves along the sweep trajectory. In theory, the
part could be sampled directly into the workspace volume to create the implicit model of the
swept surface. Performance issues dictate that the implicit model is sampled into the workspace volume. This is because it is much faster to sample the implicit model of the part rather
than the part itself, since computing the distance function from a part that may consist of tens
of thousands of cells is relatively time-consuming, compared to sampling the implicit model
V_I.

Sampling V_I is depicted in **Figure 9–33**. The sweep trajectory is defined by a series of
transformation matrices $ST = \{t_1, t_2, \ldots, t_m\}$. As the part moves along ST, interpolation
is used to compute an inbetween transformation matrix t. Sampling is achieved by inverse
transforming V_W into the local space of V_I using t. Then, similar to the probe operation

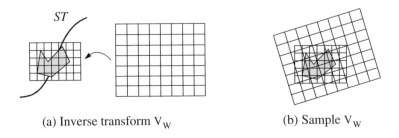

(a) Inverse transform V_W (b) Sample V_W

Figure 9–33 Generating workspace volume by sampling implicit volume.

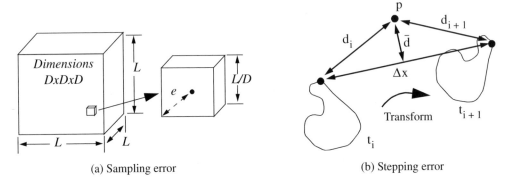

(a) Sampling error   (b) Stepping error

Figure 9–34 Computing sampling and stepping error.

described in "Probing" on page 318, the points of V_W are transformed by the inverse of the transformation matrix t^{-1}, and used to interpolate the distance values from the implicit model V_I.

Because we are dealing with an implicit modeling technique, parts with concave features can generate multiple surfaces. As discussed in "Connectivity" on page 320, the connectivity algorithm is used to separate out the swept surface. This final surface is an approximation to the actual swept surface, since we are sampling the actual geometric representation on an array of points (i.e., the implicit model), and then sampling the implicit model on another volume (i.e., the workspace volume). Also, stepping along the sweep trajectory generates errors proportional to the step size Δx.

These errors can be characterized as follows (**Figure 9–34**). Given a voxel size L/D, where L is the edge length of the volume, and D is the dimension of the volume (assumed uniform for convenience), the maximum sampling error is

$$e \leq \frac{\sqrt{3}}{2}\left(\frac{L}{D}\right)$$ **(9-20)**

The error due to stepping, which includes both translation and rotational components, is bounded by $\Delta x/2$, where Δx is the maximum displacement of any point on the implicit

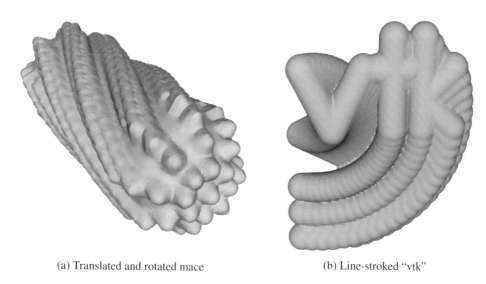

(a) Translated and rotated mace   (b) Line-stroked "vtk"

Figure 9–35 Swept surfaces. (a) Swept mace sampled at 25 locations (`sweptMac.cxx`).
(b) Swept vtk sampled at 21 locations (`sweptVtk.tcl`).

model at any given translational step. Combining these terms for sampling both volumes and the error due to stepping, the total error is

$$e_{tot} \le \frac{\sqrt{3}}{2}\left(\frac{L_I}{D_I} + \frac{L_W}{D_W}\right) + \frac{\Delta x}{2} \qquad (9\text{-}21)$$

where the subscripts I and W refer to the implicit model and workspace volume, respectively.

To show the application of this algorithm, we have generated swept surfaces for the letters "VTK" and the "mace" model as shown in **Figure 9–35**. We have purposely chosen a step size to exaggerate the stepping error. Using more steps would smooth out the surface "bumps" due to stepping. Also, the appearance of the surface varies greatly with the selected isosurface value. Larger values give rounder, smoother surfaces. If you use small values near zero (assuming positive distance function) the surface may break up. To correct this you need to use a higher resolution workspace or compute negative distances. Negative distances are computed during the implicit modeling step by negating all points *inside* the original geometry. Negative distances allow us to use a zero isosurface value or to generate internal offset surfaces. Negative distances can only be computed for closed (i.e., manifold) objects.

Visualizing Unstructured Points

Unstructured point datasets consist of points at irregular positions in 3D space. The relationship between points is arbitrary. Examples of unstructured point datasets are visualizing temperature distribution from an array of (arbitrarily) placed thermocouples, or rainfall level measured at scattered positions over a geographic region.

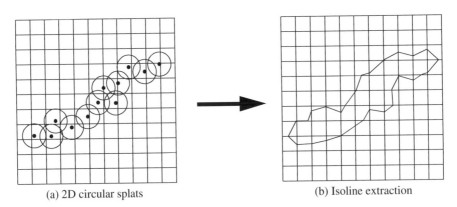

(a) 2D circular splats   (b) Isoline extraction

igure 9–36 Splatting techniques depicted in 2D. (a) Injecting points into the image dataset (circular plats). (b) Visualizing the image dataset via contouring. Any image-based visualization technique ould be used.

Unlike image data and structured grids, or even unstructured grids, unstructured point dataset have no topological component relating one point to another. For these reasons unstructured points are simple to represent but difficult to visualize. They are difficult to visualize because there is no inherent "structure" to which we can apply our library of visualization techniques. Beyond just displaying points (possibly colored with scalar value, or using oriented vector glyphs) none of the techniques discussed thus far can be used. Thus, to visualize unstructured points we have to build structure to which we can apply our visualization techniques.

There are several approaches available to build topological structure given a random set of points. One common approach samples unstructured points into an image dataset, and then visualizes the data using standard volume or surface-based rendering techniques. Another approach creates n-dimensional triangulations from the unstructured points, thereby creating topological structure. These and other common techniques are described in the following sections.

Splatting Techniques. Splatting techniques build topological structure by sampling unstructured points into a image dataset (**Figure 9–36**). The sampling is performed by creating special influence, or splatting, functions $SF(x,y,z)$ that distribute the data value of each unstructured point over the surrounding region. To sample the unstructured points, each point is inserted into a image dataset SP, and the data values are distributed through SP using the splatting functions $SF(x,y,z)$. Once the topological structure is built, any image-based visualization technique can be used (including volume rendering).

A common splatting function is a uniform Gaussian distribution centered at a point p_i. The function is conveniently cast into the form

$$SF(x, y, z) = se^{-f(r/R)^2} \tag{9-22}$$

where s is a scale factor that multiplies the exponential, f is the exponent scale factor $f \geq 0$, r is the distance between any point and the Gaussian center point (i.e., the splat point) $r = \|p - p_i\|$, and R is the radius of influence of the Gaussian, where $r \leq R$.

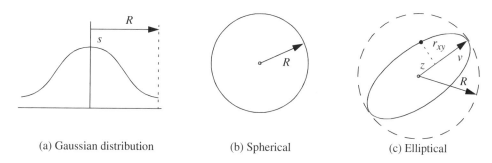

(a) Gaussian distribution   (b) Spherical   (c) Elliptical

Figure 9–37 Gaussian splatting functions. (a) one-dimensional, (b) 2D spherical, and (c) 2D elliptical.

The Gaussian function (**Figure 9–37**(a)) becomes a circle in cross section in two dimensions (**Figure 9–37**(b)) and a sphere in three dimensions. Since the value of the function is maximum when $r = 0$, the maximum value is given by the scale factor s. The parameter f controls the rate of decay of the splat. Scalar values can be used to set the value of s, so that relatively large scalar values create bigger splats than smaller values.

Splats may be accumulated using the standard implicit modeling boolean operations (**Equation 6-13**, **Equation 6-14**, and **Equation 6-15**). That is, we may choose to form a union, intersection, or difference of the splats. The union and intersection operators are used most frequently.

Another interesting variation modifies the shape of the splat according to a vector quantity such as surface normal or vector data. **Figure 9–37**(c) shows an example where the splat shape is elongated in the direction parallel to a vector. Thus, if we have a set of points and normals, we can create a polygonal surface by combining splatting with isosurface extraction.

To generate oriented splats, we modify **Equation 9-22** by introducing an eccentricity factor E and the vector $\vec{v}$.

$$SF(x, y, z) = se^{-f\left(\frac{\left(\frac{r_{xy}}{E}\right)^2 + z^2}{R^2}\right)} \tag{9-23}$$

where z and r_{xy} are computed from

$$z = \vec{v} \cdot (p - p_i), \text{ with } |\vec{v}| = 1$$

$$r_{xy} = r^2 - z^2 \tag{9-24}$$

The parameter z is the distance along the vector $\vec{v}$, and the parameter r_{xy} is the distance perpendicular to v to the point p. The eccentricity factor controls the shape of the splat. A value $E = 1$ results in spherical splats, whereas $E > 1$ yields flattened splats and $E < 1$ yields elongated splats in the direction of the vector v.

Figure 9–38(a) shows an elliptical splat with $E = 10$. (The splat surface is created by using isosurface extraction.) As expected, the splat is an ellipsoid. **Figure 9–38**(b) is an application of elliptical splatting used to reconstruct a surface from an unstructured set of points. The advantage of using an elliptical splat is that we can flatten the splat in the plane perpendicular to the point normal. This tends to bridge the space between the point samples. The surface itself is extracted using a standard isosurface extraction algorithm.

Interpolation Techniques. Interpolation techniques construct a function to smoothly interpolate a set of unstructured points. That is, given a set of n points $p_i = (x_i, y_i, z_i)$ and function values $F_i(p_i)$, a new function $F(p)$ is created that interpolates the points p_i. Once the interpolation function is constructed, we can build topological structure from the unstructured points by sampling $F(p)$ over an image dataset. We can then visualize the image data using any of the various techniques presented throughout the text.

Shepard's method is an inverse distance weighted interpolation technique [Wixom78]. The interpolation functions can be written

$$F(p) = \frac{\displaystyle\sum_{i=1}^{n} \frac{F_i}{|p - p_i|^2}}{\displaystyle\sum \frac{1}{|p - p|^2}} \qquad (9\text{-}25)$$

where $F(p_i) = F_i$. Shepard's method is easy to implement, but has the undesirable property that limits its usefulness for most practical applications. The interpolation functions generate a local "flat spot" at each point p_i since the derivatives are zero

$$\frac{\partial F}{\partial x} = \frac{\partial F}{\partial y} = \frac{\partial F}{\partial z} = 0 \qquad (9\text{-}26)$$

As a result, Shepard's method is overly constrained in the region around each point.

Shepard's method is an example of a basis function method. That is, the interpolation function $F(p)$ consists of a sum of functions centered at each data point, p_i. Other basis function methods have been developed as described by Nielson [Nielson91]. They vary in localization of the basis functions and the sophistication of the interpolation function. Localization of basis functions means that their effect is isolated to a small region. Examples of more sophisticated basis functions include quadratic polynomials and cubic splines. Please see the references for more information.

Triangulation Techniques. Triangulation techniques build topology directly from unstructured points. The points are *triangulated* to create a topological structure consisting of n-dimensional simplices that completely bound the points and linear combinations of the points (the so-called *convex hull*). The result of triangulation is a set of triangles (2D) or tetrahedra (3D), depending upon the dimension of the input data [Lawson86].

An n-dimensional triangulation of a point set $P = (p_1, p_2, p_3, ..., p_n)$ is a collection of n-dimensional simplices whose defining points lie in P. The simplices do not intersect one another and share only boundary features such as edges or faces. The Delaunay triangulation is a particularly important form [Bowyer81] [Watson81]. It has the property that the circum-

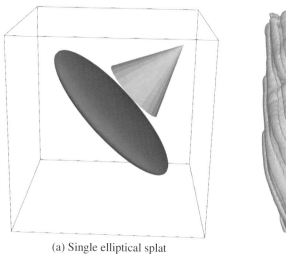

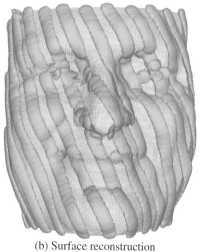

(a) Single elliptical splat   (b) Surface reconstruction

Figure 9–38 Elliptical splatting. (a) Single elliptical splat with eccentricity $E=10$. Cone shows orientation of vector (`singleSplat.cxx`). (b) Surface reconstructed using elliptical splats into 100^3 volume followed by isosurface extraction. Points regularly subsampled and overlayed on original mesh (`splatFace.tcl`).

sphere of any n-dimensional simplex contains no other points of P except the $n+1$ defining points of the simplex (**Figure 9–39**(a)).

The Delaunay triangulation has many interesting properties. In two dimensions, the Delaunay triangulation has been shown to be the optimal triangulation. That is, the minimum interior angle of a triangle in a Delaunay triangulation is greater than or equal to the minimum interior angle of any other possible triangulation. The Delaunay triangulation is the dual of the Dirichlet tessellation (**Figure 9–39**(b)), another important construction in computational geometry. The Dirichlet tessellation, also known as the Voronoi tessellation, is a tiling of space where each tile represents the space closest to a point p_i. (The tiles are called Voronoi cells.) An n-dimensional Delaunay triangulation can be constructed from the Dirichlet tessellation by creating edges between Voronoi cells that share common $n-1$ boundaries (e.g., faces in 3D and edges in 2D). Conversely, the vertices of the Dirichlet tessellation are located at the circumcenters of the Delaunay circumcircles.

The Delaunay triangulation can be computed using a variety of techniques. We describe a particularly elegant technique introduced independently by Watson [Watson81] and Bowyer [Bowyer81] (**Figure 9–40**). The algorithm begins by constructing an initial Delaunay triangulation that strictly bounds the point set P, the so-called bounding triangulation. This bounding triangulation can be as simple as a single triangle (2D) or tetrahedron (3D). Then, each point of P is injected one by one into the current triangulation. If the injected point lies within the circumcircle of any simplex, then the simplex is deleted, leaving a "hole" in the triangulation. After deleting all simplices, the $n-1$ dimensional faces on the boundary of the hole, along with the injected point, are used to construct a modified triangu-

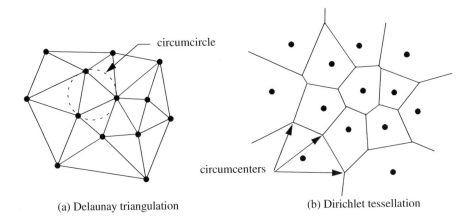

(a) Delaunay triangulation   (b) Dirichlet tessellation

Figure 9–39 The Delaunay triangulation (a) and Dirichlet tessellation (b). The circumcircle of each triangle in a Delaunay triangulation contains no other points but the three vertices of the triangle. The region surrounding each point p_i in a Dirichlet tessellation is the set of points closest to p_i.

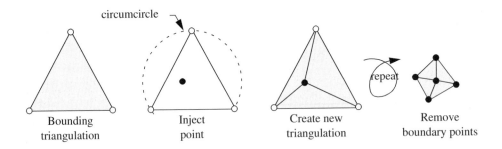

Figure 9–40 Computing the Delaunay triangulation using technique of Watson and Boyer. Points are injected into triangulation forming new Delaunay triangulations. In the final step, the initial bounding points are removed to reveal final triangulation.

lation. This is a Delaunay triangulation, and the process continues until all points are injected into the triangulation. The last step removes the simplices connecting the points forming the initial bounding triangulation to reveal the completed Delaunay triangulation.

This simplistic presentation of triangulation techniques has shown how to create topological structure from a set of unstructured points. We have ignored some difficult issues such as degeneracies and numerical problems. Degeneracies occur when points in a Delaunay triangulation lie in such a way that the triangulation is not unique. For example, the points lying at the vertices of a square, rectangle, or hexagon are degenerate because they can be triangulated in more than one way, where each triangulation is equivalent (in terms of Delaunay criterion) to the other. Numerical problems occur when we attempt to compute circumcenters, especially in higher-dimensional triangulations, or when simplices of poor aspect ratio are present.

Despite these problems, triangulation methods are a powerful tool for visualizing unstructured points. Once we convert the data into a triangulation (or in our terminology, an unstructured grid), we can directly visualize our data using standard unstructured grid techniques.

Hybrid Techniques. Recent work has focused on combining triangulation and basis function techniques for interpolating 2D bivariate data. The basic idea is as follows. A triangulation of P is constructed. Then an interpolating network of curves is defined over the edges of the triangulation. These curves are constructed with certain minimization properties of interpolating splines. Finally, the curve network is used to construct a series of triangular basis functions, or surface patches, that exhibit continuity in function value, and possibly higher order derivatives. (See [Nielson91] for more information.)

Multidimensional Visualization

The treatment of multidimensional datasets is an important data visualization issue. Each point in a dataset is described by an n-dimensional coordinate, where $n \geq 3$. Here we assume that each coordinate is an independent variable, and that we wish to visualize a single dependent variable. (Multidimensional visualization of vectors and tensors is an open research area.) An application of multidimensional data is financial visualization, where we might want to visualize return on investment as a function of interest rate, initial investment, investment period, and income, to name just a few possibilities.

There are two fundamental problems that we must address when applying multidimensional visualization. These are the problems of *projection* and *understanding*.

The problem of projection is that in using computer graphics we have two dimensions in which to present our data, or possibly three or four if we use specialized methods. Using 3D graphics we can give the illusion of three dimensions, or we can use stereo viewing techniques to achieve three dimensions. We can also use time as a fourth dimension by animating images. However, except for these limited situations, general n-dimensional data cannot be represented on a 2D computer screen.

The problem of understanding is that humans do not easily comprehend more than three dimensions, or possibly three dimensions plus time. Thus, even if we could create a technique to display data of many dimensions, the difficulty in understanding the data would impair the usefulness of the technique.

Most multidimensional visualization techniques work with some form of dimension mapping, where n dimensions are mapped to three dimensions and then displayed with 3D computer graphics techniques. The mapping is achieved by fixing all variables except three, and then applying the visualization techniques described throughout the text to the resulting data. For maximum benefit, the process of fixing independent variables, mapping to three dimensions, and then generating visualization must be interactive. This improves the effectiveness of the visualization process, allowing the user to build an internal model of the data by manipulating different parts of the data.

One novel approach to multidimensional visualization has been proposed by Inselberg and Dimsdale [Inselberg87]. This approach uses *parallel coordinate systems*. Instead of plot-

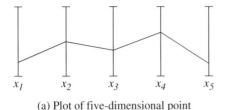 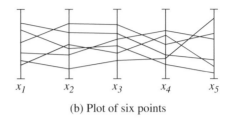

(a) Plot of five-dimensional point   (b) Plot of six points

Figure 9–41 Plotting a five-dimensional point using parallel coordinates. (a) plot of single point, (b) plot of many points.

ting points on orthogonal axes, the ith dimensional coordinate of each point is plotted along separate, parallel axes. This is shown in **Figure 9–41** for a five-dimensional point. In parallel coordinate plots, points appear as lines. As a result, plots of n-dimensional points appear as sequences of line segments that may intersect or group to form complex fan patterns. In so doing, the human pattern recognition capability is engaged. Unfortunately, if the number of points becomes large, and the data is not strongly correlated, the resulting plots can become a solid mass of black, and any data trends are drowned in the visual display.

Another useful multivariable technique uses glyphs. This technique associates a portion of the glyph with each variable. Although glyphs cannot generally be designed for arbitrary n-dimensional data, in many applications we can create glyphs to convey the information we are interested in. Refer to "Glyphs" on page 178 for more information about glyphs.

Texture Algorithms

Texturing is a common tool in computer graphics used to introduce detail without the high cost of graphics primitives. As we suggested in Chapter 7, texture mapping can also be used to visualize data. We explore a few techniques in the following sections.

Texture Thresholding. We saw earlier how to threshold data based on scalar values (see "Thresholding" on page 318). We refer to this approach as *geometric thresholding* because structural components of a dataset (e.g., points and cells) are extracted based on data value. In contrast, we can use texture mapping techniques to achieve similar results. We call this technique *texture thresholding*.

Texture thresholding conceals features we do not want to see and accentuates features that we want to see. There are many variations on this theme. A feature can be concealed by making it transparent or translucent, by reducing its intensity, or using muted colors. A feature can be accentuated by making it opaque, increasing its intensity, or adding bright color. In the following paragraphs we describe a technique that combines intensity and transparency.

Texture thresholding requires two pieces of information: a texture map and an index into the map, or texture coordinate. In the simplest case we can devise a texture map that consists of two distinct regions as shown in **Figure 9–42**(a). The first region is alternatively

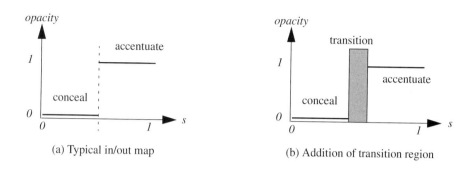

Figure 9–42 shown as:
(a) Typical in/out map

(b) Addition of transition region

Figure 9–42 1D texture map. (a) In/out map. (b) Addition of transition region to in/out map.

referred to as "conceal," "off," or "outside." The second region is referred to as "accentuate," "on," or "inside." (These different labels are used depending upon the particular application.) With this texture map in hand we can texture threshold by computing an appropriate texture coordinate. Areas that we wish to accentuate are assigned a coordinate to map into the "accentuate" portion of the texture map. Areas that we want to conceal are assigned a coordinate to map into the "conceal" portion of the texture map.

One texture threshold technique uses transparency. We can conceal a region by setting its alpha opacity value to zero (transparent), and accentuate it by setting the alpha value to one (opaque). Thus, the texture map consists of two regions: a concealed region with $\alpha = 0$ and an accentuated region with $\alpha = 1$. Of course, the effect can be softened by using intermediate alpha values to create translucent images.

An extension of this technique introduces a third region into the texture map: a transition region (**Figure 9–42**(b)). The transition region is the region between the concealed and accentuated regions. We can use the transition region to draw a border around the accentuated region, further highlighting the region.

To construct the texture map we use *intensity-alpha,* or $I\alpha$ values. The intensity modulates the underlying color, while the alpha value controls transparency (as described previously). In the accentuated region, the intensity and opacity values are set high. In the concealed region, the intensity value can be set to any value (if $\alpha = 0$) or to a lower value (if $\alpha \neq 0$). The transition region can use various combinations of α and intensity. A nice combination produces a black, opaque transition region (i.e., $I = 0$ and $\alpha = 1$).

To visualize information with the thresholding technique, we must map data to texture coordinates. As we saw previously, we can use scalar values in combination with a threshold specification to map data into the concealed, transition, and accentuated regions of the texture map. **Figure 9–43**(a) shows an example of texture thresholding applied to scalar data from a simulation of fluid flow. A scalar threshold s_T is set to show only data with scalar value greater than or equal to s_T.

Another useful texture thresholding application uses implicit functions to map point position to texture coordinate. This is similar in effect to geometric clipping (see "Clipping With Scalar Fields" on page 305). As we saw in "Implicit Functions" on page 173, implicit

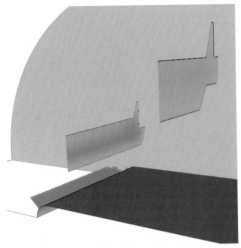
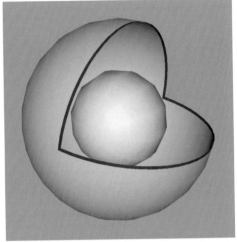

(a) Thresholding data with texture   (b) Sphere cut with transparent texture

Figure 9–43 Examples of texture thresholding. (a) Using scalar threshold to show values of flow density on plane above value of 1.5 (texThresh.tcl). (b) Boolean combination of two planes to cut nested spheres (tcutSph.cxx).

functions naturally map a (x, y, z) coordinate value into three regions: $F(x, y, z) < 0$, $F(x, y, z) = 0$, and $F(x, y, z) > 0$; or equivalently, the concealed, transition, and accentuated regions of the texture map. Using boolean combinations of implicit functions, we can create complex cuts of our data as illustrated in **Figure 9–43**(b). This figure shows two nested spheres. The outer sphere is cut by a boolean combination of two planes to show the inner sphere.

Boolean Textures. Texture thresholding can be extended into higher dimensions. That is, 2D or 3D texture coordinates can be used to map two or three data variables into a texture map. One such technique is *boolean textures*, a method to clip geometry using a 2D texture map and two implicit functions [Lorensen93].

Boolean textures extend texture thresholding for geometric clipping from 1D to 2D. Instead of using a single implicit function to label regions "in" or "out", two implicit functions are used. This results in four different regions corresponding to all possible combinations of "in" and "out." The boolean texture map is modified to reflect this as shown in **Figure 9–44**. As with 1D texture thresholding, transition regions can be created to separate the four regions.

The boolean texture map can be created with combinations of intensity and transparency values to achieve a variety of effects. By combining the four combinations of in/out (i.e., four regions of **Figure 9–44**) with the two combinations of "conceal" and "accentuate," sixteen different boolean textures are possible. **Figure 9–45**(a) illustrates these combinations expressed as boolean combinations of two implicit functions A and B. The "inside" of the implicit functions is indicated with subscript i, while the outside is indicated with subscript o.

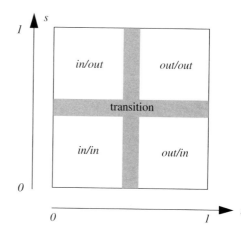

Figure 9–44 2D Boolean texture.

The boolean expressions indicate the regions that we wish to conceal, as shown by open circles. The darkened circles are the regions that are accentuated. We can see in **Figure 9–45**(b) the effects of applying these different boolean textures to a sphere. The implicit functions in this figure are two elliptical cylinders sharing a common axis, and rotated 90 degrees from one another. In addition, transition regions have been defined with I = 0 to generate the dark cut edges shown. All 16 spheres share the same texture coordinates; only the texture map changes.

Texture Animation. Time-based animation techniques can illustrate motion or temporal data variations. This process often requires relatively large amounts of computer resource to read, process, and display the data. As a result, techniques to reduce computer resources are desirable when animating data.

Texture mapping can be used to animate certain types of data. In these techniques, the data is not regenerated frame by frame, instead a time-varying texture map is used to change the visual appearance of the data. An example of this approach is texture animation of vector fields [Yamrom95].

As we saw in "Hedgehogs and Oriented Glyphs" on page 161, vector fields can be represented as oriented and scaled lines. Texture animation can transform this static representational scheme into a dynamic representation. The key is to construct a series of 1D texture maps that when applied rapidly in sequence create the illusion of motion. **Figure 9–46**(a) shows a series of sixteen such texture maps. The maps consist of intensity-alpha ($I\alpha$) values, A portion of the texture map is set fully opaque with full intensity ($I = 1$, $\alpha = 1$). This is shown as the "dark" pattern in **Figure 9–46**(a). The remainder of the map is set fully transparent with arbitrary intensity ($I = 1$, $\alpha = 0$) shown as the "white" portion. As is evidenced by the figure, the sequence of 16 texture maps scanned top to bottom generate the appearance of motion from left to right. Notice also how the texture maps are designed to wrap around to form a continuous pattern.

Along with the 1D texture map, the texture coordinate s must also be generated — on a line this is straightforward. The line origin receives texture coordinate $s = 0$, while the line terminus receives texture coordinate value $s = 1$. Any intermediate points (if the vector is a polyline) are parameterized in monotonic fashion in the interval (0,1). Texture coordinates

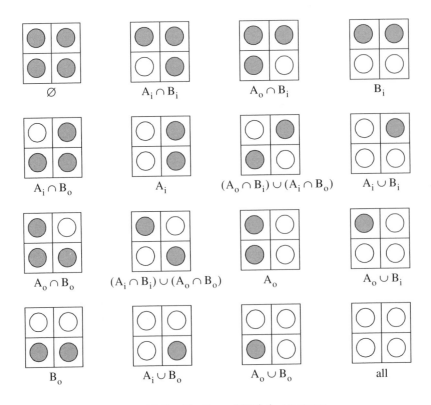

(a) Combinations of 2D in/out textures

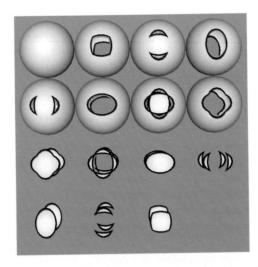

(b) Sixteen boolean textures (from above) applied to sphere (`quadricCut.cxx`)

Figure 9–45 Sixteen boolean textures. (a) Sixteen combinations of in/out. (b) Textures applied to sphere using two elliptical cylinder implicit functions.

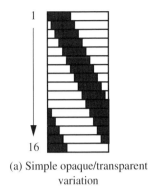

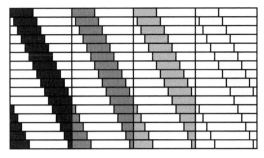

(a) Simple opaque/transparent
variation

(b) Feathered opaque/transparent
variation

Figure 9–46 Texture maps for vector animation. Sixteen textures applied in succession create effect of motion along a vector. (a) Simple map. (b) Varying intensity "feathers" effect of motion.

need only be generated once. Only the texture map is varied to generate the vector animation.

Other effects are possible by modifying the texture map. **Figure 9–46**(b) shows a texture map with a repeating sequence of opaque/transparent regions. In each opaque region the intensity is gradually reduced from left to right. The result is that this tends to "feather" the appearance of the vector motion. The resulting image is more pleasing to the eye.

9.5 Putting It All Together

With the conclusion of this chapter we have provided an overview of the basics of data visualization. In this section we show you how to use some of the advanced algorithms as implemented in the *Visualization Toolkit*.

Dividing Cubes / Point Generation

Dividing cubes is implemented in VTK with the class vtkDividingCubes. It has been specialized to operate with image datasets. Besides specifying the contour value, you must specify a separation distance between points (using the method SetDistance()). If you desire a solid appearance, pick a distance that is less than or equal to display resolution.

The separation distance controls the accuracy of point generation. It is possible to generate points that appear to form a solid surface when rendered, but are not accurately located on the contour surface. Although this usually is not an issue when viewing contour surfaces, if the accuracy of the point positions is important, the distance value must be set smaller. However, this can result in huge numbers of points. To reduce the number of points, you can use the SetIncrement() method, which specifies that every nth point is to be generated. Using this approach, you can obtain good accuracy and control the total number of points. An example where point positions are important is when the points are used to locate glyphs or as seed points for streamline generation.

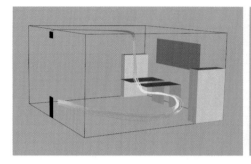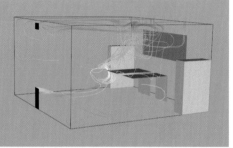

Figure 9–47 Using random point seeds to create streamlines (office.tcl).

The *Visualization Toolkit* provides other point generation techniques. The source object vtkPointSource generates a user-specified number of points within a spherical region. The point positions are random within the sphere. (Note that there is a natural tendency for higher point density near the center of the sphere because the points are randomly generated along the radius and spherical angles ϕ and θ.)

Figure 9–47 is an example use of vtkPointSource to generate streamlines. The dataset is a structured grid of dimensions $21 \times 20 \times 20$ with flow velocity and a scalar pressure field. The dataset is a CFD simulation of flow in a small office. As this picture shows, there are a couple of bookcases, desks, a window, and an inlet and outlet for the ventilation system. On one of the desks is a small, intense heat source (e.g., a cigarette). In the left image 25 streamlines are started near the inlet using a vtkPointSource point generator. The second image shows what happens when we move the point source slightly to the left. By adjusting a single parameter (e.g., the center of the point source) it is possible to quickly explore our simulation data.

Another convenient object for point generation is the class vtkEdgePoints. vtkEdgePoints generates points on an isosurface. The points are generated by locating cell edges whose points are both above and below the isosurface value. Linear interpolation is used to generate the point. Since vtkEdgePoints operates on any cell type, this filter's input type is any dataset type (e.g., vtkDataSet). Unlike vtkDividingCubes this filter will not typically generate dense point clouds that appear solid.

Clipping with Scalar Fields

Clipping is implemented in vtkClipPolyData. Each polygonal data primitive implements the operation in its Clip() method using cases tables derived in a manner similar to that of triangles described on Page 305. vtkClipPolyData has methods to control whether an implicit function provides the scalar data or whether the dataset's scalar data will be used. ComputeScalarDataOn() uses the implicit function and ComputeScalarDataOff() uses the dataset's scalar data. Two output polygonal datasets are produced. These are accessed with GetOutput() and GetClippedOutput() methods. GetOutput() returns the polygonal data that is "inside" the clipping region while GetClippedOutput() returns polygonal data that is "outside" the region. (Note that GenerateClippedOutputOn() must be enabled if you are to get the clipped output.) The meaning of inside and outside can be reversed using the InsideOutOn() method. **Figure 9–48** shows a plane of quadrilaterals clipped with a boolean implicit function.

Until recently, VTK supported clipping only for polygonal data cell types (vertices, polyvertices, line, polylines, polygons and triangle strips). Recent additions since VTK version 4.0 support clipping of 3D cells using an ordered Delaunay triangulation approach.

Swept Volumes and Surfaces

Swept surfaces can be applied in two interesting ways. First, they can be used as a modelling tool to create unusual shapes and forms. In this sense, swept surfaces are an advanced implicit modelling technique. Second, swept surfaces can be used to statically represent object motion. This is an important visualization technique in itself and has many important applications. One of these applications is design for maintainability.

When a complex mechanical system like a car engine is designed, it is important to design proper access to critical engine components. These components, like spark plugs, require higher levels of service and maintenance. It is important that these components can be easily reached by a mechanic. We've read horror stories of how it is necessary to remove an engine to change a spark plug. Insuring ready access to critical engine parts prevents situations like this from occurring.

Swept surface can assist in the design of part access. We simply define a path to remove the part (early in the design process), and then generate a swept surface. This surface (sometimes referred to as a maintenance access solid or MAS) is then placed back into the CAD system. From this point on, the design of surrounding components such as fuel lines or wiring harnesses must avoid the MAS. As long as the MAS is not violated, the part can be removed. If the MAS is violated, a reevaluation of the removal path or redesign of the part or surrounding components is necessary.

Figure 9–49 shows how to create a swept surface from a simple geometric representation. The geometry is simply a line-stroked VTK. The next step is to define a motion path. This path is defined by creating a list of transformation matrices. Linear interpolation is used to generate intermediate points along the path if necessary.

In **Figure 9–49** we also see the basic procedure to construct the swept surface. First, we must construct an implicit representation of the part by using vtkImplictModeller. This is then provided as input to vtkSweptSurface. It is important that the resolution of the implicit model is greater than or equal to that of vtkSweptSurface. This will minimize errors when we construct the surface. A bounding box surrounding the part and its motion can be defined, or it will be computed automatically. For proper results, this box must strictly contain the part as its moves. We also can set the number of interpolation steps, or allow this to be computed automatically as well. In the figure, we have chosen a small number to better illustrate the stepping of the algorithm.

Once vtkSweptSurface executes, we extract the swept surface using an isosurfacing algorithm. The isosurface value is an offset distance; thus we can create surfaces that take into account geometry tolerance. (This is particularly important if we are designing mechanical systems.) The implementation of the implicit modeller in VTK uses a positive distance function; so the isosurface value should always be positive. To create swept surfaces of zero and negative value requires a modification to the implicit modeller.

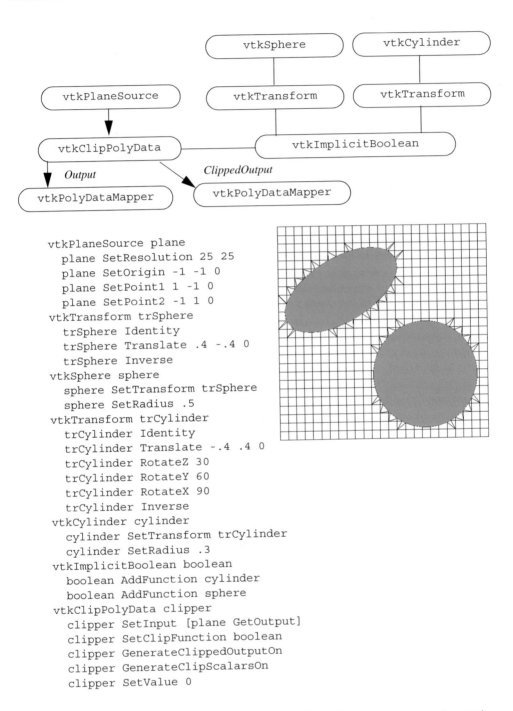

Figure 9–48 A plane clipped with a sphere and an ellipse. The two transforms place each implicit function into the appropriate position. Two outputs are generated by the clipper. (clipSphCyl.tcl).

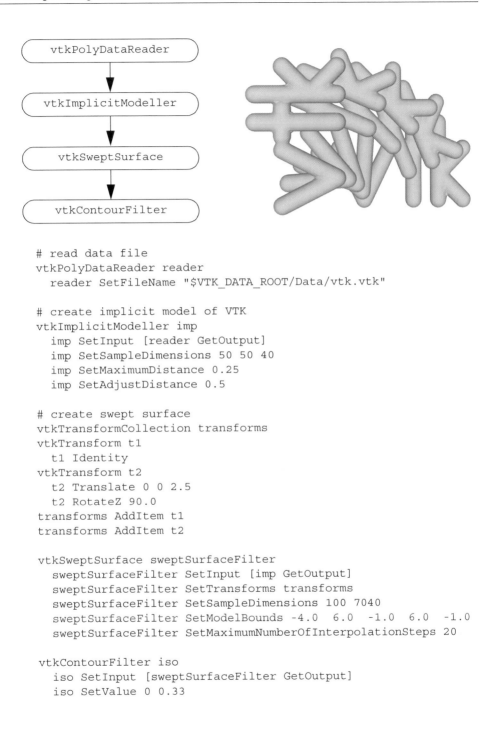

```
# read data file
vtkPolyDataReader reader
  reader SetFileName "$VTK_DATA_ROOT/Data/vtk.vtk"

# create implicit model of VTK
vtkImplicitModeller imp
  imp SetInput [reader GetOutput]
  imp SetSampleDimensions 50 50 40
  imp SetMaximumDistance 0.25
  imp SetAdjustDistance 0.5

# create swept surface
vtkTransformCollection transforms
vtkTransform t1
  t1 Identity
vtkTransform t2
  t2 Translate 0 0 2.5
  t2 RotateZ 90.0
transforms AddItem t1
transforms AddItem t2

vtkSweptSurface sweptSurfaceFilter
  sweptSurfaceFilter SetInput [imp GetOutput]
  sweptSurfaceFilter SetTransforms transforms
  sweptSurfaceFilter SetSampleDimensions 100 7040
  sweptSurfaceFilter SetModelBounds -4.0  6.0  -1.0  6.0  -1.0
  sweptSurfaceFilter SetMaximumNumberOfInterpolationSteps 20

vtkContourFilter iso
  iso SetInput [sweptSurfaceFilter GetOutput]
  iso SetValue 0 0.33
```

Figure 9–49 Generating swept surface from line-stroked "vtk" (sweptVtk.tcl).

Multidimensional Visualization

An important characteristic of multidimensional datasets is that they cannot be categorized according to any of the types defined in the *Visualization Toolkit*. This implies that source objects interfacing with multidimensional data are responsible for converting the data they interface with into one of the types defined in VTK. This can be a difficult process, requiring you to write interface code.

Other visualization systems treat this problem differently. In these systems a dataset type is defined that can represent multidimensional data. This dataset type is essentially an *n*-dimensional matrix. Additional filters are defined that allow the user to extract pieces of the dataset and assemble them into a more conventional dataset type, such as a volume or structured grid. After mapping the data from multidimensional form to conventional form, standard visualization techniques can be applied. (Future implementations of VTK may include this functionality. At the current time you must map multidimensional data into a known VTK form.)

To demonstrate these ideas we will refer to **Figure 9–50**. This is an example of multidimensional financial data. The data reflects parameters associated with monetary loans. In the file `financial.txt` there are six different variables: TIME_LATE, MONTHLY_PAYMENT, UNPAID_PRINCIPLE, LOAN_AMOUNT, INTEREST_RATE, and MONTHLY_INCOME. (Note: this is simulated data, don't make financial decisions based upon this!)

We will use Gaussian splatting to visualize this data (see "Splatting Techniques" on page 338). Our first step is to choose dependent and independent variables. This choice is essentially a mapping from multidimensional data into an unstructured point dataset. In this example we will choose MONTHLY_PAYMENT, INTEREST_RATE, and LOAN_AMOUNT as our (x, y, z) point coordinates, and TIME_LATE as a scalar value. This maps four of six variables. For now we will ignore the other two variables.

We use vtkGaussianSplatter to perform the splatting operation (i.e., conversion from unstructured points to volume dataset). This is followed by an isosurface extraction. We splat the data two times. The first time we splat the entire population. This is to show context and appears as gray/wireframe in the figure. The second time we splat the data and scale it by the value of TIME_LATE. As a result, only payments that are late contribute to the second isosurface.

The results of this visualization are interesting. First, we see that there is a strong correlation between the two independent variables MONTHLY_PAYMENT and LOAN_AMOUNT. (This is more evident when viewing the data interactively.) We see that the data falls roughly on a plane at a 45 degree angle between these two axes. With a little reflection this is evident: the monthly payment is strongly a function of loan amount (as well as interest rate and payment period). Second, we see that there is a clustering of delinquent accounts within the total population. The cluster tends to grow with larger interest rates and shrink with smaller monthly payments and loan amounts. Although the relationship with interest rate is expected, the clustering towards smaller monthly payments is not. Thus our visualization has provided a clue into the data. Further exploration into the data may reveal the reason(s), or we may perform additional data analysis and acquisition to understand the phenomena.

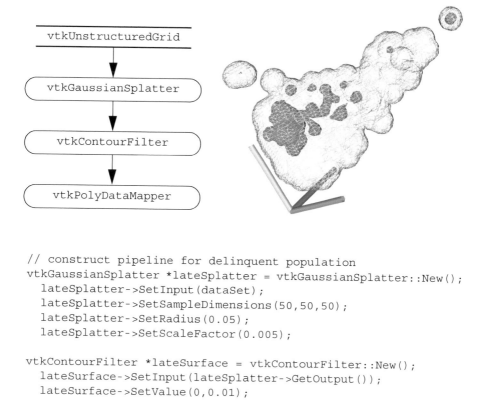

```
// construct pipeline for delinquent population
vtkGaussianSplatter *lateSplatter = vtkGaussianSplatter::New();
   lateSplatter->SetInput(dataSet);
   lateSplatter->SetSampleDimensions(50,50,50);
   lateSplatter->SetRadius(0.05);
   lateSplatter->SetScaleFactor(0.005);

vtkContourFilter *lateSurface = vtkContourFilter::New();
   lateSurface->SetInput(lateSplatter->GetOutput());
   lateSurface->SetValue(0,0.01);

vtkPolyDataMapper *lateMapper = vtkPolyDataMapper::New();
   lateMapper->SetInput(lateSurface->GetOutput());
   lateMapper->ScalarVisibilityOff();

vtkActor *lateActor = vtkActor::New();
   lateActor->SetMapper(lateMapper);
   lateActor->GetProperty()->SetColor(1.0,0.0,0.0);
```

Figure 9–50 Visualization of multidimensional financial data. Visualization network, output image, and sample C++ code are shown (finance.cxx). The gray/wireframe surface represents the total data population. The dark surface represents data points delinquent on loan payment.

One important note about multidimensional visualization. Because we tend to combine variables in odd ways (e.g., the use of MONTHLY_PAYMENT, INTEREST_RATE, and LOAN_AMOUNT as *(x, y, z)* coordinates), normalization of the data is usually required. To normalize data we simply adjust data values to lie between (0,1). Otherwise our data can be badly skewed and result in poor visualizations.

Connectivity

Many useful visualization algorithms often borrow from other fields. Topological connectivity analysis is one such technique. This technique is best categorized as a method in computational geometry, but serves many useful purposes in computer graphics and visualization.

To illustrate the application of connectivity analysis, we will use an MRI dataset generated by Janet MacFall at the Center for In Vivo Microscopy at Duke University. The dataset is a volume of dimensions 256^3 and is included on the CD-ROM. The data is of the root system of a small pine tree. Using the class vtkSliceCubes, an implementation of marching cubes for large volumes, we generate an initial isosurface represented by 351,118 triangles. (We have placed the file pine_root.tri on CD-ROM. This is a faster way of manipulating this data. If you have a large enough computer you can process the volume directly with vtkVolume16Reader and vtkMarchingCubes.)

Figure 9–51(a) shows the initial dataset. Notice that there are many small, disconnected isosurfaces due to noise and isolated moisture in the data. We use vtkConnectivityFilter to remove these small, disconnected surfaces. **Figure 9–51**(b) shows the result of applying the filter. Over 50,000 triangles were removed, leaving 299,480 triangles.

The vtkConnectivityFilter is a general filter taking datasets as input, and generating an unstructured grid as output. It functions by extracting cells that are connected at points (i.e., share common points). In this example the single largest surface is extracted. It is also possible to specify cell ids and point ids and extract surfaces connected to these.

Decimation

Decimation is a 3D data compression technique for surfaces represented as triangle meshes. We use it most often to improve rendering interactive response for large models.

Figure 9–52 shows the application of decimation to the data from the pine root example. The original model of 351,118 triangles is reduced to 81,111 triangles using a combination of decimation and connectivity. The decimation parameters are fairly conservative. Here we see a reduction of approximately 55 percent.

The most common parameters to adjust in the vtkDecimate filter are the TargetReduction, InitialError, ErrorIncrement, MaximumIterations, and InitialFeatureAngle. TargetReduction specifies the compression factor (numbers closer to one represent higher compression). Because of topological, decimation criterion, aspect ratio, and feature angle constraints this reduction may not be realized (i.e., TargetReduction is a desired goal, not a guaranteed output). The InitialError and ErrorIncrement control the decimation criterion. As the filter starts, the decimation criterion is set to InitialError. Then, for each iteration the decimation criterion is incremented by ErrorIncrement. The algorithm terminates when either the target reduction is achieved, or the number of iterations reaches MaximumIterations. The InitialFeatureAngle is used to compute feature edges. Smaller angles force the algorithm to retain more surface detail.

Other important parameters are the AspectRatio and MaximumSubIterations. AspectRatio controls the triangulation process. All triangles must satisfy this criterion or the vertex will not be deleted during decimation. A sub-iteration is an iteration where the deci-

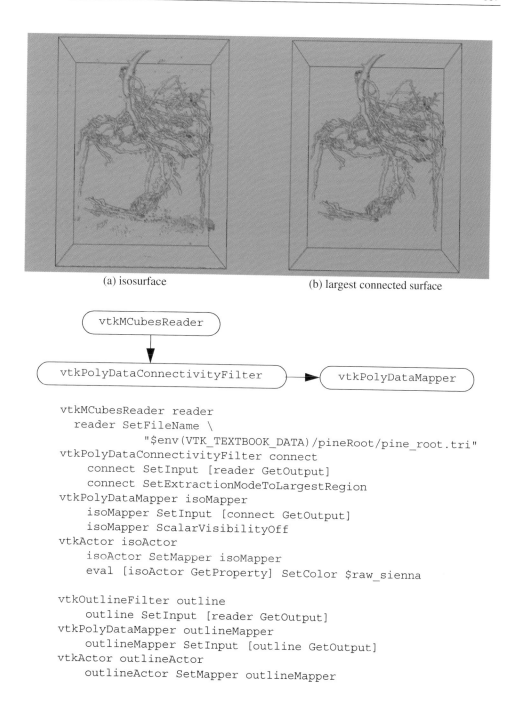

(a) isosurface   (b) largest connected surface

```
vtkMCubesReader reader
  reader SetFileName \
          "$env(VTK_TEXTBOOK_DATA)/pineRoot/pine_root.tri"
vtkPolyDataConnectivityFilter connect
    connect SetInput [reader GetOutput]
    connect SetExtractionModeToLargestRegion
vtkPolyDataMapper isoMapper
    isoMapper SetInput [connect GetOutput]
    isoMapper ScalarVisibilityOff
vtkActor isoActor
    isoActor SetMapper isoMapper
    eval [isoActor GetProperty] SetColor $raw_sienna

vtkOutlineFilter outline
    outline SetInput [reader GetOutput]
vtkPolyDataMapper outlineMapper
    outlineMapper SetInput [outline GetOutput]
vtkActor outlineActor
    outlineActor SetMapper outlineMapper
```

Figure 9–51 Applying connectivity filter to remove noisy isosurfaces (connPineRoot.tcl). Data is from 256^3 volume data of the root system of a pine tree.

mation criterion is not incremented. This can be used to coalesce triangles during rapid rates of decimation. MaximumSubIterations controls the number of sub-iterations. This parameter is typically set to two.

Texture Clipping

Texture mapping is a powerful visualization technique. Besides adding detail to images with minimal effort, we can perform important viewing and modelling operations. One of these operations is clipping data to view internal structure.

Figure 9–53 is an example of texture clipping using a transparent texture map. The motor show consists of five complex parts, some of which are hidden by the outer casing. To see the inside of the motor, we define an implicit clipping function. This function is simply the intersection of two planes to form a clipping "corner." The object vtkImplicitTextureCoords is used in combination with this implicit function to generate texture coordinates. These objects are then rendered with the appropriate texture map and the internal parts of the motor can be seen.

The texture map consists of three regions (as described previously in the chapter). The concealed region is transparent. The transition region is opaque but with a black (zero intensity) color. The highlighted region is full intensity and opaque. As can be seen from Figure 9–53, the boundaries appear as black borders giving a nice visual effect.

The importance of texture techniques is that we can change the appearance of objects and even perform modelling operations like clipping with little effort. We need only change the texture map. This process is much faster relative to the alternative approach of geometric modelling. Also, hardware support of texture is becoming common. Thus the rendering rate remains high despite the apparent increase in visual complexity.

Delaunay Triangulation

Delaunay triangulation is used to construct topology from unstructured point data. In two dimensions we generate triangles (i.e., an unstructured grid or polygonal dataset) while in three dimensions we generate tetrahedra (i.e., an unstructured grid). Typical examples of image data include points measured in space, or a dimensional subset of multidimensional data.

In the example of Figure 9–54 we show how to create a 2D Delaunay triangulation from a field of points. The points are created by generating random x and y coordinate values in the interval $[0, 1]$, and setting the z-value to a constant value (i.e., the points lie in an x-y plane). The points are then triangulated, and tubes and sphere glyphs are used to highlight the resulting points and edges of the triangulation.

One important concern regarding Delaunay triangulations is that the process is numerically sensitive. Creating triangles with poor aspect ratio (e.g., slivers) can cause the algorithm to break down. If you have a large number of points to triangulate, you may want to consider randomizing the point order. This approach tends to generate triangles with better aspect ratio and give better results. You may also want to consider other implementations of Delaunay triangulation that are more numerically robust. See [Edelsbrunner94] for an example.

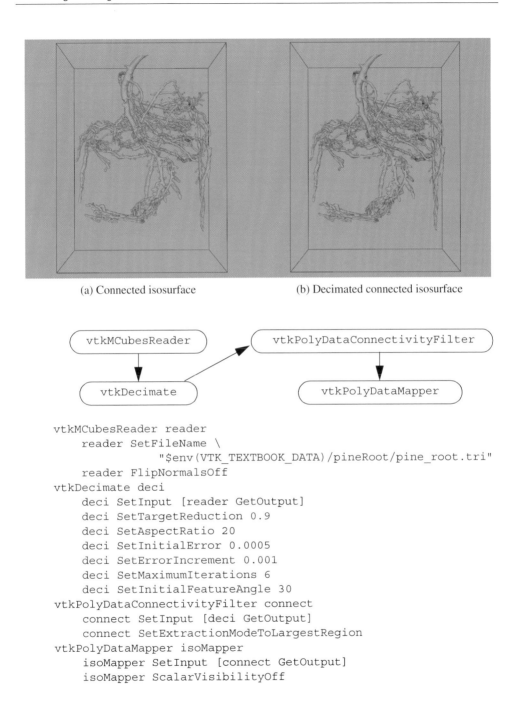

(a) Connected isosurface   (b) Decimated connected isosurface

```
vtkMCubesReader                    vtkPolyDataConnectivityFilter


vtkDecimate                        vtkPolyDataMapper
```

```
vtkMCubesReader reader
    reader SetFileName \
                "$env(VTK_TEXTBOOK_DATA)/pineRoot/pine_root.tri"
    reader FlipNormalsOff
vtkDecimate deci
    deci SetInput [reader GetOutput]
    deci SetTargetReduction 0.9
    deci SetAspectRatio 20
    deci SetInitialError 0.0005
    deci SetErrorIncrement 0.001
    deci SetMaximumIterations 6
    deci SetInitialFeatureAngle 30
vtkPolyDataConnectivityFilter connect
    connect SetInput [deci GetOutput]
    connect SetExtractionModeToLargestRegion
vtkPolyDataMapper isoMapper
    isoMapper SetInput [connect GetOutput]
    isoMapper ScalarVisibilityOff
```

Figure 9–52 Applying connectivity and decimation filters to remove noisy isosurfaces and reduce data size (deciPineRoot.tcl). Data is from 256^3 volume data of the root system of a pine tree.

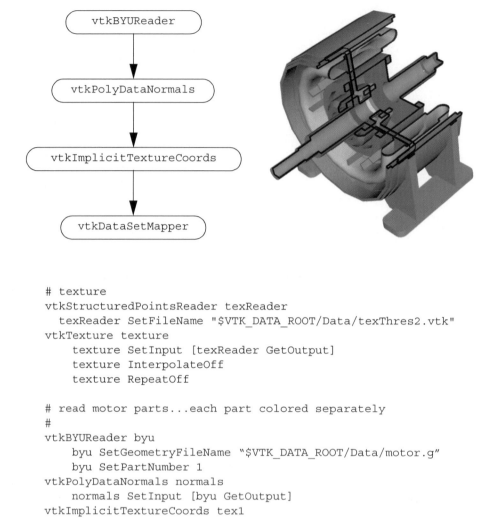

```
# texture
vtkStructuredPointsReader texReader
  texReader SetFileName "$VTK_DATA_ROOT/Data/texThres2.vtk"
vtkTexture texture
    texture SetInput [texReader GetOutput]
    texture InterpolateOff
    texture RepeatOff

# read motor parts...each part colored separately
#
vtkBYUReader byu
    byu SetGeometryFileName "$VTK_DATA_ROOT/Data/motor.g"
    byu SetPartNumber 1
vtkPolyDataNormals normals
    normals SetInput [byu GetOutput]
vtkImplicitTextureCoords tex1
    tex1 SetInput [normals GetOutput]
    tex1 SetRFunction planes
vtkDataSetMapper byuMapper
    byuMapper SetInput [tex1 GetOutput]
vtkActor byuActor
    byuActor SetMapper byuMapper
    byuActor SetTexture texture
    eval [byuActor GetProperty] SetColor $cold_grey

# other parts follow...
```

Figure 9–53 Texture cut used to reveal internal structure of a motor. Two cut planes are used in combination with transparent texture (motor.tcl).

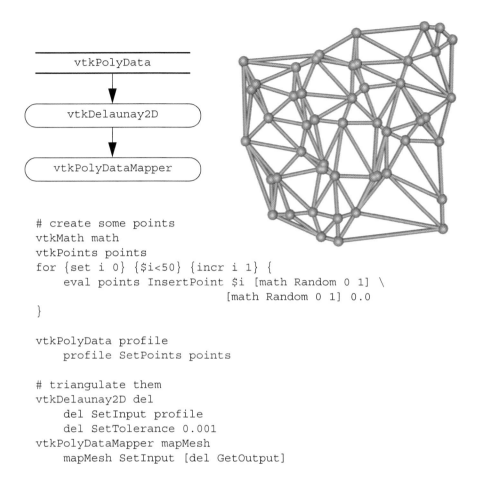

```
# create some points
vtkMath math
vtkPoints points
for {set i 0} {$i<50} {incr i 1} {
    eval points InsertPoint $i [math Random 0 1] \
                            [math Random 0 1] 0.0
}

vtkPolyData profile
    profile SetPoints points

# triangulate them
vtkDelaunay2D del
    del SetInput profile
    del SetTolerance 0.001
vtkPolyDataMapper mapMesh
    mapMesh SetInput [del GetOutput]
```

Figure 9–54 Two-dimensional Delaunay triangulation of a random set of points. Points and edges are shown highlighted with sphere glyphs and tubes (`DelMesh.tcl`). Only the pipeline to generate triangulation is shown.

9.6 Chapter Summary

Dividing cubes is a scalar contouring operation that generates points rather than surface primitives such as lines or polygons. Dense point clouds appear solid because of the limited resolution of computer images.

Vector fields have a complex structure. This structure can be visualized using streamribbons, streamsurfaces, and streampolygons. The topology of a vector field can be characterized by connecting critical points with streamlines.

Tensor fields consist of three orthogonal vector fields. The vector fields are the major, medium, and minor eigenvectors of the tensor field. Hyperstreamlines can be used to visualize tensor fields.

Dataset topology operations generate triangle strips, extract connected surfaces, and compute surface normals. Decimation is a polygon reduction algorithm that reduces the number of triangles in a triangle mesh. Implicit modelling techniques can be used to construct swept surfaces and volumes. Unstructured points are easy to represent but difficult to visualize. Splatting, interpolation, and triangulation techniques are available to construct structure for unstructured points. Multivariate visualization is required for data of dimension four and higher. Data must be mapped to three dimensions before standard visualization techniques can be used. Parallel coordinates techniques are also available to visualize multivariate data.

Modelling algorithms extract geometric structure from data, reduce the complexity of the data or create geometry. Spatial extraction selects dataset structure and associated data attributes lying within a specified region in space. Subsampling reduces data by selecting every nth data point. A related technique, data masking, selects every nth cell. Subsets of a dataset can also be selected using thresholding, which selects cells or points that lie within a range of scalar values. Probing resamples data at a set of points. The probe produces a dataset that has the topology of the probe with data values from the probed dataset. Generating triangle strips can reduce storage requirements and improve rendering speeds on some systems. If a dataset has multiple disjoint structures, a connectivity algorithm can uniquely identify the separate structures. For polygonal data that does not have vertex normals defined, normal generation algorithms can compute these values that are suitable for interpolation by Gouraud or Phong shading. Decimation, another data reduction technique, removes triangles in "flat" regions and fills the resulting gaps with new triangles. Unstructured points present a challenge because the data does not have topology. Splatting represents each point in the data with a uniform sampling and accumulates these splats using implicit modelling techniques. Triangulation techniques build topology directly from the unstructured points.

Multidimensional visualization techniques focus on data that has many scalar data values for each point. Parallel coordinates is an interesting approach that plots the scalar values for a data point along a parallel axis. The observer looks for trends and relationships between the lines that represent each point's data.

Texture algorithms use texture coordinates and texture maps to select or highlight portions of a dataset. Texture thresholding assigns texture coordinates based on a scalar value. The scalar value and texture map determine how a cell or portion of a cell is rendered. Boolean textures extend this concept to 2D and 3D. Careful design of a boolean texture map permits the "clipping" of geometry with combinations of implicit surfaces. Texture can also be used to animate vector fields.

9.7 Bibliographic Notes

Dividing cubes is an interesting algorithm because of the possibilities it suggests [Cline88]. Point primitives are extremely simple to render and manipulate. This simplicity can be used to advantage to build accelerated graphics boards, perform 3D editing, or build parallel visualization algorithms.

Many plotting and visualization systems use carpet plots extensively. Carpet plots are relatively easy to represent and render. Often 2D plotting techniques are used (i.e., lighting and perspective effects ignored). Check [Wang90] for additional information on rendering carpet plots.

In recent years a number of powerful vector visualization techniques have emerged. These techniques include streamsurfaces [Hultquist92], streampolygons [Schroeder91], vector field topology [Helman91] [Globus91], streamballs [Brill94], and vorticity visualization [Banks94]. The streamballs technique is a recent technique that combines techniques from implicit modeling. You may also wish to see references [Crawfis92] [vanWijk93] and [Max94]. These describe volume rendering and other advanced techniques for vector visualization, topics not well covered in this text.

Some abstract yet beautiful visualization images are due to Delmarcelle and Hesselink [Delmarcelle93]. Their rendering of hyperstreamlines reflect the underlying beauty and complexity of tensor fields.

Polygon reduction is a relatively new field of study. SIGGRAPH '92 marked a flurry of interest with the publication of two papers on this topic [Schroeder92a] [Turk92]. Since then a number of valuable techniques have been published. One of the best techniques, in terms of quality of results, is given by [Hoppe93], although it is limited in time and space because it is based on formal optimization techniques. Other interesting methods include [Hinker93] and [Rossignac93]. A promising area of research is multiresolution analysis, where wavelet decomposition is used to build multiple levels of detail in a model [Eck95]. The most recent work in this field stresses progressive transmission of 3D triangle meshes [Hoppe96], improved error measures [Garland97], and algorithms that modify mesh topology [Popovic97] [Schroeder97]. Most recently an extensive book on the technology is available including specialized methods for terrain simplification [Luebke02].

Triangle strip generation is an effective technique for achieving dramatic improvements in rendering speed and reductions in data handling. The reference by [Evans96] describes other triangle strip generation algorithms as well as presenting some of the most effective techniques to date.

The use of texture for visualization is relatively unexploited. This has been due in part to lack of texture support in most graphics software and hardware. This is now changing, as more vendors support texture and software systems (such as OpenGL) that provide an API for texture. Important references here include the boolean textures [Lorensen93] and surface convolution techniques [Cabral93] [Stalling95].

Unstructured or unorganized point visualization is likely to play a prominent role in visualization as the field matures and more complex data is encountered. Nielson et al. have presented important work in this field [Nielson91].

Multidimensional visualization is another important focus of visualization research [Bergeron89] [Mihalisin90]. Much real-world data is both unstructured and multidimensional. This includes financial databases, marketing statistics, and multidimensional optimization. Addressing this type of data is important to achieve future advances in understanding and application. Feiner [Feiner90] has presented a simple projection method combined with virtual reality techniques. [Inselberg87] has introduced parallel coordinates. These techniques have been shown to be powerful for many types of visual analysis.

9.8 References

[Banks94]
>   D. C. Banks and B. A. Singer. "Vortex Tubes in Turbulent Flows: Identification, Represen-
>   tation, Reconstruction." In *Proceedings of Visualization '94*. pp. 132–139, IEEE Computer
>   Society Press, Los Alamitos, CA, 1994.

[Bergeron89]
>   R. D. Bergeron and G. Grinstein. "A Reference Model for the Visualization of Multidimen-
>   sional Data." In *Proceedings Eurographics '89*. pp. 393–399, North Holland, Amsterdam,
>   1989.

[Bowyer81]
>   A. Bowyer. "Computing Dirichlet Tessellations." *The Computer Journal*. 24(2):162–166,
>   1981.

[Brill94]
>   M. Brill, H. Hagen, H-C. Rodrian, W. Djatschin, S. V. Klimenko. "Streamball Techniques
>   for Flow Visualization." In *Proceedings of Visualization '94*. pp. 225–231, IEEE Computer
>   Society Press, Los Alamitos, CA, 1994.

[Cabral93]
>   B. Cabral and L. Leedom. "Imaging Vector Fields Using Line Integral Convolution." In
>   *Proceedings of SIGGRAPH '93*, pp. 263–270, Addison-Wesley, Reading, MA, 1993.

[Cline88]
>   H. E. Cline, W. E. Lorensen, S. Ludke, C. R. Crawford, and B. C. Teeter, "Two Algorithms
>   for the Three-Dimensional Construction of Tomograms." *Medical Physics*. 15(3):320–327,
>   June 1988.

[Crawfis92]
>   R, Crawfis and N. Max. "Direct Volume Visualization of Three Dimensional Vector
>   Fields." In *Proceedings 1992 Workshop on Volume Visualization*. pp. 55–60, ACM Sig-
>   graph, New York, 1992.

[Delmarcelle93]
>   T. Delmarcelle and L. Hesselink. "Visualizing Second-Order Tensor Fields with Hyper-
>   streamlines." *IEEE Computer Graphics and Applications*. 13(4):25–33, 1993.

[Eck95]
>   M. Eck, T. DeRose, T. Duchamp, H. Hoppe, M. Lounsbery, W. Stuetzle. "Multiresolution
>   Analysis of Arbitrary Meshes." In *Proceedings SIGGRAPH '95*. pp. 173–182, Addison-
>   Wesley, Reading, MA, August 1995.

[Edelsbrunner94]
>   H. Edelsbrunner and E. P. Mucke. "Three-dimensional alpha shapes." *ACM Transactions
>   on Graphics*. 13:43–72, 1994.

[Evans96]
>   F. Evans, S. Skiena, A. Varshney. "Optimizing Triangle Strips for Fast Rendering." In *Pro-
>   ceedings of Visualization '96*. pp. 319–326, IEEE Computer Society Press, Los Alamitos,
>   CA, 1996.

[Feiner90]
>   S. Feiner and C. Beshers. "Worlds within Worlds: Metaphors for Exploring *n*-Dimensional
>   Virtual Worlds." In *Proceedings UIST '90* (ACM Symp. on User Interface Software). pp.
>   76–83, October, 1990.

[Garland97]

M. Garland and P. Heckbert. "Surface Simplification Using Quadric Error Metrics." In *Proceedings SIGGRAPH '97.* pp. 209–216, The Association for Computing Machinery, New York, August 1997.

[Globus91]

A. Globus, C. Levit, and T. Lasinski. "A Tool for Visualizing the Topology of Three-Dimensional Vector Fields." In *Proceedings of Visualization '91.* pp. 33–40, IEEE Computer Society Press, Los Alamitos, CA, 1991.

[He96]

T. He, L. Hong, A. Varshney, S. Wang. "Controlled Topology Simplification." *IEEE Transactions on Visualization and Computer Graphics.* 2(2):171–184, June 1996.

[Helman91]

J. L. Helman and L. Hesselink. "Visualization of Vector Field Topology in Fluid Flows." *IEEE Computer Graphics and Applications.* 11(3):36–46, 1991.

[Hinker93]

P. Hinker and C. Hansen. "Geometric Optimization." In *Proceedings of Visualization '93.* pp. 189–195, IEEE Computer Society Press, Los Alamitos, CA, October 1993.

[Hoppe93]

H. Hoppe, T. DeRose, T. Duchamp, J. McDonald, W. Stuetzle. "Mesh Optimization." In *Proceedings of SIGGRAPH '93.* pp. 19–26, August 1993.

[Hoppe96]

H. Hoppe. "Progressive Meshes." In *Proceedings SIGGRAPH '96.* pp. 96–108, The Association for Computing Machinery, New York, August 1996.

[Hultquist92]

J. P. M. Hultquist. "Constructing Stream Surfaces in Steady 3-D Vector Fields." In *Proceedings of Visualization '92.* pp. 171–178, IEEE Computer Society Press, Los Alamitos, CA, 1992.

[Inselberg87]

A. Inselberg and B. Dimsdale. "Parallel Coordinates for Visualizing Multi-Dimensional Geometry." In *Computer Graphics 1987 (Proceedings of CG International '87).* pp. 25–44, Springer-Verlag, 1987.

[Lawson86]

C. L. Lawson. "Properties of *n*-Dimensional Triangulations." *Computer-Aided Geometric Design.* 3:231–246, 1986.

[Lorensen93]

W. Lorensen. "Geometric Clipping with Boolean Textures." in *Proceedings of Visualization '93.* pp. 268–274, IEEE Computer Society Press, Los Alamitos, CA, Press, October 1993.

[Luebke02]

D. Luebke, M. Reddy, J. Cohen, A. Varshney, B. Watson, R. Huebner. *Level of Detail for 3D Graphics.* Morgan Kaufmann 2002. ISBN 1-55860-838-9.

[Max94]

N. Max, R. Crawfis, C. Grant. "Visualizing 3D Vector Fields Near Contour Surfaces." In *Proceedings of Visualization '94.* pp. 248–255, IEEE Computer Society Press, Los Alamitos, CA, 1994.

[Mihalisin90]
   T. Mihalisin, E. Gawlinski, J. Timlin, and J. Schwegler. "Visualizing a Scalar Field on an *n*-Dimensional Lattice." In *Proceedings of Visualization '90*. pp. 255–262, IEEE Computer Society Press, Los Alamitos, CA, October 1990.

[Nielson91]
   G. M. Nielson, T. A. Foley, B. Hamann, D. Lane. "Visualizing and Modeling Scattered Multivariate Data." *IEEE Computer Graphics and Applications*. 11(3):47–55, 1991.

[Popovic97]
   J. Popovic and H. Hoppe. "Progressive Simplicial Complexes." In *Proceedings SIG-GRAPH '97*. pp. 217–224, The Association. for Computing Machinery, New York, August 1997.

[Rossignac93]
   J. Rossignac and P. Borrel. "Multi-Resolution 3D Approximations for Rendering Complex Scenes." In *Modeling in Computer Graphics: Methods and Applications*. B. Falcidieno and T. Kunii, eds., pp. 455–465, Springer-Verlag Berlin, 1993.

[Schroeder91]
   W. Schroeder, C. Volpe, and W. Lorensen. "The Stream Polygon: A Technique for 3D Vector Field Visualization." In *Proceedings of Visualization '91*. pp. 126–132, IEEE Computer Society Press, Los Alamitos, CA, October 1991.

[Schroeder92a]
   W. Schroeder, J. Zarge, and W. Lorensen. "Decimation of Triangle Meshes." *Computer Graphics (SIGGRAPH '92)*. 26(2):65–70, August 1992.

[Schroeder92b]
   W. Schroeder, W. Lorensen, G. Montanaro, and C. Volpe. "Visage: An Object-Oriented Scientific Visualization System." In *Proceedings of Visualization '92*. pp. 219–226, IEEE Computer Society Press, Los Alamitos, CA, October 1992.

[Schroeder94]
   W. Schroeder, W. Lorensen, and S. Linthicum, "Implicit Modeling of Swept Surfaces and Volumes." In *Proceedings of Visualization '94*. pp. 40–45, IEEE Computer Society Press, Los Alamitos, CA, October 1994.

[Schroeder97]
   W. Schroeder. "A Topology Modifying Progressive Decimation Algorithm." In *Proceedings of Visualization '97*. IEEE Computer Society Press, Los Alamitos, CA, October 1997.

[Stalling95]
   D. Stalling and H-C. Hege. "Fast and Independent Line Integral Convolution." In *Proceedings of SIGGRAPH '95*. pp. 249–256, Addison-Wesley, Reading, MA, 1995.

[Turk92]
   G. Turk. "Re-Tiling of Polygonal Surfaces." *Computer Graphics (SIGGRAPH '92)*. 26(2):55–64, July 1992.

[vanWijk93]
   J. J. van Wijk. "Flow Visualization with Surface Particles." *IEEE Computer Graphics and Applications*. 13(4):18–24, 1993.

[Wang90]
   S-L C. Wang and J. Staudhammer. "Visibility Determination on Projected Grid Surfaces." *IEEE Computer Graphics and Applications*. 10(4):36–43, 1990.

[Watson81]
> D. F. Watson. "Computing the *n*-Dimensional Delaunay Tessellation with Application to Voronoi Polytopes." *The Computer Journal.* 24(2):167–172, 1981.

[Wixom78]
> J. Wixom and W. J. Gordon. "On Shepard's Method of Metric Interpolation to Scattered Bivariate and Multivariate Data." *Math. Comp.* 32:253–264, 1978.

[Yamrom95]
> B. Yamrom and K. M. Martin. "Vector Field Animation with Texture Maps." *IEEE Computer Graphics and Applications.* 15(2):22–24, 1995.

9.9 Exercises

9.1 Describe an approach to adapt dividing cubes to other 3D cell types. Can your method be adapted to 1D and 2D cells?

9.2 Discuss the advantages and disadvantages of representing surfaces with points versus polygons.

9.3 Streamribbons can be constructed by either i) connecting two adjacent streamlines with a surface, or ii) placing a ribbon on the streamline and orienting the surface according to streamwise vorticity vector. Discuss the differences in the resulting visualization.

9.4 Write the following programs to visualize velocity flow in the combustor.
a) Use vtkProbeFilter and vtkHedgeHog.
b) Use vtkProbeFilter and vtkStreamLine.
c) Use vtkProbeFilter and vtkWarpVector.
d) Use vtkProbeFilter and vtkVectorNorm.
e) Use vtkProbeFilter and vtkVectorDot.

9.5 Describe a method to extract geometry using an arbitrary dataset. (That is, extract geometry that lies within the culling dataset.) (*Hint:* how would you evaluate in/out of points?)

9.6 The filter vtkPolyDataNormals is often used in combination with the filters vtkSmoothPolyData and vtkContourFilter to generate smooth isosurfaces.
a) Write a class to combine these three filters into one filter. Can you eliminate intermediate storage?
b) How much error does vtkSmoothPolyData introduce into the isosurface? Can you think of a way to limit the error?
c) What is the difference between the surface normals created by vtkMarchingCubes and vtkPolyDataNormals?

9.7 Assume that we have a database consisting of interest rate R, monthly payment P, monthly income I, and days payment is late L.
a) If R, P, I are all sampled regularly, how would you visualize this data?
b) If all data is irregularly sampled, list three methods to visualize it.

9.8 Why do you think triangle strips are often faster to render than general polygons?

9.9   The normal generation technique described in this chapter creates consistently oriented
      surface normals.
      a) Do the normals point inside or outside of a closed surface?
      b) Describe a technique to orient normals so that they point out of a closed   surface.
      c) Can surface normals be used to eliminate visible triangles prior to
          rendering? (*Hint:* what is the relationship between camera view and surface nor-
      mal?)

9.10 Describe a technique to partially threshold a cell (i.e., to cut a cell as necessary to sat-
      isfy threshold criterion). Can an approach similar to marching cubes be used?

9.11 The class vtkRendererSource allows us to use the rendered image as a texture map (or
      image data dataset). Write a program to construct iterated textures, that is textures that
      consist of repeated images. Can the same image be generated using texture coordi-
      nates?

9.12 Describe how you would modify the decimation algorithm to treat general polygons.

9.13 Several examples in the text (e.g., deciFran.tcl and deciHawa.tcl) use the class
      vtkDecimate. Modify these examples to use the topology modifying progressive deci-
      mation algorithm (implemented in vtkDecimatePro). How much greater reduction can
      you achieve?

Image Processing

*I*n this chapter we describe the image processing components of the *Visualization Toolkit*. The focus is on key representational ideas, pipeline issues such as data streaming, and useful algorithms for improving the appearance and effectiveness of image data visualizations.

10.1 Introduction

Image processing has been a mainstay of computing since the advent of the digital computer. Early efforts focused on improving image content for human interpretation. More recently image processing has been utilized by practitioners of computer vision, the goal being the processing of image data for autonomous machine perception [Gonzalez92]. From the perspective of data visualization, image processing is used to manipulate image content to improve the results of subsequent processing and interpretation. For example, a CT or MRI scan may generate spurious signal noise or require image segmentation. Using the techniques of image processing, noise can be removed and automatic and semi-automatic segmentation can be performed on a slice by slice (i.e., image by image basis). As a result, isosurface generation, volume rendering, and other 3D techniques can be improved in appearance, accuracy, and effectiveness by applying techniques from image processing.

Since the focus of this text is on 3D graphics and visualization, this chapter treats image processing in a limited way. However, we would like to emphasize the interrelationship of image processing, computer graphics, and visualization. Often texts and courses treat these as distinctly separate disciplines, when in fact they are closely related (see "Imaging, Computer Graphics, and Visualization" on page 4).

The material presented here was selected to demonstrate a number of important points. First, the data flow or pipeline approach presented earlier is directly applicable to image processing, with the added benefit that we can easily implement data streaming and caching due to the regular nature of image data. Second, image processing algorithms can improve the results of visualization. We will show this through a number of useful examples. And finally, from a practical point of view, we wanted to demonstrate a system architecture that includes imaging, graphics, and visualization.

10.2 Data Representation

In this section we will briefly describe the data representation behind the imaging pipeline. As we saw earlier (see "The Dataset" on page 114), a dataset consists of both a structure (topology and geometry) and data attributes. Although in principle an image can be represented as a image data dataset, the special nature of image processing suggests a more complex representation, as we will soon see.

An image is typically used to refer to a 2D structured point dataset. More generally, in this chapter we will define an image as consisting of up to four dimensions: three spatial dimensions x, y, and z, and time t. The reason we add the time dimension is that images are frequently generated as a time series, and we often wish to access the data along the time axis. For example, we may plot the value at a point as a function of time.

As described in "Image Data" on page 124, an image has both regular topology and geometry. The regularity of the data lends itself to many special operations. In particular, we can support *data caching* and *streaming*, and operating on *regions of interest* in the data.

Regions of Interest

When data has a regular spatial organization, it is possible to request the data in pieces or regions of interest. For example, a mapper may need only a region of the data for its display, so loading or processing the whole dataset would be inefficient. An example of this is a two-dimensional viewer that displays only one slice of a large structured volume. By loading slices only as they are needed, disk access can be reduced, and memory conserved.

Although regions of interest can have arbitrary shapes, the regular structure of the data samples determines optimal region configurations. An image stored in a Cartesian coordinate system easily divides into smaller rectangular regions, while data sampled on a polar coordinate grid is best divided into pie-shaped regions (**Figure 10–1**). Therefore, operating on regions of data means that we process "windows" of data specified by (*min,max*) ranges of each dimension, or axis. For example, a region in a 2D image of dimensions 100 x 100 might be specified as *(25,49, 0,49)*, meaning that we would operate on a (25 x 50) window.

Streaming and Caching

The disadvantage of processing regions of interest is that the same data may be read and processed multiple times. If the viewer described above needs to cine (i.e., loop) through the

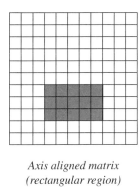

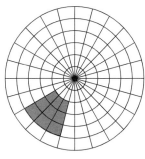

Axis aligned matrix
(rectangular region)

Polar coordinate grid
(pie-shaped region)

Figure 10–1 Axis aligned matrices naturally lend themselves to rectangular regions, and polar coordinate grids to pie-shaped regions.

slices, or interactively pan around a large image, it would be beneficial to have all the data loaded at once.

A compromise between the two extreme approaches of maintaining all data in memory or operating on small pieces is to update regions larger than requested, but not as large as the whole image. This is referred to as a data cache. Data caching anticipates future requests and works well in most cases. However, it breaks down when there is little or no coherence between subsequent requests.

With the region-processing model, the data objects can be thought of as caches that hold any number of regions. There are numerous caching strategies for saving and releasing regions that can be quite complex. The simplest strategy saves only a single region at any one time. If subsequent requests are completely contained in the cached region, no further processing is required. An alternative strategy might divide an image into tiled regions of all the same size. When a region larger than the tile is requested, multiple tiles are updated to cover the region. When designing a caching strategy, it is important to consider the overhead of copying data to change its format. Some of the advantages of complex strategies are lost when all the factors are considered.

Given the ability to operate on regions of data, it is a small step to *stream* operations on a whole dataset. Streaming is the process of pulling regions of data in a continual flow through the pipeline. For instance, a pixel histogram mapper could request single pixels as it accumulates values in its bins. Large datasets can be processed in this manner without ever having to load more than a few pixels at a time. If multiple processors are available, region processing can also be used to split a task into multiple pieces for load balancing and faster execution.

Attribute Data and Components

Unlike visualization algorithms that may generate normals, vectors, tensors, and texture coordinates, image processing algorithms generally process attribute data consisting of scalar data. Often the data is a single component (e.g., a gray-scale image), but frequently color images (three components of RGB, for example) may also be processed.

In the *Visualization Toolkit* imaging pipeline, attribute data is represented as *n*-dimensional component data. Refer to "Putting It All Together" on page 387 to see the implementation details for component data, regions of interest, streaming, and caching.

10.3 Algorithms

This section provides an overview and examples for important image processing algorithms. The importance of the algorithms is measured on their relevance to 3D data visualization. Topics include: removing noise, smoothing, reducing sampling artifacts, image enhancement, segmentation, and morphological operators such as erosion and dilation.

Image Restoration

Noise and other artifacts are inherent in all methods of data acquisition. Since artifacts can degrade the visual appearance and analysis of images, the first step of image processing is often restoration. Knowledge of the statistical properties of artifacts allows filters to selectively remove them with minimal impact on the underlying data. For example, most of the power of typical images lie in low frequencies, while white noise is evenly distributed across the frequency spectrum. In this situation, low-pass filters eliminate much of the noise, but leave most of the image intact.

A simple implementation of a low-pass smoothing filter is convolution with a kernel with all positive values. The typical kernels used for smoothing are either constant across a circular neighborhood, or have a Gaussian profile (see **Figure 10–2**). Gaussian smoothing results in better-looking images than smoothing with constant kernels, but can be more computationally expensive because of the large kernel size necessary to capture the Gaussian profile. Smoothing becomes even more expensive when it is generalized to three-dimensional datasets, and three-dimensional kernels.

One way to speed Gaussian smoothing is to decompose the filter into two 1D convolutions. Since the 2D Gaussian function is separable,

$$g(i, j) = \frac{1}{2\pi\sigma^2}\exp\left(-\frac{i^2 + j^2}{2\sigma^2}\right) = \frac{1}{\sqrt{2\pi}\sigma}\exp\left(-\frac{i^2}{2\sigma^2}\right)\frac{1}{\sqrt{2\pi}\sigma}\exp\left(-\frac{j^2}{2\sigma^2}\right) \qquad \textbf{(10-1)}$$

smoothing along the *x* axis and then along the *y* axis with 1D Gaussian kernels is equivalent to convolving with a 2D Gaussian kernel. It is also possible to approximate Gaussian smoothing by convolving with a constant binary kernel multiple times.

Nonlinear Smoothing

One problem with simple smoothing to remove noise is that edges are blurred. Although high frequencies make up a small part of images, the human visual system is acutely sensitive to high frequencies in the spatial form of edges. In fact, most of the low frequencies in an image are discarded by the visual system before it even leaves the retina. One approach to smoothing that preserves edges is anisotropic diffusion. This filter smooths relatively flat regions of an image, but does not diffuse across abrupt transitions. The diffusion is iterated until the

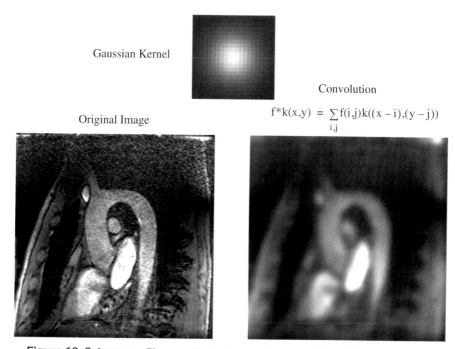

Gaussian Kernel

Convolution

Original Image

$$f*k(x,y) = \sum_{i,j} f(i,j)k((x-i),(y-j))$$

Figure 10–2 Low-pass filters can be implemented as convolution with a Gaussian kernel. The Gaussian kernel displayed on top has been magnified for this figure (GaussianSmooth.tcl).

desired level of noise reduction is reached. Two possible diffusion criteria are: Diffuse only when the gradient magnitude is below a specified value, or diffuse two pixels only when the difference between the pixels is lower than a specified constant.

A median filter also smooths while preserving edges. This filter replaces each pixel with the median value of the scalar values in a neighborhood centered on the pixel. Median filters are most effective on high amplitude noise that has a low probability of occurring (see **Figure 10–3**). There are two ways to control the amount and scale of noise removed: The size of the neighborhood can be varied, or the filter can be applied multiple times. This median filter preserves edges; however, it does round corners and remove thin lines. The hybrid median filter was developed to address this behavior. It operates on a 5 x 5 neighborhood around each pixel. The algorithm consists of two steps: first the median values of an "x"-shaped and "+"-shaped neighborhoods are computed, then the median of these two values and the center-pixel value is computed to give the final result. The hybrid median has a fixed size neighborhood, but can be applied multiple times to further reduce noise (**Figure 10–4**).

Low Frequency Artifacts

An artifact called aliasing occurs when subsampling and is often associated with stair-stepping edges. Sampling theory proves that discrete sampled signals with spacing S, completely describe continuous functions composed of frequencies less than $S/2$. When a signal is sub-

Original Image   Noisy Image

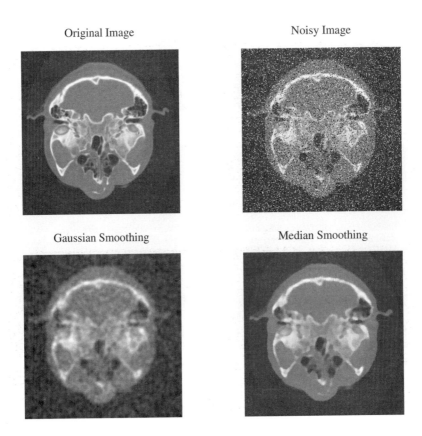

Gaussian Smoothing   Median Smoothing

Figure 10–3 Comparison of Gaussian and Median smoothing for reducing low-probability high-amplitude noise (`MedianComparison.tcl`).

sampled, its capacity to hold high frequency information is reduced. However, the high frequency energy does not disappear. It wraps around the frequency spectrum appearing as a low frequency alias artifact (**Figure 10–5**). The solution, which eliminates this artifact, is to low-pass filter before subsampling. Low-pass smoothing reduces the high frequency range of an image that would cause aliasing.

The same aliasing phenomena occurs when acquiring data. If a signal from an analog source contains high frequencies, saving the analog data in a discrete form requires subsampling that will introduce alias artifacts. For this reason, it is common practice to acquire data at high resolutions, then smooth and subsample to reduce the image to a manageable size.

Low-frequency artifacts, other than aliasing, can also occur when acquiring data. One example is base-line drift. As data is acquired over time, the average value (base line) of the signal can slowly change. This drift can be removed with a high-pass filter after data acquisition. It is also possible to acquire a second dataset that isolates the baseline. Subtracting the baseline from the primary signal removes the drift artifact. In general, it is better to measure the artifact than risk making wrong assumptions that might adversely affect the actual data.

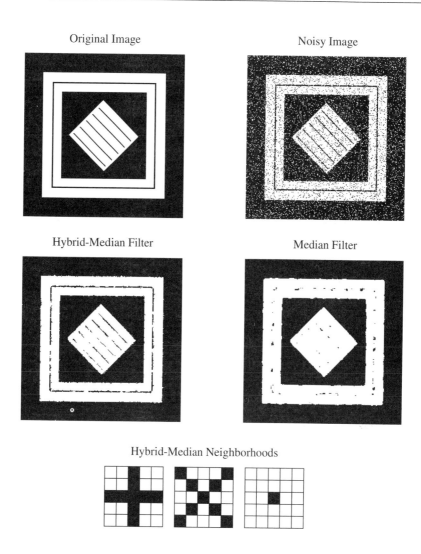

Figure 10–4 Comparison of median and hybrid-median filters. The hybrid filter preserves corners and thin lines, better than the median filter. The lower patterns represent the three neighborhoods used to compute the hybrid median (see the example Tcl script `HybridMedianComparison.tcl`).

Another gradual change across an image is caused by sensor position. The amplitude of a measured signal usually attenuates as the source moves away from the sensor. An example of this attenuation artifact is seen in surface-coil-MRI images as shown in **Figure 10–6**. If the attenuation profile is known, then the artifact can be removed by dividing the original data with the profile. Since this artifact can be characterized by a small set of parameters like sensor position and range, it is possible to automatically determine the attenuation profile from the data. Like most artifacts, nonuniform attenuation tends to hide the information in an

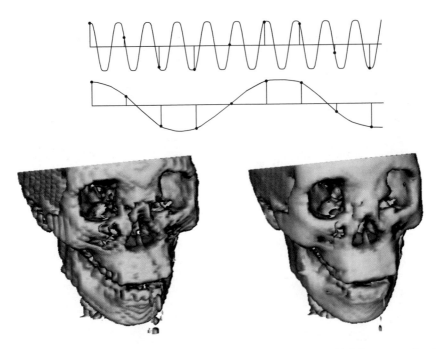

Figure 10–5 This figure demonstrates aliasing that occurs when a high-frequency signal is subsampled. High frequencies appear as low frequency artifacts. The lower left image is an isosurface of a skull after subsampling. The right image used a low-pass filter before subsampling to reduce aliasing (`IsoSubsample.tcl`).

image. Given a function that measures the amount of information in an image, gradient descent and other search strategies can find the optimal attenuation parameters.

Image Enhancement

Often datasets contain information or have dynamic range that cannot be completely displayed in a single image. X-Ray ComputedTomography (CT) datasets, for example, can have 10 times the scalar resolution of the typical computer monitor capable of displaying 256 shades of gray. One method used for conveying information buried in the large dynamic range of these medical datasets is to allow a user to interactively set the color map with a window-level transfer function. The user can then choose to display the range of data they find most important as shown in **Figure 10–7**. The slope of the transfer function determines the amount of contrast in the final image. Slopes greater than one increase contrast, and slopes less than one decrease contrast. All contrast and information is lost in the scalar ranges where the transfer function is constant and has zero slope.

The short fall of simple window-level transfer functions are their limited shape. More general nonlinear transfer functions can be more appropriate for certain datasets. One example is the logarithmic transfer function, $f(x) = K\log(1 + x)$, which can be used to display image power spectrums (**Figure 10–10**). Most of the pixels in the power spectrum represent

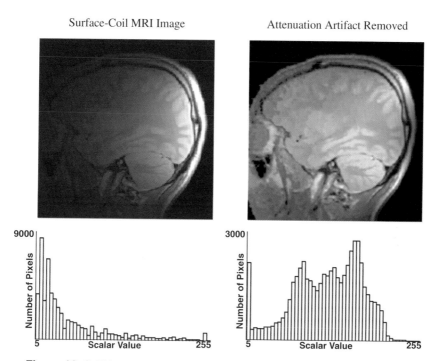

Figure 10–6 This MRI image illustrates attenuation that can occur due to sensor position. The artifact is removed by dividing by the attenuation profile determined manually. This histograms shows how the artifact hides information in the form of scalar value clusters (`Attenuation.tcl`).

high frequencies, and have small values. However the smaller population of low-frequency pixels often have large values. The logarithmic function has the largest slope near zero, and therefore leaves the most contrast for pixels with small values. However, when the constant K is chosen correctly, none of the large pixel values become completely saturated.

To take advantage of all the available display contrast, images should have a uniform distribution of intensities. For continuous images, this intensity distribution is called the *probability density function* (PDF). For discretely-sampled images with discrete scalar values, the image histogram has the same information as the PDF (**Figure 10–7**). A histogram breaks the scalar range of an image into discrete nonoverlapping bins. Each bin has a pixel count that represents the number of pixels whose scalar value falls in that bin's range.

To achieve the goal of a uniform scalar histogram, transfer functions can be used to spread out clusters in the histogram and compress scalar ranges that are under-represented in the image. To maintain the general appearance of the image, the transfer function should be monotonically increasing so that the brightness relation is maintained. To spread out clusters in the histogram, the slope of the transfer function should be large where the scalar densities are the highest, and the slope should be small in empty regions of the histogram.

Histogram equalization is an algorithm that automatically generates a tailored transfer function to increase contrast in an image. For continuous images, the transfer function is simply the cumulative distribution function (CDF) which is defined as the integral of the PDF.

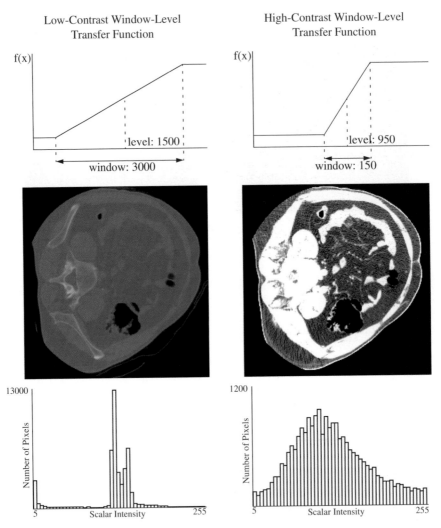

Figure 10–7 The top charts show two window-level transfer functions. The resulting images are displayed in the middle row. The bottom row shows image histograms of the images.

By definition, the CDF function has a large slope where the PDF has the largest value, and therefore gives the greatest contrast to scalar ranges that occur most frequently in an image. The result of using the CDF as a transfer function is an image with an ideal constant scalar distribution. For discrete images and image histograms, a discrete version of the CDF function can be used. However, because of the discrete approximation, the resulting image is not guaranteed to have a constant histogram (**Figure 10–8**).

High-pass filters can also be used to compress the range of an image. Since low frequencies account for much of the dynamic range of an image but carry little information, a high-pass filter can significantly decrease an image's scalar range and emphasize hidden

Original Image and Its Histogram

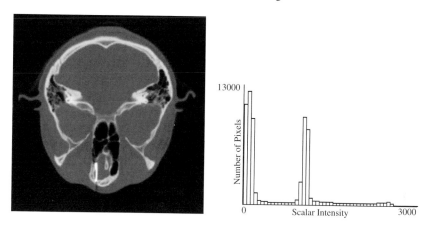

Computed Transfer Function

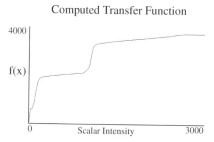

Resulting Image and Its Histogram

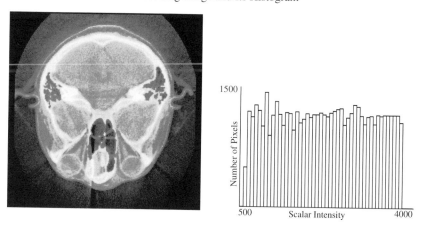

Figure 10–8 Histogram equalization automatically computes a transfer function that produces an image with a nearly constant scalar histogram (HistogramEqualization.tcl).

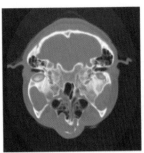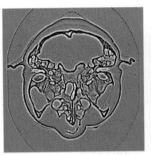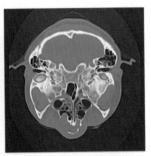

Figure 10–9 High-pass filters can extract and enhance edges in an image. Subtraction of the Laplacian (middle) from the original image (left) results in edge enhancement or a sharpening operation (right) (`EnhanceEdges.tcl`).

details. The Laplacian filter, which is a second derivative operation, is one implementation of a high-pass filter. It eliminates constant and low frequencies leaving only high-frequency edges. The output of the Laplacian can be subtracted from the original image to produce edge enhancement or sharpening of an image (**Figure 10–9**).

Frequency Domain

The Fourier transform belongs to a class of filters that fundamentally change the representation of an image without changing its information. The output of the Fourier transform is in the frequency domain. Each pixel is a complex number describing the contribution of a sinusoidal function to the original image. The magnitude of the pixel encodes the amplitude of the sinusoid, and the orientation of the complex pixel encodes the sinusoid's phase. Each pixel represents a sinusoid with different orientation and frequency. The reverse Fourier transform converts a frequency domain image back to the original spatial domain (**Figure 10–10**).

Low-pass and high-pass filtering become trivial in the frequency domain. A portion of the pixels are simply masked or attenuated. **Figure 10–11** shows a high pass Butterworth filter that attenuates the frequency domain image with the function H

$$H(u,v) = \frac{1}{1 + [C^{2n}/(u^2 + v^2)^n]} \qquad (10\text{-}2)$$

The gradual attenuation of the filter is important. The ideal high-pass filter, shown in the same figure, simply masks a set of pixels in the frequency domain. The abrupt transition causes a ringing effect in the spatial domain (as the figure illustrates).

Although any filter that operates in the frequency domain can also be implemented in the spatial domain, some operations are less computationally expensive and easier to implement in the frequency domain. To perform similar filtering of **Figure 10–11** in the spatial domain would require convolution with a large kernel and would be slow. In general, convolution with large kernels is more efficient when performed in the frequency domain. Multiplication, $\alpha\beta$, in the frequency domain, is equivalent to convolution, $a*b$, in the spatial domain

$$F(u,v) = \frac{1}{MN} \sum_{x=0}^{M-1} \sum_{y=0}^{N-1} f(x,y) \exp\left[-j2\pi\left(\frac{xv}{M} + \frac{vy}{N}\right)\right]$$

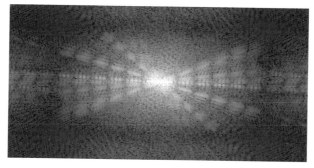

Figure 10–10 The discrete Fourier transform changes an image from the spatial domain into the frequency domain, where each pixel represents a sinusoidal function. This figure show an image and its power spectrum displayed using a logarithmic transfer function (VTKSpectrum.tcl).

(and vice versa). In these equations, α is the Fourier transform of a, and β is the Fourier transform of b.

In order to make frequency-domain processing feasible, it is first necessary to minimize the cost of transforming from the spatial to frequency domain and back. There exist fast algorithms that implement the Fourier transform and its inverse. First, the Fourier transform is decomposable, so a 2D transform can be implemented by first taking the 1D Fourier transform of all the rows, and then taking the Fourier transform of all the columns of an image. Second, the complexity of one-dimensional Fourier transforms can be reduced with an algorithm called the fast Fourier transform (FFT). It works by recursively factoring the number samples, N, into its prime components. If N is prime and not factorable, then the transform is completed in one step that is order $O(N^2)$ complexity. If N is divisible by two, the array of numbers is divided into two parts that are transformed separately and then combined. If N is a power of two, then the algorithm executes in order $O(N \log N)$ time. For this reason, it is more efficient to process images with sizes that are powers of two (e.g., 512 x 512) than other sized images. For non-power of two images it may be faster to pad the image to a size that is a power of two size before processing.

Ideal High-Pass Filter   Butterworth High-Pass Filter

$$H(u, v) = \begin{cases} 1 & if(u^2 + v^2 < C^2) \\ 0 & otherwise \end{cases}$$

$$H(u,v) = \frac{1}{1 + [C^{2n}/(u^2 + v^2)^n]}$$

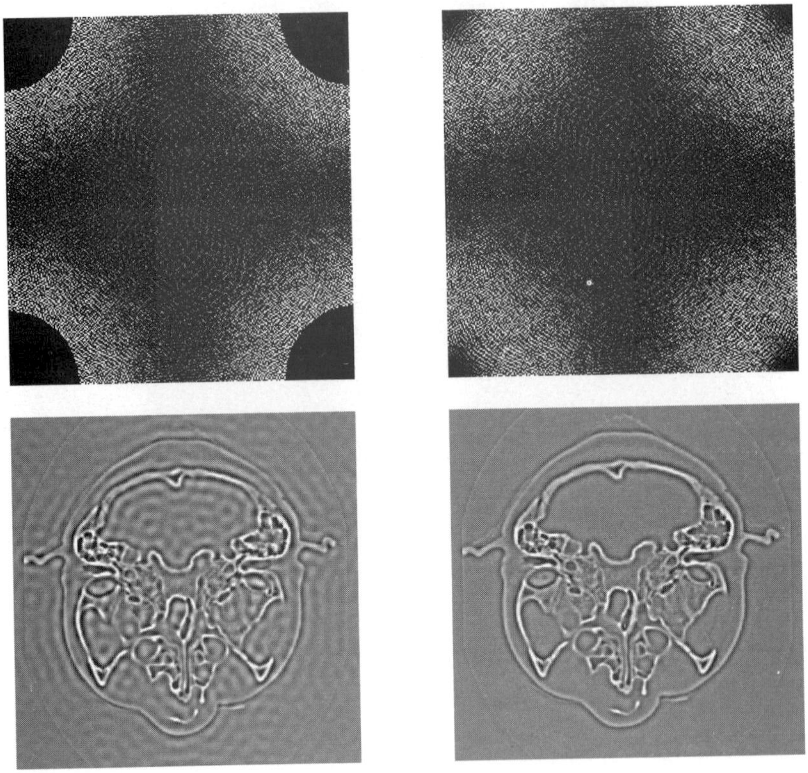

Figure 10–11 This figure shows two high-pass filters in the frequency domain. The Butterworth high-pass filter has a gradual attenuation that avoids ringing produced by the ideal high-pass filter with an abrupt transition (`IdealHighPass.tcl`).

An important point about the discrete Fourier transform is that it treats the image as a periodic function. This means the pixels on the right border are adjacent to pixels on the left border. Since there is usually no physical relationship between these pixels, the artificial horizontal and vertical edges can distort the frequency spectrum and subsequent processing. To reduce these artifacts, the original image can be multiplied by a window function that becomes zero at the borders. Another approach removes these artificial edges by smoothing only along the borders.

In both of these approaches, a portion of the original image is lost, so only the central portion of an image can be processed. If this is unacceptable, another solution is to double the

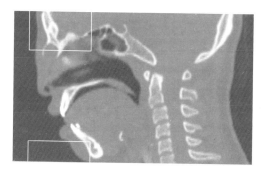

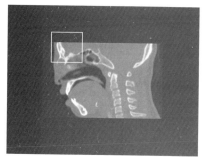 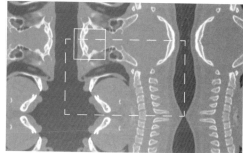

Figure 10–12 Convolution in frequency space treats the image as a periodic function. A large kernel can pick up features from both sides of the image. The lower-left image has been padded with zeros to eliminate wraparound during convolution. On the right, mirror padding has been used to remove artificial edges introduced by borders (`Pad.tcl`).

dimensions of the original image with a mirror-padding filter. The intermediate image is periodic and continuous (**Figure 10–12**).

Image Segmentation

Segmentation is the process of classifying pixels in an image or volume. It can be one of the most difficult tasks in the visualization process. One form of segmentation takes an image as input, and outputs a map that contains a classification for each pixel. The output of such a segmentation filter usually has binary or discrete values for each pixel; however, it is also possible to output a fuzzy classification where the pixel's scalar value represents a measure of confidence in the classification.

A simple example of a one-parameter segmentation is a threshold filter used to mark bone in a CT dataset. Since bone has the largest scalar value, it is easy to select a threshold that separates bone from the rest of the image.

For other tissues and other imaging modalities, segmentation is usually more difficult. Noise in the image and overlapping scalar values of tissues can decrease the effectiveness of simple threshold segmentation. By using two parameters, the threshold can segment pixels with a range of scalar values. The extra parameter allows more control over the resulting segmentation, but also doubles the complexity of selecting the parameters.

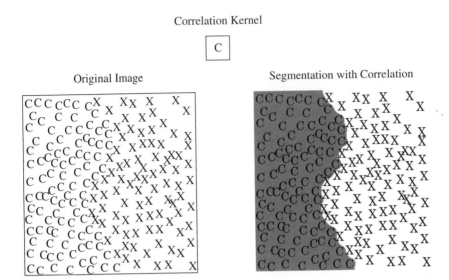

Correlation Kernel

Figure 10–13 A pipeline containing correlation, thresholding, dilation, and erosion is used here to segment a region composed of "C"s. The left image shows the original image. The right image shows the segmented region superimposed on the original image.

Images can be preprocessed to segment images based on more complex features such as textures. Sometimes textures in tissues add information useful for segmentation. Texture sensitive filters like Laplacian and gradient magnitude can discriminate between different textures. Additional filters that can be used for texture segmentation are the range, variance, and correlation filters. The range filter simply reports the difference between the maximum and minimum values in a neighborhood around each pixel, and the variance filter computes the variance of the neighborhood pixels relative to the center pixel.

Figure 10–13 shows an example of how a correlation filter can be used for segmentation. A correlation filter is similar to convolution. The kernel is shifted across the image, and for each location the dot product between the image and the kernel gives a measure of correlation between the two. The output of the correlation filter is large everywhere the pattern occurs in the image, but small at other locations. Because the resulting map is sparse, additional postprocessing is required to find a uniform, segmented region. In this example, dilation followed by erosion was used to close the gaps between the patterns. (Dilations and erosion are discussed in the next section.)

Postprocessing

Although preprocessing can do a lot to improve segmentation results, postprocessing can also be useful. Morphological filters, which operate on binary or discrete images, can be useful for manipulating the shape of the segmented regions. In this brief discussion we will only consider operations that use circular footprints, even though these morphological filters can be defined much more generally. Erosion is implemented by removing pixels within a specified distance of a border. For each pixel not in the segmented region, all the neighbors in a

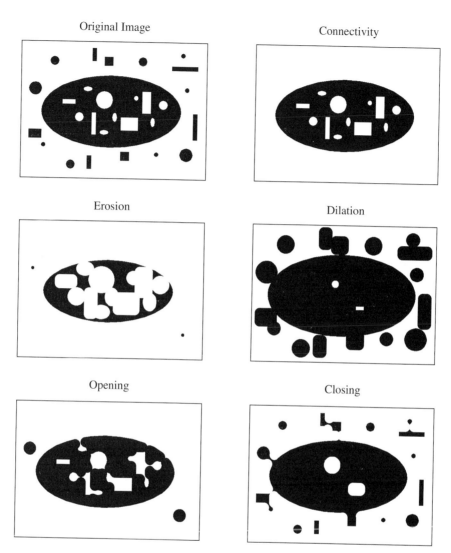

Figure 10–14 This figure demonstrates various binary filters that can alter the shape of segmented regions (`MorphComparison.tcl`).

circular region around the pixels are turned off. This erosion filter shrinks the segmented region and small isolated regions disappear.

The opposite of erosion is dilation. This filter grows the area of segmented regions. Small holes in the segmented region are completely closed. Any pixel not in the segmented region but near the region is turned on. Dilation and erosion are dual filters with nearly identical implementations. Dilating the "on" pixels is equivalent to eroding "off" pixels in a binary image (see **Figure 10–14**).

Closing is the serial application of first dilation and then erosion. When an image is dilated small holes in the map disappear. However, dilation alone also grows the boundaries of the segmented regions. When dilation is followed by erosion in a closing operation, small holes are removed; however, the boundary of the segmented regions remain in the same general location. Opening is the dual of closing. Opening removes small islands of pixels. It is implemented with an initial erosion, followed by a dilation.

Connectivity filters can also remove small regions without affecting the remaining boundaries of segmented regions. This set of filters separate the segmented pixels into equivalence classes based on a neighbor relation. Two pixels belong to the same class if they are touching. There are two common neighbor relations in two-dimensional images: four connectivity considers pixels neighbors if they are edge neighbors, and eight connectivity considers pixels neighbors if pixels share any vertex.

After the pixels have been assigned an equivalence class, various methods are used to determine which groups of pixels will pass through the filter, and which classes will be eliminated. The island-removal filter is a connectivity filter that removes groups that have too few pixels. Seed connectivity allows the user to explicitly specify which groups will pass through the filter. The user or application specifies a set of seeds. Any group that includes a seed makes it through the filter. Groups that do not contain seeds are removed. This filter is similar to the seed-connectivity filter; however, the seeds are supplied in a second image. First the intersection between the segmented image and the seed image is taken. Each remaining pixel is then added to a set of seeds.

Multispectral Segmentation

From everyday experience we know that it is easier to see structure and information in color images than in gray-scale images. This is because each pixel contains more information in the red, blue, and green components than a single component gray-scale pixel. One way to segment multispectral images is to separate the components and threshold them individually and then combine the resulting binary images with logic filters. This allows selection of rectangular patched areas in the color/component space of the pixels.

By using multiple thresholds combined with multiple levels of logic filters, it is possible to specify arbitrary areas in the component's space for segmentation. However, it can be easier and more efficient to transform the components into a different coordinate system before the threshold operation. The simplest example of this is to threshold a projection of the components. This is equivalent to a threshold after performing a dot product between the components of a pixel and a constant-direction vector. This divides the component space into two areas separated by a hyper-plane.

Another example of a coordinate transformation is conversion from red, green, blue (RGB) color component to hue, saturation, value (HSV) representation (see "Color" on page 37). Segmentation of images based on hue and color saturation is difficult in RGB space, but trivial in HSV space.

Color is not the only multispectral information that can be used for segmentation. It is possible to take advantage of multispectral segmentation even if the original dataset has only one component. Additional images can be created from spatial information of the images using spatial filters. These multiple images can then be combined into one multicomponent image, then multicomponent segmentation can proceed.

Typically, the number of free parameters in a filter is directly correlated to the dimensionality of the pixels; and although additional parameters make a filter more powerful, it also makes it more difficult to find an appropriate set of parameter values. There are supervised and unsupervised algorithms that can be used to automatically select the best set of segmentation parameters, but discussion of these is outside the scope of this book.

10.4 Putting It All Together

We suggest that you review the code accompanying the images in this chapter to see how to use the VTK imaging pipeline. In this section we will explain some of the implementation details of image data. We will also show how to mix the imaging and visualization pipelines, and how to use imaging filters to perform regression testing.

Data Representation

In the imaging pipeline, the class for representing and manipulating data is vtkImageData (see "Types of Datasets" on page 122 for more information). In addition, the data extent (topological extent specification) plays a vital role in controlling how images are processed.

vtkImageData actually represents the image data. Internally, it refers to an instance of vtkDataArray. Therefore, its native representation data type may be any one of unsigned char, char, unsigned short, short, int, float, or any concrete type of vtkDataArray. Please remember that vtkImageData can represent 1D, 2D (image), and 3D (volume) data.

There are three types of data extents in the imaging pipeline. In general, any rectangular piece of image data can be described by the extent six-vector ($i_{min},i_{max},\ j_{min},j_{max}$, k_{min},k_{max}). The WholeExtent refers to the original data size of an image and is derived from the image dimensions. The UpdateExtent is the extent that is processed by a particular filter during execution.

Extents are used to manage the streaming of data through the visualization pipeline, as well as to coordinate the multi-threaded parallel processing that the imaging pipeline uses throughout. By controlling the extents, it is possible to greatly reduce the amount of memory used by the pipeline. For more information, see *The VTK User's Guide* sold by Kitware.

In the VTK imaging pipeline, point attribute data is represented differently than in the visualization pipeline. In the imaging pipeline point attribute data is represented as n components per data point. Typically n is one for gray-scale data, or three for color data but, in general, can be any positive number.

Create an Image

This example demonstrates how to directly create an image using C++ code. Typically, you will use an image reader or procedurally create an image from a source object. The example shown here creates an vtkImageData and then fills it with an image of interfering sinusoidal grids

$$F(x, y) \ = \ \left(\sin\left(\frac{x}{10}\right) + \sin\left(\frac{y}{10}\right) \right)$$

$$(10\text{-}3)$$

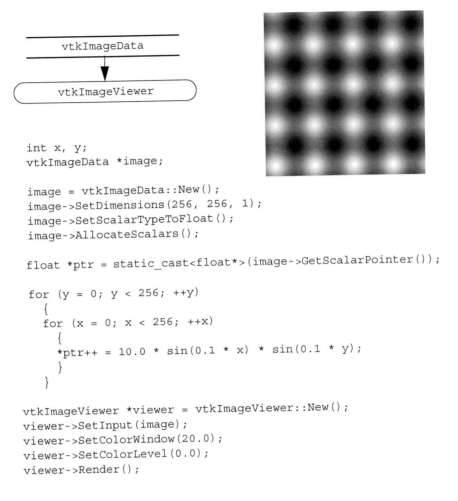

```
                int x, y;
                vtkImageData *image;

                image = vtkImageData::New();
                image->SetDimensions(256, 256, 1);
                image->SetScalarTypeToFloat();
                image->AllocateScalars();

                float *ptr = static_cast<float*>(image->GetScalarPointer());

                for (y = 0; y < 256; ++y)
                  {
                  for (x = 0; x < 256; ++x)
                    {
                    *ptr++ = 10.0 * sin(0.1 * x) * sin(0.1 * y);
                    }
                  }

                vtkImageViewer *viewer = vtkImageViewer::New();
                viewer->SetInput(image);
                viewer->SetColorWindow(20.0);
                viewer->SetColorLevel(0.0);
                viewer->Render();
```

Figure 10–15 Creating an image of two interfering sinusoidal gratings in an image dataset. The resulting image has dimensions 256^2.

Note that direct pointer access is used to fill the image. The AllocateScalars() method allocates enough memory for the dimensions provided.

Gradient Magnitude

In this example we demonstrate a lengthy imaging pipeline. The basic purpose of the pipeline is to visualize information about the image gradient. The gradient direction and magnitude are mapped into the hue and saturation components of the color HSV space, respectively. The pipeline, resulting image, and a portion of the code are shown in **Figure 10–16**.

The pipeline demonstrates some interesting tricks. The first three filters read CT data of the human head (i.e., using vtkImageReader), magnify the image by a factor of four (vtkImageMagnify), and then smooth the data (since magnification uses linear interpolation, introducing some sharp edges). The next filter actually computes the 2D gradient (vtkImageGradient), placing the *x-y* gradient components into its output.

The next series of filters is where the fun begins. First, the data is converted to polar coordinates (vtkImageEuclideanToPolar). We use this filter because we want to operate in color HSV space (see "Color" on page 37). The image magnitude is to be mapped into saturation value, while the gradient direction is mapped into hue value (remember hue is represented as an angle on the HSV color wheel). The filter vtkImageConstantPad is used to add a third component to the data, since the gradient filter only generated two components, and we need three components to represent color. The vtkImageExtractComponents is used to rearrange the components into HSV order. Finally, the data is converted back into RGB color space with vtkImageHSVToRGB. (This is necessary because the image viewer expects RGB values.)

Image Warping

In this example we combine the imaging and visualization pipelines. Imaging filters are used to read in an image (vtkBMPReader) and then convert it to grayscale (vtkImageLuminance). The data, which is a image data dataset, is then passed down the visualization pipeline as polygons using vtkImageDataGeometryFilter. Next we warp the data in the direction perpendicular to the image plane using the visualization filter vtkWarpScalar. The vtkMergeFilter is used to combine the warped geometry (now vtkPolyData) with the original image data from the reader. (Note that in this example the vtkMergeFilter takes two inputs.) The pipeline, example output, and sample code are shown in **Figure 10–17**.

Regression Testing

In our work with VTK, we often need to perform software testing. The testing may be necessary because we've added new classes or features to the system, modified old code, or are simply testing a graphics library or new piece of hardware. We use a powerful testing procedure based on processing the output of the system, which is typically an image. We refer to the testing process as regression testing.

Regression testing is based on the following procedure. A test program (typically a Tcl/Tk script) is written that exercises a portion of the code. In our example, we will assume that we are testing a feature of implicit modelling. The output of the script is an image with a fixed view, as shown in **Figure 10–18**(a). To perform the test, we compare the output of the test program with a previously stored image, or "valid" image (**Figure 10–18**(b)). The valid image was generated when we initially created the object or objects to be tested, and is assumed to be the correct output. Then, we use a the filter vtkImageDifference to compare the test image with the valid image. This filter takes into account dithering and anti-aliasing effects, and creates an output image representing the difference between the test image and valid image (**Figure 10–18**(c)). It also reports the difference in the images in terms of a pixel count. To determine whether the test is passed, we compare the pixel count with a threshold value (for example, 10 pixels).

Our regression testing procedure cannot test the original implementation of an object or objects. The developer must verify that the valid image is indeed correct. However, the pro-

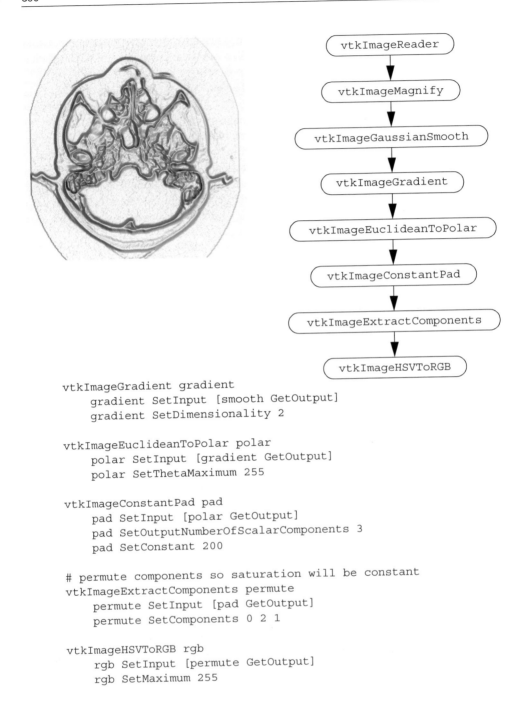

```
vtkImageGradient gradient
    gradient SetInput [smooth GetOutput]
    gradient SetDimensionality 2

vtkImageEuclideanToPolar polar
    polar SetInput [gradient GetOutput]
    polar SetThetaMaximum 255

vtkImageConstantPad pad
    pad SetInput [polar GetOutput]
    pad SetOutputNumberOfScalarComponents 3
    pad SetConstant 200

# permute components so saturation will be constant
vtkImageExtractComponents permute
    permute SetInput [pad GetOutput]
    permute SetComponents 0 2 1

vtkImageHSVToRGB rgb
    rgb SetInput [permute GetOutput]
    rgb SetMaximum 255
```

Figure 10–16 An imaging pipeline to visualize gradient information. The gradient direction is mapped into color hue value while the gradient magnitude is mapped into the color saturation (ImageGradient.tcl).

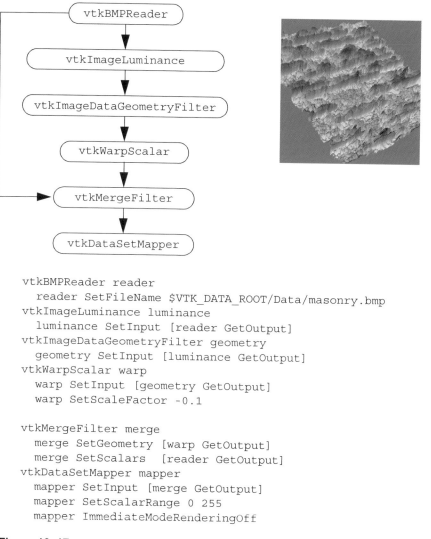

```
vtkBMPReader reader
    reader SetFileName $VTK_DATA_ROOT/Data/masonry.bmp
vtkImageLuminance luminance
    luminance SetInput [reader GetOutput]
vtkImageDataGeometryFilter geometry
    geometry SetInput [luminance GetOutput]
vtkWarpScalar warp
    warp SetInput [geometry GetOutput]
    warp SetScaleFactor -0.1

vtkMergeFilter merge
    merge SetGeometry [warp GetOutput]
    merge SetScalars  [reader GetOutput]
vtkDataSetMapper mapper
    mapper SetInput [merge GetOutput]
    mapper SetScalarRange 0 255
    mapper ImmediateModeRenderingOff
```

Figure 10–17 Combining the imaging and visualization pipelines to deform an image in the z-direction (`imageWarp.tcl`). The vtkMergeFilter is used to combine the warped surface with the original color data.

cess is invaluable for finding and correcting problems due to incremental code changes (e.g., bug fixes, enhancements, etc.) Furthermore, the test can be run as a batch process, with a simple pass/fail output, and an image to show the differences.

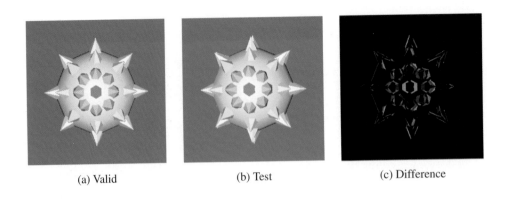

| (a) Valid | (b) Test | (c) Difference |

```
vtkRendererSource renSrc
    renSrc WholeWindowOn
    renSrc SetInput ren1

vtkPNGReader pnm
    pnm SetFileName "valid/$afile.png"

vtkImageDifference imgDiff
    imgDiff SetInput [renSrc GetOutput]
    imgDiff SetImage [pnm GetOutput]
    imgDiff Update

if {[imgDiff GetThresholdedError] < 10.0} {
    puts "Passed Test for $afile"
} else {
    puts "Failed Test for $afile with an error \
            of [imgDiff GetThresholdedError]"
    vtkPNGWriter pnmw
        pnmw SetInput [imgDiff GetOutput]
        pnmw SetFileName "$afile.error.png"
        pnmw Write
    vtkPNGWriter pnmw2
        pnmw2 SetInput [renSrc GetOutput]
        pnmw2 SetFileName "$afile.test.png"
        pnmw2 Write
}
```

Figure 10–18 Software regression testing using image processing. A test image is taken from the renderer and compared with a valid image stored on disk. (a) shows the valid image. (b) shows the test image (artificially modified by slight camera rotation). (c) shows the image difference. The code fragment above is extracted from the regression testing procedure.

10.5 Chapter Summary

Image processing can be used to improve 3D visualizations of structured point datasets (images and volumes). Important techniques include smoothing, filtering, morphological operators such as erosion and dilation, and segmentation.

Because of the regular topology and geometry of images, it is possible to design caching and streaming pipelines to reduce memory requirements. In the *Visualization Toolkit*, the imaging pipeline is integrated with the visualization pipeline. This capability enables the creation of applications that combine computer graphics, imaging, and visualization.

10.6 Bibliographic Notes

Many books are available describing imaging algorithms. Several are listed below including [Gonzalez92] and [Russ95]. The texts [Pavlidis82] and [Wolberg90] are imaging books with somewhat of a computer graphics and/or visualization slant. The text [Robb95] is an outstanding reference for medical imaging and visualization.

Technical references describing VTK's unique streaming visualization pipeline are available [Law99] [Martin01]. Using this approach, data sizes of approximately a petabyte in size have been processed.

10.7 References

[Ballard82]
> D. H. Ballard, C. M. Brown. *Compute Vision*. Prentice Hall, Inc., Englewood Cliffs, NJ, 1982.

[Davies97]
> E. R. Davies. *Machine Vision Theory Algorithms Practicalities 2d ed*. Academic Press, San Diego, CA, 1997.

[Gonzalez92]
> R. C. Gonzalez, R. E. Woods. *Digital Imaging Processing*. Addison-Wesley Publishing Co., Reading, MA, 1992.

[Law99]
> C. Charles Law, K. M. Martin, W. J. Schroeder, J. E. Temkin. A Multi-Threaded Streaming Pipeline Architecture for Large Structured Data Sets. In *Proceedings. of Visualization '99*, IEEE, October 1999.

[Martin01]
> K. M. Martin, B. Geveci, J. Ahrens, C. Law. Large Scale Data Visualization Using Parallel Data Streaming. *IEEE Computer Graphics & Applications*, July 2001.

[Niblack86]
> W. Niblack. *An Introduction to Digital Image Processing*. Prentice Hall, Inc., London, 1986.

[Pavlidis82]
> T. Pavlidis. *Algorithms for Graphics and Image Processing*. Computer Science Press, Rockville, MD, 1982.

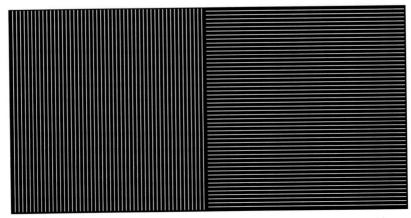

Figure 10–19 Sample image for segmentation exercise (`HVLines.tcl`)

[Robb95]
R. Robb. *Three-Dimensional Biomedical Imaging Principles and Practice*. VCH Publishers, New York, NY, 1995.

[Russ95]
J. C. Russ. *The Image Processing Handbook 2d ed.* CRC Press, Inc, Boca Raton, FL, 1995.

[Wolberg90]
G. Wolberg. *Digital Image Warping*. IEEE Computer Society Press, Los Alamitos, CA, 1990.

10.8 Exercises

10.1 Create an image pipeline that will segment the area with vertical lines in **Figure 10–19**.

10.2 Decomposition can increase the speed of an operation.
a) Prove that 3D Gaussian smoothing can be decomposed into three 1D operations.
b) Determine the complexity of the decomposed filter and the same filter implemented as a 3D convolution.
c) Under what conditions can constant smoothing be decomposed into 1D operations?

10.3 Create an image pipeline that shows the spectrum of a Gaussian image. What effect does increasing or decreasing the standard deviation have on the spectrum?

Visualization on the Web

*T*he early 1990s established the widespread use and accessibility of the World Wide Web. Once a network used primarily by researchers and universities, the Web has become something that is used by people throughout the world. The effects of this transformation have been significant, ranging from personal home pages with static images and text, to professional Web pages embedding animation and virtual reality. This chapter discusses some of those changes and describes how the World Wide Web can be used to make visualization more accessible, interactive, and powerful. Topics covered include the advantages and disadvantages of client-side versus server-side visualization, VRML, and Java3D, interwoven with demonstration examples.

11.1 Motivation

Before describing in detail how to perform visualization over the Web, it is important to understand what we expect to gain. Clearly people have been visualizing data prior to the invention of the Web, but what the Web adds is the ability for people throughout the world to share information quickly and efficiently. Like all successful communication systems, the Web enables people to interact and share information more efficiently compared to other methods. In many ways the Web shares the characteristic of computer visualization in its ability to communicate large amounts of data. For that reason, computer graphics and visualization are now vital parts of the Web, and are becoming widespread in their application.

To demonstrate these concepts we provide a simple example that illustrates the usefulness of the Web, and leads us into our first important topic: client-side versus server-side visualization.

One common problem for researchers has been how to share or publish results. Typically, this involved having one site perform the research, interact with the data, form conclusions, and then publish the results as a report. The report might include a few pictures and possibly even a short animation. Obtaining access to the report might be through a journal or conference. Subsequently, co-workers at other sites would read the report and respond via verbal communication or formal articles.

While certainly a viable means of sharing information, there are two important shortcomings in such a scenario. First, the report does not allow another researcher to interact with the visualizations. They are static pictures or pre-recorded animations. There is no opportunity to look from a different angle or change the parameters of the visualization. Second, access to the report may be limited or untimely. For example, some journals require as much as two years to accept, review, and publish an article. This time delay is too long for many technology-driven fields such as medicine, computers, or business. Such delays in receiving information can result in fruitless research or a failed business.

Using the Web this scenario changes significantly. It is now possible to create reports so that other researchers can interact directly with the data, including visualizing the results in an alternative form. The Web also provides the opportunity to publish results immediately so that anyone with Web access can view them. Additionally, results can be modified as your work progresses so that they are always up to date.

Another motivation for visualization over the Web is collaboration. If a researcher is performing a visualization of a dataset at one site, there are a number of hurdles preventing someone at another site from doing the same. For starters, the data, which could be sizable, must be copied, or sent from one site to the other. Then the software being used must be available at both sites which may not even be possible depending on the hardware available. The popularity of cross-platform systems such as AVS, IBM's Data Explorer, and VTK have helped this situation, but even then the software and data reside at both locations. This is frequently referred to as client-side visualization because all steps of the visualization are performed at the collaboration (or client) sites. In contrast, server-side visualization occurs when all of the visualization is done at one centralized location called the server. The results of the server-side visualization are then sent to collaboration sites.

The Web opens up the opportunity to perform mixed client/server visualization that has a number of benefits. First, let's consider the drawbacks to client-side only visualization. As mentioned in the preceding discussion, client-side visualization requires both the data and the software at the client. If the datasets are very large it may be impractical to transfer the data over the Web. Since the server doesn't know what the client is going to do with the data, all of the data must be sent. Additionally, the client may not have sufficient memory or performance to perform the visualization. The advantages of client-side visualization are that the user has complete control over the visualization and can interact with or modify it at will.

With server-side visualization the most significant loss is in interaction. A server-side only visualization is much like publishing a report. The clients have very little control over the images and animations it produces. The advantage is that the results are easily viewed from any client without requiring special hardware or software. As we will see in the remaining sections, the advantage of using recently developed Web technology is that we can mix server-, and client- side visualization much more readily than before, providing the benefits of both.

11.2 Early Web Visualization

While the World Wide Web received most of its attention in the early 1990s, its foundations date back decades earlier to the Internet and ARPAnet. What made the 1990s so significant was the development of some standardized visual tools for exchanging information. The most common of these are the Web browsers such as Mosaic, Netscape Navigator, and Microsoft Internet Explorer. These browsers provide a unified interface supporting many data (or content) types. The first content type to gain wide acceptance was HyperText Markup Language or HTML. HTML provides a way to format text and images in a document that can be shared across the Web. HTML also includes the ability to provide active links in one document that point to other documents on the Web. This helps to solve the problem of sharing results but it still limits the user to static images.

This problem was quickly solved as Web browsers started to support other content types including animation formats such as MPEG, AVI, and QuickTime. Now a link in a HTML document can load an animation sequence for the user to view and interact with. The next step was to allow the client to control the generation of the animation sequence on the server. To facilitate this process, a mechanism for the client to send general information to the server was introduced. The Common Gateway Interface (CGI) along with HTML forms serves this purpose. In this two-pronged approach, an HTML form collects information from the client, passes it to the server that executes a CGI-BIN script, and then finally produces a result for the client to view.

For example, consider a situation where you would like to perform an isosurface extraction from volume data and then generate a short animation rotating the camera around the isosurface. There are a number of ways to generate such an animation and create an MPEG file, which can then be linked into an HTML document. **Figure 11–1** shows one example generated from the following HTML code:

```
<HEAD><TITLE>Sample MPEG Animation Page</TITLE></HEAD>

In this page we show an MPEG animation of a visualization
of the visible woman dataset. The MPEG is stored in a file
tissue.mpg. We also have taken one frame from the animation
and stored it as a static JPEG image tissue.jpg. We
display the JPEG image so that someone visiting the site will
have an idea of what the mpeg animation will contain.

<br>
<A HREF="tissue.mpg"><IMG SRC="tissue.jpg">
<br>Click here for an MPEG Animation</A>
```

The title and text description are followed by <A HREF="tissue.mpg"> which associates the MPEG file, tissue.mpg, with whatever comes between the first <A> and the closing </A>.

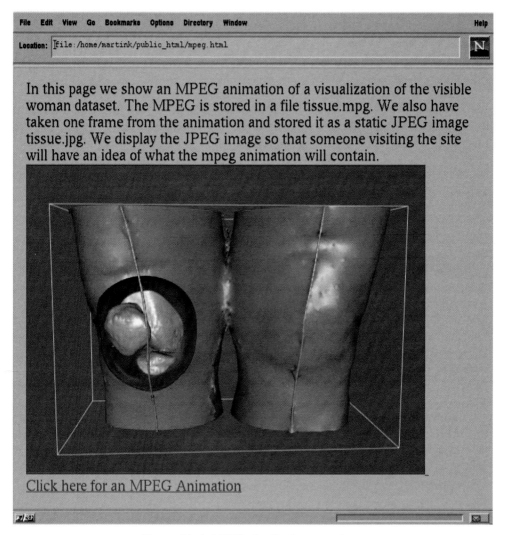

Figure 11–1 MPEG visualization example.

In this example there is a JPEG image and a line of text. Clicking on either of these will play the MPEG animation.

Now let's use CGI and an HTML form to enable the client to change the isosurface value. The first step is to obtain the desired isosurface value from the client using an HTML form such as **Figure 11–2**. The form was generated by the following HTML code:

```
<HEAD><TITLE>Sample MPEG Animation Page</TITLE></HEAD>

<FORM METHOD="POST" ACTION="/cgi-bin/makempg.csh">
```

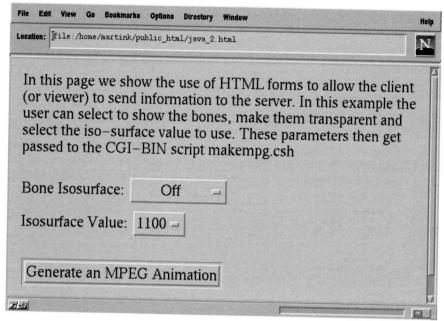

Figure 11–2 Example HTML form.

```
In this page we show the use of HTML forms to allow the client
(or viewer) to send information to the server. In this example
the user can select to show the bones, make them transparent and
select the isosurface value to use. These parameters then get
passed to the CGI-BIN script makempg.csh</P>

<P>Bone Isosurface: <SELECT NAME=iso>
<OPTION SELECTED>Off
<OPTION>On
<OPTION>Transparent
</SELECT><BR>
Isosurface Value: <SELECT NAME=isoval>
<OPTION>1400 <OPTION>1200
<OPTION SELECTED>1100
<OPTION>1000 <OPTION>900
</SELECT><BR>

<P><INPUT TYPE="submit"
VALUE="Generate an MPEG Animation"></FORM></P>
```

The FORM keyword starts the definition of the HTML form. The ACTION keyword indicates what should happen when the form is submitted. In this example the server will run a CGI-BIN script called makempg.csh when a client submits this form. Next the two pulldown menus are declared with the SELECT keyword. The NAME keyword sets up an asso-

ciation between a string name and the value for this menu. This will be used by the script
makempg.csh to access the values from the form. The OPTION and SELECTED keywords
provide a mechanism to specify the values for the menu and what value the default should be.
Finally, the last two lines create the button that will submit the form when pressed.

Once the client has submitted the form, the server will execute the CGI-BIN script and
pass it the arguments from the form. The script will then generate a new MPEG animation
based on the client's request and return it to the client.

While these examples demonstrate a closed loop of interaction between the client and
server, there are two remaining problems. First, this approach places the entire computational
load on the server. While this may be viable for some applications, some servers literally
receive millions of client requests a day, severely straining server resources. Second, while
the process is interactive, the lag time between making a change and seeing the result can be
considerable, depending on the length of the animation and the communication bandwidth.
Better solutions are now available to improve interactivity.

11.3 Virtual Reality Modeling Language (VRML)

HTML is a powerful tool for creating hypertext documents; however, it does not directly support 3D content. This limitation can be severe if we are interested in exploring 3D data, and
do not know exactly what we wish to see, or what we wish to present to a user. As a result, an
important development has been to create 3D worlds that the user can freely navigate. One
application of this technology is Web content that allows customers to preview a hotel, resort,
or vacation area by moving through a model representing the site. Such an application allows
customers to preview a prospective business and directly experience what is available without relying on preconstructed views of the site.

As a result of this need for greater interactivity, a new content type appeared referred to
as the Virtual Reality Modeling Language (VRML). The idea behind VRML was to create a
standard definition for transmitting 3D content over the Web. Having its origins in an early
system called Labyrinth, which is in turn based on Reality Lab from Rendermorphics, it
quickly evolved to the VRML 1.0 specification based on Open Inventor from Silicon Graphics.

A VRML 1.0 file (typically with a .wrl extension, abbreviated from world) contains a
scene graph representation of a 3D world (e.g., a scene). Consider **Figure 11–3** which shows
a simple scene. It is a directed graph that is traversed depth first from top to bottom with the
content of the graph in its nodes (the circles). In this figure the top node is a group node that
collects child nodes together. The light is a directional light node and the second group node
represents an isosurface. The isosurface group node is represented by three children nodes:
one to control the material properties, a general transformation, and finally the 3D geometry.
VRML and Open Inventor support many different types of nodes including some support for
animation. (See also "Alternative Visual Programming Models" on page 95.)

The basic idea behind VRML 1.0 is that the 3D content can be downloaded from the
server and then interacted with the client. There are many Web browsers that support VRML
and most take advantage of client-side graphics hardware if available. This helps address
both the server-load problem and the interaction lag time associated with the earlier approach

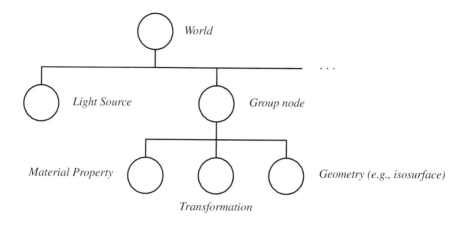

Figure 11–3 A simple scene graph.

of server-generated MPEG animations. Like HTML, VRML supports active links so that navigating through a door in one VRML world can send you to new VRML (or HTML) sites.

To address many of the limitations in VRML 1.0, significant changes were made resulting in the VRML 2.0 standard. Where VRML 1.0 was primarily a static scene description with some very limited behaviors, VRML 2.0 adds audio, video, and integration with Web scripting languages and more. It is still essentially a data file, but with the capabilities of simulating much more realistic and immersive environments. Many visualization systems, including VTK, support exporting scenes as VRML files. Consider the following example:

```
vtkRenderer ren1
vtkRenderWindow renWin
    renWin AddRenderer ren1

# create pipeline
#
vtkPLOT3DReader pl3d
    pl3d SetXYZFileName "$VTK_DATA_ROOT/Data/combxyz.bin"
    pl3d SetQFileName "$VTK_DATA_ROOT/Data/combq.bin"
    pl3d SetScalarFunctionNumber 100
    pl3d SetVectorFunctionNumber 202
vtkContourFilter iso
    iso SetInput [pl3d GetOutput]
    iso SetValue 0 .38
vtkPolyDataNormals normals
    normals SetInput [iso GetOutput]
    normals SetFeatureAngle 45
vtkPolyDataMapper isoMapper
    isoMapper SetInput [normals GetOutput]
    isoMapper ScalarVisibilityOff
vtkActor isoActor
```

```
      isoActor SetMapper isoMapper
      eval [isoActor GetProperty] SetColor 0.3 0.4 0.5

vtkStructuredGridOutlineFilter outline
      outline SetInput [pl3d GetOutput]
vtkPolyDataMapper outlineMapper
      outlineMapper SetInput [outline GetOutput]
vtkActor outlineActor
      outlineActor SetMapper outlineMapper

# Add the actors to the renderer, set the background and size
#
ren1 AddActor outlineActor
ren1 AddActor isoActor
renWin SetSize 500 500
ren1 SetBackground 0.1 0.2 0.4
```

This is a typical program within VTK that extracts an isosurface and bounding outline from a structured grid dataset. To export this result to a VRML data file we can use the vtkVRMLExporter as shown below:

```
vtkVRMLExporter exp
      exp SetRenderWindow renWin
      exp SetFileName Combustor.wrl
      exp Write
```

These four lines create an instance of vtkVRMLExporter, set its input to renWin (an instance of vtkRenderWindow), set a file name, and finally write out the result. This is different from previous examples where data was written out using vtkPolyDataWriter or other subclasses of vtkWriter. vtkVRMLExporter is a subclass of vtkExporter, not vtkWriter. The significant difference is that a writer takes a vtkDataSet as input and is responsible for writing out a single dataset. An exporter takes a vtkRenderWindow as input and is responsible for writing out an entire scene, possibly containing multiple actors, lights, textures, and material properties, in addition to any datasets.

If you consider a continuum from a static data file to a fully interactive visualization program, vtkWriter would be at one end, vtkExporter in the middle, and a VTK program at the other. VRML 1.0 would fall at the same place as vtkExporter and VRML 2.0 would fall between vtkExporter and an actual program due to its added support for behavior and script interaction. What VRML lacks from a visualization perspective is algorithms. VRML is a 3D multimedia content format and lacks direct support for applying visualization techniques or algorithms.

11.4 A VRML Visualization Server

We can improve on the earlier MPEG visualization server example by creating a VRML visualization server. The primary limitations of the MPEG approach were that the processing burden was on the server, and the client-side interaction was limited to requesting that a dif-

ferent MPEG animation be generated. In our improved example, the basic idea is the same as
before. That is, we use a HTML form to define parameters for a visualization, which then
spawns off a CGI-BIN script. The difference is that in this example the server will generate a
VRML data file that is returned to the client. The client can then control the viewpoint and
rendering of the VRML result. The data and visualization software still reside on the server,
so the client is only required to have a VRML compatible Web browser.

The HTML form is essentially the same as the one used to generate **Figure 11–2**. What
changes is that the CGI-BIN script now needs to produce a VRML file instead of an MPEG.
So instead of the form invoking makempg.csh, it will invoke a C++ executable named
VRMLServer. This executable will parse the inputs from the form and then write out a
VRML file to its standard output. The first part of the program parses the arguments from the
form. The server passes these arguments as a single string to the program's standard input. At
the same time an environment variable named CONTENT_LENGTH is set to the length of
this input. In this example there are two values passed from the form: iso and isoval. According to convention they are separated by a "&" when passed to the CGI-BIN script. The following C++ code extracts these values from the input string and performs some quick error
checking.

```
// first get the form data
env = getenv("CONTENT_LENGTH");
if (!env) return -1;
int inputLength = atoi(env);
// a quick sanity check on the input
if ((inputLength > 40)||(inputLength < 17)) return -1;
cin >> arg1;

if (strncmp(arg1,"isoval=",7) == 0)
  {
  isoval = atof(arg1 + 7);
  strcpy(isoType,arg1 + 11);
  }
else
  {
  isoval = atof(arg1 + inputLength - 4);
  strncpy(isoType,arg1 + 4,inputLength - 16);
  isoType[inputLength - 16] = '\0';
  }
```

This code is specific to the parameters in this example, but generic argument extraction routines such as cgic (see http://www.boutell.com/cgic/) can be used. Once the form
data has been obtained, it can be used to set up the visualization pipeline as usual. In the following code, an isosurface is added to the renderer based on the isoType input from the form.
Likewise if isoType is set to "Transparent" then that actor's opacity is set to 0.5.

```
// should we do the isosurface
if (strcmp(isoType,"Off"))
  {
  ren1->AddActor( isoActor );
```

```
    }
if (strcmp(isoType,"Transparent") == 0)
    {
    isoActor->GetProperty()->SetOpacity( 0.5 );
    }
```

Once the pipeline is set up, the last step is to generate the proper headers and VRML output. The header is the keyword Content-type: followed by the keyword x-world/x-vrml that is the specification for VRML content. This is often followed by a pragma indicating that the client browser should not cache the data, typically because of the memory it would consume.

```
// Send out vrml header stuff
fprintf(stdout,"Content-type: x-world/x-vrml\n");
fprintf(stdout,"Pragma: no-cache\n\n");

// write out VRML 2.0 file
vtkVRMLExporter *writer = vtkVRMLExporter::New();
writer->SetInput( renWin );
writer->SetFilePointer( stdout );
writer->Write();
```

Finally an instance of vtkVRMLExporter is created, assigned an instance of vtkRenderWindow as input, and set to write to standard output. When the Write() method is applied, the exporter updates the visualization pipeline and produces the VRML output. The vtkRenderWindow is never rendered and no windows appear on the server. There is no need for an interactor because the interaction will be handled by the client's VRML browser. This program simply reads in a string of input (the parameters from the form) and then produces a string of output (the VRML data). It is also important to remember that CGI-BIN scripts are typically run from a different user id and environment than your own; file names and paths should be fully specified.

11.5 Visualization with Java

The examples discussed so far have addressed Web-based visualization in a number of ways. We have seen how to present preconstructed content such as images and animations using HTML, as well as creating interactive worlds with VRML. Each technique has its benefits but lacks the flexibility found in a custom-developed program. This is where Java stands out. Java's origins trace back to an embedded control language for small appliances and personal digital assistants. As such it was designed to work on a wide variety of hardware without recompilation and with high reliability. These same qualities are valuable to Web programming where a single program must run on many different machines without fail.

Since Java is a full programming language, any visualization application written in Java will run on any Java-compliant system. In addition, Java provides the flexibility to perform the visualization on the server, on the client, or even a mixture of both. A number of early Java programs (a.k.a., applets) have emerged that render simple geometry or play back image sequences. Unfortunately Java provides no direct support for using accelerated 3D hardware and this limits the types of visualizations that can be done.

There are two common approaches to utilizing graphics hardware from Java. The first approach is to access an existing toolkits capabilities from within Java. Fortunately, the <Emphasis>Visualization Toolkit has been interfaced with Java so that it can be used from Java in a manner similar to its use in Tcl/Tk (see Chapter 11 for more information on Tcl/Tk). The second is to use Java3D which is a native 3D extension to Java that supports hardware rendering and a rich scene graph based API.

While Java is a portable byte-compiled language, its designers realized it was important to have a mechanism for developers to make calls to C or C++ routines. This mechanism is called the Java Native Interface, or JNI for short. The JNI provides a clean, well-defined way for native code such as C and C++ to work with Java. This allows a visualization system such as VTK to be used, which in turn provides a mechanism to access 3D graphics hardware (if available). Native code also allows performance critical functions to be handled in optimized C or C++ code instead of Java.

The downside to using Java3D or native code is that it sacrifices Java's portability somewhat. Where a pure Java program can be byte-compiled and run on any machine that supports Java, a program that relies on Java3D or native code requires that the compiled Java3D or native code support be installed on the client. For each type of machine you want to support, you will need a compiled version of the native code. For a toolkit like VTK this means that the client would have to download the native VTK support (e.g., an object library) before being able to run VTK-Java applications. Once that is done, most applications described in this book can be made into a Web-based visualization. Depending on the needs of the application, the data can be left on the server and the results sent to the client, or the data could be sent to the client for both processing and viewing.

The following example outlines how to use Java and VTK to display vibrational modes of a rectangular plate. In the preceding examples an HTML form was used to obtain input from the client. With Java we can construct a customized client-side user interface to obtain the required information.

The first step in this example creates the HTML code that in turn launches the Java applet.

```
<title>Vibrational Modes of a Rectangular Plate</title>
<h2>Vibrational Modes of a Rectangular Plate</h2>
This Java applet downloads a VTK data file into a Java String. It
then uses the InputString method of the VTK data reader to use this
string as its data. Then it creates a filter pipeline that takes
the original geometry and warps it according to the vector data.
There are four sets of vector data in this example. They correspond
to the first, second, fourth and eighth vibrational modes. The
geometry is color based on the amount of displacement.
<hr>
<applet code=App2.class width=400 height=500>
<param name=model value=plate.vtk>
</applet>
<hr>
```

The key lines are near the end where the applet keyword is used to start the App2 Java applet with a default window size of 400 by 500. Parameters are passed to the applet using the param keyword followed by key-value pairs. When the client encounters the applet keyword, it then requests that Java applet from the server and starts executing it. We will consider the Java code in App2 from a visualization perspective. A more complete introduction to Java programming can be found in numerous books (see "Bibliographic Notes" on page 417).

The applet will have a standard structure starting by importing other classes that this application will use.

```
import vtk.*;
import java.awt.*;
import java.applet.*;
etc...
```

Next comes the class definition for App2. As with most Java applets, this class extends the Applet class. It has a number of instance variables including many VTK objects that will be used to set up the visualization pipeline.

```
public class App2 extends Applet
    {
    vtkPolyDataReader pr = null;
    vtkWarpVector warp = null;
    vtkGeometryFilter ds2poly = null;
    vtkCleanPolyData clean = null;
    vtkPolyDataNormals normals = null;
    vtkVectorDot color = null;
    vtkDataSetMapper plateMapper = null;
    vtkPanel panel = null;
    etc...
```

The init() method handles applet initialization. This is where parameters from the HTML page will be processed and the visualization pipeline and user interface will be set up. To place the rendering window within the user interface, we use the vtkPanel class that is a subclass of the Java Canvas class. This way the rendering window can be treated as if it were just another piece of the user interface.

```
public void init()
    {
    GridBagLayout grid = new GridBagLayout();

    this.setLayout(grid);
    panel = new vtkPanel();
    panel.resize(400,400);
    constrain(this,panel,0,0,8,8);
```

Next, this method checks to see if the model parameter is set, and opens a stream connection to the server that is used to download the data file into a Java string. This is then passed to a vtkPolyDataReader at which point the data is now available to the native VTK code on the

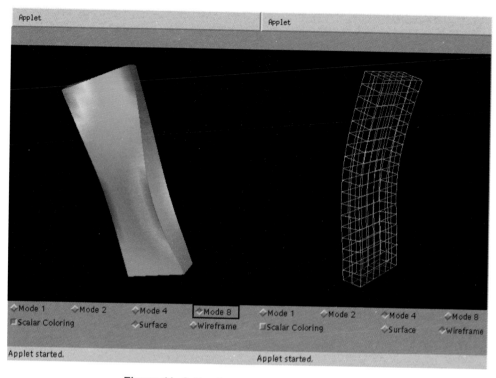

Figure 11–4 Two images from a Java (JNI) applet.

client. The rest of the pipeline is set up as usual with the exception that a Java syntax is used instead of C++ or Tcl. (Due to VTK's object-oriented design the variations from one language to another are minor.) At this point in the init() method the rest of the pipeline is set up along with some checkboxes and event handlers for the user interface. The vtkPanel has a method that returns the RenderWindow that can then be acted on as usual. For example:

```
panel.GetRenderer().AddActor(a);
```

The resulting applet is shown in **Figure 11–4**.

This demonstrates one of the advantages of using Java for Web visualization. VRML would require that the geometry of each vibrational mode be sent to the client for viewing. With Java and VTK the geometry can be sent once along with a set of scalar displacements for each vibrational mode. Then as the client switches between modes, the geometry can be modified quickly by the client without any additional network traffic. In fact the client could mix vibrational modes or perform an animation showing the vibration of the plate all without having to go back to the server, and without requiring much more data than a single VRML model of the plate. If the client decided to examine another geometry, say the vibrational modes of a disc, then it would likely return to the server for the new data. This is the flexibility that Java provides.

11.6 Java3D

Similar to a native code implementation (such as a VTK implementation) Java3D provides access to hardware accelerated 3D graphics. Java3D provides both scene graph rendering similar to VRML, and high-level immediate mode rendering. The immediate mode rendering support is not as complete as libraries like OpenGL or DirectX, but it does provide a good subset of its functionality. Java3D does share some of the limitations of native code implementations in that the client must have a version of Java3D for their operating system installed for it to work. There are also some limitations in how both Java3D and native interfaces interact with lightweight GUI components such as swing.

To better understand the Java3D API, we'll walk through an example applet distributed with the original 1.0 specification. In this example, a colored cube is rendered as it rotates at a fixed rate.

First, let's consider the definition of the cube. Some of the details have been left out for brevity. The complete description of the cube is stored in a Java class we'll call ColorCube. It contains two class variables (verts and colors) that store the vertex positions and RGB colors. It has an instance of the Shape3D class that will be used by Java3D and a method, getShape(), to access it. Finally, ColorCube has a constructor that creates a QuadArray, inserts the verts and colors into it, and assigns it to the Shape3D instance variable.

```
public class ColorCube extends Object
   {
   private static final float[] verts =
      {
      // front face
      1.0f, -1.0f,  1.0f, 1.0f,  1.0f,  1.0f,
      -1.0f,  1.0f,  1.0f, -1.0f, -1.0f,  1.0f,
   . . .
      // bottom face
      -1.0f, -1.0f,  1.0f, -1.0f, -1.0f, -1.0f,
      1.0f, -1.0f, -1.0f, 1.0f, -1.0f,  1.0f,
      };
   private static final float[] colors = {
      // front face (red)
      1.0f, 0.0f, 0.0f, 1.0f, 0.0f, 0.0f,
      1.0f, 0.0f, 0.0f, 1.0f, 0.0f, 0.0f,
   . . .
      // bottom face (cyan)
      0.0f, 1.0f, 1.0f, 0.0f, 1.0f, 1.0f,
      0.0f, 1.0f, 1.0f, 0.0f, 1.0f, 1.0f,
      };
   private Shape3D shape;
   public ColorCube() {
      QuadArray cube = new QuadArray(24,
                  QuadArray.COORDINATES | QuadArray.COLOR_3);
      cube.setCoordinates(0, verts);
      cube.setColors(0, colors);
      shape = new Shape3D(cube, new Appearance());
```

```
    }
  public Shape3D getShape() {
    return shape;
    }
  }
```

Having defined the geometry, the entry point for a Java3D application is the applet. The HelloUniverse class extends the Applet class and provides the initialization code for this application. The constructor for this applet creates a Canvas3D object that is where the 3D information will be rendered. It then calls the createSceneGraph() method that performs the detailed setup of the scene graph including creating an instance of ColorCube. Then the constructor creates an instance of a UniverseBuilder given the Canvas3D and attaches the scene graph to the Universe. The UniverseBuilder is mostly boiler-plate code that handles setting up the view location (or platform) and attaching it to the Canvas3D.

```
  public class HelloUniverse extends Applet
    {
    public HelloUniverse()
      {
      setLayout(new BorderLayout());
      Canvas3D c = new Canvas3D(graphicsConfig);
      add("Center", c);
      // Create a simple scene and attach it to the virtual universe
      BranchGroup scene = createSceneGraph();
      UniverseBuilder u = new UniverseBuilder(c);
      u.addBranchGraph(scene);
      }
    }
```

It is worth noting that in the createSceneGraph() method, the use of the previously defined ColorCube class and its insertion into the scene graph via the BranchGroup class. The setCapability() method is used to enable the cube's transform to be modified and underlies an important concept. To achieve the highest rendering rate, Java3D performs a number of optimizations on the scene graph. Many of these optimizations only work if certain properties of the nodes are guaranteed to not change. So by default most properties of a node are set to be "read only." To modify them after creation requires the specific call shown below.

```
  public BranchGroup createSceneGraph()
    {
    // Create the root of the branch graph
    BranchGroup objRoot = new BranchGroup();
    // Create the transform group node and initialize it to the
    // identity.  Enable the TRANSFORM_WRITE capability so that
    // our behavior code can modify it at runtime.  Add it to the
    // root of the subgraph.
    TransformGroup objTran = new TransformGroup();
    objTran.setCapability(TransformGroup.ALLOW_TRANSFORM_WRITE);
    objRoot.addChild(objTran);
    // Create a simple shape leaf node, add it to the scene graph.
```

```
objTran.addChild(new ColorCube().getShape());
// Create a new Behavior object that will perform the desired
// operation on the specified transform object and add it into
// the scene graph.
Transform3D yAxis = new Transform3D();
Alpha rotationAlpha = new Alpha(
    -1, Alpha.INCREASING_ENABLE, 0, 0, 4000, 0, 0, 0, 0, 0);
RotationInterpolator rotator =
new RotationInterpolator(rotationAlpha, objTran, yAxis,
        0.0f, (float) Math.PI*2.0f);
BoundingSphere bounds =
    new BoundingSphere(new Point3d(0.0,0.0,0.0), 100.0);
rotator.setSchedulingBounds(bounds);
objTran.addChild(rotator);
return objRoot;
}

public void addBranchGraph(BranchGroup bg) {
    locale.addBranchGraph(bg);
}
```

11.7 VRML, Java, and the EAI

The External Authoring Interface (EAI) provides VRML with the same combination of power and flexibility that Java3D has. The EAI provides a communication interface that allows Java and VRML to interact with each other. This is particularly powerful in that a Java applet can create a VRML world, add and delete nodes from the scene graph, and a VRML scene graph can invoke Java code or Java Script in response to an event. In many ways this is similar to the Java3D solution with the exception that VRML is being used for the rendering instead of the Java3D rendering engine. Both solutions have the benefit of Java as a general purpose language for handling programmatic and user-interface issues.

There are a number of ways to organize a visualization that uses the EAI. We will consider the most general method that starts with an HTML page that loads both a VRML world file and a Java applet in the traditional way. This example is loosely derived from work by David Brown. The Java applet starts by importing a number of classes including some VRML specific ones and then defining the instance variables that it will be using.

```
import java.awt.*;
import java.applet.*;
import java.lang.*;
import vrml.external.field.*;
import vrml.external.Node;
import vrml.external.Browser;
import vrml.external.exception.*;

public class visApplet extends Applet
    {
```

```
// The Browser
Browser browser = null;
// Various UI widgets
Button grow_button, shrink_button;

// Various stuff in the VRML scene we hang on to
Node root_node, sphere_node;
EventInSFVec3f setScale = null;
float currentScale = (float)1.0;
```

Next, the applet defines the init() method that will request a reference to the browser, invoke initScene() to build the VRML interface, and create the user interface. In this case the user interface is just two buttons on a white background.

```
/** Initialize the Applet */
public void init()
    {
    // Connect to the browser
    browser = Browser.getBrowser(this);
    if (browser == null) {
      die("init: NULL browser!");
    }
    System.out.println("Got the browser: "+browser);

    // Initialize some VRML stuff
    initScene();

    // Build a simple UI
    grow_button = new Button("Grow Sphere");
    add(grow_button);
    shrink_button = new Button("Shrink Sphere");
    add(shrink_button);
    // Misc other UI setup
    Color c = Color.white;
    System.out.println("Setting bg color to: " + c);
    setBackground(c);
    }
```

There is a simple error handling routine defined.

```
/** Handle a fatal error condition */
public void die(String s)
    {
    System.out.println("visApplet: FATAL ERROR!");
    System.out.println("--> " + s);
    System.out.println("visApplet: Aborting...\n");
    }
```

The initScene() method sets up the VRML scene and relies heavily on the EAI. For synchronization reasons, this method starts off by waiting a few seconds to assure that the VRML browser has time to initialize and read the VRML file specified by the HTML. Then it uses the browser.getNode("aName") method to obtain nodes from the scene graph. These nodes must be named using the DEF keyword in the VRML file. The first node it gets is the SPHERE node that happens to be a VRML transform. It uses the getEventIn() method to obtain a handle to the scale instance variable of this transform which will be used later.

```
/** Set up some stuff in the VRML scene */
public void initScene()
    {
    System.out.println("initScene()...");

    // wait a couple seconds
    try {
        Thread.currentThread().sleep(5000);
        }
    catch(InterruptedException e) {}

    // Get the "SPHERE" node
    try {
        sphere_node = browser.getNode("SPHERE");
        }
    catch(InvalidNodeException e){
        System.out.println("InvalidNodeException: " + e);
        die("initScene: SPHERE node not found!");
        return;
        }

    System.out.println("- Got the SPHERE node: " + sphere_node);
    try {
        setScale = (EventInSFVec3f)
        sphere_node.getEventIn("set_scale");
        }
    catch (InvalidEventInException e) {
        die("initScene: InvalidEventInException " + e);
        return;
        }
```

Then the same techniques are used to obtain the ROOT node of the scene graph. If you scan the VRML file that follows this example, you will see that the ROOT node is just an empty Group. After obtaining the node we request handles to its addChildren() and removeChildren() methods.

```
// Get the "ROOT" node (a Group which we add to)
try {
    root_node = browser.getNode("ROOT");
    }
catch(InvalidNodeException e){
```

```
    System.out.println("InvalidNodeException: " + e);
    die("initScene: ROOT node not found!");
    return;
    }
  System.out.println("- Got the ROOT node: " + root_node);

  // Get the ROOT node's add/removeChildren EventIns
  EventInMFNode addChildren;
  EventInMFNode removeChildren;
  try {
    addChildren = (EventInMFNode)
    root_node.getEventIn("addChildren");
    removeChildren = (EventInMFNode)
    root_node.getEventIn("removeChildren");
    }
  catch (InvalidEventInException e) {
    die("initScene: InvalidEventInException " + e);
    return;
    }
```

Using the EAI, VRML can be created from a Java string as shown in the following code. This allows us to create geometry on the fly and add it to the scene graph using the addChildren() handle obtained above. The handles support matching setValue() and getValue() methods that modify and interrogate the scene graph respectively.

```
  // Create the VRML for a purple sphere
  Node[] shape;
  String purple_sphere =
    "#VRML V2.0 utf8\n" +
    "Transform {\n" +
    "  children Shape {\n" +
    "    appearance Appearance {\n" +
    "      material Material {\n" +
    "        diffuseColor 0.8 0.2 0.8\n" +
    "      }\n" +
    "    }\n" +
    "    geometry Sphere {}\n" +
    "  }\n" +
    "  translation 0 3 0" +
    "}\n";
  try {
    shape = browser.createVrmlFromString(purple_sphere);
    }
  catch (InvalidVrmlException e) {
    die("initScene: InvalidVrmlException: " + e);
    return;
    }
  // Add the sphere to the ROOT group
  addChildren.setValue(shape);
  System.out.println("initScene: done.");
```

```
}
```

The events for the two buttons are processed in the action() method. One increases the scale of the sphere and the other decreases it. This is done using the handle to the SPHERE node's scale that was obtained in the initScene() method, and invoking the setValue() method with the appropriate arguments.

```
/** Handle actions from AWT widgets */
public boolean action(Event event, Object what)
  {
  if (event.target instanceof Button) {
  Button b = (Button) event.target;
  if (b == grow_button) {
    currentScale = currentScale * (float)1.2;
    float ascale[] = new float[3];
    ascale[0] = currentScale;
    ascale[1] = currentScale;
    ascale[2] = currentScale;
    setScale.setValue(ascale);
    }
  else if (b == shrink_button) {
    currentScale = currentScale / (float)1.2;
    float ascale[] = new float[3];
    ascale[0] = currentScale;
    ascale[1] = currentScale;
    ascale[2] = currentScale;
    setScale.setValue(ascale);
    }
  } // event.target instanceof Button
  return true;
  }
```

The last method in the applet draws a border around the two buttons when the applet needs to be repainted.

```
/** Override paint() to get more control over how we're drawn */
public void paint(Graphics g)
  {
  int w = size().width;
  int h = size().height;

  // Draw a simple border
  g.drawRect(0, 0, w-1, h-1);
  g.drawRect(1, 1, w-3, h-3);
  super.paint(g);
  }
}
```

An excerpt from the VRML file has been included below. Note the use of the DEF keyword to name nodes that can then be accessed from Java. The resulting Java/VRML example can be seen in **Figure 11–5**.

```
#VRML V2.0 utf8
#
Group {
  children [
    #
    # Some objects
    #
    DEF ROOT Group {}
    DEF SPHERE Transform {
      childrenShape {
        appearanceAppearance {
          materialMaterial {
            ambientIntensity0.283774
            diffuseColor0.0846193 0.56383 0.0595097
            specularColor0.13092 0.87234 0.0920716
            emissiveColor0 0 0
            shininess0.2
            transparency0
          }
        }
        geometrySphere {}
      }
      translation-4 0 0
    }
  ]
}
```

11.8 The Future of Web Visualization

In the previous sections we provided an overview of some of the technologies important to applying visualization on the World Wide Web. Since Web-based technologies, computer graphics, and visualization are all rapidly growing fields, the likelihood of new development and change is high. However, we are confident that these technologies will remain important to the future. Eventually we expect 3D graphics and data visualization to become as pervasive as 2D graphical user interfaces and presentations are today. The main barriers to this development is the limited bandwidth of the Web, lack of familiarity (and difficulty of use) of 3D graphics and visualization, and limitations in computer hardware and software. We believe that technological advances will eventually minimize bandwidth and computer hardware limitations, while systems like VTK will make 3D graphics and visualizations easier to use.

One of the benefits of systems like VTK is that they are driven by their algorithmic content. The systems we have seen earlier such as OpenGL, HTML, VRML and Java, are implementations of a system or information protocol. Algorithmic systems, on the other

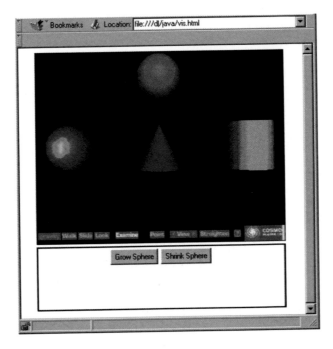

Figure 11–5 Java and VRML combined using the EAI.

hand, implement mathematical, logical, and design relationships that change much more slowly than system implementations. As a result, systems like VTK will remain vital for years to come, although the underlying implementation language and interface may change. To track future changes to VTK visit our Web pages at `http://www.vtk.org`.

11.9 Chapter Summary

Visualization over the Web opens up many forms of collaborative development, entertainment, and publishing that were previously restricted to a few individuals with access to custom software. There are many ways to perform visualization over the Web ranging from simple HTML pages with pictures, to complete Java-based applications. Deciding on the correct solution for Web visualization depends on three key factors: 1) the amount of interaction and control you want to provide to the user or client, 2) performance issues related to data size and client/server load balancing, 3) how much complexity you are willing to deal with. While the Java-based solutions can provide interaction, control, and load balancing, this involves added complexity. It may be that producing a static VRML file for your Web page is sufficient. Either way there are a host of tools available and more are on the way. The greatest challenge will likely be to create a future standard for the Web that includes not just 3D viewing but also visualization.

11.10 Bibliographic Notes

For a general introduction to HTML and CGI consider [Morris95] or [Graham95]. Both books provide a good introduction and include coverage for both UNIX and MS Windows-based systems. For more detailed coverage of CGI programming consider [Gundavaram96]. Mark Pesce [Pesce95] provides a n excellent introduction to VRML including its early genesis. [Ames96] is also a great VRML resource. *The Inventor Mentor* by Josie Wernecke [Wernecke94] is an excellent book for learning about Open Inventor and scene graphs. *Java in a Nutshell* [Flanagan96] is a good reference for Java and for someone who already knows how to program in another language For documentation on the Java Native Interface or Java3D, visit Sun's Web site at `http://java.sun.com`.

11.11 References

[Ames96]
> A. Ames, D. Nadeau, and J. Moreland. *The VRML Sourcebook.* John Wiley & Sons, Inc., New York, NY, 1996.

[Flanagan96]
> David Flanagan. *Java in a Nutshell.* O'Reilly & Associates, Inc., Sebastopol, CA, 1996.

[Graham95]
> I. S. Graham. *The HTML Sourcebook.* John Wiley & Sons, Inc., New York, NY, 1995.

[Gundavaram96]
> S. Gundavaram. *CGI Programming on the World Wide Web.* O'Reilly & Associates, Inc., Sebastopol, CA, 1996.

[Morris95]
> M. E. S. Morris. *HTML for Fun and Profit.* SunSoft Press, Prentice Hall PTR, Englewood Cliffs, NJ, 1995.

[Pesce95]
> M. Pesce. *VRML - Browsing and Building Cyberspace.* New Riders Publishing, Indianapolis, IN, 1995.

[Wernecke94]
> J. Wernecke. *The Inventor Mentor.* Addison-Wesley, Reading MA,1994.

Applications

We have described the design and implementation of an extensive toolkit of visualization techniques. In this chapter we examine several case studies to show how to use these tools to gain insight into important application areas. These areas are medical imaging, financial visualization, modelling, computational fluid dynamics, finite element analysis, and algorithm visualization. For each case, we briefly describe the problem domain and what information we expect to obtain through visualization. Then we craft an approach to show the results. Many times we will extend the functionality of the *Visualization Toolkit* with application-specific tools. Finally, we present a sample program and show resulting images.

The visualization design process we go through is similar in each case. First, we read or generate application-specific data and transform it into one of the data representation types in the *Visualization Toolkit*. Often this first step is the most difficult one because we have to write custom computer code, and decide what form of visualization data to use. In the next step, we choose visualizations for the relevant data within the application. Sometimes this means choosing or creating models corresponding to the physical structure. Examples include spheres for atoms, polygonal surfaces to model physical objects, or computational surfaces to model flow boundaries. Other times we generate more abstract models, such as isosurfaces or glyphs, corresponding to important application data. In the last step we combine the physical components with the abstract components to create a visualization that aids the user in understanding the data.

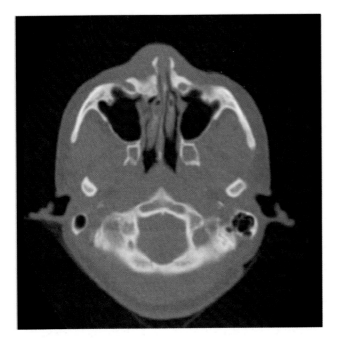

Figure 12–1 A CT slice
through a human head.

12.1 3D Medical Imaging

Radiology is a medical discipline that deals with images of human anatomy. These images come from a variety of medical imaging devices, including X-ray, X-ray Computed Tomography (CT), Magnetic Resonance Imaging (MRI), and ultrasound. Each imaging technique, called an imaging modality, has particular diagnostic strengths. The choice of modality is the job of the radiologist and the referring physician. For the most part, radiologists deal with two-dimensional images, but there are situations when three-dimensional models can assist the radiologist's diagnosis. Radiologists have special training to interpret the two dimensional images and understand the complex anatomical relationships in these two-dimensional representations. However, in dealing with referring physicians and surgeons, the radiologist sometimes has difficulty communicating these relationships. After all, a surgeon works in three-dimensions during the planning and execution of an operation; moreover, they are much more comfortable looking at and working with three-dimensional models.

This case study deals with CT data. Computed tomography measures the attenuation of X-rays as they pass through the body. A CT image consists of levels of gray that vary from black (for air), to gray (for soft tissue), to white (for bone). **Figure 12–1** shows a CT cross section through a head. This slice is taken perpendicular to the spine approximately through the middle of the ears. The gray boundary around the head clearly shows the ears and bridge of the nose. The dark regions on the interior of the slice are the nasal passages and ear canals. The bright areas are bone. This study contains 93 such slices, spaced 1.5 mm apart. Each slice has 256^2 pixels spaced 0.8 mm apart with 12 bits of gray level.

Our challenge is to take this gray scale data (over 12 megabytes) and convert it into information that will aid the surgeon. Fortunately, our visualization toolkit has just the right techniques. We will use isocontouring techniques to extract the skin and bone surfaces and display orthogonal cross-sections to put the isosurface in context. From experience we know that a density value of 500 will define the air/skin boundary, and a value of 1150 will define the soft tissue/bone boundary.

In VTK terminology, medical imaging slice data is image data. Recall from Chapter 5 that for image data, the topology and geometry of the data is implicitly known, requiring only dimensions, an origin, and the data spacing.

The steps we follow in this case study are common to many three-dimensional medical studies.

1. Read the input.

2. For each anatomical feature of interest, create an isosurface.

3. Transform the models from patient space to world space.

4. Render the models.

This case study describes in detail how to read input data and extract anatomical features using isocontouring. Orthogonal planes will be shown using a texture-based technique. Along the way we will also show you how to render the data. We finish with a brief discussion of medical data transformations. This complete source code for the examples shown in this section are available from Medical1.cxx, Medical2.cxx, and Medical3.cxx.

Read the Input

Medical images come in many flavors of file formats. This study is stored as flat files without header information. Each 16-bit pixel is stored with little-endian byte order. Also, as is often the case, each slice is stored in a separate file with the file suffix being the slice number of the form prefix.1, prefix.2, and so on. Medical imaging files often have a header of a certain size before the image data starts. The size of the header varies from file format to file format. Finally, another complication is that sometimes one or more bits in each 16-bit pixel is used to mark connectivity between voxels. It is important to be able to mask out bits as they are read.

VTK provides several image readers including one that can read raw formats of the type described above—vtkVolume16Reader. To read this data we instantiate the class and set the appropriate instance variables as follows.

```
vtkVolume16Reader *v16 = vtkVolume16Reader::New();
    v16->SetDataDimensions (64,64);
    v16->SetImageRange (1,93);
    v16->SetDataByteOrderToLittleEndian();
    v16->SetFilePrefix ("headsq/quarter");
    v16->SetDataSpacing (3.2, 3.2, 1.5);
```

The FilePrefix and FilePattern instance variable work together to produce the name of files in a series of slices. The FilePattern—which by default is %s.%d—generates the filename to read by performing a C-language sprintf() of the FilePrefix and the current file number into the FilePattern format specifier.

Create an Isosurface

We can choose from three techniques for isosurface visualization: volume rendering, marching cubes, and dividing cubes. We assume that we want to interact with our data at the highest possible speed, so we will not use volume rendering. We prefer marching cubes if we have polygonal rendering hardware available, or if we need to move up close to or inside the extracted surfaces. Even with hardware assisted rendering, we may have to reduce the polygon count to get reasonable rendering speeds. Dividing cubes is appropriate for software rendering. For this application we'll use marching cubes.

For medical volumes, marching cubes generates a large number of triangles. To be practical, we'll do this case study with a reduced resolution dataset. We took the original 256^2 data and reduced it to 64^2 slices by averaging neighboring pixels twice in the slice plane. We call the resulting dataset *quarter* since it has 1/4 the resolution of the original data. We adjust the DataSpacing for the reduced resolution dataset to 3.2 mm per pixel. Our first program will generate an isosurface for the skin.

The flow in the program is similar to most VTK applications.

1. Generate some data.

2. Process it with filters.

3. Create a mapper to generate rendering primitives.

4. Create actors for all mappers.

5. Render the results.

The filter we have chosen to use is vtkMarchingCubes. We could also use vtkContourFilter since it will automatically create an instance of vtkMarchingCubes as it delegates to the fastest subclass for a particular dataset type. The class vtkPolyDataNormals is used to generate nice surface normals for the data. vtkMarchingCubes can also generate normals, but sometimes better results are achieved when the normals are directly from the surface (vtkPolyDataNormals) versus from the data (vtkMarchingCubes). To complete this example, we take the output from the isosurface generator vtkMarchingCubes and connect it to a mapper and actor via vtkPolyDataMapper and vtkActor. The C++ code follows.

```
vtkContourFilter *skinExtractor = vtkContourFilter::New();
  skinExtractor->SetInput((vtkDataSet *) v16->GetOutput());
  skinExtractor->SetValue(0, 500);
vtkPolyDataNormals *skinNormals = vtkPolyDataNormals::New();
  skinNormals->SetInput(skinExtractor->GetOutput());
  skinNormals->SetFeatureAngle(60.0);
vtkPolyDataMapper *skinMapper = vtkPolyDataMapper::New();
  skinMapper->SetInput(skinNormals->GetOutput());
  skinMapper->ScalarVisibilityOff();
vtkActor *skin = vtkActor::New();
  skin->SetMapper(skinMapper);

vtkOutlineFilter *outlineData = vtkOutlineFilter::New();
  outlineData->SetInput((vtkDataSet *) v16->GetOutput());
vtkPolyDataMapper *mapOutline = vtkPolyDataMapper::New();
```

```
    mapOutline->SetInput(outlineData->GetOutput());
  vtkActor *outline = vtkActor::New();
    outline->SetMapper(mapOutline);
    outline->GetProperty()->SetColor(0,0,0);

  vtkCamera *aCamera = vtkCamera::New();
    aCamera->SetViewUp (0, 0, -1);
    aCamera->SetPosition (0, 1, 0);
    aCamera->SetFocalPoint (0, 0, 0);
    aCamera->ComputeViewPlaneNormal();

  aRenderer->AddActor(outline);
  aRenderer->AddActor(skin);
  aRenderer->SetActiveCamera(aCamera);
  aRenderer->ResetCamera ();
  aCamera->Dolly(1.5);

  aRenderer->SetBackground(1,1,1);
  renWin->SetSize(640, 480);

  aRenderer->ResetCameraClippingRange ();

  // Initialize the event loop and then start it.
  iren->Initialize();
  iren->Start();
```

To provide context for the isosurface an outline is created around the data. An initial view is set up in a window size of 640×480 pixels. Since the dolly command moves the camera towards the data, the clipping planes are reset to insure that the isosurface is completely visible. **Figure 12–2** shows the resulting image of the patient's skin.

We can improve this visualization in a number of ways. First, we can choose a more appropriate color (and other surface properties) for the skin. We use the vtkProperty method SetDiffuseColor() to set the skin color to a fleshy tone. We also add a specular component to the skin surface. Next, we can add additional isosurfaces corresponding to various anatomical features. Here we choose to extract the bone surface by adding an additional pipeline segment. This consists of the filters vtkMarchingCubes, vtkPolyDataMapper, and vtkActor, just as we did with the skin. Finally, to improve rendering performance on our system, we create triangle strips from the output of the contouring process. This requires adding vtkStripper. **Figure 12–3** shows the resulting image, and the following is the C++ code for the pipeline.

```
    vtkActor *skin = vtkActor::New();
    skin->SetMapper(skinMapper);
    skin->GetProperty()->SetDiffuseColor(1, .49, .25);
    skin->GetProperty()->SetSpecular(.3);
    skin->GetProperty()->SetSpecularPower(20);
    skin->GetProperty()->SetOpacity(1.0);

  vtkContourFilter *boneExtractor = vtkContourFilter::New();
    boneExtractor->SetInput((vtkDataSet *) v16->GetOutput());
```

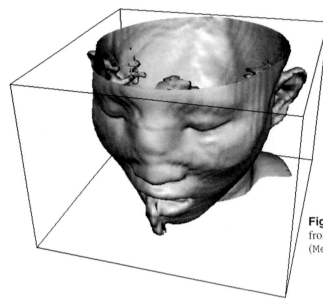

Figure 12–2 The skin extracted from a CT dataset of the head (Medical1.cxx).

```
boneExtractor->SetValue(0, 1150);
vtkPolyDataNormals *boneNormals = vtkPolyDataNormals::New();
   boneNormals->SetInput(boneExtractor->GetOutput());
   boneNormals->SetFeatureAngle(60.0);
vtkStripper *boneStripper = vtkStripper::New();
   boneStripper->SetInput(boneNormals->GetOutput());
vtkPolyDataMapper *boneMapper = vtkPolyDataMapper::New();
   boneMapper->SetInput(boneStripper->GetOutput());
   boneMapper->ScalarVisibilityOff();
vtkActor *bone = vtkActor::New();
   bone->SetMapper(boneMapper);
   bone->GetProperty()->SetDiffuseColor(1, 1, .9412);
```

The *Visualization Toolkit* provides other useful techniques besides isocontouring for exploring volume data. One popular technique used in medical imaging is to view orthogonal slices, or planes, through the data. Because computer graphics hardware supports texture mapping, an approach using texture mapping gives the best result in terms or interactive performance.

We will extract three orthogonal planes corresponding to the axial, sagittal, and coronal cross sections that are familiar to radiologists. The axial plane is perpendicular to the patient's neck, sagittal passes from left to right, and coronal passes from front to back. For illustrative purposes, we render each of these planes with a different color lookup table. For the sagittal plane, we use a gray scale. The coronal and axial planes vary the saturation and hue table, respectively. We combine this with a translucent rendering of the skin (we turn off the bone with the C++ statement bone->VisibilityOff()). The following VTK code creates the three lookup tables that is used in the texture mapping process.

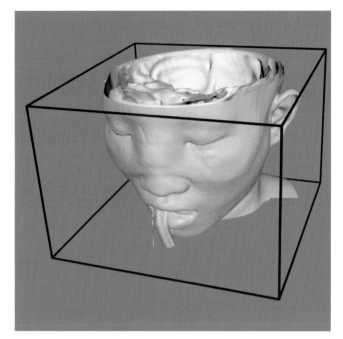

Figure 12–3 Skin and bone isosurfaces (`Medical2.cxx`).

```
vtkLookupTable *bwLut = vtkLookupTable::New();
    bwLut->SetTableRange (0, 2000);
    bwLut->SetSaturationRange (0, 0);
    bwLut->SetHueRange (0, 0);
    bwLut->SetValueRange (0, 1);

  vtkLookupTable *hueLut = vtkLookupTable::New();
    hueLut->SetTableRange (0, 2000);
    hueLut->SetHueRange (0, 1);
    hueLut->SetSaturationRange (1, 1);
    hueLut->SetValueRange (1, 1);

  vtkLookupTable *satLut = vtkLookupTable::New();
    satLut->SetTableRange (0, 2000);
    satLut->SetHueRange (.6, .6);
    satLut->SetSaturationRange (0, 1);
    satLut->SetValueRange (1, 1);
```

The image data is mapped to colors using the filter vtkImageMapToColors in combination with the lookup tables created above. The actual display of the slice is performed with vtkImageActor (see "Assemblies and Other Types of vtkProp" on page 75 for more information). This class conveniently combines a quadrilateral, polygon plane with a texture map. vtkImageActor requires image data of type unsigned char, which the class vtkImageMapToColors conveniently provides. To avoid copying the data and to specify the 2D texture to use, the DisplayExtent of each vtkImageActor is set appropriately. The C++

code is as follows:

```
// saggital
vtkImageMapToColors *saggitalColors =
        vtkImageMapToColors::New();
  saggitalColors->SetInput(v16->GetOutput());
  saggitalColors->SetLookupTable(bwLut);
vtkImageActor *saggital = vtkImageActor::New();
  saggital->SetInput(saggitalColors->GetOutput());
  saggital->SetDisplayExtent(32,32, 0,63, 0,92);

// axial
vtkImageMapToColors *axialColors =
        vtkImageMapToColors::New();
  axialColors->SetInput(v16->GetOutput());
  axialColors->SetLookupTable(hueLut);
vtkImageActor *axial = vtkImageActor::New();
  axial->SetInput(axialColors->GetOutput());
  axial->SetDisplayExtent(0,63, 0,63, 46,46);

// coronal
vtkImageMapToColors *coronalColors =
        vtkImageMapToColors::New();
  coronalColors->SetInput(v16->GetOutput());
  coronalColors->SetLookupTable(satLut);
vtkImageActor *coronal = vtkImageActor::New();
  coronal->SetInput(coronalColors->GetOutput());
  coronal->SetDisplayExtent(0,63, 32,32, 0,92);

aRenderer->AddActor(outline);
aRenderer->AddActor(saggital);
aRenderer->AddActor(axial);
aRenderer->AddActor(coronal);
aRenderer->AddActor(bone);
aRenderer->AddActor(skin);
```

Figure 12–4 shows the resulting composite image.

In this example, the actor named skin is rendered last because we are using a translucent surface. Recall from "Transparency and Alpha Values" on page 201 that we must order the polygons composing transparent surfaces for proper results. We render the skin last by adding it to aRenderer's actor list last.

We need to make one last point about processing medical imaging data. Medical images can be acquired in a variety of orders that refer to the relationship of consecutive slices to the patient. Radiologists view an image as though they were looking at the patient's feet. This means that on the display, the patient's left appears on the right. For CT there are two standard orders: top to bottom or bottom to top. In a top to bottom acquisition, slice i is farther from the patient's feet than slice i - 1. Why do we worry about this order? It is imperative in medical applications that we retain the left / right relationship. Ignoring the slice acquisition order can result in a flipping of left and right. To correct this, we need to trans-

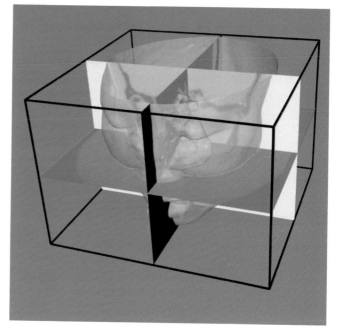

Figure 12–4 Composite image of three planes and translucent skin (Medical3.cxx).

form either the original dataset or the geometry we have extracted. (See "Exercises" on page 464.) Also, you may wish to examine the implementation of the classes vtkVolume16Reader and vtkVolumeReader (the superclass of vtkVolume16Reader). These classes have special methods that deal with transforming image data.

12.2 Creating Models from Segmented Volume Data

The previous example described how to create models from gray-scale medical imaging data. The techniques for extracting bone and skin models is straightforward compared to the task of generating models of other soft tissue. The reason is that magnetic resonance and, to some extent, computed tomography, generates similar gray-scale values for different tissue types. For example, the liver and kidney in a medical computed tomography volume often have overlapping intensities. Likewise, many different tissues in the brain have overlapping intensities when viewed with magnetic resonance imaging. To deal with these problems researchers apply a process called *segmentation* to identify different tissues. These processes vary in sophistication from almost completely automatic methods to manual tracing of images. Segmentation continues to be a hot research area. Although the segmentation process itself is beyond the scope of this text, in this case study we show how to process segmented medical data.

For our purposes we assume that someone (or many graduate students) have laboriously labeled each pixel in each slice of a volume of data with a tissue identifier. This identifier is an integer number that describes which tissue class each pixel belongs to. For example, we may be given a series of MRI slices of the knee with tissue numbers defining the meniscus, femur, muscles, and so forth. **Figure 12–5** shows two representations of a slice from a volume acquired from a patient's knee. The image on the left is the original MRI slice; the image on the right contains tissue labels for a number of important organs. The bottom image is a composite of the two images.

Notice the difference in the information presented by each representation. The original slice shows gradual changes at organ borders, while the segmented slice has abrupt changes. The images we processed in the previous CT example used marching cubes isocontouring algorithm and an intensity threshold to extract the isosurfaces. The segmented study we present has integer labels that have a somewhat arbitrary numeric value. Our goal in this example is to somehow take the tissue labels and create grayscale slices that we can process with the same techniques we used previously. Another goal is to show how image processing and visualization can work together in an application.

The Virtual Frog

To demonstrate the processing of segmented data we will use a dataset derived from a frog. This data was prepared at Lawrence Berkeley National Laboratories and is included with their permission on the CD-ROM accompanying this book. The data was acquired by physically slicing the frog and photographing the slices. The original segmented data is in the form of tissue masks with one file per tissue. There are 136 slices per tissue and 15 different tissues. Each slice is 470 by 500 pixels. (To accommodate the volume readers we have in VTK, we processed the mask files and combined them all in one file for each slice.) We used integer numbers 1–15 to represent the 15 tissues. **Figure 12–6** shows an original slice, a labeled slice, and a composite of the two representations.

Before we describe the process to go from binary labeled tissues to gray-scale data suitable for isosurface extraction, compare the two images of the frog's brain shown in **Figure 12–7**. On the left is a surface extracted using a binary labeling of the brain. The right image was created using the visualization pipeline that we will develop in this example.

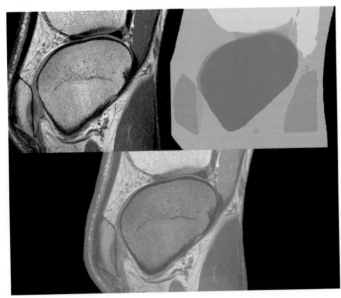

Figure 12–5 Magnetic Resonance Image of a knee (left); segmented tissue (right); composite (bottom). (Data and segmentation courtesy of Brigham and Women's Hospital Surgical Planning Lab.)

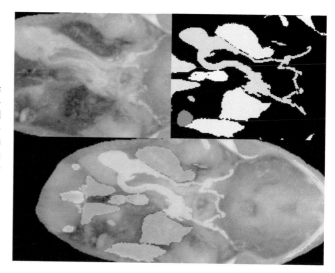

Figure 12–6 Photographic slice of frog (upper left), segmented frog (upper right) and composite of photo and segmentation (bottom). The purple color represents the stomach and the kidneys are yellow (frogSlice.tcl).

Developing a Strategy

In the last example, we used C++ and created a program that was tailored to extract two surfaces: one of the skin and one of the bone. All the parameters for the surface extraction were hard-coded in the source. Since our frog has 15 different tissues; we seek a more general solution to this problem. We may have to experiment with a number of different parameters for a number of visualization and imaging filters. Our goal is to develop a general pipeline that will work not only our 15 tissues but on other medical datasets as well. We'll design the program to work with a set of user-specified parameters to control the elements of the pipeline. A reasonable description might look like:

```
SLICE_ORDER hfsi
ROWS 470
COLUMNS 500
STUDY ../frogMasks/frogTissue
PIXEL_SIZE 1
SPACING 1.5
```

plus possibly many more parameters to control decimation, smoothing, and so forth. Working in C++, we would have to design the format of the file and write code to interpret the statements. We make the job easier here by using Tcl interpreter. Another decision is to separate the modelling from the rendering. Our script will generate models in a "batch" mode. We will run one VTK Tcl script for each tissue. That script will create a .vtk output file containing the polygonal representation of each tissue. Later, we can render the models with a separate script.

Overview of the Pipeline

Figure 12–8 shows the design of the pipeline. This generic pipeline has been developed over the years in our laboratory and in the Brigham and Women's Hospital Surgical Planning Lab.

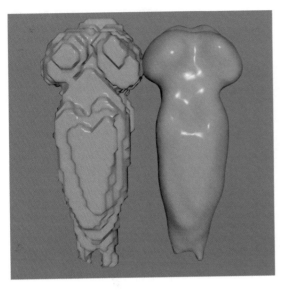

Figure 12–7 The frog's brain. Model extracted without smoothing (left) and with smoothing (right).

We find that it produces reasonable models from segmented datasets. Do not be intimidated by the number of filters (twelve in all). Before we developed VTK, we did similar processing with a hodgepodge of programs all written with different interfaces. We used intermediate files to pass data from one filter to the next. The new pipeline, implemented in VTK, is more efficient in time and computing resources.

We start by developing Tcl scripts to process the volume data. In these scripts, we use the convention that user-specified variables are in capital letters. First we show the elements of the pipeline and subsequently show sample files that extract 3D models of the frog's tissues.

Read the Segmented Volume Data

We assume here that all the data to be processed was acquired with a constant center landmark. In VTK, the origin of the data applies to the lower left of an image volume. In this pipeline, we calculate the origin such that the x,y center of the volume will be (0,0). The DataSpacing describes the size of each pixel and the distance between slices. DataVOI selects a volume of interest (VOI). A VOI lets us select areas of interest, sometimes eliminating extraneous structures like the CT table bed. For the frog, we have written a small C program that reads the tissue label file and finds the volume of interest for each tissue.

The SetTransform() method defines how to arrange the data in memory. Medical images can be acquired in a variety of orders. For example, in CT, the data can be gathered from top to bottom (superior to inferior), or bottom to top (inferior to superior). In addition, MRI data can be acquired from left to right, right to left, front-to-back (anterior to posterior) or back-to-front. This filter transforms triangle vertices such that the resulting models will all "face" the viewer with a view up of (0,-1,0), looking down the positive z axis. Also, proper left-right correspondence will be maintained. That means the patient's left will always be left on the generated models. Look in `SliceOrder.tcl` to see the permutations and rotations for each order.

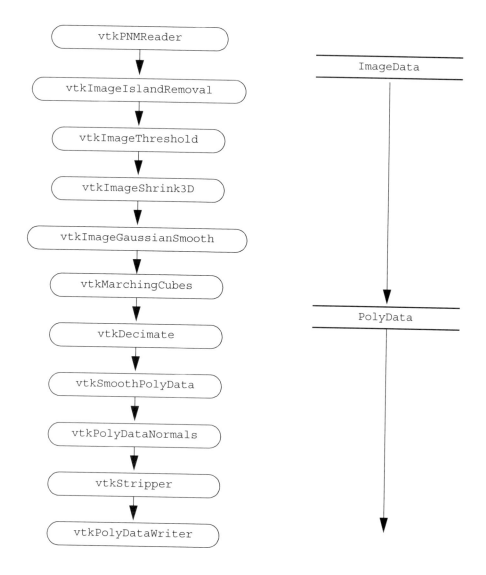

Figure 12–8 The segmented volume to triangle pipeline. Volume passes through image pipeline before isosurface extraction (`frogSegmentation.tcl`).

All the other parameters are self-explanatory except for the last. In this script, we know that the pipeline will only be executed once. To conserve memory, we invoke the ReleaseDataFlagOn() method. This allows the VTK pipeline to release data once it has been processed by a filter. For large medical datasets, this can mean the difference between being able to process a dataset or not.

```
set originx [expr ( $COLUMNS / 2.0 ) * $PIXEL_SIZE * -1.0]
set originy [expr ( $ROWS / 2.0 ) * $PIXEL_SIZE * -1.0]
vtkPNMReader reader
   reader SetFilePrefix $STUDY
   reader SetDataSpacing $PIXEL_SIZE $PIXEL_SIZE $SPACING
   reader SetDataOrigin $originx $originy
[expr $START_SLICE * $SPACING]
   reader SetDataVOI $VOI
   reader SetTransform $SLICE_ORDER
   [reader GetOutput] ReleaseDataFlagOn
```

Remove Islands

Some segmentation techniques, especially those that are automatic, may generate islands of misclassified voxels. This filter looks for connected pixels with the ISLAND_REPLACE label, and if the number of connected pixels is less than ISLAND_AREA, it replaces them with the label TISSUE. Note that this filter is only executed if ISLAND_REPLACE is positive.

```
set lastConnection reader
if {$ISLAND_REPLACE >= 0} {
   vtkImageIslandRemoval2D islandRemover
      islandRemover SetAreaThreshold $ISLAND_AREA
      islandRemover SetIslandValue $ISLAND_REPLACE
      islandRemover SetReplaceValue $TISSUE
      islandRemover SetInput [$lastConnection GetOutput]
   set lastConnection islandRemover
}
```

Select a Tissue

The rest of the pipeline requires gray-scale data. To convert the volume that now contains integer tissue labels to a gray-scale volume containing only one tissue, we use the threshold filter to set all pixels with the value TISSUE (the tissue of choice for this pipeline) to 255 and all other pixels to 0. The choice of 255 is somewhat arbitrary.

```
vtkImageThreshold selectTissue
   selectTissue ThresholdBetween $TISSUE $TISSUE
   selectTissue SetInValue 255
   selectTissue SetOutValue 0
   selectTissue SetInput [$lastConnection GetOutput]
```

Resample the Volume

Lower resolution volumes produce fewer polygons. For experimentation we often reduce the resolution of the data with this filter. However, details can be lost during this process. Averaging creates new pixels in the resampled volume by averaging neighboring pixels. If averaging is turned off, every SAMPLE_RATE pixel will be passed through to the output.

```
vtkImageShrink3D shrinker
    shrinker SetInput [selectTissue GetOutput]
    eval shrinker SetShrinkFactors $SAMPLE_RATE
    shrinker AveragingOn
```

Smooth the Volume Data

To this point, unless we have resampled the data, the volume is labeled with a value of 255 in pixels of the selected tissue and 0 elsewhere. This "binary" volume would produce stepped surfaces if we did not blur it. The Gaussian kernel specified in this filter accomplishes the smoothing we require to extract surfaces. The amount of smoothing is controlled by GAUSSIAN_STANDARD_DEVIATION that can be independently specified for each axis of the volume data. We only run this filter if some smoothing is requested,

```
set lastConnection shrinker
if {$GAUSSIAN_STANDARD_DEVIATION != "0 0 0"} {
  vtkImageGaussianSmooth gaussian
  gaussian SetDimensionality 3
  gaussian SetStandardDeviation $GAUSSIAN_STANDARD_DEVIATION
  gaussian SetRadiusFactor 1
  gaussian SetInput [shrinker GetOutput]
  set lastConnection gaussian
}
```

Generate Triangles

Now we can process the volume with marching cubes just as though we had obtained gray-scale data from a scanner. We added a few more bells and whistles to the pipeline. The filter runs faster if we turn off gradient and normal calculations. Marching cubes normally calculates vertex normals from the gradient of the volume data. In our pipeline, we have concocted a gray-scale representation and will subsequently decimate the triangle mesh and smooth the resulting vertices. This processing invalidates the normals that are calculated by marching cubes.

```
vtkMarchingCubes mcubes
mcubes SetInput [toStructuredPoints GetOutput]
mcubes ComputeScalarsOff
mcubes ComputeGradientsOff
mcubes ComputeNormalsOff
eval mcubes SetValue 0 $VALUE
[mcubes GetOutput] ReleaseDataFlagOn
```

Reduce the Number of Triangles

There are often many more triangles generated by the isosurfacing algorithm than we need for rendering. Here we reduce the triangle count by eliminating triangle vertices that lie within a user-specified distance to the plane formed by neighboring vertices. We preserve any edges of triangles that are considered "features."

```
vtkDecimate decimator
  decimator SetInput [mcubes GetOutput]
  eval decimator SetInitialFeatureAngle $DECIMATE_ANGLE
  eval decimator SetMaximumIterations $DECIMATE_ITERATIONS
  decimator SetMaximumSubIterations 0
  decimator PreserveEdgesOn
  decimator SetMaximumError 1
  decimator SetTargetReduction $DECIMATE_REDUCTION
  eval decimator SetInitialError $DECIMATE_ERROR
  eval decimator SetErrorIncrement $DECIMATE_ERROR_INCREMENT
  [decimator GetOutput] ReleaseDataFlagOn
```

Smooth the Triangle Vertices

This filter uses Laplacian smoothing described in "Mesh Smoothing" on page 331 to adjust triangle vertices as an "average" of neighboring vertices. Typically, the movement will be less than a voxel. Of course we have already smoothed the image data with a Gaussian kernel so this step may not give much improvement; however, models that are heavily decimated can sometimes be improved with additional polygonal smoothing.

```
vtkSmoothPolyDataFilter smoother
  smoother SetInput [decimator GetOutput]
  eval smoother SetNumberOfIterations $SMOOTH_ITERATIONS
  eval smoother SetRelaxationFactor $SMOOTH_FACTOR
  eval smoother SetFeatureAngle $SMOOTH_ANGLE
  smoother FeatureEdgeSmoothingOff
  smoother BoundarySmoothingOff;
  smoother SetConvergence 0
  [smoother GetOutput] ReleaseDataFlagOn
```

Generate Normals

To generate smooth shaded models during rendering, we need normals at each vertex. As in decimation, sharp edges can be retained by setting the feature angle.

```
vtkPolyDataNormals normals
  normals SetInput [smoother GetOutput]
  eval normals SetFeatureAngle $FEATURE_ANGLE
  [normals GetOutput] ReleaseDataFlagOn
```

Generate Triangle Strips

Triangle strips are a compact representation of large numbers of triangles. This filter processes our independent triangles before we write them to a file.

```
vtkStripper stripper
  stripper SetInput [normals GetOutput]
  [stripper GetOutput] ReleaseDataFlagOn
```

Write the Triangles to a File

Finally, the last component of the pipeline writes the triangles strips to a file.

```
vtkPolyDataWriter writer
  writer SetInput [stripper GetOutput]
  eval writer SetFileName $NAME.vtk
```

Execute the Pipeline

If you have gotten this far in the book, you know that the *Visualization Toolkit* uses a demand-driven pipeline architecture and so far we have not demanded anything. We have just specified the pipeline topology and the parameters for each pipeline element.

```
writer Update
```

causes the pipeline to execute. In practice we do a bit more than just Update the last element of the pipeline. We explicitly Update each element so that we can time the individual steps. The script frogSegmentation.tcl contains the more sophisticated approach.

Specifying Parameters for the Pipeline

All of the variables mentioned above must be defined for each tissue to be processed. The parameters fall into two general categories. Some are specific to the particular study while some are specific to each tissue. For the frog, we collected the study-specific parameters in a file frog.tcl that contains:

```
set SLICE_ORDER hfsi
set ROWS 470
set COLUMNS 500
set STUDY ../frogMasks/frogTissue
set PIXEL_SIZE 1
set SPACING 1.5
set VALUE 511.5
set SAMPLE_RATE "1 1 1"
set DECIMATE_REDUCTION .95
set DECIMATE_ITERATIONS 5
set DECIMATE_ERROR .0002
set DECIMATE_ERROR_INCREMENT .0002
set SMOOTH_ITERATIONS 0
set SMOOTH_FACTOR .01
set FEATURE_ANGLE 60
```

There is a specific file for each tissue type. This tissue-specific file reads in the frog-specific parameters, sets tissue-specific parameters, and then reads the pipeline script (we call it frogSegmentation.tcl). For example, liver.tcl contains:

```
source frog.tcl
set NAME liver
set TISSUE 10
set START_SLICE 25
```

```
set END_SLICE 126
set VOI "167 297 154 304 $START_SLICE $END_SLICE"
source frogSegmentation.tcl
```

Parameters in `frog.tcl` can also be overridden. For example, `skeleton.tcl` overrides the standard deviation for the Gaussian filter.

```
source frog.tcl
set NAME skeleton
set TISSUE 13
set VALUE 368.5
set START_SLICE 1
set END_SLICE 136
set ZMAX [expr $END_SLICE - $START_SLICE]
set VOI "23 479 8 473 0 $ZMAX"
set GAUSSIAN_STANDARD_DEVIATION "1.5 1.5 1"
source frogSegmentation.tcl
```

Note that both of these examples specify a volume of interest. This improves performance of the imaging and visualization algorithms by eliminating empty space.

Another script, `marchingFrog.tcl`, uses similar parameters but processes the original gray-scale volume rather than the segmented volume. This script is used in `skin.tcl` to extract the skin. The file `marchingFrog.tcl` does not have the island removal or threshold pipeline elements since the data is already has gray-scale information.

Once the models are generated with the process just outlined, they can be rendered using the following tcl script called `ViewFrog.tcl`. First we create a Tcl procedure to automate the creation of actors from the model files. All the pipeline elements are named consistently with the name of the part followed by the name of the pipeline element. This makes it easy for the user to identify each object in more sophisticated user interfaces.

```
proc mkname {a b} {return $a$b}
# proc to make actors and create pipeline
proc MakeActor { name r g b} {
  set filename  [eval mkname $name .vtk]
  set reader  [eval mkname $name PolyDataReader]
  vtkPolyDataReader $reader
    $reader SetFileName $filename
  set mapper [eval mkname $name PolyDataMapper]
  vtkPolyDataMapper $mapper
    $mapper SetInput [$reader GetOutput]
      $mapper ScalarVisibilityOff
  set actor [ eval mkname $name Actor]
  vtkLODActor $actor
  $actor SetMapper $mapper
  eval [$actor GetProperty] SetDiffuseColor $r $g $b
  eval [$actor GetProperty] SetSpecularPower 50
  eval [$actor GetProperty] SetSpecular .5
  eval [$actor GetProperty] SetDiffuse .8
  return $actor
}
```

After the familiar code to create required rendering objects, a single statement for each part creates an actor we can add to the renderer:

```
# Now create the RenderWindow, Renderer and Interactor
vtkRenderer ren1
vtkRenderWindow renWin
    renWin AddRenderer ren1
vtkRenderWindowInteractor iren
    iren SetRenderWindow renWin
# Add the actors to the renderer using the MakeActor proc#
ren1 AddActor [eval MakeActor lung $powder_blue]
ren1 AddActor [eval MakeActor heart $tomato]
ren1 AddActor [eval MakeActor liver $pink]
ren1 AddActor [eval MakeActor duodenum $orange]
ren1 AddActor [eval MakeActor blood $salmon]
ren1 AddActor [eval MakeActor brain $beige]
ren1 AddActor [eval MakeActor eye_retna $misty_rose]
ren1 AddActor [eval MakeActor eye_white $white]
ren1 AddActor [eval MakeActor ileum $raspberry]
ren1 AddActor [eval MakeActor kidney $banana]
ren1 AddActor [eval MakeActor l_intestine $peru]
ren1 AddActor [eval MakeActor nerve $carrot]
ren1 AddActor [eval MakeActor spleen $violet]
ren1 AddActor [eval MakeActor stomach $plum]
ren1 AddActor [eval MakeActor skeleton $wheat]
```

The rest of the script defines a standard view.

```
ren1 SetBackground 0.2 0.3 0.4
renWin SetSize 450 450
[ren1 GetActiveCamera] SetViewUp 0 -1 0
[ren1 GetActiveCamera] Azimuth 30
[ren1 GetActiveCamera] Elevation 30
[ren1 GetActiveCamera] Dolly 1.75
iren Initialize
iren SetUserMethod {wm deiconify .vtkInteract}
# prevent the tk window from showing up
wm withdraw .
```

Figure 12–9 shows four views of the frog generated with `ViewFrog.tcl`.

This lengthy example shows the power of a comprehensive visualization system like the *Visualization Toolkit*.

- We mixed image processing and computer graphics algorithms to process data created by an external segmentation process.

- We developed a generic approach that allows users to control the elements of the pipeline with a familiar scripting language, tcl.

- We separated the task into a "batch" portion and an "interactive" portion.

Other Frog-Related Information

The folks at Lawrence Berkeley National Laboratory have an impressive Web site that fea-

All frog parts and
translucent skin.

The complete frog without skin.

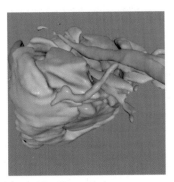

No skin or skeleton.

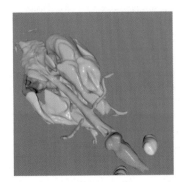

A view from the top. How good
is your biology?

Figure 12–9 Various frog images generated with `ViewFrog.tcl`.

tures the frog used in this example. The site describes how the frog data was obtained and also permits users to create mpeg movies of the frog. There are also other datasets available. Further details on "The Whole Frog Project" can be found at `http://www-itg.lbl.gov/Frog`. Also, the Stanford University Medical Media and Information Technologies (SUMMIT) group has on-going work using the Berkeley frog. They are early VTK users. Enjoy their *Virtual Creatures* project at: `http://summit.stanford.edu/creatures`.

12.3 Financial Visualization

The application of 3D visualization techniques to financial data is relatively new. Historically, financial data has been represented using 2D plotting techniques such as line, scatter plots, bar charts, and pie charts. These techniques are especially well suited for the display of price and volume information for stocks, bonds, and mutual funds. Three-dimensional techniques are becoming more important due to the increased volume of information in recent years, and 3D graphics and visualization techniques are becoming interactive. Interactive rates mean that visualization can be applied to the day-to-day processing of data. Our belief is that this will allow deeper understanding of today's complex financial data and other more timely decisions.

In this example we go through the process of obtaining data, converting it to a form that we can use, and then using visualization techniques to view it. Some of the external software tools used in this example may be unfamiliar to you. This should not be a large concern. We have simply chosen the tools with which we are familiar. Where we have used an Awk script, you might choose to write a small C program to do the same thing. The value of the example lies in illustrating the high-level process of solving a visualization problem.

The first step is to obtain the data. We obtained our data from a public site on the World Wide Web (WWW) that archives stock prices and volumes for many publicly traded stocks. (This Web site has closed down since publication of the first edition. The data for this example are available on the CD-ROM.)

Once we have obtained the data, we convert it to a format that can be read into VTK. While VTK can read in a variety of data formats, frequently your data will not be in one of those. The data files we obtained are stored in the following format:

```
930830   49.375   48.812   49.250   1139.2   56.1056
930831   49.375   48.938   49.125   1360.4   66.8297
930902   49.188   48.688   48.750   1247.2   60.801
. . .
```

Each line stores the data for one day of trading. The first number is the date, stored as the last two digits of the year, followed by a two-digit month and finally the day of the month. The next three values represent the high, low, and closing price of the stock for that day. The next value is the volume of trading in thousands of shares. The final value is the volume of trading in millions of dollars.

We used an Awk script to convert the original data format into a VTK data file. (See the *VTK User's Guide* for information on VTK file formats; or refer to the Web page http:/ /www.vtk.org/VTK/pdf/file-formats.pdf.) This conversion could be done using many other approaches, such as writing a C program or a Tcl script.

```
BEGIN {print "# vtk DataFile Version 2.0\n
Data values for stock\nASCII\n\nDATASET POLYDATA"}
{count += 1}
{ d = $1%100}
{ m = int(($1%10000)/100)}
{ if (m == 2) d += 31}
{ if (m == 3) d += 59}
{ if (m == 4) d += 90}
{ if (m == 5) d += 120}
{ if (m == 6) d += 151}
{ if (m == 7) d += 181}
{ if (m == 8) d += 212}
{ if (m == 9) d += 243}
{ if (m == 10) d += 273}
{ if (m == 11) d += 304}
{ if (m == 12) d += 334}
{ d = d + (int($1/10000) - 93)*365}
```

```
{dates[count] = d; prices[count] = $4; volumes[count] = $5}
END {
    print "POINTS " count " float";
    for (i = 1; i <= count; i++) print dates[i] " " prices[i] " 0 ";
    print "\nLINES 1 " (count + 1) " " count;
    for (i = 0; i < count; i++) print i;
    print "\nPOINT_DATA " count "\nSCALARS volume float";
    print "LOOKUP_TABLE default";
    for (i = 1; i <= count; i++) print volumes[i];
    }
```

The above Awk script performs the conversion. Its first line outputs the required header information indicating that the file is a VTK data file containing polygonal data. It also includes a comment indicating that the data represents stock values. There are a few different VTK data formats that we could have selected. It is up to you to decide which format best suits the data you are visualizing. We have judged the polygonal format (vtkPolyData) as best suited for this particular stock visualization.

The next line of the Awk script creates a variable named count that keeps track of how many days worth of information is in the file. This is equivalent to the number of lines in the original data file.

The next fourteen lines convert the six digit date into a more useful format, since the original format has a number of problems. If we were to blindly use the original format and plot the data using the date as the independent variable, there would be large gaps in our plot. For example, 931231 is the last day of 1993 and 940101 is the first day of 1994. Chronologically, these two dates are sequential, but mathematically there are (940101–931231=) 8870 values between them. A simple solution would be to use the line number as our independent variable. This would work as long as we knew that every trading day was recorded in the data file. It would not properly handle the situation where the market was open, but for some reason data was not recorded. A better solution is to convert the dates into numerically ordered days. The preceding Awk script sets January 1, 1993, as day number one, and then numbers all the following days from there. At the end of these 14 lines the variable, d, will contain the resulting value.

The next line in our Awk script stores the converted date, closing price, and dollar volume into arrays indexed by the line number stored in the variable count. Once all the lines have been read and stored into the arrays, we write out the rest of the VTK data file. We have selected the date as our independent variable and x coordinate. The closing price we store as the y coordinate, and the z coordinate we set to zero. After indicating the number and type of points to be stored, the Awk script loops through all the points and writes them out to the VTK data file. It then writes out the line connectivity list. In this case we just connect one point to the next to form a polyline for each stock. Finally, we write out the volume information as scalar data associated with the points. Portions of the resulting VTK data file are shown below.

```
# vtk DataFile Version 2.0
Data values for stock
ASCII
```

```
DATASET POLYDATA
POINTS 348 float
242 49.250 0
243 49.125 0
245 48.750 0
246 48.625 0
. . .

LINES 1 349 348
0
1
2
3
. . .

POINT_DATA 348
SCALARS volume float
LOOKUP_TABLE default
1139.2
1360.4
1247.2
1745.4
. . .
```

Now that we have generated the VTK data file, we can start the process of creating a visualization for the stock data. To do this, we wrote a Tcl script to be used with the Tcl-based VTK executable. At a high level the script reads in the stock data, sends it through a tube filter, creates a label for it, and then creates an outline around the resulting dataset. Ideally, we would like to display multiple stocks in the same window. To facilitate this, we designed the Tcl script to use a procedure to perform operations on a per stock basis. The resulting script is listed below.

```
package require vtk
# this is a tcl script for the stock case study
# Create the RenderWindow, Renderer and both Actors
vtkRenderer ren1
vtkRenderWindow renWin
  renWin AddRenderer ren1
vtkRenderWindowInteractor iren
  iren SetRenderWindow renWin

#create the outline
vtkAppendPolyData apf
vtkOutlineFilter olf
  olf SetInput [apf GetOutput]
vtkPolyDataMapper outlineMapper
  outlineMapper SetInput [olf GetOutput]
vtkActor outlineActor
  outlineActor SetMapper outlineMapper
```

```
set zpos 0

# create the stocks
proc AddStock {prefix name x y z} {
  global zpos

  # create labels
  vtkTextSource $prefix.TextSrc
    $prefix.TextSrc SetText "$name"
    $prefix.TextSrc SetBacking 0
  vtkPolyDataMapper $prefix.LabelMapper
    $prefix.LabelMapper SetInput [$prefix.TextSrc GetOutput]
  vtkFollower $prefix.LabelActor
    $prefix.LabelActor SetMapper $prefix.LabelMapper
    $prefix.LabelActor SetPosition $x $y $z
    $prefix.LabelActor SetScale 0.25 0.25 0.25
    eval $prefix.LabelActor SetOrigin
                  [$prefix.LabelMapper GetCenter]
  # create a sphere source and actor
  vtkPolyDataReader $prefix.PolyDataRead
    $prefix.PolyDataRead SetFileName
                "../../../vtkdata/$prefix.vtk"
  vtkTubeFilter $prefix.TubeFilter
    $prefix.TubeFilter SetInput [$prefix.PolyDataRead GetOutput]
    $prefix.TubeFilter SetNumberOfSides 8
    $prefix.TubeFilter SetRadius 0.5
    $prefix.TubeFilter SetRadiusFactor 10000
  vtkTransform $prefix.Transform
    $prefix.Transform Translate 0 0 $zpos
    $prefix.Transform Scale 0.15 1 1
  vtkTransformPolyDataFilter $prefix.TransformFilter
    $prefix.TransformFilter SetInput
                    [$prefix.TubeFilter GetOutput]
    $prefix.TransformFilter SetTransform $prefix.Transform
  # increment zpos
  set zpos [expr $zpos + 10]
  vtkPolyDataMapper $prefix.StockMapper
    $prefix.StockMapper SetInput
            [$prefix.TransformFilter GetOutput]
  vtkActor $prefix.StockActor
    $prefix.StockActor SetMapper $prefix.StockMapper
    $prefix.StockMapper SetScalarRange 0 8000
    [$prefix.StockActor GetProperty] SetAmbient 0.5
    [$prefix.StockActor GetProperty] SetDiffuse 0.5

  apf AddInput [$prefix.TransformFilter GetOutput]

  ren1 AddActor $prefix.StockActor
  ren1 AddActor $prefix.LabelActor
  $prefix.LabelActor SetCamera [ren1 GetActiveCamera]
```

```
}

# set up the stocks
ddStock GE "GE" 94 46 4
AddStock GM "GM" 107 39 14
AddStock IBM "IBM" 92 70 16
AddStock DEC "DEC" 70 19 26

# Add the actors to the renderer, set the background and size
#
ren1 AddActor outlineActor
ren1 SetBackground 0.1 0.2 0.4
renWin SetSize 1200 600

# render the image
[ren1 GetActiveCamera] SetViewAngle 10
ren1 ResetCamera
[ren1 GetActiveCamera] Zoom 2.8
[ren1 GetActiveCamera] Elevation 90
[ren1 GetActiveCamera] SetViewUp 0 0 -1
iren Initialize

# prevent the tk window from showing up then start the event loop
wm withdraw .
```

The first part of this script consists of the standard procedure for renderer and interactor creation that can be found in almost all of the VTK Tcl scripts. The next section creates the objects necessary for drawing an outline around all of the stock data. A vtkAppendPolyData filter is used to append all of the stock data together. This is then sent through a vtkOutlineFilter to create a bounding box around the data. A mapper and actor are created to display the result.

In the next part of this script, we define the procedure to add stock data to this visualization. The procedure takes five arguments: the name of the stock, the label we want displayed, and the *x*, *y*, *z* coordinates defining where to position the label. The first line of the procedure indicates that the variable ren1 should be visible to this procedure. By default the procedure can only access its own local variables. Next, we create the label using a vtkTextSource, vtkPolyDataMapper, and vtkFollower. The names of these objects are all prepended with the variable "$prefix." so that the instance names will be unique. An instance of vtkFollower is used instead of the usual vtkActor, because we always want the text to be right-side up and facing the camera. The vtkFollower class provides this functionality. The remaining lines position and scale the label appropriately. We set the origin of the label to the center of its data. This insures that the follower will rotate about its center point.

The next group of lines creates the required objects to read in the data, pass it through a tube filter and a transform filter, and finally display the result. The tube filter uses the scalar data (stock volume in this example) to determine the radius of the tube. The mapper also uses the scalar data to determine the coloring of the tube. The transform filter uses a transform object to set the stock's position based on the value of the variable zpos. For each stock, we will increment zpos by 10, effectively shifting the next stock over 10 units from the current

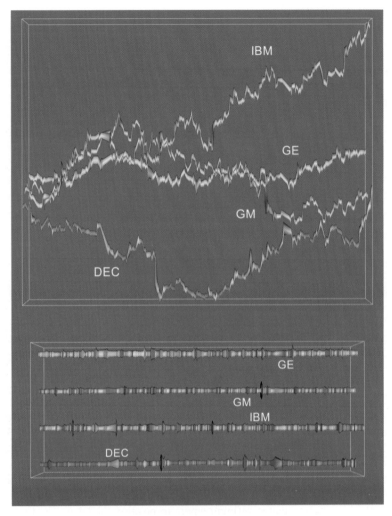

Figure 12–10 Two views from the stock visualization script. The top shows closing price over time; the bottom shows volume over time (`stocks.tcl`).

stock. This prevents the stocks from being stacked on top of each other. We also use the transform to compress the *x*-axis to make the data easier to view. Next, we add this stock as an input to the append filter and add the actors and followers to the renderer. The last line of the procedure sets the follower's camera to be the active camera of the renderer.

Back in the main body of the Tcl script, we invoke the AddStock procedure four times with four different stocks. Finally, we add the outline actor and customize the renderer and camera to produce a nice initial view. Two different views of the result are displayed in **Figure 12–10**. The top image shows a history of stock closing prices for our four stocks. The color and width of these lines correspond to the volume of the stock on that day. The lower image more clearly illustrates the changes in stock volume by looking at the data from above.

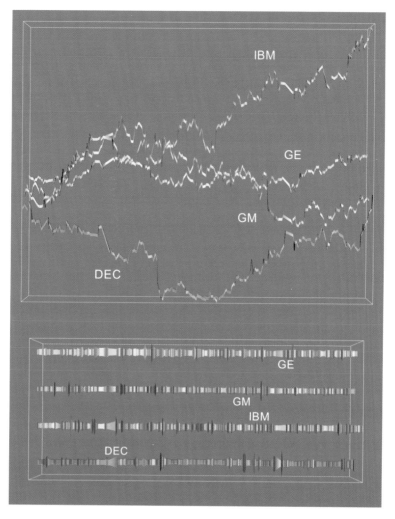

Figure 12–11   Two more views of the stock case study. Here the tube filter has been replaced by a ribbon filter followed with a linear extrusion filter.

A legitimate complaint with **Figure 12–10** is that the changing width of the tube makes it more difficult to see the true shape of the price verses the time curve. We can solve this problem by using a ribbon filter followed by a linear extrusion filter, instead of the tube filter. The ribbon filter will create a ribbon whose width will vary in proportion to the scalar value of the data. We then use the linear extrusion filter to extrude this ribbon along the *y*-axis so that it has a constant thickness. The resulting views are shown in **Figure 12–11**.

12.4 Implicit Modelling

The *Visualization Toolkit* has some useful geometric modelling capabilities. One of the most powerful features is implicit modelling. In this example we show how to use polygonal descriptions of objects and create "blobby" models of them using the implicit modelling objects in VTK. This example generates a logo for the *Visualization Toolkit* from polygonal representations of the letters *v*, *t*, and *k*.

We create three separate visualization pipelines, one for each letter. **Figure 12–12** shows the visualization pipeline. As is common in VTK applications, we design a pipeline and fill in the details of the instance variables just before we render. We pass the letters through a vtkTransformPolyDataFilter to position them relative to each other. Then we combine all of the polygons from the transformed letters into one polygon dataset using the vtkAppendPolyData filter. The vtkImplicitModeller creates a volume dataset of dimension 64^3 with each voxel containing a scalar value that is the distance to the nearest polygon. Recall from "Implicit Modelling" on page 177, that the implicit modelling algorithm lets us specify the region of influence of each polygon. Here we specify this using the SetMaximumDistance() method of the vtkImplicitModeller. By restricting the region of influence, we can significantly improve performance of the implicit modelling algorithm. Then we use vtkContourFilter to extract an isosurface that approximates a distance of 1.0 from each polygon. We create two actors: one for the blobby logo and one for the original polygon letters. Notice that both actors share the polygon data created by vtkAppendPolyData. Because of the nature of the VTK visualization pipeline (see "Implicit Control of Execution" on page 99), the appended data will only be created once by the portion of the pipeline that is executed first. As a final touch, we move the polygonal logo in front of the blobby logo. Now we will go through the example in detail.

First, we read the geometry files that contain polygonal models of each letter in the logo. The data is in VTK polygonal format, so we use vtkPolyDataReader.

```
vtkPolyDataReader *letterV = vtkPolyDataReader::New();
  letterV->SetFileName ("v.vtk");

vtkPolyDataReader *letterT = vtkPolyDataReader::New();
  letterT->SetFileName ("t.vtk");

vtkPolyDataReader *letterK = vtkPolyDataReader::New();
  letterK->SetFileName ("k.vtk");
```

We want to transform each letter into its appropriate location and orientation within the logo. We create the transform filters here, but defer specifying the location and orientation until later in the program.

```
vtkTransform *VTransform = vtkTransform::New();
vtkTransformPolyDataFilter *VTransformFilter =
    vtkTransformPolyDataFilter::New();
    VTransformFilter->SetInput (letterV->GetOutput());
```

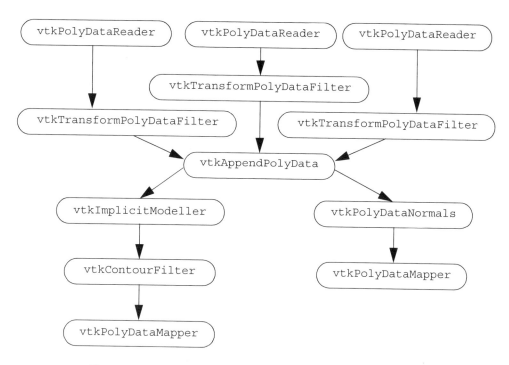

Figure 12–12 The visualization pipeline for the VTK blobby logo.

```
VTransformFilter->SetTransform (VTransform);

vtkTransform *TTransform = vtkTransform::New();
vtkTransformPolyDataFilter *TTransformFilter =
     vtkTransformPolyDataFilter::New();
   TTransformFilter->SetInput (letterT->GetOutput());
   TTransformFilter->SetTransform (TTransform);

vtkTransform *KTransform = vtkTransform::New();
vtkTransformPolyDataFilter *KTransformFilter =
     vtkTransformPolyDataFilter::New();
   KTransformFilter->SetInput (letterK->GetOutput());
   KTransformFilter->SetTransform (KTransform);
```

We collect all of the transformed letters into one set of polygons by using an instance of the class vtkAppendPolyData.

```
vtkAppendPolyData *appendAll = vtkAppendPolyData::New();
appendAll->AddInput (VTransformFilter->GetOutput());
appendAll->AddInput (TTransformFilter->GetOutput());
appendAll->AddInput (KTransformFilter->GetOutput());
```

Since the geometry for each letter did not have surface normals, we add them here. We use vtkPolyDataNormals. Then we complete this portion of the pipeline by creating a mapper and an actor.

```
// create normals
vtkPolyDataNormals *logoNormals = vtkPolyDataNormals::New();
    logoNormals->SetInput (appendAll->GetOutput());
    logoNormals->SetFeatureAngle (60);

// map to rendering primitives
vtkPolyDataMapper *logoMapper = vtkPolyDataMapper::New();
    logoMapper->SetInput (logoNormals->GetOutput());

// now an actor
vtkActor *logo = vtkActor::New();
    logo->SetMapper (logoMapper);
```

We create the blobby logo with the implicit modeller, and then extract the logo with vtkContourFilter. The pipeline is completed by creating a mapper and an actor.

```
// now create an implicit model of the letters
vtkImplicitModeller *blobbyLogoImp = vtkImplicitModeller::New();
    blobbyLogoImp->SetInput (appendAll->GetOutput());
    blobbyLogoImp->SetMaximumDistance (.075);
    blobbyLogoImp->SetSampleDimensions (64,64,64);
    blobbyLogoImp->SetAdjustDistance (0.05);

// extract an iso surface
vtkContourFilter *blobbyLogoIso = vtkContourFilter::New();
    blobbyLogoIso->SetInput (blobbyLogoImp->GetOutput());
    blobbyLogoIso->SetValue (1, 1.5);

// map to rendering primitives
vtkPolyDataMapper *blobbyLogoMapper = vtkPolyDataMapper::New();
    blobbyLogoMapper->SetInput (blobbyLogoIso->GetOutput());
    blobbyLogoMapper->ScalarVisibilityOff ();

// now an actor
vtkActor *blobbyLogo = vtkActor::New();
    blobbyLogo->SetMapper (blobbyLogoMapper);
    blobbyLogo->SetProperty (banana);
```

To improve the look of our resulting visualization, we define a couple of organic colors. Softer colors show up better on some electronic media (e.g., VHS video tape) and are pleasing to the eye.

```
vtkProperty *tomato = vtkProperty::New();
    tomato->SetDiffuseColor (1, .3882, .2784);
    tomato->SetSpecular (.3);
    tomato->SetSpecularPower (20);
```

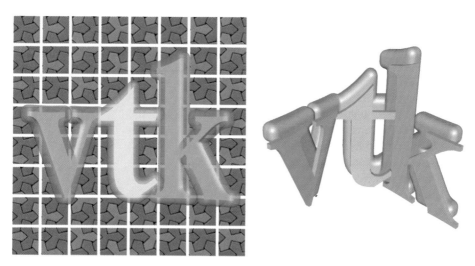

Figure 12–13 A logo created with `vtkImplicitModeller` (`vtkLogo.cxx`).

```
vtkProperty *banana = vtkProperty::New();
    banana->SetDiffuseColor(.89, .81, .34);
    banana->SetDiffuse (.7);
    banana->SetSpecular(.4);
    banana->SetSpecularPower(20);
```

These colors are then assigned to the appropriate actors.

```
    logo->SetProperty (tomato);

    blobbyLogo->SetProperty (banana);
```

And finally, we position the letters in the logo and move the polygonal logo out in front of the blobby logo by modifying the actor's position.

```
    VTransform->Translate (-16,0,12.5);
    VTransform->RotateY (40);
    KTransform->Translate (14, 0, 0);
    KTransform->RotateY (-40);

    // move the polygonal letters to the front
    logo->SetPosition(0,0,6);
```

An image made from the techniques described in this section is shown in **Figure 12–13**. Note that the image on the left has been augmented with a texture map.

12.5 Computational Fluid Dynamics

Computational Fluid Dynamics (CFD) visualization poses a challenge to any visualization toolkit. CFD studies the flow of fluids in and around complex structures. Often, large amounts of supercomputer time is used to derive scalar and vector data in the flow field. Since CFD computations produce multiple scalar and vector data types, we will apply many of the tools described in this book. The challenge is to combine multiple representations into meaningful visualizations that extract information without overwhelming the user.

CFD analysts often employ finite difference grids. A finite difference grid represents the discretization of the problem domain into small computational cells. The grid allows the analyst to create a large system of equations that can then be solved on a computer. The grid is topologically uniform in *i-j-k* space, but the corresponding physical coordinates need not be uniformly distributed. This is what we call a structured grid dataset in VTK.

There are a number of techniques we can use when we first look at the complex data presented by CFD applications. Since we need to apply several algorithms to the data, and since there will be many parameter changes for these algorithms, we suggest using the Tcl interpreter rather than C++ code. Our strategy for visualizing this CFD data includes the following:

1. Display the computational grid. The analyst carefully constructed the finite difference grid to have a higher density in regions where rapid changes occur in the flow variables. We will display the grid in wireframe so we can see the computational cells.

2. Display the scalar fields on the computational grid. This will give us an overview of where the scalar data is changing. We will experiment with the extents of the grid extraction to focus on interesting areas.

3. Explore the vector field by seeding streamlines with a spherical cloud of points. Move the sphere through areas of rapidly changing velocity.

4. Try using the computational grid itself as seeds for the streamlines. Of course we will have to restrict the extent of the grid you use for this purpose. Using the grid, we will be able to place more seeds in regions where the analyst expected more action.

For this case study, we use a dataset from NASA called the LOx Post. It simulates the flow of liquid oxygen across a flat plate with a cylindrical post perpendicular to the flow [Rogers86]. This analysis models the flow in a rocket engine. The post promotes mixing of the liquid oxygen.

We start by exploring the scalar and vector fields in the data. By calculating the magnitude of the velocity vectors, we derive a scalar field. This study has a particularly interesting vector field around the post. We seed the field with multiple starting points (using points arranged along a curve, referred to as a *rake*) and experiment with parameters for the streamlines. Streampolygons are particularly appropriate here and do a nice job of showing the flow downstream from the post. We animate the streamline creation by moving the seeding line or rake back and forth behind the post.

Following our own advice, we first display the computational grid. The following Tcl code produced the right image of **Figure 12–14**.

```
# read data
```

```
vtkPLOT3DReader pl3d
  pl3d SetXYZFileName "$env(VTK_TEXTBOOK_DATA)/postxyz.bin"
  pl3d SetQFileName "$env(VTK_TEXTBOOK_DATA)/postq.bin"
  pl3d IBlankingOn
  pl3d Update

# computational planes: the floor
vtkStructuredGridGeometryFilter floorComp
  floorComp SetExtent 0 37 0 75 0 0
  floorComp SetInput [pl3d GetOutput]
vtkPolyDataMapper floorMapper
  floorMapper SetInput [floorComp GetOutput]
  floorMapper ScalarVisibilityOff
vtkActor floorActor
  floorActor SetMapper floorMapper
  [floorActor GetProperty] SetColor 0 0 0
  [floorActor GetProperty] SetRepresentationToWireframe

# the post
vtkStructuredGridGeometryFilter postComp
  postComp SetExtent 10 10 0 75 0 37
  postComp SetInput [pl3d GetOutput]
vtkPolyDataMapper postMapper
  postMapper SetInput [postComp GetOutput]
  postMapper ScalarVisibilityOff
vtkActor postActor
  postActor SetMapper postMapper
  [postActor GetProperty] SetColor 0 0 0
  [postActor GetProperty] SetRepresentationToWireframe

# plane upstream of the flow
vtkStructuredGridGeometryFilter fanComp
  fanComp SetExtent 0 37 38 38 0 37
  fanComp SetInput [pl3d GetOutput]
vtkPolyDataMapper fanMapper
  fanMapper SetInput [fanComp GetOutput]
  fanMapper ScalarVisibilityOff
vtkActor fanActor
  fanActor SetMapper fanMapper
  [fanActor GetProperty] SetColor 0 0 0
  [fanActor GetProperty] SetRepresentationToWireframe

# outline
vtkStructuredGridOutlineFilter outline
  outline SetInput [pl3d GetOutput]
vtkPolyDataMapper outlineMapper
  outlineMapper SetInput [outline GetOutput]
vtkActor outlineActor
  outlineActor SetMapper outlineMapper
  [outlineActor GetProperty] SetColor 0 0 0
```

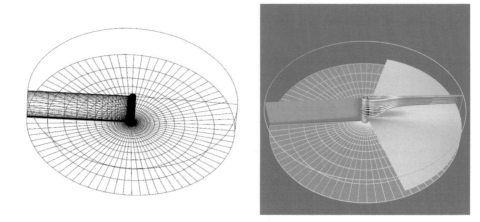

Figure 12–14 Portion of computational grid for the LOx post (LOxGrid.tcl).

```
# Create graphics stuff
vtkRenderer ren1
vtkRenderWindow renWin
    renWin AddRenderer ren1
vtkRenderWindowInteractor iren
    iren SetRenderWindow renWin

# Add the actors to the renderer, set the background and size
#
ren1 AddActor outlineActor
ren1 AddActor floorActor
ren1 AddActor postActor
ren1 AddActor fanActor
```

To display the scalar field using color mapping, we must change the actor's representation from wireframe to surface, turn on scalar visibility for each vtkPolyDataMapper, set each mapper's scalar range, and render again, producing the right image of **Figure 12–14**.

```
postActor SetRepresentationToSurface
fanActor SetRepresentationToSurface
floorActor SetRepresentationToSurface

postMapper ScalarVisibilityOn
postMapper SetScalarRange [[pl3d GetOutput] GetScalarRange]
fanMapper ScalarVisibilityOn
fanMapper SetScalarRange [[pl3d GetOutput] GetScalarRange]
floorMapper ScalarVisibilityOn
floorMapper SetScalarRange [[pl3d GetOutput] GetScalarRange]
```

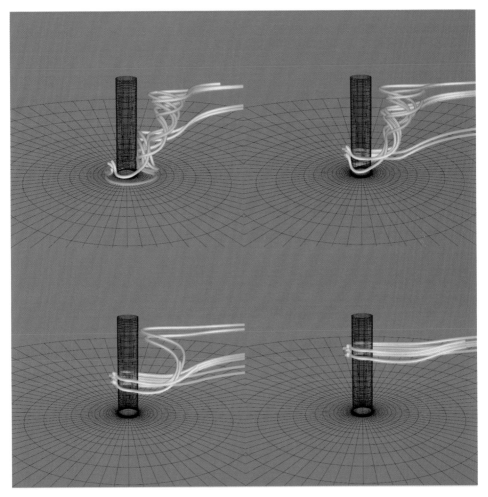

Figure 12–15 Streamlines seeded with spherical cloud of points. Four separate cloud positions are shown.

Now, we explore the vector field using vtkPointSource. Recall that this object generates a random cloud of points around a spherical center point. We will use this cloud of points to generate streamlines. We place the center of the cloud near the post since this is where the velocity seems to be changing most rapidly. During this exploration, we use streamlines rather than streamtubes for reasons of efficiency. The Tcl code is as follows.

```
# spherical seed points
vtkPointSource rake
    rake SetCenter -0.74 0 0.3
    rake SetNumberOfPoints 10
vtkStreamLine streamers
    streamers SetInput [pl3d GetOutput]
```

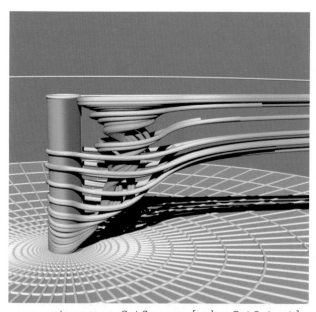

Figure 12–16 Streamtubes created by using the computational grid just in front of the post as a source for seeds (LOx.tcl).

```
   streamers SetSource [rake GetOutput]
   streamers SetMaximumPropagationTime 250
   streamers SpeedScalarsOn
   streamers SetIntegrationStepLength .2
   streamers SetStepLength .25
vtkPolyDataMapper mapTubes
   mapTubes SetInput [streamers GetOutput]
   eval mapTubes SetScalarRange [[pl3d GetOutput] GetScalarRange]
vtkActor tubesActor
   tubesActor SetMapper mapTubes
```

Figure 12–15 shows streamlines seeded from four locations along the post. Notice how the structure of the flow begins to emerge as the starting positions for the streamlines are moved up and down in front of the post. This is particularly true if we do this interactively; the mind assembles the behavior of the streamlines into a global understanding of the flow field.

For a final example, we use the computational grid to seed streamlines and then generate streamtubes as is shown in **Figure 12–16**. A nice feature of this approach is that we generate more streamlines in regions where the analyst constructed a denser grid. The only change we need to make is to replace the rake from the sphere source with a portion of the grid geometry.

```
vtkStructuredGridGeometryFilter seedsComp
   seedsComp SetExtent 10 10 37 39 1 35
   seedsComp SetInput [pl3d GetOutput]
streamers SetSource [seedsComp GetOutput]
# create tubes
vtkTubeFilter tubes
    tubes SetInput [streamers GetOutput]
    tubes SetNumberOfSides 8
```

```
      tubes SetRadius .08
      tubes SetVaryRadiusOff
# change input to streamtubes
mapTubes SetInput [tubes GetOutput]
```

There are a number of other methods we could use to visualize this data. A 3D widget such as the vtkLineWidget could be used to seed the streamlines interactively (see "3D Widgets and User Interaction" on page 241). As we saw in "Point Probe" on page 293, probing the data for numerical values is a valuable technique. In particular, if the probe is a line we can use it in combination with vtkXYPlotActor to graph the variation of data value along the line. Another useful visualization would be to identify regions of vorticity. We could use **Equation 9-12** in conjunction with an isocontouring algorithm (e.g., vtkContourFilter) to creates isosurfaces of large helical-density.

12.6 Finite Element Analysis

Finite element analysis is a widely used numerical technique for finding solutions of partial differential equations. Applications of finite element analysis include linear and nonlinear structural, thermal, dynamic, electromagnetic, and flow analysis. In this application we will visualize the results of a blow molding process.

In the extrusion blow molding process, a material is extruded through an annular die to form a hollow cylinder. This cylinder is called a *parison*. Two mold halves are then closed on the parison, while at the same time the parison is inflated with air. Some of the parison material remains within the mold while some becomes waste material. The material is typically a polymer plastic softened with heat, but blow molding has been used to form metal parts. Plastic bottles are often manufactured using a blow molding process.

Designing the parison die and molds is not easy. Improper design results in large variations in the wall thickness. In some cases the part may fail in thin-walled regions. As a result, analysis tools based on finite element techniques have been developed to assist in the design of molds and dies.

The results of one such analysis are shown in **Figure 12–17**. The polymer was molded using an isothermal, nonlinear-elastic, incompressible (rubber-like) material. Triangular membrane finite elements were used to model the parison, while a combination of triangular and quadrilateral finite elements were used to model the mold. The mold surface is assumed to be rigid, and the parison is assumed to attach to the mold upon contact. Thus the thinning of the parison is controlled by its stretching during inflation and the sequence in which it contacts the mold.

Figure 12–17 illustrates 10 steps of one analysis. The color of the parison indicates its thickness. Using a rainbow scale, red areas are thinnest while blue regions are thickest. Our visualization shows clearly one problem with the analysis technique we are using. Note that while the nodes (i.e., points) of the finite element mesh are prevented from passing through the mold, the interior of the triangular elements are not. This is apparent from the occlusion of the mold wireframe by the parison mesh.

To generate these images, we used a Tcl script shown in **Figure 12–18** and **Figure 12–19**. The input data is in VTK format, so a vtkUnstructuredGridReader was used as a source

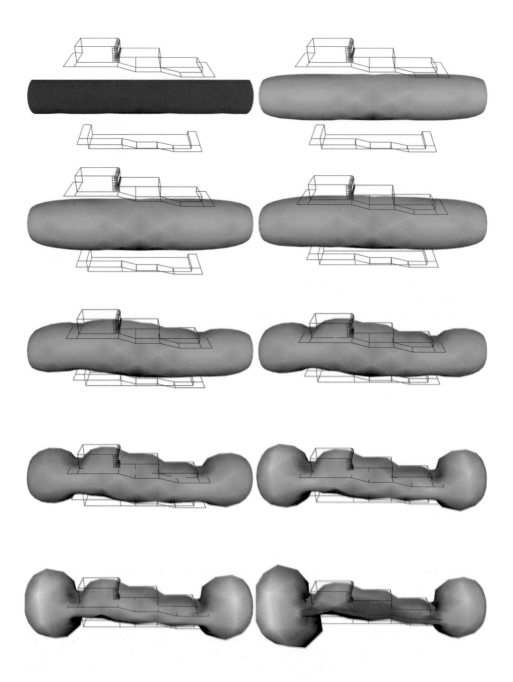

Figure 12–17 Ten frames from a blow molding finite element analysis. Mold halves (shown in wireframe) are closed around a parison as the parison is inflated. Coloring indicates thickness—red areas are thinner than blue (blow.tcl)

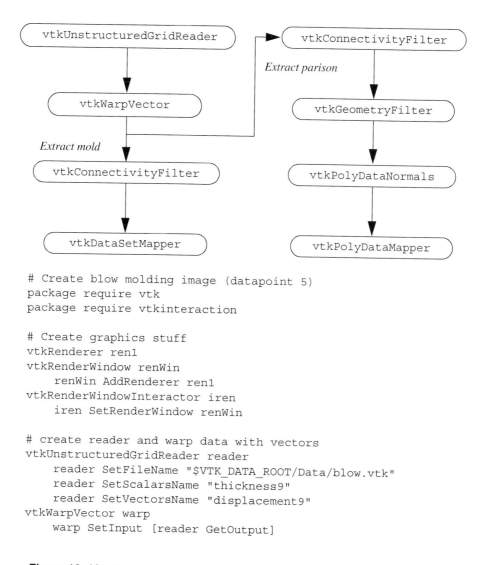

Figure 12–18 Tcl script to generate blow molding image. Network topology and initial portion of script are shown (Part one of two).

object. The mesh displacement is accomplished using an instance of vtkWarpVector. At this point the pipeline splits. We wish to treat the mold and parison differently (different properties such as wireframe versus surface), but the data for both mold and parison is combined. Fortunately, we can easily separate the data using two instances of class vtkConnectivityFilter. One filter extracts the parison, while the other extracts both parts of the mold. Finally, to achieve a smooth surface appearance on the parison, we use a vtkPolyDataNormals filter. In order to use this filter, we have to convert the data type from vtkUnstructuredGrid (output of vtkConnectivityFilter) to type vtkPolyData. The filter

```
# extract mold from mesh using connectivity
vtkConnectivityFilter connect
    connect SetInput [warp GetOutput]
    connect SetExtractionModeToSpecifiedRegions
    connect AddSpecifiedRegion 0
    connect AddSpecifiedRegion 1
vtkDataSetMapper moldMapper
    moldMapper SetInput [connect GetOutput]
    moldMapper ScalarVisibilityOff
vtkActor moldActor
    moldActor SetMapper moldMapper
    [moldActor GetProperty] SetColor .2 .2 .2
    [moldActor GetProperty] SetRepresentationToWireframe


# extract parison from mesh using connectivity
vtkConnectivityFilter connect2
    connect2 SetInput [warp GetOutput]
    connect2 SetExtractionModeToSpecifiedRegions
    connect2 AddSpecifiedRegion 2
vtkGeometryFilter parison
    parison SetInput [connect2 GetOutput]
vtkPolyDataNormals normals2
    normals2 SetInput [parison GetOutput]
    normals2 SetFeatureAngle 60
vtkLookupTable lut
    lut SetHueRange 0.0 0.66667
vtkPolyDataMapper parisonMapper
    parisonMapper SetInput [normals2 GetOutput]
    parisonMapper SetLookupTable lut
    parisonMapper SetScalarRange 0.12 1.0
vtkActor parisonActor
    parisonActor SetMapper parisonMapper


# Add the actors to the renderer, set the background and size
ren1 AddActor moldActor
ren1 AddActor parisonActor
ren1 SetBackground 1 1 1
renWin SetSize 750 400


iren Initialize
iren AddObserver UserEvent {wm deiconify .vtkInteract}

# prevent the tk window from showing up then start the event loop
wm withdraw .
```

Figure 12–19 Tcl script to generate blow molding image (Part two of two).

```
// Recursive solution of Towers of Hanoi. Parameters are number
// of disks,originating peg, final peg, and intermediate peg.
static void Hanoi (int n, int peg1, int peg2, int peg3)
{
  if ( n != 1 )
    {
    Hanoi (n-1, peg1, peg3, peg2);
    Hanoi (1, peg1, peg2, peg3);
    Hanoi (n-1, peg3, peg2, peg1);
    }
  else
    {
    MovePuck (peg1, peg2);
    }
}
```

Figure 12–21 C++ code for recursive solution of Towers of Hanoi (Hanoi.cxx).

vtkGeometryFilter does this nicely.

12.7 Algorithm Visualization

Visualization can be used to display algorithms and data structures. Representing this information often requires creative work on the part of the application programmer. For example, Robertson et al. [Robertson91] have shown 3D techniques for visualizing directory structures and navigating through them. Their approach involves building three dimensional models (the so-called "cone trees") to represent files, directories, and associations between files and directories. Similar approaches can be used to visualize stacks, queues, linked lists, trees, and other data structures.

In this example we will visualize the operation of the recursive Towers of Hanoi puzzle. In this puzzle there are three pegs (**Figure 12–20**). In the initial position there are one or more disks (or pucks) of varying diameter on the pegs. The disks are sorted according to disk diameter, so that the largest disk is on the bottom, followed by the next largest, and so on. The goal of the puzzle is to move the disks from one peg to another, moving the disks one at a time, and never placing a larger disk on top of a smaller disk.

The classical solution to this puzzle is based on a divide-and-conquer approach [AhoHopUll83]. The problem of moving n disks from the initial peg to the second peg can be thought of as solving two subproblems of size $n-1$. First move $n-1$ disks from the initial peg to the third peg. Then move the nth disk to the second peg. Finally, move the $n-1$ disks on the third peg back to the second peg.

The solution to this problem can be elegantly implemented using recursion. We have shown portions of the C++ code in **Figure 12–21** and **Figure 12–22**. In the first part of the solution (which is not shown in **Figure 12–21**) the table top, pegs, and disks are created using the two classes vtkPlaneSource and vtkCylinderSource. The function Hanoi() is then called to begin the recursion. The routine MovePuck() is responsible for moving a disk from one

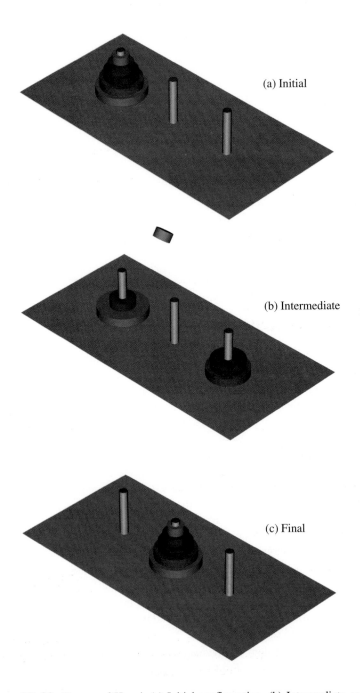

Figure 12–20 Towers of Hanoi. (a) Initial configuration. (b) Intermediate configuration. (c) Final configuration (`Hanoi.cxx`).

```
// Routine is responsible for moving disks from one peg to the next
//.
void MovePuck (int peg1, int peg2)
{
  float distance, flipAngle;
  vtkActor *movingActor;
  int i;

  NumberOfMoves++;
  // get the actor to move
  movingActor = (vtkActor *)pegStack[peg1].Pop();
  // get the distance to move up
  distance = (H - (L * (pegStack[peg1].GetNumberOfItems() -1)) + rMax
              / NumberOfSteps;
  for (i=0; i<NumberOfSteps; i++)
    {
    movingActor->AddPosition(0,distance,0);
    Renwin->Render();
    }
  // get the distance to move across
  distance = (peg2 - peg1) * D / NumberOfSteps;
  flipAngle = 180.0 / NumberOfSteps;
  for (i=0; i<NumberOfSteps; i++)
    {
    movingActor->AddPosition(distance,0,0);
    movingActor->RotateX(flipAngle);
    Renwin->Render();
    }
  // get the distance to move down
  distance = ((L * (pegStack[peg2].GetNumberOfItems() - 1)) - H -
  rMax) / NumberOfSteps;
  for (i=0; i<NumberOfSteps; i++)
    {
    movingActor->AddPosition(0,distance,0);
    Renwin->Render();
    }
  pegStack[peg2].Push(movingActor);
}
```

Figure 12–22 Function to move disks from one peg to another in the Towers of Hanoi example. The resulting motion is in small steps with an additional flip of the disk.

peg to another. It has been jazzed up to move the disk in small, user-specified increments, and to flip the disc over as it moves from one peg to the next. This gives a pleasing visual effect and adds the element of fun to the visualization.

Because of the clear relationship between algorithm and physical reality, the Towers of Hanoi puzzle is relatively easy to visualize. A major challenge facing visualization research-ers is to visualize more abstract information, such as information on the Internet, the structure of documents, or the effectiveness of advertising/entertainment in large market segments. This type of visualization, known as information visualization, is likely to emerge in the future as an important research challenge.

12.8 Chapter Summary

This chapter presented several case studies covering a variety of visualization techniques. The examples used different data representations including polygonal data, volumes, structured grids, and unstructured grids. Both C++ and Tcl code was used to implement the case studies.

Medical imaging is a demanding application area due to the size of the input data. Three-dimensional visualization of anatomy is generally regarded by radiologists as a communication tool for referring physicians and surgeons. Medical datasets are typically image data—volumes or layered stacks of 2D images that form volumes. Common visualization tools for medical imaging include isosurfaces, cut planes, and image display on volume slices.

Next, we presented an example that applied 3D visualization techniques to financial data. In this case study, we began by showing how to import data from an external source. We applied tube filters to the data and varied the width of the tube to show the volume of stock trading. We saw how different views can be used to present different pieces of information. In this case, we saw that by viewing the visualization from the front, we saw a conventional price display. Then, by viewing the visualization from above, we saw trade volume.

In the modelling case study we showed how to use polygonal models and the implicit modelling facilities in VTK to create a stylistic logo. The final model was created by extracting an isosurface at a user-selected offset.

Computational fluid dynamics analysts frequently employ structured grid data. We examined some strategies for exploring the scalar and vector fields. The computational grid created by the analyst serves as a starting point for analyzing the data. We displayed geometry extracted from the finite difference grid, scalar color mapping, and streamlines and streamtubes to investigate the data.

In the finite element case study, we looked at unstructured grids used in a simulation of a blow molding process. We displayed the deformation of the geometry using displacement plots, and represented the material thickness using color mapping. We saw how we can create simple animations by generating a sequence of images.

We concluded the case studies by visualizing the Towers of Hanoi algorithm. Here we showed how to combine the procedural power of C++ with the visualization capabilities in VTK. We saw how visualization often requires our creative resources to cast data structures and information into visual form.

12.9 Bibliographic Notes

The case studies presented in the chapter rely on having interesting data to visualize. Sometimes the hardest part of practicing visualizing is finding relevant data. The Internet is a tremendous resource for this task. Paul Gilster [Gilster94] has written an excellent introduction to many of the tools for accessing information on the Internet. There are many more books available on this subject in the local bookstore.

In the stock case study we used a programming tool called AWK to convert our data into a form suitable for VTK. More information on AWK can be found in *The AWK Programming Language* [Aho88]. Another popular text processing languages is Perl [Perl95].

If you would like to know more about information visualization you can start with the references listed here [Becker95] [Ding90] [Eick93] [Feiner88] [Johnson91] [Robertson91]. This is a relatively new field but will certainly grow in the near future.

12.10 References

[Aho88]

A. V. Aho, B. W. Kernighan, and P. J. Weinberger. *The AWK Programming Language*. Addison-Wesley, Reading, MA, 1988.

[AhoHopUll83]

A. V. Aho, J. E. Hopcroft, and J. D. Ullman. *Data Structures and Algorithms*. Addison-Wesley, Reading, MA, 1983.

[Becker95]

R. A. Becker, S. G. Eick, and A. R. Wilks. "Visualizing Network Data." *IEEE Transactions on Visualization and Graphics*. 1(1):16–28,1995.

[deLorenzi93]

H. G. deLorenzi and C. A. Taylor. "The Role of Process Parameters in Blow Molding and Correlation of 3-D Finite Element Analysis with Experiment." *International Polymer Processing*. 3(4):365–374, 1993.

[Ding90]

C. Ding and P. Mateti. "A Framework for the Automated Drawing of Data Structure Diagrams." *IEEE Transactions on Software Engineering*. 16(5):543–557, May 1990.

[Eick93]

S. G. Eick and G. J. Wills. "Navigating Large Networks with Hierarchies." In *Proceedings of Visualization '93*. pp. 204–210, IEEE Computer Society Press, Los Alamitos, CA, October 1993.

[Feiner88]

S. Feiner. "Seeing the Forest for the Trees: Hierarchical Displays of Hypertext Structures." In *Conference on Office Information Systems*. Palo Alto, CA, 1988.

[Gilster94]

P. Gilster. *Finding It on the Internet: The Essential Guide to Archie, Veronica, Gopher, WAIS, WWW (including Mosaic), and Other Search and Browsing Tools*. John Wiley & Sons, Inc., 1994.

[Johnson91]

B. Johnson and B. Shneiderman. "Tree-Maps: A Space-Filling Approach to the Visualization of Hierarchical Information Structures." In *Proceedings of Visualization '91*. pp. 284–291, IEEE Computer Society Press, Los Alamitos, CA, October 1991.

[Perl95]

D. Till. *Teach Yourself Perl in 21 Days*. Sams Publishing, Indianapolis, Indiana, 1995.

[Robertson91]
    G. G. Robertson, J. D. Mackinlay, and S. K. Card. "Cone Trees: Animated 3D Visualiza-
    tions of Hierarchical Information." In *Proceedings of ACM CHI '91 Conference on Human
    Factors in Computing Systems*. pp. 189–194, 1991.

[Rogers86]
    S. E. Rogers, D. Kwak, and U. K. Kaul, "A Numerical Study of Three-Dimensional Incom-
    pressible Flow Around Multiple Post." in *Proceedings of AIAA Aerospace Sciences Con-
    ference*. vol. AIAA Paper 86-0353. Reno, Nevada, 1986.

12.11 Exercises

12.1 The medical example did nothing to transform the original data into a standard coordinate system. Many medical systems use RAS coordinates. R is right/left, A is anterior/
posterior and S is Superior/Inferior. This is the patient coordinate system. Discuss and
compare the following alternatives for transforming volume data into RAS coordinates.
a) vtkActor transformation methods.
b) vtkTransformFilter.
c) Reader transformations.

12.2 Modify the last example found in the medical application (Medical3.cxx) to use
vtkImageDataGeometryFilter instead of vtkImageActor. Compare the performance of
using geometry with using texture. How does the performance change as the resolution
of the volume data changes?

12.3 Modify the last medical example (Medical3.cxx) to use vtkTexture and
vtkPlaneSource instead of vtkImageActor.

12.4 Change the medical case study to use dividing cubes for the skin surface.

12.5 Combine the two scripts frogSegmentation.tcl and marchingFrog.tcl into one
script that will handle either segmented or grayscale files. What other parameters and
pipeline components might be useful in general for this application?

12.6 Create polygonal / line stroked models of your initials and build your own logo. Experiment with different transformations.

12.7 Enhance the appearance of Towers of Hanoi visualization.
a) Texture map the disks, base plane, and pegs.
b) Create disks with central holes.

12.8 Use the blow molding example as a starting point for the following.
a) Create an animation of the blow molding sequence. Is it possible to interpolate
between time steps? How would you do this?
b) Create the second half of the parison using symmetry. What transformation matrix
do you need to use?

12.9 Start with the stock visualization example presented in this chapter.
a) Modify the example code to use a ribbon filter and linear extrusion filter as described
in the text. Be careful of the width of the generated ribbons.
b) Can you think of a way to present high/low trade values for each day?

 **Glossary**

3D Widget. An interaction paradigm enabling manipulation of scene objects (e.g., lights, camera, actors, and so on). The 3D widget typically provides a visible representation that can be intuitively and interactively manipulated.

API. An acronym for application programmer's interface.

Abstract Class. A class that provides methods and data members for the express purpose of deriving subclasses. Such objects are used to define a common interface and attributes for their subclasses.

Abstraction. A mental process that extracts the essential form or unifying properties of a concept.

Alpha. A specification of opacity (or transparency). An alpha value of one indicates that the object is opaque. An alpha value of zero indicates that the object is completely transparent.

Ambient Lighting. The background lighting of unlit surfaces.

Animation. A sequence of images displayed in rapid succession. The images may vary due to changes in geometry, color, lighting, camera position, or other graphics parameters. Animations are used to display the variation of one or more variables.

Antialiasing. The process of reducing aliasing artifacts. These artifacts typically result from undersampling the data. A common use of antialiasing is to draw straight lines that don't have the jagged edges found in many systems without antialiasing.

Azimuth. A rotation of a camera about the vertical (or view up) axis.

Attribute. A named member of a class that captures some characteristic of the class. Attributes have a name, a data type, and a data value. This is the same as a data member or instance variable.

Base Class. A superclass in C++.

Binocular Parallax. The effect of viewing the same object with two slightly different viewpoints to develop depth information.

Boolean Texture. A texture map consisting of distinct regions used to "cut" or accentuate features of data. For example, a texture map may consist of regions of zero opacity. When such a texture is mapped onto the surface of an object, portions of its interior becomes visible. Generally used in conjunction with a quadric (or other implicit function) to generate texture coordinates.

C++. A compiled programming language with roots in the C programming language. C++ is an extension of C that incorporates object-oriented principles.

CT (Computed Tomography). A data acquisition technique based on X-rays. Data is acquired in a 3D volume as a series of slice planes (i.e., a stack of n^2 points).

Cell. The atoms of visualization datasets. Cells define a topology (e.g., polygon, triangle) in terms of a list of point coordinates.

Cell Attributes. Dataset attributes associated with a cell. See also *point attributes*.

Class. An object that defines the characteristics of a subset of objects. Typically, it defines methods and data members. All objects instantiated from a class share that class's methods and data members.

Clipping Plane. A plane that restricts the rendering or processing of data. Front and back clipping planes are commonly used to restrict the rendering of primitives to those lying between the two planes.

Color Mapping. A scalar visualization technique that maps scalar values into color. Generally used to display the variation of data on a surface or through a volume.

Compiled System. A compiled system requires that a program be compiled (or translated into a lower-level language) before it is executed. Contrast with *interpreted systems*.

Composite Cell. A cell consisting of one or more primary cells.

Concrete Class. A class that can be instantiated. Typically, abstract classes are not instantiated but concrete classes are.

Connectivity. A technique to extract connected cells. Cells are connected when they share common features such as points, edges, or faces.

Contouring. A scalar visualization technique that creates lines (in 2D) or surfaces (in 3D) representing a constant scalar value across a scalar field. Contour lines are called isovalue lines or isolines. Contour surfaces are called isovalue surfaces or isosurfaces.

Constructor. A class method that is invoked when an instance of that class is created. Typically the constructor sets any default values and allocates any memory that the instance needs. See also *destructor*.

Critical Points. Locations in a vector field where the local vector magnitude goes to zero and the direction becomes undefined.

Cutting. A visualization technique to slice through or cut data. The cutting surface is typically described with an implicit function, and data attributes are mapped onto the cut surface. See also *boolean texture*.

Dataset. The general term used to describe visualization data. Datasets consist of structure (geometry and topology) and dataset attributes (scalars, vectors, tensors, etc.).

Dataset Attributes. The information associated with the structure of a dataset. This can be scalars, vectors, tensors, normals, and texture coordinates, or arbitrary data arrays that may be contained in the field.

Data Extraction. The process of selecting a portion of data based on characteristics of the data. These characteristics may be based on geometric or topological constraints or constraints on data attribute values.

Data Flow Diagram. A diagram that shows the information flow and operations on that information as it moves throughout a program or process.

Data Object. An object that is an abstraction of data. For example, a patient's file in a hospital could be a data object. Typical visualization objects include structured grids and volumes. See also *process object*.

Data Member. A named member of a class that captures some characteristic of the class. Data members have a name, a data type, and a data value. This is the same as an attribute or instance variable.

Data Visualization. The process of transforming data into sensory stimuli, usually visual images. Data visualization is a general term, encompassing data from engineering and science, as well as information from business, finance, sociology, geography, information management, and other fields. Data visualization also includes elements of data analysis, such as statistical analysis. Contrast with *scientific visualization* and *information visualization*.

Decimation. A type of polygon reduction technique that deletes points in a polygonal mesh that satisfies a co-planar or co-linear condition and replaces the resulting hole with a new triangulation.

Delaunay Triangulation. A triangulation that satisfies the Delaunay circumsphere criterion. This criterion states that a circumsphere of each simplex in the triangulation contains only the points defining the simplex.

Delegation. The process of assigning an object to handle the execution of another object's methods. Sometimes it is said that one object forwards certain methods to another object for execution.

Demand-driven. A method of visualization pipeline update where the update occurs only when data is requested and occurs only in the portion of the network required to generate the data.

Derived Class. A class that is more specific or complete than its superclass. The derived class, which is also known as the subclass, inherits all the members of its superclass. Usually a derived class adds new functionality or fills in what was defined by its superclass. See also *subclass*.

Destructor. A class method that is invoked when an instance of that class is deleted. Typically the destructor frees memory that the instance was using. See also *constructor*.

Device Mapper. A mapper that interfaces data to a graphics library or subsystem.

Diffuse Lighting. Reflected light from a matte surface. Diffuse lighting is a function of the relative angle between the incoming light and surface normal of the object.

Displacement Plots. A vector visualization technique that shows the displacement of the surface of an object. The method generates scalar values by computing the dot product between the surface normal and vector displacement of the surface. The scalars are visualized using color mapping.

Display Coordinate System. A coordinate system that is the result of mapping the view coordinate system onto the display hardware.

Divergence. In numerical computation: the tendency of computation to move away from the solution. In fluid flow: the rapid motion of fluid particles away from one another.

Dividing Cubes. A contour algorithm that represents isosurfaces as a dense cloud of points.

Dolly. A camera operation that moves the camera position towards (*dolly in*) or away (*dolly out*) from the camera focal point.

Double Buffering. A display technique that is used to display animations more smoothly. It consists of using two buffers in the rendering process. While one buffer is being displayed, the next frame in the animation is being drawn on the other buffer. Once the drawing is complete the two buffers are swapped and the new image is displayed.

Dynamic Memory Model. A data flow network that does not retain intermediate results as it executes. Each time the network executes, it must recompute any data required as input to another process object. A dynamic memory model reduces system memory requirements but places greater demands on computational requirements.

Dynamic Model. A description of a system concerned with synchronizing events and objects.

Effective Stress. A mathematical combination of the normal and shear stress components that provide a measure of the stress at a point. Effective stress is a scalar value, while stress is represented with a tensor value. See *stress*.

Eigenfields. Vector fields defined by the eigenvectors of a tensor.

Eigenvalue. A characteristic value of a matrix. Eigenvalues often correspond to physical phenomena, such as frequency of vibration or magnitude of principal components of stress.

Eigenvector. A vector associated with each eigenvalue. The eigenvector spans the space of the matrix. Eigenvectors are orthogonal to one another. Eigenvectors often correspond to physical phenomena such as mode shapes of vibration.

Elevation. A rotation of a camera about the horizontal axis.

Entity. Something within a system that has identity. Chairs, airplanes, and cameras are things that correspond to physical entities in the real world. A database and isosurface algorithm are examples of nonphysical entities.

Event-driven. A method of visualization pipeline update where updates occur when an event affects the pipeline, e.g., when an object instance variable is set or modified. See also *demand-driven*.

Execution. The process of updating a visualization network.

Explicit Execution. Controlling network updates by performing explicit dependency analysis.

Exporter. An object that saves a VTK scene definition to a file or other program. (A scene consists of lights, cameras, actors, geometry, properties, texture, and other pertinent data.) See also *importer.*

Fan-in. The flow of multiple pieces of data into a single filter.

Fan-out. The flow of data from a filter's output to other objects.

Feature Angle. The angle between surface normal vectors, e.g., the angle between the normal vectors on two adjacent polygons.

Filter. A process object that takes at least one input and generates at least one output.

Finite Element Method (FEM). A numerical technique for the solution of partial differential equations. FEM is based on discretizing a domain into elements (and nodes) and constructing basis (or interpolation) functions across the elements. From these functions a system of linear equations is generated and solved on the computer. Typical applications include stress, heat transfer, and vibration analysis.

Finite Difference Method. A numerical technique for the solution of partial differential equations (PDEs). Finite difference methods replace the PDEs with truncated Taylor series approximations. This results in a system of equations that is solved on a computer. Typical applications include fluid flow, combustion, and heat transfer.

Flat Shading. A shading technique where the lighting equation for a geometric primitive is calculated once, and then used to fill in the entire area of the primitive. This is also known as faceted shading. See also *gouraud shading* and *phong shading.*

Functional Model. The description of a system based on what it does.

Generalization. The abstraction of a subset of classes to a common superclass. Generalization extracts the common members or methods from a group of classes to create a common superclass. See also *specialization* and *inheritance.*

Geometry. Used generally to mean the characteristic position, shape, and topology of an object. Used specifically (in tandem with topology) to mean the position and shape of an object.

Glyph. A general visualization technique used to represent data using a meaningful shape or pictorial representation. Each glyph is generally a function of its input data and may change size, orientation, and shape; or modify graphics properties in response to changes in input.

Gouraud Shading. A shading technique that applies the lighting equations for a geometric primitive at each vertex. The resulting colors are then interpolated over the areas between the vertices. See also *flat shading* and *Phong shading.*

Hedgehog. A vector visualization technique that represents vector direction and magnitude with oriented lines.

Height Field. A set of altitude or height samples in a rectangular grid. Height fields are typically used to represent terrain.

Hexahedron. A type of primary 3D cell. The hexahedron looks like a "brick." It has six faces, 12 edges, and eight vertices. The faces of the hexahedron are not necessarily planar.

Homogeneous Coordinates. An alternate coordinate representation that provides more flexibility than traditional Cartesian coordinates. This includes perspective transformation and combined translation, scaling, and rotation.

Hyperstreamline. A tensor visualization technique. Hyperstreamlines are created by treating the eigenvectors as three separate vectors. The maximum eigenvalue/eigenvector is used as a vector field in which particle integration is performed (like streamlines). The other two vectors control the cross-sectional shape of an ellipse that is swept along the integration path. See also *streampolygon*.

Image Data. A dataset whose structure is both geometrically and topologically regular. Both geometry and topology are implicit. A 3D image dataset is known as a volume. A 2D image dataset is known as a pixmap.

Image-Order Techniques. Rendering techniques that determine for each pixel in the image plane which data samples contribute to it. Image-order techniques are implemented using ray casting. Contrast with *object-order techniques*.

Implicit Execution. Controlling network updates by distributing network dependency throughout the visualization process objects. Each process object requests that its input be updated before it executes. This results in a recursive update/execution process throughout the network.

Implicit Function. A mathematical function of the form $F(x, y, z) = c$, where c is a constant.

Implicit Modelling. A modelling technique that represents geometry as a scalar field. Usually the scalar is a distance function or implicit function distributed through a volume.

Importer. An object that interfaces to external data or programs to define a complete scene in VTK. (The scene consists of lights, cameras, actors, geometry, properties, texture, and other pertinent data.) See also *exporter*.

Information Visualization. The process of transforming information into sensory stimuli, usually visual images. Information visualization is used to describe the process of visualizing data without structure, such as information on the World Wide Web; or abstract data structures, like computer file systems or documents. Contrast with *scientific visualization* and *data visualization*.

Inheritance. A process where the attributes and methods of a superclass are bestowed upon all subclasses derived from that superclass. It is said that the subclasses inherit their superclasses' methods and attributes.

Instance. An object that is defined by a class and used by a program or application. There may be many instances of a specific class.

Instance Variable. A named member of a class that captures a characteristic of the class. Instance variables have a name, a data type, and a data value. The phrase, instance variable, is often abbreviated as ivar. This is the same as an attribute or data member.

Intensity. The light energy transferred per unit time across a unit plane perpendicular to the light rays.

Interpolate. Estimate a value of a function at a point p, given known function values and points that bracket p.

Interpolation Functions. Functions continuous in value and derivatives used to interpolate data from known points and function values. Cells use interpolation functions to compute data values interior to or on the boundary of the cell.

Interpreted System. An interpreted system can execute programs without going through a separate compilation stage. Interpreted systems often allow the user to interact and modify the program as it is running. Contrast with *compiled systems*.

Irregular Data. Data in which the relationship of one data item to the other data items in the dataset is arbitrary. Irregular data is also known as unstructured data.

Iso-parametric. A form of interpolation in which interpolation for data values is the same as for the local geometry. Compare with *sub-parametric* and *super-parametric*.

Isosurface. A surface representing a constant valued scalar function. See *contouring*.

Isovalue. The scalar value used to generate an isosurface.

Jacobian. A matrix that relates one coordinate system to another.

Line. A cell defined by two points.

MRI (Magnetic Resonance Imaging). A data acquisition technique based on measuring variation in magnetic field in response to radio-wave pulses. The data is acquired in a 3D region as a series of slice planes (i.e., a stack of n^2 points).

Mapper. A process object that terminates the visualization network. It maps input data into graphics libraries (or other devices) or writes data to disk (or a communication device).

Manifold Topology. A domain is manifold at a point p in a topological space of dimension n if the neighborhood around p is homeomorphic to an n-dimensional sphere. Homeomorphic means that the mapping is one to one without tearing (i.e., like mapping a rubber sheet from a square to a disk). We generally refer to an object's topology as manifold if every point in the object is manifold. Contrast with *nonmanifold topology*.

Marching Cubes. A contouring algorithm to create surfaces of constant scalar value in 3D. Marching cubes is described for volume datasets, but has been extended to datasets consisting of other cell types.

Member Function. A member function is a function or transformation that can be applied to an object. It is the functional equivalent to a data member. Member functions define the behavior of an object. Methods, operations, and member functions are essentially the same.

Method. A function or transformation that can be applied to an object. Methods define the behavior of an object. Methods, operations, and member functions are essentially the same.

Modal Lines. Lines on the surface of a vibrating object that separate regions of positive and negative displacement.

Mode Shape. The motion of an object vibrating at a natural frequency. See also *eigenvalues* and *eigenvectors*.

Model Coordinate System. The coordinate system that a model or geometric entity is defined in. There may be many different model coordinate systems defined for one scene.

Motion Blur. An artifact of the shutter speed of a camera. Since the camera's shutter stays open for a finite amount of time, changes in the scene that occur during that time can result in blurring of the resulting image.

Morph. A progressive transformation of one object into another. Generally used to transform images (2D morphing) and in some cases geometry (3D morphing).

Multiple Input. Process objects that accept more than one input.

Multiple Output. Process objects that generate more than one output.

Multidimensional Visualization. Visualizing data of four or more variables. Generally requires a mapping of many dimensions into three or fewer dimensions so that standard visualization techniques can be applied.

Nonmanifold Topology. Topology that is not manifold. Examples include polygonal meshes, where an edge is used by more than two polygons, or polygons connected to each other at their vertices (i.e., do not share an edge). Contrast with *manifold topology.*

Normal. A unit vector that indicates perpendicular direction to a surface. Normals are a common type of data attribute.

Object. An abstraction that models the state and behavior of entities in a system. Instances and classes are both objects.

Object Model. The description of a system in terms of the components that make up the system, including the relationship of the components one to another.

Object-Order Techniques. Rendering techniques that project object data (e.g., polygons or voxels) onto the image plane. Example techniques include ordered compositing and splatting.

Object-Oriented. A software development technique that uses objects to represent the state and behavior of entities in a system.

Octree Decomposition. A technique to decompose a cubical region of three-dimensional space into smaller cubes. The cubes, or octants, are related in tree fashion. The root octant is the cubical region. Each octant may have eight children created by dividing the parent in half in the x, y, and z directions.

Object Factory. An object used to construct or instantiate other objects. In VTK, object factories are implemented using the class method New().

OMT. *Object Modelling Technique.* An object-oriented design technique that models software systems with object, dynamic, and functional diagrams.

Operation. A function or transformation that can be applied to an object. Operations define the behavior of an object. Methods and member functions implement operations.

Overloading. Having multiple methods with the same name. Some methods are overloaded because there are different versions of the same method. These differences are based on argument types, while the underlying algorithm remains the same. Contrast with *polymorphic.*

Painter's Algorithm. An object-order rendering technique that sorts rendering primitives from back to front and then draws them.

Parametric Coordinates. A coordinate system natural to the geometry of a geometric object. For example, a line may be described by the single coordinate *s* even though the line may lie in three or higher dimensions.

Parallel Projection. A mapping of world coordinates into view coordinates that preserves all parallel lines. In a parallel projection an object will appear the same size regardless of how far away it is from the viewer. This is equivalent to having a center of projection that is infinitely far away. Contrast with *perspective projection*.

Particle Trace. The trajectory that particles trace over time in fluid flow. Particle traces are everywhere tangent to the velocity field. Unlike streamlines, particle lines are time-dependent.

Pathline. The trajectory that a particle follows in fluid flow.

Perspective Projection. A mapping of world coordinates into view coordinates that roughly approximates a camera lens. Specifically, the center of projection must be a finite distance from the view plane. As a result closer, objects will appear larger than distant objects. Contrast with *parallel projection*.

Phong Shading. A shading technique that applies the lighting equations for a geometric primitive at each pixel. See also *flat shading* and *Gouraud shading*.

Pitch. A rotation of a camera's position about the horizontal axis, centered at its viewpoint. See also *yaw* and *roll*. Contrast with *elevation*.

Pixel. Short for picture element. Constant valued elements in an image. In VTK, a two-dimensional cell defined by an ordered list of four points.

Point. A geometric specification of position in 3D space.

Point Attributes. Data attributes associates with the points of a dataset.

Polygon. A cell consisting of three or more co-planar points defining a polygon. The polygon can be concave but without imbedded loops.

Polygonal Data. A dataset type consisting of arbitrary combinations of vertices, polyvertices, lines, polylines, polygons, and triangle strips. Polygonal data is an intermediate data form that can be easily rendered by graphics libraries, and yet can represent many types of visualization data.

Polygon Reduction. A family of techniques to reduce the size of large polygonal meshes. The goal is to reduce the number of polygons, while preserving a "good" approximation to the original geometry. In most techniques topology is preserved as well.

Polyline. A composite cell consisting of one or more lines.

Polymorphic. Having many forms. Some methods are polymorphic because the same method in different classes may implement a different algorithm. The semantics of the method are typically the same, even though the implementation may differ. Contrast with *overloading*.

Polyvertex. A composite cell consisting of one or more vertices.

Primary Cell. A cell that is not defined in terms of other cells.

Probing. Also known as sampling or resampling. A data selection technique that selects data at a set of points.

Process Object. A visualization object that is an abstraction of a process or algorithm. For example, the isosurfacing algorithm marching cubes is implemented as a process object. See also *data object.*

Progressive Mesh. A representation of a triangle mesh that enables incremental refinement and derefinement. The data representation is compact and is useful for transmission of 3D triangle meshes across a network. See also *polygon reduction.*

Properties. A general term used to describe the rendered properties of an actor. This includes lighting terms such as ambient, diffuse, and specular coefficients; color and opacity; shading techniques such as flat and Gouraud; and the actor's geometric representation (wireframe, points, or surface).

Pyramid. A type of primary 3D cell. The pyramid has a quadrilateral base connected to a single apex point. It has five faces, eight edges, and five vertices. The base face of the pyramid is not necessarily planar.

Quadric. A function of the form
$$f(x, y, z) = a_0 x^2 + a_1 y^2 + a_2 z^2 + a_3 xy + a_4 yz + a_5 xz + a_6 x + a_7 y + a_8 z + a_9 \quad . \qquad \text{The}$$
quadric equation can represent many useful 3D objects such as spheres, ellipsoids, cylinders, and cones.

Quadratic Edge. A type of primary 1D cell with a quadratic interpolation function. The quadratic edge is defined by three points: two end points and a mid-edge node.

Quadratic Triangle. A type of primary 2D cell with quadratic interpolation functions. The quadratic triangle is defined by six points: three corner points and three mid-edge nodes.

Quadratic Quadrilateral. A type of primary 2D cell with quadratic interpolation functions. The quadratic quadrilateral is defined by eight points: four corner points and four mid-edge nodes.

Quadratic Tetrahedron. A type of primary 3D cell with quadratic interpolation functions. The quadratic tetrahedron is defined by ten points: four corner points and six mid-edge nodes.

Quadratic Hexahedron. A type of primary 3D cell with quadratic interpolation functions. The quadratic edge is defined by twenty points: eight corner points and twelve mid-edge nodes.

Quadrilateral (Quad). A type of primary 2D cell. The quadrilateral is four sided with four vertices. The quadrilateral must be convex.

Reader. A source object that reads a file or files and produces a data object.

Reference Counting. A memory management technique used to reduce memory requirements. Portions of memory (in this case objects) may be referenced by more than one other object. The referenced object keeps a count of references to it. If the count returns to zero, the object deletes itself, returning memory back to the system. This technique avoids making copies of memory.

Region of Interest. A portion of a dataset that the user is interested in visualizing. Sometimes abbreviated ROI.

Regular Data. Data in which one data item is related (either geometrically or topologically) to other data items. Also referred to as structured data.

Rendering. The process of converting object geometry (i.e., geometric primitives), object properties, and a specification of lights and camera into an image. The primitives may take many forms including surface primitives (points, lines, polygons, splines), implicit functions, or volumes.

Resonant Frequency. A frequency at which an object vibrates.

Roll. A rotation of a camera about its direction of projection. See also *azimuth, elevation, pitch,* and *yaw.*

Sampling. Selective acquisition or sampling of data, usually at a regular interval. See also *probing.*

Scalar. A single value or function value. May also be used to represent a field of such values.

Scalar Range. The minimum and maximum scalar values of a scalar field.

Scalar Generation. Creating scalar values from other data such as vectors or tensors. One example is computing vector norm.

Scene. A complete representation of the components required to generate an image or animation including lights, cameras, actors. properties, transformations, geometry, texture, and other pertinent information.

Scene Graph. A hierarchical, acyclic, directed tree representation of a scene. The graph order (depth first) controls when objects are processed by the graphics system.

Scientific Visualization. The process of transforming data into sensory stimuli, usually visual images. Generally used to denote the application of visualization to the sciences and engineering. Contrast with *data visualization* and *information visualization.*

Searching. The process of locating data. Usually the search is based on spatial criteria such as position or being inside a cell.

Segmentation. Identification and demarcation of tissue types. Segmentation is generally applied to CT and MRI data to associate soft tissue with a particular body organ or anatomical structure.

Simplex. The convex combination of n independent vectors in n-space forms an n-dimensional simplex. Points, lines, triangles, and tetrahedra are examples of simplices in 0D, 1D, 2D, and 3D.

Source. A process object that produces at least one output. Contrast with *filter.*

Specialization. The creation of subclasses that are more refined or specialized than their superclass. See also *generalization* and *inheritance.*

Specular Lighting. Reflected lighting from a shiny surface. Specular lighting is a function of the relative angle between the incoming light, the surface normal of the object, and the view angle of the observer.

Splatting. A method to distribute data values across a region. The distribution functions are often based on Gaussian functions.

State Diagram. A diagram that relates states and events. Used to describe behavior in a software system.

Static Memory Model. A data flow network that retains intermediate results as it executes. A static memory model minimizes computational requirements, but places greater demands on memory requirements.

Strain. A nondimensional quantity expressed as the ratio of the displacement of an object to its length (normal strain), or angular displacement (shear strain). Strain is a tensor quantity. See also *stress*.

Stress. A measure of force per unit area. Normal stress is stress normal to a given surface, and is either compressive (a negative value) or tensile (a positive value). Shear stress acts tangentially to a given surface. Stress is related to strain through the linear proportionality constants E (the modulus of elasticity), ν (Poisson's ratio), and G (modulus of elasticity in shear). Stress is a tensor quantity. See also *strain*.

Streakline. The set of particles that have previously passed through a particular point.

Streamline. Curves that are everywhere tangent to the velocity field. A streamline satisfies the integral curve $\frac{d}{ds}\vec{x} = \vec{v}(x, t')$ at some time t'.

Streampolygon. A vector and tensor visualization technique that represents flow with tubes that have polygonal cross sections. The method is based on integrating through the vector field and then sweeping a regular polygon along the streamline. The radius, number of sides, shape, and rotation of the polygon are allowed to change in response to data values. See also *hyperstreamline*.

Streamribbon. A vector visualization technique that represents vectors with ribbons that are everywhere tangent to the vector field

Streamsurface. A surface that is everywhere tangent to a vector field. Can be approximated by generating a series of streamlines along a curve and connecting the lines with a surface.

Streamwise Vorticity. A measure of the rotation of flow around a streamline.

Structured Data. Data in which one data item is related (either geometrically or topologically) to other data items. Also referred to as regular data.

Structured Grid. A dataset whose structure is topologically regular but whose geometry is irregular. Geometry is explicit and topology is implicit. Typically, structured grids consist of hexahedral cells.

Structured Points. *Preferred term is* Image Data. A dataset whose structure is both geometrically and topologically regular. Both geometry and topology are implicit. A 3D structured point dataset is known as a volume. A 2D structured point dataset is known as a pixmap.

Subclass. A class that is more specific or complete than its superclass. The subclass, which is also known as the derived class, inherits all the members of its superclass. Usually a subclass will add some new functionality or fill in what was defined by its superclass. See also *derived class*.

Sub-parametric. A form of interpolation in which interpolation for data values is of higher order than that for the local geometry. Compare with *iso-parametric* and *super-parametric*.

Subsampling. Sampling data at a resolution at less than final display resolution.

Superclass. A class from which other classes are derived. See also *base class*.

Super-parametric. A form of interpolation in which interpolation for data values is of lower order than that for the local geometry. Compare with *iso-parametric* and *sub-parametric*.

Surface Rendering. Rendering techniques based on geometric surface primitives such as points, lines, polygons, and splines. Contrast with *volume rendering*.

Swept Surface. The surface that an object creates as it is swept through space.

Swept Volume. The volume enclosed by a swept surface.

Tcl. An interpreted language developed by John Ousterhout in the early 1980s.

Tk. A graphical user-interface toolkit based on Tcl.

Tensor. A mathematical generalization of vectors and matrices. A tensor of rank k can be considered a k-dimensional table. Tensor visualization algorithms treat 3×3 real symmetric matrix tensors (rank 2 tensors).

Tensor Ellipsoid. A type of glyph used to visualize tensors. The major, medium, and minor eigenvalues of a 3×3 tensor define an ellipsoid. The eigenvalues are used to scale along the axes.

Tetrahedron. A 3D primary cell that is a simplex with four triangular faces, six edges, and four vertices.

Texture Animation. Rapid application of texture maps to visualize data. A useful example maps a 1D texture map of varying intensity along a set of lines to simulate particle flow.

Texture Coordinate. Specification of position within texture map. Texture coordinates are used to map data from Cartesian system into 2D or 3D texture map.

Texture Map. A specification of object properties in a canonical region. These properties are most often intensity, color, and alpha, or combinations of these. The region is typically a structured array of data in a pixmap (2D) or in a volume (3D).

Texture Mapping. A rendering technique to add detail to objects without requiring extensive geometric modelling. One common example is to paste a picture on the surface of an object.

Texture Thresholding. Using texture mapping to display selected data. Often makes use of alpha opacity to conceal regions of minimal interest.

Thresholding. A data selection technique that selects data that lies within a range of data. Typically scalar thresholding selects data whose scalar values meet a scalar criterion.

Topology. A subset of the information about the structure of a dataset. Topology is a set of properties invariant under certain geometric transformation such as scaling, rotation, and translation.

Topological Dimension. The dimension or number of parametric coordinates required to address the domain of an object. For example, a line in 3D space is of topological dimension one because the line can be parametrized with a single parameter.

Transformation Matrix. A 4×4 matrix of values used to control the position, orientation, and scale of objects.

Triangle Strip. A composite 2D cell consisting of triangles. The triangle strip is an efficient representation scheme for triangles where $n + 2$ points can represent n triangles.

Triangle. A primary 2D cell. The triangle is a simplex with three edges and three vertices.

Triangular Irregular Network (TIN). An unstructured triangulation consisting of triangles. Often used to represent terrain data.

Triangulation. A set of nonintersecting simplices sharing common vertices, edges, and/or faces.

Type Converter. A type of filter used to convert from one dataset type to another.

Type Checking. The process of enforcing compatibility between objects.

Uniform Grid. A synonym for image data.

Unstructured Data. Data in which one data item is unrelated (either geometrically or topologically) to other data items. Also referred to as irregular data.

Unstructured Grid. A general dataset form consisting of arbitrary combinations of cells and points. Both the geometry and topology are explicitly defined.

Unstructured Points. A dataset consisting of vertex cells that are positioned irregularly in space, with no implicit or explicit topology.

Visualization. The process of converting data to images (or other sensory stimuli). Alternatively, the end result of the visualization process.

Vector. A specification of direction and magnitude. Vectors can be used to describe fluid velocity, structural displacement, or object motion.

Vector Field Topology. Vector fields are characterized by regions flow diverges, converges, and/or rotates. The relationship of these regions one to another is the topology of the flow.

Vertex. A primary 0D cell. Is sometimes used synonymously with point or node.

View Coordinate System. The projection of the world coordinate system into the camera's viewing frustrum.

View Frustrum. The viewing region of a camera defined by six planes: the front and back clipping planes, and the four sides of a pyramid defined by the camera position, focal point, and view angle (or image viewport if viewing in parallel projection).

Visual Programming. A programming model that enables the construction and manipulation of visualization applications. A typical implementation is the construction of a visualization pipeline by connecting execution modules into a network.

Visualization Network. A series of process objects and data objects joined together into a dataflow network.

Volume. A regular array of points in 3D space. Volumes are often defined as a series of 2D images arranged along the *z*-axis.

Volume Rendering. The process of directly viewing volume data without converting the data to intermediate surface primitives. Contrast with *surface rendering*.

Vorticity. A measure of the rotation of fluid flow.

Voxel. Short for volume element. In VTK, a primary three-dimensional cell with six faces. Each face is perpendicular to one of the coordinate axes.

Warping. A scalar and vector visualization technique that distorts an object to magnify the effects of data value. Warping may be used on vector data to display displacement or velocity, or on scalar data to show relative scalar values.

Wedge. A type of primary 3D cell. The wedge has two triangular faces connected with three quadrilateral faces. It has five faces, nine edges, and six vertices. The quadrilateral faces of the wedge are not necessarily planar.

World Coordinate System. A three-dimensional Cartesian coordinate system in which the main elements of a rendering scene are positioned.

Writer. A type of mapper object that writes data to disk or other I/O device.

Yaw. A rotation of a camera's position about the vertical axis, centered at its viewpoint. See also *pitch* and *roll*. Contrast with *azimuth*.

Z-Buffer. Memory that contains the depth (along the view plane normal) of a corresponding element in a frame buffer.

Z-Buffering. A technique for performing hidden line (point, surface) removal by keeping track of the current depth, or *z* value for each pixel. These values are stored in the *z*-buffer.

Zoom. A camera operation that changes the field of view of the camera. Contrast with *dolly*.

Index

parametric coordinates 260

R

radial-edge structure 281, 297
rake 309
raster hardware 52
rasterization **56–57**
ray casting
  volume rendering 207–214
ray-tracing 34, 207
reader 86, *474*
  interfacing to data 97
reader object 86
rectilinear grid 125
  example 140
  implementation 132
  representation 133
red-blue stereo 235
  implementation 245
reference counting 94, *474*
region of interest **257**, 370, *475*
  in volume rendering 228–229
regression testing
  example 389
regular data 111, *475*
  structured data 112
rendering **33–36**, *475*
  image-order **35–36**, *470*
  object-order **35–36**, *472*
  stereo **233–236**
  surface **36**, *477*
  volume 36, **206–220**, *479*
representation
  implementation 135
  in visualization 81
resonant frequency *475*
RGB **37**, 52, 59, 204
  and opacity 204
ROI, see region of interest
roll 45, *475*
rotation
  about a vector 75
  and actor 72

S

sample 335
sampling 320, 338, *475*
  in ray casting 212
scalar **121**, *475*

relationship to color 275–277
scalar algorithms 150, **151–161**
  301–307
  carpet plots **304–305**
  clipping with scalars **305–307**
  color mapping **151–153**
  contouring **154–161**
  dividing cubes **301–304**
  marching cubes **154–159**
scalar attributes 121
scalar generation **159–161**, *475*
scalar range *475*
scan conversion
  to generate discrete rays 213
scene *475*
scene graph **95**, 95
  475
scientific visualization *475*
  versus data visualization 1
  versus information visualization 2
searching **273–274**, *475*
  image data 279
  implementation 288–290
segmentation 383–384, 427, *475*
  multi-spectral 386–387
segmented volume data
  application 427–438
sensor position
  image artifact 374, 375
server
  VRML 402–404
shading **56–57**
  flat 56, *469*
  Gouraud 56
  gouraud *469*
  Phong 56
  phong *473*
shear strain 310
shear-warp 219–220
Shepard's method 340
simple point 327
simplex **271**, 341, *475*
Single Image Random Dot Stereograms 235
sink object 82
SIRDS 235
Smalltalk 28, 29
smoothing 372
  mesh 331–334
  non-linear 372
software

Programming Resources

The Visualization Toolkit (VTK) is an open-source, freely available system for 3D computer graphics, image processing, and visualization. VTK is used around the world in commercial, academic, and research applications. http://www.vtk.org

Insight Segmentation and Registration Toolkit (ITK) is an open-source system for image processing, segmentation, and registration. Sponsored by the National Library of Medicine, ITK employs leading-edge segmentation and registration algorithms in two, three, and more dimensions. http://www.itk.org

CMake is a cross-platform, open-source build system. CMake controls the software compilation process using simple platform and compiler independent configuration files. CMake generates native makefiles and workspaces that can be used in the compiler environment of your choice. http://www.cmake.org

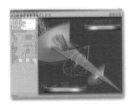

ParaView is a turn-key application for parallel, large data visualization built on top of the VTK visualization system. ParaView is portable across operating systems and supports run-time extension via Tcl scripts and XML configuration files. Other features include distributed parallel processing support with MPI. http://www.paraview.org

Open Source Software

Visit http://www.kitware.com
for more information

Kitware

Leaders in Visualization Technology

Kitware provides a variety of support services for its open-source software systems. ***The VTK User's Guide*** is used by users and developers to create VTK-based applications and to extend VTK. The book is updated frequently to reflect changes to the software base.

VolView is an intuitive, interactive system for volume visualization that allows researchers and clinicians to quickly explore complex 3D medical or scientific images. Features include filtering, contouring, measuring, histograms, and annotation.

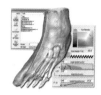

ActiViz is a family of software products that allows you to embed active visualization tools into Microsoft documents. Depending on your requirements, you can use C# or Visual Basic to extend such applications as Word, Excel, PowerPoint, and Internet Explorer.

PolyViz is a powerful, easy-to-use application and Active-X control for geometric viewing, annotating, and editing. As an Active-X control or end-user application, PolyViz can be used without the need for programming or scripting. Just drop in the control and go!

Kitware offers **Professional Support & Training** for its open-source products. Custom consulting contracts are available to design, enhance and/or implement applications or to adapt existing applications such as VolView, ParaView, or PolyViz to customer requirements.

Commercial Solutions

Contact kitware@kitware.com
for purchasing information